List of contributors

Dr Rohin Francis MBBS BSc (Hons) MRCP
Cardiology Registrar
Papworth Hospital
Cambridge
UK

Dr Parag R Gajendragadkar MA MPhil
MRCP(UK)
Cardiology Registrar
Papworth Hospital
Cambridge
UK

Dr James C P Harper MBChB BSc MRCP
Registrar in Respiratory Medicine
Wellington Regional Hospital
Wellington
New Zealand

Dr Martin D Knolle MB BChir PhD MRCP
Consultant in Respiratory Medicine
Cambridge University Hospitals NHS
Foundation Trust
Cambridge
UK

Dr Ioannis Merinopoulos BSc MSc
MRCP
Cardiology Registrar
Norfolk and Norwich University Hospitals
NHS Foundation Trust
Norwich
UK

Dr Abdul M Mozid BMedSci MD FRCP
Consultant Cardiologist
Bristol Heart Institute
Bristol
UK

Dr Paul R Roberts MD FRCP
Consultant Cardiologist
University Hospital Southampton NHS
Foundation Trust
Southampton
UK

Dr Mark G Slade FRACP FRCP
Consultant Respiratory Physician
Cheltenham General Hospital
Cheltenham
UK

Dr Henry J Steer BMedSci PhD FRCP
Consultant Respiratory Physician
Gloucestershire Royal Hospital
Gloucester
UK

Acknowledgements

The third edition of Medical Masterclass has been produced by a team. The names of those who have written and edited are clearly indicated, and along with all these contributors I gratefully acknowledge the contributions of those who wrote and edited the first and second editions. This third edition is based on their foundations, and some of their material has been retained. But my acknowledgements must not stop there, because the Medical Masterclass would not have been published without the efforts of many other people. Naming names is risky, but I must name Claire Daley, who has worked as editor of the third edition with a wonderful combination of quietness and efficiency, and with an attention to detail that has made me feel triumphant if I have ever spotted a misplaced comma in a proof.

Dr John Firth DM FRCP
Medical Masterclass Editor-in-Chief

© 2008, 2010, 2018 Royal College of Physicians of London

Cover image courtesy of: KTS Design / Science Photo Library

Published by:
Royal College of Physicians of London
11 St Andrews Place
Regent's Park
London NW1 4LE
United Kingdom

Typeset by Manila Typesetting Company, Makati City, Philippines

Printed by The Lavenham Press Limited, Suffolk

First edition published 2001
Reprinted 2004
Second edition published 2008
Updated and reprinted 2010
Third edition published 2018

ISBN: 978-1-86016-658-7 (this book)
eISBN: 978-1-86016-659-4 (this book)
ISBN: 978-1-86016-670-9 (set)
eISBN: 978-1-86016-671-6 (set)

Royal College of Physicians of London
11 St Andrews Place
Regent's Park
London NW1 4LE
United Kingdom
Tel: +44 (0)20 3075 1379
Email: medical.masterclass@rcplondon.ac.uk
Web: www.rcplondon.ac.uk/medicalmasterclass

Contents

Respiratory medicine

Medical Masterclass third edition

Editor-in-Chief

Dr John D Firth DM FRCP
Consultant Physician and Nephrologist
Addenbrooke's Hospital
Cambridge
UK

Cardiology and respiratory

Editors

Dr Paul R Roberts MD FRCP
Consultant Cardiologist
University Hospital Southampton NHS Foundation Trust
Southampton
UK

Dr Mark G Slade FRACP FRCP
Consultant Respiratory Physician
Cheltenham General Hospital
Cheltenham
UK

Third edition

Disclaimer

Although every effort has been made to ensure that drug doses and other information are presented accurately in this publication, the ultimate responsibility rests with the prescribing physician. Neither the publishers nor the authors can be held responsible for any consequences arising from the use of information contained herein. Any product mentioned in this publication should be used in accordance with the prescribing information prepared by the manufacturers.

The information presented in this publication reflects the opinions of its contributors and should not be taken to represent the policy and views of the Royal College of Physicians of London, unless this is specifically stated.

Every effort has been made by the contributors to contact holders of copyright to obtain permission to reproduce copyrighted material. However, if any have been inadvertently overlooked, the publisher will be pleased to make the necessary arrangements at the first opportunity.

Preface

This third edition of Medical Masterclass is produced and published by the Royal College of Physicians of London. It comprises 12 books and an online question bank. Its aim is to interest and help doctors in their first few years of training, to enable them to improve their medical knowledge and skills, and to pass postgraduate medical examinations, most particularly the MRCP(UK): Part 1, Part 2 and PACES (the practical assessment of clinical examination skills that is the final part of the exam).

The 12 textbooks are divided as follows: two cover the scientific background to medicine; one is devoted to general clinical skills, including medicine for older people, palliative care and specific guidance on exam technique for PACES; one deals with acute medicine; and the other eight cover the range of medical specialties.

The medical specialties are dealt with in eight sections:

> Case histories – you are presented with letters of referral that are commonly received in each specialty and led through the ways in which the patients' histories should be explored, and what investigations and/or treatments should follow, as in Station 2 of PACES.

> Physical examination scenarios – these emphasise solid and reliable clinical method, logical analysis of physical signs and sensible clinical reasoning ('having found this, what would you want to do next?'), as in Stations 1 and 3 of PACES.

> Communication and ethical scenarios – you are presented with difficult issues that can arise in each specialty. What should you actually say in response to the 'frequently asked (but nonetheless tricky) questions', as required in Station 4 of PACES?

> Brief clinical consultations – how should you take a focused history and perform a focused examination of a patient who has a medical problem when there isn't much time? This section explains how to do this while working as a medical registrar on take, or in Station 5 of PACES.

> Acute presentations – what are your priorities if you are the doctor seeing a patient in the emergency department or the medical admissions unit? The material in this section is relevant to all parts of the MRCP(UK) exam.

> Diseases and treatments – concise structured notes that are of particular relevance to the Part 1 and Part 2 exams.

> Investigations and practical procedures – short and concise notes.

> Self-assessment questions – in the form used in the Part 1 and Part 2 exams.

The online question bank, which is continually updated, enables you to take mock Part 1 and Part 2 exams, or to be selective in the questions that you tackle (if you want to do 10 questions on cardiology, or any other specialty, then you can do so). You can see how your scores compare with those of others who have attempted the same questions, which helps you to know where to focus your learning.

I hope that you enjoy using the Medical Masterclass to learn more about medicine. I know that medicine is tough at the moment, with hospital services under unprecedented pressure and the medical registrar bearing more than their fair share of the burden. But careers are a long game, and being a physician is a wonderful occupation. It is sometimes intellectually and/or emotionally very challenging, but with these challenges come great rewards, and few things give more substantial satisfaction than being a doctor who provides good care for a patient. The Medical Masterclass should help you do to that, as well as to pass the MRCP(UK) exam along the way.

Dr John Firth DM FRCP
Medical Masterclass Editor-in-Chief

Key features

We have created a range of icon boxes that sit among the text of the various Medical Masterclass books. They are there to help you identify key information and to make learning easier and more enjoyable. Here is a brief explanation:

This icon is used to highlight points of particular importance.

Key point

A patient with a normal physical examination, a normal ECG and a normal echocardiogram is at very low risk of significant arrhythmia.

This icon is used to indicate common or important drug interactions, pitfalls of practical procedures, or when to take symptoms or signs particularly seriously.

Hazard

Acute lymphoblastic leukaemia may present in an identical manner to infectious mononucleosis.

Case examples / case histories are used to demonstrate why and how an understanding of the scientific background to medicine helps in the practice of clinical medicine.

Case history

A man with a renal transplant is immunosuppressed with ciclosporin, azathioprine and prednisolone. He develops recurrent gout and is started on allopurinol.

Cardiology

Authors

Dr R Francis, Dr P Gajendragadkar, Dr I Merinopoulos, Dr A Mozid and Dr P Roberts

Editor

Dr P Roberts

Editor-in-Chief

Dr JD Firth

The cardiology section of the second edition of Medical Masterclass was written by Dr B Chandrasekaran, Dr PWX Foley, Dr PR Kalra, Dr N Melikian, Dr R Sharma and Dr PR Roberts (editor). This third edition of Medical Masterclass contains entirely new material, but many sections from the second edition have been retained and updated, and we gratefully acknowledge the contribution of these authors.

Cardiology: Section 1

1 PACES stations and acute scenarios

1.1 History taking

1.1.1 Palpitations with dizziness

Letter of referral for urgent assessment in the cardiology clinic

Dear Doctor,

Re: Mr Matthew Carney, aged 57 years

Please assess this retired policeman who has a 2-month history of rapid palpitations. Initially he was well during the episodes, but more recently he has noticed that he is dizzy when they go on for more than 20 seconds. He came to see me today as he nearly blacked out this morning. He has previously been very well and this is the first time he has asked to see a doctor. Examination today was unremarkable but I am quite concerned about the pre-syncopal episode today and would value your opinion. Does he require detailed cardiac investigation?

Yours sincerely,

Introduction

Your main concern is that this patient gives a history of presyncope, which places him in a higher risk category for life-threatening arrhythmia. The main objective must be to exclude a significant ventricular arrhythmia. With the little information available, it is apparent that the palpitations are directly related to the presyncope, which

would be consistent with the diagnosis of ventricular tachycardia (VT).

It is vital to ensure that the patient is safe while a diagnosis is being established. He should thus be admitted from clinic for investigation and monitoring. It is essential to document his heart rhythm during an episode. Some patients with VT are asymptomatic, whereas others are extremely symptomatic from only short runs of VT. Both groups are at risk of cardiac arrest as a result of VT or the VT degenerating into ventricular fibrillation.

History of the presenting problem

What is the relationship of the presyncope and palpitations?
It is important to determine the order of symptoms; many patients with presyncope or syncope will have a reactive sinus tachycardia after the event that might cause a feeling of palpitation. In this case it is clear that the presyncope is occurring with more prolonged episodes of palpitation.

Aside from ventricular arrhythmia, consider other causes of palpitations and syncope:

> bradyarrhythmias

> atrial flutter with 1:1 conduction

> atrial fibrillation (AF) and Wolff–Parkinson–White syndrome

> aortic stenosis.

And do not forget the following:

> vasovagal syncope – the most common cause of presyncope and syncope

> epilepsy – a common cause of syncope, but there seem to be no features here to support that diagnosis

> acute blood loss – this will usually be obvious, but it is a mistake to miss the fact that the patient has had melaena.

Key point

Cardiac arrhythmias that can cause syncope:

> VT/fibrillation

> bradyarrhythmias

> atrial flutter with 1:1 conduction

> AF and Wolff–Parkinson–White syndrome.

Other relevant history

Ischaemic heart disease is a common cause of VT. In this situation there appears to be no previous history, but it is important to clarify whether or not there is a previous history of angina or myocardial infarction. If not, then specific symptoms of angina should be sought: 'What is the most exercise that you do? Have you had any tightness in your chest when you've been doing that recently?' It will also be appropriate to ask about risk factors for ischaemic heart disease.

Cardiomyopathy: most forms of this can cause VT. It is important to find out whether there is a history of breathlessness, lethargy or recent viral illness. An alcohol history should be taken, both for the current time and for the past.

Drugs (prescribed and non-prescribed): drug toxicity can provoke VT, eg digoxin, quinidine and catecholamines. Check the datasheet or *British National Formulary* for details of any drug that the patient is taking. Is arrhythmia reported as a side effect? Recreational drugs such as cocaine and ecstasy are associated with arrhythmias.

Family history: this is particularly pertinent in young patients presenting with arrhythmias. Always enquire if anyone in the family has had a similar problem, or if anyone has died suddenly and unexpectedly.

VT may be part of a primary electrophysiological disturbance or secondary to any pathology that produces structural changes in the ventricles. Any 'cardiac history' could therefore be relevant, eg valvular heart disease, congenital heart disease, right ventricular dysplasia or previous cardiac surgery.

Epilepsy: the history in this case points very clearly to a cardiac arrhythmia, but it would be sensible to enquire briefly to ensure that the patient does not have epilepsy and confirm that there are no features to suggest that this might be responsible for the current episodes

(such as aura, tongue biting or urinary incontinence).

Plan for investigation and management

Note: This must be explained to the patient in terms that they can understand.

In this case, examination of the patient was normal. You would plan as follows.

Electrocardiogram (ECG) – obtaining an ECG during an episode is a key objective in establishing a diagnosis (Fig 1). Beware of confusing VT and supraventricular tachycardia with aberrant conduction (see Section 3.1).

Key point

A broad complex tachycardia should always be treated as VT until proven otherwise.

Ambulatory monitoring – if the diagnosis is not apparent, monitoring for longer periods may be necessary (see Section 3.3).

Electrophysiological study – if symptoms are infrequent or doubt exists as to the diagnosis, then provocation of the rhythm during an electrophysiological study will provide definitive evidence (see Section 3.2).

Other – if VT is suspected, investigations to identify possible causes should be considered. Specifically, investigations should be orientated around identifying any structural cardiac abnormality (Table 1).

Further discussion

The patient is likely to be having presyncope associated with VT. Management will consist of treating any immediate episodes of VT (direct current (DC) shock / pharmacological cardioversion) and identification of the cause of the arrhythmia (see Section 2.2.2). If possible, the underlying cause should be corrected and the risk of arrhythmia then reassessed. In this case, it may turn out that the patient has significant coronary artery disease that warrants revascularisation, either

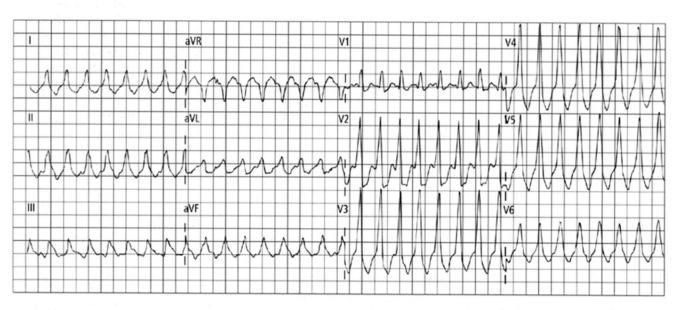

Fig 1 Twelve-lead ECG of VT. Note broad complexes and concordance across chest leads. Right bundle branch block (RBBB) morphology suggests left ventricular origin.

Table 1 Investigations to be considered to identify cardiac abnormality that may provoke ventricular arrhythmias

Investigation	Looking for
Chest X-ray	Cardiomegaly, cardiac silhouette and pulmonary oedema (Fig 2)
Electrolytes	Abnormalities of potassium or magnesium can be associated with arrhythmia
Echocardiogram	Cardiac function, valve structure/function and intracardiac masses (Fig 3)
Exercise ECG	Exercise-induced arrhythmias
Ischaemia study (stress echo/MRI or myocardial perfusion scan)	Looking for myocardial ischaemia
Coronary angiography if ischaemia identified	Coronary atherosclerosis and valvular function
CT or MRI	Mediastinal pathology and pericardial/myocardial disease

CT, computerised tomography; ECG, electrocardiogram; MRI, magnetic resonance imaging.

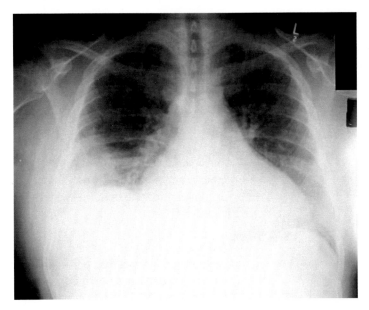

Fig 2 Chest radiograph of patient with dilated cardiomyopathy. The cardiothoracic ratio is increased. There is a pleural effusion at the right base.

with percutaneous intervention or coronary artery bypass grafting. Following this it would be important to reassess left ventricular function and consider an electrophysiological study to determine whether or not recurrent VT was likely (see Section 3.2). All patients with VT should be assessed to see whether they would benefit from an implantable cardioverter defibrillator (ICD) (see Section 3.4).

In those patients who do not have an indication for an ICD, either catheter ablation or pharmacological therapy

may be considered. It is essential to monitor the patient to ensure suppression of the arrhythmia; symptomatology is not always adequate because the drugs may slow but not prevent the VT, thus making it better tolerated or unnoticed. Monitoring will usually be by ambulatory ECG recording, but exercise testing if the arrhythmia is exercise induced or provocation at electrophysiological study may be appropriate in some cases.

1.1.2 Breathlessness and ankle swelling

Letter of referral to the cardiology outpatient clinic

Dear Doctor,
Re: Professor Freddie Walsh, aged 48 years

Thank you for seeing this professor of mathematics who has a 3-month history of progressive exertional dyspnoea, fatigue and peripheral oedema. He has generally been fit and well without prior history. His father died in his 40s of 'a large heart'. He is not taking routine medication, although I have started him today on furosemide 40 mg once a day. Please assess the cause of his symptoms.

Yours sincerely,

Introduction

These symptoms are most commonly caused by cardiac or pulmonary disease. The cause usually becomes apparent early in the history: subsequent questions, examination and investigation should be directed to providing confirmatory details.

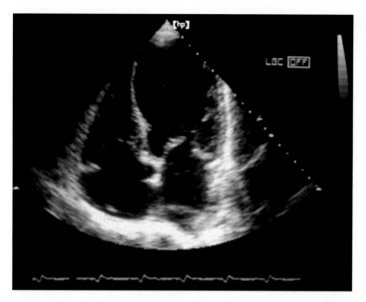

Fig 3 Echocardiogram demonstrating dilated cardiomyopathy. This is a 'four-chamber' view with both ventricles dilated, particularly the left ventricle (seen in the centre at the top).

The common differential diagnoses are given in Table 2. Consider the main causes of chronic heart failure when taking the history. It is important to assess the impact of symptoms on general daily activities, including work.

Poor rate control of atrial fibrillation is also a relatively common cause of breathlessness and ankle oedema. It is well known that patients with atrial fibrillation might not experience palpitations but can present with decompensated cardiac failure.

History of the presenting problem

If the following do not emerge spontaneously, make specific enquiry about them:

> Chest pain: if present, does this sound like ischaemic cardiac pain or like pleurisy?

> Cough/sputum: has it been present and has there been haemoptysis?

> Wheeze: but note that this is not synonymous with airway disease – it may occur in pulmonary oedema when it is known as 'cardiac asthma'.

Hazard
Asthma is not the only cause of wheezing.

Cardiovascular system
Progressive breathlessness associated with orthopnoea, paroxysmal nocturnal dyspnoea and cough productive of clear, frothy sputum would suggest a cardiac cause. The ankle swelling in cardiac failure is usually bilateral and symmetrical, but it is not uncommon for one ankle to swell initially.

A preceding episode of severe central chest pain at rest, particularly if occurring against a background of stable angina, would suggest a precipitating myocardial infarction (MI). A 'really bad episode of indigestion' may have been something different.

Has the patient been started on diuretic therapy: has this helped? A good response would support but not prove a cardiac cause for the symptoms.

Is there any history of palpitations?

Table 2	Differential diagnosis of ankle swelling and breathlessness
Cardiac	**Left ventricular dysfunction** **Valvular heart disease** Atrial fibrillation Pericardial effusion/constriction Cyanotic congenital heart disease High-output cardiac failure secondary to anaemia
Pulmonary	**Chronic airway or parenchymal lung disease (cor pulmonale)** Chronic thromboembolic pulmonary disease Primary pulmonary hypertension
Gastrointestinal	Liver failure Protein-losing enteropathy
Renal	Nephrotic syndrome Chronic renal failure
Endocrine	Hypothyroidism

Note: Most common causes are in bold.

Respiratory system

The development of increasing breathlessness and ankle swelling may indicate the development of cor pulmonale in a man with long-standing respiratory disorder. His symptoms are said to have started only 3 months ago, but what was he like before then? What is the most vigorous exercise he ever took? Three months ago was his breathing more laboured than that of his wife, family or friends?

Stepwise progression (sudden deterioration followed by periods of stability) should raise the suspicion of multiple recurrent pulmonary embolism (PE), even in the absence of pleuritic chest pain or haemoptysis.

Other relevant history

It is clearly important to establish any history of cardiovascular or respiratory disease. Ask about the following:

> rheumatic fever or history of a cardiac murmur

> recurrent asthma/bronchitis or any other respiratory problem

> smoking, which is obviously a substantial risk factor for both chronic airway disease and ischaemic heart disease

> alcohol intake, which is a risk factor for cardiomyopathy – ask: 'How much alcohol do you drink now? Have you ever been a heavy drinker in the past?'

> previous blood pressure (BP) measurements: untreated hypertension can lead to left ventricular failure

> previous cardiac surgery might be suggestive of impaired left ventricular function or constrictive pericarditis.

While the general practitioner's (GP's) letter has stated that the patient was not taking any regular medication, it is essential to confirm this and ensure that he has not been taking non-prescribed treatment that may be causing or exacerbating his symptoms, eg non-steroidal anti-inflammatory drugs (NSAIDs).

A detailed family history is particularly important in this case. His father died at a young age of presumed cardiomyopathy ('a large heart'). This might reflect a familial dilated cardiomyopathy or alternatively premature coronary artery disease.

Plan for investigation and management

Note: This must be explained to the patient in terms that they can understand.

After explaining to the patient that you would normally complete a full examination, plan the following baseline investigation.

ECG

A routine ECG is very helpful. If it is completely normal this would be against a diagnosis of chronic heart failure. Other abnormalities may help elucidate the aetiology of the patient's symptoms:

> a dominantly negative P wave in lead V1, reflecting left atrial hypertrophy – an indirect sign of left heart dysfunction (Fig 4)

> right ventricular hypertrophy (right bundle branch block (RBBB) with dominant R waves in V1) secondary to any cause of pulmonary hypertension

> low voltages and electrical alternans, which occur with a large pericardial effusion

> atrial arrhythmias: common in both cardiac and pulmonary disease

> previous MI, left bundle branch block (LBBB) or poor R-wave progression indicating left ventricular disease.

Chest radiograph

In the context of an elevated jugular venous pressure (JVP):

> A large heart should prompt echocardiography (Fig 5).

> Are there signs of pulmonary oedema?

> If the heart size is normal, inspect the lung fields closely for evidence of chronic obstructive airway disease or parenchymal lung disease.

> If the heart size and lung fields are both normal, consider PE or pericardial constriction.

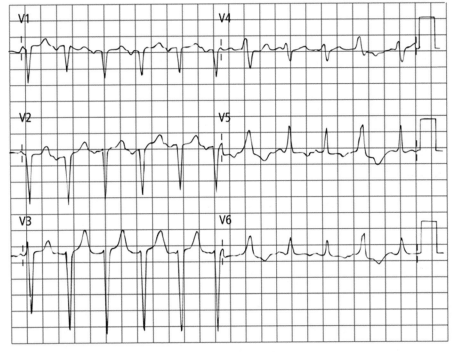

Fig 4 ECG showing left atrial strain (inverted P wave in V1) and partial LBBB in a patient with severe congestive cardiac failure secondary to alcoholic cardiomyopathy.

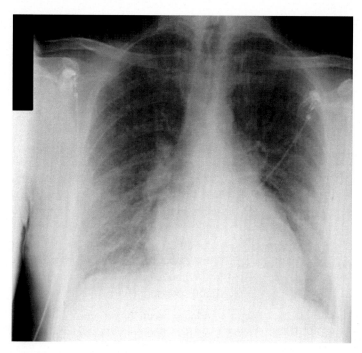

Fig 5 Chest radiograph showing cardiomegaly and pulmonary oedema in a patient with congestive cardiac failure caused by severe mitral regurgitation. Note cardiomegaly and enlarged left atrium.

If chronic heart failure is suspected and supported by initial investigations, eg abnormal ECG and chest radiograph, then initial management might include the adjustment of diuretic dose and commencement of an angiotensin-converting enzyme inhibitor (ACEI). According to the patient's symptoms and ejection fraction further medications can also be added such as, beta-blockers, aldosterone antagonists (spironolactone or eplerenone) and ivabradine (if sinus rhythm and heart rate >70 beats per minute). The patient should be reviewed with results in due course, but remember that renal function should be monitored in the interim. This should occur approximately 1–2 weeks after starting ACEI treatment (Section 2.3), with advice given to the GP to stop the ACEI if serum creatinine rises by more than 20%.

Further discussion

The impact of symptoms on daily living are very important. Recommendations regarding work and exercise should all be discussed. Education with particular emphasis on the rationale for treatment may help compliance. Involvement of a specialist heart-failure nurse is extremely helpful. The role of the specialist heart-failure nurse is (1) to educate the patients further and help them manage with their chronic condition in the community and (2) to up-titrate the medications to their maximum tolerated doses.

If the patient were to deteriorate despite full medical therapy then cardiac resynchronisation therapy (+/- implantable cardioverter defibrillator – see Section 3.4 – or referral for transplant assessment might be required – see Section 2.3).

Blood tests

Check the full blood count (FBC), electrolytes and renal, liver and thyroid function tests and brain natriuretic peptide (BNP), if available.

Urinalysis

Do not forget this simple test. If there is significant proteinuria on dipstick testing (>2++), then nephrotic syndrome is possible. In this case check serum albumin and urinary albumin:creatinine ratio or 24-hour urinary protein excretion. Remember that proteinuria of up to 1 g/day (occasionally more) can be caused by severe cardiac failure.

Echocardiogram

This is most useful for ruling out significant valvular or left ventricular disease. If a pericardial effusion is found, then careful clinical and echocardiographic assessment is required to judge whether this is contributing to his symptoms. Assessment of right heart function is largely subjective, but reasonably accurate indirect measurements of pulmonary artery systolic pressure can be obtained. Echocardiography may suggest pericardial constriction or restrictive cardiomyopathy, which requires further investigation such as magnetic resonance imaging (MRI) and/or cardiac catheterisation for confirmation.

Other more specialist investigations may be required and will be directed by the clinical features and initial investigations. These include cardiac catheterisation (for coronary artery anatomy and valvular dysfunction) and spiral computerised tomography (CT) scanning (for PE).

1.1.3 Breathlessness and exertional presyncope

Dear Doctor,

Re: Miss Susan Ward, aged 38 years

Thank you for seeing this accountant who is currently out of work. Over the last few months she has complained of gradually worsening fatigue and exertional dyspnoea. A year ago she was fit and active but is now unable to jog or attend her usual exercise classes. There has been no improvement with bronchodilator therapy.
She is extremely anxious about an episode last week when she nearly fainted while hurrying for a train to a job interview. Please advise on further management.

Yours sincerely,

Introduction
There are suggestions in this history that stress or anxiety may be contributing to this patient's symptoms, but your primary concern should be to exclude the significant organic conditions that can present insidiously like this, shown in Table 3.

> **!** **Hazard**
> Exertional syncope or presyncope is a symptom to be taken seriously. It usually indicates an inability to increase the cardiac output appropriately as a result of a fixed obstruction or ventricular dysfunction.

Table 3 Differential diagnoses of exertional dyspnoea and presyncope

Pathophysiology	Specific conditions
Left ventricular outflow tract obstruction	HCM Aortic subvalvular/valvular/supravalvular stenosis
Pulmonary hypertension	Primary pulmonary hypertension Secondary, eg to respiratory disease, pulmonary thromboembolism or mitral valve disease (see Section 2.12.2)
RV outflow tract obstruction	Infundibular/pulmonary stenosis
Left ventricular dysfunction	See Section 2.3
Pericardial compromise of cardiac filling	Effusion Constriction
Anaemia	–
Sustained arrhythmia	Atrial fibrillation Complete heart block

HCM, hypertrophic cardiomyopathy; RV, right ventricular.

Although not usually associated with exertional dyspnoea, other causes of syncope and sudden cardiac death in young subjects such as arrhythmogenic right ventricular (RV) dysplasia and QT prolongation should also be considered. An accurate and detailed family history is imperative.

Fatigue is a non-specific symptom of multi-factorial aetiology, but is a common limiting symptom in patients with heart failure and valvular disease.

History of the presenting problem
Ask the patient the following:

> 'Are you limited by fatigue (this may indicate low cardiac output), breathlessness or by something else (if so what?)'

> 'How far can you walk/run?' 'How many flights of stairs can you climb?' Be specific about this, and try to get a feeling for the pace of progression by asking: 'How does this compare with last Christmas / during your summer holidays?'

> 'Have there been any other instances of syncope/presyncope, and exactly what were the circumstances?' It is important to establish the environment in which they occurred (eg warm and not having eaten, or following alcohol might suggest vagal component) and as to whether there was any warning.

Ask specifically about the following associated symptoms:

> Chest pain: if present, is this pleuritic or anginal? This woman is young for ischaemic heart disease, but anginal pain can be associated with pulmonary hypertension. This is thought to originate from the hypertrophied (and therefore relatively hypoxic) RV. Rare other causes include anomalous origins of coronary arteries.

> Haemoptysis: a feature of pulmonary hypertension, but could also indicate PE.

> Cough/wheeze/sputum: features that would suggest chronic lung disease.

- Orthopnoea/paroxysmal nocturnal dyspnoea: suggests incipient pulmonary oedema.

- Palpitations: see Sections 1.1.1 and 1.1.2.

- Ankle oedema / calf swelling or tenderness: unilateral problems raise the possibility of venous thromboembolism; bilateral swelling suggests RV failure.

- Raynaud's phenomenon: this may be present in autoimmune rheumatic disease and also in 10% of women with primary pulmonary hypertension (PPH).

- Any features that would suggest autoimmune rheumatic disease, eg joint pains and rashes.

Other relevant past history

Enquire specifically about a history of the following:

- venous thromboembolism

- rheumatic fever or 'heart murmur'

- any problems during a previous pregnancy (if relevant, see below)

- chest trauma or tuberculosis – these may lead to pericardial problems

- respiratory disease.

Also ask about the following:

- smoking

- alcohol

- pregnancy – many previously silent cardiorespiratory conditions manifest themselves in pregnancy because of the physiological changes it engenders

- other risk factors for ischaemic heart disease (eg hypertension, smoking, hypercholesterolaemia, family history and diabetes)

- other risk factors for PE (eg immobility and clotting abnormalities).

Drug history

Ask her directly about the use of the following:

- Oral contraceptive: this carries a risk factor for thromboembolism.

- Appetite suppressants: these have been implicated in valve disease and pulmonary hypertension.

- Cardiotoxic chemotherapy.

- Cocaine: this can cause left ventricular dysfunction and pulmonary hypertension.

Family history

A detailed family history is important. Ask broad questions such as 'has anyone in your family died suddenly at a young age?', and specifically consider:

- premature ischaemic heart disease

- PE

- hypertrophic cardiomyopathy (HCM)

- pulmonary hypertension.

Social history

Stress may be a contributory factor. Ask questions regarding work (financial consequences of currently being unemployed), the implications of looking for a new job and about her general home circumstances.

Plan for investigation and management

Note: This must be explained to the patient in terms that they can understand.

 Key point

The echocardiogram is the key investigation in the patient with dyspnoea and syncope on exertion.

Explain that you would carry out a full clinical examination before conducting the following investigations.

ECG

Note the rhythm, axis, and any atrial or ventricular hypertrophy (see Section 3.1). LBBB is commonly associated with a dilated left ventricle (LV).

Chest radiograph

Note the heart size and shape, pulmonary arteries, lung fields and any valve calcification or pleural effusions.

Echocardiography

Enables visualisation of ventricular dimensions, hypertrophy and function, together with outflow tracts and valves (with gradients) and any intracardiac shunt or pericardial effusion. If there is significant pulmonary hypertension, a dilated, hypertrophied RV – compressing the LV into a D shape (Fig 6) – can usually be seen and the presence of tricuspid regurgitation enables the estimation of pulmonary artery pressure.

Ambulatory monitoring

To exclude tachyarrhythmias, particularly if structural abnormalities are found on echo.

Oxygen saturation

Check pulse oximetry. Perform arterial blood gases if the oxygen saturation is <95% or the patient looks cyanosed.

Blood tests

Check FBC, electrolytes, renal and liver function, glucose, cholesterol and inflammatory markers – C-reactive protein (CRP) and erythrocyte sedimentation rate (ESR). Other tests for autoimmune rheumatic disease may be indicated.

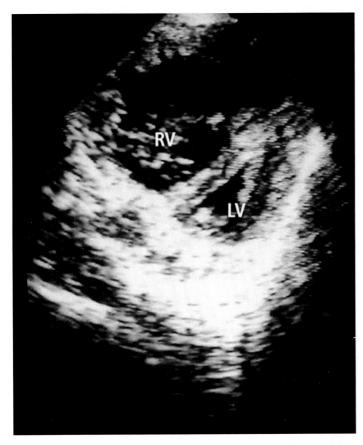

Fig 6 Short axis echocardiographic view of a patient with PPH showing the high pressure, dilated right ventricle (RV) compressing the left ventricle (LV) into a characteristic D shape. (Courtesy of Dr LM Shapiro.)

encourage the patient to maintain activity. Make sure you retain an open mind and keep her under review on at least one further occasion. If exercise limitation persists, then an exercise test (with monitoring of arterial oxygen saturation) can be valuable in providing reassurance that it is safe to resume previous levels of activity.

Further discussion

Exertional breathlessness is a common reason for referral to cardiology clinics. Identifying patients with significant pathology can sometimes be difficult, and even if patients do have genuine pathology, anxiety may influence how their symptoms are manifested. Exertional syncope should be taken seriously even in a young, apparently fit individual; in rare cases it can precede sudden cardiac death. Initial investigations should be ordered on an urgent basis, particularly if the ECG is abnormal.

If hypertrophic obstructive cardiomyopathy (HOCM) is diagnosed, it will be important to ask about children and other family members because issues of screening will need to be considered and discussed. This is generally best performed via a specialist service with trained counsellors.

Urinalysis
Look specifically for protein, blood and glucose. Could there be a multisystem inflammatory condition?

Others
If the echocardiogram suggests pulmonary hypertension but no cause is apparent, further investigations are needed (see Section 2.12.1). These should initially be directed towards excluding secondary causes of pulmonary hypertension. If a cause is

not discovered and the diagnosis of PPH is made, other investigations, eg right heart catheterisation, are used to determine prognosis and optimise treatment. Consider pulmonary function tests.

Further management will depend on the specific diagnosis. Urgent referral for specialist care is required if a structural cardiac abnormality is found, eg HCM or pulmonary hypertension. By contrast, if examination and investigations are normal, provide reassurance and

> **!** **Hazard**
> Do not forget that a diagnosis of HOCM or other genetic condition has implications for the rest of the family – not just for the patient in front of you.

1.1.4 Dyspnoea, ankle oedema and cyanosis

Dear Doctor,
Re: Mr Rob Owen, aged 45 years

Many thanks for assessing this reclusive 45-year-old man. Despite having been registered at the practice for over 10 years, he has recently presented for the first time. His major complaint was ankle swelling that has prevented him from putting on his shoes on. I was, however, surprised to find that he was centrally cyanosed and moderately dyspnoeic. Many thanks for your urgent help in investigating his symptoms.

Yours sincerely,

Introduction

Cyanosis can be of cardiac (right-to-left shunting) or respiratory origin, or (very rarely) associated with abnormal haemoglobin. If cyanosis develops over a long period it can be reasonably well tolerated, but may lead to other complications (see Section 2.7). The list of differential diagnoses for this patient includes:

> respiratory failure and cor pulmonale most commonly secondary to chronic obstructive pulmonary disease (COPD), but also bronchiectasis, pulmonary fibrosis or hypoventilation syndromes

> Eisenmenger's syndrome (see Section 2.7.3)

> primary pulmonary hypertension (not likely in a middle-aged man, see Section 2.12.1)

> secondary pulmonary hypertension of another cause (see Section 2.12)

> other congenital heart disease: patients with Ebstein's anomaly or mild cases of uncorrected tetralogy of Fallot may survive to middle age.

You need to determine the cause of his cyanosis by looking for evidence of respiratory disease, pulmonary hypertension and intracardiac shunts.

Key point

Causes of cyanosis in an adult:

> respiratory failure and cor pulmonale

> Eisenmenger's syndrome

> pulmonary hypertension – primary or secondary

> other congenital heart disease

> abnormal haemoglobin (very rare).

History of the presenting problem

Enquire about the duration and severity of the presenting symptoms, remembering that some patients – perhaps such as this man – may not be reliable witnesses, tending to deny ill health and generally play down the issues. Ask the following questions.

> How long has his ankle swelling been going on for?

> Has he noticed that he has become blue and, if so, when? Has he been a 'funny colour' for as long as he can remember? Have others commented on his complexion changing? If this has been very long standing, it suggests a cardiac rather than a respiratory explanation.

> Is he limited by breathlessness? Quantify his functional status: how

far can he go on the flat? Can he go up stairs? How many times does he have to stop?

Ask about the following.

> Has he suffered from dizziness, headache, visual disturbance or paraesthesiae? These could be symptoms of hyperviscosity, probably indicating secondary polycythaemia in this case.

> Has he had any episodes of syncope or presyncope? These are worrying signs in patients with pulmonary hypertension.

> Does he find it difficult to stay awake sometimes? Has he ever fallen asleep during the day when he was not trying to, eg when driving a car? Has anyone ever complained that he snores excessively when he sleeps? Does he wake up with headaches in the mornings? Any of these features would make you think that he might have obstructive sleep apnoea.

> Does he smoke? Does he have chronic cough, sputum or wheeze? Is there any history of asbestos exposure? These may suggest chronic lung disease.

Ask about features that would suggest thromboembolic disease:

> asymmetrical calf swelling or tenderness

> pleuritic chest pain

> haemoptysis.

Other relevant history

Ask specifically about the following.

> Does he know if he was a blue baby? Has he ever been told he has a heart murmur? Did he have rheumatic fever (try St Vitus' dance) as a child or as a young man?

> Tuberculosis and whooping cough: these would put him at risk of bronchiectasis.

> Did any of his siblings die young? If so, consider cystic fibrosis.

Also ask about the following.

> Symptoms of autoimmune rheumatic disease, which can be associated with interstitial lung disease.

> Use of prescribed medications and other drugs: are any associated with chronic lung disease or pulmonary hypertension?

> History of stroke or transient ischaemic attack. These would be uncommon in a patient aged 45 years, but may be attributable to paradoxical embolism from right-to-left shunting in this case.

Plan for investigation and management

Note: This must be explained to the patient in terms that they can understand.

 Key point
Cardiac cyanosis will not improve with maximal inspired oxygen, whereas respiratory cyanosis generally will.

Explain that after examining him you would want to organise the following tests.

Oxygen saturation and arterial blood gas
Check his pulse oximetry. Check arterial blood gases for PO_2 and PCO_2 when the patient is breathing air and (monitoring him continuously in case he retains CO_2 and is dependent on

hypoxic drive) after 10 minutes on high-flow oxygen.

ECG
Look for evidence of right-axis deviation, right atrial enlargement (P pulmonale) and right ventricular hypertrophy (RVH) (see Section 3.1).

Chest radiograph
Look for signs of pulmonary hypertension and chronic lung disease, in particular the hyperexpansion of COPD and the interstitial shadowing of parenchymal lung disease.

Blood tests
Check his FBC: is the patient polycythaemic? Check his electrolytes, renal and liver function. Chronically elevated right heart pressures can cause hepatic congestion and even cirrhosis. Other tests, eg for autoimmune rheumatic disorders, may be indicated in some cases.

Echocardiography
This is a key investigation to assess right ventricular (RV) function, assess RVH and pulmonary pressures and examine the heart valves. Care should be taken to look specifically for congenital abnormalities such as septal defects, abnormal anatomy and shunts.

Pulmonary function tests
Does the patient have severe obstructive or restrictive lung disease? Check spirometry, lung volumes and gas transfer.

Depending on the initial results consider the following:

> high-resolution CT scan of the chest (see Section 3.9)

> transoesophageal echocardiography for atrial septal defect if there is pulmonary hypertension and a shunt is suspected, but not

seen on transthoracic echo (see Section 3.11)

> ventilation–perfusion scan or CT pulmonary angiogram scan if pulmonary thromboembolism is considered possible (see Section 3.9)

> MRI of the heart to define anatomy more clearly (see Section 3.8.2).

Management depends on the underlying condition. Note that in all patients with pulmonary hypertension, great care must be taken with the use of diuretics for oedema. The risk of this is that overzealous fluid removal can lead to reduction in RV filling pressure and thereby cause circulatory collapse.

 Hazard
> Swollen ankles do not always mean diuretics are indicated.

> Be *very* careful with diuretics in patients with pulmonary hypertension: overzealous fluid removal can cause circulatory collapse.

Further discussion
The optimal management of severe pulmonary hypertension requires early referral to a specialist clinic. Patients with Eisenmenger's syndrome should be referred to a cardiologist with an interest in adult congenital heart disease; other patients may benefit from referral to a specialist pulmonary hypertension service. If anticoagulation is required it will be important to ensure that the patient will be compliant with monitoring and understand the key importance of this.

1.1.5 Chest pain and recurrent syncope

Dear Doctor,

Re: Mr John Morris, aged 65 years

This man works as a farmer and presents with a 3-month history of syncopal episodes and exertional chest pain. He has been seen in the practice over the last few years with a number of minor ailments, but has no significant past medical history.

I would be grateful if you would see him and advise on further investigation and management.

Yours sincerely,

Introduction

The history of syncope and exertional chest pain strongly suggests a cardiac problem, with syncope due to outflow tract obstruction or arrhythmia and pain due to cardiac ischaemia. Severe pain can sometimes cause vasovagal syncope, and patients on vasodilatory medications can develop orthostatic syncope. However, neither of these would seem likely from the history given.

Key point

Cardiac causes of syncope:

> vasovagal
> arrhythmia
> aortic stenosis
> hypertrophic obstructive cardiomyopathy
> orthostatic hypotension.

History of the presenting problem

Syncope

Ask the patient for as detailed an account of the syncopal episodes as they can give.

> Outflow tract obstruction resulting from vasodilatation and reflex bradycardia usually occurs on exertion.

> Arrhythmias can occur at any time, although some may be provoked by exertion due to ischaemia or increased release of catecholamines. Was the patient aware of his heart beating in an unusual way at any time?

> Orthostatic hypotension can occur after variable periods of standing and may be prominent after exertion.

> Vasovagal syncope is typically preceded by a definite prodrome of worsening nausea and sweating.

Chest pain

Confirm the nature of the pain: it is important to be clear that he is experiencing angina rather than any other pain. Establish quickly its character, radiation etc.

Other features

Ask directly if any witnesses have told the patient what happened when he collapsed. Did he change colour? If so, this suggests a cardiac cause. Did anyone check his pulse? This may firmly establish the diagnosis if done by a reliable witness. And were there any features to suggest epilepsy (aura, limb shaking, tongue biting and urinary incontinence)? But remember that seizures can occasionally be secondary to a cardiac cause of collapse.

Other relevant history

Does the patient have a history of ischaemic heart disease, valvular heart disease or arrhythmia?

Has he ever had a heart attack? Has he ever seen a specialist for his heart? Has he ever been aware of his heart beating fast or abnormally?

Does he have any risk factors for ischaemic heart disease? Does he smoke? Is there a family history of this condition? Does he have diabetes or high blood cholesterol?

Ask specifically about rheumatic fever. This usually occurs in childhood and may have involved a sore throat, prolonged bed rest and aching joints. Also, although clearly not relevant in this case, note if a patient has congenital heart disease such as Fallot's, which can be associated with exertional syncope.

At the age of 65 years and with the history of chest pain the following conditions are not likely, but check if there is any family history of sudden death, especially at a young age. If there is, this may suggest hypertrophic obstructive cardiomyopathy, long QT syndrome with associated arrhythmias, Brugada syndrome or arrhythmogenic right ventricular dysplasia.

Plan for investigation and management

Note: This must be explained to the patient in terms that they can understand.

The diagnosis will be aided by the examination and confirmed by the following investigations.

ECG

Is it normal? Is there any evidence of heart block or other arrhythmia? Measure the PR interval and QRS durations. Is there evidence of left ventricular hypertrophy (LVH) (Fig 7a)? This could suggest aortic stenosis, hypertrophic obstructive cardiomyopathy or dilated cardiomyopathy, or a previous myocardial infarct, which may predispose to ventricular arrhythmia (Fig 7b). Are there other abnormalities such as delta waves or long QT interval (Fig 7c)?

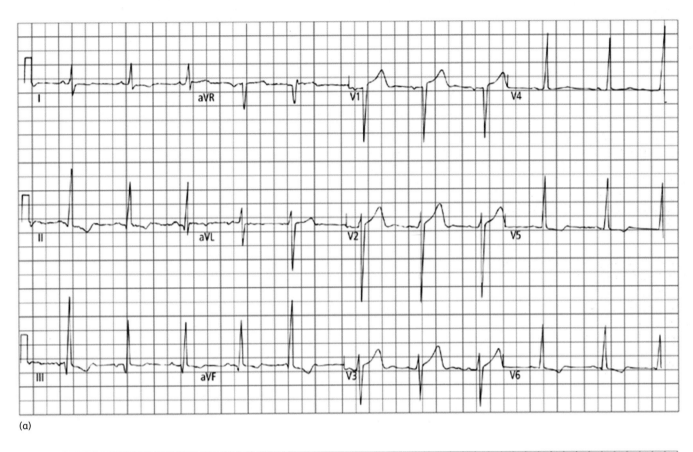

(a)

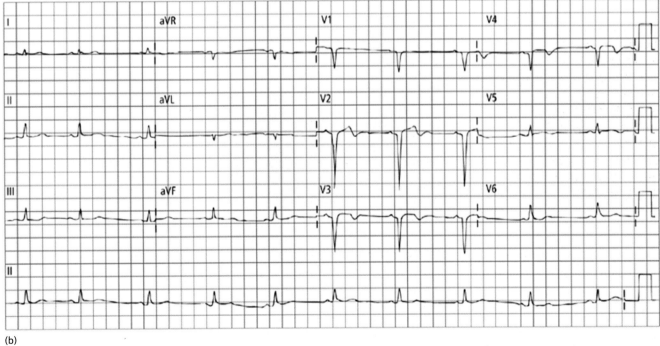

(b)

Fig 7 Twelve-lead ECGs: **(a)** LVH; **(b)** old anterior myocardial infarction.

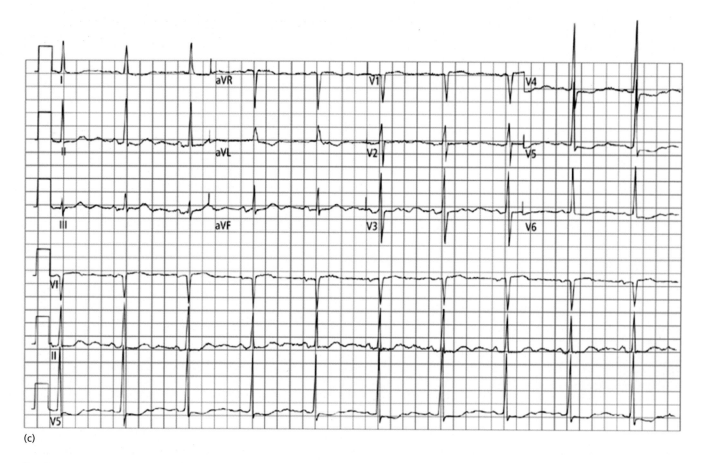

(c)

Fig 7 cont Twelve-lead ECGs: **(c)** long QT.

Chest radiograph
Look for increased cardiothoracic ratio (>0.5) suggestive of cardiomegaly and for evidence of aortic valve calcification.

Echocardiography
This will determine the presence of aortic valve stenosis, left ventricular outflow obstruction and the left ventricular function, which if poor may predispose to ventricular arrhythmias (Fig 8).

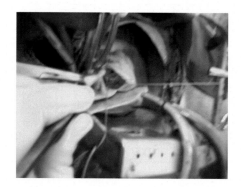

Fig 8 Stenotic aortic valve seen at operation prior to replacement.

Exercise testing
Physiological stress testing with ECG monitoring on a treadmill/bike with or without echocardiography can provide valuable information regarding aetiology of symptoms and risk stratify patients. Note that patients with hypertrophic cardiomyopathy who demonstrate a hypotensive responsive to exercise are at increased risk of sudden death.

Ambulatory ECG monitoring
Prolonged monitoring, initially with a
24-hour tape, may pick up ventricular or
other arrhythmias, which can sometimes
be revealed on standard 12-lead
recordings (Fig 9).

Blood tests
These are not likely to be critical
investigations in this case, but anaemia
may worsen the symptoms of ischaemic
heart disease or aortic valve disease,
and assessment of cardiovascular risk

factors (glucose and cholesterol) would
be appropriate.

If doubt as to the diagnosis remains,
then further tests to be considered
would including tilt-table testing
(vasovagal syncope may be provoked,
with either bradycardia or hypotension
initiating the event) and coronary
angiography.

If you consider that the patient may
be at risk of ventricular arrhythmias

then consider admitting him for
further investigation and management
(see Section 1.1.2).

Further discussion

Driving
Patients with syncope cannot drive
until they satisfy the Driver and
Vehicle Licensing Agency (DVLA – UK)
that recurrence is unlikely (see
Section 2.19).

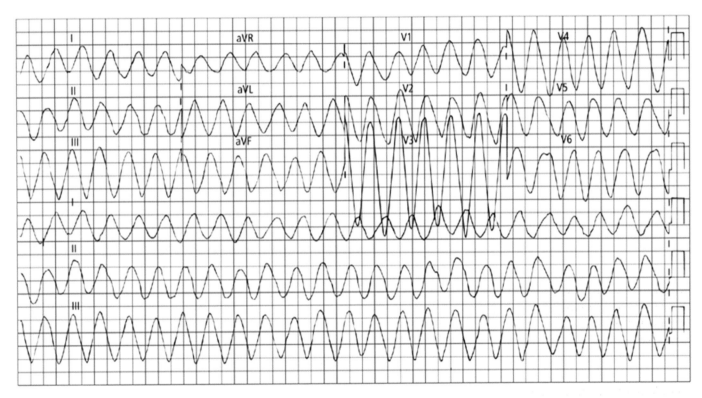

Fig 9 Twelve-lead ECG showing ventricular tachycardia.

General advice

Advise the patient to avoid heavy lifting and vigorous exercise until a diagnosis is made and treatment established.

1.1.6 Hypertension found at routine screening

Dear Doctor,

Re: Mrs Joy King, aged 30 years

This African-Caribbean woman attended the family planning clinic to obtain a prescription for the oral contraceptive pill (OCP). However, her blood pressure (BP) readings on numerous occasions are typically around 180/100 mmHg. She smokes between 10 and 20 cigarettes a day but drinks minimal amounts of alcohol. She has no other known medical problems, but there is strong family history of high BP with her mother, older sister and one maternal aunt all being treated for the condition. Her father died from a haemorrhagic stroke when she was a child. On examination she is overweight with a body mass index (BMI) of 31 kg/m^2 (normal range 18–25). Please can you advise on further investigation and management?

Yours sincerely,

Introduction

Hypertension is a common problem, especially in the African-Caribbean population. Although there may be multiple causes for her father's death from a haemorrhagic stroke,

uncontrolled and unrecognised hypertension is certainly a possibility. The initial approach in managing this patient should be directed towards confirming the diagnosis of hypertension (ie to ensure there is no element of 'white coat' hypertension) and, if hypertension is confirmed, treating the BP. This should then be followed by an assessment of whether there are secondary causes for her hypertension, followed by advice and management of her other vascular risk factors (her being overweight and smoking) and a decision regarding prescribing the OCP.

The differential diagnosis of this woman's high BP reading is summarised in Table 4.

History of the presenting problem

Hypertension is usually asymptomatic until there is progression to end-organ damage. Some patients, on being given a diagnosis of hypertension, will ascribe many different and varied complaints to it. A multitude of symptoms, eg headache, epistaxis, tinnitus, dizziness and fainting, are often blamed on an elevated BP, but probably occur with similar frequency in those whose BP is normal.

It is important to elicit any potential complications of untreated hypertension:

Cardiovascular system

Hypertension initially results in left ventricular hypertrophy (LVH), followed by diastolic and finally systolic left ventricular dysfunction. Pursue a history of shortness of breath on exertion or at rest, as well as one of pulmonary oedema. Enquire about swelling of ankles. Other non-specific symptoms can include palpitations and potentially chest pain (if associated with ischaemic heart disease, although this is unlikely in this patient).

Table 4 Differential diagnosis of hypertension	
Comment	**Diagnosis**
Common	Essential hypertension False elevation as a result of inadequate BP cuff size Isolated clinic ('white coat') hypertension
Must consider	Renal hypertension Renovascular hypertension Primary hyperaldosteronism (Conn's syndrome)[1] Phaeochromocytoma[1] Coarctation of the aorta[1]
Other causes[2]	Cushing's syndrome Acromegaly Polycystic ovarian syndrome Pre-eclampsia (must be considered when hypertension develops in pregnancy)

BP, blood pressure.
1 Rare or very rare.
2 Hypertension not likely to be the dominant feature of these conditions.

Neurological system

Ask about any transient or prolonged episodes of weakness in any of her limbs, or problems with her speech or eye sight. The answers to these questions can rule out transient ischaemic attacks or a stroke. Ask whether the patient has had any episodes of loss of vision or blurred vision that may have been caused by retinal bleeds.

Peripheral vascular system

Ask about symptoms that might indicate intermittent claudication, although this would be extremely unlikely in a 30-year-old woman.

Other relevant history

Could there be a secondary cause of hypertension?

It is important to address specific symptoms which may point towards a secondary cause of high BP (Table 5).

In most cases, however, a secondary cause is not found and hypertension is classified as primary or 'essential'. A strong family history of hypertension would support the diagnosis of essential hypertension, therefore a detailed family history must always be pursued, or confirmed when it is stated (as in this case).

Cardiovascular risk factors

In any patient presenting with hypertension it is very important to assess other cardiovascular risk factors, including the following:

> smoking

> diabetes

> hyperlipidaemia

> family history of cardiovascular events

> alcohol consumption.

Plan for investigation and management

Note: This must be explained to the patient in terms that they can understand.

Key point

When investigating the patient with hypertension consider:

> Is there a secondary cause?

> Is there evidence of end-organ damage?

After examining her your strategy for investigation should be directed towards detecting secondary causes and identifying evidence of end-organ complications (see Section 2.17).

Table 5 Possible secondary causes of hypertension and relevant questions to be asked in the history	
Cause of hypertension	**History to be elicited**
Atheromatous renovascular disease	The presence of other atheromatous complications such as peripheral vascular disease and cerebrovascular disease increase the likelihood of renovascular hypertension. Ask: > Does she get pain in the legs on walking? > Has she had any neurological symptoms?
Renal parenchymal disease	> Has she ever had tests on her urine or kidneys (for instance during pregnancy or for insurance purposes)? > Has she ever been told that she had a problem with her kidneys? > Is there any family history of kidney disease? > Has she noticed any blood in her urine, or ever had bad swelling in her legs?
Phaeochromocytoma	> Ask about intermittent episodes of panic attacks (anxiety), sweating, tremors, palpitations and chest pain.
Primary hyperaldosteronism (Conn's syndrome)	There are no specific symptoms, but a history of muscle cramps secondary to low potassium levels, and possibly polyuria and polydipsia, may be relevant.
Cushing's syndrome	> Has she gained weight? > Has she noticed striae, or thinning of her hair or skin? > Does she bruise easily? > Any changes in menstrual cycle? > Has she been prescribed steroids?
Acromegaly	> Any change in her hand or foot size? > Has anyone commented on change in her facial appearance? > Has she noticed any change in vision? > Does she have any joint problems?
Drugs	> Has she taken any prescribed or non-prescribed medication? > Has she been eating lots of liquorice?

Note: It is very rare for a secondary cause of hypertension to be diagnosed from history alone, but the history can provide useful clues to follow.

ECG
Look particularly for evidence of LVH.

Urine
Dipsticks for proteinuria and haematuria. If positive for protein, quantification with a spot urine albumin:creatinine ratio or 24-hour collection is required. The presence of proteinuria and/or haematuria would be consistent with the patient having a renal disorder with secondary hypertension, or with renal damage caused by hypertension.

Blood tests
Check the FBC, electrolytes, renal and liver function, uric acid, fasting glucose and lipid profile. The most common cause of hypokalaemia is diuretic treatment, but low values are often found in untreated accelerated phase hypertension and in primary hyperaldosteronism (suspect only if patients are on no diuretic treatment). Is her renal function normal? Does she have glucose intolerance or diabetes? Is her cholesterol elevated?

Chest radiograph
Assess heart size and look for pulmonary oedema and possible (but very unlikely) radiographic signs of coarctation (Fig 10).

Echocardiography
This is more sensitive than the ECG at detecting LVH, especially if patients are of African-Caribbean descent (Fig 11). Look for evidence of diastolic and systolic left ventricular impairment.

Other tests may be appropriate depending on the findings of those detailed above:

Ambulatory blood pressure monitoring
This may be needed to confirm the diagnosis and exclude 'white coat' hypertension, the latter being suspected particularly in cases where the BP recorded in clinic is very high, but there seems to be no evidence of end-organ damage.

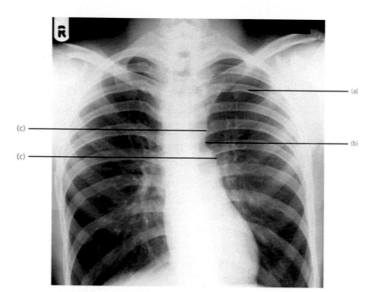

Fig 10 Chest X-ray of patient with coarctation of the aorta, showing **(a)** rib notching, **(b)** site of coarctation and **(c)** prestenotic and poststenotic dilation. (Reproduced with permission from Ray KK, Ryder REJ and Wellings RM, *An aid to radiology for the MRCP*. Oxford: Blackwell Science, 1999.)

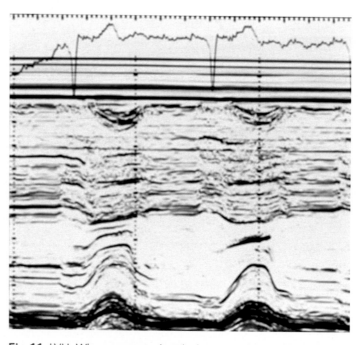

Fig 11 LVH. When compared with the normal parasternal M-mode (see Fig 119) it is evident that the interventricular septum is grossly thickened in this patient. (Courtesy of Dr J Chambers.)

Other specific tests may be required as dictated by the clinical setting to diagnose primary renal disease (serological tests or renal biopsy), renovascular disease (renal ultrasound and Doppler examination, or MRI angiography), Conn's syndrome (plasma renin and aldosterone levels) or phaeochromocytoma (24-hour urinary and blood catecholamine levels). See Section 2.17.

Management will consist of treating any underlying secondary cause of hypertension if present. Otherwise a stepwise approach to antihypertensive medication is most likely.

Further discussion

Do not forget to offer advice and treatment (where possible) to reduce other cardiovascular risk factors. Decisions regarding the treatment of hypertension (or hypercholesterolaemia) should never be taken in isolation. For example, in this case it is important that any treatment for high BP is combined with general lifestyle measures (in her case to stop smoking, to increase physical activity and to try and lose weight). Should she have an abnormal lipid profile this should also be actively managed with dietary advice (and possibly review by a dietitian) and statin therapy. It is only after addressing these issues that the choice of an OCP or other methods of contraception should be made on the basis of overall cardiovascular risk and benefits.

1.2 Clinical examination

1.2.1 Congestive heart failure

Instruction

This 78-year-old man has a 6-week history of progressive breathlessness, orthopnoea and swollen ankles – please examine his cardiovascular system.

General features

Look for cyanosis, anaemia, stigmata of chronic liver disease or nicotine-stained fingers.

Are there any features to suggest previous cardiac interventions, such as a sternotomy scar or presence of a pacemaker?

Although this is not a respiratory station, note the shape of the chest and whether it seems to expand normally as the patient breathes. Do appearances suggest chronic airways disease? If they do, and particularly if you find signs other than basal crackles when you listen to the patient's lungs, then a respiratory cause of breathlessness and oedema is likely (consider right heart failure of cor pulmonale).

Expose both arms fully to ensure that there are no fistulae present.

> **!** **Hazard**
> Oedema of the hands and face is a feature of hypoalbuminaemia and very rarely the result of congestive cardiac failure (Fig 12).

Cardiovascular examination

Key points to look for on cardiovascular examination are:

Signs of cardiac dysfunction

> Pulse – rate, rhythm, volume and character: a sinus tachycardia may be caused by anxiety or cardiac failure; consider specifically: is this man in atrial fibrillation (AF)? A low-volume pulse might indicate

cardiac failure or alternatively severe mitral regurgitation, but is there anything about the character to suggest either aortic stenosis or incompetence?

> BP – including pulsus paradoxus, which suggests pericardial effusion/ tamponade.

> JVP – is this raised? Check for the features of JVP, including the effect of respiration (eg increasing with inspiration in constrictive pericarditis and 'CV' waves in tricuspid regurgitation).

> Apex beat – is this displaced? Is it hyperdynamic, in keeping with a volume overloaded left ventricle (eg mitral or aortic incompetence)?

> Heart sounds – is there an S3 gallop? Are there murmurs (especially diastolic)?

> Lungs – are there basal crepitations? But remember that these are not specific for pulmonary oedema and cardiac failure.

Signs of pulmonary hypertension
This is suggested by the following:

> raised JVP

> left parasternal heave (palpable right ventricle (RV))

> loud pulmonary component of the second heart sound.

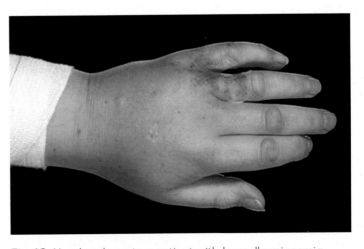

Fig 12 Hand oedema in a patient with hypoalbuminaemia.

It is very important to note the patient's weight, which is probably the most useful way to monitor the effect of treatment.

Also note whether one leg is much more swollen than the other, which might indicate deep venous thrombosis.

Key point

Examination of the JVP:

> Do not finish your examination until you have found out where the JVP is. Make sure that you correctly position the patient, ensuring that they are at 45 degrees with their head well supported by a pillow, thereby relaxing the neck muscles. Good lighting will help. Look for position, waveform characteristics (if in AF then large waves must be v waves) and the effect of respiration.

> Remember that it is possible to miss a markedly elevated JVP: if you cannot see it and the neck appears 'full', then look again when the patient is sitting up at 90 degrees.

Further discussion

Clinical diagnosis of heart failure can be difficult. Although any individual sign (eg elevated JVP) has a relatively low positive predictive value for the diagnosis, finding a constellation of signs makes left ventricular impairment much more likely. The diagnosis should always be confirmed by an objective assessment of cardiac function, generally in the form of an echocardiogram. Along with an ECG and a chest radiograph, this would be the first-line investigation to request in this case.

The following are important factors when considering the case of a patient with possible congestive cardiac failure.

> The presence of bilateral basal crackles on auscultation of the chest has a very poor positive predictive value for the presence of pulmonary oedema – a chest radiograph is much more accurate.

> Remember that marked abnormality of renal and liver function tests commonly occurs in cases of congestive cardiac failure, and does not necessarily indicate primary disease in these organs. Starting appropriate treatment (diuretics, angiotensin-converting enzyme inhibitors (ACEIs), beta-blockers, aldosterone antagonists etc) unloads the heart, improves the cardiac output and frequently results in improvement of renal and liver function tests.

> The severity of left ventricular dysfunction on echocardiography correlates poorly with the severity of the clinical syndrome of heart failure, but normal systolic left ventricular function on echocardiography should prompt a review of a diagnosis of heart failure.

Hazard

When the cause of breathlessness is not obvious, consider chronic thromboembolic pulmonary disease, which is a commonly missed diagnosis. Multiple small pulmonary emboli lead to progressive occlusion of the pulmonary arteriolar bed, classically presenting with breathlessness that becomes more severe in a stepwise manner. Pulmonary hypertension eventually leads to RV failure and ankle swelling. Prominent pulmonary arteries may be the only finding on a chest radiograph. Diagnosis is made by a lung ventilation–perfusion scan or a spiral CT of the chest.

1.2.2 Mechanical valve

Instruction

This man has had cardiac surgery – please examine his cardiovascular system.

General features

From the foot of the bed, can you hear the characteristic clicking sound of a ball and cage valve? Look for pallor or jaundice, which may be caused by haemolysis from a failing valve. Also check for bruising, which could suggest problems with anticoagulation use. Aside from the scar of cardiac surgery, look for scars on the upper chest suggestive of a pacemaker (atrioventricular block is more common following aortic valve surgery) and on the legs suggestive of vein harvest for coronary artery bypass grafting. Remember also to look for a mitral valvotomy under the left breast. Does the patient have any phenotypic features of conditions that are associated with aortic valve pathology, eg Marfan syndrome?

Cardiovascular examination

The key points to look for in the cardiovascular examination are:

> Pulse: check rate and rhythm – is the patient in sinus rhythm? Atrial fibrillation is very common after cardiac surgery. A collapsing pulse suggests significant aortic regurgitation (AR) and valve failure. A slow rising pulse suggests valvular stenosis.

> BP: a wide pulse pressure suggests AR and a narrow pulse pressure outflow tract obstruction (offer to check this at the end of your examination).

> Signs of congestive cardiac failure: an elevated JVP, displaced or prominent apex beat, parasternal heave, added heart sounds, basal crackles and ankle swelling may be a result of prosthetic valve failure.

> Mechanical aortic valve: if present the second heart sound will be prosthetic and loud. There will always be abnormal forward flow with a mechanical valve and therefore an ejection systolic murmur will be present, the intensity of which has no bearing on the function (or dysfunction) of the valve. Listen carefully for an early diastolic murmur suggestive of valve failure and remember that a shorter duration of the diastolic murmur indicates severe regurgitation.

> Mechanical mitral valve (MV): if present the first heart sound will be prosthetic and a diastolic flow murmur may be heard. However, these are not typically as loud as the prosthetic sound and flow murmur associated with a mechanical aortic valve. A systolic mitral regurgitant murmur may be due to a prosthetic or paraprosthetic leak.

> Biological valves: these do not produce the harsh metallic sounds of mechanical valves.

Further discussion

Prosthetic aortic or MVs can be mechanical or biological (Table 6).

Key point

All patients with mechanical valves require:

> lifelong anticoagulation

> advice regarding prevention of endocarditis.

All mechanical heart valves need anticoagulation to prevent valve thrombosis and the resulting complications. Currently, only warfarin has been proven to be a safe and effective anticoagulant in this setting. However, despite the best anticoagulation control

Table 6 Types of prosthetic heart valves	
Mechanical	**Biological**
Ball and cage (Starr–Edwards) Single disc (Björk–Shiley or Medtronic Hall) Bileaflet (St Jude or Carbomedics)	Porcine (Carpentier–Edwards) Pericardial Homograft Autologous (pulmonary autograft)

the incidence of systemic emboli is 1% per patient year. The recommended international normalised ratio (INR) range is 2.0–3.0 for bileaflet valves and 2.5–3.5 for other disc and Starr–Edwards valves. Risks of thrombosis are higher in the lower flow mitral area than in the higher flow aortic area.

Endocarditis is a feared complication of all prosthetic valves. The greatest risk of infection is immediately following surgery: from 12 months onwards the annual incidence is 0.4%. The causative organisms are most likely to be coagulase-negative staphylococci and *Staphylococcus aureus* in the early period (see Fig 72). The mortality from prosthetic valve endocarditis is 60% and the condition is difficult to treat with medical therapy alone, therefore urgent referral to a cardiothoracic centre is required. Recent UK guidance on endocarditis prophylaxis suggested that other than taking precautions regarding endocarditis prevention (good oral health, care during body piercing / tattooing), further antibiotic prophylaxis was not needed. This is a controversial area with many strong and differing views and guidelines may change in the future.

Haemolysis from mechanical valves is more common than from bioprosthetic valves. It may be acute or chronic, and may be related to valve failure. Presentation is typically with anaemia and mild jaundice. Blood films show a microangiopathic haemolytic picture. Infective endocarditis must be excluded. Management may vary from regular transfusions to repeating the valve surgery.

Replacement of a prosthetic valve should only be considered in patients who are symptomatic with objective evidence of valve failure. It is a high-risk procedure and may not provide a better outcome than an expectant approach in both old people and those with significant comorbidity.

1.2.3 Pansystolic murmur

Instruction

This man has a murmur – please examine his cardiovascular system.

General features

Comment on the patient's general appearance and in particular if he appears short of breath at rest, cyanosed or has a phenotype suggesting a particular valvular abnormality, eg Marfan syndrome (this can be associated with mitral regurgitation as well as aortic regurgitation). Look carefully for surgical scars, remembering especially that the left thoracotomy scar of mitral valvotomy is easy to miss (especially in women when they can be hidden under the fold of the breast).

Cardiovascular examination

Check for stigmata of endocarditis. Pay attention to dental hygiene. Check if patient is in atrial fibrillation. Look for signs of heart failure, in particular elevation of the JVP and displacement of the apex. Do not forget to examine for a parasternal heave suggesting pulmonary hypertension. Remember the following when trying to decide the cause of the pansystolic murmur:

> Mitral regurgitation: a thrusting displaced apex beat suggests volume overload of the left ventricle, which means that the murmur is probably mitral. The murmur will typically be loudest in expiration, most prominent at the apex and radiate to the axilla. A soft first heart sound and loud third sound would support the diagnosis.

> Ventricular septal defect (VSD): you should suspect this condition if the murmur is loudest in inspiration and best heard over the lower left sternal edge. In cases of VSD the apex is undisplaced, the first sound normal and no third heart sound is heard.

> Tricuspid regurgitation (TR): typically the murmur is loudest over the lower left sternal edge during inspiration. Giant v waves will be present and a pulsatile liver edge. The apex is not displaced and a third sound not heard.

Key point

Differential diagnosis of a pansystolic murmur:

> mitral regurgitation
> ventricular septal defect (VSD)
> tricuspid regurgitation (TR).

Further discussion

The commonest causes of mitral regurgitation are mitral valve (MV) prolapse and ischaemic heart disease. Other causes are rheumatic heart disease, previous mitral valvotomy and dilated cardiomyopathy.

Features of the examination that would suggest severe mitral regurgitation include a third heart sound, displaced apex beat, signs of heart failure and

signs of pulmonary hypertension. An echocardiogram will confirm diagnosis and (probably) aetiology, as well as the severity by giving information regarding the haemodynamic consequences of the mitral leak. This is particularly the case for left ventricular dilatation, impaired left ventricular systolic function and pulmonary hypertension.

Follow-up recommendations vary and are dependent on the severity of the mitral regurgitation, aetiology, left ventricular function as well as the overall potential for further intervention (eg valve replacement/repair). Patients with moderate disease should be reviewed annually in a cardiac clinic. All patients should be given advice regarding preventative measures to avoid endocarditis. Many patients with mitral regurgitation will require lifelong anticoagulation due to coexisting atrial fibrillation.

Surgery is indicated in those with severe mitral regurgitation and symptoms. For asymptomatic cases, surgery (to improve prognosis) is recommended if there is evidence of left ventricular dilatation, impaired left ventricular systolic function or pulmonary hypertension. The outcome is generally better if the MV can be repaired rather than replaced, but suitability for repair will depend on the complexity of the valvular disease. Coronary angiography is required prior to surgery to look for coexistent coronary artery disease for which concomitant bypass surgery may be considered.

1.2.4 Mitral stenosis

Instruction

This woman has had increasing shortness of breath over the past 6 months – please examine her cardiovascular system.

General features

Comment on the patient's general wellbeing and in particular if she is short of breath at rest or cyanosed. Look for surgical scars, in particular a mitral valvotomy under the left breast. Does the patient have a malar flush?

Cardiovascular examination

Check for stigmata of endocarditis. Pay attention to dental hygiene. In mitral stenosis (MS) the following may be seen:

> Pulse – atrial fibrillation (AF) is very common in MS.

> Signs of heart failure – elevated JVP and giant v waves due to secondary tricuspid incompetence (also hepatomegaly, ascites and ankle oedema).

> Apex beat – tapping (palpable first heart sound) that is not displaced.

> Parasternal heave – suggests pulmonary hypertension.

> Accentuation of first heart sound may occur when leaflets are flexible.

> Loud pulmonary second heart sound due to pulmonary hypertension.

> Opening snap (OS) – caused by sudden tensing of the valve leaflets after they have completed their opening excursion; the time from second heart sound to OS varies inversely with the severity of the stenosis (shorter duration = more severe stenosis).

> Mid-diastolic rumbling murmur (with pre-systolic accentuation if the patient is in sinus rhythm) localised to the apex and heard loudest in expiration with the patient in the left lateral position. This low-pitched murmur is best heard using the bell of the stethoscope. The severity of the stenosis is related to the duration of the murmur, not intensity (more severe = longer duration).

> A Graham Steell early diastolic murmur due to secondary pulmonary regurgitation may be heard.

Further discussion

By far the commonest cause of MS is rheumatic heart disease. The murmur of MS may be difficult to hear, so be alert for clues prior to auscultation. If a patient in PACES is in AF and their face looks as though it has a malar flush, then MS is much more likely to be the diagnosis than it might be in routine clinical practice. Note that the murmur of MS is accentuated with exercise, but tachycardia may make it more difficult to hear. The presence of an opening snap suggests the mitral valve (MV) is still pliant. The closer the murmur is to the second heart sound, the more severe the stenosis. AF can exacerbate and worsen symptoms (particularly in the setting of a rapid ventricular response) due to a shortened diastolic filling period and loss of atrial kick, therefore adequate rate control is important.

Transthoracic echocardiography confirms the diagnosis and allows an assessment of severity (see Section 2.5.3).

Patients with mild or moderate disease should be reviewed annually in a cardiac clinic. All patients should be given advice regarding good dental hygiene. All patients with MS require lifelong anticoagulation with warfarin unless there are very pressing contraindications.

Surgery is indicated for severe MS with limiting symptoms, embolic events or an episode of pulmonary oedema. If this is planned, a transoesophageal echocardiogram should be performed to assess the degree of valve calcification, to check for the presence of mitral incompetence and to examine for thrombus in the left atrial appendage. Patients with minimal MV calcification –

no more than mild mitral regurgitation and no left atrial appendage thrombus – should be considered for percutaneous mitral valvotomy. Otherwise, the patient requires MV replacement. In general, mechanical and not tissue MV prostheses are required (Table 6). Coronary angiography is required prior to surgery to look for coexistent coronary artery disease.

1.2.5 Aortic stenosis

Instruction

This woman has chest tightness on effort – please examine her cardiovascular system.

General features

Comment on patient's general wellbeing and in particular if she is short of breath at rest or cyanosed. Look carefully for surgical scars.

Cardiovascular examination

Check for stigmata of endocarditis. Pay attention to dental hygiene. Check for signs of heart failure, noting particularly that in cases of aortic stenosis the following may be observed:

> Pulse: this will be regular, slow rising and small volume due to narrow pulse pressure. Reduced arterial compliance in older patients may negate these findings. Atrial fibrillation is less common than with mitral valve disease.

> BP: narrow pulse pressure.

> JVP: prominent a-wave.

> Apex: this is usually undisplaced and heaving; it may have a double beat due to additional left atrial impulse. Displacement suggests left ventricular dilatation. A systolic thrill may be

palpable over the aortic region and carotids.

> Heart sounds: the dominant feature is likely to be a harsh-ejection systolic murmur in the aortic region, radiating to the neck and loudest in expiration. Typically the murmur quietens across the precordium and becomes loud again at the apex (Galliverdin's sign). Diminished or absent A2 (soft second heart sound) suggests severe aortic stenosis. An opening snap suggests a bicuspid aortic valve. Fourth heart sound maybe present due to atrial contraction on a poorly compliant ventricle.

In late presentation, classic signs may lessen and left ventricular failure and secondary pulmonary hypertension dominate.

Hazard

In aortic stenosis the murmur is not a guide to severity – look for clinical signs that reflect the haemodynamic significance.

Further discussion

The differential diagnosis of aortic stenosis include:

> Innocent systolic murmur, eg aortic sclerosis.

> Pulmonary stenosis: dominant indications of this are a murmur loudest in inspiration, palpable right ventricular heave and signs of right heart failure. Usually congenital in origin, eg Fallot's tetralogy. Always consider in a cardiac patient who looks cyanosed.

> Hypertrophic cardiomyopathy (HCM): if you suspect this look for jerky impulse and a double apex beat. The patients who suffer from HCM are often young.

Key point

Features present in aortic stenosis that would not be expected in aortic sclerosis:

> low pulse pressure

> slow rising pulse

> carotid thrill

> radiation of murmur to neck

> abnormal heart sounds – particularly a soft second heart sound

> forceful/displaced apex (unless there is another possible explanation, eg hypertension).

Symptoms of aortic stenosis include angina, shortness of breath and syncope. Transthoracic echocardiography confirms the diagnosis and enables an assessment of severity (see Section 2.5.1). Note, however, that the aortic valve gradient will be underestimated in patients with heart failure, so a dynamic assessment may be required with dobutamine stress in this situation. Coronary angiography is required prior to surgery to look for coexistent coronary artery disease.

Patients with mild or moderate disease should be reviewed annually in a cardiac clinic. All patients should be given advice regarding good dental hygiene.

All patients with symptoms due to aortic stenosis require aortic valve replacement because the prognosis is poor for symptomatic patients who remain untreated. In particular, the onset of heart failure is a very poor prognostic sign and such patients should be considered for urgent valve replacement. Mechanical valve prostheses (Table 6) are generally preferred unless the patient is an older person, increased risks of bleeding on anticoagulation are present or the patient is a young

woman who wishes to get pregnant in the future. In the latter situation patients will often elect to have a tissue valve: this eliminates the need for teratogenic warfarin during their child-bearing years but they accept that the valve replacement may need to be performed again at a later date. Patients previously deemed inoperable or at high risk of mortality from conventional surgical aortic valve replacement can now be considered for transcatheter aortic valve implantation (TAVI) which has been shown to reduce 1-year mortality compared to medical therapy alone.

1.2.6 Aortic regurgitation

Instruction

This woman is short of breath – please examine her cardiovascular system.

General features

Comment on the patient's general wellbeing and in particular if she is short of breath at rest or cyanosed. Look for previous surgical scars. Look for a

Marfanoid habitus or features of arthropathy, especially ankylosing spondylitis.

Cardiovascular examination

Check for visible carotid pulsation from the end of the bed (Corrigan's). Examine for stigmata of endocarditis. Pay attention to dental hygiene. Check for signs of heart failure, noting particularly that in aortic regurgitation (AR) the following may be observed.

> Pulse: this would be regular, collapsing in nature and large volume. Atrial fibrillation is less common than with mitral valve (MV) disease. The collapsing or 'water hammer' pulse is a specific sign but requires some practice to detect. Using the flat of the fingers, palpate the radial or brachial pulse and quickly elevate the arm. The 'water hammer' will strike the fingers forcefully.

> BP: wide pulse pressure. This may be associated with a number of eponymous signs (Table 7).

> Apex: thrusting and displaced (volume overload). A systolic thrill may be palpable over the aortic region and carotids.

Table 7	Clinical signs of a wide pulse pressure seen in AR
Sign	**Clinical observation**
De Musset's	Head nods with each pulsation
Quincke's	Capillary pulsation visible in nail beds
Duroziez's	Femoral artery compressed and auscultation proximal to this reveals a diastolic murmur
Corrigan's	Visible carotid neck pulsations
Muller's	Pulsating uvula
Hill's	Popliteal BP greater than brachial BP by more than 20 mmHg when lying flat
Gerhard's	Systolic pulsation of the spleen
Rosenbach's	Systolic pulsation of the liver
Traube's	Pistol shot sounds over femoral arteries

AR, aortic regurgitation; BP, blood pressure.

> Heart sounds: the dominant finding is an early diastolic murmur best heard over the lower left sternal edge during expiration with the patient sitting forward. It becomes prolonged in more severe AR. There is almost always an accompanying ejection systolic murmur which represents a large stroke volume. An Austin–Flint murmur, which needs to be distinguished from the murmur of mitral stenosis, is a rumbling mid-diastolic murmur caused by the aortic regurgitant jet hitting the MV leaflets. The second heart sound is single (no aortic component), but P2 may be normal or loud. The third heart sound may be heard.

Further discussion

Key point

Causes and associations of AR.

Chronic:

> bicuspid aortic valve

> hypertension and aortic root dilatation

> Marfan syndrome

> infective endocarditis

> rheumatic heart disease

> arthritides – ankylosing spondylitis, rheumatoid and Reiter's

> syphilis.

Acute:

> dissection of aorta

> infective endocarditis

> failure of prosthetic valve

> acute rheumatic fever.

Symptoms of AR include shortness of breath, lethargy and, less commonly, angina. Transthoracic echocardiography confirms the diagnosis (see Section 2.5.2), may reveal the aetiology and enables an assessment of severity. Key parameters are AR severity, left ventricle (LV) diastolic and systolic volumes and LV systolic function. If there is a suggestion of significant dilatation of the proximal aorta from chest radiograph or echocardiography, a cardiac MRI should be considered. Coronary angiography is required prior to surgery to look for coexistent coronary artery disease.

Patients with mild or moderate disease should be reviewed annually in a cardiac clinic. Asymptomatic patients with severe AR should be considered for surgery if there is evidence of declining left ventricular systolic function or left ventricular dilatation. The onset of heart failure is a poor prognostic sign.

Aortic valve surgery (predominantly replacement) is indicated for symptomatic patients with severe AR, asymptomatic patients with severe AR and LV ejection fraction under 50% or deteriorating LV dimensions.

Mechanical valve prostheses (Table 6) are generally preferred unless the patient has a high bleeding risk due to frailty or old age or if they have a bleeding disorder. The patient may be a young woman who wishes to get pregnant in the future. Both mechanical and bioprosthetic (tissue) valves can be considered in this scenario; patients will often elect to have a tissue valve: this eliminates the need for subcutaneous low-molecular-weight heparin or teratogenic warfarin during child-bearing years but the patient accepts that a valve replacement will need to be performed again at a later date.

In acute AR there is often no murmur to hear due to very rapid equalisation of pressures between the aorta and the LV in early diastole. The only murmur that sounds like AR is pulmonary regurgitation, which can be distinguished because it is louder in inspiration and usually associated with signs of right heart compromise.

1.2.7 Tricuspid regurgitation

Instruction

This man has a murmur – please examine his cardiovascular system.

General features

Comment on the patient's general wellbeing and in particular if short of breath at rest or cyanosed. Chronic right-sided heart failure may present as cachexia, cyanosis or icterus. Look for previous scars on the chest and more widely over the skin for evidence of intravenous (IV) drug abuse or dialysis fistulae.

Cardiovascular examination

Check for stigmata of endocarditis. Pay attention to dental hygiene. Check if the patient is in atrial fibrillation. Note that with tricuspid regurgitation (TR) the following may be observed:

> JVP: often significantly elevated with giant v waves. Make sure to look up to the level of the ear. To avoid confusion with carotid pulsation, examine the waveform (double versus sharp, single pulsation) or change venous return with the hepatojugular reflux or inspiration. The carotid will not move.

> Apex: undisplaced with right ventricular (RV) parasternal heave.

> Heart sounds: a pansystolic murmur that is loudest in inspiration and typically most prominent at the lower left sternal edge. A loud pulmonary component of the second heart sound would suggest pulmonary hypertension.

> The liver may be enlarged, tender and pulsatile. Occasionally a systolic murmur or thrill can be detected over the liver.

> Other signs: sacral and peripheral oedema. Check for pleural effusions and (less common) ascites. Look for evidence of chronic lung disease as TR may be caused by cor pulmonale.

Further discussion

Key point

Causes of tricuspid regurgitation (TR):

> functional TR due to right ventricular (RV) dilatation:

> > mitral valve (MV) disease

> > pulmonary hypertension

> > intracardiac shunt

> > RV infarction.

> infective endocarditis (IV drug abuse, in-dwelling lines, dialysis)

> carcinoid syndrome

> congenital, eg Ebstein's anomaly

> trauma (pacemaker lead complication)

> myxomatous change.

The character of the JVP establishes the presence of TR, but the examiner will expect you to be able to discuss the differential diagnosis of a pansystolic murmur: mitral regurgitation, ventricular septal defect and TR (see Section 1.2.6).

An echocardiogram will confirm the diagnosis and severity of TR. It is possible to estimate the pulmonary artery pressure from the velocity of the tricuspid regurgitant jet. If pulmonary hypertension is suspected to be the cause of TR, then chest radiography, lung function tests and lung ventilation–perfusion scanning (or CT pulmonary angiography) should be pursued.

Diuretics are frequently used but oedema can prove refractory. If secondary TR, the underlying cause should be treated.

Surgery is rarely indicated, even for severe TR. However, when the cause is endocarditis it should be considered if there is a large-vegetation (bigger than 1 cm), persistent sepsis despite the patient taking antibiotics or evidence of embolisation. In patients undergoing MV surgery, tricuspid annuloplasty is sometimes performed in the presence of severe TR and dilatation of the annulus (larger than 5.0 cm).

1.2.8 Eisenmenger's syndrome

Instruction

This woman has become breathless on minimal exertion. A doctor noted that she had a murmur as a child. Please examine her heart.

General features

A large left-to-right shunt causes increased pulmonary blood flow, which in turn causes increased pulmonary vascular resistance and right ventricular (RV) hypertrophy. Eventually the pulmonary resistance exceeds the systemic resistance, and the blood flow is reversed causing a right-to-left shunt with resulting cyanosis.

Look for cyanosis and evidence of stroke in a young person. Is there a sputum pot? Look specifically for haemoptysis.

Cardiovascular examination

Look specifically for:

> cyanosis

> clubbing – seen more dramatically in cyanotic congenital heart disease than in any other context

> pulse – atrial fibrillation or flutter are common

> JVP – this will always be significantly raised; are there flutter waves?

> RV heave

> listen for RV gallop rhythm and loud P2

> pulmonary or tricuspid regurgitation

> ankle oedema.

Once Eisenmenger's syndrome has developed the murmur of the original shunt will have disappeared.

Further discussion

Eisenmenger's syndrome is a clinical diagnosis aided by ECG (particularly for RV hypertrophy), chest radiograph (for cases of prominent pulmonary arteries and peripheral pruning), echocardiography and cardiac catheterisation. Echocardiography enables the shunt to be visualised and an assessment of RV pressure to be made.

Optimal treatment of patients with Eisenmenger's syndrome is provided by a congenital heart disease specialist service, and may involve the following.

> Continuous oxygen, which acts as a vasodilator.

> Aspirin for patients with polycythaemia to reduce the risk of stroke.

> Venesection for symptomatic polycythaemia.

> Atrial arrhythmias: these are common, but may be lethal and can often be treated with catheter ablation (see Section 3.4).

> Ventricular arrhythmias: patients at high risk may require an implantable cardioverter defibrillator (see Section 3.4).

> Transplantation is an option in selected cases.

> Counselling: this can include advice regarding pregnancy and delivery risks for both mother and fetus. Contraceptive advice is also important. In a case where the patient is pregnant, the early opinion of a fetal medicine obstetrician and congenital heart disease specialist are vital.

> Antibiotic prophylaxis: patients with shunts need antibiotic prophylaxis prior to dental procedures or other instrumentation.

Early detection and closure of haemodynamically significant left-to-right shunts is important to prevent Eisenmenger's syndrome from developing. Other options include pulmonary artery banding to limit the flow to the lungs and prevent the development of pulmonary hypertension.

When Eisenmenger's syndrome is established, the 10-year survival rate is 80% and the 25-year survival rate is 40%. Poor prognostic features are syncope, low cardiac output, hypoxaemia and RV failure.

Key point

Patients with Eisenmenger's syndrome should be told to avoid volume depletion, systemic vasodilators, altitude, heavy exertion and pregnancy. They should also be advised to take antibiotics before dental or other procedures.

Key point

Who was Eisenmenger?

In 1897, Eisenmenger reported the case of a 32-year-old man who had showed exercise intolerance, cyanosis, heart failure and haemoptysis prior to death. At post-mortem a large ventricular septal defect and an over-riding aorta were found. Eisenmenger described the link between a large congenital cardiac shunt defect and the development of pulmonary hypertension for the first time.

1.2.9 Dextrocardia

Instruction

This patient has a congenital heart condition – please examine his heart.

General features

This instruction raises many possibilities, making general inspection from the end of the bed particularly important in this case. Are there any obvious dysmorphic features that may indicate a well-known congenital condition? Is the patient cyanosed, which may indicate a cyanotic congenital heart lesion or Eisenmenger's syndrome (see Section 2.7.3)? Are there any obvious surgical scars? Look carefully all over their torso.

Cardiovascular examination

You will need to keep an open mind as you approach this case and may need to focus on particular aspects of the examination depending on what you discover. Key points to look for are:

> Pulse: check all peripheral pulses to ensure that they are present and equal. Previous surgery may cause absent pulses, and coarctation of the aorta or stenoses may cause delayed or weakened pulses. Is the pulse irregular and/or tachycardic? Atrial arrhythmias are very common in patients with congenital cardiac conditions, especially if they have been surgically corrected.

> JVP: this may be significantly elevated with right heart conditions or pulmonary hypertension. Tricuspid regurgitation (TR) may be evident (giant v wave).

> Praecordium: examine for thrills and heaves.

> Apex beat: identify the location and nature of the apex beat – if you cannot feel it in the normal position, percuss the area of cardiac dullness and remember to feel the right side of the chest to identify dextrocardia.

> Heart sounds: careful auscultation will reveal any added sounds/murmurs (see Table 8). If you suspect dextrocardia, auscultate over the right side of the chest as well as the left.

> Signs of congestive heart failure: is there any evidence of pulmonary oedema? Is there peripheral oedema or hepatic enlargement, or a pulsatile liver of TR? This is not an uncommon finding with complex congenital conditions.

Further discussion

This patient had a relatively rare condition of dextrocardia with no other associated cardiac abnormalities.

Keeping an open mind to examination would have led to a successful outcome in this instance when the apex beat was difficult to feel and the heart sounds very quiet. This was the only abnormality to find on examination and so the case would easily confuse you if you had missed the abnormal apex beat. There are increasing numbers of patients with surgically corrected complex congenital conditions surviving to adulthood. With a methodical approach to the examination it should be possible to identify many of the clinical signs. It is not always necessary to obtain the exact diagnosis, as the complexity of some of these cardiac conditions can be exceptional.

1.3 Communication skills and ethics

1.3.1 Resistance of inappropriate investigations

Scenario

Role: you are the core medical trainee in a cardiology outpatient clinic.

Scenario: Miss Jenny Pinto, aged 28 years, has been referred to the clinic for investigation of palpitations. She had previously not been worried about these symptoms, but recent knowledge of the deaths of two relatives following sudden collapses has made her very concerned. At her first appointment it became clear from her history that the palpitations were consistent with ventricular ectopic beats. Examination was normal, as was a routine 12-lead ECG. Echocardiography showed her heart to be normal and a 24-hour ECG demonstrated ectopic beats when she was symptomatic. She is keen to have further investigations, but these would not be appropriate.

Your task: to reassure Miss Pinto that her condition is benign and explain that further investigations are not necessary.

Key issues to explore

What is the patient's main concern? Why does she want further investigation? Does her desire stem from the actual symptoms or the perceived risk from the condition in view of her family history?

Table 8 Key clinical signs with congenital heart disease

Congenital condition	Clinical signs
Dextrocardia	Quiet/absent sounds on left side of chest. Area of cardiac dullness shifted. Apex felt on the right side
VSD	Palpable thrill at left sternal edge. Loud pansystolic murmur
ASD	Wide fixed splitting of second heart sound (does not vary with respiration) and soft ejection systolic murmur over pulmonary area
PS	RV heave and thrill in second right space. Split second heart sound (not fixed) and systolic click may be heard
Coarctation of the aorta	Systemic hypertension, reduced lower limb or left arm pulses and radio-femoral delay
Surgically corrected transposition of the great arteries	Mustard or Senning operations are indicated by RV heave, single second heart sound and pansystolic murmur of TR. Switch operation patients may have ejection systolic murmurs of supravalvular PS or aortic stenosis
Congenitally corrected transposition	Raised JVP and pansystolic murmur of TR. Signs of systemic (right in this situation) ventricular dysfunction
Ebstein's anomaly	JVP often normal even with severe TR. First and second heart sounds widely split. Often third and fourth heart sounds present
Eisenmenger's syndrome	Cyanosed and clubbed. Will have clinical features of underlying shunt, ie ASD, VSD or patent ductus arteriosus, although these may not be apparent if the shunt has reversed

Note: Some patients will have extensive surgical scars.
ASD, atrial septal defect; JVP, jugular venous pressure; PS, pulmonary stenosis; RV, right ventricular; TR, tricuspid regurgitation; VSD, ventricular septal defect.

Key points to establish

Reassure the patient that the diagnosis of ectopics is certain, as her symptoms have been clearly correlated with ectopics on the 24-hour ECG. Additional reassurance is often provided when patients understand that most people have ectopic beats at some stage every day, the majority of whom are unaware of them. Some people have a lot more ectopics than others do, but this does not signify anything if the heart is normal. In this case we know from investigations that her heart is normal and no further tests will add anything to this.

Key point

It is important that the patient understands her symptoms are not being dismissed. An explanation that ectopic beats can be very debilitating in some people can reassure. Further qualification that knowing the symptom is benign often leads to a significant improvement in the degree of intensity and awareness the patient feels from it.

Appropriate responses to likely questions

Patient: what can I do to make them go away?

Doctor: in many cases they will just settle down without needing to do anything. Some people find that they are worse after alcohol or after drinks containing caffeine. It might be worthwhile trying to reduce your intake of these to see whether the symptoms improve. Other people find relaxation tricks such as taking a few deep breaths or lying down can be helpful.

Patient: are there any tablets that you can give me to help with them?

Doctor: there are drugs that can help suppress the symptoms … but these ectopic beats are, essentially, a normal heart rhythm. We would not generally advise patients to take any medication unless absolutely necessary … because you can end up with more symptoms from the side effects of the medication than the actual palpitations themselves. If you are desperate to take something for these then beta-blockers may help. I can explain how they work and what side effects they might cause.

Patient: am I likely to die suddenly like my relatives?

Doctor: it is difficult to answer this question without further knowledge of exactly what was responsible for the deaths of your two relatives. However, we have very carefully assessed your heart and can find no problems that would give us cause for concern at all. I can certainly reassure you that the palpitations will not cause you to die.

Patient: I am really worried about these symptoms. Would it be possible to have a second opinion?

Doctor: of course you can. Either your GP or I can organise this for you … but I would emphasise that all of the investigations have been reassuring and we know that these ectopic beats, while unpleasant, are not in any way life-threatening … but if you'd like to have a second opinion, then I can help arrange this.

1.3.2 Explanation of uncertainty of diagnosis

Scenario

Role: you are the core medical trainee working on a general medical ward.

Scenario: a 65-year-old man is admitted to your ward from the emergency department following an unexplained syncope while shopping. There have been no previous episodes and since his arrival on the ward he has been alert and orientated with normal observations. Physical examination and investigations including ECG, chest radiography and blood tests (including troponin at 12 hours after the collapse) have been normal. His telemetry up to this point has shown no abnormalities.

The plan agreed after consultant review on the post-take ward round is to discharge him home, with arrangements for an outpatient 24-hour tape and echocardiogram.

Your task: to explain to his wife the uncertainty of the diagnosis and what the management plan is likely to be.

Key issues to explore

What is the wife's current level of understanding of events? What are her concerns and expectations regarding her husband's condition and treatment?

Key points to establish

Firstly establish that you have the patient's consent to talk to his wife about his condition. Explain that the cause of the collapse is uncertain, but initial assessment has so far been reassuringly normal, as have the appropriate investigations. Reassure her that this is a common presentation and the vast majority of syncopal episodes have a benign cause.

Key point

Explain that sometimes an exact diagnosis is not determined, and the importance of investigations is to rule out the more serious causes for which there are effective treatments rather than to pinpoint the specific cause.

Appropriate responses to likely questions

Wife: what caused my husband to collapse?

Doctor: at the moment it is not possible to give an exact cause ... but the most common cause of collapse is a simple faint. We will make a plan to do further tests, mainly to rule out other causes.

Wife: does this mean that this will never happen again?

Doctor: unfortunately there is no guarantee that the symptoms will not reoccur ... but the fact that he is well now, that there are no abnormalities when we examine him, and that the initial tests, the ECG (an electrical tracing of his heart), a chest X-ray and blood tests, are all normal ... makes it less likely that there is a serious underlying cause.

Wife: you said he needed more tests: what are these?

Doctor: it's very unlikely that they will show anything worrying, but to be on the safe side we plan to organise for a 24-hour tape recording of his heart beat to check that it doesn't go too fast or too slow at any time, and an echocardiogram – that's a special scan – to look at the heart in more detail than you can see on the chest X-ray. We plan to do these with your husband as an outpatient.

Wife: can't these tests be done before he goes home?

Doctor: it's sometimes better to get these tests done when he's doing his usual activities. We wouldn't discharge him if it wasn't safe; your husband seems well now and when the consultant saw him earlier on we agreed that we didn't need to keep him in hospital and could do the tests as an outpatient.

Wife: can he drive?

Doctor: not at the moment. However, if he has no recurrence of his symptoms then he can return to driving in 4 weeks if we are happy that it wasn't a problem with his heart that caused this episode [see Section 2.19]. However, if there are any further symptoms then he should await the results of his remaining investigations and clinic review before recommencing driving.

Wife: will a pacemaker help?

Doctor: at this stage there is no evidence that a pacemaker would be helpful. All procedures have some risk and so we wouldn't want to expose him to any risk unless absolutely necessary. The results of his tests will help decide whether this needs to be considered in the future.

Wife: what happens if he collapses again at home?

Doctor: as I've explained, we don't think that this is likely or we wouldn't be suggesting that he goes home. If he does collapse, then – the same as if you or I were to collapse – you would need to call the doctor or an ambulance.

1.3.3 Discussion of screening relatives for an inherited condition

Scenario

Role: you are the core medical trainee in a cardiology outpatient clinic.

Scenario: Mr Patrick McDonagh is a 37-year-old builder and father of three who was admitted on the medical take with a syncopal episode 2 months ago. He has been previously fit and well. Examination on admission had revealed a normal pulse rate, but his BP was elevated persistently at 160/95 mmHg. There was a soft ejection systolic murmur over the left sternal edge. His ECG was normal apart from large voltage complexes consistent with left ventricular hypertrophy. He had been discharged and prescribed atenolol for his hypertension, and arrangements have also been made for him to have a 24-hour ECG and an echocardiogram as an outpatient. The 24-hour ECG was normal but the echocardiogram has demonstrated severe hypertrophic cardiomyopathy (HCM) with an outflow tract gradient of 50 mmHg, following which an urgent appointment for the cardiac clinic has been made. His GP has told him that the condition can affect the family, and he is concerned about this.

HCM is typically an autosomal dominant disorder with very variable manifestations: some people with the condition have no problems, but others die suddenly. Further investigation, eg exercise testing and possibly electrophysiological studies, will be advised.

Your task: to explain the diagnosis of HCM and the potential genetic implications of the condition.

Key issues to explore

Has the patient had any further symptoms since discharge? What does he understand about his condition and what are his main concerns regarding his family?

Key points to establish

Key point

Establish that there are two main issues to be explored: firstly, the impact of HCM on the patient and the potential need for him to have further investigations; secondly, the hereditary nature of the condition.

It is important to understand precisely why the patient is concerned about the impact of the diagnosis on his family: is his main concern the impact of his health (or ill health) on the family; has he understood the genetic aspect of the condition; or are both issues of concern to him? Both are very important, but an understanding of the patient's main concern will allow for a more productive consultation.

Appropriate responses to likely questions

Patient: I feel great now. Does this mean I don't need any further tests?

Doctor: that is really good news and an excellent sign, but it is important that we do further tests of your heart as some patients with this condition can have very serious problems later on.

Patient: does this mean I am going to die?

Doctor: that's not what I said, but a small number of patients with this condition are at risk of dangerous heart rhythm problems and sudden blackouts. The further tests will help us assess whether you are at risk of this. If you are, then there are a number of ways that we can reduce this risk.

Patient: have I given this to my children?

Doctor: I assume that none of your children have had any heart problems so far? [Patient confirms that they haven't.] But yes, this condition can be passed on to your children.

Patient: what are the chances that my children have it?

Doctor: because of the way it runs in the family the chances for each child are about 50/50. So at some stage it will be important for you to have your children seen by a specialist, when a simple test like an ultrasound scan of the heart may allow the diagnosis to be made. However, it's not always possible to say that a child definitely does not have the condition.

Patient: is there a blood test that will enable a diagnosis to be made?

Doctor: at the moment there is no single test that will give a definite diagnosis. There have been a lot of advances in the genetic testing of blood samples that may allow us to get this answer in the future, and we can refer you to a clinical geneticist who will be able to give you more information on the inherited aspect of the condition.

1.3.4 Communicating news of a patient's death to a spouse

Scenario

Role: you are the core medical trainee on a coronary care unit.

Scenario: Mr Smith, a 40-year-old man, is admitted from work with a large anterior myocardial infarct, which is treated with percutaneous coronary intervention (PCI). Unfortunately he arrests in the catheter laboratory and, despite prolonged attempts at resuscitation, he dies. His wife arrives 5 minutes after he dies.

Your task: to inform Mrs Smith that Mr Smith is dead.

Key issues to explore

What does the patient's wife know already? She will be more prepared for bad news if she knows he is gravely ill than if she doesn't know why he is in hospital. Explaining an unexpected death is one of the most difficult communication tasks that a medical professional has to perform: if it is done with compassion and sensitivity it can ease the inevitable distress that family and friends will go through.

Key points to establish

Find a quiet room, if possible a relatives' room, and ask the nurse looking after the patient to accompany you. Leave your pager with someone else so that you are free of interruptions. There is no hiding from the fact that you must inform Mrs Smith that her husband has had a heart attack and unfortunately has not survived this. State that you and the team did what you could, and say how sorry the whole team is. Demonstrate empathy: if it feels appropriate hold her hand or touch a non-threatening area, such as the arm or the shoulder.

Key point

Wait until asked to explain details, but keep it simple. Allow her to cry with dignity, such as by handing her some tissues. Do not be afraid of silence, but if this becomes uncomfortable it is often helpful to make an open statement, eg 'this must have come as a shock'.

In finishing the discussion, explain that should she think of questions later you will be happy to answer them. Also say that you will have to notify the coroner, which is a routine practice following any unexpected death, and that the nursing staff or bereavement office will provide her with information about practical matters such as death certification.

Appropriate responses to likely questions

Wife: what's happened?

Doctor: [after ascertaining that she knows that her husband was brought into hospital as an emergency, but not that he has died; and speaking quietly, slowly and deliberately to let the information sink in.] Your husband was brought to the hospital as an emergency. He was very unwell when he was admitted. He had suffered a big heart attack. We gave him the best treatment we could – a procedure called angioplasty, to open up the blocked artery – but I'm afraid his heart did not recover. The damage to his heart was too great, it couldn't beat properly and, despite us doing everything we could, he passed away.

Wife: you mean he's dead?

Doctor: yes. I'm very sorry, but I'm afraid your husband has died.

Wife: why did this happen?

Doctor: I don't know why it happened, but he had a very large heart attack. This happens when an artery supplying the heart blocks off. This normally means it had narrowed over time and the heart attack occurred when it blocked completely.

Wife: but people can survive heart attacks, why didn't he?

Doctor: you're right, many people do survive heart attacks, but sadly many don't. Sometimes the heart attack is so big that it damages too much of the heart muscle for the heart to work at all; and sometimes the heart attack affects the electrical system of the heart meaning it stops beating properly. I'm very sorry to say that both of these things happened in your husband's case.

Wife: why couldn't you bring him back to life?

Doctor: we did absolutely everything we could to open up the artery, but the damage caused by the heart attack was too severe. When his heart stopped, we tried everything we could to resuscitate him, but I'm afraid that it didn't work.

Wife: did he suffer?

Doctor: no: it was very quick and he was not conscious, so he wasn't aware of what was going on and he would not have suffered.

Wife: will he have a post-mortem?

Doctor: it is unlikely that he will have to have a post-mortem. We will need to inform the coroner, which is something that we have to do after any unexpected death, and very occasionally they will insist on a post-mortem. However, I think it unlikely that they will do so in this case, because we know why your

husband died. If you would like further information about his health and how he died then we can request a hospital post-mortem, but I understand it may be difficult for you to discuss this now. We can talk about this again later if you want to.

Remember to end the discussion with a reiteration that you are sorry for her loss.

1.3.5 Explanation to a patient of the need for investigations

Scenario

Role: you are the core medical trainee working on a cardiology ward.

Scenario: Mr Hugh Jones, aged 23 years, has congenital heart disease. He was admitted from clinic for further investigations into the cause of his breathlessness. The view of the cardiac team is that it will not be possible to give best advice about prognosis and treatment without information from a cardiac catheterisation study, but he is refusing to consent.

Your task: to determine what concerns Mr Jones has and explain the purpose of further investigation.

Key issues to explore

First find out what the patient knows about his condition: he may be concerned that nothing can be done or be in denial about the seriousness of the problem. Then establish what he knows about cardiac catheterisation and his fears about the procedure: some patients are worried about pain and discomfort, whereas others worry about complications. Try and put any such fears in perspective. Explain any alternative investigative strategies that are available, but also why a cardiac catheterisation study is needed to give him best advice about his condition. If possible offer him information booklets and if there is a specialist nurse available, ask him or her to speak with the patient.

Key points to establish

Key point

Mr Jones does not have to undergo any investigation or treatment unless he agrees to it. He will still receive care even if he does not undergo the investigations recommended, but a proper investigation may improve the care that can be given to him and thus alleviate some of his symptoms.

Appropriate responses to likely questions

Patient: I feel fine.

Doctor: I hear what you say, but you went to the doctor because your breathing isn't as good as it should be and it looks as though this is due to a problem with your heart.

Patient: but the problem isn't very bad.

Doctor: I know that things aren't terrible at the moment, but we have found a problem with the heart that could be serious and which may get worse. It may be that treatment now can improve things so that they don't get any worse, or the rate of any deterioration can be slowed down so that you will feel well for longer.

Patient: will you treat me differently if I don't have it?

Doctor: we will never force you to have any test and will treat you as best we can at all times. The decision to have the test is yours. However, it is our job to explain that this test may help us give you better treatment.

Patient: can you guarantee that the problem can be sorted?

Doctor: no, I'm afraid that I can't. Until we know exactly what the problem is, we won't be able to tell you.

Patient: I still don't like the idea of a cardiac catheter. Is there an alternative?

Doctor: we can and will do scans that will give us some information. However, cardiac catheterisation gives us the most important information, such as the amount of oxygen in the chambers of the heart, which we cannot get in any other way. We recommend this test because it is the best way to understand what is happening with your heart.

Patient: will it hurt?

Doctor: the procedure may be uncomfortable while the local anaesthetic is being given. Patients report it feels like a bee sting, it lasts a few minutes and after this it goes numb and should not be uncomfortable.

Patient: could I die during the procedure?

Doctor: that's extremely unlikely. This is a routine procedure, although as you can imagine any procedure involving the heart carries a small risk – but it is very small. The risk of death is one in 4,000, which means that 3,999 survive out of 4,000 people undergoing the procedure.

1.3.6 Explanation to a patient who is reluctant to receive treatment

Scenario

Role: you are the core medical trainee in a medical outpatient clinic.

Scenario: Mrs Jessica Yelland, aged 30 years, has been found to be significantly hypertensive when she came to her GP's family planning clinic. Her BP has been measured on several occasions and found to be consistently in the region of 180/100 mmHg. It has been explained to her that she has high BP that requires investigation and treatment, but she feels well and only wants a prescription for the oral contraceptive pill, not any tests or medication.

Your task: to inform Mrs Yelland why investigations and treatment are required.

Key issues to explore

The key to a successful outpatient consultation will be to understand the reason why the patient does not want further investigation or treatment. Does she feel that investigation and treatment are unnecessary because she feels well? Is she afraid of what may be found? Is she concerned about the effects of treatment?

Key points to establish

It is very important to establish a rapport with this woman so that she will trust you and thus hopefully follow the recommended management plan. Explain to her that hypertension is a common and often asymptomatic condition that is frequently picked up on routine screening, or incidentally as part of investigations for other medical problems.

She will need reassurance and an explanation that investigations are necessary to exclude a secondary cause of high BP, which might mean that the hypertension can be cured and that she would not need long-term treatment. If no specific cause for hypertension is found, then simple changes to her lifestyle may be adequate to treat her BP. But in some situations this is not enough and she may require medication.

Your advice should be accompanied by a provision of reading material and help with associated programmes for smoking cessation, weight loss and dietary advice. But remember that most patients diagnosed with hypertension perceive themselves as being healthy and lead a normal lifestyle with no day-to-day limitations, therefore starting treatment and addressing lifestyle issues can be difficult and in some cases unacceptable.

Appropriate responses to likely questions

Patient: I feel very well and only went to the doctor for a prescription, so I can't have much of a problem, can I?

Doctor: high blood pressure is a very common condition that can affect up to 20% (one in five) of people. As in your case, high blood pressure is often discovered when someone has their blood pressure measured for an entirely unrelated problem. The fact that it was discovered for that reason does not mean that having high

blood pressure is unimportant. People can have conditions without knowing about them but it doesn't mean they aren't important.

Patient: what will happen if I have nothing done?

Doctor: over a period of many years high blood pressure can result in serious damage to many important organs in the body. For example, if left untreated it can lead to major heart problems and strokes, and very rarely it can result in problems with the eyes that can affect normal vision and in extreme cases may result in blindness. However, all these problems can be avoided by achieving good blood pressure control. In your case, we can use a calculator to try to estimate what your risks are (www.jbs3risk.com/pages/risk_calculator.htm).

Patient: what causes high blood pressure?

Doctor: a good question, and I wish I could give you a good answer. For most patients we don't know, but in some cases it can be caused by problems with the kidneys or glands so we will recommend some tests – blood tests and urine tests – to see if this might be the case for you.

Patient: how can you tell if high blood pressure is causing damage to the body?

Doctor: by examining you and doing tests. For instance: we can look in your eyes to see if it is having an effect on the blood vessels at the back of the eye; we can do an ECG – an electrical tracing of the heart – or an echocardiogram – a special scan of the heart – and see if it is having an effect there; and we can do urine and blood tests to check kidney function.

Patient: what is the treatment likely to consist of?

Doctor: the first thing is for us to look at your lifestyle to see whether we can help you make it more healthy to bring your blood pressure down. Examples of things that can help are ensuring you take regular exercise, stopping smoking and looking at your diet. In the future, it may be that tablets are needed.

Patient: am I always going to have high blood pressure?

Doctor: not everyone who is started on medication for blood pressure continues with high blood pressure for the rest of their life. In some situations the changes to their lifestyle may mean that they do not need to continue taking medication long term. The treatment is something that your doctor will want to review on a regular basis.

Patient: will one tablet cure me?

Doctor: it might do, but a significant number of patients actually require a combination of tablets. We will start you off on one tablet and then review your blood pressure, and only add in additional tablets if required.

Patient: what if I get side effects from the pills?

Doctor: there are lots of different sorts of blood pressure pills, and we want to make sure that we get one that suits you. If you do get side effects from the first one that we try, I'd like you to tell me so that we can try and find one that suits you better.

Patient: can I still take the oral contraceptive pill?

Doctor: yes, as long as we can get your blood pressure under control.

1.3.7 Communicating with a patient and family to discuss deactivating an implantable cardioverter defibrillator

Scenario

Role: you are the core medical trainee on a cardiac ward.

Scenario: Mrs Rogers is an 87-year-old woman who had coronary artery bypass grafting 12 years ago. She had heart failure and a collapse with ventricular tachycardia 2 years later and an implantable cardioverter defibrillator (ICD) was implanted. Over the last 12 months she has had three admissions with severe heart failure and has been admitted again with cardiogenic shock. She and her husband have questioned whether it is appropriate for her ICD to be active.

Her ICD has fired on one occasion. The view of the cardiology consultant is that it would be appropriate for the shock therapy capacity of the ICD to be deactivated.

Your task: to explore with Mrs Rogers and her husband the issues of continuing with ICD therapy or not.

Key issues to explore

It will be important to explore with Mrs Rogers and her husband whether they understand the role of the ICD, and what the potential effect of turning it off will be. It will be important to confirm, as stated in the scenario, whether the ICD has delivered shock therapy previously for ventricular arrhythmias.

Key points to establish

Find a quiet room, if possible a relatives' room, and ask the nurse looking after the patient to accompany you. Leave your pager with someone else so that you are free of interruptions. This is an important decision and therefore the discussion needs to be conducted in the appropriate environment.

Key point

The most important issue is, have they made a decision that she no longer wishes to be resuscitated in the event of a cardiac arrest?

It is also important to establish that therapies can be switched on again in the future if Mrs Rogers changes her mind.

It is clearly important to establish that Mrs Rogers understands the implications of this important decision, ie has capacity. If there is any doubt about this, it would be important to have a conversation with her GP to ensure that you have as much information as possible about her.

Appropriate responses to likely questions

Patient: *I've been talking with my husband about things, and we've decided that we want the shock thing turned off ... can that be done?*

Doctor: yes, it's certainly possible to do that ... but before doing anything, I need to be sure that you understand the implications.

Patient: *what do you mean?*

Doctor: well, having an implanted defibrillator – the thing that delivers the shock – is a bit like having a cardiac arrest team permanently with you, although it doesn't do everything that a cardiac arrest team can do. Have you decided whether, if you were to collapse, you would want to be resuscitated?

Patient: *yes, I have decided ... I don't want to be resuscitated ... and I've*

talked with my husband about it, and he's happy ... no, happy's not the right word ... he accepts my decision.

Patient: *how long after you switch off my ICD will I die?*

Doctor: your ICD monitors your heart continuously and only delivers life-saving treatment if your heart goes into a very dangerous rhythm. [You can outline how often that has happened, if at all, having reviewed her ICD history beforehand.] You will not notice that we have switched it off, but it would mean that if you had a dangerous heart rhythm, the ICD would not deliver a shock and this might mean that you pass away.

Patient: *how am I going to die then with the ICD switched off?*

Doctor: your heart muscle is very weak and this is why you have been unwell and needed to come into hospital. Eventually the heart stops working. This means that it might just get very weak over a period of time and so you would gently pass away. In other times a dangerous heart rhythm occurs. If this were to happen then you would pass away quickly over a few minutes.

Patient: *is there anything that you can do to help?*

Doctor: yes, I can arrange for you and your husband to be seen by the palliative care team ... they will be able to talk to you about future plans ... where you would want to be, what nursing care might be needed, and about helping with symptoms such as breathlessness.

Patient: *when I die I want to be cremated. Will this be OK?*

Doctor: it is usual practice for ICDs to be removed prior to cremation. This is a very minor procedure that is done either in hospital or at a funeral directors.

Further discussion

From a technical point of view it would also important to identify the precise type of ICD that the patient has. If this is a cardiac resynchronisation therapy defibrillator (CRT-D) device, it would be normal practice to leave the biventricular pacing function on, and it would be appropriate to explain this.

Doctor: although we are going to switch the shock function off, we are not going to change the way that the device helps the heart to beat more strongly.

1.3.8 Recommendation against intervention

Scenario

Role: you are the core medical trainee working on the cardiology ward.

Scenario: Mr Dixon is an 80-year-old man admitted 2 days earlier with chest pain, no significant ECG changes, and a borderline positive troponin level. He has significant cognitive impairment due to Alzheimer's disease and also significantly limited mobility due to arthritis. He has stage III chronic kidney disease. He has not complained of any further chest pain since admission and the consultant ward round decision was made to manage him medically. His daughter, who works as a nurse, would like to see you to discuss why her father is not being referred for angiography with a view to coronary intervention.

Your task: to explain to Mr Dixon's daughter the recommendation against an invasive approach.

Key issues to explore

What is the daughter's main concern? Why would she like her father to undergo an invasive procedure? Is she concerned that her father is not being given the appropriate treatment?

Key points to establish

Reassure the daughter that her father is receiving optimal medical care for his condition. Explain that not all patients with an acute coronary syndrome benefit from an invasive approach to management and the risks of the procedure may in this case outweigh the potential benefits.

Key point

It is important that she understands the medical decision is being made in the best interests of her father, taking into account comorbidities and weighing up the risks of possible intervention.

Explain that if he has further symptoms such as angina or repeat admissions with chest pain then the decision for an invasive approach can be reconsidered. It is important to clearly document the discussion in the medical notes.

Appropriate responses to likely questions

Daughter: *why is my father not being referred for an angiogram?*

Doctor: your father has suffered a small heart attack and has been started on all the appropriate medications for this. He has not had any further chest pain since admission and appears to be stable on the medications.

Daughter: *so why not go ahead and do an angiogram now that things have settled down?*

Doctor: I agree that this could be done, but what we're trying to do is to balance benefits and risks ... we could discharge him on medical therapy and follow up in clinic to assess symptoms – which is what we think is the best thing to do – or we could go ahead with an angiogram to assess his heart arteries ... but at the moment we feel the risks of an angiogram, including worsening of kidney function, outweigh the potential benefits. We feel he should be assessed in the clinic in a few weeks' time and if he is experiencing chest pain then we could reconsider the need for an angiogram at that stage.

Daughter: *you are only saying this because doing an angiogram would be expensive.*

Doctor: I agree that angiograms and other tests like that are expensive ... but that's not the reason for our decision ... given that his pain has settled down, and that all the evidence is that he's had a small heart attack and not a big one, we think that there's more chance of an angiogram doing harm than good.

Daughter: *is my father likely to have another heart attack?*

Doctor: he has now been started on all appropriate medical therapy, including antiplatelet therapy which – as you know – thins the blood and reduces the risk of a heart attack, so we hope that the risk of a further heart attack has been lowered. If there are problems despite the medical therapy then the need for an angiogram with a view to intervention can be reconsidered.

Daughter: *what will happen now?*

Doctor: your father has remained well from a cardiac point of view since admission and is now on the right drugs. We are planning to discharge him home and he will be followed up in the cardiology clinic in a few weeks.

1.3.9 Explanation to a patient of the recommendation for (percutaneous coronary) intervention

Scenario

Role: you are the core medical trainee working in a cardiology clinic.

Scenario: Mrs Daphne Gilbert is a mentally alert and active 80-year-old woman who presented with chest pain and underwent a stress-perfusion cardiac MRI scan which demonstrated she had a large area of inducible ischaemia in her left ventricular wall. A CT coronary angiogram showed a significant lesion in her proximal left anterior descending artery.

At a previous outpatient appointment the consultant had said to Mrs Gilbert that percutaneous coronary intervention (PCI) might be indicated. The clinic nurses have told you that Mrs Gilbert is not happy about this.

Your task: to explain to Mrs Gilbert that your recommendation is to undergo PCI to treat her coronary artery disease.

Key issues to explore

Ascertain what Mrs Gilbert already knows about her heart condition. Explain that the non-invasive testing done so far has suggested a significant narrowing in the blood vessel supplying the front of the heart. Explain that the chest pain (angina) she experienced is likely to be due to this narrowing. The location of the narrowing is prognostically significant, ie treating it should reduce her chance of having a heart attack, improve her survival and reduce further chest pain.

Key issues to establish

Key point

Why is the patient reluctant to have intervention?

Explain that consideration has been given to all possible ways of treating her chest pain, including options that do not require invasive procedures. Reassure that there is no intention to force her to have treatment against her will, but that the medical team needs to be sure that she has the right information to make the best decision, and is not making a decision on the basis of incomplete understanding of the issues.

Appropriate responses to likely questions

Doctor: we need to talk about the treatment for your heart problem … at the last clinic the consultant explained that they thought the best thing to do might be to have what we call percutaneous coronary intervention, where a catheter is used to open up the narrowing in an important blood vessel in your heart … but the clinic nurses tell me that you're not happy about that … is that right?

Patient: *yes … I don't like the idea of it at all.*

Doctor: why's that?

Patient: *well, I only get the pain very occasionally now … and I'm 80 years old … so can't I just go home … I'll take any tablets that you want.*

Doctor: of course you can go home … we are not going to give you any treatment against your will … but we do want to be sure that you have the right information to make your decision.

Patient: *what are the treatment options?*

Doctor: the problem you've got is caused by narrowing of one of the main arteries in your heart … this can be treated by 'revascularisation', which is restoring adequate flow to the muscle, or by using medication. Sometimes both options are reasonable choices, but in your case we recommend revascularisation using stenting.

Patient: *why?*

Doctor: the narrowing is at a very important location in your heart's blood supply. The two scans you have had tell us that a big part of the heart muscle is at risk. If the narrowing blocks off, we think you will have a very big heart attack … one that you probably would not survive. Revascularisation is better than just tablets alone in terms of controlling symptoms … although I know you haven't got a lot of these now, probably because you're taking things easy … and in terms of life expectancy, for this type of narrowing.

Patient: *what does 'revascularisation' involve?*

Doctor: for your type of heart disease, the best results are achieved with what we call angioplasty and stenting. This is a procedure that opens up the narrowed artery and keeps it open using a special tube that's left inside.

Patient: *how do you do it?*

Doctor: we normally use the wrist or the top of the leg to enter an artery. After cleaning the area, local anaesthetic is used to numb the area. It will sting when it goes in but after this the rest of the procedure should not be painful. A very thin tube is pushed up the artery to the heart, and we then inject dye into the arteries and take pictures using an X-ray machine. When we have identified the narrowing, a very thin wire is passed across it and we can then stretch open the artery using small balloons and put the special tube – called a stent – inside the artery, where it will stay and keep the artery open. The whole business usually takes about an hour.

Patient: what are the risks?

Doctor: any procedure inside the body has a small risk, but for angioplasty this risk is very low … in about 1% of cases there are serious problems … by which I mean stroke, heart attack or – very rarely – death … but 99 out of a 100 people don't have these. Other complications, which are usually minor, include bleeding from the site where the tube goes in or internally, and the X-ray dye can sometimes cause an allergic reaction or damage to the kidneys. These risks are clearly important to be aware of, but we feel the risk of leaving the narrowing untreated is greater.

Patient: I don't like the idea of these risks … what about just staying on tablets?

Doctor: I agree that there are risks, and that you could just stay on tablets … but what we're trying to do here is to balance benefits and risks … and we think that, overall, the risks of continuing on just tablets are greater than the risks of having an angioplasty and stent.

Patient: what happens afterwards?

Doctor: the procedure can often be performed as a day case and you can return home the same day. You will need to take some additional medication – tablets designed to stop the stent from narrowing or blocking – some of these tablets will be for life, and one will normally be continued for 1 year.

Further discussion

Indications for PCI are prognostically significant lesions (left main stem, proximal left anterior descending) or symptomatic coronary artery disease despite maximal tolerated medical therapy. Patients with more complex coronary disease affecting two or three vessels may be more appropriately treated with coronary artery bypass grafting.

It is important to establish bleeding risk. Most patients will receive drug-eluting coronary stents, which perform better than bare metal stents. However, drug-eluting stents require a year of therapy with two antiplatelet agents, such as aspirin and clopidogrel. Patients with a high bleeding risk (peptic ulcer disease, coagulopathies, frail patients on anticoagulant therapy) may be offered a bare metal stent, which only requires 1 month of dual antiplatelet therapy, after which point one agent could stop. All patients will normally remain on aspirin life long.

1.4 Brief clinical consultations

1.4.1 Paroxysmal palpitations

Scenario

Mrs Jane Evans, aged 28 years

This woman with no significant past medical history has presented to the emergency department having experienced sudden onset palpitations lasting 2 hours. By the time she had been triaged her symptoms had settled, observations were normal, and a 12-lead ECG was unremarkable. What is the likely diagnosis, and how would you manage her?

Introduction

The symptom of palpitations (abnormal awareness of the heart beat) can be caused by a range of clinical conditions from the very benign to the potentially life threatening. Approach the patient with this in mind. It is unusual to see someone during a symptomatic episode, so as much information as possible should be gained from the history, with a main aim being to assess the patient's potential risk from life-threatening ventricular arrhythmias.

You should always have in the back of your mind a list of the possible causes of palpitations (Table 9). In most situations it will be essential to have investigations during a symptomatic episode. Remember that the severity of symptoms does not always reflect the seriousness of the underlying problem: some patients in sinus rhythm may experience severe palpitations, whereas others may be asymptomatic when in ventricular tachycardia (VT).

> **!** **Hazard**
> Severe symptoms do not necessarily mean a dangerous arrhythmia and minor symptoms do not necessarily mean a benign arrhythmia.

Beginning the encounter

Doctor: hello, my name is Dr A, I understand that you have experienced palpitations: is that right?

Patient: yes.

Doctor: before we get onto the details of that, can you tell me if you have any major medical problems? Any problems with the heart?

Table 9 Potential causes of palpitations

Type of palpitation	Cause
No arrhythmia	Anxiety Panic attacks Depression
Extrasystoles	Atrial Ventricular
Bradyarrhythmia	Atrioventricular block Sinus node disease
Tachyarrhythmia	VT AF/flutter AVNRT AVRT Sinus tachycardia

AF, atrial fibrillation; AVNRT, atrioventricular nodal re-entry tachycardia; AVRT, atrioventricular re-entry tachycardia; VT, ventricular tachycardia.

Patient: [gives list (with doctor politely but firmly discouraging lengthy detail).]

Doctor: and are you on any tablets or medications?

Patient: [gives details (and will probably have been asked to produce a written list).]

These introductory questions will provide useful clinical context and may immediately give a clue to the likely diagnosis as well as allowing risk stratification, eg a patient with known ischaemic heart disease and/or previous myocardial infarction with palpitations is more likely to have a clinically significant arrhythmia than a patient with no prior medical history.

Focused history

Doctor: please describe what you mean by palpitations – the characteristics of the palpitations can provide valuable clues in making the diagnosis.

Doctor: can you tap out the abnormality that you experienced? Was it regular or irregular? How do the palpitations start, what brings them on and how do they stop? Do you get any warning at all? Do they come on gradually or suddenly? [Palpitations that come on and go

away gradually are most likely to be due to sinus tachycardia.]

Specific questions about symptoms that would be helpful in this case are:

> Are there accompanying symptoms? Are they associated with chest pain or shortness of breath? Do you feel faint or dizzy with them? Have you ever collapsed? Arrhythmias causing these symptoms are more likely to be of a serious (potentially life-threatening) cause and clearly mandate thorough investigation. Some patients with supraventricular tachycardia (SVT) develop polyuria as a result of atrial stretch causing the release of atrial natriuretic peptide.

> How frequent are the palpitations? Palpitations that occur infrequently are likely to be difficult to catch on simple ambulatory monitoring.

> What treatments have been tried already? An SVT may be terminated by a Valsalva manoeuvre.

> Do they feel the palpitations in their neck? These are suggestive of cannon waves, indicating simultaneous atrial and ventricular contraction. This can occur in atrioventricular (AV) block, AV dissociation associated with ventricular tachycardia (VT) or

atrioventricular nodal re-entry tachycardia (AVNRT).

> Has anyone in your family had heart problems, or collapsed or dropped dead suddenly? A positive family history should alert to genetic conditions such as hypertrophic cardiomyopathy.

Focused examination

Physical examination is usually unremarkable in a patient presenting with self-limiting palpitations. However, a patient with an abnormal cardiovascular examination is more likely to have a clinically significant arrhythmia.

Cardiovascular – check the following:

> cardiac surgical scars (sternotomy or mini-thoracotomy)

> pulse rate and rhythm

> JVP

> cardiac apex (but not formally counting down rib spaces)

> heart sounds and murmurs (quick auscultation at apex, aortic area and neck – not a full examination).

Thyroid – exclude thyrotoxicosis:

> tremor

> goitre

> exophthalmos.

Questions from the patient

[Assuming no clear diagnosis from history, and no abnormal findings on cardiovascular examination:]

Patient: *what caused the palpitations?*

Doctor: at the moment, I'm not sure … your heart rhythm is now normal, and the ECG – the electrical tracing of your heart – is normal. Both of these things are reassuring, but you could have been experiencing an episode where the heart rhythm was abnormal. We will need to do some tests to try to work out what, if anything, was going on.

Patient: *what tests do you mean?*

Doctor: the most important will be to arrange for you to have a monitor to record your heart beat over a period of time, an ultrasound scan of your heart, and some blood tests, which can very occasionally help to explain why the pulse goes racing away.

Patient: *do I have to stay in hospital for these tests?*

Doctor: no, we'll get the blood tests taken now … but then I'm happy for you to go home … and I will discuss with the cardiology team so that you get sent an appointment to have the heart monitor and scan of your heart.

Questions from the examiner

Examiner: *what would you be looking for specifically on the ECG?*

Doctor: when assessing the 12-lead ECG of a patient with palpitations:

> Look for sinus bradycardia or tachycardia.

> Check if there are features suggestive of a cardiac structural abnormality, eg P mitral or left ventricular hypertrophy (LVH, Fig 13).

> Measure the PR interval.

> Check if there is an AV block.

> Are there delta waves? (Fig 14).

> Has the patient had a previous myocardial infarction (Q wave or T wave changes)?

> Measure the QT interval and calculate the QT correction (QTc, QT adjusted for rate).

> Are there any atrial or ventricular extrasystoles?

However, if an ECG has been recorded during symptoms and documents an arrhythmia, it may not be necessary to investigate further because this alone may enable a precise diagnosis to be made.

Examiner: *what blood tests would you like to request?*

Doctor: I'd want to exclude electrolyte abnormalities, particularly abnormal levels of serum potassium, and check for hyperthyroidism.

Examiner: *what exactly are the tests and follow-up that you would organise?*

Doctor: I would organise follow-up with an ambulatory ECG monitoring (eg 24-hour tape) and an echocardiogram, with follow-up in a cardiology clinic.

Ambulatory monitoring – see Section 3.3. An example of an arrhythmia captured on an ambulatory monitor record is shown in Fig 15.

Echocardiogram – this is an important test to help stratify the patient's risk. If the echo shows the patient to have a structurally and functionally normal heart it puts them into a very low risk group. However, it is important not to discount the possibility of significant arrhythmia just because the echo is normal, particularly in a patient with a potentially significant family history.

Key point

A patient with a normal physical examination, a normal ECG and a normal echocardiogram is at very low risk of significant arrhythmia.

Further discussion

In many cases a benign arrhythmia is detected, such as ventricular or atrial ectopy, and occasionally symptoms are clearly associated with sinus rhythm. In most cases explanation and positive reassurance to the patient are all that is required. Only in rare instances, where the patient is very debilitated, should a beta-blocker be prescribed.

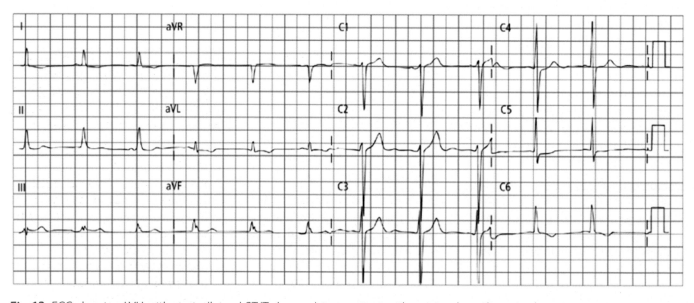

Fig 13 ECG showing LVH with strain (lateral ST/T changes) in a patient with previously undiagnosed aortic stenosis.

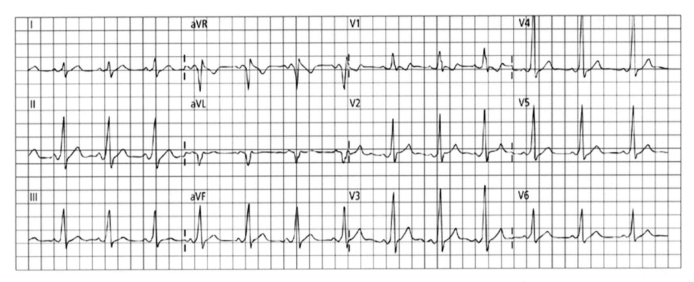

Fig 14 Twelve-lead ECG of patient with the Wolff–Parkinson–White syndrome. Note the short PR interval and delta waves.

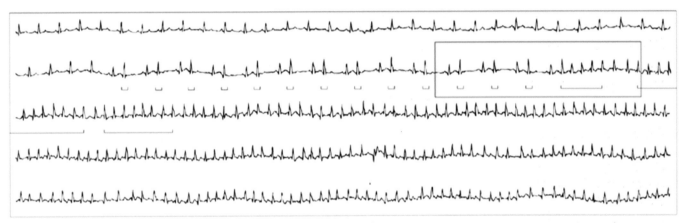

Fig 15 Ambulatory monitor of a patient with SVT. Sinus tachycardia is followed by ventricular bigeminy before the sudden onset of SVT.

Significant symptoms can occasionally be associated with sinus tachycardia. In these circumstances it is important to exclude causes of sinus tachycardia, the most common being anxiety, before attributing the arrhythmia to inappropriate sinus node function.

If an arrhythmia has been found to be associated with symptoms, the management will be tailored to the individual and the specific arrhythmia. In different situations this may require reassurance, antiarrhythmic medication or referral to a specialist

electrophysiologist for consideration of catheter ablation (see Section 3.4).

1.4.2 Murmur in pregnancy

Scenario

Mrs Rose Berry, aged 23

This woman is 29 weeks pregnant and has been noted to have a systolic murmur at a routine antenatal visit. This is her first pregnancy and there have been no other problems. Is her murmur of any significance?

Introduction

Your major concern will be to differentiate an innocent murmur from one that suggests underlying pathology (Table 10). Can you reassure the patient or, if there is a structural cardiac lesion, can you predict and prevent problems that might arise during the pregnancy?

The most common diagnosis will be an innocent systolic murmur due to the hyperdynamic circulation of pregnancy, requiring no further intervention. Mitral or aortic valve disease, hypertrophic cardiomyopathy (HCM) and congenital abnormalities, such as a ventricular septal defect, are likely to require at

Table 10 Differential diagnosis of a systolic murmur during pregnancy

Comment	Diagnosis
Common	Innocent systolic murmur Mitral valve prolapse (Fig 16)
Must consider	MV disease (regurgitation/mixed/stenosis with tricuspid regurgitation) Aortic valve disease (stenosis/mixed/regurgitation with flow murmur) HCM Atrial or ventricular septal defect
Other causes	Peripartum cardiomyopathy

HCM, hypertrophic cardiomyopathy; MV, mitral valve.

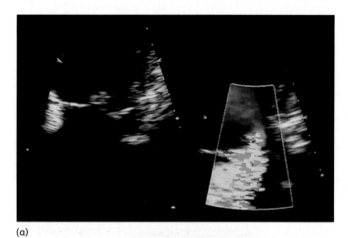
(a)

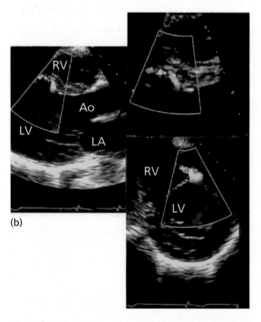
(b)

Fig 16 **(a)** Mitral valve prolapse: in the two-dimensional image on the left, the anterior mitral valve leaflet is seen to bow into the left atrium. The effect of this can be seen in the colour flow mapping in the image on the right – a broad regurgitant jet can be seen. **(b)** Ventricular septal defect: in these parasternal long and short axis views, a small jet of orange colour represents the abnormal blood flow across the septum from the left to right ventricle. LA, left atrium; LV, left ventricle; RV, right ventricle; Ao, aorta. (Courtesy of Dr J Chambers.)

least careful monitoring. Occasionally, rare and severe conditions such as cardiomyopathy of pregnancy can present in the third trimester.

Beginning the encounter

Doctor: hello, my name is Dr A, I understand that you are 29 weeks pregnant and the reason why you are here is that someone heard a murmur while examining you? Is that right?

Patient: yes.

Doctor: before we get onto the details of that, can you tell me if you have any major medical problems? Any problems with the heart?

Patient: [gives list (with doctor politely but firmly discouraging lengthy detail).]

Doctor: and are you on any tablets or medications?

Patient: [gives details (and will probably have been asked to produce a written list).]

The initial brief questions will just confirm the points from the letter and ensure you are along the right lines of questioning.

Focused history

Doctor: going back to the murmur, just some general questions. Have you felt particularly short of breath? Have you had any dizzy spells or blackouts? Have you noticed a lot of ankle swelling?

Most patients who present in this way will be asymptomatic. The presence of symptoms should raise the suspicion of significant pathology, but bear in mind that some weakness, exertional dyspnoea, dizziness and peripheral oedema are quite common during pregnancy and are a result of physiological adaptation rather than intrinsic cardiac disease. Be sure to gauge the precise severity of the symptoms and relate it to the stage of the pregnancy.

Ask some general questions:

> Have you been getting out of breath more easily?

> How far can you walk?

> Have you woken up breathless at night?

> Have you had any chest pains?

> Have you had any palpitations, when your heart seems to beat with an unusual rate or rhythm? When do you get them?

> Have you experienced any blackouts? What were you doing at the time?

> Do you ever feel as if you are going to pass out?

Doctor: now more specifically, before you became pregnant, had a doctor ever mentioned that you had a murmur? If so, when, and what did they say about it?

Enquire about any previous cardiac history. Sometimes a minor abnormality will have been documented in infancy or childhood, and the patient may have been told that she has a murmur, 'hole'

or 'sound' in her heart. Ask about any difficulties before the pregnancy that might also suggest a congenital abnormality. Also ask about any heart problems in other family members – a history of sudden death at a young age might raise the possibility of a hereditary cardiomyopathy or Marfan syndrome.

Focused examination

Remember to maintain patient privacy and dignity as much as is practical.

Cardiovascular – check the following:

> pulse rate and rhythm

> pulse character: check at brachial or carotid – is it slow rising?

> BP: ask the examiner for this, don't forget pre-existing hypertension/pre-eclampsia

> JVP

> cardiac apex (but not formally counting down rib spaces)

> heart sounds and murmurs (auscultation in all four areas and radiation and neck).

Key point

'Innocent' murmurs are usually soft-sounding, relatively short, mid-systolic, don't obscure normal heart sounds, and usually don't radiate significantly. Harsh-sounding or diastolic murmurs, or those associated with abnormal pulses, are more concerning and need further investigation.

If further concerns, check:

> lung bases for evidence of fluid overload

> ankles for evidence of significant oedema.

Ask the examiners for an ECG: minor flattening of the T waves or axis shift are common in normal pregnancy, as are sinus tachycardia and ectopic beats. Look for evidence of atrial enlargement, left or right ventricular hypertrophy, or conduction abnormalities (Fig 17).

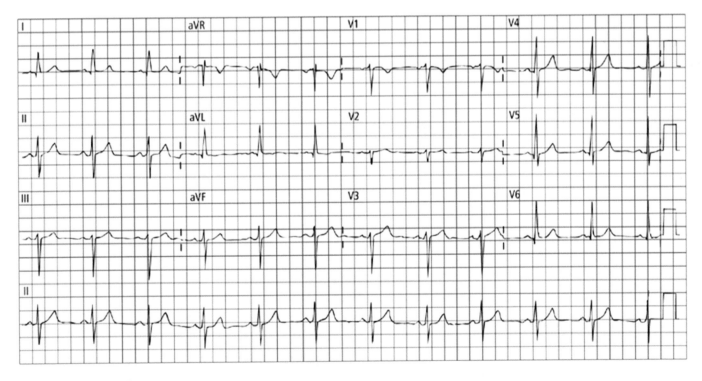

Fig 17 ECG: axis shift in pregnant woman.

Questions from the patient

Patient: why have I got a murmur?

Doctor: [assuming it is innocent] a murmur is just a noise caused by blood flowing through the heart. In your case, I don't think there is anything wrong with your heart, the murmur is just because there is more blood flowing through your heart than normal because you are pregnant. You don't have any other problems and I don't think there is much more we need to do.

Patient: do I need any more tests?

Doctor: [innocent murmur] I don't think you do – many pregnant women have murmurs because of increased blood flow. You don't have any other problems and I haven't found anything worrying while examining you. I am happy that you are healthy. [Alternative] Because of [xxx], I will arrange for you to have an echocardiogram … this is a simple test to look at the heart, and it is completely harmless … it uses ultrasound waves similar to those you have had when you have had scans on your baby.

Patient: will my baby also have a murmur?

Doctor: [innocent murmur] I don't think your murmur is caused by any problem with your heart and so it shouldn't have any bearing on whether or not your baby has a murmur. [More concerning murmur] I'm not sure … it's a bit early to tell … we need to do more investigations such as the echocardiogram and we will take things from there.

Questions from the examiner

Examiners: if you did find a concerning murmur with a structural lesion confirmed on echocardiography, in general terms, what management issues would you consider?

Doctor: this would depend on the specific lesion and its severity. Patients with structural heart disease would need joint management by a cardiologist and the obstetric team. The timing and frequency of the follow-up would depend on exactly what the problem was, and whether or not the patient was symptomatic. Planning the timing and specific nature of the delivery, for example a planned early caesarean section, would be crucial.

Examiners: which structural cardiac conditions presenting with murmurs would you be worried about detecting in a pregnant woman?

Doctor: in general, any severe valvular condition – particularly aortic or mitral stenosis. Any condition causing significant pulmonary hypertension would also be very concerning. A new diagnosis of Marfan syndrome because of the high risk of aortic dissection would also be worrying.

Further discussion

Congenital heart disease in pregnancy is the third commonest cause of maternal death. It will become an increasing problem as more patients survive with complex congenital cardiac abnormalities: the recurrence rate for most (non-syndromic) congenital abnormalities in the offspring is 5%.

Mild lesions may get worse or ventricular function may deteriorate as pregnancy progresses, therefore careful monitoring with specialist input is necessary. In some patients careful consideration will need to be given to advising termination of their pregnancy on medical grounds, and – when that pregnancy is over – patients with high-risk and intermediate cardiac lesions should be offered advice about contraception (Table 11).

Patients with significant cardiac lesions undergoing vaginal delivery require antibiotic prophylaxis to prevent endocarditis. Warfarin is teratogenic; therefore special arrangements (usually conversion to low-molecular-weight heparin) are required for those who need anticoagulation during pregnancy.

Table 11 The risks of pre-existing heart disease in pregnancy		
High risk	**Intermediate risk**	**Low risk**
Pulmonary hypertension Mitral stenosis Aortic and pulmonary stenosis Marfan syndrome	Coarctation of aorta HCM Cyanotic congenital heart disease without pulmonary hypertension	Well-tolerated valvular regurgitation Septal defects without pulmonary hypertension Totally corrected congenital heart disease Prosthetic valves

HCM, hypertrophic cardiomyopathy.

1.4.3 Irregular pulse

Scenario

Mrs Edith Peters, aged 57 years

This woman has presented to the emergency department with irregular palpitations. She was well by the time she was assessed, but the emergency department staff have asked for a medical opinion. What is the likely diagnosis, and how should she be managed?

Introduction

What causes irregular palpitations? The most common cause will be atrial fibrillation, but the differential will also include ectopic beats. It will be important to establish the exact nature of the palpitations from the patient in order to distinguish the two.

If this is atrial fibrillation what else should be considered?

There are many conditions associated with atrial fibrillation (Table 12) and so these should all be thought about in the approach to this patient. Are there any general features that would support one of these diagnoses? Look for a history of surgery (eg thoracotomy or pacemaker / implantable cardioverter defibrillator), evidence of hypercholesterolaemia (xanthelasma or tendon xanthomata) and the characteristic skin colour of chronic amiodarone use (see Fig 18). It will be important to assess this patient's risk of stroke if she has atrial fibrillation.

Beginning the encounter

Doctor: hello, my name is Dr A, I understand that the problem is that you have had some palpitations that led you to come to the hospital: is that right?

Patient: yes.

Table 12	Causes of AF
System	**Cause**
Cardiac	**Hypertension** **Ischaemic heart disease** **Non-ischaemic cardiomyopathy** MV disease Pericardial disease Endocarditis Atrial myxoma
Respiratory	**Chest infection**[1] Pulmonary infarction Bronchial carcinoma
Other	Hyperthyroidism Alcohol Haemochromatosis Sarcoidosis Recreational drug use

Note: Common causes are in bold.
1 Common in routine clinical practice but not in PACES.
AF, atrial fibrillation; MV, mitral valve.

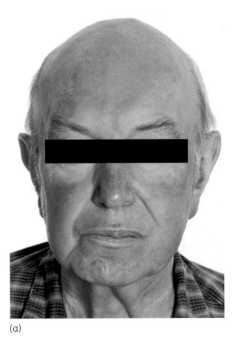 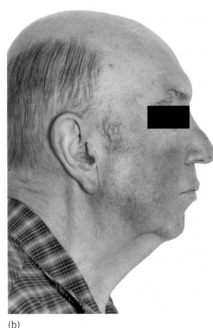

(a) (b)

Fig 18 Typical slate-grey skin colouration associated with long-term amiodarone treatment.

Doctor: before we get onto the details of that, can you tell me if you have any major medical problems? Any problems with the heart? Or other illnesses before? Have you been unwell recently?

Patient: [gives list (with doctor politely but firmly discouraging lengthy detail).]

Doctor: and are you on any tablets or medications?

Patient: [gives details (and will probably have been asked to produce a written list).]

These introductory questions will provide useful clinical context and may immediately give a clue to the likely diagnosis, eg has she had this before, are there other conditions that may predispose to atrial fibrillation?

Focused history

Doctor: now please tell me exactly what you experienced with the palpitations … what were you doing before it happened? [Be very particular in your enquiries. Ask her to tap out the palpitations so that you can establish whether it was slow or fast, or just momentary, which may suggest ectopic beats.] Were there any other associated symptoms such as dizziness or breathlessness?

Doctor: have you had this before?

And if the patient has had more than one episode:

> How long have these episodes being going on for and how many have you had?

> Are the episodes becoming more frequent?

> Is there anything that brings on the symptoms?

> Are there any other associated symptoms?

Specific questions that you will need to ask if you think this is atrial fibrillation surround your assessment of her risk of stroke (ie CHA_2DS_2-VASc score – see below):

> Are you diabetic?

> Have you been treated for hypertension?

> Have you ever had a stroke or a mini stroke?

> Have you had any other problems with your heart or circulation?

Focused examination

Look quickly for evidence of any coexisting conditions such as thyroid abnormalities.

Cardiovascular – check the following:

> Pulse – rate and rhythm. Is there an arrhythmia now? Are the hands cool and the pulse of small volume suggestive of low cardiac output?

> Signs of heart failure – look for evidence of congestive heart failure or tricuspid regurgitation by examining the JVP. Is the apex beat displaced? What is the character of the apex beat? Is there evidence of pulmonary oedema or right-sided heart failure?

> Heart sounds – careful auscultation should reveal any valve abnormalities. Particular focus should be on the mitral valve (MV) as there is an increased incidence of AF with mitral stenosis or regurgitation. Mitral regurgitation is common in patients with impaired, dilated left ventricles (LVs). Is there an ejection systolic murmur that might suggest hypertrophic cardiomyopathy?

Thyroid – check the following:

> tremor?

> sweating?

> anxious?

Questions from the patient

Patient: what caused this episode?

Doctor: [on the assumption that the history and examination have not revealed a clear cause] I'm not sure … the commonest cause for irregular palpitations is an abnormal rhythm of the heart called atrial fibrillation … one in five women over the age of 40 will suffer from this at some stage in their life (one in four men). We will need to try and identify exactly what caused your symptoms and this will require some tests on your heart.

Patient: is this dangerous?

Doctor: if this is atrial fibrillation then it does make you more susceptible to strokes than you would be if the pulse was regular. We will need to look into this in more detail. If we find that you are at increased risk then there are treatments that significantly reduce this risk.

Patient: I feel fine now, can I go home?

Doctor: it's good that you feel well enough to go home now, but I'd like to see the results of a few simple tests before you do … in particular I'd like to see the results of an ECG, an electrical tracing of your heart … this might give a clue to the rhythm of your heart or any other problems with your heart. We will also arrange a few simple blood tests. If these are all OK then we can let you go home, but will need to organise a couple of other tests of the heart and then see you in the outpatient clinic to review matters.

Questions from the examiner

Examiner: what features would lead you to a diagnosis of ectopic beats rather than atrial fibrillation?

Doctor: this would depend on getting an impression of the exact nature of the palpitations. Atrial fibrillation tends to be very fast and chaotic. Ectopic beats might be described as an occasional extra beat or even a missed beat.

Examiner: you mentioned doing some other tests … what were you intending to do?

Doctor: if her 12-lead ECG was normal, then I'd want to follow up by organising a 24-hour tape to see if she was getting bursts of atrial fibrillation, and I'd want to organise an echocardiogram to see if there was any underlying structural heart disease.

Examiner: your patient has another episode of palpitation while in the emergency department prior to going home and the monitor confirms atrial fibrillation. How are you going to treat her?

Doctor: she requires medication to prevent further episodes and an assessment of her stroke risk.

Examiner: what drug are you going to prescribe?

Doctor: I would use a beta-blocker such as bisoprolol in the first instance, providing she doesn't have a contraindication. If her risk assessment of stroke is high then I would consider either recommending warfarin or a novel oral anticoagulant.

Examiner: if her ECG showed occasional ectopics while she was having symptoms what would you tell her?

Doctor: providing I had established that there were no other significant coexisting conditions or cardiac abnormality then I would reassure her that ectopic beats are common and not dangerous.

Further discussion

An irregular pulse may obviously be the cause of her symptoms, and to confirm the diagnosis of an arrhythmia an ECG will clearly be the first investigation to perform. If the pulse is rapid and regular then it is either going to be a sinus tachycardia, supraventricular tachycardia (SVT) or ventricular tachycardia (VT). In a formal examination such as PACES it is highly improbable that the patient will be in VT, although SVT is possible, eg atrial flutter with a pulse of 150 beats per minute. If the pulse is irregularly irregular then it is either AF or sinus rhythm with frequent ectopics. A regularly irregular rhythm will either be sinus rhythm with regular ectopic beats, eg ventricular trigeminy, or heart block, such as Wenckebach.

Patients with structural cardiac abnormalities are more likely to have arrhythmias: specific conditions to look for are impaired LV function, valvular abnormalities and cardiomyopathies. Many cardiomyopathies may just have features of impaired left or right ventricular function, but some may have very specific findings, eg HCM. A chest radiograph and echocardiogram would clearly be the first-line investigations to look for structural cardiac lesions.

Hazard

Remember that in routine clinical practice many patients who complain of palpitations do not have a pathological arrhythmia: anxiety can lead to an increased awareness of sinus rhythm or normal ectopic beats.

Key point

CHA$_2$DS$_2$-VASc score – this evaluates ischaemic stroke risk in patients with atrial fibrillation

Congestive heart failure	+1
Hypertension	+1
Age >75	+2
Diabetes mellitus	+1
Stroke or transient ischaemic attack (TIA)	+2
Vascular disease	+1
Age 65–74	+1
Sex category – female	+1

In general a score of 0 is low risk for stroke, 1 is moderate risk (unless the score is only for being female), and any score above 1 is high risk.

1.4.4 Hypertension

Scenario

Mrs Lucy Jones, aged 40

This woman has been referred to cardiology clinic after being found to be hypertensive by her GP. The GP sent some routine blood tests which were normal. Please take a focused history, do a focused examination and formulate an initial management plan.

Introduction

Hypertension is a very common clinical encounter (see Table 13 for differential diagnosis). The assessment of a patient with hypertension should aim to:

1 identify any potential causes of secondary hypertension

2 identify any end-organ damage

3 assess the patient's cardiovascular risk

4 initiate appropriate management.

Most patients with hypertension have primary or idiopathic hypertension, but causes of secondary hypertension should be considered in the appropriate clinical setting.

Beginning the encounter

Doctor: hello, my name is Dr A, I understand that the problem you have is high blood pressure. Is that right?

Patient: yes.

Doctor: before we get into the details of that, can you tell me if you have any other major medical problems? Any problems with the heart or the kidneys?

Patient: [gives list (with doctor politely but firmly discouraging lengthy detail).]

Table 13   Differential diagnosis of hypertension

Comment	Diagnosis	Clinical clues
Common	Essential hypertension	No other cause found
	'White coat' hypertension	Hypertension in clinic but not at home
Must consider	Renovascular hypertension	Deterioration in renal function after ACEI/ARB, asymmetric kidneys on imaging, diffuse atherosclerosis, recurrent 'flash' pulmonary oedema, renal bruits
	Primary kidney disease	Chronic kidney disease and abnormal urinalysis
	Phaeochromocytoma	Headaches, palpitations, sweating
	Coarctation of aorta	Radio-femoral delay
	Primary aldosteronism	Unexplained hypokalaemia, but remember that more that 50% of patients have normal serum potassium. Check plasma renin and aldosterone
	NSAIDs, steroids, oral contraceptive pill, chemotherapeutic agents	
	Sleep apnoea	Daytime somnolence, apnoeic episodes, morning headaches
Other causes	Cushing's syndrome	Cushingoid facies, proximal weakness, thin skin, easy bruising, long-term steroids
	Hypothyroidism/hyperthyroidism	Abnormal TFTs
	Acromegaly	Appropriate general appearance (check old pictures)

ACEI, angiotensin-converting enzyme inhibitor; ARB, angiotensin receptor blocker; NSAID, non-steroidal anti-inflammatory drug; TFT, thyroid function test.

Doctor: are you on any tablets or medications?

Patient: [gives details (and will probably have been asked to produce a written list).]

These introductory questions will provide useful clinical context and may immediately give a clue to the likely diagnosis, eg the antihypertensives drugs that the patient takes, are there any drugs that might exacerbate hypertension (eg steroids, non-steroidal anti-inflammatory, oral contraceptive pill)?

Focused history

Enquire about the possible effects of hypertension to end organs (heart, brain etc).

Doctor: now, please tell me, have you got any symptoms? [Ask specifically about exertional chest pain, breathlessness on exertion, palpitations, orthopnoea, ankle oedema, headaches or visual disturbance.]

Enquire about possible causes of hypertension.

Doctor: how much salt do you put in your food?

Doctor: are there any other members of your family with high blood pressure? [and if yes] how old were they when they developed this?

Doctor: do you suffer from headaches, palpitations or excessive sweating? [This is the classic triad that points towards phaeochromocytoma.]

Doctor: do you suffer from headaches, weakness of your arms/thighs and easy bruising? Have you been taking oral steroids for a long time? [These questions aim to identify Cushing's syndrome.]

Doctor: do you suffer from increased tiredness, morning headaches, excessive snoring? Has your partner told you that sometimes you seem to stop breathing at night?

[These questions aim to identify obstructive sleep apnoea.]

Doctor: do you suffer from palpitations, sweating? Have you had any weight loss or diarrhoea? Have you noticed any increased fatigue, weight gain, ankle swelling or constipation? [These questions aim to identify hyperthyroidism or hypothyroidism, both of which can cause hypertension.]

Focused examination

General appearance
Look quickly for any evidence for Cushing's syndrome, sleep apnoea, acromegaly.

Cardiovascular examination
Pay particular attention to the following:

> BP – In this scenario you should obviously offer to measure the patient's BP, but it is unlikely that the examiners will actually allow you to do so because of the time constraints

of the station. However, if they do, make sure you do it properly. The patient is likely to have been lying on a couch for some time, but remember that they should be recumbent for at least 3 minutes before taking a reading and that the arm should be supported at the level of the heart when making the measurement. Make sure you use an appropriately sized cuff and offer to measure the BP in both arms (which will almost certainly be declined).

> JVP, apex beat, heaves, heart sounds and lungs. Examine these for any evidence of left ventricular hypertrophy or heart failure. Remember to consider neck circumference as an indicator of risk of sleep apnoea in the correct clinical context.

> Peripheral pulses – examine carefully, in particular for the radio-femoral delay of coarctation of the aorta. Also assess the presence and volume of all pulses as the patient may have peripheral vascular disease.

> Abdomen – feel for an abdominal aortic aneurysm and listen over the renal arteries for bruits.

> Fundi – offer to examine for evidence of hypertensive retinopathy (again this will probably be declined by the examiners in view of the time constraints).

Questions from the patient

Patient: why is my BP elevated?

Doctor: [on the assumption that history and examination have not revealed a clear cause] I have not found a specific cause to explain your high blood pressure. The commonest cause is called essential (idiopathic) hypertension, which means that we can't find any particular underlying reason.

Patient: why do I need to take medications for my hypertension when I feel fine?

Doctor: most patients with hypertension don't have any symptoms, but untreated hypertension causes gradual damage to organs such as the heart, the retina (back of the eyes), arteries and kidneys … and it does increase the risk of heart attacks and strokes. The reason for wanting to control blood pressure is to stop damage to the heart and other organs, and reduce the risk of heart attacks and strokes in the long term.

Questions from the examiner

Examiner: how would you initially investigate this patient if you were the medical registrar assessing the patient in clinic?

Doctor: I would request a 12-lead ECG.

Examiner: suppose that this was normal?

Doctor: I would request a transthoracic echocardiogram.

Examiner: what would you be looking for on the echocardiogram?

Doctor: I would look for evidence of left ventricular hypertrophy, atrial dilatation or valvular abnormalities.

Examiner: how would you confirm and assess further the degree of the patient's hypertension?

Doctor: I would request 24-hour BP monitoring. Based on 24-hour BP monitoring, hypertension is classified as stage 1 if average BP is above 135/85 mmHg, and stage 2 if average BP is above 150/95 mmHg. Severe hypertension is defined as clinic systolic BP of over 180 mmHg or a clinic diastolic BP of over 110 mmHg.

Examiner: what would you do if her BP was still not well controlled on 24-hour BP monitoring despite four antihypertensive medications and all initial investigations were normal?

Doctor: I would suspect either a secondary cause of hypertension, or a medicine compliance issue.

Examiner: so what would you do?

Doctor: at this point I think I'd want to ask for advice from a hypertension specialist, but investigation for secondary causes of hypertension would be tailored according to the clinical clues and index of suspicion.

Further discussion

You should be able to discuss the secondary causes of hypertension and in particular any obvious cause that you may have elicited from the examination. Particular emphasis may be placed on the subsequent treatment of the patient's hypertension, including lifestyle changes, risk factor modification and medical management (see Section 2.17).

Key point

When examining a patient with hypertension, consider the following:

> Essential hypertension – if the patient has elevated BP, evidence of left ventricular hypertrophy or hypertensive retinopathy, and there are no pointers to a secondary cause.

> Isolated clinic hypertension – look for anxiety, eg tachycardia. Is the BP lower when measured by the clinic nurse or the GP, or at place of work or at home? There must be no evidence of target organ damage.

> Renovascular disease – are there abdominal or vascular bruits, abdominal aortic aneurysm, or other evidence of atherosclerosis?

> Coarctation – look for absent femoral pulses and radio-femoral delay, collaterals in the back muscles and a widespread systolic murmur heard best over the back.

1.4.5 Syncope

Scenario

Mrs Helen Diver, aged 65

This woman has presented to the emergency department after she collapsed when out shopping earlier today. When the paramedic team arrived at the scene she was alert and orientated, and all observations were normal and have remained so. What is the most likely diagnosis, and how should she be managed?

Introduction

How common are unexplained collapses?

These are a very common clinical problem, and account for up to 3% of attendances at emergency departments and 1% of hospital admissions. A difficult aspect of managing patients such as this is that there are many causes of syncope, both cardiac and non-cardiac (Table 14).

Who are the high-risk patients?

Untreated cardiac-related syncope has a 1-year mortality rate of 20–30%, making it of paramount importance to identify this group of patients as early as possible. A carefully taken history may eliminate high risk in many patients, and a meticulous examination may elicit the cause. A history from a witness should be obtained if at all possible – it might be invaluable.

Key point

Syncope is a transient disturbance of consciousness. The differential diagnosis of sudden collapse is more extensive, including diagnoses such as aortic dissection, pulmonary embolism, cardiac tamponade and sub-arachnoid haemorrhage. The patient who has recovered fully and has normal observations is not likely to have suffered such a catastrophe.

Beginning the encounter

Doctor: hello, my name is Dr A, I understand that the problem is that you collapsed in the street earlier today: is that right?

Patient: *yes.*

Doctor: before we get onto the details of that, can you tell me if you have any major medical problems? Any problems with the heart? Or with fits or faints before?

Patient: [gives list (with doctor politely but firmly discouraging lengthy detail).]

Doctor: and are you on any tablets or medications?

Patient: [gives details (and will probably have been asked to produce a written list).]

These introductory questions will provide useful clinical context and may immediately give a clue to the likely diagnosis, eg are there any drugs that might predispose to syncope (eg diuretics that could cause postural hypotension) or agents that might predispose to arrhythmia?

Focused history

Doctor: now please tell me what you can remember about the collapse … what were you doing before it happened? [Be very particular in your enquiries. Do not accept: 'I was out shopping'. Ask: 'Were you walking, or standing still, or sitting down?' … 'Had you just got up?']

Doctor: did anyone else see what happened? What did they tell you? [Obtaining a history from a witness would be of highest importance in routine clinical practice.]

Did the woman really have a syncopal episode or did she just trip up?

Specific questions about symptoms that would suggest a cardiac cause are:

> Did you feel sweaty or nauseous before the episodes?

> Did you get palpitations ('a feeling that the heart was beating oddly'), chest pain or breathlessness beforehand?

Seizures are associated with the following:

> tongue biting

> incontinence

> unconsciousness for less than 5 minutes ('how long were you out for?')

> drowsiness and disorientation for a variable length of time on recovery

Type	Cause
Table 14	Causes of syncope
Non-cardiac	Seizures[1]
	Postural hypotension[1]
	Situational (micturition, defecation, cough and swallow)[1]
	Cerebrovascular (TIA, stroke)[2]
	Psychogenic (anxiety, panic, somatisation and depression)
Cardiac	Bradyarrhythmias (including vasovagal)[1]
	Tachyarrhythmias[1]
	Left ventricular outflow obstruction (aortic stenosis and HCM)
	Rarities, eg atrial myxoma

HCM, hypertrophic cardiomyopathy; TIA, transient ischaemic attack.
1 Commonest causes.
2 Patients with syncope should not be diagnosed as having had a TIA or stroke in the absence of a clear history or physical signs of focal neurological deficit.

(did you come round straight away? What's the next thing that you can remember?).

And if the patient has had more than one episode:

> How long have these episodes being going on for and how many have you had?
> Are the episodes becoming more frequent?
> Have you had fits of any sort before?
> Is there anything that brings on the symptoms?

Focused examination

Look for evidence of injury caused by the syncope ('did you hurt yourself anywhere?'), and concentrate specifically on cardiovascular and neurological assessment (first examining the system that seems most relevant, which is likely to be the cardiovascular system).

Cardiovascular – check the following:

> pulse rate and rhythm
> pulse character: check at brachial or carotid – is it slow rising?
> BP: ask the examiner for this, and if there is a postural drop (this may lead the examiner to show you an observation chart)
> JVP
> cardiac apex (but not formally counting down rib spaces)
> heart sounds and murmurs (quick auscultation at apex, aortic area and neck – not a full examination).

Neurological – check the following:

> mouth and tongue – injuries from biting during seizure
> arms out with palms facing up ... close your eyes ... touch your nose with this finger (touch one of the patient's index fingers) ... arm back out ... now with this finger (touching the index finger of the

patient's other hand) – rapid screening for weakness or sensory disorder in the arms
> gait – rapid screening for weakness or sensory disorder in the legs (examiner is likely to tell you that you don't need to do this for reasons of time).

Other relevant examination:

> Ask the patient to move her neck through its full range of movement: if this provokes feelings of presyncope or dizziness, then this suggests vertebrobasilar ischaemia as a possible cause for her syncope.

Questions from the patient

Patient: why did I collapse?

Doctor: [on the assumption that the history and examination have not revealed a clear cause] I'm not sure ... the commonest reasons are that there's been a problem with the heart going too slow or too fast, or with the blood pressure dropping, or with a fit of some sort ... but I haven't found anything obvious from what you've told me about what happened, and I didn't find anything worrisome when I examined you.

Patient: I feel fine now, can I go home?

Doctor: it's good that you feel well enough to go home now, but I'd like to see the results of a few simple tests before you do ... in particular I'd like to see the results of an ECG, an electrical tracing of your heart ... this might give a clue if your heart is likely to have gone too slow or too fast.

Questions from the examiner

Examiner: how do you differentiate between seizures and cardiac syncope?

Doctor: the key thing is to get a history from a reliable witness.

Seizures are associated with the following:

> blue face (not pale)
> convulsive movements (usually, but not always)

> tongue biting
> incontinence
> unconsciousness for less than 5 minutes
> drowsiness and disorientation for a variable length of time on recovery.

Cardiac syncope is associated with the following:

> known heart rhythm abnormality
> known structural heart disease (aortic stenosis, hypertrophic cardiomyopathy)
> abnormal cardiac examination
> family history of sudden cardiac death.

Examiner: if you were the medical registrar in the emergency department, how would you manage this woman?

Doctor: [on the assumption that the history and examination have not revealed a clear cause] the first thing I'd want to do is look at a 12-lead ECG.

Examiner: supposing that was entirely normal?

Doctor: I'd want a chest radiograph.

Examiner: supposing that was entirely normal?

Doctor: as she's collapsed in the street, and we don't know why, I'd want to admit her overnight for observation ... and further tests that would be most useful would be ambulatory monitoring – 24-hour Holter monitoring and patient-activated devices to look for tachyarrhythmias and bradyarrhythmias [Fig 19] – and echocardiography, which may indicate structural [Fig 20] or functional cardiac disease.

Examiner: what should you do if no cause for syncope is established and the patient is asking to go home?

Doctor: if, after 24 hours, there has been no recurrence of presyncope or syncope, the patient has 'mobilised' satisfactorily on the ward and serial

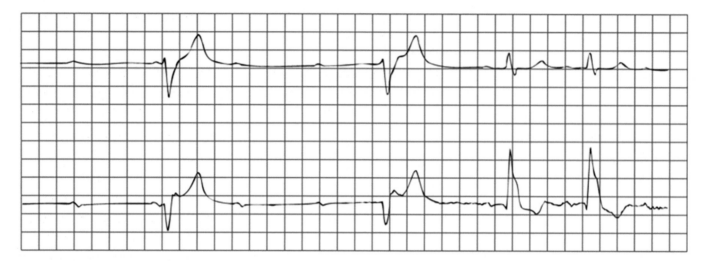

Fig 19 Complete heart block demonstrated on a Holter monitor.

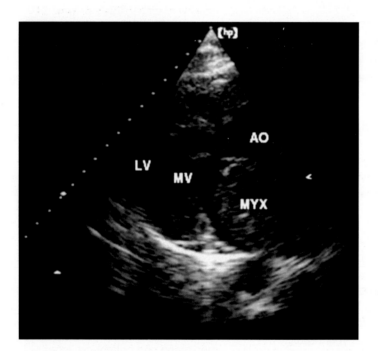

Fig 20 Transthoracic echocardiogram of an atrial myxoma. The myxoma (MYX) is seen to occupy most of the left atrium and is almost prolapsing through the mitral valve (MV) into the left ventricle (LV). The aorta (AO) is seen above the left atrium. This would be an exceedingly rare cause of syncope.

12-lead ECGs show no change, then I'd let them go home … I'd give reassurance that nothing terrible has been found, but also a clear statement that no firm diagnosis had been made … I'd tell them to report recurrence of presyncope or syncope immediately … and I'd make arrangements for 24-hour ambulatory monitoring and echocardiography if it had not been possible to obtain these during the patient's admission.

Further discussion

ECG – 10% of patients with cardiac syncope will have an identifiable abnormality on their 12-lead ECG to suggest a cause. Look for the following:

> sinus rate

> PR interval

> QRS axis

> QRS width

> QT interval (long QT syndrome)

> left ventricular hypertrophy

> right ventricular hypertrophy

> P-wave morphology

> evidence of pre-excitation (Wolff–Parkinson–White syndrome)

> evidence of acute (or old) myocardial infarction

> Brugada syndrome (partial right bundle branch block (RBBB) and ST elevation V1–V3).

Chest radiograph – look for the following:

> cardiac size and shape

> prominent pulmonary vasculature

> pulmonary oedema.

Blood tests – these are rarely useful in the diagnosis of syncope, but cardiac enzymes, FBC, electrolytes, renal and liver function tests, and inflammatory markers will often be requested as a 'screen'. Electrolyte disturbance (particularly hypokalaemia) might predispose to arrhythmia and syncope.

Recurrent unexplained syncope – consider referral for specialist investigations such as tilt-table testing and electrophysiological tests.

Key point

Most patients will be aware of the serious nature of most cardiac causes of syncope. It is essential to be aware of the psychological needs of such patients. Reassurance and appropriate information at an early stage may prevent problems at a later stage in their management.

1.4.6 Acute chest pain

Scenario
Mr Alex McTanner, aged 55

This Glaswegian merchant seaman has presented to the emergency department with chest tightness after unloading his ship of heavy goods. A 12-lead ECG done on arrival in the emergency department shows no clear abnormalities. What is the likely diagnosis, and how should he be managed?

Introduction

If the patient was still in pain, the first concern would be to rule out life-threatening emergencies such as myocardial infarction (MI) or aortic dissection where treatment can be life saving. Quickly assess the patient's haemodynamic status, including checking for bradycardia and tachycardia, and measuring the BP. Obtain an initial brief history and conduct a quick examination (in routine clinical practice but not in PACES) while the ECG is being recorded, but the obvious concern in this case is that the patient has had ischaemic cardiac pain.

Beginning the encounter

Doctor: hello, my name is Dr A, I understand you've had some chest tightness. Have you still got it now / are you still in pain?

Patient: it's gone now … the ambulance crew gave me something for it …

Doctor: that's good news, before I get into the specifics, do you have any major medical problems or anything you take regular tablets for?

Patient: [gives list.]

Doctor: please let me or one of the nursing staff know if that feeling of pain or chest tightness comes back.

Patient: OK.

These introductory questions will provide useful clinical context regarding how urgent the situation is and may hint towards a diagnosis.

Focused history

Doctor: let's go back to the chest tightness … what were you doing when it came on, and what did you feel?

This patient's pain was associated with heavy exertion, but it is important to determine answers to the following questions if they do not emerge spontaneously.

> When did it start?

> What were you doing when it started?

> What was it like? Characteristically ischaemic pain is described as tight, squeezing or crushing, whereas pleuritic chest pain is sharp and stabbing. It may be helpful to offer suggestions, but it is important to realise that patients may find it difficult to describe pain, especially if it is severe.

> How bad was the pain? Severity should be recorded out of 10.

> How long did it last? Pains that last for only a few seconds, or are

constant for days, are unlikely to be cardiac.

> Did it start suddenly? If so then consider aortic dissection, although this is also typical of non-cardiac pain related to anxiety. Or did it build up rapidly over minutes? That is more typical of cardiac ischaemia.

> Did the pain go anywhere else? In particular, did it radiate in a manner typical of ischaemic cardiac pain?

> Has the patient experienced unusual breathlessness or chest tightness on exertion previously? Ischaemic pain at rest sometimes builds up with a crescendo of similar pain on ever decreasing amounts of exertion.

> Beware of pain which comes on at rest or during sleep – both unstable angina and acute coronary syndromes (ACSs) may occur at rest.

Associated symptoms – ask about breathlessness, sweating, nausea, faintness and whether the pain was frightening, all of which are features of cardiac ischaemia.

Key point

A patient with stable angina who then presents with increasing frequency and severity of angina ('crescendo angina') is likely to have an unstable plaque and should be admitted, even if pain free when seen.

Doctor: have you had any heart trouble before? – [Does the patient have known coronary disease? Ask about history of angina, MI and cardiac catheterisation/revascularisation procedures (percutaneous coronary intervention or coronary artery bypass surgery). If not, are they at high risk of coronary disease? Note previous vascular events – does the patient have a history of stroke or peripheral vascular disease? Consider risk factors for coronary disease, including family history, smoking, diabetes mellitus, hypercholesterolaemia and hypertension.]

Consider differential diagnoses:

> Aortic dissection. A sudden onset of severe pain radiating to the back, which may be described as 'tearing', should ring alarm bells and the patient should be evaluated for dissection. This is more likely in patients with known hypertension. Always be concerned about patients presenting with odd neurological symptoms and chest pain (carotid artery involvement from aortic arch dissection).

> Digestive pain – reflux oesophagitis or peptic ulceration. Ask whether the pain was associated with the bringing up of wind or an acid taste into the mouth. Also enquire about any previous history of indigestion, use of treatments for indigestion ('Do you take antacids?') or previous investigations for indigestion ('Have you ever had a barium meal or endoscopy test?'). Remember that severe epigastric pain can be caused by myocardial ischaemia as well as the abdominal conditions usually considered (peptic ulceration, biliary pain, pancreatitis and intestinal ischaemia). Patients may describe chest pain but the pain is actually in the abdomen; pointing to where the pain was experienced is very useful.

> Musculoskeletal. This tends to be very localised ('Can you point to the pain with one finger?') and affected by the position of the sufferer, unlike ischaemic pain that is not. It may occur after strenuous exertion, which often leads to anxiety that this has 'brought on a heart attack'.

> Pericarditis. This is unlikely in this case, but ask about whether the patient has had any flu-like symptoms. The pain tends to be sharper than ischaemic cardiac pain and is usually eased by sitting forward.

> Anxiety. This can manifest itself as pain, but severe pain may cause patients to become anxious, so beware of dismissing the patient's symptoms. Patients may develop tingling in the fingers due to hyperventilation in response to chest pain. This is generally a diagnosis of exclusion.

Focused examination

All patients with chest pain need prompt, rapid assessment. How does the patient look: well, ill, very ill or about to die? Patients with MI usually look very ill (or worse).

After checking vital signs, examine particularly for epigastric tenderness and guarding: patients with perforations or pancreatitis may present in this way and be misdiagnosed. Where the patient does not have a life-threatening condition, palpation for tenderness that reproduces the pain is useful.

Cardiovascular examination

This is frequently normal in patients with acute central chest pain. Features that would be diagnostically useful:

> Pulses. Unequal radial pulses and unequal BPs in the arms may indicate aortic dissection.

> Heart sounds. An early diastolic murmur of aortic regurgitation may indicate dissection; a pericardial rub would suggest pericarditis.

> Basal crackles suggesting pulmonary oedema. These would indicate left ventricular dysfunction, probably caused by ischaemia.

Questions from the patient

Patient: have I had a heart attack?

Doctor: I don't know … I can't say for certain at the moment, but it is something I am considering. The pain you had certainly sounds suspicious, but the heart tracing doesn't show anything definite, and you aren't in pain now. We need to see how things go, and

check a blood test for markers of damage to the heart.

Patient: if the blood test is normal can I go home?

Doctor: if you haven't had any more pain, further heart tracings are normal, and the blood tests are OK, then we won't need to keep you in hospital … but there is something going on that's given you this chest pain, and we will almost certainly recommend that you have more tests as an outpatient and see you in clinic.

Patient: what about work?

Doctor: it's a bit early to give any advice as we haven't worked out what's going on yet. Let's wait and see what we find and we can discuss things again.

Patient: what happens if I have had a heart attack? Do I need to have bypass surgery?

Doctor: if you have had a heart attack we would keep you in for observation and consider performing a test called an angiogram, where we take pictures of the arteries supplying blood to the heart. If we find narrowings or blockages that need treating, we may be able to do this without an operation, but sometimes bypass surgery is needed. But we're getting ahead of ourselves here … we need to find out if you have had a heart attack first.

Patient: can I go outside to phone my wife?

Doctor: we can arrange for you to talk to your wife, but I don't want you to go outside. You've just had a bad episode of chest pain, so it's important that you stay connected to the monitor so that if anything changes suddenly with your heart rhythm we can deal with it quickly. I think you ought to stay here until we know exactly what is going on.

Questions from the examiner

Examiner: *as the medical registrar, how would you manage this patient?*

Doctor: given the characteristic history, he needs further investigation prior to discharge.

Examiner: *why have you kept him on a cardiac monitor?*

Doctor: there is a risk of life-threatening ventricular arrhythmias such as ventricular tachycardia (VT) and ventricular fibrillation (VF) which could be treated promptly if he is monitored appropriately.

Examiner: *if he had further pain with dynamic ECG changes, how would you manage the patient?*

Doctor: I'd give him analgesia – morphine and an antiemetic – followed by antiplatelet therapy … aspirin 300 mg and clopidogrel 300 mg if they hadn't already been given … and I'd want to discuss with the on-call cardiology team. An

intravenous nitrate infusion may help the pain, but I suspect he would need a glycoprotein IIb/IIIa inhibitor such as tirofiban and transfer to the local interventional cardiology centre for angiography.

Further discussion

Investigations

Appropriate investigations are the key to proving a diagnosis of an ACS.

ECG

Hazard

An entirely normal ECG at presentation does not exclude serious underlying coronary disease.

Look in particular for:

> ST segment elevation / left bundle branch block (MI) (Fig 21)

> ST segment depression (non-ST elevation MI (NSTEMI) or unstable angina) (Fig 22)

> T wave inversion (NSTEMI or unstable angina)

> concave ST segment elevation in multiple leads that do not conform to a single coronary artery territory, or PR segment depression (pericarditis).

Biochemical markers

Troponins should be measured at specified time intervals depending on the assay to see if there has been myocyte necrosis to diagnose MI (see Section 3.7). High sensitivity troponins allow rapid detection of myocyte necrosis and if not elevated are increasingly used as 'rule-out' tests in many hospital departments. They can be elevated in a variety of cardiac and non-cardiac conditions. However, they are not the only diagnostic criteria for diagnosing MI.

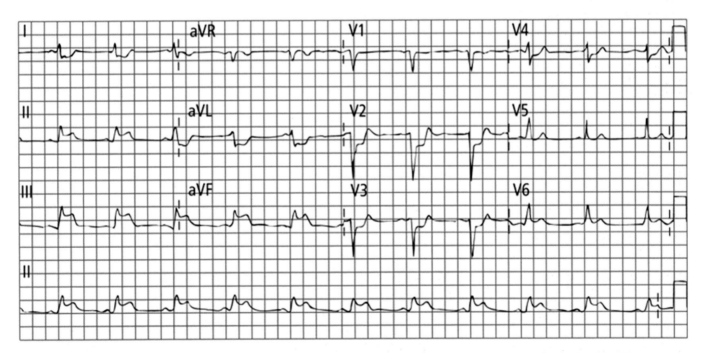

Fig 21 Acute inferior MI. The ECG shows ST segment deviation in the inferior leads (II, III and aVF). ST segment depression in leads V2 and V3 may indicate posterior extension.

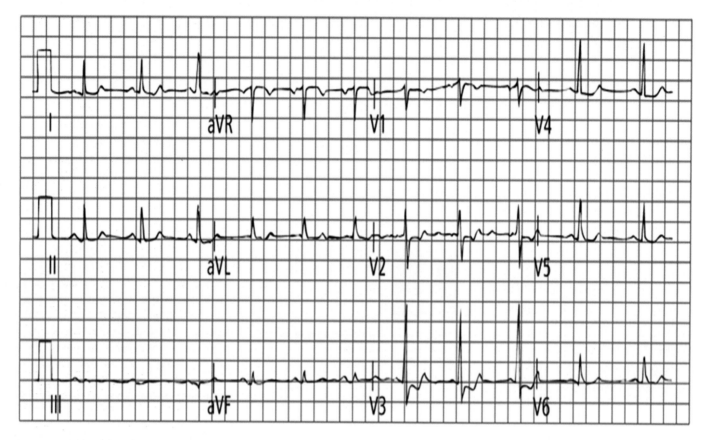

Fig 22 ECG showing anterior ST depression in a patient presenting with chest pain. Antithrombotics should be commenced and urgent angiography considered.

A good history and ECG findings make up the other components of the commonly used diagnostic tests.

Other blood tests

Should include FBC (extreme anaemia can cause myocardial ischaemia and troponin rise), creatinine and electrolytes, glucose, cholesterol and, in patients with epigastric pain, serum amylase.

Chest radiograph

Is the mediastinum widened (aortic dissection) or is there pulmonary oedema?

Management

Ischaemic cardiac pain

Patients will usually already have received 300 mg aspirin. Give oxygen and analgesia if the patient is still in pain. Further management will depend on the diagnosis:

> unstable angina/NSTEMI (see Section 2.1.2).
> ST-elevation MI (see Section 2.1.3).

Persisting pain without ECG abnormalities and no other clear diagnosis

Reassure the patient, give them analgesia and admit them for observation with repeat ECGs and serial troponin measurements.

Key point

Do not discharge patients who present with undiagnosed chest pain without a further ECG and interval troponin – unstable ischaemic heart disease can be difficult to diagnose clinically and is easily missed.

Pain resolved but diagnosis uncertain

Patients who attend hospital with chest pain that is not clearly musculoskeletal should stay for further assessment with a troponin and ECG. A negative troponin will not rule out important coronary disease, so a test to look for ischaemia (such as stress echocardiography) should be arranged as an outpatient. The patient should be advised to seek medical help immediately if the pain recurs after discharge.

Hazard

Oesophageal pain is difficult to distinguish from cardiac pain. Cardiac pain may be relieved by belching. It is inadvisable to discharge a high-risk patient with a clinical diagnosis of oesophageal pain without a period of observation and measurement of serum troponin.

Hazard

Difficult cases of chest pain may be due to coronary vasospasm (see Fig 23). Features of spasm include:

> normal coronary angiogram or 'minor irregularities'

> paroxysms of crushing central chest pain at rest

> affects postmenopausal women the most

> relieved by glyceryl trinitrate (GTN)

> does not limit exercise

> may be associated with syncope

> usually benign unless associated with ECG changes or ventricular arrhythmias.

1.4.7 Pleuritic chest pain

Scenario

Mrs Pamela Evers, aged 50 years

This woman has presented to the emergency department with a 1-day history of left-sided pleuritic chest pain and progressive breathlessness on minimal exertion. Routine observations reveal temperature 37.9°C, pulse 80/minute, BP 130/80 mmHg and respiratory rate 18/minute. What is the likely diagnosis, and how should she be managed?

Introduction

The differential diagnosis of the patient presenting with pleuritic pain is shown in Table 15. The two most important acute diagnoses to consider in this case are obviously pulmonary embolus (PE) and pneumonia; although pneumothorax also needs to be considered. A chest radiograph will easily rule out a pneumothorax and an infection if the infective process is advanced to have formed pulmonary changes.

Hazard

Beware of the following in a patient with pleuritic chest pain:

> A low-grade fever (<38°C) does not necessarily indicate infection: it can be associated with inflammation of any cause – including pulmonary infarction.

> Pneumonia may present in a variety of ways and sputum production is not generally an early feature.

> Rib fracture tends to be associated with a clearly memorable episode of trauma and is therefore not usually a diagnostic difficulty, but remember the possibility of pathological fracture.

Beginning the encounter

Doctor: hello, my name is Dr A, I understand that the problem is that you feel breathless and have chest pain since yesterday. Is that right?

Patient: yes.

Doctor: before we get onto the details of that, can you tell me if you have any major medical problems? Any problems with the heart or lungs?

Patient: [gives list (with doctor politely but firmly discouraging lengthy detail).]

Doctor: and are you on any tablets or medications?

Patient: [gives details (and will probably have been asked to produce a written list).]

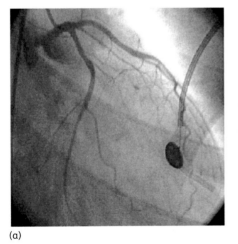

(a)

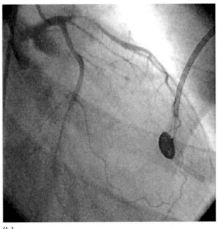

(b)

Fig 23 Left coronary angiogram demonstrating coronary vasospasm. This 34-year-old woman presented with chest pain and anterior ST segment elevation on the ECG. Shortly afterwards, she had a ventricular fibrillation arrest. After resuscitation, the ECG returned to normal. **(a)** Initial angiography showed a normal left coronary artery. **(b)** Intra-coronary ergometrine induced localised spasm of the proximal left anterior descending coronary artery, and reproduced the chest pain with ECG changes.

Table 15	Differential diagnosis of patient presenting with pleuritic chest pain
Common causes	PE Pneumothorax Pneumonia Musculoskeletal: rib fracture, costochondritis, Bornholm myalgia (Coxsackie B virus, self-limiting), non-specific
Less common causes	Autoimmune/rheumatic disease Pericarditis Neoplasia: primary or secondary Herpes zoster ('shingles' difficult to diagnose before the rash)

PE, pulmonary embolism.

These introductory questions will provide useful clinical context and may immediately give a clue to the likely diagnosis, eg previous relevant medical history such as PE or pneumothorax, or recently started on antibiotics by her GP.

Focused history

Bear in mind the diagnoses listed in Table 15 when taking the history – which is most likely?

Doctor: now please tell me about your chest pain and breathlessness.

Doctor: how would you describe your chest pain? When did it start? What makes it better or worse? Does it radiate anywhere?

It is important to establish that the pain is definitely pleuritic: sharp, localised and exacerbated by deep inspiration and coughing.

Doctor: tell me more about how the pain started. Was it sudden and associated with coughing or straining [indicating pneumothorax or PE] or gradual? Did it follow a flu-like illness [suggesting pneumonia or Bornholm myalgia] or an incident of chest trauma [suggesting pneumothorax or rib fracture]?

Doctor: tell me more about the pain itself … where is it, and does anything make it better or worse?

It is also important to identify the location of the pain and any radiation. Is the pain better or worse on leaning forwards or backwards (which would suggest pericarditic pain)?

Doctor: when did your breathlessness start? Was it before or after the pain? And how bad is it?

A sudden onset of pain and breathlessness together supports PE, although different timing does not exclude it. How severe is the breathlessness: 'at rest' / 'can't walk' / 'can't hurry'. It will be even better if the patient can estimate their exercise tolerance, although this is sometimes difficult.

Doctor: have you been coughing? Have you coughed anything up? Have you been sweating or having any high temperatures with shivering?

Cough is a non-specific symptom. Haemoptysis would point strongly towards PE. The production of purulent sputum indicates likely infection, but sputum production is a late feature of pneumonia in patients with a normal chest. Fever, sweats, rigors and temperature >38.5°C would suggest pneumonia.

Doctor: have you had any recent leg pain, swelling or tenderness?

Any of these would be suggestive of venous thrombosis and strongly support the diagnosis of PE in this clinical context.

Specific questions that would be helpful in this case include:

> Have there been similar previous episodes? This is always a good question to ask: the patient may tell you the diagnosis! Enquire specifically about previous history of pneumothorax, PE or deep venous thrombosis and autoimmune/ rheumatic disease.

> Pursue other risk factors for PE – recent immobility, surgery, travel, dehydration, smoking and a family history of PE, and deep venous thrombosis or hypercoagulable states. In a woman, ask about pregnancy or use of the oral contraceptive / hormone replacement therapy.

> Consider risk factors for pneumothorax (chronic respiratory disease, recent flights or diving) and for pneumonia (exposure to others with the condition and travel, which is especially relevant for atypical pneumonias such as *Legionella*).

Focused examination

General features
The first priority is always to establish how unwell the patient is:

> Is she breathless at rest?

> Does she look cyanosed? Check pulse oximetry.

> Can she speak easily?

> Check peripheral perfusion and confirm pulse, BP, respiratory rate and temperature.

In this case the routine observations do not indicate that the patient is severely compromised, although she clearly has significant symptoms: examination can therefore be completed before a decision regarding investigation. In patients who appear very unwell with cardiorespiratory compromise, history taking, examination, investigations and treatment would all begin concurrently.

Note any of the following:

> Habitus. Tall thin 'marfanoid' young men have an increased risk of spontaneous pneumothorax.

> Labial herpes. This is often seen in pneumonia.

> Signs of autoimmune or rheumatic disease, eg joint deformity in rheumatoid arthritis or butterfly rash in systemic lupus erythematosus (SLE).

Cardiovascular

Note particularly the following:

> Pulse: rate and rhythm. Tachycardia would be expected in these circumstances and is non-specific. Atrial fibrillation can occur secondary to PE or pneumonia, but is once again non-specific.

> Signs of right ventricular (RV) dysfunction, such as elevated JVP, left parasternal heave, loud P2 and pansystolic murmur of tricuspid regurgitation. Any or all of these would support the diagnosis of a large PE, but a patient presenting with a small peripheral PE causing lung infarction and pleurisy (as perhaps in this case) would not be expected to have any of these findings.

> Heart sounds: is there pericardial rub?

> Calf swelling and tenderness: measure both sides. A difference of >2 cm may indicate venous thrombosis and would strongly support the diagnosis of PE in this clinical context, but an absence of swelling does not rule out a deep vein thrombosis (DVT)/PE.

Respiratory and other systems
Thoracic wall tenderness or rib crepitus

Exquisite local tenderness clearly suggests a musculoskeletal cause, but there can be local tenderness with pleurisy. Rib crepitus proves that a rib has been broken.

Expansion, percussion and auscultation of the chest

Is there a pleural rub? These can be very localised. Ask the patient to put a finger on the place that hurts most and listen at this point and just around it. In pneumothorax expansion may be reduced, the percussion note may be hyper-resonant and breath sounds may be diminished on the affected side. However, with a small pneumothorax examination may be normal. If there is consolidation secondary to an infection, percussion will be dull and localised coarse crackles and/or bronchial breathing may be heard.

If you suspect a PE, examine the abdomen for masses and organomegaly, along with the breasts in a woman and the testes in a man (time will not permit this in PACES).

Key point

To listen for a pleural rub, ask the patient to point to the place that hurts most and listen to it and just around it – you may miss it if you do not take care to do this.

Questions from the patient
Patient: *why do I feel breathless and have chest pain?*

Doctor: [assuming that the most likely diagnosis is PE] I'm not sure at the moment, but the most likely reason is that there is a blood clot in the lung … a pulmonary embolus … and this is causing the chest pain and breathlessness. We need some tests to find out if this is the right diagnosis.

Patient: *what's going to happen now?*

Doctor: well, because I think that the chances of you having a blood clot in the lungs are very high, I'm going to ask the nurses to give you an injection of something to thin the blood right away … that's to try to stop any more clots forming … and then I'm going to organise a scan of your chest to see if there is a clot there.

Patient: *if I have got a clot in my lungs, then what's the treatment?*

Doctor: the treatment for PE is to thin the blood … anticoagulation will reduce the risk of the clot getting bigger, and it will get broken down in the body. Given that this is the first time you've had problems with a blood clot, we will recommend that you have anticoagulation for 6 months.

Patient: *I've heard about that … it's rat poison, isn't it?*

Doctor: yes, the usual way of giving anticoagulation is with warfarin, and that can be used as a rat poison … but we control the level of thinning of the blood by measuring it with blood tests and adjusting the dose … the nurses in the anticoagulation clinic will explain the details.

Patient: *someone told me that you didn't have to take rat poison nowadays … is that right?*

Doctor: it's true that there are some new medications that can thin the blood … and they have advantages and disadvantages over warfarin. They don't need the blood tests that are required with warfarin … but on the other hand we don't have antidotes for them if there's serious bleeding.

Questions from the examiner

Examiner: *do you think that a D-dimer would be helpful in this case?*

Doctor: no, I don't think it would … a D-dimer has a high negative predictive value but a poor positive predictive value. If a patient has a low clinical probability … as might be judged by the Wells score … a negative D-dimer is very useful for excluding PE. But in a patient with a high clinical probability of PE – such as this case – a D-dimer is not recommended because a negative D-dimer will not exclude PE and imaging is going to be required whatever the D-dimer result.

Examiner: *what further work-up would you consider in a patient with an unprovoked PE?*

Doctor: about 10% of patients with unprovoked PE will have or develop cancer, usually within 1–2 years after the PE, so I'd want to take a thorough history and perform a thorough examination. I'd also want to do some routine screening tests … a chest X-ray … blood tests – FBC, serum calcium, liver function tests … and urinalysis. And I'd have a low threshold for further imaging.

Further discussion

Investigation
Imaging

The most important investigations in making the diagnosis will be imaging of the chest. Look at the chest radiograph carefully for features listed in Table 16.

Key point

If a confident diagnosis cannot be made to explain the pleuritic pain and breathlessness, then ventilation–perfusion lung scanning (see Section 3.9) or CT pulmonary angiography (see Section 3.9) is required.

Table 16   Signs to look for on the chest radiograph in the patient with pleuritic chest pain

Radiological sign	Comment
Pneumothorax	Look very carefully at the lung apex and bases – is there an area within the chest that does not have any lung markings? Can you see a line indicating the edge of the lung? Are you absolutely sure?
Lobar oligaemia	A rare sign, but suggesting large PE
Pleural effusion	This may be small and visible only as blunting of the costophrenic angle. This would be consistent with the diagnosis of PE or pneumonia
Wedge-shaped peripheral infarcts	Typical of PE (but rare)
Consolidation	Typical of pneumonia
Ribs and bony structures	Look carefully at anterior and posterior aspects of ribs for fracture lines and more obvious displacement

PE, pulmonary embolism.

ECG

Look for arrhythmia, RV strain and pericarditis (see Section 3.1). Remember that the ECG is most likely to be normal in someone with PE, and also that pain and fear are the most common causes of sinus tachycardia in a patient presenting to hospital (sinus tachycardia will be the most likely finding in this case).

Blood tests

Full blood count, electrolytes, renal and liver function tests and a clotting screen would be routine in all cases with this presentation. Blood cultures, atypical respiratory serology screen, inflammatory markers and tests for autoimmune rheumatic disease may all be indicated in some patients.

Key point

Measurement of D-dimers is *not* an appropriate investigation when the clinical probability of PE is high. It is a good test for ruling out PE when the clinical probability of PE is low.

Arterial blood gases

If the patient is unwell or pulse oximetry indicates oxygen saturation <95%, check arterial blood gases. Typical findings in cases of PE where the patient presents with pleurisy are normal PO_2 (but there may be hypoxia) and reduced PCO_2 as a result of hyperventilation.

Sputum

If present, sputum should be sent for microscopy, culture and sensitivity, and also for cytology and acid-fast bacilli (indicating tuberculosis) if the clinical picture is appropriate.

Management

Key point

If the probable diagnosis is PE, then give anticoagulation (low-molecular-weight heparin) immediately while you are waiting for confirmatory investigations.

This depends on the specific diagnosis:

> PE

> pneumothorax

> pneumonia

> musculoskeletal pain: analgesia and reassurance. Particularly in the case of rib fracture, adequate analgesia is essential to allow the patient to inspire fully and avoid hypostatic pneumonia. Local intercostal nerve blocks can be very effective

> pericarditis: see Section 2.6.

1.4.8 Chest pain after a flu-like illness

Scenario

Mr Patrick Green, aged 55 years

This man has presented to the emergency department with chest pain that developed following an episode of flu-like symptoms. What is the likely diagnosis, and how would you manage him?

Introduction

The recent flu-like illness in association with chest pain clearly suggests a post-viral cardiac problem. Pericarditis generally has a very favourable prognosis, whereas the presence of myocarditis in association with acute pericarditis (myo-pericarditis) can be more serious. You should seek to establish which diagnosis is more likely.

Classic pericarditic pain may occur in pericarditis or myo-pericarditis, but the presence of shortness of breath and palpitations suggests the latter. Both typically present 1–2 weeks after a flu-like illness. Most of the time a specific virus is not identified. A reduction in cardiac function or elevation in cardiac biomarkers indicates myocarditis.

Prognosis is excellent for pericarditis but for myocarditis can vary widely. Most patients will have a significant improvement or a full resolution, but a few will have long-term cardiac symptoms or deteriorate further.

Other causes of chest pain following a flu-like illness include pleurisy in association with an incompletely resolved chest infection, or costochondritis.

Beginning the encounter

Doctor: hello, my name is Dr A, I understand you have been getting some chest pain?

Patient: yes.

Doctor: before I ask you more about that, can you tell me if you have any major medical problems? Have you ever had any heart trouble?

Patient: [gives list (with doctor politely but firmly discouraging lengthy detail).]

Doctor: and are you on any tablets or medications?

Patient: [gives details (and will probably have been asked to produce a written list).]

Focused history

Doctor: how long have you had the pain? Can you describe it to me? Does anything make it better? Does anything make it worse?

Pericarditic pain is typically a sharp pain that is exacerbated by lying flat and breathing in deeply. Patients prefer to sit upright, leaning forward.

Doctor: have you been feeling short of breath? Any ankle swelling? Have you felt your heart racing or skipping beats?

Symptoms of heart failure or palpitations would suggest myocarditis.

Doctor: I understand that you've recently had a flu-like illness … is that right? Could you tell me about it? How long did it last? Have you felt completely well since?

Patients will often describe a non-productive cough, fever or malaise which has resolved. Most cases are idiopathic.

Specific questions that would be helpful in this case are:

> any rheumatological problems (systemic lupus erythematosus, rheumatoid fever)

> any use of non-steroidal anti-inflammatory drugs (NSAIDs) such as ibuprofen.

Focused examination

Cardiovascular system: check the following:

> Pulse: arrhythmia would be unusual in pericarditis.

> Auscultation: pericardial rub. Scratchy, high-pitched sound heard with stethoscope diaphragm. Location is variable, but often parasternal. Often described as 'crunching in fresh snow'. Distinguished from a pleural rub by the fact that it occurs with the frequency of the heart beat rather than the respiratory rate.

> Signs of heart failure: raised JVP, displaced apex, peripheral oedema would all suggest significant cardiac impairment from coexisting myocarditis.

> Quiet heart sounds might suggest a pericardial effusion.

Respiratory system: check the following:

> Palpate intercostals to assess any tenderness.

> Auscultate lung fields.

Questions from the patient

Patient: why have I got chest pain?

Doctor: [assuming pericarditis is the most likely diagnosis] From what you've told me and what I find, I think you've got something called pericarditis … this is an inflammation of the lining around the heart … it's almost always caused by a virus, and the fact you felt like you had the flu a few days ago is very typical. Patients often feel unwell, get better and then develop this sort of chest pain.

Patient: *is it serious?*

Doctor: no, it's very unlikely to be serious … nearly all patients with pericarditis make a full recovery with no long-term effects.

Patient: *is there any treatment?*

Doctor: this is something that will get better on its own, but we can give tablets to help cut down the inflammation and help the pain.

Questions from the examiner

Examiner: *what investigations would you like to do?*

Doctor: I would like to start by performing an ECG … it may be normal, but there's typically significant ST elevation, concave upwards. I would like to organise blood tests to look for active inflammation and cardiac biomarker elevation. A chest radiograph and echocardiography might be useful to look for a pericardial effusion. Reduced systolic function on the echocardiogram would suggest myo-pericarditis.

Examiner: *how would you differentiate between pericarditis and acute coronary syndrome based solely on the ECG?*

Doctor: both can produce ST elevation, but rather than being confined to one coronary artery territory, pericarditis typically produces widespread saddle-shaped ST elevation … also, in pericarditis there won't be reciprocal changes, and the PR segment may be depressed.

Examiner: *is a pericardial effusion a bad sign?*

Doctor: many patients will have a small effusion in acute pericarditis, and for most it isn't of any significance … if there is no haemodynamic compromise, the patient could be discharged with a follow-up echocardiogram and review … but care should be taken to exclude tamponade clinically and on echocardiography.

Examiner: *how would you treat this?*

Doctor: NSAIDs and colchicine are the standard treatments. NSAIDs are generally given for a few days, in combination with gastric protection. Colchicine might be given for longer.

1.5 Acute scenarios

1.5.1 Stroke and a murmur

Scenario

A 58-year-old woman who is married with two sons and works as a part-time teacher, presents with a left-sided hemiparesis of sudden onset. She had previously been fit and well. However, a murmur had been noted, but not investigated, when she was 45 years old and undergoing a minor gynaecological procedure. There is no past medical history or family history of note. She is on no medication.

Introduction

A stroke can be a devastating condition with high morbidity and mortality. It is not possible at presentation to predict accurately the degree of recovery that this woman will make. However, it is important to identify whether or not she is at high risk of further events, and in particular

whether she is at risk of cardiac embolic stroke. Most strokes are related to cerebrovascular atheromatous disease and not to cardiac disease, but most cardiac causes of embolic stroke are treatable meaning that further events in that group are potentially preventable. History taking or examination will detect most cases where there is a cardiac cause for stroke.

Key point

Consider the causes of cardiac embolic strokes when taking a history and examining a patient who has had a stroke:

> 'non-valvular' atrial fibrillation (AF)

> acute myocardial infarction (MI) with mural thrombus

> mechanical prosthetic valves

> rheumatic heart disease

> dilated cardiomyopathy

> infective endocarditis

> paradoxical embolism

> left atrial myxoma

> calcific aortic stenosis

> aortic arch atheroma.

History of the presenting problem

The first priority will be to confirm the diagnosis of stroke, then to focus on possible causes. With regard to identification of cardiac causes of stroke, establish whether there have been any previous thromboembolic events. Is the patient known to have any cardiac condition? Does she have any cardiac symptoms? Specifically, is there a history of palpitations suggestive of AF?

Other relevant history

In most cases it will be obvious if there is any pre-existing cardiac condition, but ask the patient the following:

> Are you known to have an irregular pulse?

> Have you had angina or a heart attack?

> Have you had rheumatic fever?

> Have you had any heart operations?

> Has a murmur ever been heard?

> Did you have a 'hole in the heart' as a child?

Examination: general features

In the absence of previous cardiac conditions and with an entirely normal clinical examination, the likelihood of stroke being cardiac in origin is small. It is therefore vital that the examination of the cardiovascular system is thorough. A patient with a recent stroke may have difficulty in cooperating with you during the examination, eg rolling the patient on to the side to listen for mitral stenosis (MS) may be difficult if he or she has a hemiparesis. However, it is important not to compromise the quality of your examination – seek help in moving the patient if necessary.

It is unlikely that there will be many signs from a general examination that will help in establishing whether or not the cause was cardiac:

> The patient with a previous MI or dilated cardiomyopathy might be dyspnoeic as a result of cardiac failure, but there are many other causes of breathlessness, including aspiration pneumonia, in someone who has just suffered a stroke.

> The patient with infective endocarditis or atrial myxoma may have fever and peripheral stigmata, but these are uncommon conditions (see Sections 2.8.1 and 2.9).

> Look carefully for any signs of previous cardiac surgery, particularly if the patient is unable to give a history. Do not forget to examine the back and the breast crease where there may be scars from previous mitral surgery (valvuloplasty).

Examination: cardiovascular system

Take careful note of the following:

> Pulses. Check the rhythm and character: in particular, is there AF? Is it possible that this woman has had an aortic dissection?

> BP. This is often elevated in someone who has just had a stroke.

> Heart sounds. This woman is said to have a murmur – listen carefully for both MS and aortic incompetence, which are easy murmurs to miss. You are most unlikely ever to hear the 'tumour plop' of an atrial myxoma, but it is absolutely certain that you will not if you never listen!

Consider non-thromboembolic cardiovascular causes for her stroke, eg aortic dissection involving the carotid arteries or vasculitis of the cerebral vessels (very rare).

Investigation

In most cases, simple non-invasive investigations will provide the information needed to establish a cardiac cause of a stroke.

ECG and chest radiograph

Every patient who has a stroke should have a 12-lead ECG and chest radiograph. The ECG may provide valuable clues to the aetiology of thrombus (Fig 24).

Echocardiogram

This should be requested if there is a clinical, ECG or chest radiographic indication of cardiac abnormality (Fig 25). If the heart is structurally normal on transthoracic echocardiography and no other cause of stroke found, a transoesophageal echocardiogram should be requested to look for aortic arch atheroma, patent foramen ovale (PFO, Fig 26) or left atrial appendage thrombus (Fig 27). CT or MRI of the chest may rarely be required to define a structural abnormality.

Blood tests

FBC (if polycythaemia or thrombocytosis are possible), electrolytes, renal and liver function tests, inflammatory markers (if these are raised and there is no other mundane explanation, consider endocarditis, myxoma and vasculitis, and perform appropriate specialist blood tests) and blood cultures (if any suspicion of endocarditis).

CT scan brain

This is required to exclude haemorrhage, aneurysm or tumour. Evidence of multiple cortical infarcts in different vascular territories and a structurally normal heart on transthoracic echo should raise the possibility of PFO if carotid artery disease is not found.

Management

It is important to involve the acute stroke team at the soonest possible opportunity so that the patient can be assessed for suitability for thrombolysis or any other acute intervention where time may be of vital importance. The patient will require care appropriate to the disability produced by their stroke. Particular attention to

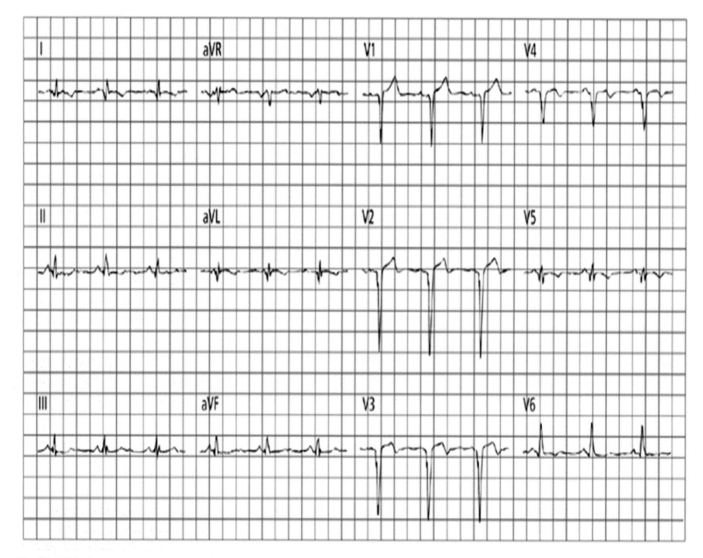

Fig 24 ECG demonstrating anterior Q-waves and poor R-wave progression across the chest leads. This is most probably secondary to a previous large anterior MI. Left ventricular mural thrombus is possible in this scenario.

anticoagulation, restoration of sinus rhythm (in some cases) and surgical correction of cardiac lesions (in rare cases) will be required in patients with a cardiac cause for stroke.

Anticoagulation
Consider if the stroke is confirmed as ischaemic on CT brain scan and a cardiac cause has been identified. The balance of benefit versus risk in the acute setting is difficult: leaving the patient without anticoagulation keeps her at risk of further thromboembolism, but anticoagulation puts her at increased risk of haemorrhagic transformation of a cerebral infarct. There are no good data to determine when anticoagulation should be started. Assuming that the patient is recovering from their stroke, most physicians would begin with heparin (intravenous or low-molecular-weight) at some time between 7 and 14 days, with a view to long-term anticoagulation therapy if the thromboembolic risk persists.

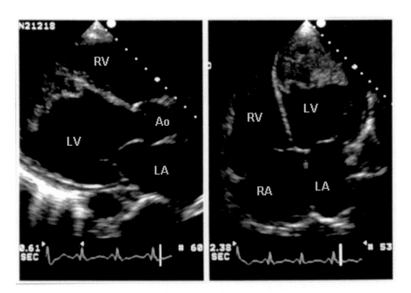

Fig 25 Transthoracic echocardiogram of an apical thrombus after MI. Ao, aorta; LA, left atrium; LV, left ventricle; RA, right atrium; RV, right ventricle.

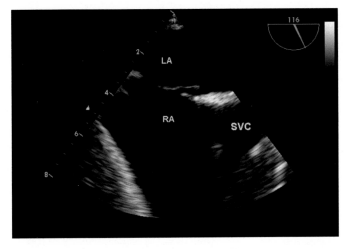

Fig 26 Transoesophageal echocardiogram of a PFO. LA, left atrium; RA, right atrium; SVC, superior vena cava.

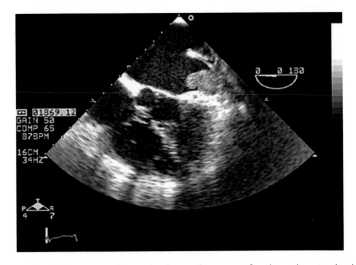

Fig 27 Transoesophageal echocardiogram of a thrombus in the left atrial appendage.

Key point
> Strokes may be haemorrhagic, even in those at risk of thromboembolism.

> Some features are more likely with cerebral haemorrhage than with infarction, such as nausea/vomiting, cerebral irritation and depressed conscious level.

> Ischaemic and haemorrhagic strokes cannot be distinguished with certainty on clinical grounds and a CT brain scan should always be performed before commencing anticoagulation.

Antiarrhythmics
After anticoagulation, management of atrial fibrillation should be the priority. In some instances, where the patient has haemodynamic impairment then restoration of sinus rhythm should be the primary target. In others that are well from a cardiovascular perspective then control of the heart rate may be appropriate. Pharmacological cardioversion is preferable to direct current (DC) cardioversion in this context because of the risk of a general anaesthetic after recent stroke (see Section 2.2.2).

Closure of patent foramen ovale
Percutaneous closure may be recommended if no other cause of stroke is found, there are recurrent episodes despite anticoagulation and a large PFO is demonstrated by echocardiography. Patients should be referred to a centre that specialises in this procedure for assessment.

Surgical correction of cause
Repair of an aortic dissection, replacement of an infected valve or removal of an atrial myxoma may be necessary immediately. There is high risk of further cerebral insult when the patient goes on cardiac bypass, but this

has to be balanced against the potential risk of not treating the underlying condition. In those with valvular pathology, it is usual to allow time for the patient to make as complete a recovery as possible from the stroke before considering surgery.

1.5.2 Hypotension following acute myocardial infarction

Scenario

Mr Jones is a 60-year-old man who was admitted with an acute inferior myocardial infarction (MI), which was treated with aspirin, prasugrel and primary percutaneous coronary intervention (PCI) to the right coronary artery via the right femoral artery with 8,000 U of heparin given during the PCI procedure. He was reviewed the following morning once the coronary care team were happy with his progress. His creatine kinase (CK) was 4,010 IU/mL, troponin I >50 IU/mL (both grossly elevated) and an angiotensin-converting enzyme inhibitor (ACEI) was prescribed. However, the coronary care nurses ask you to review him before giving the first dose of the ACEI because his systolic BP has fallen to 70 mmHg.

Introduction

Hypotension after MI requires rapid assessment and intervention. The combination of clinical examination, ECG, chest radiography and transthoracic echocardiography will usually determine the diagnosis.

History of the presenting problem

Pay particular attention to the following:

> How quickly did the hypotension arise? Sudden onset of hypotension usually indicates a catastrophic event, whereas pump failure is more gradual.

> Does the patient have chest pain? This may indicate reinfarction or cardiac rupture.

> Drugs are rarely the cause of severe hypotension unless the patient is fluid deplete, but look for a temporal relationship.

> Breathlessness. This may indicate pulmonary oedema or, more rarely in this situation, pulmonary embolism (PE).

> Volume depletion. Has the patient over-used diuretics? Examine the fluid charts.

Examination: general features

Assess the general condition. If the patient appears on the verge of arresting, call the resuscitation team immediately: do not wait until the heart has definitely stopped. Check the Glasgow Coma Scale to confirm the baseline. Assess pain level (if any).

Examination: cardiovascular system

The following are important:

> Peripheral circulation. Does the patient have cold feet and hands? How far up the arms and legs is perfusion impaired? Severe peripheral shut down indicates a poor prognosis.

> BP. Recheck the measurement, and record in the left arm as well as the right. Could the patient have an aortic dissection presenting with an inferior myocardial infarct?

> JVP. If it is grossly elevated consider right ventricular (RV) infarction, ventricular septal defect (VSD), tamponade or PE.

> Heart sounds. A gallop rhythm suggests left ventricular failure.

A new pansystolic murmur suggests a VSD or mitral regurgitation from chordal or papillary muscle rupture.

> The groin. Could the patient be bleeding into the leg or abdomen from the femoral puncture?

> Urine output. An essential aid for assessment of end-organ perfusion.

Investigations

Routine investigations will help establish the diagnosis:

> ECG: arrhythmia or re-infarction?

> Chest radiograph. Look for pulmonary oedema, and also for widening of the mediastinum.

> Arterial blood gases. These will confirm oxygenation and ventilation. Hypoxia in the presence of a normal chest radiograph suggests PE.

> Other blood tests. Creatinine and electrolytes will document renal function; and FBC will be used to assess for blood loss (could the patient be having a retroperitoneal bleed following femoral artery puncture?) or sepsis (unlikely in this context).

> Echocardiography. This is essential to assess left ventricular function, RV function, mitral regurgitation, VSD and tamponade.

When contemplating the results of these investigations, consider the diagnoses listed in Table 17.

Management

Rapid assessment and diagnosis is vital: delay can be disastrous. Early consultant advice is important. Continuous monitoring of rhythm and BP, and of hourly urine output is essential. Serum creatinine and

Table 17 Differential diagnosis of sudden hypotension following MI	
Differential diagnosis	**Features**
RV infarction	Inferior MI High JVP with hypotension Clear chest radiograph
Acute mitral regurgitation	Pansystolic murmur – although this may be absent if there is a rapid equalisation of pressure between left atrium and left ventricle Severe pulmonary oedema Echocardiography will be diagnostic (Fig 28) A PA catheter may confirm this diagnosis by revealing a giant v wave
Acquired VSD	Very high JVP Pansystolic murmur Pulmonary oedema, but less severe than acute mitral regurgitation Echocardiography will pick up the location
Intermittent ischaemia from severe ischaemic heart disease	Severe coronary disease (especially critical left main stem disease) Recurrent chest pain associated with widespread ischaemic changes on the ECG High risk of death – refer patient for urgent revascularisation
Pump failure	Raised JVP Pulmonary oedema Echocardiogram shows poor left ventricular function, but no evidence of VSD or mitral regurgitation PA catheter may be helpful if there is doubt about left ventricular filling. In general fill with cautious boluses of fluid until PA wedge pressure is 15 mmHg; if the patient is hypotensive and anuric despite PA wedge over 15 mmHg, start inotropes
Retroperitoneal bleeding	This may be spontaneous in response to the thrombolytic and antiplatelet agents, but may also occur from a leaking femoral artery puncture site after angiography and PCI Tachycardia Low BP and JVP Good BP response to fluids Evidence of dropping haemoglobin on serial tests Consultant advice should be taken regarding urgent CT scanning of the abdomen, and stopping glycoprotein IIb/IIIa antagonists
Gastrointestinal bleeding	Recognised complication of thrombolytic and antiplatelet agents Tachycardia Low BP and JVP Good BP response to fluids Evidence of dropping haemoglobin on serial tests Watch for melaena

BP, blood pressure; CT, computerised tomography; ECG, electrocardiogram; JVP, jugular venous pressure; MI, myocardial infarction; PA, pulmonary artery; PCI, percutaneous coronary intervention; RV, right ventricular; VSD, ventricular septal defect.

> Attempt to chemically cardiovert new onset atrial fibrillation by correcting potassium and magnesium levels, and administering intravenous amiodarone. These patients should receive therapeutic heparin.

> Most patients are not under filled after MI, but in a hypotensive patient with clear lung fields who is not hypoxic it is reasonable to give a fluid bolus such as 250 mL 0.9% saline intravenously and then reassess. This can be repeated if necessary. However, if there is no response it is important to seek further advice and consider inserting a pulmonary artery (PA) catheter to guide fluid management. Note, patients with confirmed RV infarction will require intravenous fluid to improve and maintain an adequate filling pressure.

> The combination of pulmonary oedema and hypotension indicates a poor prognosis. If there is evidence of pulmonary oedema you must not administer fluid, as this could be fatal. Give intravenous furosemide as 80 mg bolus. Central venous access should be obtained, inotropes started and consultant advice sought. Intra-aortic balloon pumping may be helpful, particularly if revascularisation may be feasible in the future. Notify the intensive care unit, as ventilation may be required.

Further comments

Hypotension after MI is a serious problem with high mortality. Remember that the patient must be kept as comfortable as possible: explain what needs to be done and why, and give analgesia in small doses (eg diamorphine 2.5 mg intravenously (IV) as often as needed. The patient's relatives should be contacted.

electrolytes should be checked at least daily.

> Stop drugs which cause hypotension, excepting beta-blockers in patients with heart failure who have been taking them long term, as there is a risk of deterioration on rapid cessation.

> Monitor pulse oximetry and give high-flow oxygen.

> Assess and treat the underlying condition if possible: patients with VSD or mitral regurgitation require urgent cardiothoracic surgical referral.

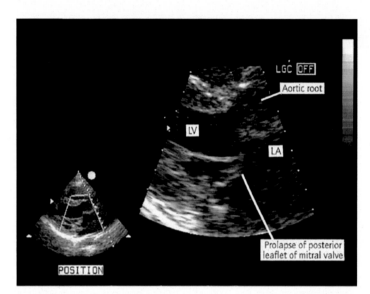

Fig 28 Transoesophageal echocardiogram showing prolapse of the posterior mitral valve leaflet (indicated) into the left atrium (LA) after papillary muscle rupture. LV, left ventricle.

1.5.3 Breathlessness and collapse

Scenario

A 55-year-old woman is brought to hospital by an ambulance. Her husband called 999 this morning when he found her acutely breathless at home. She had a brief syncopal episode on being moved into the ambulance, but is now conscious, although extremely dyspnoeic. Her BP is only 80 mmHg systolic. You are bleeped urgently by the emergency department to assess and instigate initial management.

Introduction

What is the differential diagnosis in this patient? Common causes (Table 18) should be considered as you assess and resuscitate the patient. Preliminary assessment will direct specific investigations and treatment. Pulmonary embolism (PE) should be high on the list of diagnoses for a patient such as the one described, particularly if there is no prior history of cardiorespiratory disease. The episode of syncope is of particular concern and confirms the life-threatening nature of this presentation.

Key point

In cases of breathlessness and collapse, always consider tension pneumothorax.

History of the presenting problem

If you can obtain a history from the patient and/or her husband, ask particularly about the following, doing so at the same time as you examine and organise initial investigations such as ECG, arterial blood gases and chest radiography.

> Did the breathlessness have sudden or gradual onset? Sudden onset suggests pneumothorax, massive PE, acute valve dysfunction, dissection or arrhythmia.

> Is there central chest or interscapular pain? This suggests myocardial infarction (MI) or ascending aorta dissection and descending aorta dissection, respectively.

> Presence of pleuritic chest pain or haemoptysis: suggests smaller PEs preceding a larger one.

> Are there any symptoms suggestive of pulmonary oedema, such as orthopnoea, paroxysmal nocturnal dyspnoea or pink frothy sputum?

Table 18 Differential diagnoses of acute dyspnoea and haemodynamic collapse

General cause	Comment	Specific cause
Cardiac	Common	MI/complications (acute mitral regurgitation, VSD, acute left ventricular failure) Arrhythmia (VT)
	Less common	Aortic dissection Cardiac tamponade Acute aortic regurgitation
Cardiorespiratory	Common	Massive PE (occluding >50% pulmonary vasculature)
Respiratory	Common	Acute life-threatening asthma
	Less common	Tension pneumothorax[1]
Other	Common	Sepsis
	Less common	Intra-abdominal catastrophe Severe haemorrhage ('air hunger') Anaphylaxis

MI, myocardial infarction; PE, pulmonary embolism; VSD, ventricular septal defect; VT, ventricular tachycardia.
1 Remember that, although tension pneumothorax is uncommon, this diagnosis should be considered before all others because immediate treatment is life-saving.

> Does the patient have a history of asthma, and has it been getting worse?

> Has the patient suffered from abdominal pain, vomiting, haematemesis or melaena: could there have been an intra-abdominal catastrophe?

> Symptoms suggestive of sepsis: the most common infective cause of hypotension and breathlessness would be septicaemia and acute respiratory distress syndrome, but with flu-like illness also consider pericardial effusion with sudden decompensation.

> Exposure to a known allergen.

> Drugs – illicit or prescribed.

Key point

When dealing with patients who are very ill, history taking, examination, investigations and treatment should all begin together – just finishing taking a very complete history at the same time as the patient expires it to be avoided!

Other relevant history

This is not the time for a lengthy past medical history, but in critically ill patients sometimes the small, relevant details can play a crucial role. Therefore, remember to ask about the following:

> PE or deep venous thrombosis and the relevant risk factors (see Section 2.18)

> cardiac: MI, angina, previously undiagnosed anginal pain, valve disease, rheumatic fever, 'heart murmur' (and if so any recent dental work or surgery – could she have acute valve dysfunction caused by infective endocarditis?) and hypertension (risk factor for ischaemic heart disease and aortic dissection)

> respiratory: asthma, chronic airflow obstruction and pneumothorax

> abdominal: peptic ulcers, pancreatitis and gallstones

> anaphylaxis: allergy to anything?

> drugs: a useful rapid check of past medical history in this context.

If no history is available, check bags and pockets for inhalers, glyceryl trinitrate etc.

Key point

Try to establish the functional status of the patient prior to becoming unwell. This is very important and will play a significant role for decisions such as ceiling of care and involvement of intensive care unit.

Examination: general features

How does the patient look?

Key point

If the patient looks *in extremis*, call for intensive care unit help or the cardiac resuscitation team immediately. Do not wait until she has a cardiac arrest if she looks as though she is deteriorating.

The ABCDE (Airway, Breathing, Circulation, Disability, Exposure) approach is a very good starting point which will provide a structure in your assessment. Remember that you need everyone's help as many things have to happen as soon as possible. Ask the accident and emergency (A&E) team to help you with organisation of blood tests, chest X-ray +/– other scan as needed.

Hopefully, when you arrive in resus the vital signs (SaO_2, BP, heart rate, respiratory rate, temperature) have already been checked and the patient is on a cardiac monitor.

Airway

> Is it open or compromised?

> Is there cyanosis? Check pulse oximetry (but do not remove the high-flow oxygen to 'check value on air' in someone who is desperately ill). Ask for arterial blood gas (ABG).

> Is there swelling of the lips and tongue (anaphylaxis)?

Breathing

> Is there evidence of tension pneumothorax? Look for asymmetry of the chest, shift of trachea from midline and silent chest on one side. These signs are not subtle, but they require a clear head to recognise in the context of a patient who is desperately ill. This should still be detected and treated before the chest X-ray.

> Are there reasonable breath sounds in both lung fields? If lots of crackles and/or bronchial breathing, consider pulmonary oedema, pneumonia or adult respiratory distress syndrome.

Circulation

> Does the pulse become impalpable on inspiration? This indicates severe paradox, so consider life-threatening asthma or tamponade.

> Where is the JVP? A high JVP suggests a cardiac or respiratory cause for collapse, whereas a low one suggests bleeding, intra-abdominal catastrophe or sepsis.

> Specifically look for evidence of massive PE: high JVP, right ventricular (RV) heave and tricuspid regurgitation.

> Heart sounds – is there a pansystolic murmur? If so, consider acute mitral regurgitation or VSD (see Section 1.5.2).

> Check the legs for oedema and any signs of DVT.

> Ask for secure venous access, blood tests, blood cultures and ECG.

Disability

> What is the Glasgow Coma Scale score?

> What is the glucose?

Exposure

> Is there any rash?

Abdominal

Peritonism indicates an intra-abdominal catastrophe. Feel deliberately for an abdominal aortic aneurysm. FAST (focused assessment with sonography in trauma) scan by A&E will also be helpful.

Investigation (most of these should happen simultaneously with the assessment)

The following investigations are required immediately in all patients who present with severe hypotension and breathlessness:

Blood tests

Check finger-prick blood glucose immediately in anyone who is severely ill. Check arterial gases. Take samples for FBC, electrolytes, renal and liver function tests, cardiac enzymes and blood cultures.

ECG

Look for the following (and repeat after 1 hour, but sooner if clinically indicated):

> arrhythmia (see Section 2.2)

> localised ST segment elevation of acute MI (see Section 2.1.3)

> ECG changes compatible with acute PE, the most common being sinus tachycardia and T wave inversion in leads V1–V4. The 'typical' right-axis deviation and 'S1Q3T3' are actually quite unusual (see Section 2.18)

> generalised low voltages of pericardial effusion (see Section 2.6).

Chest radiograph

Look for pneumothorax, pulmonary oligaemia (resulting from PE), pulmonary oedema, consolidation, effusions, heart size, mediastinal shift and the widened mediastinum of aortic dissection.

Hazard

A normal mediastinal width on the chest radiograph does not exclude aortic dissection.

Echocardiogram

This is the examination of choice to look for effusion, valve regurgitation and VSD, and to assess ventricular function. Remember that right ventricular dysfunction in the context of acute severe dyspnoea and hypoxia is highly suspicious of massive PE.

Other investigations

As determined by clinical assessment and the findings of preliminary tests: eg CT pulmonary angiography for suspected massive PE, or CT abdomen if an abdominal cause is likely.

Management (most of these should happen simultaneously with the assessment)

Key priorities when you reach the patient are:

> Resuscitate (Airway, Breathing and Circulation) and secure venous access while taking their history.

> Give high-flow oxygen and adjust as per ABG.

> If tension pneumothorax clinically – insert a large bore cannula into the silent side of the chest (second intercostal space, mid-clavicular line or mid-axillary line, above the level of the nipple)

> If acute MI with definitive ECG changes then follow the local protocol either for ST elevation myocardial infarction (STEMI) or non-ST elevation myocardial infarction (NSTEMI) according to the ECG changes.

'General supportive measures' will be required by all patients, in particular rapid restoration of intravascular volume in those who are volume deplete (low JVP and postural hypotension when lying and sitting, as standing will clearly not be possible).

Specific management will depend on the diagnosis:

> PE: the two major treatment options for massive PE with haemodynamic collapse are thrombolysis and surgical embolectomy (see Section 2.18)

> arrhythmia (see Sections 1.1.1, 1.1.2, 1.1.3 and 2.2)

> complications of MI (see Section 2.1)

> tamponade: urgent pericardiocentesis (see Section 2.6.2)

> asthma

> intra-abdominal catastrophe. Call for surgical help immediately; resuscitate the patient while considering surgery – do not say you will resuscitate the patient and then call the surgeons

> anaphylaxis.

And, if you do not know the diagnosis, give broad-spectrum antibiotics to cover sepsis.

Arrange for the patient to be transferred to an appropriate high-dependency area for continuing management (high-dependency unit, critical care unit or intensive care unit).

Further comments

Communication

After making your clinical assessment, performing immediate investigations and initiating management, you will need to speak to the patient's husband to explain the situation.

1.5.4 Fever, weight loss and a murmur

Scenario

A 26-year-old man with a previous history of intravenous drug abuse presents with a 6-week history of recurrent sweats and weight loss. He comes to the emergency department because he is feeling increasingly unwell. On examination he is tachycardic, has a swollen, hot and tender left knee joint, and a faint pansystolic murmur at the left sternal edge. You are called to assess him.

Introduction

Possible causes of this presentation are shown in Table 19. However, in the presence of a murmur, whether new or not, the diagnosis of infective endocarditis (IE) must be the number one

differential diagnosis. This remains the case even though the patient is said, according to the scenario, to no longer use intravenous drugs and may be septic from a primary infection of his knee joint. A careful history and examination are essential to help rule out other non-infective and non-cardiac causes for his symptoms, although these would clearly be very unlikely in this case.

History of the presenting problem

The history (and examination) will be dominated by consideration of the most likely diagnosis, infective endocarditis, but clues may emerge that take you off on another tack. Bear the diagnoses listed in Table 19 in mind as you take the history and go on to examine the patient.

Gauge the severity of the patient's debilitation. In acute IE, the fever is high with rigors and prostration. Ask: 'have you had attacks of really bad shivering and shaking?' and 'have you sweated so much that you had to change your clothes or the sheets on the bed?' The current history is more suggestive of a subacute presentation, which is associated with a low-grade fever, malaise and weight loss.

It is clearly critical to explore whether the patient has been injecting drugs at any point over the past 2–3 months,

emphasising the point that even a single episode may be enough to result in a very dangerous infection. Also enquire about dental procedures or medical investigations (particularly if invasive), which are other well-recognised risk factors for endocarditis.

Ask the patient about symptoms of heart failure: has he been getting breathless walking, at rest or when lying flat at in bed at night? Have his ankles become swollen? These signs may be insidious. If present they raise the possibility of haemodynamic compromise from aortic or mitral regurgitation. Sudden episodes of pulmonary oedema may be suggestive of significant valve degeneration.

Ask about chest pain and haemoptysis: myocardial infarction is rare in endocarditis, but can arise from coronary artery embolism. Pleuritic chest pain and/or haemoptysis would suggest pulmonary abscess or infarction, commonly from tricuspid valve endocarditis. In this patient, where tricuspid endocarditis is a real possibility, there might be mycotic pulmonary emboli from the right side of the heart. Remember that pulmonary tuberculosis (TB) and (very much less likely in this case) other lung pathologies, such as malignancies, can also present with haemoptysis.

Table 19	Differential diagnosis of 6 weeks' fever and weight loss	
Category	**Common example**	**In presence of a murmur**
Infective	Infective endocarditis TB Liver abscess Primary joint infection / osteomyelitis Soft tissue infection Rheumatic fever (very unlikely in UK)	Infective endocarditis is the most likely
Autoimmune disorders and/or vasculitis	SLE Rheumatoid arthritis Polymyalgia rheumatica Potentially any other vasculitic condition	SLE (also some other rheumatic disorders) can affect the heart valves and cause substantial diagnostic difficulty
Malignancy	Lymphoma Hypernephroma	Atrial myxoma possible, but extremely rare Marantic endocarditis is possible

SLE, systemic lupus erythematosus; TB, tuberculosis.

Other relevant history

Endocarditis has a very wide range of extracardiac manifestations (see Section 2.8), therefore many other aspects of the history could be relevant. For instance, the swollen knee joint could be secondary to infective seeding from bacteraemia or the result of a mycotic embolus from the heart (for the latter, the infection would have to affect a left-sided cardiac valve). Ask about systemic manifestations of other conditions on the differential diagnosis list in Table 19, especially autoimmune disorders, TB and, in this case because of the knee problem, joint/bone infections.

The following can be seen with both IE as well as autoimmune disorders: skin rashes, changes in the nails, blood in the urine, back or abdominal pain, changes in vision, sudden periods of arm or leg weakness, or episodes of difficulty speaking.

Although uncommon, vasculitic rashes can occur with IE, but they are not specific and may occur with several of the differential diagnoses. Also rare, but much more suggestive, are transient changes in the hands and feet, which may be painful lesions in the finger or toe pulps (Osler's nodes), or painless ones in the palms or soles (Janeway spots or lesions).

The glomerulonephritis that may accompany IE or autoimmune conditions often results in microscopic haematuria, which goes unnoticed by the patient, although macroscopic haematuria (a symptom that can also be caused by renal infarction or hypernephroma) is also possible.

Back pain may simply result from myalgia, but severe loin pain suggests renal infarction, abscess or tumour, although the latter is not normally painful. Similarly, pain in the left hypochondrium radiating to the left shoulder may result from splenic infarction or abscess.

Regarding other infective causes, ask the patient:

> Have you had a cough? Does this produce any phlegm or blood?
> Have you travelled abroad recently?
> Have you ever had TB? Have you been in contact with anyone who has TB?
> Have you had any injuries to your knee?
> Did your cough or knee injury start before or after your sweats and temperature?
> Have you had any swollen glands? Have you had any problems with the blood or the lymph glands in the past?
> Have you had arthritis?
> Have you had any odd illnesses in the past?

Concerning past history, ask the patient:

> Has anyone ever told you that you have a 'murmur' or 'hole' in your heart?
> Have you had rheumatic fever?
> Have you had any antibiotics recently? Are you absolutely sure about that? A common reason for negative blood cultures in endocarditis is partial treatment with antibiotics, which render the blood cultures sterile but do not cure the condition.

Examination: general features

Just as the history may be relatively non-specific, the examination findings may also be so. As always, get an overall impression. Patients with IE are likely to look unwell, although older patients presenting atypically may simply be confused.

General points must include:

> Temperature. A fever of <39°C is typical of endocarditis, although higher is occasionally seen.
> Pallor and anaemia. These can suggest chronic disease.
> Look at the hands, feet, skin, conjunctiva and mucous membranes for splinters / vasculitic manifestations of endocarditis.

Key point

When examining a patient with chronic fever, malaise and weight loss:

> How does the patient look?
> A thorough examination of all systems is essential.
> Look carefully for skin rashes and nail changes.
> Look carefully for signs of embolic phenomena.
> Is there lymphadenopathy?
> Is there evidence of significant valvular regurgitation?
> Can you feel the patient's spleen?

Examination: cardiovascular

Take particular note of the following:

> Peripheral perfusion.

> Pulse – check rate (often tachycardic as in this case), rhythm and character ('collapsing' pulse in significant aortic regurgitation).

> JVP. This may be elevated if there is tricuspid valve regurgitation (often seen in right heart infectious endocarditis) and/or heart failure.

> Apex. Will be hyperdynamic in sepsis and if displaced is suggestive of long-standing heart disease.

> Heart sounds. Are there any murmurs or added sounds? The pansystolic murmur could be tricuspid or mitral regurgitation, but take care to listen carefully for aortic and/or pulmonary incompetence. Be aware that a difficult murmur / funny sound could, extremely rarely, be a 'tumour plop'.

Examination: other systems

Check specifically for the following:

> Lymphadenopathy – this is not a feature of endocarditis and would point towards another infective cause or a lymphoproliferative condition.

> Chest. Are there any signs at all? Consider TB, but remember, as stated previously, that right heart IE may give rise to pulmonary mycotic emboli.

> Abdomen. Can you feel the spleen? The splenic tip or a mildly enlarged spleen can be felt in endocarditis, but a moderately or grossly enlarged spleen would favour lymphoma as the diagnosis. Is the liver palpable or tender (consider liver abscess),

and can you feel a renal mass (hypernephroma)?

> Neurological. Are there any focal signs? These are likely to have been caused by emboli from an infected valve in this clinical situation.

> Fundi. Is there any evidence of endocarditic lesions (see Section 2.8)?

Investigations

Key point

The critical investigations in the patient with chronic fever, malaise and weight loss are:

> Blood cultures: at least three taken 1 hour apart from separate well-cleaned sites.

> FBC, erythrocyte sedimentation rate (ESR) and C-reactive protein (CRP): is there evidence of systemic inflammation?

> Urine: look for haematuria and proteinuria, which suggest glomerulonephritis (autoimmune, vasculitic or endocarditic).

> Chest radiograph: look for TB, lung abscess or lymphadenopathy.

> Echocardiography: check for evidence of endocarditis.

The following are the key investigations in the patient with chronic fever, malaise and weight loss:

Blood cultures

These are the single most important investigation and should be carried out as soon as possible. Three or more blood samples should be taken from separate sites at different times, ideally over 24 hours. Seriously ill patients thought to have endocarditis should

have samples taken over 1–2 hours and then be given antibiotics.

Other blood tests

FBC, inflammatory markers (ESR and CRP), electrolytes, renal, liver and bone function in all cases. A range of further studies, in particular serological tests for other infective conditions or autoimmune disease, may be indicated if there are appropriate clues from the history or examination.

Urine

Dipsticks for haematuria and proteinuria in all cases; microscopy (to look for casts indicating renal inflammation), culture and sensitivity if dipsticks show abnormality.

ECG

Look particularly for evidence of conduction disturbance such as a prolonged PR interval (consider aortic root abscess in this context) and atrial fibrillation.

Chest radiograph

Look for pulmonary oedema, heart contour, pulmonary abscess, pneumonia, mediastinal lymphadenopathy or (unlikely here) lung tumour (Fig 29).

Echocardiogram

This is crucial for the detection of vegetations (or cardiac tumours) and the assessment of valvular regurgitation and paravalvular abscesses. Transoesophageal echocardiography may be needed (Fig 30) if good views cannot be obtained on transthoracic echocardiography. This is particularly relevant if the patient has prosthetic heart valves or the clinical suspicion for endocarditis is high even if the transthoracic echo is completely normal.

Management

This depends on the specific diagnosis:

> IE: see Section 2.8.1.

> Left atrial myxoma: see Section 2.9.

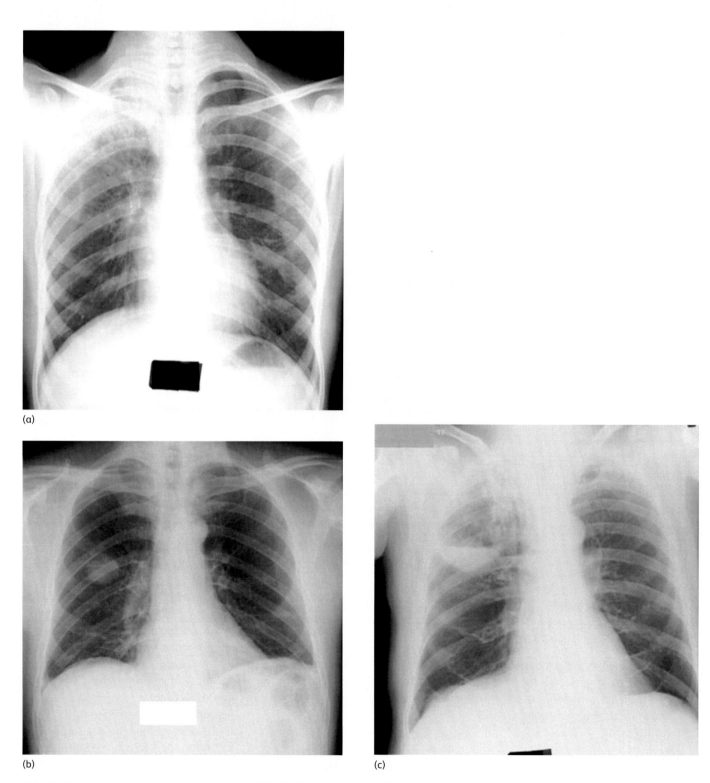

Fig 29 Chest radiographs demonstrating **(a)** TB, **(b)** lung tumour and **(c)** abscess.

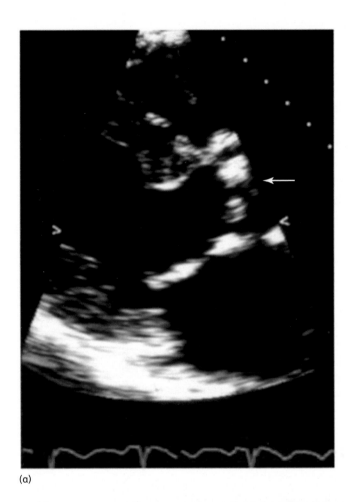

(a)

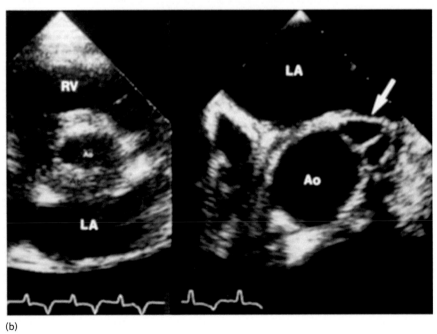

(b)

Fig 30 (a) aortic vegetation and **(b)** para-aortic abscess (indicated by arrow). Ao, aorta; LA, left atrium; RV, right ventricle. (Courtesy of Dr J Chambers.)

2 Diseases and treatments

2.1 Coronary artery disease

Coronary artery disease (CAD) is the leading cause of death in both the UK and worldwide. It is responsible for 73,000 deaths in the UK each year. About one in six men and one in 10 women die from CAD.

2.1.1 Stable angina

Aetiology/pathophysiology/pathology

Atheromatous plaques in the coronary arteries reduce blood flow. The myocardial oxygen supply cannot meet the demand resulting in myocardial ischaemia and chest pain (angina pectoris).

Epidemiology

The prevalence of angina in the UK is estimated at 2,000,000.

Clinical presentation

Common

> predictable exertional central chest tightness

> worse in cold weather and after meals

> may radiate to jaw or the left arm

> pain resolves with rest.

Uncommon

> Exertional dyspnoea (angina equivalent). This is more common in females.

> Decubitus angina – chest pain when lying down.

Physical signs

Examinations are often normal, but look out for signs of aortic stenosis and anaemia, and check the peripheral pulses and BP.

Investigations

See algorithm (Fig 31).

> Resting ECG – this is often normal and does not exclude coronary disease.

> Exercise ECG – this may show exercise-induced ischaemic changes, confirming the diagnosis and giving objective evidence of exercise capacity and prognosis (see Section 3.1). This test is used less frequently now as functional studies of ischaemia (stress imaging) are considered more valuable.

> Stress imaging includes myocardial nuclear perfusion, stress echocardiography and magnetic resonance stress imaging. This may be used in patients unable to exercise as pharmacological stress may be used instead of treadmill exercise (see Sections 3.8.2 and 3.10). These tests can be used in patients with left bundle branch block (LBBB).

> Cardiac catheterisation (see Section 3.12).

> Blood tests – full blood count (FBC) and fasting lipids.

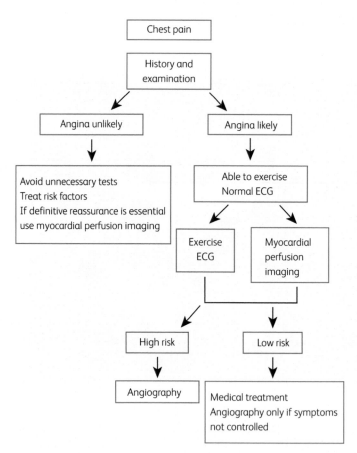

Fig 31 Algorithm for patients presenting with suspected stable angina.

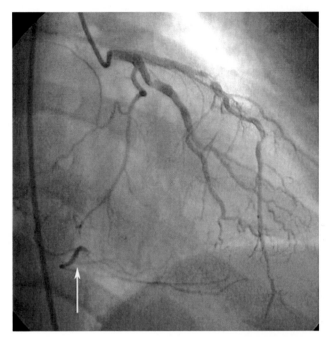

Fig 32 Left coronary arteriogram demonstrating major stenosis in two major vessels with retrograde filling of a blocked right coronary artery (indicated by arrow) via collaterals. This patient has three-vessel coronary disease.

Patients who have chest pain without diagnostic ECG changes during exercise testing may have important coronary disease. It is important to stratify patients by their presentation and risk factors into low- and high-risk groups. Patients at high risk of CAD with exertional chest pain but without diagnostic ischaemic changes should proceed directly to diagnostic cardiac catheterisation (Fig 32). Those at low risk of ischaemic heart disease should undergo stress imaging to look for ischaemia. If these investigations demonstrate ischaemia then cardiac catheterisation should be considered.

Treatment

Lifestyle advice
Encourage regular exercise. Prophylactic sublingual glyceryl trinitrate (GTN) administered before exertion may be helpful. Stress the importance of stopping smoking.

Medical therapy
First-line therapy is with aspirin, GTN spray, beta-blockers and statin. Angiotensin-converting enzyme inhibitors should be prescribed to patients with normal left ventricular function and ischaemic heart disease.

Revascularisation
There are two methods of revascularisation – coronary artery bypass grafting (CABG) and percutaneous coronary intervention (PCI – angioplasty and stenting). Currently, the evidence is that CABG confers prognostic advantage in certain groups:

> complex three-vessel coronary artery disease

> diabetic patients with multi-vessel coronary artery disease.

PCI is carried out more commonly than CABG, and is currently indicated for symptomatic stenoses greater than 70%. The haemodynamic significance of intermediate stenoses (40–70%) can be assessed during coronary catheterisation using pressure wire technology. PCI improves symptoms in patients with stable angina compared to medical therapy alone but at present an improvement in life expectancy has not been demonstrated. Patients with stable angina who undergo PCI will require dual antiplatelet therapy for variable time periods depending on stent type (1 month for bare metal stents, 6–12 months for drug eluting stents). Patients who are unfit for CABG may be considered for PCI. See algorithm for investigation (Fig 33).

Prognosis
Generally stable coronary artery disease confers a good prognosis. Cardiac catheterisation of patients identified to be at high risk by non-invasive stress testing will identify those patients with prognostically important disease.

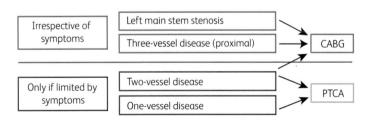

Fig 33 Interventional treatment of coronary artery disease. PTCA, percutaneous coronary angioplasty.

Key point

Important information for patients:

> The condition is stable.

> There are important narrowings in the arteries.

> Continue exercise but avoid strenuous exertion, especially heavy lifting.

> GTN before exertion may be helpful.

> Chest pain at rest continuing for longer than 15 minutes despite GTN warrants immediate hospital admission.

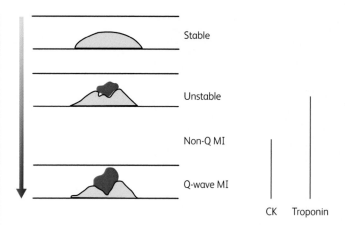

Fig 34 Schematic diagram illustrating the sequence of events within a coronary artery during an acute coronary syndrome. Fissuring or erosion of an atherosclerotic plaque (yellow) leads to thrombosis (red), a rapid reduction in coronary blood flow and MI. Sustained occlusion of the coronary artery leads to Q-wave (transmural) infarction. Highly sensitive troponin assays can detect microembolic heart muscle damage, enabling identification of those that are at higher risk of further infarction. CK, creatine kinase; MI, myocardial infarction.

2.1.2 Unstable angina and non-ST elevation myocardial infarction (NSTEMI)

Aetiology/pathophysiology/pathology

An atheromatous plaque within a coronary artery reduces the blood flow to such an extent that there is ischaemia at rest (unstable angina). The plaque may fissure or erode exposing the dense lipid core. The lipid is very thrombogenic, causing platelets to clump on it. If the thrombus is not sufficient to occlude the artery, it reduces blood flow downstream and pieces of the thrombus may break off and pass downstream to lodge in small end vessels, causing NSTEMI (Fig 34).

Clinical presentation

> Rapid onset of central chest pain at rest, unrelieved by glyceryl trinitrate (GTN).

> Pain may escalate, and occur with increasing frequency and severity (crescendo angina).

> Pain may radiate to jaw and arm.

> Severe breathlessness may reflect pulmonary oedema due to transient impairment of left ventricular function.

Physical signs

Often there are no abnormalities on examination, but other causes of chest pain may be excluded.

Investigation

> ECG – often normal, but look for ST segment changes and T wave inversion; T wave inversion alone has no prognostic significance

> cardiac biomarkers (see Section 3.7)

> cardiac catheterisation (Fig 35) (see Section 3.12).

Differential diagnosis

After excluding an ST segment elevation myocardial infarction (STEMI) other diagnoses should be considered. These are the same as the differentials listed for a STEMI.

Treatment

The aim of treatments is to limit myocardial damage by 'pacifying' the vulnerable plaque with medication. Patients who fall into high-risk groups undergo cardiac catheterisation.

Emergency

> Aspirin, sublingual GTN followed by an infusion, beta-blocker, low-molecular-weight heparin and statin. Chronic obstructive pulmonary disease and peripheral vascular disease are not contraindications to beta-blockers, and these groups benefit greatly from cardioselective beta-blockers.

> P2Y12 inhibiting antiplatelet agent, eg clopidogrel, ticagrelor or prasugrel, depending on local guidelines.

> Glycoprotein IIb/IIIa antagonists, eg tirofiban or eptifibatide, are recommended for patients with unstable symptoms and a positive troponin assay who are planned to undergo early coronary angiography with a view to percutaneous coronary intervention.

In-hospital management

Continue antianginals and antithrombotics.

Patients who do not have elevated troponin are diagnosed with unstable angina and do not require urgent

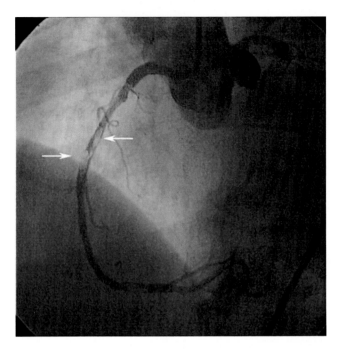

Fig 35 Right coronary angiogram in a patient with an NSTEMI. There is extensive thrombus present, seen as filling defects within the lumen (indicated by arrows).

cardiac catheterisation with a view to revascularisation unless they fall into a high-risk group as follows:

> positive troponin assay
> ongoing ischaemic pain
> ST segment changes with pain
> recurrent unstable angina
> ventricular arrhythmias.

Long-term treatment
Patients admitted with unstable angina are treated medically, and if the pain settles they are assessed in the same way as patients with stable angina. Medication should be continued, and if the troponin is positive dual antiplatelet therapy is continued for 1 year.

Complications
Common

> recurrent angina
> myocardial infarction (MI).

Uncommon

> pulmonary oedema
> ventricular arrhythmias.

Prognosis
The risk of death or non-fatal MI is 7% at 6 months with appropriate revascularisation of high-risk cases.

2.1.3 ST elevation myocardial infarction (STEMI)

Aetiology/pathophysiology/pathology
Rupture of an atheromatous plaque exposes the rich lipid core to the circulating platelets and fibrin, which forms thrombus, occluding the artery. Occlusion will lead to a full thickness muscle necrosis. Transient occlusion leads to limited heart muscle death.

Epidemiology

> Approximately 25,000 STEMIs occur every year in the UK.

> One-quarter of patients do not reach hospital.
> Death rates are declining.

Clinical presentation
Common

> rapid onset, severe and crushing central chest pain radiating to the jaw / left arm that is unrelieved by glyceryl trinitrate (GTN) or oxygen
> acute breathlessness (pulmonary oedema)
> cardiac arrest (ventricular fibrillation (VF)).

Uncommon

> epigastric, arm or back pain
> collapse
> vomiting and sweating without pain
> painless infarct (diabetics and older people).

Physical signs
Common
Examination may be normal. Patients are commonly pale, sweaty and often appear to be in pain. The patient may be hypotensive or hypertensive. Listen for pulmonary oedema. Patients presenting late after symptom onset may have signs of complications of myocardial infarction such as acute mitral regurgitation or ventricular septal defect.

Uncommon
Epigastric tenderness.

Investigations

> ECG – ST segment elevation and new left bundle branch block are indications for reperfusion treatment (Fig 36)
> biochemical markers (see Section 3.7)
> cholesterol (level may drop after 24 hours for up to 3 months)
> echocardiogram – indicated in cardiogenic shock.

Differential diagnosis

Consider the following:

> unstable angina / non-ST elevation myocardial infarction (NSTEMI)

> thoracic aortic dissection

> pulmonary embolism

> musculoskeletal pain

> pain of gastric/oesophageal origin.

Treatment

Emergency

Primary percutaneous coronary intervention (PCI) is now the treatment of choice for acute STEMI and has largely replaced thrombolysis in most parts of the UK. Thrombolysis should only be considered for those who are unable to access primary PCI within 2 hours of calling for help. When compared to thrombolysis, primary PCI is associated with improved short- and long-term mortality due to a higher rate of successful recanalisation of the occluded coronary artery and reduced major bleeding events.

Key point

Indications for primary PCI:

> Typical chest pain within 24 hours of onset.

> ST segment elevation >1 mm in the standard leads, >2 mm in the chest leads or new BBB.

> Take history while obtaining intravenous access.

> Simultaneous recording of ECG and observations by nursing staff.

> Oxygen, opiate analgesia and antiemetic.

> Activate primary PCI pathway as soon as STEMI is confirmed on the ECG.

> Quickly examine the patient and ensure there are no contraindications to antiplatelet therapy and primary PCI.

> Aspirin 300 mg if no contraindications.

> Clopidogrel 150 mg, prasugrel 60 mg or ticagrelor 180 mg (depending on local guidelines).

> Ensure timely transfer to cardiac catheter laboratory.

> Transfer to coronary care unit after primary PCI.

> Intravenous insulin for diabetics, or where BM is >11.

See Figs 31, 32 and 37.

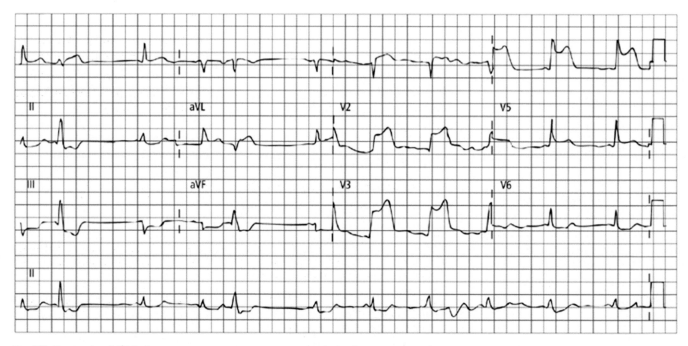

Fig 36 Twelve-lead ECG showing an acute anterior myocardial infarction.

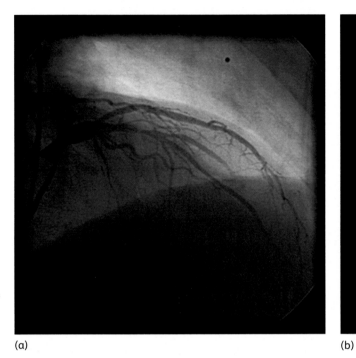

(a)

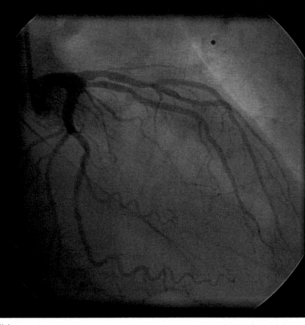

(b)

Fig 37 Left coronary arteriogram showing a severe stenosis in the left anterior descending artery. **(a)** This patient had a prolonged VF arrest due to an anterior myocardial infarct that was initially thrombolysed. **(b)** The stenosis has been stented.

> **Key point**
>
> **Contraindications to primary PCI**
> Consultant cardiologist advice should be sought prior to transfer to a catheter laboratory.
>
> > unable to take antiplatelet therapy
>
> > severe peripheral vascular disease making femoral or radial catheterisation impossible
>
> > active bleeding – preventing administration of antiplatelets
>
> > thrombocytopenia
>
> > severe allergy to iodine (contrast contains iodine)
>
> > inability to lie flat – intubation may be necessary if the patient has resistant pulmonary oedema.

Short term
Standard treatment should include:

> aspirin should be started straightaway and continued long term

> potent P2Y12 inhibiting antiplatelet agent such as clopidogrel,

prasugrel or ticagrelor for 12 months

> beta-blocker – taken orally within 24 hours and continued indefinitely

> angiotensin-converting enzyme inhibitor (ACEI) is of particular benefit in patients with left ventricular (LV) impairment, but improves the prognosis of all patients

> statin – for all patients unless contraindicated

> eplerenone should be prescribed in patients with signs and symptoms of LV failure with ejection fraction of <40% on echocardiography

> sliding insulin scale for patients with a blood sugar >11 or known diabetics

> warfarin – indicated for patients with atrial fibrillation (AF), severe LV dysfunction due to risk of LV thrombus, or who exhibit presence of LV thrombus (Fig 38)

> consider early staged intervention of significant coronary disease in non-culprit vessels seen during the index angiogram.

Long term
Continued secondary prevention is important.

Glucose tolerance testing should be considered as a high proportion of patients have diabetes mellitus (30% of these patients are missed when fasting glucose alone is tested).

Complications
Common

> haemorrhage induced by thrombolysis – transfuse as required

> haemorrhage from arterial puncture site – apply direct pressure, transfuse as required

> VF/tachycardia – cardiovert promptly

> AF

> complete heart block

> pulmonary oedema

> cardiogenic shock – seek expert advice

> post-infarct unstable angina

> reinfarction

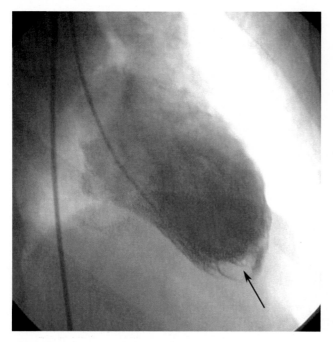

Fig 38 Left ventriculogram showing apical mural thrombus (indicated by arrow) after anterior MI.

> post-infarct pericarditis – usually benign and responds to non-steroidal anti-inflammatory drugs; echocardiogram is needed to exclude contained rupture

> stroke – urgent CT of head required

> deep vein thrombosis / pulmonary embolus.

Uncommon

> LV rupture (Fig 39)

> ventricular septal defect

> severe mitral regurgitation from papillary muscle rupture or ischaemia

> Dressler's syndrome – fever, pleuropericarditis, anaemia, raised erythrocyte sedimentation rate, usually 1–4 weeks after infarct.

Prognosis

This is determined by LV function, comorbidity and whether the patient has been revascularised. Patients with poor LV function undergo repeat echocardiography at 6 weeks to see if remodelling has occurred.

> 25% of patients treated conservatively develop unstable angina.

> 10% of patients treated conservatively have a further infarct.

> 25% of patients with a first myocardial infarction (MI) do not reach hospital alive.

> 10% of patients die before discharge.

> 10% of patients die in the year after discharge.

Secondary prevention

Prevention involves regular exercise, a healthy diet and stopping smoking. Other measures include:

> Aspirin, beta-blocker, ACEI, statin long term for all patients if no side effects.

> Patients with poor LV function (ejection fraction <35%) undergo repeat echocardiography at 6 weeks to see if remodelling has occurred. If the LV remains poor, an implantable cardioverter defibrillator may be indicated (see Section 3.4).

> Patients with poor LV may be treated with spironolactone or eplerenone.

Key point
Advice to patients
On admission inform the patient:

> that they are having a heart attack and effective treatment is available

> that the risk of treatment is less than the risk of the heart attack

> that the main risk is of bleeding, and that thrombolysis carries the risk of stroke.

On discharge advise the patient about the following:

> A good recovery is expected.

> Cardiac rehabilitation. Patients are seen prior to discharge by the specialist nurses, an exercise programme is arranged and support to help them stop smoking is offered. Car drivers must cease driving for 4 weeks, and heavy goods drivers must inform the driver and vehicle licensing agency (DVLA – UK) and satisfy requirements prior to re-licensing (see Section 2.19).

> The usual advice regarding fitness for sexual activity is that the patient should be able to climb one flight of stairs prior to intercourse.

> Smoking cessation is vital – it reduces risk of reinfarction by 50%.

> Always carry GTN, even if free of angina.

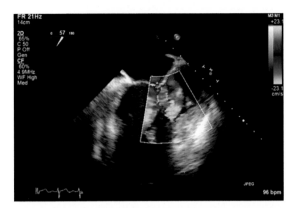

(a)

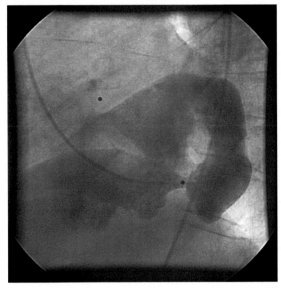

(b)

(c)

Fig 39 Rupture of the inferior–posterior wall of the LV after an acute MI.
(a) Transoesophageal echocardiogram showing flow through the defect in the LV wall; **(b)** left ventriculogram – a pigtail catheter has been passed through the defect, outlining the LV, the defect and the pericardium; **(c)** the LV at operation showing a hole on the inferior–posterior surface of the ventricle.

2.2 Cardiac arrhythmia

2.2.1 Bradycardia

Aetiology

Virtually any condition that has a pathophysiological effect on the heart might affect normal electrophysiological properties and thus cause bradycardias. The more common conditions are listed in Table 20.

Pathology/pathophysiology

Sinoatrial dysfunction

> abnormality of neurohormonal input to sinoatrial (SA) node, eg sympathetic/parasympathetic

> abnormality of SA node leading to slow or failed conduction to atrial tissue.

Atrioventricular block

> abnormality in conduction through atrioventricular (AV) node

> failure to conduct rapidly throughout the ventricles.

Classification of bradycardias

Bradycardias can be divided clinically into SA dysfunction and AV block (Table 21).

Clinical presentation

Common

> dizziness (presyncope)

> syncope.

Uncommon

> dyspnoea

> exertional fatigue

> heart failure.

Rare

> palpitations are unusual.

Physical signs

These include the following:

> slow regular / irregular pulse

> cannon waves in complete heart block

Table 20 Possible causes of bradycardia

Sinoatrial disease	Atrioventricular block
Ischaemic heart disease	Ischaemic heart disease
Idiopathic fibrosis	Aortic stenosis
Infective	Cardiomyopathy
Pericardial disease	Infection
Post-radiotherapy	Sarcoidosis
Post-cardiac surgery	Congenital
Trauma	Connective tissue disease
Amyloidosis	Antiarrhythmic drugs
	Post-radiotherapy
	Post-cardiac surgery
	Trauma
	Hypothermia

Table 21 Clinical classifications of bradycardias

Sinoatrial dysfunction	Atrioventricular block
Sinus bradycardia	First degree
Vasovagal syndrome	Second degree: Möbitz I (Wenckebach's)
Carotid sinus hypersensitivity	Second degree: Möbitz II
Junctional rhythm	Third degree: complete

> beat-to-beat variation in intensity of first heart sound in complete heart block

> hypotension

> pulmonary oedema.

Consider carotid sinus massage to induce bradycardia. Do not perform this in patients who have had a stroke or are known to have atherosclerotic carotid disease.

Investigations

In most cases the diagnosis will be made with one of the following:

> 12-lead ECG: see Section 3.1

> Holter monitor: see Section 3.3

> patient-activated device

> tilt-table testing.

Treatment

Emergency/short term

In a patient with haemodynamic compromise consider the following:

> intravenous atropine

> temporary pacing: transvenous or transcutaneous (short-term measure)

Address any potential reversible causes of bradycardia:

> hypothyroidism

> drugs (Fig 40)

> hypothermia

> electrolyte imbalance.

Long term

Consider whether permanent pacemaker implantation is appropriate (see Section 3.5).

2.2.2 Tachycardia

For practical purposes it is easiest to divide tachyarrhythmias into:

> atrial tachycardia

> atrial fibrillation (AF) / atrial flutter

> atrioventricular nodal re-entry tachycardia (AVNRT) and atrioventricular re-entry tachycardias (AVRT)

> ventricular tachycardias (VT).

Aetiology/epidemiology

Atrial tachycardia

Atrial tachycardia is caused by an ectopic source of atrial tissue firing in a rhythmical manner faster than the sinus node. It is a rare cause of tachycardia. On an ECG it may look similar to sinus tachycardia but with abnormal P wave morphology.

Atrial fibrillation/flutter

Atrial fibrillation (AF) affects 0.4% of the whole population, rising to 2–4% in people aged over 60 years and >11% in those over 75 years. A male's lifetime risk over the age of 40 years is one in four and for a female one in five. Patients with AF may also have atrial flutter and vice versa. Atrial flutter may be seen after patients have had AF ablation and often are of the 'atypical' variety.

The causes of AF/atrial flutter are numerous:

> hypertension

> ischaemic heart disease

> congestive heart failure

> valvular heart disease

> thyroid dysfunction

> pulmonary abnormalities, eg pulmonary embolism

> pericardial disease.

AVNRT/AVRT

This is the result of the presence of an additional conducting pathway, allowing a re-entry mechanism. In most cases, the electrical impulse is conducted antegradely (atrium to ventricle) via the atrioventricular node and retrogradely through the accessory pathway (concealed accessory pathway). If conduction is in an antegrade direction through the pathway, eg the Wolff–Parkinson–White syndrome, pre-excitation is seen on the surface ECG (delta wave and short PR interval).

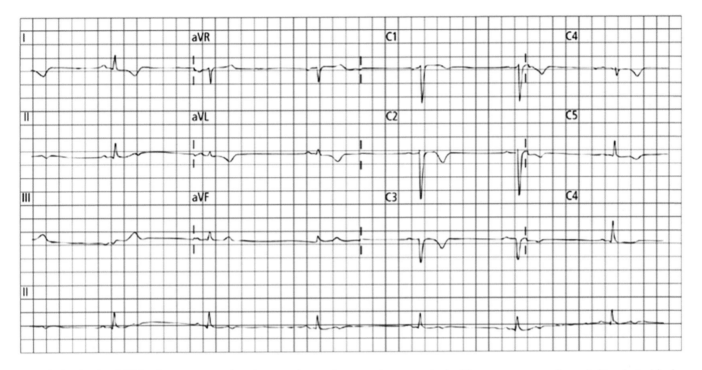

Fig 40 Twelve-lead ECG of a patient with ischaemic heart disease who presented with presyncope and was taking beta-blockers. Heart rate is <40/min.

Ventricular tachycardia (VT)

Almost any pathological process affecting the ventricles may predispose to VT:

> myocardial infarction (MI) (acute/chronic)

> dilated cardiomyopathy

> hypertrophic cardiomyopathy

> valvular heart disease (especially aortic stenosis and mitral prolapse)

> hypertension

> congenital heart disease

> long QT syndrome

> cardiac tumours.

Pathophysiology/pathology

Tachyarrhythmias occur as a result of:

> abnormal automaticity, eg VT after an MI

> triggered activity, eg VT with long QT syndrome

> re-entry, eg AF, AVRT/AVNRT, VT/ventricular fibrillation (VF).

Clinical presentation

Common

> palpitations

> presyncope/syncope

> breathlessness

> chest pain.

Uncommon

> Patients may complain only of lethargy.

Rare

> Thromboembolism is unusual, except in AF.

Physical signs

Examination of sinus rhythm may be unremarkable. However, during tachycardia some physical signs may help to establish a diagnosis.

Atrial fibrillation/flutter

For the physical signs of AF/atrial flutter, see Table 22.

AVNRT/AVRT

Physical signs are not especially helpful in making the diagnosis:

> regular pulse

> jugular venous pressure (JVP) may be raised, but waveform is normal

> constant intensity of first heart sound.

Table 22 Clinical features distinguishing AF from atrial flutter

	AF	Atrial flutter
Pulse	Irregularly irregular	May be regular
JVP	Absence of 'a' waves	Rapid flutter waves
First heart sound	Variation in intensity	Constant intensity

AF, atrial fibrillation; JVP, jugular venous pressure.

Ventricular tachycardias

Patients may or may not be significantly compromised, physical signs include:

> hypotension

> cannon waves.

Investigations

Investigations aim to exclude a structural thoracic/cardiac or metabolic cause: aside from an ECG, a chest radiograph, echocardiogram, thyroid function tests, renal function and electrolytes are appropriate in most cases.

Twelve-lead ECG

Documenting the arrhythmia with a 12-lead ECG will, in most cases, establish the diagnosis (see Section 3.1). In some cases where there is evidence of pre-excitation, the diagnosis can be relatively confidently made in sinus rhythm. Distinguishing some arrhythmias can be difficult:

> Atrial flutter versus AF: look for characteristic flutter waves. Flutter waves may not be so obvious in cases of atypical flutter (Figs 41 and 42).

> AVNRT versus AVRT: distinguishing these is rarely of clinical importance because, in most cases, the management is similar (Fig 43).

> VT versus AVNRT/AVRT with aberrant conduction: see Section 3.1.

Ambulatory monitoring

Documentation of an infrequent rhythm may be possible using 24-hour Holter monitoring or patient-activated devices (see Section 3.3). In patients where symptoms are occasional, implantable loop recorders (ILR) may be appropriate.

Electrophysiological studies

See Section 3.2.

Treatment

There are many different classifications of antiarrhythmic agents. The Vaughan Williams classification is the most commonly used and is based on the cellular action of the drug (Table 23).

Emergency
Atrial tachycardia

Most patients will not be compromised. Direct current (DC) cardioversion or intravenous amiodarone will restore sinus rhythm in the majority.

Atrial fibrillation/flutter

If the patient is compromised, consider DC cardioversion or intravenous amiodarone.

AVNRT/AVRT

Most will respond to intravenous adenosine.

Ventricular tachycardias

For resuscitation, see the *Acute medicine* book of Medical Masterclass, Section 1.3.1.

Short term
Atrial tachycardia

Consider the following:

> bisoprolol (beta-blocker)

> diltiazem or verapamil (calcium antagonist)

> flecainide (class I agent)

> amiodarone (class III agent).

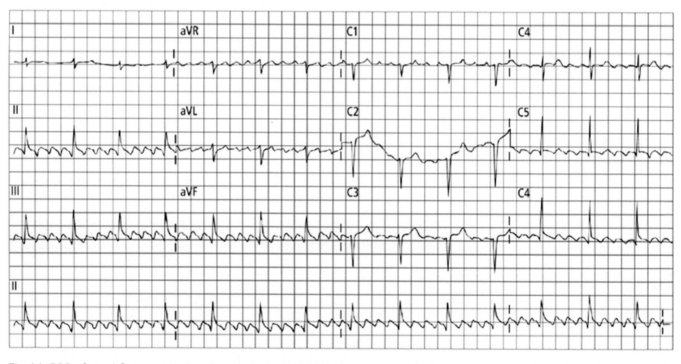

Fig 41 ECG of atrial flutter: note the characteristic saw-tooth appearance of the baseline.

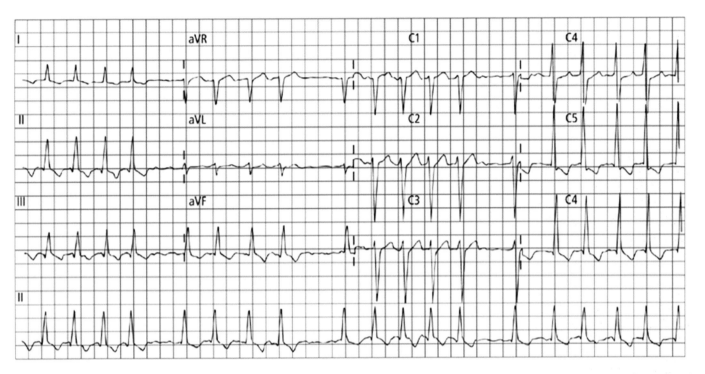

Fig 42 ECG of AF. Notice the 'chaotic' baseline in comparison to Fig 41 and the complete irregularity of QRS complexes.

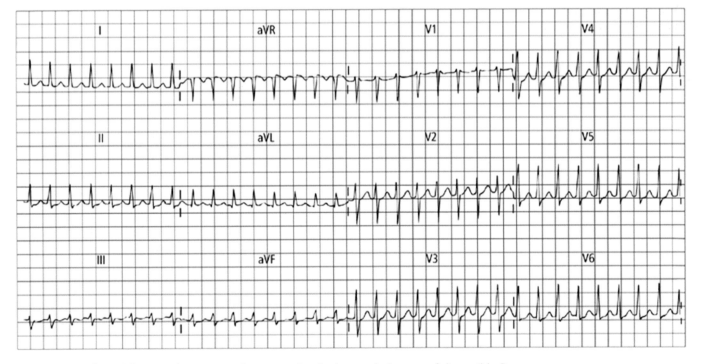

Fig 43 ECG of AVNRT. Note the very rapid rate, regular rhythm and absence of discernible P waves.

Table 23 Vaughan Williams classification of antiarrhythmic drugs (not all of these drugs are readily available in all hospital pharmacies)

Category	Action	Example
1	A Prolong action potential B Shorten action potential C Slow conduction	Quinidine, procainamide, disopyramide Lidocaine, mexiletine Propafenone, flecainide
2	Block β-adrenergic receptors	Propranolol, atenolol, metoprolol
3	K$^+$ channel blockers, prolong repolarisation	Sotalol, amiodarone, dronedarone
4	Block slow calcium channels	Verapamil, diltiazem

Note class 1C drugs are generally avoided where patients may have coronary artery disease.

Atrial fibrillation/flutter

The main aim of treatment is to prevent complications and alleviate symptoms. This will involve making a decision on anticoagulation and then deciding whether to control the heart rate or restore sinus rhythm. In new onset AF restoration of sinus rhythm should be considered.

Consider the following:

> anticoagulation

> DC cardioversion

> beta-blocker / calcium antagonist / digoxin (rate control only)

> amiodarone (class III agent)

> flecainide (class I agent).

AVNRT/AVRT
Consider:

> bisoprolol (beta-blockers)

> verapamil (calcium antagonist)

> flecainide (class 1 agent)

> sotalol or amiodarone (class III).

Ventricular tachycardias
Consider:

> bisoprolol (beta-blockers)

> amiodarone (class III)

> temporary pacing may prevent VT in patients with bradycardia-induced VT or long QT syndrome.

Long term
Most short-term drugs may be used long term, but more definitive therapies should be considered. Particular caution should be applied to committing any patient to long-term use of amiodarone. Its side-effect profile is worse with long-term use.

Atrial tachycardia
The focal origin of these arrhythmias makes them particularly suited to catheter ablation.

Atrial fibrillation/flutter
Consider the following:

When deciding on rate versus rhythm control, rate control should be the first line of therapy unless:

> There is a reversible cause to the AF.

> There is heart failure secondary to AF.

> Atrial flutter is present and suitable for ablation.

> In patients where rhythm control would be more suitable based upon clinical judgement eg a young patient.

Therefore, consider:

> anticoagulation with novel oral anticoagulant (NOAC) or vitamin K antagonist (warfarin) based upon CHA$_2$DS$_2$-VASc score

> antiarrhythmics for rate or rhythm control

> ablation for atrial flutter (see Section 3.4.1)

> ablation for AF (see Section 3.4.1)

> ablation of atrioventricular node and permanent pacemaker for AF not controlled with drugs (see Section 3.4.1).

AVNRT/AVRT
Consider ablation (see Section 3.4.1).

Ventricular tachycardias
Consider referral for ablation / implantable cardioverter defibrillator (see Section 3.4).

Key point
Cardioversion of AF/atrial flutter

The following can be used as guidelines for anticoagulation:

> duration <48 hours: proceed without anticoagulation

> duration >48 hours: therapeutic anticoagulation for 4 weeks before cardioversion, and for 4 weeks afterwards

> duration >48 hours and no evidence of intracardiac thrombus on transoesophageal echocardiography: proceed without anticoagulation.

Sinus rhythm is achieved in approximately 85% of cases of AF/atrial flutter, but recurrence rates may be high (up to 75% at 12 months).

Key point

CHA$_2$DS$_2$-VASc score

C	Congestive heart failure	1 point
H	Hypertension	1 point
A$_2$	Age ≥75 years	2 points
D	Diabetes	1 point
S$_2$	Stroke or TIA	2 points
V	Vascular disease	1 point
A	Age 65–74 years	1 point
Sc	Sex category, female	1 point

Offer anticoagulation to patients with a score of 2 or more (consider in men with a score of 1 or more).

Complications

Atrial fibrillation/flutter
Thromboembolism is the most significant and devastating condition.

AVNRT/AVRT
Complications are uncommon but, with the Wolff–Parkinson–White syndrome, rapid conduction of AF down an accessory pathway may precipitate VF.

Ventricular tachycardias
Haemodynamic collapse and death is a potential risk in many cases of VT.

Prevention
Primary and secondary prevention of stroke/transient ischaemic attack (see Section 2.14.1).

2.3 Cardiac failure

Aetiology/pathophysiology/pathology
The common causes of heart failure are listed in Table 24.

Left ventricular (LV) systolic dysfunction is commonly associated with ventricular dilatation. Other causes include viral myocarditis, toxins (eg alcohol, cocaine and chemotherapeutic agents), metabolic abnormalities (eg thyroid disease and acromegaly) and inflammatory conditions

(eg sarcoidosis and connective tissue disorders). In patients with idiopathic dilated cardiomyopathy, around 25% are thought to have a familial origin.

After a single episode of cardiac damage, eg a myocardial infarction (MI), LV dysfunction is often progressive even in the absence of further cardiac insults. This appears to result from the neurohumoral response to reduced cardiac output, which is initially compensatory but becomes detrimental in the long term (Fig 44).

Epidemiology
The prevalence of heart failure is approximately 1–2% of the adult population in developed countries and increases to >10% among persons >70 years old. Heart failure is the primary diagnosis in about 4% of general medical admissions to hospital.

Increasing prevalence is the result of:

> an ageing population

> better survival after MI

> better survival with heart failure.

Clinical presentation
Patients suffering from heart failure commonly present with the following:

> exertional breathlessness

> fatigue

> paroxysmal nocturnal dyspnoea

> cough productive of clear, frothy sputum

> ankle swelling

> orthopnoea.

Table 24   Causes of heart failure (with approximate relative frequency)

Cause	Relative frequency (%)
Ischaemic heart disease	50
Valve disease	10
Hypertension	5
Dilated cardiomyopathy / unknown (see text)	35

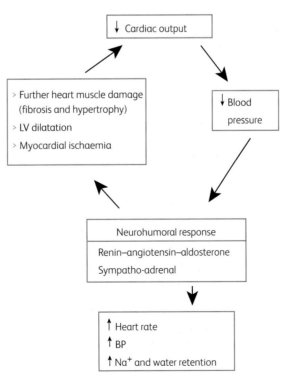

Fig 44 The vicious cycle of progressive left ventricular damage.

Key point

Severity of breathlessness in heart failure is graded according to the New York Heart Association (NYHA) classes:

> NYHA I: impaired LV function but asymptomatic on ordinary activity

> NYHA II: symptoms resulting in slight limitation of ordinary activity

> NYHA III: symptoms on minimal exertion, eg walking around the house

> NYHA IV: symptoms present at rest.

Physical signs

The physical signs may include the following:

> pulse – tachycardia or atrial fibrillation (AF)

> JVP – elevated (if it is up to angle of the jaw, then suspect tricuspid regurgitation (TR); check for any systolic v waves that coincide with contralateral carotid; also check for pulsatile liver)

> left parasternal heave (usually right ventricular hypertrophy, occasionally the result of greatly enlarged left atrium)

> heart sounds – third heart sound (probably the most sensitive and specific physical sign for LV dysfunction, but it has poor reproducibility). Pansystolic murmur of functional mitral regurgitation (other murmurs may be present and relate to aetiology)

> basal lung crackles

> bilateral ankle oedema ± ascites.

Investigations

ECG

A completely normal ECG is rare in heart failure. Look for:

> rhythm (eg AF)

> LV hypertrophy

> previous MI

> left bundle branch block (LBBB)

> left-axis deviation.

Chest radiograph

In addition to excluding lung pathology, look for:

> heart size

> pulmonary oedema

> pleural effusions.

Blood tests

> urea and electrolytes: associated hyponatraemia, hypokalaemia (diuretic treatment) and renal dysfunction

> liver function tests: often mildly deranged in chronic heart failure

> thyroid function tests (aetiology)

> haemoglobin: mild anaemia common and associated with adverse outcomes. If present check haematinics

> brain natriuretic peptide (see Section 3.7): a normal value virtually excludes a diagnosis of heart failure.

Echocardiography

Gold standard for diagnosis of heart failure; use for assessment of LV systolic function, filling pressures and valvular function (see Section 3.10).

Differential diagnosis

Consider the following:

> cor pulmonale

> nephrotic syndrome

> renal failure

> liver failure.

Treatment

Emergency

In someone suffering from acute pulmonary oedema:

> Sit them up.

> Give them oxygen (monitor blood gases).

> Give them intravenous diamorphine (venodilator).

> Offload with intravenous infusion of nitrate titrated to maximum tolerated dose (but keep BP >90 mmHg systolic).

> Give intravenous furosemide in small aliquots (eg 40–80 mg).

> Check FBC, urea and electrolytes, and cardiac enzymes.

> Monitor clinical response including urine output (urinary catheter).

> Consider ventilatory support (continuous positive airway pressure or intubation) and/or inotropic support where appropriate.

> Invasive monitoring may be required if the patient gives a poor response (arterial line and central venous line, or pulmonary artery catheter).

> Identify and treat any cause that might have precipitated the exacerbation of heart failure.

Short term

Hospital treatment of decompensated chronic heart failure:

> Monitor fluid balance, daily weight (aim to lose 0.5–1 kg daily) and daily urea and electrolytes.

> No-added-salt diet.

> Intravenous loop diuretic, eg furosemide once or twice daily (dose will depend on prior exposure).

> Angiotensin-converting enzyme inhibitor (ACEI – angiotensin II receptor blocker can be used if the ACEI not tolerated) – monitor renal function.

> In patients not already on beta-blockers, introduce beta-blockers as soon as possible after stabilisation and up-titrate as blood pressure and heart rate allow.

> In patients not already on aldosterone antagonists (spironolactone or eplerenone), introduce as soon as possible after stabilisation and monitor renal function.

> Consider anticoagulation (AF and LV thrombus).

> Avoid calcium antagonists and non-steroidal anti-inflammatory drugs.

If there is a good response, change to oral diuretics when approaching euvolaemia. Aim to continue hospital treatment until their oedema is clearly improved and the patient is stable on oral therapy for 48 hours. In patients with impaired renal function it may be necessary to accept some residual oedema rather than precipitate acute-on-chronic renal failure. Do not use the JVP as the sole guide for treatment because this is often persistently elevated as a result of TR.

If weight loss is not satisfactory on twice daily furosemide, consider furosemide infusion (eg 5–10 mg/hour). If diuresis remains unsatisfactory, consider adding a thiazide diuretic (bendroflumethiazide 2.5 mg or metolazone 2.5–5 mg daily) but watch the renal function closely. Remember that this combination of diuretics is very potent (usually only needed for 2–3 days) and needs daily monitoring of renal function and electrolytes. Sometimes, only

a single dose of metolazone is enough to produce good diuresis. Fluid restriction should be held in reserve for resistant cases. Rarely, inotropes (dopamine or dobutamine) are required for a few days to assist diuresis.

Following discharge an early review is important to prevent re-decompensation. Ensure a referral has been made to the heart-failure nurse. Check renal function and up-titrate medication.

Long term

Key point

'You are a physician, doctor. You would promise life to a corpse if he could swallow pills' (Napoleon Bonaparte).

Counselling a patient with heart failure can be very difficult as the prognosis may be poor. Education is key to enhancing patient compliance. It is important to judge each case individually and not to give the patient unrealistic expectations.

Figure 45 shows long-term treatment options for those with heart failure. The following improve symptoms and life expectancy:

> ACEI for all patients, unless contraindicated (titrate to maximum tolerated dose).

> Beta-blocker, eg bisoprolol, carvedilol or nebivolol, in patients with stable NYHA II–IV symptoms. Only start when clinically stable and euvolaemic – start low, go slow. Titrate to maximum tolerated dose. Hypotension may be avoided by reducing other drugs including diuretics where possible. If fluid retention occurs increase the loop diuretic. Try to continue the beta-blocker if at all possible, because side effects are usually transient.

> Spironolactone in patients with NYHA III–IV, creatinine <200 μmol/L and K$^+$ <5.5 mmol/L. Check electrolytes weekly for 2 weeks and stop spironolactone if K$^+$ >6.0 mmol/L. If patient cannot tolerate spironolactone, then an angiotensin receptor blocker (ARB) can be added to ACEI (the combination of ACEI and ARB reduces morbidity but not mortality). If patient cannot

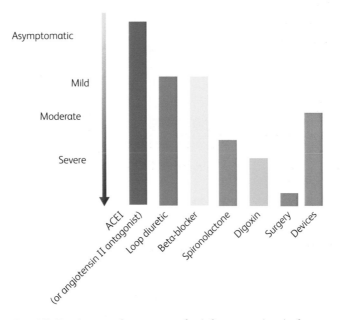

Fig 45 Escalation of treatment for left ventricular dysfunction.

tolerate at all ACEI, ARB or aldosterone antagonists then the combination of hydralazine with isosorbide mononitrate can be used.

> If still symptomatic, NYHA II–IV, left ventricular ejection fraction (LVEF) <35% and patient is in sinus rhythm with a heart rate of >70 beats per minute, then add ivabradine.

> Digoxin does not prolong life, but improves symptoms and reduces hospital admissions in more severe cases of heart failure.

> Cardiac resynchronisation therapy (dual chamber pacemaker with additional LV lead) may be considered in symptomatic patients with poor LV function and broad QRS (see Section 3.4.2).

> Implantable cardioverter defibrillators (see Section 3.4.2) in selected patients.

Surgical intervention may be beneficial in carefully evaluated patients with valvular disease and those with ischaemic aetiology and ongoing angina. Cardiac transplantation (of which there are around 200 a year in UK) is indicated for the following.

> Acute heart failure not responding to ventilation and inotropic support. A ventricular assist device (VAD – an artificial heart) may be used as a 'bridge to transplantation' if a suitable donor is not immediately available (Fig 46). The function of the heart may improve (and transplantation be avoided) when it is 'rested' by one of these devices. However, use of a VAD is frequently complicated by thromboembolism and infection.

> Chronic progressive heart failure in young patients with very poor prognosis and no comorbidity.

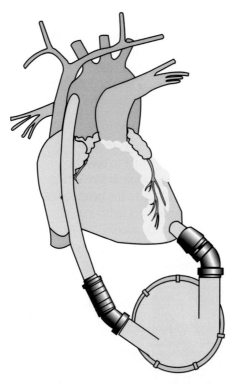

Fig 46 Left ventricular assist device (VAD).

Key point
'it is infinitely better to transplant a heart than to bury it so it can be devoured by worms' (Christiaan N Barnard)

Complications

> AF

> ventricular tachycardia

> sudden death

> progressive heart failure

> renal impairment.

Prognosis

> mortality related to ejection fraction and NYHA class

> chronic stable heart failure: overall annual mortality rate = 10%

> following hospitalisation annual mortality rate = 30–50%

> mortality rate of NYHA IV up to 60% in 1 year.

Prevention

Primary

> prevention of MI (see Section 2.1)

> prompt reperfusion therapy for acute MI

> avoid excess alcohol.

Secondary
ACEIs, beta-blockers and spironolactone all reduce progression of heart failure and mortality.

Key point
Important information for patients:

> advice about no-added-salt diet

> moderation of alcohol intake

> avoid heavy lifting (potentially arrhythmogenic)

> may feel worse for a few days after starting beta-blocker, or if the dose is increased

> they must weigh themselves daily and report to their GP or increase the amount of diuretic they are taking if they gain weight (>1–2 kg in 3 days or >2.5 kg in 2 weeks)

> education and monitoring ideally performed in conjunction with a specialist heart-failure nurse.

2.4 Diseases of heart muscles

2.4.1 Hypertrophic cardiomyopathy

Aetiology/pathophysiology/pathology

Hypertrophic cardiomyopathy (HCM) is defined by the presence of increased left ventricular (LV) wall thickness (for adults, >15 mm in one or more LV myocardial segments) that is not solely explained by abnormal loading conditions (eg hypertension).

Up to 60% of the cases are due to mutations in genes that encode sarcomeric proteins, such as the beta-myosin heavy chain, the myosin-binding protein C, troponin I and T (autosomal dominant). Five to ten per cent of the cases are due to other genetic disorders including inherited metabolic and neuromuscular diseases (eg Friedreich's ataxia, amyloidosis and mitochondrial diseases).

The degree and distribution of hypertrophy is very variable (eg septal, apical, mid-cavity). Depending upon the severity and extent of the hypertrophy, patients with HCM can develop LV outflow tract obstruction (LVOTO), diastolic dysfunction, myocardial ischaemia or mitral regurgitation.

In the classic form of obstructive HCM, the obstruction occurs at the level of the LVOT by a combination of septal hypertrophy and systolic anterior movement of the anterior mitral valve (Fig 47) (Venturi effect due to the high velocities in the LVOT). In other morphologic variants of HCM, obstruction at the mid-cavity can also occur.

Epidemiology

The prevalence of hypertrophic cardiomyopathy (HCM) is one in 500 and it is the most common single-gene cardiac disorder.

Clinical presentation

Common

> exertional chest pain and breathlessness
> palpitations
> asymptomatic murmur
> abnormal ECG on screening.

Uncommon

> syncope.

Rare

> sudden death.

Physical signs

There may be no abnormal findings.

Common

> jerky pulse
> prominent apical impulse.
> systolic murmur at left lower sternal edge/apex.

Uncommon

> Fourth heart sound: often easier to feel (as a double apical impulse) than hear.

Investigations

The ECG and echocardiogram must be interpreted together because they provide complementary information.

ECG

The ECG is sensitive but not very specific. It varies from T wave inversion to overt left ventricular hypertrophy (LVH).

Echocardiography

Echocardiography is specific but less sensitive than the ECG. Classically, there is asymmetrical septal hypertrophy with systolic anterior motion of the mitral valve leaflet, LVOTO and secondary mitral regurgitation. Alternative patterns include apical, free wall or concentric LVH.

LVOTO is defined as a peak instantaneous Doppler LVOT gradient of >30 mmHg, but the threshold for invasive treatment is usually >50 mmHg.

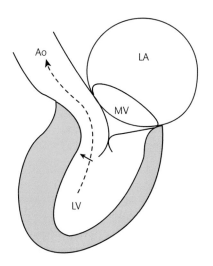

Early systole

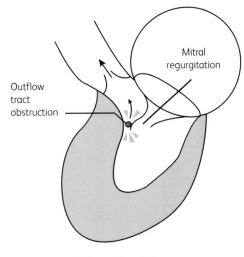

Late systole anterior motion of mitral valve

Fig 47 Effect of asymmetrical septal hypertrophy in HCM. In late systole the septum contracts down on the outflow tract, obstructing flow and generating a gradient. This generates a negative pressure (Venturi effect) just proximal to the obstruction, sucking the MV anteriorly (systolic anterior motion) and producing mitral regurgitation. Ao, aorta; LA, left atrium; LV, left ventricle; MV, mitral valve.

Ambulatory monitoring

This is used to identify the cause of palpitations or detect asymptomatic arrhythmia.

Exercise ECG

This is used to provoke arrhythmia and assess the BP response (important for prognosis or for vocational driving licence).

Magnetic resonance imaging

MRI may confirm the diagnosis if echocardiographic images are not clear (Fig 48).

> **!** **Hazard**
> It is possible to have HCM without any hypertrophy. The diagnosis may be made on the family history plus an abnormal ECG.

Differential diagnosis

> Hypertensive cardiac hypertrophy: a concentric pattern of hypertrophy with documented hypertension.

> Athlete's heart: differentiation may be difficult because some highly trained athletes, especially weight-lifters, rowers and cyclists, have an identical pattern of physiological hypertrophy. However, this will regress if training is discontinued. A septal thickness of >1.6 cm is likely to be pathological.

Treatment

Patients with LVOTO

By consensus, symptomatic patients with LVOTO should be treated with non-vasodilating beta-blockers. If beta-blockers are not tolerated or ineffective, then disopyramide, verapamil or diltiazem can be used.

Low-dose loop or thiazide diuretics can be considered with caution to improve breathlessness but remember that avoiding hypovolaemia is very important.

Patients who remain symptomatic with LVOTO >50 mmHg, NYHA class III–IV and/or recurrent exertional syncope despite maximum tolerated medical therapy should be considered for invasive treatment. The main invasive methods for relieving LVOTO are surgical myomectomy or septal alcohol ablation.

> Surgical septal myomectomy (Morrow procedure): a rectangular trough is created from the basal septum below the aortic valve until beyond the point of the mitral leaflet–septal contact. At the same time realignment of the papillary muscle or mitral valve repair can also happen. The mortality rate is 1–2%.

> Septal alcohol ablation (Fig 49): a localised septal scar is created following selective injection of alcohol into a septal perforator artery. This relieves the LVOTO but potential issues with the papillary muscles or the mitral valve cannot be addressed. The mortality rate is similar to surgical myomectomy with the main complications being atrioventricular (AV) block (7–20%).

Patients without LVOTO

The main therapy includes beta-blockers, verapamil or diltiazem to improve symptoms.

Symptoms of heart failure should be treated according to standard guidelines. ACE inhibitors (ACEIs) and mineralocorticoid receptor antagonists are indicated if ejection fraction (EF) <50%.

All patients should be assessed for risk of sudden cardiac death (SCD) according to the HCM Risk-SCD calculator. The variables needed to assess the risk are: age, family history of SCD, unexplained syncope, LV outflow gradient, maximum LV wall thickness, left atrial diameter and non-sustained ventricular tachycardia (NSVT). The general advice is that:

> Implantable cardioverter defibrillator (ICD) is not indicated if the 5-year risk is <4%.

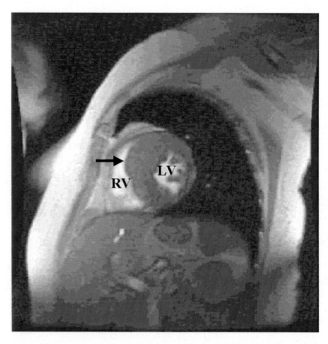

Fig 48 MRI of the heart in the short axis, showing asymmetrical hypertrophy of the interventricular septum in HCM (indicated by arrow). LV, left ventricular cavity; RV, right ventricular cavity.

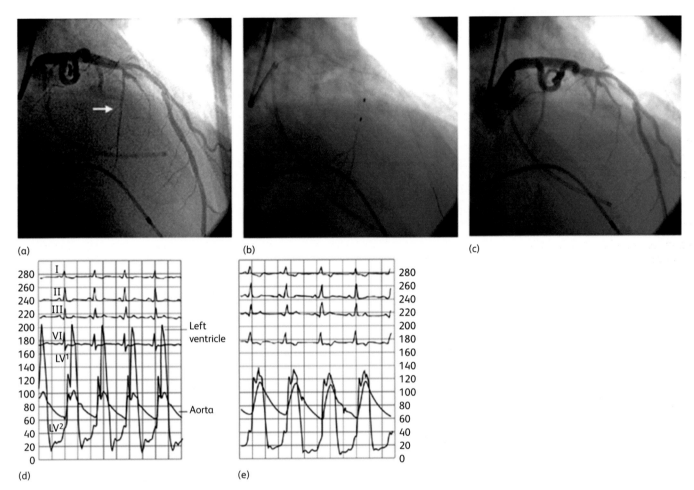

Fig 49 Septal ablation in hypertrophic obstructive cardiomyopathy. **(a)** A wire is passed through a coronary guide catheter into the target septal artery, indicated by arrow. A balloon catheter is passed, the wire is removed and the balloon inflated to occlude the artery. **(b)** Dye is injected down the lumen of the balloon catheter into the distal septal artery to confirm correct positioning. **(c)** Absolute alcohol is then injected to destroy selectively the septal artery, leaving a stump. Simultaneous pressure recordings reveal a left ventricular outflow tract gradient (peak ventricular minus peak aortic pressure) of approximately 100 mmHg **(d)** before the procedure, falling to **(e)** 15 mmHg afterwards.

> ICD may be considered if 5-year risk is 4–6%.

> ICD should be considered if 5-year risk is >6%.

Complications

Common

Atrial fibrillation (AF): always anticoagulate because there is a high risk of thromboembolism. Do not use the CHA_2DS_2-VASc score as these patients were not included in the clinical trials. Patients with HCM and AF have high incidence of stroke and should be anticoagulated (in general lifelong, even if sinus rhythm has been restored). Atrial fibrillation (AF) is often poorly tolerated, so consider cardioversion along with antiarrhythmic drugs to maintain sinus rhythm. Note that digoxin is contraindicated if there is significant LV outflow tract (LVOT) gradient (>30 mmHg), so use a beta-blocker or calcium antagonist for rate control.

Uncommon

> Ventricular tachycardia (VT): sustained VT is associated with high risk of sudden death and requires an implantable cardioverter defibrillator (ICD) (see Section 3.4).

> Progression to dilated cardiomyopathy: documented in up to 15% of early series, but certainly less common than this in modern practice.

> Sudden death.

Rare

> endocarditis.

Prognosis

Risk of premature death associated with the following:

> cardiac arrest or sustained VT

> syncope (especially when recurrent or associated with exertion)

> strong family history of sudden early death

> diagnosis of HCM in childhood

> VT on 24-hour ECG monitoring

> BP drop on exercise

> presence of certain high-risk mutations

> extreme LVH (>3 cm).

Disease associations

Friedreich's ataxia and the Wolff–Parkinson–White syndrome.

Key point

Important information for patients

Explain the following:

> It is an inherited condition.

> There is a 50% chance of transmission to their children.

> It is benign in most cases, so reassure them it is low risk if appropriate.

> Continue as far as possible with a normal life, but avoid competitive physical sports.

> Seek medical advice in the event of palpitations, dizziness or blackouts.

> Carefully discuss the matter before you begin screening – no treatment is indicated in the absence of symptoms and knowledge of the diagnosis will adversely affect life insurance, mortgages, etc.

Occupational aspects

Patients should not be professionals in sports requiring vigorous physical exertion. They may still hold vocational driving licences if they meet the Driver and Vehicle Licensing Agency (DVLA – UK) criteria (see Section 2.19).

2.4.2 Dilated cardiomyopathy

Aetiology/pathophysiology/pathology

This is a chronic progressive disorder characterised by dilatation and systolic dysfunction of the left (and sometimes the right) ventricle. There are various causes but frequently no cause is found and it is classified as idiopathic:

> idiopathic: 50%

> myocarditis: 9%

> ischaemic heart disease: 7%

> infiltrative disease: 5%

> peripartum cardiomyopathy: 4%

> hypertension: 4%

> HIV: 4%

> connective tissue disease: 3%

> substance abuse: 3%

> other: 10%.

Familial dilated cardiomyopathy caused by mutations in cytoskeletal proteins has been described in up to 50% of patients with idiopathic dilated cardiomyopathy. Mutations in more than 30 genes have been identified that could cause dilated cardiomyopathy.

Clinical presentation

This condition presents with congestive cardiac failure or arrhythmia (atrial or ventricular).

Investigations

> ECG – often shows poor R-wave progression or left bundle branch block.

> Echocardiography – dilated left ventricle with globally impaired contraction. Focal areas of hypokinesia suggest ischaemic damage or prior myocarditis.

> Cardiac catheterisation / stress imaging to ensure that there is no occult coronary disease and confirm diagnosis (see Sections 3.12, 3.8.2 and 3.10).

Treatment/prognosis

See Section 2.3.

2.4.3 Restrictive cardiomyopathy

Aetiology/pathophysiology/pathology

This is a chronic progressive condition characterised by excessively rigid ventricular walls that impair ventricular filling (diastolic dysfunction). Contractile (systolic) function is preserved.

According to the European Society of Cardiology (ESC) consensus statement, the causes of restrictive cardiomyopathy can be classified into:

> familial (familial – unknown gene, sarcomeric protein mutations, familial amyloidosis, desminopathy, pseudoxanthoma elasticum, haemochromatosis, Anderson–Fabry disease, glycogen storage disease)

> non-familial (amyloid, scleroderma, endomyocardial fibrosis – hypereosinophilic syndrome, carcinoid heart disease, radiation, drugs).

Epidemiology

This condition is rare in Western countries. Endomyocardial fibrosis is common in the tropics, particularly in Africa.

Clinical presentation

Symptoms

> breathlessness

> fatigue

> ankle swelling.

Signs

> elevated JVP, which rises on inspiration (Kussmaul's sign)

> third and/or fourth heart sound

> peripheral oedema

> ascites.

Investigations

Chest radiograph
The heart size may be normal or increased due to atrial enlargement. Pericardial calcification suggests constrictive pericarditis rather than restrictive cardiomyopathy (see Section 2.6.3).

Echocardiography
Ventricular cavities are usually not dilated, but atrial cavities are often greatly enlarged. Rapid ventricular filling may be seen at the onset of diastole, which stops abruptly in early diastole.

Cardiac catheterisation
May be diagnostic in restrictive cardiomyopathy. Rapid ventricular filling in early diastole produces a 'square root sign' appearance of the left ventricular diastolic pressure trace, which is also seen in pericardial constriction. However, other catheter data help differentiate the two conditions (Table 25).

Myocardial biopsy
Biopsy is sometimes useful to identify the cause of a restrictive cardiomyopathy.

Differential diagnosis
Restrictive cardiomyopathy must be distinguished from pericardial constriction, which is readily treated by surgery. Table 25 gives distinguishing features, but in up to 25% of patients it is not possible to tell and in these circumstances exploratory surgery may be justified.

Treatment
There is no specific treatment for idiopathic restrictive cardiomyopathy. If there is an underlying disease causing the restrictive cardiomyopathy, then this should be treated accordingly.

Heart failure should be treated according to standard guidelines, even though there are very few data specifically for restrictive cardiomyopathy. The response of patients to medical treatment of heart failure is often poor. Successful combined heart and liver transplantation has been described in amyloid cardiomyopathy.

Prognosis
The disease is generally relentlessly progressive with a high mortality.

2.4.4 Arrhythmogenic right ventricular cardiomyopathy

Aetiology/pathophysiology/pathology
Arrhythmogenic right ventricular cardiomyopathy (ARVC) is a disease of primarily the right ventricular (RV) myocardium. It is characterised by myocyte death and replacement with fibro-fatty tissue often confined to the 'triangle of dysplasia' (RV inflow, outflow and apex). In some cases the left ventricle is also involved.

The typical anatomic findings include localised or generalised RV dilatation and myocardial thinning. It has been shown that most of the mutations in ARVC involve proteins that make up desmosomes which provide mechanical support between the cardiac myocytes. The most current hypothesis for the pathogenesis of ARVC supports that the impaired desmosome function in combination with mechanical stress causes myocyte detachment and death. The impaired cell adhesion hypothesis explains some of the characteristic features of ARVC such as the predilection for the thinnest parts of the RV and the fact that athletes have more severe disease, which is probably the result of the increased stress on the heart.

At least 30% of cases are familial. There are two patterns of inheritance: an autosomal dominant which is the most common and an autosomal recessive in which ARVC is part of a cardiocutaneous syndrome including woolly hair and hyperkeratosis of palms and soles.

Clinical presentation
This condition usually presents with palpitations, syncope, atypical chest pain, ventricular arrhythmias or sudden death and affects young adults. The ventricular arrhythmias arise from the RV (commonly left bundle branch block morphology). In later stages there may be progressive RV dilatation leading to right heart failure and in some cases biventricular failure.

Table 25 Differing features of restrictive cardiomyopathy and pericardial constriction

	Restrictive cardiomyopathy	Pericardial constriction
Third heart sound	Present	Absent
Pericardial calcification	Absent	In 50%
CT of the chest	Normal pericardium	Thickened pericardium
PA systolic pressure	Usually >50 mmHg	<50 mmHg
Diastolic pressure	LV>RV	LV = RV

CT, computerised tomography; LV, left ventricular; PA, pulmonary artery; RV, right ventricular.

Investigations

ECG

It can be normal in 50% of cases at presentation but eventually all patients with ARVC develop an abnormal ECG as disease progresses. ECG abnormalities to look for include: QRS prolongation particularly in V1, incomplete or complete right bundle branch block (RBBB), epsilon wave and inversion of T wave in right precordial leads (V1–3).

Echocardiography

It might show RV akinesia, dyskinesia, aneurysm or dilatation of the right ventricular outflow tract (RVOT).

MRI

This is the best method of demonstrating fatty infiltration of the RV. It might show global and regional ventricular dilatation or dysfunction, intramyocardial fat, late gadolinium enhancement and focal wall thinning.

Electrophysiological studies

May be used to induce ventricular arrhythmias (see Section 3.2).

Diagnosis is often difficult if the ECG and imaging are not conclusive. For diagnosis, the 2010 revised Task Force Criteria should be used. The main differential diagnosis is benign right outflow tract tachycardia which can respond to beta-blockers.

Treatment

The main treatment goal is to prevent sudden cardiac death.

> Because of the association between exercise and induction of ventricular arrhythmias, patients with ARVC should not participate in competitive sports and should also avoid any activity that causes symptoms such as palpitations, presyncope or syncope.

> Beta-blockers to reduce the arrhythmic risk.

> ICD implantation for secondary prevention and for primary prevention in certain high-risk patients (extensive RV disease, LV involvement or unexplained syncope consistent with tachyarrhythmia).

Heart failure is treated in the usual way (see Section 2.3).

2.4.5 Left ventricular non-compaction

Aetiology/pathophysiology/pathology

This rare cardiomyopathy is characterised by an altered myocardial wall with prominent left ventricular (LV) trabeculae and deep intertrabecular recesses. The result is a thin, compacted epicardial layer and a thickened endocardial layer of non-compacted myocardium which communicates with the LV cavity but does not communicate with the coronary circulation. The exact pathogenesis is not well understood. It is believed that it could be either the result of either intrauterine arrest of compaction of the fetal myocardial primordium or the result of abnormal persistence of the trabecular layer.

Clinical presentation

It can be diagnosed at any age, from childhood to adulthood. Usually it presents with heart failure, arrhythmias (atrial and ventricular), syncope or thromboembolic events.

Investigations

ECG

It is usually abnormal but changes are non-specific.

Echocardiography

Used as the main diagnostic tool in order to demonstrate the compacted and non-compacted layers, communication of the deep intertrabecular recesses with the LV cavity and prominent trabecular meshwork. The Jenni echocardiographic criteria are the most widely accepted for diagnosis.

Cardiac MRI

It is the investigation of choice when echocardiography is inconclusive.

Treatment/prognosis

There is no specific treatment for LV non-compaction. Management should be guided towards the specific presentation (heart failure, arrhythmia, thromboembolism).

See Section 2.3.

2.5 Valvular heart disease

2.5.1 Aortic stenosis

Aetiology/pathophysiology/pathology

Senile: calcific/degenerative

This is the most common form of aortic stenosis, especially in those aged >65 years. Diabetes, hypercholesterolaemia and chronic renal failure are predisposing factors. Coexistent coronary artery disease is common.

Congenital bicuspid valve

Symptoms usually appear at the age of 40–50 years. There is a male predominance. Bicuspid valves are more susceptible to endocarditis than trileaflet valves. They are associated with aortopathies, ie dissection and/or aneurysm.

Rheumatic heart disease

This is an unusual cause of aortic stenosis.

Stenosis results from a combination of fibrosis and calcification, with additional commissural fusion and reduced cusp separation. The increased left ventricular (LV) pressure load results in compensatory left ventricular hypertrophy (LVH) and diastolic dysfunction. Subendocardial ischaemia and fibrosis is common. Untreated, LV dilatation and failure will occur. There is an increased risk of ventricular arrhythmia. Atrial arrhythmias are usually poorly tolerated.

Clinical presentation

Common

Common symptoms are exertional angina, dyspnoea and syncope, and occasionally palpitations. There are symptoms of LV failure if presentation is late.

Uncommon

> embolic phenomena from calcific emboli

> gastrointestinal bleeding (idiopathic/ angiodysplasia)

> infective endocarditis (IE).

Physical signs

See Section 1.2.5.

Investigations

ECG

Look for LVH (85% cases) and, rarely, conduction disturbance.

Chest radiograph

May be normal. Post-stenotic aortic dilatation may be seen. Suspect aortic (or mitral) regurgitation or LV dilatation if cardiomegaly present.

Echocardiography

Echocardiography determines whether the valve is tricuspid, bicuspid or rheumatic in appearance. The degree of valve thickening, leaflet mobility and calcification (Fig 50) can be determined. Continuous-wave Doppler enables estimation of the pressure drop across the aortic valve and the aortic valve area (Table 26). LVH and dilatation with reduced systolic function will be seen with severe disease.

Coronary angiography

Coronary angiography will be required in most cases to assess the coronary arteries before surgery. The peak–peak withdrawal gradient across the aortic valve can also be determined.

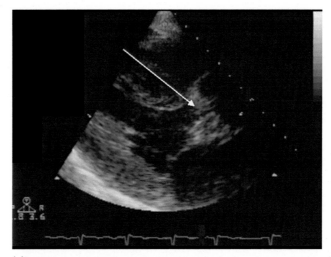

(a)

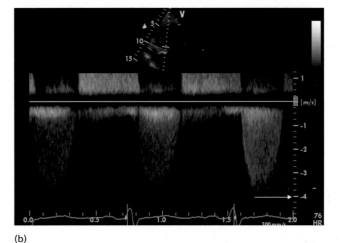

(b)

Fig 50 (a) Calcific aortic stenosis. In this parasternal long-axis view, the aortic valve cusps (indicated by arrow) appear markedly thickened and calcified. Note the hypertrophy of the septum and posterior wall. **(b)** The peak velocity across the valve is 4 m/s. The calculated peak valve gradient is 64 mmHg.

Table 26	Grading of aortic stenosis by aortic valve gradient and area	
Aortic stenosis	Peak aortic valve gradient (mmHg)	Aortic valve area (cm^2)
Mild	<50	>1.5
Moderate	50–70	1.1–1.5
Severe	>70	<0.8–1.0

Key point

Consider the following in your differential diagnosis:

> innocent systolic murmur: pregnancy, fever, anaemia and thyrotoxicosis
> aortic sclerosis
> mitral regurgitation
> hypertrophic obstructive cardiomyopathy
> atrial or ventricular septal defect
> pulmonary stenosis.

Treatment

Key point

Severe aortic stenosis is associated with peak gradient of >70 mmHg and mean gradient of >40 mmHg. However, with LV impairment the aortic valve gradient may underestimate the degree of stenosis. In this situation, valve area (severe <1 cm²) is a more reliable measurement and a dynamic assessment of the valve gradient with dobutamine stress may be required.

Emergency
Admit the patient if there is heart failure and treat with diuretics with a view to early inpatient valve replacement. Try to avoid the use of inotropes. Exercise great caution with angiotensin-converting enzyme inhibitors and other vasodilators, and never use them if the patient is hypotensive.

Long term
Follow moderate disease with repeat echocardiography at yearly intervals. Severe stenosis requires closer supervision to detect onset of symptoms. Valve replacement should be considered in all patients with severe aortic stenosis who

become symptomatic. It is also indicated in asymptomatic patients who develop LV dysfunction or prior to non-cardiac surgery. Antibiotic prophylaxis is no longer routinely recommended in patients with native valvular heart disease undergoing dental and endoscopy procedures (NICE guidance 2008).

Patients previously deemed inoperable or at high risk of mortality from conventional surgical aortic valve replacement can now be considered for transcatheter aortic valve implantation (TAVI) which has been shown to reduce 1-year mortality compared to medical therapy alone. The number of TAVI procedures is increasing rapidly and providing therapy for a group of patients who would previously not have been considered for an intervention. Clinical trials are now underway comparing TAVI to open surgical valve replacement in patients who are at moderate to low risk from surgery. TAVI is also the treatment of choice in patients who have degenerative tissue valve disease where a re-do valve operation carries significant risk.

Complications
The following are associated with aortic stenosis:

> cardiac failure and pulmonary hypertension
> sudden death
> IE
> embolic disease
> complete heart block.

Prognosis
Symptoms occur only after the stenosis has become severe. Mild aortic stenosis progresses to being severe in about 20% of cases, two-thirds remaining unchanged. On average, the valve gradient will increase by 4–8 mmHg per year. Extensive valve calcification, the presence of a bicuspid valve and coexistent coronary artery disease predispose those affected to

more rapid stenosis progression. Asymptomatic patients have an excellent prognosis. In symptomatic disease, the average survival with angina or syncope is 2–3 years, and with heart failure 1 year.

2.5.2 Aortic regurgitation
Aetiology/pathophysiology/pathology
Aortic regurgitation (AR) may result from primary disease of the valve leaflets, dilatation of the aortic root, loss of commissural support or failure of valve prosthesis – either alone or in combination. The result is the addition of a regurgitant volume to the normal inflow from the left atrium.

Key point
Aetiology of AR

Dilatation of the aortic root
> degenerative (senile)
> cystic medial necrosis: isolated/ associated with Marfan syndrome
> aortic dissection
> systemic hypertension
> connective tissue diseases, eg ankylosing spondylitis, rheumatoid arthritis, giant cell aortitis
> syphilitic aortitis.

Primary disease of valve leaflets
> rheumatic heart disease
> infective endocarditis
> bicuspid valve
> myxomatous degeneration with prolapse
> trauma.

Loss of support of the aortic valve cusps
> high ventricular septal defect
> Fallot's tetralogy.

Failure of a prosthetic valve

Clinical presentation

The patient may present with the following:

> exertional dyspnoea, orthopnoea and paroxysmal nocturnal dyspnoea

> lethargy

> palpitations

> angina.

Physical signs

See Section 1.2.6.

Investigations

ECG

Look for the following:

> normal/left ventricular (LV) hypertrophy

> left atrial enlargement

> prolongation of PR interval

> non-specific ST segment and T-wave changes.

Chest radiograph

This is normal or shows cardiomegaly, which may be gross. There is pulmonary oedema in acute cases. Look out for evidence of aortic dilatation or dissection.

Echocardiography

Echocardiography may enable diagnosis of the aetiology from the anatomy of the aortic valve and root. Severity assessment is semiquantitative and derived from colour and continuous wave Doppler (Fig 51). LV dilatation and reduced ejection fraction occur with untreated severe disease. Transoesophageal echocardiography may be required to exclude dissection and endocarditis.

Coronary angiography

Coronary angiography will be required before surgery to assess the coronary arteries in most cases. The AR can be assessed with an aortogram.

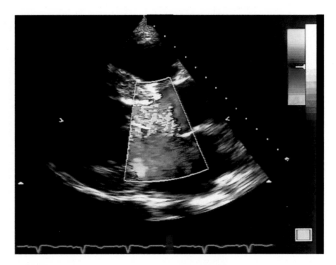

Fig 51 Parasternal long-axis view showing severe AR with colour flow mapping. In early diastole there is a broad-based regurgitant jet (yellow–blue) filling the whole of the left ventricular outflow tract.

Differential diagnosis

Consider pulmonary regurgitation and mitral stenosis with Graham Steell murmur.

Treatment

Emergency

In patients with acute severe AR or severe decompensated chronic AR, treat heart failure aggressively with diuretics, vasodilators and inotropes. Look for the underlying cause and plan early for emergency valve replacement.

Long term

Patients with asymptomatic mild/moderate AR with normal ventricular function require annual clinical and echocardiography assessment. All patients with severe symptomatic AR should be considered for surgery. Early surgery is indicated if there is evidence of LV dilatation or LV systolic dysfunction. Patients with coexistent aortic root dilatation >5 cm and AR of any severity should have aortic root reconstruction and valve resuspension or replacement. Antibiotic prophylaxis is no longer routinely recommended in patients with native valvular heart disease undergoing dental and endoscopy procedures (NICE guidance 2008).

Complications

Complications commonly encountered include the following:

> progressive heart failure

> mitral regurgitation

> atrial fibrillation

> sudden death.

Prognosis

The risk of developing symptoms and/or LV dysfunction in severe AR with normal LV function is 4% per year. If there is LV dysfunction, the risk is >25% per year. Prognosis is excellent in mild or moderate disease. In symptomatically severe AR the yearly mortality rate is >10%.

2.5.3 Mitral stenosis

Aetiology

Most mitral stenosis (MS) is acquired through rheumatic heart disease. It is more common in women, presenting in developed countries in the fourth or fifth decades of life.

Clinical presentation

MS commonly presents with the following:

> exertional dyspnoea

> orthopnoea

> paroxysmal nocturnal dyspnoea

> haemoptysis

> palpitations

> fatigue

> weight loss

> embolic phenomena in up to 15%.

Physical signs

See Section 1.14.

Investigations

ECG

> normal

> left atrial enlargement or atrial fibrillation (AF)

> right ventricular hypertrophy.

Chest radiograph

> normal

> straightening of left cardiac border as a result of dilated left atrial appendage

> pulmonary oedema

> atrial double shadow along right cardiac border (Fig 52).

Echocardiography

This enables visualisation of leaflet mobility and calcification. Quantification of the valve area and mean gradient (Table 27) are derived from continuous wave Doppler. Left atrial size and right ventricle (RV) function should be assessed. Left ventricle (LV) size is usually small and LV systolic function normal. Doppler echocardiography allows estimation of the pulmonary artery pressure (PAP). A transoesophageal study is usually required to assess the suitability for valvuloplasty if this is being considered (Fig 53).

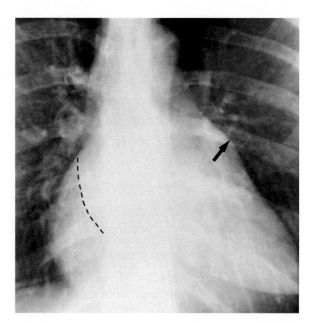

Fig 52 Chest radiograph showing left atrial enlargement in a patient with mitral valve (MV) disease: note the double atrial shadow (left atrial border indicated by broken line) and dilatation of the left atrial appendage (indicated by arrow). (Reproduced from Axford (ed.) *Medicine*. Oxford: Blackwell Science, 1996.)

Table 27 Severity of mitral stenosis assessed by mean gradient and mitral valve area		
Severity	**Mean gradient (mmHg)**	**Mitral valve area (cm^2)**
Mild	0–6	>1.5
Moderate	6–11	1.0–1.5
Severe	>12	<1.0

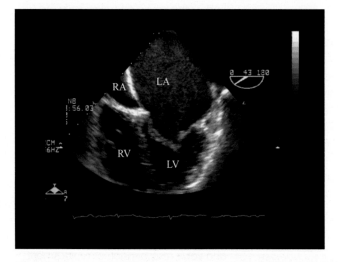

Fig 53 Rheumatic MS: note thickening of the leaflet tips and subvalvular apparatus causing marked restriction of leaflet excursion in diastole. There is marked left atrial enlargement with a relatively small left ventricular cavity. Spontaneous echo contrast (smoky appearance) can be seen in left atrium suggestive of a prothrombotic state. LA, left atrium; LV, left ventricle; RA, right atrium; RV, right ventricle.

Cardiac catheterisation

This is advisable when patient symptoms and echocardiographic findings are discordant or coexistent coronary artery disease is suspected. The mean mitral valve (MV) gradient can be calculated from the difference between the left ventricular end diastolic pressure and pulmonary artery wedge pressure recorded simultaneously.

Dynamic assessment

Some symptomatic patients may only have evidence of mild or moderate MS at rest. However, during exercise the rate of mitral inflow increases, which may cause the transvalvular gradient to increase significantly. Diastolic filling time may also be reduced causing raised left atrial pressure. Exercise echocardiography should therefore be considered in patients who are symptomatic with apparent mild or moderate disease only, and no other explanation for their symptoms (eg anaemia, other valvular disease or coronary artery disease). An increase in mean MV gradient to >15 mmHg or PAP to >60 mmHg with exercise is considered significant.

Differential diagnosis

Consider the following:

> Austin Flint murmur (of aortic regurgitation)

> left atrial myxoma

> tricuspid stenosis.

Treatment

Emergency

Treat acute pulmonary oedema with diuretics.

Short term

Beta-blockers or rate-limiting calcium antagonists may help symptoms.

Atrial fibrillation (AF) requires adequate ventricular rate control. Regular oral diuretics are often required. (see Section 2.2.2).

Long term

Formal anticoagulation with warfarin is required. Intervention is required if there is severe stenosis and symptoms. If the MV has minimal calcification, no more that mild mitral regurgitation, and there is no evidence of left atrial thrombus, then percutaneous mitral balloon valvuloplasty (PMBV) should be considered. Otherwise, open valvuloplasty or MV replacement is required. Antibiotic prophylaxis is no longer routinely recommended in patients with native valvular heart disease undergoing dental and endoscopy procedures (NICE guidance 2008).

Complications

The following are possible:

> AF

> pulmonary hypertension or infarction

> chest infections

> tricuspid regurgitation

> RV failure

> thromboembolic disease.

Prognosis

In severe MS, 5-year survival rates range from 62% with New York Heart Association class III symptoms to 15% with class IV. After surgery, 5-year survival rates are between 90% and 96%.

2.5.4 Mitral regurgitation

Aetiology/pathophysiology/pathology

Abnormalities of the mitral valve (MV) annulus, valve leaflets, chordae tendineae, papillary muscles or adjacent left ventricular wall may cause mitral regurgitation.

Key point

Common causes of mitral regurgitation in the adult:

> idiopathic mitral valve prolapse (MVP) is the most common cause

> after myocardial infarction (MI):

  > papillary muscle dysfunction (ischaemia or rupture)

  > ruptured chordae tendineae

  > annular dilatation (ischaemic heart disease or dilated cardiomyopathy)

> rheumatic heart disease

> infective endocarditis (IE)

> atrial septal defect

> failure of valve prosthesis / paraprosthetic leak.

Epidemiology

The prevalence of MVP varies from 1% to 6%, and is twice as common in women. After MI, the prevalence is 20%.

Clinical presentation

Common symptoms include exertional dyspnoea, orthopnoea, fatigue and lethargy. Occasionally, there are palpitations and, in severe acute mitral regurgitation, the patient may be very unwell with severe dyspnoea.

Physical signs

In mild disease, there are few signs apart from an apical pansystolic murmur radiating to the axilla. In more haemodynamically significant regurgitation, there can be the following:

> atrial fibrillation (AF)

> laterally displaced, hyperdynamic apex beat with systolic thrill

> left parasternal late systolic heave (atrial filling) in severe mitral regurgitation

> soft first heart sound, wide splitting of the second heart sound, and a third heart sound

> late systolic murmur in association with a systolic click suggests MVP.

In acute severe mitral regurgitation, there is poor perfusion with pulmonary oedema. A murmur may not be heard due to very rapid equalisation of pressures between the left atrium and left ventricle (LV) during early diastole.

See Section 1.2.3.

Investigations

ECG
This may be normal, but look for AF, left atrial enlargement or LV hypertrophy.

Chest radiograph
This can be normal, or may show cardiomegaly with left atrial enlargement. Mitral annular calcification (Fig 54) may be seen. There is pulmonary oedema in acute mitral regurgitation.

Echocardiography
The presence of excess leaflet motion, restricted leaflet motion and annular size must be carefully assessed with both transthoracic echo and transoesophageal echocardiography. In the case of prolapse, a precise assessment of the scallops involved is required. Severity assessment is semiquantitative from colour and continuous wave Doppler. Measurements are required for left and right ventricular size, systolic function and pulmonary artery pressure (Fig 55).

Coronary angiography
Coronary angiography may be required if there is a suspicion of coronary artery disease.

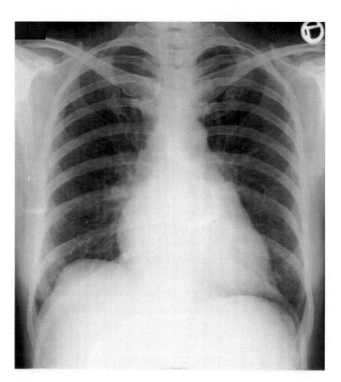

Fig 54 Mitral annular calcification: a ring of calcification can be seen within the heart shadow.

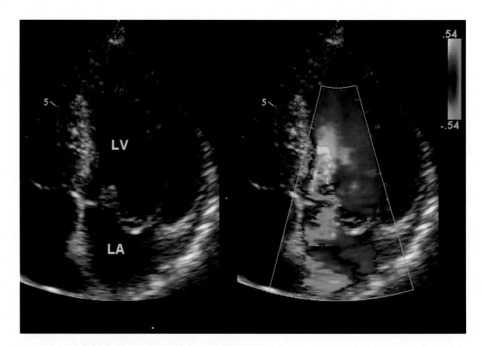

Fig 55 Apical four chamber view of a patient with prolapse of the posterior MV leaflet. An anteriorly directed jet of mitral regurgitation can be seen with colour flow mapping (coloured green).

Medical Masterclass Third edition

Dynamic assessment

In patients with ischaemic mitral regurgitation, baseline mitral regurgitation may only be mild to moderate. However, during exercise ischaemia of the papillary muscles and adjacent myocardium may cause the mitral regurgitation to become severe. Exercise (stress) echo should therefore be considered in patients with ischaemic heart disease and severe cardiac symptoms that cannot be explained by baseline mitral regurgitation or any other cause.

Treatment

Emergency

Treat acute pulmonary oedema and shock. Vasodilator therapy reduces the afterload and is of benefit. Intravenous nitroprusside may be life saving. Urgent surgery is required.

Short term

Symptomatic patients with severe mitral regurgitation who are awaiting surgery should receive diuretic and vasodilator therapy. Digoxin is of particular benefit in the treatment of AF. Anticoagulation will be required.

Long term

Mild to moderate disease requires annual monitoring only. All patients with symptomatic severe mitral regurgitation require surgery. Asymptomatic patients with severe mitral regurgitation should be referred once LV function starts to decline or LV dilatation occurs. Generally, surgical outcome is better with MV repair than replacement. Asymptomatic patients with severe mitral regurgitation secondary to MV prolapse can be considered for surgery if there is a high likelihood of successful repair of the valve without need for replacement. Symptomatic patients with severe mitral regurgitation who are felt to be high-risk surgical candidates can be considered for percutaneous treatment with MitraClip. Antibiotic prophylaxis is no longer

routinely recommended in patients with native valvular heart disease undergoing dental and endoscopy procedures (NICE guidance 2008).

Key point

Indications for surgery in severe mitral regurgitation:

> If surgical repair is possible, it should be considered in all patients aged <75 years who have a flail leaflet or persistent AF.

> Deteriorating ventricular function (ejection fraction <60% or end-systolic diameter >45 mm).

> The presence of symptoms, although careful consideration of the aetiology and severity of LV dysfunction is needed in older patients.

Complications

The following are possible:

> LV failure

> AF

> IE

> pulmonary hypertension

> right ventricular failure

> thromboembolism (more common in MVP)

> sudden death (more common in flail leaflet).

Prognosis

Progression of mitral regurgitation depends on the aetiology, but it develops in 15% of patients with MVP over a 10–15-year period. Without surgery, patients with severe mitral regurgitation have a 5-year survival rate as low as 45%. After surgery, the 5-year survival rates vary from 40% in mitral regurgitation caused by ischaemic heart disease to over 75% in cases of rheumatic MV disease.

2.5.5 Tricuspid valve disease

Aetiology/pathophysiology/pathology

Tricuspid regurgitation (TR) is usually secondary to a combination of right ventricular (RV) dilatation and high pressure resulting from severe pulmonary hypertension. Tricuspid stenosis (TS) is almost invariably rheumatic in origin, and accompanies mitral stenosis. Carcinoid is a rare cause of tricuspid valve stenosis/ regurgitation. Intravenous drug users are susceptible to developing *Staphylococcus aureus* bacteraemia with large tricuspid valve vegetations and severe TR.

See Section 1.2.7.

Clinical presentation

This is usually asymptomatic, and in the case of TR is usually discovered secondary to other more significant cardiac pathology. TR and TS may cause a sensation of neck pulsation, right upper quadrant discomfort and peripheral oedema. Occasionally, a low cardiac output syndrome comprising fatigue, weight loss and syncope may be present.

Physical signs

TR causes prominent 'v' waves in the JVP, whereas TS causes prominent 'a' waves in sinus rhythm. In more severe cases, both cause pulsatile hepatomegaly, ascites and peripheral oedema. In TR, a pansystolic murmur that increases on inspiration and is heard best at the lower left sternal edge is usual. The corresponding murmur in TS is a presystolic murmur in sinus rhythm with a mid-diastolic murmur.

See Section 1.2.7.

Investigations

ECG

This is usually normal, but right atrial enlargement is a feature of tricuspid valve disease. There is evidence of RV hypertrophy in TR.

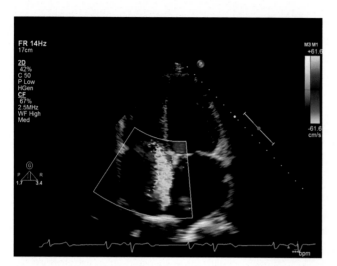

Fig 56 TR: a broad band seen mainly as blue extends back into the right atrium. (Courtesy of Dr J Chambers.)

Chest radiograph

> Often normal, but there may be an enlarged right atrium and superior vena cava in both TR and TS.

> RV enlargement may be evident in TR.

Echocardiography
This gauges the severity (from colour and continuous wave Doppler) and enables calculation of pulmonary artery pressure from a TR jet (Fig 56).

Treatment
Both TR and TS are usually well tolerated irrespective of their severity. When TR is the result of a correctable left-sided cause, eg mitral valve disease, annuloplasty at the time of surgery is corrective. TS rarely requires valvotomy.

2.5.6 Pulmonary valve disease
Aetiology/pathophysiology/pathology
Pulmonary stenosis (PS) is usually congenital in origin, and may form part of Fallot's tetralogy. Rarely, it may be the result of rheumatic fever or the carcinoid syndrome. Pulmonary regurgitation (PR) invariably results from dilatation of the pulmonary annulus, which may occur with pulmonary hypertension, leading to right ventricular hypertrophy (RVH) and right atrial hypertrophy (RAH).

Clinical presentation
Both pulmonary regurgitation and mild PS are asymptomatic. More severe disease presents with a low cardiac output syndrome and right heart failure.

Physical signs
There is a characteristic harsh ejection systolic murmur at the left sternal edge in the second intercostal space, which is louder on inspiration. Other signs include the following:

> prominent 'a' wave in JVP

> thrill over pulmonary area, right ventricular (RV) heave

> soft pulmonary second heart sound

> RV fourth heart sound.

Pulmonary regurgitation is characterised by a decrescendo early diastolic murmur heard in the pulmonary area (Graham Steell murmur).

Investigations
ECG
This is normal, or there is right axis deviation (RAD) and RVH.

Chest radiograph
This is normal, or shows right atrial and ventricular enlargement.

Treatment
Pulmonary valvotomy may be necessary in severe PS. Severe pulmonary regurgitation may require surgery if the patient is symptomatic.

2.6 Pericardial disease

2.6.1 Acute pericarditis
Aetiology/pathophysiology/pathology
There are many causes of acute pericarditis (Table 28). In the developed world the cause of many cases is never established (idiopathic), but a viral cause is often suspected – coxsackie B being most often incriminated. Tuberculosis

Table 28 Possible causes of pericarditis	
Acute idiopathic pericarditis	Unknown
Infectious	Viral TB Other bacteria Fungi
Inflammatory	Post myocardial infarction / cardiotomy Autoimmune rheumatic disorder
Other	Neoplastic Uraemia Trauma Aortic dissection Hypothyroidism Irradiation Drugs, eg hydralazine

TB, tuberculosis.

(TB) is a major cause in the developing world. It is not mandatory to search for the aetiology in all patients, especially in countries with a low prevalence of TB. Common causes of pericarditis are often associated with a relatively benign course and have a low yield of diagnostic investigations.

There is inflammation of the pericardium with infiltration of polymorphonuclear leukocytes, increased pericardial vascularity and deposition of fibrin. Inflammation can involve the superficial myocardium and fibrinous adhesions may form between the pericardium and epicardium, and between the pericardium, adjacent sternum and pleura. The visceral pleura may exude fluid, leading to pericardial effusion. Recurrences affect around 30% of patients within 18 months of a first episode of pericarditis.

Clinical presentation
See Section 1.4.8.

Common

> Chest pain: usually retrosternal or left precordial in location, radiating to the neck. The pain is aggravated by supine posture, coughing, deep inspiration and swallowing; it is eased by sitting up and leaning forward. It may be preceded by a few days of malaise.

> Fever.

Uncommon

> dyspnoea
> symptoms of any underlying cause
> acute epigastric pain mimicking an acute abdomen
> anginal type pain
> cardiac tamponade.

Physical signs
The patient may present with the following:

> pericardial friction rub
> fever

> atrial fibrillation
> evidence of an underlying disease
> signs associated with tamponade.

Investigations

Key point
The diagnosis of acute pericarditis is based on the presence of two of the following four features:

> typical chest pain
> pericardial friction rub
> classical ECG changes (widespread ST elevation or PR depression)
> pericardial effusion (new or worsening).

ECG
The ECG may be normal. There is an initial, widespread (not V1 or aVr), upwardly concave ST elevation, followed by return of the ST segments to baseline and flattened T waves. PR depression is often seen. T waves then become inverted before returning to normal over 1 week. It is necessary to distinguish these changes from those of acute myocardial infarction, in which ST elevation is convex and regional, R waves are lost, Q waves form and conduction abnormalities may develop (Fig 57). Acute pericarditis generally affects the ECG more extensively, with little in the way of 'reciprocal changes' compared to those seen with ST segment elevation myocardial infarct. Changes in the ECG imply inflammation of the epicardium, since the parietal pericardium itself is electrically inert.

Blood tests
Look for the following:

> elevated white cell count, erythrocyte sedimentation rate and C-reactive protein (CRP)

> blood culture, atypical bacterial antibody and viral titres
> renal function to exclude uraemia
> serial cardiac enzymes which may show a modest rise if a degree of myocarditis is present
> as directed by suspicion of underlying cause (Table 28).

Chest radiograph
This is often normal, but look for evidence of pericardial effusion, malignancy, TB or aortic dissection.

Echocardiography
Echocardiography is useful to exclude pericardial effusion or suspicion of aortic dissection.

Differential diagnosis
Consider the following:

> acute coronary syndrome
> aortic dissection
> pulmonary embolism
> musculoskeletal pain.

Treatment
Emergency
Pericardiocentesis if there is cardiac tamponade.

Short term
Admit if there is severe pain or large effusion, or for treatment of underlying condition. Treatment should include restriction of activity beyond normal sedentary life until full resolution of symptoms and normalisation of CRP for patients not involved in competitive sports. Oral non-steroidal anti-inflammatory drugs (NSAIDs) are given for symptomatic relief (usually aspirin or ibuprofen with gastroprotection). Colchicine is recommended as a first-line therapy for acute pericarditis in conjunction with aspirin/NSAID therapy to prevent recurrences. Consider corticosteroids as a second-line therapy in patients with contraindications and failure

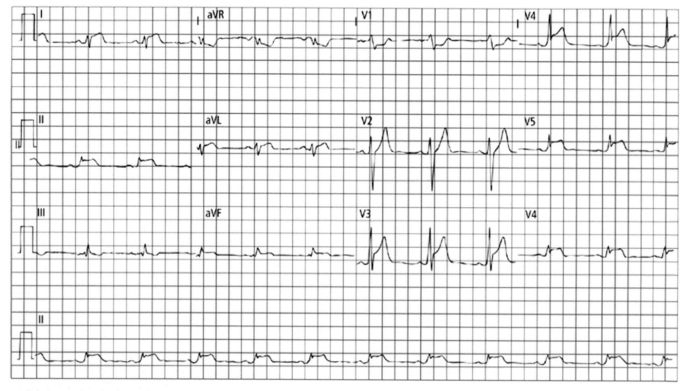

Fig 57 ECG showing changes of acute pericarditis.

of aspirin/NSAIDs. In this scenario, use them in conjunction with colchicine at low to moderate doses. The initial dose should be maintained until resolution of symptoms and normalisation of CRP, then tapered.

> **!** **Hazard**
> In cases of acute pericarditis stop any oral anticoagulants because of the risk of intrapericardial haemorrhage and tamponade.

Long term
The recurrence rate after a single episode of pericarditis is between 15% and 30% but may increase to 50% in those not treated with colchicine and particularly in those treated with corticosteroids. A common cause of recurrence is inadequate treatment of the first episode of pericarditis.

Further treatment with aspirin/NSAIDs and colchicine is usually considered with 'triple therapy' with corticosteroids in specific situations (avoided in infective causes and favoured systemic inflammatory aetiologies). In particularly difficult cases, other biological and immunosuppressive therapies may be considered.

Complications
Beware of the following:

> pericardial effusion and tamponade (early disease)

> recurrent pericarditis

> in patients with concurrent myocarditis (myopericarditis), risk of sudden death after strenuous exertion in active phase of disease

Prognosis
There is complete resolution within 3 months in 80% of patients. Cardiac tamponade may cause death if

untreated, as may some of the precipitating conditions. Constrictive pericarditis is not usually seen despite multiple relapses of acute pericarditis.

2.6.2 Pericardial effusion

Aetiology/pathophysiology/pathology
Pericardial effusion may develop in cases of acute pericarditis from any cause. The normal pericardial space contains 15–50 mL fluid and can only accommodate a rapid increase in pericardial volume to 150–200 mL before the intrapericardial pressure (IPP) starts to rise. Once the IPP exceeds the intracardiac pressure, left ventricular filling and cardiac output decline. With a gradual accumulation of fluid, volumes of up to 2 L may be present before left ventricular filling becomes compromised.

Acute cardiac tamponade typically follows cardiac trauma (which may be iatrogenic), aortic dissection, spontaneous bleeding or cardiac rupture after a myocardial infarction. The aetiology of chronic pericardial effusions remains idiopathic in developed countries (up to 50%), while other common causes include malignancy (10–25%), infections (15–30%), iatrogenic causes (15–20%) and connective tissue diseases (5–15%), whereas TB is the dominant cause in developing countries (>60%), where TB is endemic.

Iatrogenic causes include cardiothoracic surgery, implanted cardiac devices (pacemakers and ICDs) and catheter ablation procedures, eg atrial fibrillation ablation.

Clinical presentation
Common
In chronic cases the patient may be asymptomatic despite a large effusion. Typical symptoms include shortness of breath, orthopnoea and mild chest discomfort.

Uncommon
In a large pericardial effusion without tamponade, compression of adjacent structures may lead to the following:

> dysphagia (oesophagus)

> cough (bronchus/trachea)

> hiccups (phrenic nerve)

> hoarseness (laryngeal nerve)

> abdominal bloating and nausea (abdominal viscera).

Physical signs
In most patients, the examination will be normal. In large effusions without tamponade, there may be muffled heart sounds, crackles (compression of lung parenchyma) or Ewart's sign (patch of dullness below the angle of the left scapula caused by compression of the base of the left lung). There may also be pericardial friction rub or signs of cardiac tamponade. Cardiac tamponade

should be suspected in a shocked patient with apparent clear lung fields and elevated JVP.

Key point
Cardiac tamponade may present in three ways:

1 cardiac arrest

2 a severely ill patient who is stuporous or agitated and restless (survivor of acute tamponade)

3 with dyspnoea, chest pain, weight loss, anorexia and weakness (more slowly developing tamponade).

Rapid recognition of the clinical signs of tamponade is essential:

> tachypnoea and tachycardia

> pulsus paradoxus (pulse becomes impalpable on inspiration in severe cases)

> elevated JVP with prominent systolic x descent and absence of diastolic y descent

> rarely, normal JVP in severe dehydration.

If you suspect the diagnosis – organise an urgent echocardiogram.

Investigations
ECG
This is usually normal, although changes of acute pericarditis may be present. There may be a non-specific reduction in QRS voltage and T-wave flattening. Electrical alternans is suggestive of a large effusion.

Chest radiograph
This is often normal; although a large effusion may cause an enlarged globular cardiac silhouette with clear lung fields. Look for separation of the pericardial fat lines and a left-sided pleural effusion (Fig 58).

Echocardiography
Echocardiography is the most sensitive test for detection of pericardial fluid (as little as 20 mL). This appears as an echo-free space around the heart (Fig 58b). Diastolic left and right heart collapse, marked decrease in mitral inflow with inspiration and a dilated inferior vena cava that fails to collapse with inspiration suggest tamponade. It is also possible to see if an effusion is circumferential or loculated.

Differential diagnosis
In chronic cases consider the following:

> constrictive pericarditis.

> restrictive cardiomyopathy.

In those with tamponade, consider causes of circulatory collapse – in particular massive pulmonary embolus (PE) and severe asthma.

Treatment
Consider the following:

> Urgent pericardiocentesis is essential in cardiac tamponade. It is also needed for diagnosis if there is a suspicion of purulent or tuberculous pericarditis, or prolonged and otherwise unexplained illness.

> Symptom relief as for acute pericarditis (see Section 2.6.1).

> Recurrent or persistent symptomatic effusions may require balloon pericardiostomy or surgical pericardiectomy.

Complications
Common
Complications arise more commonly from the underlying conditions than from the effusion, although chronic pericardial effusion lasting more than 6 months may be seen. This is more likely after idiopathic, uraemic, myxoedematous or malignant pericarditis.

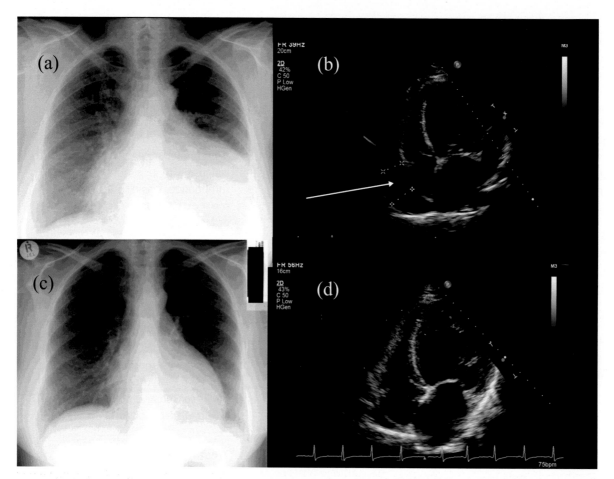

Fig 58 **(a)** Chest X-ray demonstrating enlarged globular-shaped heart. **(b)** Transthoracic echocardiography confirmed this was due to a large pericardial effusion seen as an echo-free space around the heart (indicated by arrow) in apical four-chamber view. **(c)** After drainage of the effusion, cardiomegaly resolved on chest X-ray, **(d)** and an effusion can no longer be seen around the heart at echocardiography.

Uncommon

Uncommon complications are cardiac tamponade and constrictive pericarditis.

2.6.3 Constrictive pericarditis

Aetiology/pathophysiology/pathology

Constrictive pericarditis is characterised by an abnormally thickened and non-compliant pericardium, which abruptly limits ventricular filling in mid- to late diastole. This results in elevated end-diastolic cardiac filling pressures and the equalisation of pressure in all four chambers at end diastole. As cardiac filling is compromised, cardiac output is reduced. The clinical features are secondary to systemic venous congestion.

Before the 1960s, tuberculous constrictive pericarditis was the most common cause of pericardial constriction worldwide. In the developed world, its importance has declined, and the aetiology is usually idiopathic, post-radiotherapy or post-surgical.

Clinical presentation

Common

Oedema, abdominal swelling and discomfort caused by ascites or hepatic congestion are most frequent. Vague abdominal symptoms such as postprandial fullness, dyspepsia, flatulence and anorexia may also be present.

Cachexia and fatigue suggest a reduced cardiac output.

Uncommon

Exertional dyspnoea and orthopnoea may occur when ventricular pressures become severely elevated, as may platypnoea (dyspnoea in upright position).

Physical signs

Common

Elevation of the JVP with prominent *x* and *y* descents is the most important clinical sign, plus the following:

> atrial fibrillation (AF)

> Kussmaul's sign (inspiratory rise in JVP)

> pericardial knock (third heart sound)

> hepatosplenomegaly, ascites and peripheral oedema

> cachexia.

Uncommon
Pulsus paradoxus and signs of severe liver failure.

Investigations

ECG
This may be normal or show non-specific generalised T-wave changes, low-voltage complexes or AF.

Chest radiograph
This is usually normal, but the cardiac silhouette may be either reduced or enlarged. Left atrial enlargement, pleural effusions and pericardial calcification are non-specific findings.

Echocardiography
Echocardiography shows pericardial thickening. Septal motion is abnormal and the left ventricular posterior wall flattens abruptly in early diastole due to rapid equalisation of left ventricular and right ventricular pressure. During inspiration there is a marked reduction in diastolic mitral inflow (Fig 59).

Cardiac catheterisation
This is usually needed to confirm the diagnosis, with characteristic equalisation of end-diastolic pressures in the two ventricles, persisting with respiration and fluid challenge (Fig 60).

CT/MRI
These imaging techniques may be used to demonstrate the extent and distribution of pericardial thickening (Fig 61).

Differential diagnosis
Consider the following:

> chronic pericardial effusion

> restrictive cardiomyopathy: see Section 2.4.3

> superior vena caval obstruction: excluded if there is a pulsatile waveform in JVP

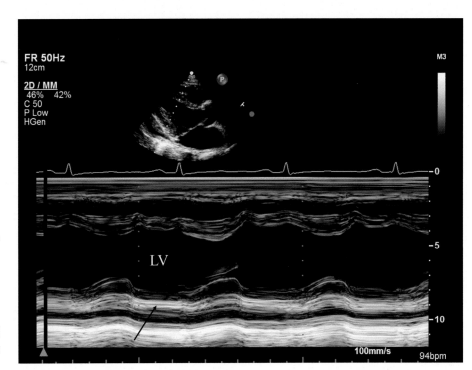

Fig 59 M-mode parasternal long-axis view of a patient with pericardial constriction demonstrating thickened pericardium with small effusion. Note the notching of the septum and abrupt flattening of the posterior wall in diastole. Both these features are due to abrupt equalisation of the left and right ventricular pressures in early diastole with cessation of further cardiac filling.

> congestive cardiac failure

> nephrotic syndrome

> malignant hepatic or intra-abdominal disease.

Treatment

A minority of patients may be managed medically with diet and diuretic therapy. Most will require pericardiectomy: an early operation is recommended.

Complications

Severe venous congestion with chronic hepatic impairment is common. Death results from the consequences of an inadequate cardiac output.

Prognosis

Morbidity
Without treatment, most patients deteriorate progressively with severely limiting symptoms.

With pericardiectomy, 90% improve and 50% may gain complete relief of symptoms.

Mortality
The outlook in untreated cases is poor. Hospital mortality rate after pericardiectomy is 5–16%, and 5-year survival rate after surgery is between 74% and 87%.

2.7 Congenital heart disease

Advances in paediatric cardiology over the past three decades have resulted in the survival of a large number of individuals with congenital heart disorders into adulthood. Management of these patients is a challenging area of cardiology with over 100 separate diagnostic conditions. Congenital cardiac abnormalities can be associated with genetic syndromes or other diseases

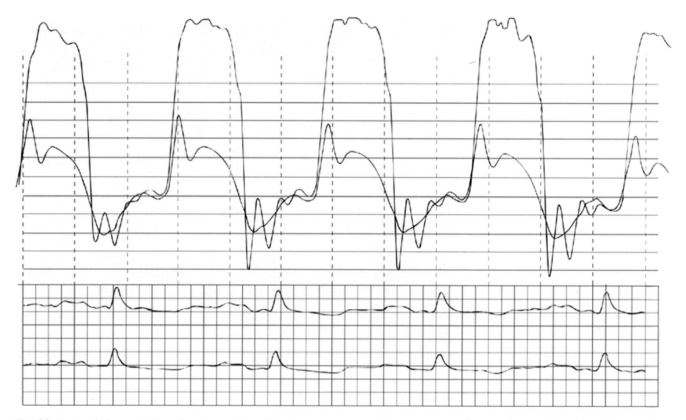

Fig 60 Pericardial constriction: the top section of the image contains pressure tracings from catheters placed simultaneously in the left and right ventricles. The pressures from the two chambers are seen to equalise at the end of diastole. (Courtesy of E Tomsett.)

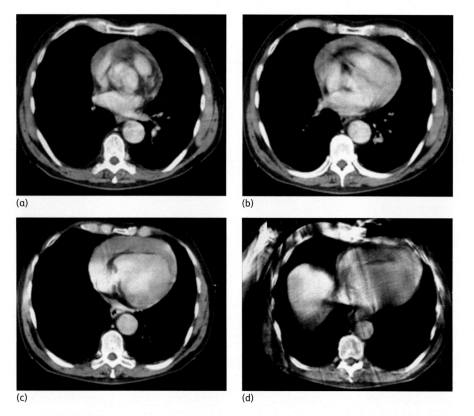

(a)

(b)

(c)

(d)

Fig 61 Pericardial thickening: these sections (a, b, c and d) through the heart show a markedly thickened pericardium.

(Table 29). Abnormalities are divided into cyanotic and acyanotic conditions (although most acyanotic conditions can progress to cyanosis later in life if untreated). The most common conditions are reviewed in this section (Table 30).

Diagnosis of these conditions is dependent on accurate imaging of underlying cardiac abnormalities. This is increasingly performed using non-invasive techniques including echocardiography and cardiac MRI (CMR). Both diagnostic tests can also be used to calculate intracardiac shunts, which play an important part in determining treatment. As a consequence, cardiac catheterisation is performed less frequently. All patients will remain under lifelong follow-up in a specialist grown-up congenital heart disease (GUCH) clinic.

See also cardiomyopathy (Section 2.4) and muscular dystrophies.

Table 29 Examples of genetic diseases affecting the cardiovascular system

Syndrome	Inheritance	Cardiac manifestations	Management
Marfan	AD	Aortic root dilatation/rupture	Echo surveillance, beta-blockade and elective aortic root repair when >5.5 cm in diameter
Turner's		Coarctation of the aorta and bicuspid aortic valve	Echo surveillance of valve and surgery for coarctation
Noonan's	AD	Pulmonary stenosis most common	
Down's		Atrioventricular canal defects	Surgical
DiGeorge	AD or sporadic	Conotruncal	Surgical
Williams		Supravalvular aortic stenosis	Echo surveillance
Holt–Oram	AD	Septal defects (hand–heart)	See Sections 2.7.1.1 and 2.7.1.2
Muscular dystrophies	Various	Conduction defects. Cardiomyopathy may also be seen in female carriers of X-linked dystrophies	Pacing for heart block, standard treatment for LV dysfunction, echocardiography and ECG screening of carriers

AD, autosomal dominant; ECG, electrocardiogram; LV, left ventricular.

Key point

In congenital heart disease particular care should be taken to prevent infective endocarditis associated with dental or surgical procedures using appropriate prophylactic antibiotics. The highest risk is associated with uncorrected cyanotic disease and high-pressure jets of blood:

> tetralogy of Fallot

> Ebstein's anomaly

> ventricular septal defect (VSD)

> patent ductus arteriosus

> coarctation of the aorta.

Table 30 Common congenital heart disorders

Cyanotic	Acyanotic
Tetralogy of Fallot	Atrial septal defect
Complete transposition of the great arteries	Ventricular septal defect
Ebstein's anomaly	Patent ductus arteriosus
	Coarctation of the aorta

2.7.1 Acyanotic congenital heart disease

2.7.1.1 Atrial septal defect

Anatomy/pathophysiology/pathology

Atrial septal defects (ASDs) may be ostium primum, secundum or sinus venosus in type (Fig 62). The haemodynamic consequences depend on the size of the defect. In larger

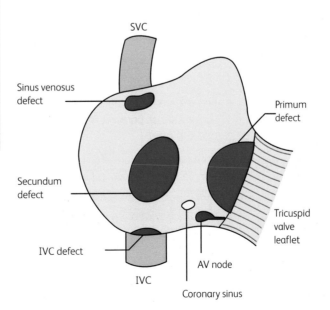

Fig 62 Sites of defects in the atrial septum seen from the right atrium. AV, atrioventricular; IVC, inferior vena cava; SVC, superior vena cava.

defects blood can shunt from the left atrium to the right because the right ventricle (RV) is more compliant than the left. As a result, over a period of time the RV may dilate and fail leading to the development of pulmonary hypertension and possibly Eisenmenger's syndrome (Section 2.7.3).

Key point

A patent foramen ovale is common, occurring in 25–30% of people. It does not permit left-to-right shunting but allows right-to-left shunting when right atrial pressure exceeds left (eg Valsalva manoeuvre). This can result in an increased risk of stroke as a result of paradoxical embolism of a venous thrombus.

Epidemiology

ASDs are the most common congenital heart abnormality and account for around 30% of all congenital heart defects in adults. Seventy-five per cent of ASDs are ostium secundum defects, which are defects in the foramen ovale and occur more frequently in females (female:male = 2:1). Primum defects account for about 20% and occur when the primum septum does not join the endocardial cushion and the ASD is normally larger.

Clinical presentation

In most adults, ASDs are asymptomatic and discovered incidentally as a result of other investigations. Symptoms are more likely if there is a left-to-right shunt and include:

> atrial arrhythmias (including atrial fibrillation, atrial flutter and sick sinus syndrome)

> exertional fatigue or dyspnoea

> right heart failure

> stroke / other arterial territory infarcts (eg lower limbs) secondary to paradoxical embolism

> migraine-type headache, although relationship is unclear.

Physical signs

> Increasing flow through the right heart causes an ejection systolic pulmonary flow murmur.

> Wide fixed splitting of S2 (equalisation of RV and LV stroke volumes throughout the respiratory cycle) can be heard.

> Signs of pulmonary hypertension: RV heave with large shunts. Tricuspid regurgitation may be present.

Hazard

Beware there is no murmur across an ASD itself (velocity and turbulence are too low).

Investigations

ECG

Look for the following:

> first-degree heart block (more suggestive of primum ASD, but can occur in any)

> right-axis deviation and right bundle branch block in secundum defects

> left-axis deviation in ostium primum defects

> atrial arrhythmias.

Chest radiograph

Look for cardiomegaly (from right atrial and RV enlargement), dilated pulmonary arteries and pulmonary plethora indicating increasing pulmonary blood flow.

Echocardiography

Transthoracic echocardiography and transoesophageal echocardiography (TOE) can be used for confirmation of diagnosis. TOE with microbubble contrast study is ideal to visualise shunting (Fig 63). The direction of shunt and the pulmonary-to-systemic flow ratio should be calculated. Look for associated abnormalities of cardiac anatomy (VSD) and assess pulmonary artery pressure.

Treatment

Surgical and percutaneous closure are both possible. Haemodynamically non-significant ASDs do not require closure unless to prevent paradoxical emboli. Closure is indicated for asymptomatic patients with pulmonary-to-systemic ratio of >1.5:1, RV overload or mild to moderate pulmonary hypertension. Severe and irreversible pulmonary hypertension or Eisenmenger's syndrome is a contraindication to closure.

Prognosis

Shunt <1.5:1 – excellent long-term outcome.

Shunt >1.5:1 – if untreated, life expectancy is fifth decade (RV failure, rarely Eisenmenger's syndrome). Good long-term outcome if ASD is closed before development of pulmonary hypertension. Small, asymptomatic defects are tolerated well in pregnancy.

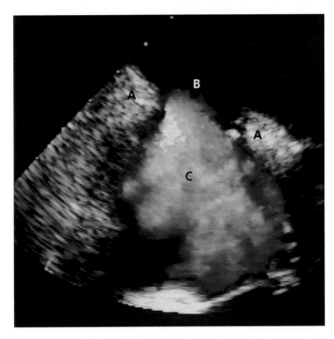

Fig 63 Transoesophageal echo image of left-to-right flow across a large atrial septal defect. A denotes the atrial septum, B the left atrium and C the flow into the right atrium. (Courtesy of Dr LM Shapiro.)

2.7.1.2 Isolated ventricular septal defect

Anatomy/pathophysiology/pathology

Defects can occur at any level in the ventricular septum. A small defect causes a high-pressure left-to-right jet but no haemodynamic abnormality. Large defects with a shunt can cause pulmonary hypertension and eventually result in Eisenmenger's syndrome (Section 2.7.3). Small defects in the membranous part of the septum noted during childhood often close by the age of 2 years.

Epidemiology

Ventricular septal defects (VSDs) are the second most common congenital malformation of the heart accounting for 10% of all congenital malformations (many close spontaneously in childhood). They can be single or multiple and although there are several specific types, the most common in the West are membranous and muscular defects.

Clinical presentation

Small defects with no shunt are usually asymptomatic and picked up incidentally, secondary to the identification of a cardiac murmur. Defects with a significant shunt present with progressive dyspnoea, reduced exercise tolerance and eventually cyanosis in adult life. The dyspnoea is caused by LV dilatation and failure or pulmonary hypertension.

Physical signs

> Pansystolic murmur and thrill at the lower-left sternal edge, but often audible across the praecordium. Smaller defects produce louder murmurs.

> Signs of pulmonary hypertension: RV heave with large shunts. Tricuspid regurgitation may be present.

> Clubbing and cyanosis in Eisenmenger's syndrome. The VSD murmur may be completely obliterated.

> Aortic regurgitation is associated with some VSDs.

Investigations

ECG

In a small VSD it is often normal. However, with progressive worsening of the shunt there may be atrial arrhythmias (eg atrial fibrillation), right-axis deviation and right ventricular hypertrophy.

Chest radiograph

Normal in small defects. With progressive shunts there are radiographic signs of pulmonary hypertension including cardiomegaly, enlarged pulmonary trunk and reduced lung markings in the periphery.

Echocardiography

Used to confirm diagnosis and classify the location and type of defect. Check for any coexisting lesions and assess LV function and size. Shunt is not usually determined with echocardiography, but jet velocity can be calculated.

Treatment

If closure is indicated, surgical closure of the defect remains the normal practice but percutaneous closure is increasing in frequency. Small VSDs without a shunt do not need closure. VSDs with a haemodynamically significant shunt (shunt ratio and LV function are used in decision making) should be closed if pulmonary hypertension is not severe and/or reversible.

Prognosis

Untreated, small VSDs normally remain asymptomatic and have a superb prognosis. They also pose no risk to pregnancy. Long-term outcome in patients who have successful closure of their VSD prior to development of pulmonary hypertension is also excellent.

2.7.1.3 Patent ductus arteriosus

Anatomy/pathophysiology/pathology

The patent ductus arteriosus (PDA) is part of the lung bypass circuit in the fetal circulation (connecting the left pulmonary artery (PA) to the descending aorta) that ensures oxygenated blood from the right heart is delivered directly to the systemic circulation. The ductus normally closes soon after birth. However, in a small number of people it can remain patent resulting in a left-to-right shunt, which leads to left ventricular enlargement and eventually pulmonary hypertension.

Epidemiology

PDAs account for 10% of all congenital heart cases. They occur more frequently with maternal rubella and in pre-term infants. Incidence is increasing as more premature babies are surviving into childhood and beyond, but remains low at 0.05%.

Clinical presentation

> Small PDA: patients are asymptomatic and PDA detected incidentally from murmur or cardiac imaging for other causes.

> PDA with moderate or large shunts: patients present with progressive fatigue, dyspnoea, palpitations or eventually Eisenmenger's syndrome.

> Infective endocarditis is a risk and may be the first presentation.

Physical signs

> Continuous machinery murmur in the second left intercostal space.

> Significant shunt – wide pulse pressure, hyperdynamic apex and signs of left ventricular (LV) failure (in large shunts).

> Pulmonary hypertension – machinery murmur shortens (as proportion of cardiac cycle during which pulmonary pressure is lower than systemic pressure reduces) and eventually disappears.

Investigations

ECG

Normal in small PDA. With large shunts there is evidence of left atrial and LV hypertrophy.

Chest radiograph

Normal in small PDA. With large shunts there is initially left-sided and then right-sided cardiomegaly, prominent proximal pulmonary arteries/ascending aorta and pulmonary plethora.

Echocardiogram

Can be used to identify defect, calculate extent of the shunt, assess LV function and estimate pulmonary arterial pressures.

Treatment

Both surgical (very low mortality <0.5% as does not require cardiopulmonary bypass) and percutaneous closure (if anatomy suitable) of PDAs are possible. Closure of all clinically detectable PDAs (in the absence of irreversible pulmonary hypertension) is recommended. Antibiotic prophylaxis is not recommended for unrepaired PDAs unless Eisenmenger's has arisen.

Prognosis

Excellent outcome if PDA closed before development of any complications. Without closure, one-third of patients will be dead by the age of 40 and two-thirds by 60 years. Potential complications include:

> infective PA endarteritis and consequent septic pulmonary emboli

> heart failure

> pulmonary hypertension

> ductal aneurysm and calcification can also occur with risk of rupture.

2.7.1.4 Coarctation of the aorta

Anatomy/pathophysiology/pathology

Aortic coarctation is the result of a flow-limiting narrowing in the aorta at the site of the fetal ductus arteriosus (Section 2.7.1.3), most commonly just distal to the left subclavian artery (may also be positioned more proximally in the aortic arch; Fig 64). With time an arterial supply to the lower body is

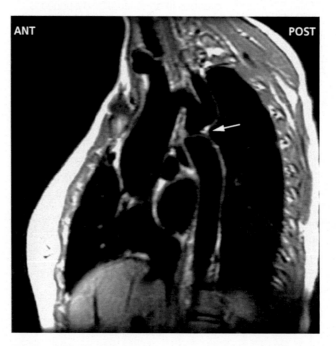

Fig 64 MRI of coarctation of the aorta (indicated by arrow).

achieved by extensive collateralisation. Often hypertension develops during childhood. The most recent data show that approximately 70% of patients with coarctation also have a bicuspid aortic valve. Another association is intracranial aneurysms in the Circle of Willis (10%).

Epidemiology

This condition is more common in males than in females (60:40). It accounts for about 5% of all congenital cardiac defects. Ten per cent of patients with Turner syndrome will have coarctation.

Clinical presentation

Common

> asymptomatic: incidental finding of murmur or systolic hypertension in the upper limbs.

Uncommon

> symptoms of hypertension (epistaxis, headache and haemorrhagic stroke)

> palpitations

> claudication in the legs

> heart failure.

Physical signs

> Systolic BP is usually greater in the arms than in the legs.

> Radio-femoral delay (leg pulses may be near impalpable).

> Due to most coarcts occurring distal to the left subclavian artery, radio-radial delay is far less common but can occur with more proximal lesions. A very small proportion have all four limbs affected.

> Left sternal edge and/or interscapular systolic murmur emanating from the coarctation.

> May be an associated bicuspid aortic valve.

Investigations

ECG

Often normal, but there may be evidence of left ventricular (LV) hypertrophy.

Chest radiograph

Rib notching of posterior third to eighth ribs (from enlarged intercostal arteries because of collateral flow – Fig 10). Pre- and post-stenotic dilatation of the aorta can give rise to the '3 sign' appearance.

Echocardiography

Can be used for diagnosis of coarctation and calculation of gradient across stenosis.

MRI and CT scan

Both can be used to assess anatomy of coarctation and the entire aorta (Fig 65). Collaterals can be seen.

Cardiac catheterisation

May aid in diagnosis, but not normally required. Performed if endovascular treatment such as stent placement is warranted.

Treatment

> Results from any form of repair are best if performed early in childhood.

> Surgical repair is often the first-line treatment if the trans-coarct gradient is >30 mmHg.

> Percutaneous dilatation with or without stent deployment is also possible. However, routine current use is confined to treatment of paediatric or adolescent cases and for the dilation of re-coarctation cases. Percutaneous treatment in adults is uncommon.

> Aggressive medical treatment of hypertension.

Complications

These may include the following:

> LV failure

> aortic aneurysm (pre or post treatment) and dissection/rupture

> premature coronary disease and myocardial infarction

> endocarditis

> intracerebral haemorrhage.

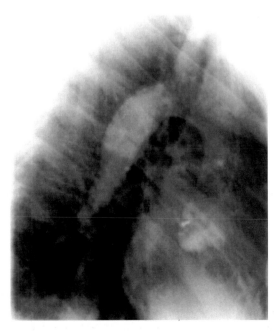

Fig 65 Angiogram showing coarctation of aorta, which can be seen to taper just after the arch. On a plain radiograph the feature to look for is rib notching (see Fig 10) produced by collateral vessels.

Prognosis

> Uncorrected: mean survival is around 35 years and 75% will die by the age of 50 years.

> Corrected: survival depends on the age at surgery – the younger the better. A risk of re-coarctation remains.

2.7.2 Cyanotic congenital heart disease

Patients with cyanotic congenital heart disease are chronically hypoxaemic. This causes a number of physiological adaptive changes leading to complications. These adaptive changes are common to all patients in this group with significant cyanosis regardless of the underlying anatomical abnormality. These changes must be treated accordingly as detailed below.

Polycythaemia and hyperviscosity syndrome

Polycythaemia increases oxygen delivery but the resultant hyperviscosity can result in multiple symptoms including headaches, altered mental activity, fatigue, myalgia and visual problems. Dehydration can worsen the situation. Recurrent venesection is one possible treatment.

Iron deficiency anaemia

This is often a result of excessive venesection, but can also occur secondary to haemoptysis and epistaxis.

Stroke

Arterial thrombosis may be associated with polycythaemia. Alternatively thrombotic strokes may occur secondary to paradoxical emboli. Haemorrhagic strokes are also possible as coagulation pathways may be deranged, thereby increasing the risk of bleeding.

Bleeding abnormalities

There is a range of presentations ranging from easy bruising to epistaxis and haemoptysis. Bleeding can be catastrophic.

Renal impairment

Overt renal failure is rare and often associated with increased uric acid absorption from excessive erythrocyte degradation.

2.7.2.1 Tetralogy of Fallot

Anatomy/pathophysiology/pathology

Four anatomical defects contribute to this abnormality (Fig 66). These include:

1 large ventricular septal defect (VSD)

2 overriding of the aorta (the origin of the aorta is deviated to the right)

3 right ventricular outflow tract obstruction (RVOTO)

4 compensatory right ventricular hypertrophy (RVH).

The large VSD results in equal left and right ventricular pressures. However, there is right-to-left shunting (cyanosis) as result of the RVOTO. Shunting (and therefore level of cyanosis) increases with any decrease in systemic vascular resistance. Before the era of total surgical repair, techniques to divert blood into the pulmonary circulation were employed, most commonly the Blalock–Taussig shunt (Fig 66), which connects the subclavian artery to the pulmonary artery.

Epidemiology

This is the most common cyanotic congenital heart defect to occur after infancy and accounts for around 10% of all congenital heart abnormalities.

Clinical presentation

> Patients who have had no correction present with cyanosis from birth or early infancy and become progressively more short of breath on exertion as their age increases.

> Patients with partial correction develop increasing cyanosis in adult life as RVOTO increases.

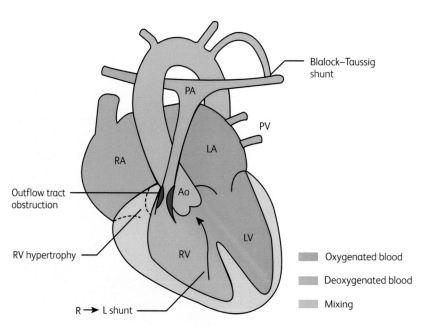

Fig 66 Tetralogy of Fallot with left Blalock–Taussig shunt. Ao, aorta; LA, left atrium; LV, left ventricle; PA, pulmonary artery; PV, pulmonary veins; RA, right atrium; RV, right ventricle.

> Patients who have had total correction can present later in life with palpitations and syncope (from atrial and ventricular arrhythmias) as well as heart failure as pulmonary and/or aortic valve regurgitation develops.

> All patients have complications of cyanosis.

Physical signs

> cyanosis

> clubbing (Fig 67)

> there may be unequal upper limb pulses in patients with Blalock–Taussig shunts

> right ventricle (RV) heave and right ventricular outflow tract (RVOT) systolic thrill

> normal S1, inaudible P2

> RVOT ejection systolic murmur.

Investigations

ECG
Can illustrate right-axis deviation, RVH and right bundle branch block.

Chest radiograph
Will detect boot-shaped heart.

Echocardiogram
Demonstrates all anatomical features which constitute the condition. Approximately 40% of cases will have additional associated cardiac abnormalities.

Cardiac MRI
As with echocardiography can be used to identify anatomical abnormalities, but has the added advantage of identifying other thoracic (pulmonary vascular and aortic) anomalies.

Cardiac catheterisation
Useful pre-operatively to identify coronary arterial abnormalities.

Treatment
Most patients today have a complete surgical repair often using a patch to close the VSD and dilating the RVOT to relieve the obstruction. In adulthood most of these individuals will require repeat surgical procedures for repair of recurrent VSDs and regurgitation in the RVOT / pulmonary valve and/or aortic valve. Adults who have had partial repair (eg Blalock–Taussig shunt) should be considered for complete repair in adult life as cyanosis worsens or other complications develop. Surgical repair is still recommended for adults who have had no form of correction. This is now extremely rare in the developed world.

Complications
These are often seen in patients who have complete correction as a child:

> ventricular arrhythmias

> atrial fibrillation and/or flutter

> pulmonary regurgitation with RV dilatation and failure

> recurrent RVOTO

> aortic dilatation and aortic regurgitation.

Prognosis

> Without surgical repair, the survival rate is 66% at age 1 and 10% at age 20 years.

> With complete surgical correction, outcomes are excellent with over 94% of patients surviving for at least 25 years.

> The main causes of death as a late complication are arrhythmias and heart failure.

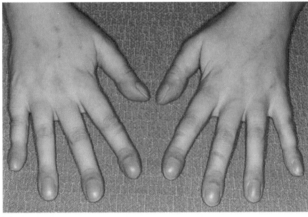

(a)

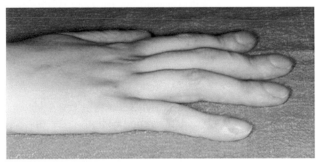

(b)

Fig 67 Example of digital clubbing in a patient with cyanotic heart disease.

2.7.2.2 Complete transposition of great arteries

Anatomy/pathophysiology/pathology

In patients with complete transposition of the great arteries (TGA) the pulmonary and systemic circulations are connected in parallel. The aorta arises anteriorly from the right ventricle (RV, the systemic ventricle) and the pulmonary artery (PA) from the left ventricle (LV). As a result the two circulations are completely separate. A communication (eg patent foramen ovale, patent ductus arteriosus (PDA) or atrial septal defect / ventricular septal defect) between the two circulations is necessary for survival (Fig 68). Other anatomical variants such as congenitally corrected TGA (CCTGA) also exist, which describe a scenario where the aorta arises from the RV and the PA from the LV. Seventy to eighty per cent of patients with CCTGA also have a VSD.

Clinical presentation

The majority of patients who survive to adulthood will have had a surgical corrective procedure soon after birth.

> Cyanosis is present from birth.

> Heart failure and valvular regurgitation (secondary to degenerative changes) are commonly seen in adults who have had corrective surgery.

Physical signs

> cyanosis

> signs of heart failure

> single loud S2 (the aorta is closer to the chest wall)

> pansystolic murmur if VSD present.

Investigations

ECG

Findings are variable and depend on exact anatomy and type of surgical correction. They include: normal traces, atrial arrhythmias, RV hypertrophy and right bundle branch block.

Chest radiograph

Narrow vascular pedicle and cardiomegaly.

Echocardiogram

Can demonstrate anatomical changes, calculate shunts and valvular abnormalities post repair.

Cardiac MRI

Very effective at demonstrating anatomical abnormalities and useful in monitoring patients postoperatively.

Treatment

Emergency

Mixing of blood between the pulmonary and systemic circulation is vital for survival at birth. This can be achieved pharmacologically with prostaglandin E to maintain patency of a PDA and/or balloon atrial septostomy.

Surgery

Multiple complex surgical procedures have been developed.

Atrial switch procedures (Mustard or Senning procedures)

Blood is re-directed at the level of the atria using a baffle made from either Dacron, pericardium (Mustard procedure) or atrial flaps (Senning procedure) to restore physiological circulation. Blood from the pulmonary veins is directed through the mitral valve and blood from the systemic venous return through the tricuspid valve. However, the RV remains the systemic ventricle and commonly fails in adult life (Fig 68).

Arterial switch procedures

Blood is re-directed at the arterial level by switching the position of the aorta and the PA. Therefore, the LV is connected to the aorta and the RV to the PA.

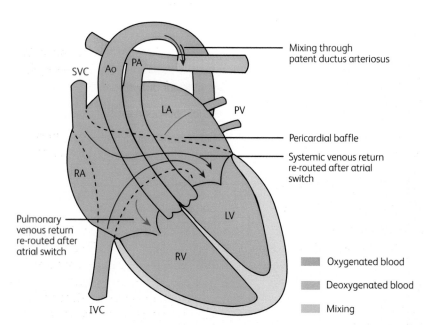

Fig 68 Transposition of the great arteries (TGA) with the circulations mixing through a PDA. The effect of an atrial switch operation is shown in dashed lines, re-routing the venous return to the correct great vessel. In the arterial switch, the great vessels are transected above the valves and switched, with reimplantation of the coronaries. Ao, aorta; IVC, inferior vena cava; LA, left atrium; LV, left ventricle; PA, pulmonary artery; PV, pulmonary veins; RA, right atrium; RV, right ventricle; SVC, superior vena cava.

Heart transplantation

Potential option for patients with significant heart failure subsequent to corrective surgery.

Prognosis

> Without intervention the mortality rate is around 90% by 6 months.

> Life expectancy is shortened in most patients even if they do have surgical correction. Only 70% of patients survive more than 20–30 years after corrective surgery.

2.7.2.3 Ebstein's anomaly

Anatomy/pathophysiology/pathology

An abnormal tricuspid valve (regurgitant or stenotic) is displaced down into the right ventricle (RV), leaving a small functional RV and a large 'atrium'. Eighty per cent of patients have other associated cardiac abnormalities including atrial septal defect or patent foramen ovale (most common – seen in 50% of cases), aberrant conduction pathways, ventricular septal defect, coarctation of the aorta, PDA and, on rare occasions, other more complex abnormalities. If the abnormality is mild most patients remain asymptomatic well into their adult life. Right-to-left shunting secondary to rising right atrial pressure (Fig 69) leads to symptoms.

Clinical presentation

There is a wide spectrum of presentation:

> In mild disease patients remain entirely asymptomatic well into adult life and diagnosis is made incidentally.

> Progressive dyspnoea, reduced exercise tolerance and palpitations can occur in the event of a worsening shunt.

> In rare instances sudden death can occur as a result of conduction abnormalities.

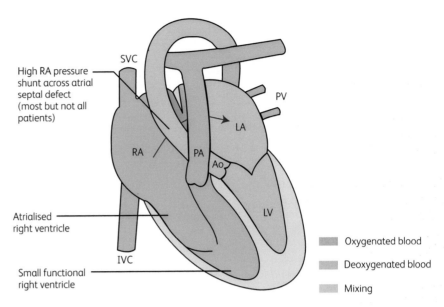

Fig 69 Ebstein's anomaly with shunting across an associated atrial septal defect. Ao, aorta; IVC, inferior vena cava; LA, left atrium; LV, left ventricle; PA, pulmonary artery; PV, pulmonary veins; RA, right atrium; SVC, superior vena cava.

> Arrhythmias are frequent, and normally from aberrant conduction pathways (eg Wolff–Parkinson–White syndrome).

Physical signs

> V waves may be seen from severe tricuspid regurgitation (TR), but occasionally JVP is low with absent v waves secondary to a large compliant right atrium.

> First and second heart sounds widely split with right bundle branch block.

> Pansystolic murmur of tricuspid regurgitation (may get quieter with increasing severity).

> Pulsatile hepatomegaly.

> Cyanosis depending on extent of right-to-left shunt.

Investigations

ECG

An ECG may be normal, but common abnormalities include: tall/broad P waves, right bundle branch block, first-degree heart block, delta waves if abnormal conduction pathways present and atrial arrhythmias (atrial fibrillation and flutter).

Chest radiograph

Convex right heart border secondary to right atrial enlargement. Cardiomegaly is also a possibility.

Echocardiogram and cardiac MRI

Both can be used to make diagnosis and outline other associated cardiac abnormalities.

Treatment

> Repair of the anatomical abnormality should be considered if there are progressive symptoms, cyanosis or heart failure. Multiple surgical procedures are available depending on the exact anatomy including tricuspid valve repair/replacement and more complex surgical corrective procedures.

> Complications (such as heart failure and arrhythmias) should be treated conventionally.

> Atrial arrhythmias can be treated with radiofrequency ablation.

Prognosis

Patients with no symptoms have a good prognosis without surgical correction and can survive well into adult life. The medium-term prognosis for patients who have undergone successful surgery is good, but they require long-term follow-up to ensure symptoms do not recur.

2.7.3 Eisenmenger's syndrome

Aetiology/pathophysiology/pathology

A large left-to-right shunt causes increased pulmonary blood flow and pressure. Over time this can result in vascular obstructive disease leading to pulmonary hypertension and right ventricular hypertrophy (RVH). As the pulmonary arterial pressures approach and exceed systemic pressures, the original left-to-right shunt becomes bidirectional and then reverses (right to left). This shunt reversal results in cyanosis. These changes and their associated complications are known as Eisenmenger's syndrome and can complicate both 'simple' (eg atrial septal defect and ventricular septal defect) as well as more 'complex' congenital cardiac abnormalities such as tetralogy of Fallot. Shunt reversal often takes many years and typically occurs in the third decade (Fig 70).

Clinical presentation

> cyanosis

> limiting exertional dyspnoea

> palpitations secondary to atrial (atrial fibrillation and flutter) and ventricular (ventricular tachycardia) arrhythmias

> haemoptysis

> syncope and sudden death

> congestive heart failure.

Physical signs

> central cyanosis

> clubbing

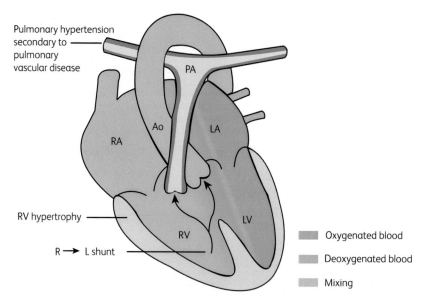

Fig 70 Eisenmenger's syndrome secondary to ventricular septal defect. Ao, aorta; LA, left atrium; LV, left ventricle; PA, pulmonary artery; RA, right atrium; RV, right ventricle.

> signs of pulmonary hypertension: right ventricular (RV) heave, RV outflow tract thrill, loud P2, pulmonary ejection flow murmur and high-pitched early diastolic murmur of pulmonary regurgitation (Graham Steell murmur)

> signs of tricuspid regurgitation (TR; elevated JVP and pansystolic murmur of TR).

> **! Hazard**
> Warning – in Eisenmenger's syndrome the murmur of the original shunt will have disappeared.

Investigations

ECG

Peaked P waves (right atrial enlargement), RVH and atrial arrhythmias.

Chest radiograph

Prominent central pulmonary arteries and 'pruning' of peripheral pulmonary vessels.

Echocardiogram

Can be used to identify the anatomic site and direction of the shunt. The shunt can also be quantified.

Cardiac catheterisation

Pulmonary pressure and saturations can be measured directly. It also allows assessment of pulmonary vascular resistance (PVR) which may determine the success of future surgical procedure.

Treatment

The main management principle in this group of patients is to avoid any factors which may destabilise the circulation and to treat any complications. In reactive pulmonary vessels surgical correction of the underlying shunt may be of value. In the remainder of patients a combination of oxygen therapy, prostacyclin and/or calcium channel blockers may provide variable levels of disease stability and marginal symptom improvement. Lung and/or heart and lung transplantation may be required.

Prognosis

After diagnosis, the 10-year survival is 80% and the 25-year survival 40%. A poor prognosis is associated with the following:

> syncope

> signs of RV failure

> low cardiac output

> severe hypoxaemia

> more complex underlying congenital abnormalities.

Prevention

Early closure of haemodynamically significant left-to-right shunts and/or protective pulmonary artery banding will reduce pulmonary flow and can avoid development of pulmonary vascular disease.

2.8 Infective disease of the heart

2.8.1 Infective endocarditis

Aetiology/pathophysiology/pathology

Microbial infection of the endocardium develops as a result of a two-stage process:

Stage 1 Non-bacterial thrombotic endocarditis (NBTE). A sterile mass arises from the deposition of platelets and fibrin on areas of endocardium injured from exposure to:

> high-velocity jets

> flow from high- to low-pressure chambers

> flow across a narrow orifice.

Stage 2 Bacteraemia with organisms that have the capacity to adhere to the NBTE result in the formation of infected vegetation. Bacteraemia rates are higher in the presence of diseased mucosa, especially if infected.

The consequences of infective endocarditis (IE) vary from trivial to catastrophic valvular and paravalvular tissue destruction.

Risk factors for IE could be cardiac or non-cardiac and are summarised in Table 31.

Epidemiology

The incidence of IE is about three to 10 cases/100,000 person-years but there is variability from country to country. The risk of IE increases with age and it is more common in men. However, the risk profile of IE patients has changed over the past decade. Rheumatic heart disease is no longer the leading cause of IE and has been replaced by increasing cases of IE occurring secondary to intravenous drug abuse, implantation of intracardiac devices, haemodialysis and increasing age.

Clinical presentation and physical signs

IE can present rapidly (acute IE), or insidiously (subacute IE) over a number of days to weeks. Clinical features of IE are varied and can at times be difficult to initially differentiate from other chronic medical conditions (Fig 71):

> features of systemic sepsis – fever and rigors, sweats, general malaise, anorexia and weight loss

> local cardiac manifestations – new cardiac murmur, heart failure, pericarditis and conduction abnormalities

> features of immune complex deposition:

>> dermatological – petechiae (most common), splinter haemorrhages, Osler's nodes and Janeway lesions

>> ophthalmological – Roth spots, conjunctival and retinal haemorrhage

Table 31	Risk factors for IE		
Cardiac	High risk	Prosthetic heart valves	
		Aortic and mitral (especially regurgitation) valve disease	
		Cyanotic congenital heart disease	
		Uncorrected left-to-right shunts (except ASD)	
	Moderate risk	MVP / isolated mitral stenosis	
		Tricuspid and pulmonary valve disease	
		Hypertrophic cardiomyopathy	
	Low risk	Isolated ASD	
		MVP with no regurgitation	
		Corrected left-to-right shunt	
		Atrial myxoma	
		Cardiac pacemakers	
Non-cardiac		Recurrent bacteraemia (intravenous drug misuse and periodontal disease)	
		Medical conditions increasing risk of infection (eg diabetes, renal failure and immunosuppression)	

ASD, atrial septal defect; IE, infective endocarditis; MVP, mitral valve prolapse.

> renal – features of glomerulonephritis and renal impairment

> embolic events. Septic emboli seen in 20–40% of cases including:

  > cerebral leading to abscess formation and focal neurological abnormalities

  > spleen leading to pain secondary to infarction

  > renal resulting in renal failure

  > pulmonary causing lung abscess or pneumonia

  > other arterial territories including joints and soft tissue infections.

Key point

Infective endocarditis (IE) must always be considered in a patient presenting with chronic fever, weight loss and malaise, irrespective of the presence of a murmur. Older patients may present with little apart from confusion. The absence of the much over-emphasised 'classic' signs of Janeway's lesions etc does not exclude the diagnosis.

Investigations

Definite pathological diagnosis can be achieved only via isolation or culture of the bacteria from material obtained from a vegetation or abscess. This is not possible in most patients, and diagnosis depends on a combination of clinical criteria. The modified Duke Criteria (Table 32) based on a number of major and minor clinical and microbiological features is designed to assist diagnosis of IE. Cases are defined as:

> definite IE: presence of two major criteria, one major and three minor criteria or five minor criteria.

> possible IE: presence of one major and one minor criteria or three minor criteria

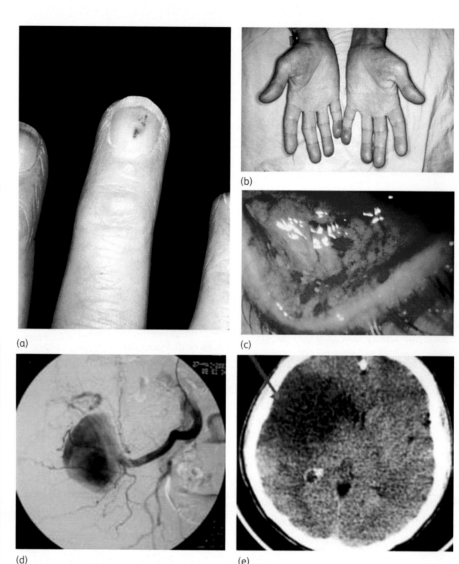

(a) (b) (c) (d) (e)

Fig 71 Peripheral manifestations of IE including **(a)** finger splinter haemorrhage, **(b)** Osler's nodes, **(c)** conjunctival petechiae, **(d)** angiogram demonstrating large mycotic aneurysm of the iliac artery and **(e)** CT brain scan showing cerebral infarction in a patient with staphylococcal endocarditis. (Adapted from *N Eng J Med* 2001;345:1318–1330 and *Heart* 2006;92:124–130.)

Table 32	Duke Criteria for the diagnosis of IE
Major criteria	Microbiologic – typical micro-organism isolated from two separate blood cultures or persistently positive blood cultures
	Evidence of cardiac involvement – echocardiographic evidence of new native or prosthetic valve regurgitation, vegetation and/or intracardiac abscess
Minor criteria	Presence of risk factor predisposing to IE (see Table 31)
	Fever >38˚C
	Vascular complications
	Immune complications
	Microbiological findings that do not meet major criteria

IE, infective endocarditis.

> unlikely diagnosis: presence of firm alternative diagnosis, or sustained resolution of clinical features with less than 4 days of antibiotic therapy.

Blood tests
FBC

> mild-to-moderate normochromic/normocytic anaemia

> neutrophil leucocytosis is usual in acute IE

> thrombocytopenia in chronic infections.

Biochemical profile

> Renal function (urea and creatinine) may be deranged.

> Liver function tests may be abnormal especially alkaline phosphatase and gamma-glutamyl transpeptidase.

Acute phase markers

> C-reactive protein (CRP) and erythrocyte sedimentation rate (ESR) are typically elevated.

Immunology

> polyclonal increase in serum immunoglobulins

> reduced complement levels

> positive rheumatoid factor.

Microbiology
Blood culture

> Take at least three to four sets of blood cultures from different sites leaving around 60 minutes between each puncture.

> Remember that the bacteraemia in IE is constant. This means that there is no need to wait for the patient to spike a temperature to obtain the blood cultures. It also implies that all blood cultures obtained prior to initiation of antibiotics should be positive. Interpret with a caution a single positive blood culture before establishing the diagnosis of IE especially if the micro-organism is consistent with potential 'contaminants'.

> Discuss cultures with microbiology to ascertain if there is a need for prolonged cultures and the use of specific culture media for infections caused by fastidious organisms and fungi.

Serum

> For immunological tests of atypical organisms including *Aspergillus* precipitins, *Candida* antibodies, rising *Brucella* agglutinins (two samples

required) and *Chlamydia* complement fixation tests.

Micro-organisms
Streptococci and staphylococci are responsible for 80% of cases but the actual proportion of each micro-organism varies according to valve (native versus prosthetic), age, comorbidities and source of infection. More recently staphylococci have become the most frequent cause of several types of IE probably because of the increased frequency of healthcare-associated IE Fig 72 shows the incidence of IE according to age and micro-organism.

Chest radiograph
This is usually normal. There may be evidence of pulmonary oedema and areas of infarction or consolidation from septic emboli (often associated with involvement of the right-sided heart valves).

ECG
Important to look for prolongation of the PR interval or higher levels of atrioventricular (AV) block indicating involvement of the conduction system (commonly associated with aortic root abscess).

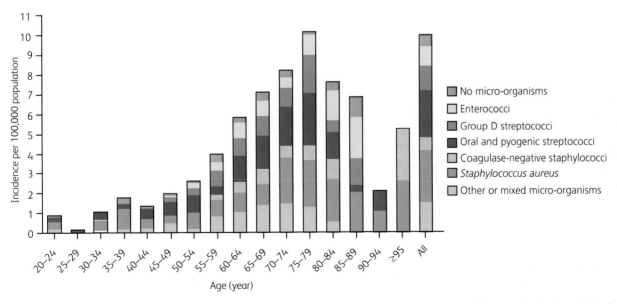

Fig 72 Incidence of infective endocarditis according to age and micro-organism. (Adapted from Hoen B, Duval X. Infective Endocarditis. *New England Journal of Medicine* 2013;368:1425–33, © 2013 Massachusetts Medical Society, reprinted with permission from Massachusetts Medical Society; and Selton-Suty C. Preeminence of Staphylococcus aureus in Infective Endocarditis: A 1-Year Population-Based Survey. *Clinical Infectious Diseases* 2012;54:1230–9, by permission of Oxford University Press.)

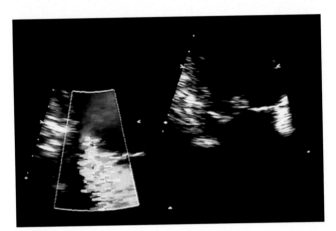

Fig 73 Transoesophageal echocardiogram demonstrating (on the right) a vegetation attached to the atrial side of a native MV and (on the left) associated mitral regurgitation.

Urinalysis
Microscopic haematuria ± proteinuria are common. Heavy proteinuria and red cell casts indicate glomerulonephritis.

Echocardiography
Transthoracic echocardiography is the first-line investigation for native valve IE looking for evidence of new valve regurgitation and/or vegetations. If inadequate, negative or non-diagnostic in a patient with a high suspicion of IE, transoesophageal echocardiography (TOE) should be performed. TOE is more sensitive for imaging of the aortic root (especially detection of an abscess) and the mitral valve (MV). TOE is the investigation of choice in suspected prosthetic valve IE (Fig 73).

Hazard

A normal echocardiogram does not exclude a diagnosis of IE.

Treatment

Medical treatment
Antibiotics are the main treatment. 'Blind' treatment (see Table 33 for a sample protocol) should be started as soon as a clinical diagnosis of IE is suspected (after multiple blood cultures have been taken!). Early discussion with microbiology and cardiothoracic teams is important. Identification of the infective organism is invaluable and antibiotic treatment should be modified according to sensitivities. Duration of therapy varies according to the severity of infection and organism. Often a total antibiotic course of around 4–6 weeks is required, with the first 2 weeks administered intravenously.

All patients must be closely monitored to chart their response to treatment including:

> daily monitoring for clinical signs of ongoing infection, such as persistent fever, changing and/or new cardiac murmurs, and embolic signs

> regular monitoring of changes in acute phase markers (CRP and ESR)

> regular urinalysis

> twice-weekly ECG looking for conduction abnormalities

> weekly echocardiogram

> monitoring antibiotic levels (especially for aminoglycoside antibiotics and vancomycin).

Surgical treatment
There are various indications for surgery in IE. In general surgery is indicated for:

> heart failure due to valve destruction refractory to treatment

> uncontrolled infection (eg abscess, false aneurysm, fistula, enlarging vegetation)

> prevention of embolism if very large vegetations.

Prognosis

Endocarditis is a serious medical condition with a high mortality rate. Prognosis is variable and depends on the infective organism and clinical scenario. In an uncomplicated streptococcal native valve endocarditis, the mortality rate is <10%, whereas *Aspergillus* prosthetic valve endocarditis is associated with virtually a 100% mortality rate.

Table 33 'Blind' antibiotic treatment for infective endocarditis: modify when microbiological sensitivities are known (adapted from *European Heart Journal* (2009) 30, 2369–2413)

Presentation	Antibiotic regime
Native valve	Ampicillin-sulbactam or amoxicillin-clavulanate (12 g/day IV in four doses) and gentamicin 3 mg/kg/day in two to three doses
Native valves (patient unable to tolerate beta-lactams)	Vancomycin 30 mg/kg/day IV in two doses and gentamicin 3 mg/kg/day in two to three doses and ciprofloxacin 1 g/day PO in two doses or 800 mg/day IV in two doses
Prosthetic valves (early, <12 months post-surgery)	Vancomycin 30 mg/kg/day in two doses and gentamicin 3 mg/kg/day in two to three doses and rifampicin 1.2 g/day orally in two doses
Prosthetic valves (late, >12 months post-surgery)	Same as for native valves

IV, intravenous; PO, *per os* (by mouth).

2.8.2 Rheumatic fever

Aetiology/pathophysiology/pathology

Rheumatic fever results from an abnormal immune response to pharyngeal infection with group A β-haemolytic streptococci. There is evidence of a genetic predisposition with specific B-cell antibody D8/17 in >90%, and linkage with HLA-DR1, -2, -3 and -4.

Characteristic perivascular Aschoff's nodules have a widespread distribution in the connective tissues of joints, tendons and blood vessels. A pancarditis may develop, with endocardial inflammation affecting valve leaflets, chordae tendineae and papillary muscles. Fusion of leaflets and chordae leads most commonly to mitral stenosis, which is worsened further by the progressive fibrosis and eventual calcification that occur after the acute episode. Mitral regurgitation may occur and tricuspid involvement is seen in 10% of rheumatic fever cases. Aortic valve involvement more commonly leads to aortic regurgitation (Fig 74).

Epidemiology

Rheumatic fever is rare in developed countries, with an incidence of less than five per 100,000 people per year, with the affected usually between the ages of 4–18.

Table 34 Duckett–Jones criteria for diagnosis of rheumatic fever

Major	Minor
Carditis	Fever
Migrating polyarthritis	Previous rheumatic fever
Chorea	Raised CRP or ESR
Erythema marginatum	Arthralgia
Subcutaneous nodules	Long PR interval

Diagnosis is based on evidence of antecedent streptococcal infection – eg positive throat swab for group A β-haemolytic streptococci (GAS), elevated streptococcal antibodies or a history of recent scarlet fever – together with either two or more major criteria, or one major plus two minor criteria. CRP, C-reactive protein; ESR, erythrocyte sedimentation rate.

Clinical presentation / physical signs / investigations
See Table 34.

Blood cultures
These help to exclude infective endocarditis (IE).

Blood tests
Look for the following:

> anaemia and leucocytosis

> elevated erythrocyte sedimentation rate and CRP

> streptococcal serology.

ECG

> Normal.

> May show prolonged PR interval.

Chest radiograph
This is either normal or shows cardiomegaly, pericardial effusion, pulmonary oedema or increased pulmonary vascularity.

Echocardiography
Echocardiography helps to exclude IE, valvular abnormalities, myocardial dysfunction, pericarditis and pericardial effusion.

Key point

Consider the following in your differential diagnosis:

> IE

> viral infection ± congenital cardiac abnormality

> non-rheumatic acute streptococcal infections

> juvenile chronic arthritis

> systemic lupus erythematosus

> traumatic or septic arthritis

> gout.

Treatment
Emergency
Treat heart failure (see Section 2.3). Severe valve lesions with deteriorating cardiac function may require valve replacement in rare instances.

Fig 74 Rheumatic mitral valve disease. The thickened and contracted mitral valve leaflets with the fish-mouth valve orifice can be seen in this post-mortem specimen.

Short term

Bed rest eases joint pains. A 10-day course of oral/intramuscular penicillin (erythromycin in allergic patients) will eradicate the organism. Treatment with salicylates or steroids is symptomatic and does not affect the outcome.

Long term

Duration of anti-inflammatory therapy varies from 1 month in mild cases to 2–3 months in more severe ones. Taper steroid therapy at the end of the course with the substitution of aspirin to reduce rebound inflammation.

Prognosis

Joint pain and fever usually settle within 2 weeks. The risk of residual heart disease increases with the severity of the initial carditis, as does the risk of further damage during any rheumatic recurrence.

2.9 Cardiac tumours

Aetiology/pathophysiology/pathology

Most cardiac tumours are secondary deposits. The most common primary cardiac tumour is a myxoma. More than 75% of primary cardiac tumours are benign. Cardiac metastasis occurs most commonly with lung and breast carcinomas and melanosarcomas. Eighty per cent of myxomas occur in the left atrium, the remainder occur in the right atrium and ventricle. Myxomas usually arise from the endocardium at the border of the fossa ovalis as a pedunculated mass. This may prolapse through the mitral valve (MV) mimicking mitral stenosis (MS).

Renal cell carcinoma may invade the inferior vena cava (IVC) into the right heart, resulting in signs of right heart failure. Carcinoid tumours may embolise

to the tricuspid valve resulting in regurgitation.

Epidemiology

The prevalence is estimated at two instances per 100,000 people. The female to male ratio is 2:1, and occurrences are most commonly in people aged 30–60.

Clinical presentation

Myxomas are discovered when their sufferers present with constitutional upset, the effect of MV obstruction, or as an incidental finding. Symptoms include fever, malaise, exertional dyspnoea and weight loss. Transient pulmonary oedema, paroxysmal nocturnal dyspnoea, haemoptysis, dizziness and syncope may occur. The first presentation may be due to embolic phenomenon.

Malignant tumours usually present acutely with haemorrhagic pericardial effusions or heart block. Renal cell cancer invading the IVC may present with signs of right heart failure and a renal mass. Carcinoid metastasis to the tricuspid valve may present with facial flushing and bronchospasm.

Physical signs

Fever, finger clubbing and anaemia of chronic disease reflect the chronic nature of myxomas. A tumour 'plop' may be heard, or auscultatory findings of MS ± regurgitation may be present. The murmur varies with posture, unlike in cases of valvular disease.

Investigations

Blood tests

In myxomas these typically show the anaemia of chronic disease, raised inflammatory markers (erythrocyte sedimentation rate and C-reactive protein) and γ-globulins.

Chest radiograph

The tumour may distort the cardiac silhouette. Sudden cardiac or pericardial enlargement, mediastinal

lymphadenopathy or an irregular/indistinct cardiac border may be seen. Intracardiac calcification may occur in myxomas (Fig 75).

Echocardiography

Usually diagnostic transoesophageal echocardiography may be required (Fig 76).

Differential diagnosis

Consider endocarditis and MV disease.

Treatment

Urgent surgical resection of myxomas is required – delay risks embolisation ('never let the sun go down on a myxoma'). Most malignant tumours are treated palliatively, although renal cell tumours invading the IVC may be excised. Palliative chemotherapy may be appropriate for certain tumour types.

Complications

Myxomas may embolise or cause pulmonary oedema due to MV obstruction. Malignant disease may cause tamponade, heart block, arrhythmias and heart failure. Recurrent pericardial effusions are treated with a pericardial window.

Prognosis

Once removed, the prognosis for patients with myxoma is a normal lifespan.

Disease associations

Myxomas can be familial (Carney syndrome or 'syndrome myxoma'), with autosomal dominant transmission in 10% of cases. This is associated with endocrine hyperactivity, lentigines and myxomas elsewhere in the body. Multiple tumours occur in approximately 50% of familial cases, and are more common in the ventricle. The mean age of presentation of familial cases is 25 years, and for sporadic cases it is 56 years.

(a)

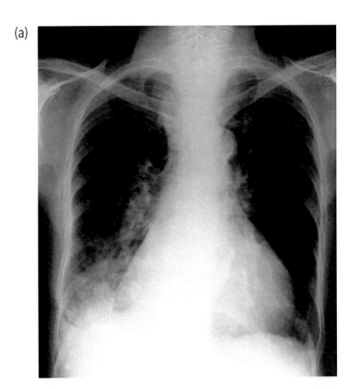

(b)

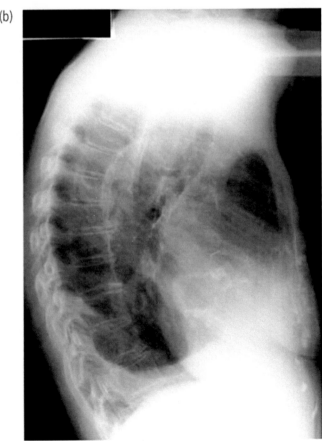

Fig 75 Intracardiac calcification. **(a)** Posterior anterior and **(b)** lateral views illustrating visible deposition of calcium within the heart.

2.10 Traumatic heart disease

Traumatic heart disease is often fatal. Rapid diagnosis and intervention are vital to reduce both mortality and morbidity.

Aetiology

> road traffic accident

> assault (non-penetrating or penetrating, including stab wounds and gunshot wounds)

> sports injuries

> falls

> iatrogenic (catheter, pacing / implantable cardioverter defibrillator lead or pericardiocentesis induced, or post cardiopulmonary resuscitation (CPR).

Pathophysiology/pathology

Virtually all cardiac components may be affected by thoracic trauma. Trauma may affect the following:

Myocardium
Contusion (approximately 20% of patients after blunt trauma), and laceration / pericardial tamponade or rupture (ventricles >atria and interventricular septum may be affected). Eighty per cent of stab wounds will present with tamponade. As little as 100 mL of blood is required in the acute situation to cause tamponade.

Pericardium
Pericarditis, laceration or post-pericardiotomy syndrome.

Endocardium
Ruptured chordae/papillary muscles or valve leaflets/cusps.

Coronary arteries
Injury/rupture/thrombosis (the left anterior descending artery most commonly).

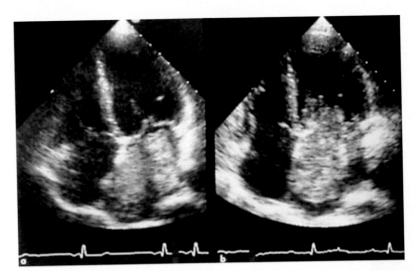

Fig 76 Echocardiography: left atrial myxoma. (Courtesy of Dr J Chambers.)

Conduction system

Bundle branch block, atrioventricular (AV) block or atrial/ventricular arrhythmias.

Thoracic vessels

Trauma to the aorta carries a very high mortality (see Table 35).

Clinical presentation

The initial insult is usually obvious and leads directly to presentation. Occasionally apparent minor trauma causes significant mediastinal injury, leading to a more insidious presentation:

> chest pain (including angina)

> presyncope/syncope.

Physical signs

Look for the following:

> hypotension

> pulsus paradoxus

> 'muffled' heart sounds

> pulmonary oedema

> murmur/thrill of mitral regurgitation

> diastolic murmur of aortic regurgitation if ascending aorta involved

> absent or abnormal peripheral pulses.

Investigations

ECG
Look specifically for the following:

> ST/T changes (may be non-specific, ST elevation secondary to pericarditis or acute myocardial infarction)

> conduction abnormalities (bundle branch block or any degree of AV block)

> arrhythmias (sinus tachycardia, atrial fibrillation, ectopic beats or ventricular arrhythmias).

Cardiac enzymes
Commonly raised following cardiac trauma but only has prognostic relevance if related to coronary artery trauma:

> elevated troponin (see Section 3.7).

Chest radiograph

> widened mediastinum (Fig 77)

> ribs/sternal fracture

> haemothorax.

Echocardiography (transthoracic and transoesophageal)

> pericardial effusion

> abnormal wall motion (coronary artery involvement)

> transoesophageal echocardiography is best for identifying myocardial injury and valvular involvement. It is contraindicated in the following circumstances:

> severe facial trauma

> cervical spinal injury

> possible oesophageal injury.

Table 35	Key features of aortic trauma
Prognosis	80% will die at scene, and of those that survive >50% die within 48 hours
Site of injury	80–90% between left subclavian and ligamentum arteriosum
Mechanism of injury	Usually blunt trauma with severe deceleration, eg road traffic accident
Symptoms	Retrosternal or interscapular pain
Signs	Hypotension, decreased pulses and systolic murmur
Chest X-ray	Widened mediastinum (>8 cm) and oesophageal/tracheal deviation
Treatment	Maintain systolic BP <120 mmHg but may require volume if hypotensive Consider intravenous beta-blockers if hypertensive Urgent cardiothoracic surgical input
Complications	Paraplegia and renal failure

BP, blood pressure.

Medical Masterclass Third edition

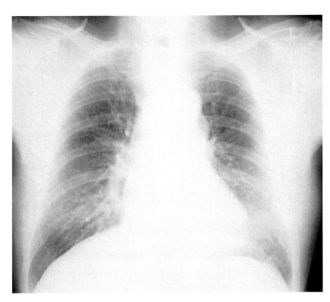

Fig 77 Chest radiograph of patient with traumatic aortic rupture. Note the widened mediastinum and abnormal descending aortic outline.

2.11 Disease of systemic arteries

2.11.1 Aortic dissection

Aetiology/pathophysiology/pathology

The aortic intima tears, exposing a diseased media that is split in two longitudinally by the force of the blood flow. This dissection usually progresses distally for a variable distance. Medial degeneration is often idiopathic but may be the result of cystic medial necrosis, especially in Marfan syndrome. There is also an association with the following:

> hypertension (history of hypertension in 80% of cases)

> pregnancy

> trauma

> increasing age.

Aortic dissection is classified according to whether or not there is involvement of the ascending aorta (Stanford classification – see Fig 79). This has practical and prognostic implications.

Cross-sectional imaging

Aortography was historically considered the 'gold standard' for diagnosing aortic trauma (Fig 78). Cross-sectional imaging is now more commonly used as it is helpful in identifying surrounding haematoma and evaluating other sites of potential trauma. CT is generally performed as the scan is quicker than MRI. Damage is most commonly seen in the upper descending aorta – the site of the ligamentum arteriosum.

Treatment

Each patient must be individually assessed. Patients can be broadly separated as follows:

> low risk – minor trauma and normal/abnormal ECG

> high risk – major trauma with associated thoracic or extrathoracic injuries and normal/abnormal ECG.

Emergency

If there is haemodynamic compromise, consider urgent pericardiocentesis/operative intervention for pericardial tamponade. If there is any doubt, seek immediate contact with a cardiothoracic surgical centre.

If all investigations demonstrate no need for surgical intervention then gentle mobilisation is encouraged. If there is evidence of possible coronary artery/conduction system injury, then these will need evaluating further.

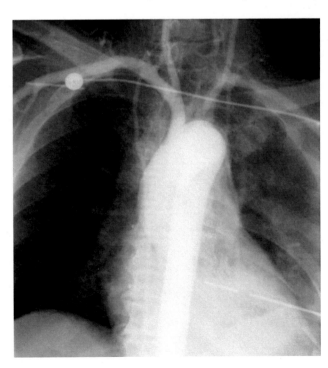

Fig 78 Aortogram of aortic rupture/trans-section. The aortic outline is clearly irregular, representing aortic rupture.

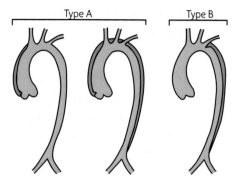

Fig 79 Stanford classification of aortic dissection. Type A refers to dissection of the ascending aorta, with or without involvement of the descending aorta. In type B, dissection is confined to the descending aorta. This classification has implications for prognosis and treatment.

Epidemiology

> peak age = 60 years

> male:female = 2:1

> incidence three per 100,000.

Clinical presentation
Common

There is central chest pain in 90% of cases – classically a 'tearing' pain that migrates to the back (interscapular) as dissection proceeds. A dissected aorta found incidentally in a patient without pain is usually chronic and therefore low risk. Thoracic back pain of sudden onset is also common.

Uncommon

> syncope

> stroke

> acute pulmonary oedema

> pulseless electrical activity arrest.

Physical signs
Common

> hypotension

> unequal radial pulses or brachial BPs (found in 50% of proximal dissections)

> aortic regurgitation (AR)

> pericardial rub

> pleural effusion

> tamponade (see Section 2.6.2)

> hemiplegia.

Investigations
ECG

The ECG may reveal inferior myocardial infarction (MI), if dissection extends to the right coronary artery. Anterior infarction is rarely seen, perhaps because occlusion of the left main coronary artery results in such a big infarct that the patient does not reach hospital alive.

Chest radiograph

This may show widened mediastinum (Fig 80), but an absence of this does not rule out aortic dissection. Blood in the pleural space from a leaking aorta may show as an effusion.

Echocardiography

The diagnosis is suggested by the following:

> dilated aortic root

> AR

> pericardial effusion

> dissection flap in the ascending aorta (unusual).

Other investigations
Consider the following:

> CT scan of the chest with contrast

> aortography

> MRI

> transoesophageal echocardiography (Fig 81).

Key point
The differential diagnosis of aortic dissection should include the following:

> acute coronary syndrome

> thoracic vertebral pathology, eg fracture and discitis

> pulmonary embolism.

Treatment
Emergency

> Do not await confirmation of diagnosis before starting medical treatment.

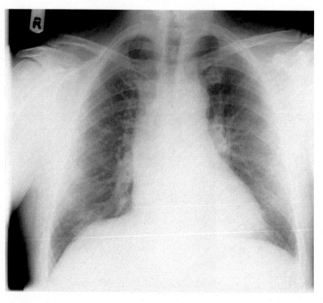

Fig 80 Chest radiograph showing widened mediastinum. Blood in the pleural space from a leaking aorta may show as an effusion.

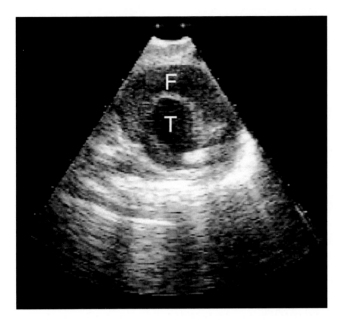

Fig 81 Transoesophageal echocardiogram of aortic dissection demonstrating the true (T) and false (F) lumina in the descending aorta. (From Armstrong P, Wastie ML. *Diagnostic imaging* (4th edn). Oxford: Blackwell Science, 1998.)

> Transfer to the coronary care unit.

> Lower systolic BP to <120 mmHg with intravenous labetalol or sodium nitroprusside.

> If confirmatory imaging cannot be obtained quickly, or when diagnosis is confirmed, arrange urgent transfer to cardiothoracic centre.

> Type A dissection requires emergency repair unless chronic (>2 weeks). Depending on the extent, a complete root or arch replacement might be performed.

> Type B dissection is generally managed medically because the risks of surgery outweigh the benefits. Consider surgery if there is a rupture or vital organ/limb ischaemia. More recently endovascular stenting has been used with some success in selected patients who were poor candidates for surgery.

Short term

After 24 hours, begin transfer of BP control to an oral agent, eg beta-blocker, angiotensin-converting enzyme inhibitor or calcium antagonist. Long-term BP control should be aggressive.

Complications

Death caused by aortic rupture or tamponade is common. Occlusion of any of the major aortic branches may occur, producing the following:

> hemiplegia

> acute renal failure

> mesenteric ischaemia

> lower limb ischaemia.

Prognosis

There is an early mortality rate of 1% per hour if left untreated. The mortality rate in the first 2 weeks is about 80%, after which a dissection would be classed as chronic.

2.12 Disease of pulmonary arteries

2.12.1 Primary pulmonary hypertension

Primary pulmonary hypertension (PPH) is defined as a sustained elevation of pulmonary artery pressure (PAP) to a mean of more than 25 mmHg at rest or 30 mmHg with exercise, in the absence of a demonstrable cause. Recent developments have highlighted that there is some overlap between PPH and secondary pulmonary hypertension in their histological features and response to treatment. The World Health Organization (WHO) latest classification uses five groups defined by their mechanism (see Table 36).

| Table 36 | Classification of pulmonary hypertension |
Classification	Subgroups
Pulmonary arterial hypertension	Idiopathic Familial Associated (collagen, congenital shunt, portal hypertension, HIV, drugs and others)
Pulmonary hypertension with left heart disease	Atrial/ventricular Valvular
Pulmonary hypertension with lung disease	Chronic obstructive pulmonary disease Interstitial Sleep disorder Alveolar hypoventilation High altitude Developmental
Pulmonary hypertension due to thromboembolism	Proximal pulmonary arteries Distal pulmonary arteries Non-thrombotic embolism
Miscellaneous	Sarcoid, tumour, compression etc.

Aetiology/pathophysiology/pathology

The aetiology is unknown. The following have been suggested causes:

> genetic: 10% of cases are familial (localised to chromosome 2) with autosomal dominant inheritance

> autoimmune: associated with a number of collagen vascular disorders

> infection: human herpes virus 8 causes Kaposi's sarcoma

> pulmonary vascular endothelial dysfunction.

Increased pulmonary vascular resistance is produced by:

> vasoconstriction

> vascular wall remodelling (medial hypertrophy and smooth muscle)

> thrombosis *in situ*.

This results in right ventricular hypertrophy (RVH) and then failure, as a result of the increased afterload.

Epidemiology

Incidence is about one per million per year, with the use of appetite suppressants associated with a greater than 20-fold increased risk. Female:male ratio is 2:1, with most diagnoses made in the fourth decade.

Clinical presentation

Early symptoms of PPH are non-specific.

Common

> exertional dyspnoea

> fatigue

> angina (right ventricular (RV) ischaemia)

> syncope/presyncope, especially exertional.

Uncommon

> peripheral oedema

> Raynaud's phenomenon – mostly in women

> haemoptysis.

Physical signs

> left parasternal heave

> loud P2 (pulmonary component of second heart sound)

> S4 originating from the RV (pressure overload)

> pansystolic murmur, prominent jugular v waves and pulsatile liver of tricuspid regurgitation

> peripheral oedema and elevated JVP.

Key point

Clubbing is not a feature of PPH and, if present, may indicate lung disease or cyanotic congenital heart disease as the underlying cause of the pulmonary hypertension.

Investigations

To confirm pulmonary hypertension, determine prognosis and guide therapy.

Echocardiogram
Will indicate:

> dilated and/or hypertrophied right heart (Fig 82)

> measurement of PAP

> exclusion of shunts

> assessment of left heart valvular and ventricular disease

> a transoesophageal study may be necessary to see an atrial septal defect.

ECG
Look for (Fig 83):

> tall P waves

> right-axis deviation

> RV hypertrophy and strain.

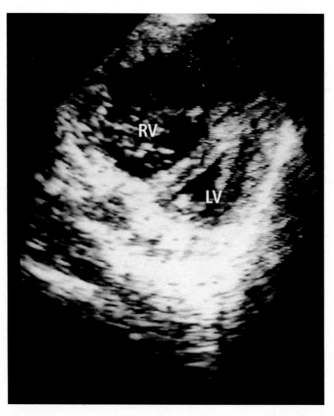

Fig 82 Short-axis echo view of a patient with PPH showing the high-pressure dilated right ventricle (RV) compressing the left ventricle (LV) into a characteristic D shape. (Courtesy of Dr LM Shapiro.)

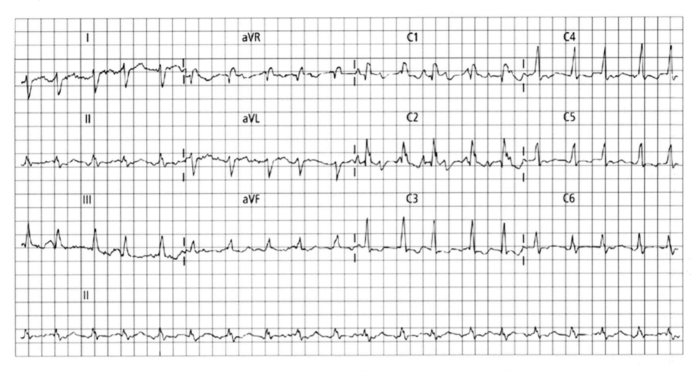

Fig 83 ECG of patient with pulmonary hypertension, showing RVH and right-axis deviation. The patient is also in atrial fibrillation. (Courtesy of the Pulmonary Vascular Disease Unit at Papworth Hospital.)

Chest radiograph
Look for prominent pulmonary arteries with peripheral pruning, and for features of underlying lung disease (Fig 84).

Cardiac catheterisation
Measure pressures and saturations (for prognosis and shunt calculation) and assess response to acute vasodilators such as prostacyclin, adenosine or inhaled nitric oxide.

Other investigations
The following are important to exclude secondary causes:

> blood: FBC (for secondary polycythaemia), liver function tests, erythrocyte sedimentation rate, rheumatoid factor and autoantibody screen, and consider an HIV test

> pulmonary function tests to exclude obstructive or restrictive lung disease

> sleep study if there is a suspicion of obstructive sleep apnoea

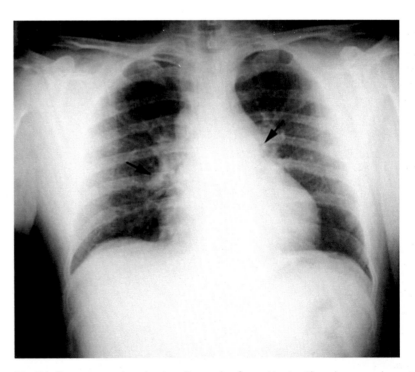

Fig 84 Posteroanterior chest radiograph of a patient with pulmonary hypertension, showing prominent pulmonary arteries (indicated by arrows) and cardiomegaly. (Courtesy of the Pulmonary Vascular Disease Unit at Papworth Hospital.)

> exclusion of pulmonary thromboembolism by ventilation–perfusion scan, spiral CT scan of the chest with contrast or pulmonary angiography (Fig 85).

Key point

PPH – consider the following in your differential diagnosis:

> secondary pulmonary hypertension

> left ventricular outflow tract obstruction

> ischaemic heart disease.

Treatment

> anticoagulation

> diuretics with daily weight checks to avoid excessive fluid depletion

> long-term oxygen for hypoxaemia

> high-dose calcium channel blockers in those patients who have a significant fall in pulmonary vascular resistance on acute vasodilator testing.

In patients who fail to respond to acute vasodilator therapy and have a poor functional class the following should be considered:

> endothelin antagonists: bosentan (monitoring of liver function tests (LFTs) is needed)

> prostacyclin analogues: intravenous/ nebulised prostacyclin therapy

> phosphodiesterase type 5 antagonists (PDE5): sildenafil or tadalafil

> atrial septostomy to decompress the RV and improve left-sided filling pressures

> lung or heart–lung transplantation in those who fail to respond to any other treatment.

Prognosis

Survival depends on RV function. Overall the 5-year survival rate is 20%, but the subgroup with adverse haemodynamics have a 20% 3-year survival rate. Responders to chronic calcium channel blocker therapy have a 95% 5-year survival rate.

Anticoagulation, prostacyclin and heart–lung transplantation (5-year survival rate of 50–60%) all confer a survival benefit. Bosentan and sildenafil have been shown to improve haemodynamics and exercise capacity.

Key point

Important information for patients – strongly advise against pregnancy. Avoid the oral contraceptive pill if possible – it may exacerbate pulmonary hypertension.

2.12.2 Secondary pulmonary hypertension

Secondary pulmonary hypertension is defined as sustained elevation of the mean pulmonary artery pressure (PAP) to >25 mmHg at rest or 30 mmHg on exercise, with an identified cause.

Aetiology/pathophysiology

Causes of secondary pulmonary hypertension are shown in Table 37.

Vascular wall remodelling and vasoconstriction increase pulmonary vascular resistance and therefore PAP, with resulting right ventricular hypertrophy (RVH) and right ventricular failure (RVF). When the primary cause is respiratory, this is known as cor pulmonale.

Clinical presentation

> ankle oedema

> dyspnoea (may be associated with the underlying primary condition)

> the primary condition.

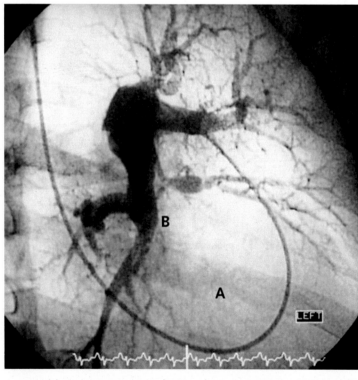

Fig 85 Left pulmonary angiogram of a patient with thromboembolic pulmonary hypertension, showing (B) the characteristic bands and cut-offs of vessel occlusion and (A) lack of perfusion in the left lower lobe. (Courtesy of the Pulmonary Vascular Disease Unit at Papworth Hospital.)

Table 37 Causes of secondary pulmonary hypertension

Mechanism	Cause
Increased left atrial pressure	Aortic/mitral valve disease Left ventricular dysfunction
Left-to-right shunts	ASD, VSD and PDA
Chronic pulmonary disease	COPD Bronchiectasis Pulmonary fibrosis
Chronic venous thromboembolism	
Chronic hypoventilation/hypoxia	Kyphoscoliosis Respiratory muscle weakness Obstructive sleep apnoea

ASD, atrial septal defect; COPD, chronic obstructive pulmonary disease; PDA, patent ductus arteriosus; VSD, ventricular septal defect.

Physical signs

The signs of the primary condition, including cyanosis if present, and then of pulmonary hypertension, RVH, dilatation and failure:

> left parasternal heave

> loud P2

> elevated JVP with prominent v wave

> pansystolic murmur of tricuspid regurgitation

> pulsatile liver

> ankle oedema.

Investigations

See Section 2.12.1.

Differential diagnosis

Consider left ventricular dysfunction and primary pulmonary hypertension.

Treatment

General

> optimise treatment of the underlying condition

> diuretics

> calcium channel blockers

> consideration of prostacyclin therapy, bosentan and

phosphodiesterase type 5 inhibitors in appropriate cases

> lung or heart–lung transplantation.

Specific

Shunts

Consideration of defect closure or pulmonary artery banding (some protection of pulmonary vasculature against high right-sided flow), if the pulmonary hypertension is not already too severe.

Chronic obstructive pulmonary disease

Long-term oxygen therapy benefits selected patients with chronic obstructive pulmonary disease (COPD).

Thromboembolism

Anticoagulation and consideration of inferior vena cava filter or pulmonary thromboendarterectomy.

Ventilatory disorders

Consideration of nocturnal continuous positive airway pressure or nasal positive pressure ventilation.

Prognosis

The prognosis is related to the underlying condition and the severity of

the pulmonary hypertension. The 5-year survival rate of COPD with oedema is 30%.

2.13 Cardiac complications of systemic disease

2.13.1 Thyroid disease

Clinical presentation

Hyperthyroidism

A patient with hyperthyroidism may have:

> sinus tachycardia

> sustained or paroxysmal atrial fibrillation (AF) (5–15% of cases)

> hyperdynamic left ventricle.

Hypothyroidism

A patient with hypothyroidism may have:

> bradycardia with prolonged QT interval

> cardiac enlargement

> pericardial effusion

> associated hypercholesterolaemia.

Treatment

Hyperthyroidism

Short term

Beta-blockers for symptomatic relief until rendered euthyroid (propranolol); AF generally reverts to sinus rhythm with treatment of thyroid disease.

Long term

Cardioversion after anticoagulation if AF persists.

Hypothyroidism

Treat with thyroxine, starting in very small doses to avoid precipitation of myocardial ischaemia in patients with cardiovascular disease. Effusions generally resolve and drainage is hardly ever required.

Key point

Amiodarone and thyroid dysfunction
Amiodarone is rich in iodine and maintenance therapy is commonly associated with abnormal thyroid function tests. Thyrotoxicosis may occur and is confirmed by elevated levels of T4 and T3 with suppressed thyroid-stimulating hormone. Hypothyroidism is treated with discontinuation of drugs (where possible) and thyroxine replacement.

2.13.2 Diabetes

Aetiology and pathophysiology

Accelerated atherogenesis
This is the result of the following:

> dyslipidaemia: increased low-density lipoprotein and triglyceride and decreased high-density lipoprotein

> hypercoagulable state and increased platelet aggregation

> hyperinsulinaemia (in type 2 diabetes) promoting vascular smooth muscle proliferation

> glycosylated proteins promoting the production of oxidants

> hypertension is very common in type 2 diabetes and leads to a disproportionate rise in risk of cardiovascular event

> endothelial dysfunction is the likely common final pathway resulting in macrovascular disease.

Autonomic neuropathy
This causes impairment of the protective sensation of angina (silent ischaemia) and may lead to prolonged ischaemia, arrhythmias and sudden death.

Diabetic cardiomyopathy
Impairment of systolic and diastolic function independent of macroscopic coronary artery disease, possibly secondary to microvascular disease.

Epidemiology
In people with diabetes the risk of acute myocardial infarction (MI) is increased by 50% for men and 150% for women. The rate of major complications is increased and associated with higher mortality rates.

Clinical presentation
Silent ischaemia may lead to atypical presentations, eg acute MI as ketoacidosis.

Treatment

Acute myocardial infarction
Standard treatment plus an insulin infusion ('sliding scale'). The absolute benefit of all standard interventions is greater in people with diabetes.

Coronary revascularisation
Diabetic coronary disease is in general more diffuse and distal, so that both coronary artery bypass grafting and percutaneous coronary intervention (PCI) have poorer outcomes than in people without diabetes (appreciating that their untreated risk is greater). However, a number of studies have indicated that coronary stenting (particularly drug-eluting stents) plus the use of a glycoprotein IIb/IIIa receptor blocker (antiplatelet) may improve results.

Prevention

Primary
Good glycaemic and BP control (<130/80 mmHg), and avoidance of smoking.

Secondary
Treatment with a statin and an angiotensin-converting enzyme inhibitor, though most of this high-risk group should now be on these drugs as primary prevention.

2.13.3 Autoimmune rheumatic diseases

Clinical presentation
The autoimmune rheumatic diseases have the following cardiac associations.

Systemic lupus erythematosus

> premature atherosclerosis: important to differentiate from coronary vasculitis (also present in cases of systemic lupus erythematosus – SLE) because the latter needs steroids

> pericarditis and effusion: clinically in 30%; at post-mortem examination in 60%

> sterile valvular vegetations (Libman–Sacks) in 60%, rarely clinically significant

> myocarditis

> conduction defects.

Primary antiphospholipid syndrome

> pulmonary thromboembolism (also in SLE if anticardiolipin antibody positive)

> degenerative mitral valve disease.

Rheumatoid arthritis

> increasingly recognised as a potent risk factor for atherosclerotic vascular disease (inflammatory state)

> pericarditis: often clinically silent but may lead to symptomatic effusion or constriction

> rheumatoid nodules causing valvular regurgitation and atrioventricular block

> coronary vasculitis (rare).

Systemic sclerosis

> pulmonary hypertension: the major cause of death in systemic sclerosis

> pericarditis and chronic effusions

> myocardial fibrosis causing ventricular dysfunction and conduction abnormalities.

Investigations

Coronary angiography
Coronary angiography may help to distinguish between vasculitis and atheromatous disease.

Echocardiography
Transoesophageal echocardiography should be used if necessary for close inspection of valve abnormalities.

Treatment
Pericarditis
Non-steroidal anti-inflammatory drugs and steroids are used if necessary for symptomatic relief. Tamponade requires immediate pericardiocentesis followed by steroids.

Myocarditis
The standard management of left ventricular dysfunction (see Section 2.3).

Pulmonary hypertension
The standard management (see Section 2.12).

2.13.4 Renal disease
Aetiology and pathophysiology
Features of end-stage renal failure / renal replacement include:

> hypertension
> elevated serum calcium and phosphate product
> anaemia
> dyslipidaemia
> uraemia
> electrolyte imbalance
> amyloidosis (β_2 microglobulin).

These result in the following cardiovascular complications via the mechanisms shown in Fig 86:

> left ventricular hypertrophy (LVH)
> myocardial ischaemia
> impaired ventricular function
> ventricular arrhythmias and sudden death
> valvular calcification, aortic more than mitral, with rapidly progressive stenosis in a small proportion of cases, and the risk of endocarditis.

Key point

The heart in renal failure
Abnormal cardiac structure is virtually uniform in patients with end-stage renal disease. LVH is present in 70–80% of patients approaching dialysis, and is linked to anaemia and hypertension. Left ventricular (LV) dilatation and impairment of systolic and diastolic function are common. These are of course influenced by fluid loading and change, at least in part, following dialysis. Cardiovascular disease is also the major cause of late mortality in renal transplant recipients.

Epidemiology
Cardiovascular disease is much commoner in patients receiving renal replacement than in the general population and is the most common cause of death in people from that group (>50%). Those whose renal failure is associated with diabetes and atherosclerotic renovascular disease are at particularly high risk.

Investigations
> Myocardial ischaemia: coronary angiography or stress echo/MRI may be of value if intervention or renal transplantation is being considered. Exercise testing (abnormal ECG) and nuclear perfusion imaging have reduced predictive value in these patients.
> Echocardiography for assessment of valves, LV function and pericardial effusion.

Treatment
Optimise haemoglobin and BP. If symptomatic coronary artery disease is present, bypass grafting is the treatment of choice as the post-angioplasty re-stenosis and coronary event rates are very high. The indications for surgery in calcific valve disease and endocarditis are the same as in a patient without renal disease. Uraemic pericarditis is

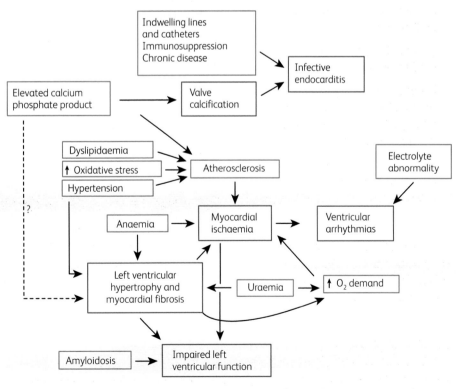

Fig 86 The pathogenesis of cardiac complications of renal failure.

an indication for dialysis. Cardiac tamponade (of any cause) requires immediate pericardiocentesis. Recurrent effusions may warrant pericardiectomy (a 'window' to enable drainage into the pleural space).

> **Hazard**
> > Prescribing in renal failure.
> > Be aware that a patient on dialysis may have large fluctuations in serum potassium, with effects on antiarrhythmic therapy.

Prognosis

The presence of LV dysfunction in a dialysis patient reduces the 2-year survival rate from 80% to 33%. Acute myocardial infarction and cardiac surgery have a higher mortality than in the general population, but when indicated coronary artery bypass grafting and valve surgery still have an acceptable risk.

Prevention

Careful control of phosphate and calcium phosphate product reduces valve calcification. Good aseptic technique is essential when inserting and using dialysis catheters to minimise the risk of infective endocarditis. Aim for good control of BP and serum cholesterol, and maintenance of haematocrit. It is important the patient stops smoking!

2.14 Systemic complications of cardiac diseases

2.14.1 Stroke

Aetiology

Approximately 20% of all ischaemic strokes are cardiogenic in cause. Cardiac causes can be divided into a direct source of embolus or a substrate for embolus formation. Direct sources of embolus include left ventricular (LV) apical thrombus in an akinetic LV territory after myocardial infarction (MI), left atrial appendage thrombus in patients with atrial fibrillation (AF), prosthetic valve thrombus in a patient with inadequate anticoagulation, valve vegetations, aortic dissection and cardiac tumours (especially atrial myxoma). Cardiac substrates for embolus formation include patent foramen ovale (PFO), aortic arch atheroma, LV non-compaction, dilated left atrium or dilated cardiomyopathy.

Physical signs

Common

> AF (in up to 25% of patients who have a cerebrovascular accident)

> murmurs (particularly mitral predisposing to left atrial enlargement and subsequent AF).

Uncommon

> pulmonary oedema

> added hearts sounds.

Investigations

ECG

There is a significant chance that, if there is underlying cardiac pathology resulting in thromboembolism, the ECG will be abnormal.

> **Key point**
> When examining an ECG for cardiac cause of stroke look for:

> AF

> previous myocardial infarction (MI) (in 90% of cases the MI is anterior)

> persistent ST elevation suggestive of LV aneurysm

> LV hypertrophy suggestive of hypertension or aortic stenosis.

Chest radiograph

Look for abnormal cardiac shape/size, pulmonary oedema and wide mediastinum suggestive of enlarged aorta.

Echocardiography

If any possible cardiac cause has been identified from the history, examination or ECG/chest radiograph, it is reasonable to examine the structure and function of the heart with echocardiography. Contrast administration aids in the diagnosis of LV thrombus. Transoesophageal echocardiography should be performed to assess for aortic arch atheroma, left atrial appendage thrombus and function, and the presence of a PFO. For the diagnosis of a PFO, the patient is asked to perform the Valsalva manoeuvre and agitated saline or microbubble solution is injected peripherally. Upon Valsalva release, immediate passage of bubbles from right atrium to left atrium suggests a PFO.

Treatment

Correct the underlying abnormality and aim for restoration of sinus rhythm where possible (see Section 2.2.2).

Percutaneous closure of a PFO is recommended in young patients with any of the following:

> stroke / transient ischaemic attack (TIA) where no other cause can be found

> recurrent embolic events despite medical treatment

> cerebral embolic events in more than one carotid territory.

In some patients who are unable to take anticoagulants a device can be implanted percutaneously in the left atrial appendage – left atrial appendage occlusion device (LAAOD).

Complication

The risk of haemorrhage into an ischaemic stroke if anticoagulated initially outweighs benefits, so patients receive 300 mg aspirin od for 2 weeks before switching to warfarin.

Prevention

See Section 2.2.2 for anticoagulation with atrial fibrillation.

2.15 Pregnancy and the heart

Aetiology

Normal physiological changes in pregnancy include the following:

> decrease in systemic and pulmonary vascular resistance

> increase in heart rate, blood volume (large shifts after delivery) and cardiac output

> no significant change in BP

> anaemia (caused by increased blood volume and/or haematinic deficiency).

These can all cause problems in women with cardiovascular disease.

Clinical presentation

Fatigue, mild dyspnoea, ankle oedema, palpitations (usually ectopics) and postural dizziness are all common in normal pregnancy, but likely to be more severe in those with cardiac disease.

Physical signs

The following are common in a normal pregnancy:

> third heart sound

> soft systolic flow murmur at the lower left sternal edge

> mild ankle oedema.

Look for signs of worsening cardiac failure and/or exacerbation of the physical signs of particular cardiac lesions.

Investigations

To exclude cardiac disease conduct the following.

Echocardiography

To check for ventricular function and valvular abnormalities.

ECG/24-hour tape

Looking for arrhythmias.

Chest radiograph

Rarely clinically needed, but should be performed if indicated because the dose to a screened fetus is negligible.

Key point

In pregnant women a 12-lead ECG may show a minor axis shift or non-specific ST changes in the left-sided precordial leads. These usually resolve after pregnancy, but may recur in subsequent pregnancies.

Prognosis/treatment

In a patient with pre-existing cardiac disease the ability to tolerate pregnancy is related to the following:

> cyanosis

> pulmonary hypertension

> haemodynamic significance of the lesion

> pre-pregnancy functional status.

High risk

Primary pulmonary hypertension / Eisenmenger's syndrome

There is a 50% maternal mortality rate and patients should be strongly advised to consider sterilisation.

Mitral stenosis

This may present for the first time in pregnancy with pulmonary oedema secondary to increased cardiac output or an episode of atrial fibrillation. Treatment consists of diuretics to clear the pulmonary oedema, and digoxin or beta-blockers to control heart rate and thereby improve atrial emptying. Mitral valvuloplasty may be necessary during pregnancy on rare occasions.

Aortic/pulmonary stenosis

Gradients are exacerbated by decreased vascular resistance. There is no effective medical therapy other than supportive.

Marfan syndrome

There is an increased risk of aortic dissection; those who already have echocardiographic evidence of aortic root dilatation >4.5 cm should be advised against pregnancy.

Intermediate risk

> coarctation of the aorta (risk of aortic dissection)

> hypertrophic cardiomyopathy

> cyanotic congenital heart disease without pulmonary hypertension – note increased risk (40%) of fetal death if mother is cyanotic.

Low risk

> well-tolerated valvular regurgitation

> septal defects without pulmonary hypertension

> totally corrected congenital heart disease

> prosthetic valves: bioprostheses do not require anticoagulation, but pregnancy reduces their lifespan. There is no consensus of opinion on the optimum management of anticoagulation in pregnant women with mechanical valves. There is the concern that heparin is not as effective as warfarin in preventing valve thrombosis.

Key point

Antibiotic prophylaxis is recommended for vaginal delivery in cases at high risk of endocarditis (prosthetic valves, prior episode of infective endocarditis, complex cyanotic congenital heart disease and surgical shunts) and for instrumented delivery in any cardiac lesion, but not for caesarean section.

New cardiac disease in pregnancy

Thromboembolic disease
Thrombolysis should be used for a massive life-threatening pulmonary embolus, as in the non-pregnant patient.

Myocardial infarction
This is rare in pregnancy but is associated with considerable mortality. Atheroma is responsible for less than half of instances and coronary artery dissection is more common than in the normal population. Ideally the treatment should be urgent coronary angiography and intervention if needed. Aspirin, nitrates and beta-blockers may be used. Angiotensin-converting enzyme inhibitors and statins should be avoided.

Peripartum cardiomyopathy
This presents as dilated cardiomyopathy in the third trimester or in the first 6 months postpartum.

Hypertension
Hypertension may be chronic (ie predates the pregnancy or develops before 20 weeks) or pregnancy induced (part of a spectrum that includes pre-eclampsia).

Key point

Important information for patients

Recurrence risk of non-syndromic congenital heart disease in the baby is 3–5%.

2.16 General anaesthesia in heart disease

Pathophysiology
Assessment for fitness for anaesthetic involves understanding the effects it has on cardiovascular physiology, the direct effects of the anaesthetic agents and the effects of artificial ventilation as well as the effect of surgery. Anaesthesia tends to cause:

> hypotension

> reduced preload

> hypoxaemia

> hypercapnia

> acidosis.

Patients with congenital cyanotic heart disease or pulmonary hypertension are at particularly high risk from general anaesthesia (GA). These patients cannot adapt to reduced preload and develop severe systemic hypotension.

Epidemiology
The risk of reinfarction during an anaesthetic after a myocardial infarction (MI) is:

> within 3 months 6%

> between 3 and 6 months 2%.

Clinical presentation
The key to assessing fitness for anaesthesia is exercise ability. Good exercise performance suggests anaesthesia will be tolerated well. Patients with unstable symptoms are likely to be at risk.

Investigation
These may help decide on the suitability for anaesthetic.

Exercise testing
Objective evidence of exercise ability and ischaemia is obtained.

Echocardiography
This is unlikely to be of routine help. Patients with severe left ventricular impairment and good exercise tolerance are likely to have a good outcome from anaesthesia. Patients with suspected aortic stenosis should have echocardiography, as the risk of complication from GA is high.

ECG
A history of syncope and evidence of trifascicular block indicates the need for permanent pacing. Generally, asymptomatic bifascicular and trifascicular block do not require temporary transvenous pacing prior to GA.

Coronary angiography
Generally, patients with ischaemic heart disease who require urgent/emergency surgery should be treated medically with beta-blockers, which may be given intravenously if required. Revascularisation prior to non-cardiac surgery has been shown to carry a higher risk than medical treatment with beta-blockade. There is a high risk of fatal stent thrombosis within the first 2 weeks after percutaneous coronary intervention (PCI). Patients undergoing emergency surgery soon after PCI should continue antiplatelet therapy.

Key point

The following are considered high-risk groups if they are undergoing surgery with cardiac disease:

> MI within the last 6 months

> congestive cardiac failure

> aortic stenosis

> aged >70 years

> undergoing emergency operation

> metabolic abnormality

> congenital cyanotic heart disease

> pulmonary hypertension.

These patients should be managed postoperatively in a high dependency unit with invasive haemodynamic monitoring. Close liaison between surgeon, anaesthetist and cardiologist is vital.

2.17 Hypertension

Aetiology/pathophysiology/pathology

Over 90% of all cases of hypertension are of unknown aetiology (essential hypertension), reflecting deranged interaction between multiple genetic and environmental factors on the homeostatic mechanisms of the body (including abnormalities of the renin–angiotensin and autonomic nervous systems, endothelial dysfunction and sodium intake). Secondary causes of hypertension are much more uncommon (Table 38). However, treatment of the underlying cause can often cure the resultant high BP.

Epidemiology

BP is a continuous variable, so hypertension is difficult to define. Up to one-quarter of adults in Western populations are found to have a BP of >140/90 mmHg at screening. This proportion increases with age, rising from 4% in those aged 18–29 years to 65% in those >80 years. However, despite a recognition of the high prevalence of hypertension and its dangers it remains inadequately treated with estimates that <30% of recognised hypertensive patients have adequate BP control.

Clinical presentation

Common

Essential hypertension is usually asymptomatic until complications (eg cardiac failure) arise. Hypertension is commonly detected 'opportunistically' when a patient attends with some complaint and the doctor or nurse takes the opportunity to measure their BP. It may also be detected at a routine health screening, or as part of a deliberate assessment of a patient's cardiovascular risk (eg when presenting with symptoms that might indicate cardiovascular disease such as ischaemic heart disease, stroke / transient ischaemic attack or peripheral vascular disease). A number of complaints are commonly associated with hypertension, but are non-specific: These include:

> headache (occipital and present on waking, settling gradually during the day)
> epistaxis
> nocturia.

Uncommon

Presentation with symptoms suggestive of a secondary cause apart from those attributable to hypertension:

> phaeochromocytoma – anxiety, diaphoresis, tremor, epigastric and chest pain, and dyspnoea

> primary hyperaldosteronism – symptoms suggestive of marked hypokalaemia: cramps, muscle weakness, polydipsia, polyuria and/or nocturia

> Cushing's syndrome – weight gain, characteristic facial appearance, easy bruising, thinning of hair and skin, striae and muscle weakness

> other less common features include symptoms suggestive of thyroid disease.

Physical signs

Apart from elevated BP, commonly there are no other abnormal signs. In moderate or severe hypertension, a loud aortic second sound may be heard. Look for evidence of the following:

> left ventricular hypertrophy (LVH)

> hypertensive retinopathy (Fig 87):

> grade I – light reflex from the arterial wall is increased as a result of thickening

> grade II – the arterial light reflex is wider, giving rise to a 'silver wire' appearance. Nipping of the veins is an optical illusion caused by the inability to see the blood within the vein through the thickened arterial wall. There is a generalised reduction in the diameter of arteries compared with veins

> grades III and IV – associated with accelerated hypertension (Section 2.17.1)

> signs of associated vascular disease: vascular bruits and absent pulses.

Investigations

The following should be considered:

Blood tests

FBC, electrolytes, renal function, fasting glucose and lipids.

Table 38 Secondary causes of hypertension	
Presentation	**Cause**
Commonly present with hypertension	Renal disease Renal artery stenosis, atherosclerotic or fibromuscular dysplasia Coarctation of the aorta Phaeochromocytoma Primary hyperaldosteronism (Conn's syndrome)
Rarely present with hypertension as the dominant feature, but may be associated with it	Cushing's syndrome Exogenous steroids Hyperthyroidism Myxoedema Acromegaly Excessive liquorice consumption

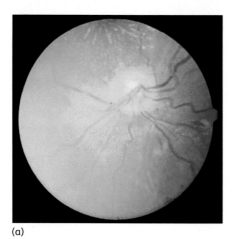

(a)

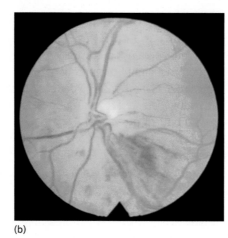

(b)

Fig 87 Hypertensive retinopathy: **(a)** grade IV showing mild papilloedema, hard exudates (12 o'clock), cotton-wool spots and flame haemorrhages (4 o'clock); **(b)** grade III showing extensive flame-shaped haemorrhages. (Courtesy of Professor J Ritter.)

Urine
A clean mid-stream urine should be tested for blood, protein and glucose. In the presence of haematuria or proteinuria, the sample should be sent for microscopy and culture.

ECG
The ECG may be normal. Look for signs of LVH and/or coronary artery disease.

Chest radiograph
This may be normal. Look for cardiomegaly, pulmonary oedema and coarctation (Fig 88).

Other baseline investigations
Other tests may be required in some cases.

> To determine whether hypertension is present in patients with no evidence of end-organ damage. Arrange 24-hour ambulatory BP measurement to have a better understanding of the pattern of change in the patient's BP and its control in their normal environment (at home and work). This will also be useful to rule out isolated clinic ('white coat') hypertension.

> To assess end-organ damage secondary to hypertensive retinopathy. Conduct transthoracic echocardiography and look for LVH, systolic or diastolic failure.

Investigations for secondary hypertension
In suspected cases of secondary hypertension further investigations led by the clinical suspicion will be required.

Indications for investigating secondary causes of hypertension:

> any evidence of underlying cause in history or examination (Table 38)

> accelerated (malignant) hypertension

> hypokalaemia (not diuretic induced)

> young age (<35 years)

> resistant hypertension (uncontrolled by three drugs).

Possible investigations include:

> 24-hour urine collection. Measure catecholamine levels and look for features of renal disease (eg creatinine clearance and urinary protein excretion).

> Renal ultrasound and Doppler. The presence of two small kidneys indicates chronic renal disease. Marked asymmetry of renal size (>2 cm difference in length) increases the probability of renal artery stenosis. Doppler ultrasound of the renal arteries can accurately diagnose renal artery stenosis.

> MRI of the renal arteries. An alternative accurate method of diagnosis for renal artery stenosis.

> Test of plasma renin and aldosterone.

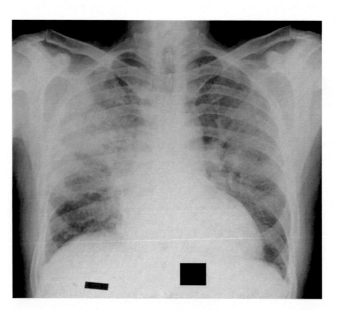

Fig 88 Chest radiograph demonstrating pulmonary oedema.

Differential diagnosis

Consider the following:

> essential hypertension

> secondary hypertension

> erroneous reading of elevated BP as a result of an inadequate cuff size

> isolated clinic hypertension ('white coat' hypertension).

Treatment

Newer recommendations suggest commencing treatment as part of a package of measures to address 'lifetime risk' of cardiovascular disease. Cardiovascular disease risk appears to be related to long-term and combined exposure to risk factors (eg smoking and having hypertension). Calculators (eg www.jbs3risk.com) can estimate both risk from cardiovascular disease and competing diseases such as cancer.

Essential hypertension

Treatment of both systolic and diastolic blood pressure (DBP) are equally important across all age groups. Having diagnosed hypertension, pharmacological therapy should be combined with advice on lifestyle changes. The following are considered recommendations for pharmacological treatment of hypertension:

> patients with persistent high BP of 160/100 mmHg or more

> patients with raised cardiovascular risk (10-year risk of coronary heart disease ≥20%, existing cardiovascular disease, diabetes or evidence of target organ damage) with a persistent BP of 140/90 mmHg or more.

The choice of antihypertensive therapy should be tailored to the patient's medical requirements. In patients who do not respond to single and/or two-agent therapy, low-dose combination therapy must be considered. A recommended treatment pathway is outlined in Fig 89.

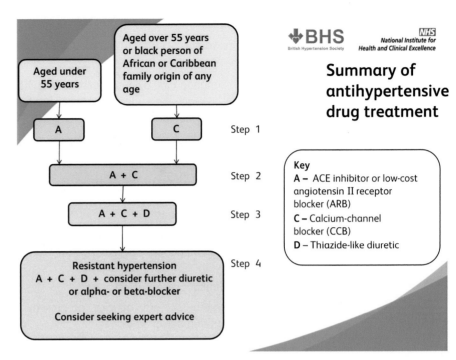

Step 1
Step 2
Step 3
Step 4

Summary of antihypertensive drug treatment

Key
A – ACE inhibitor or low-cost angiotensin II receptor blocker (ARB)
C – Calcium-channel blocker (CCB)
D – Thiazide-like diuretic

Fig 89 Treatment algorithm recommended by NICE for essential hypertension. (© NICE 2011 *Hypertension in adults: diagnosis and management Clinical guideline* (CG127), www.nice.org.uk/guidance/cg127. All rights reserved. NICE guidance is prepared for the NHS in England. All NICE guidance is subject to regular review and may be updated or withdrawn. NICE accepts no responsibility for the use of its content in this product/publication.) ACEI, angiotensin-converting enzyme inhibitor; ARB, angiotensin receptor.

Secondary hypertension

Treatment should be directed towards management of the underlying cause.

Key point

Advice regarding lifestyle modifications for patients with hypertension:

> stop smoking

> lose weight as appropriate

> moderation of alcohol intake (<14 units/week)

> dietary changes – consume a lower amount of saturated fat, and increase oily fish, fruit and vegetable intake

> limit salt intake

> sensible regular exercise.

Complications

These are often seen if BP remains untreated or poorly managed:

> retinopathy and retinal haemorrhages

> renal impairment

> left ventricular hypertrophy and cardiac failure (both systolic and diastolic)

> vascular events – stroke, myocardial infarction and peripheral arterial disease

> worsening hypertension (especially if poorly treated).

Prognosis

Morbidity

Essential hypertension increases the risk of stroke six-fold, of coronary artery disease and heart failure three-fold, and doubles the risk of peripheral vascular disease. Renal failure usually occurs only in cases of malignant hypertension, but elevated BP increases the progression of renal failure from other causes. Treatment of hypertension is well established to reduce the incidence of cardiovascular disease.

Mortality

> At an age <50 years, both diastolic and systolic hypertension are risk factors for cardiovascular death. A reduction of 5–6 mmHg in diastolic pressure is associated with a 12% reduction in mortality rate over 5 years.

> At an age >50 years, evidence suggests that the systolic BP is the important determinant of risk and that it has an inverse relationship with DBP, ie the greater the pulse pressure for a given value of systolic pressure, the higher the risk.

2.17.1 Hypertensive emergencies

Aetiology/pathology

A hypertensive crisis is defined as a severe elevation in BP (systolic blood pressure >200 mmHg, diastolic blood pressure >120 mmHg). Rate of change in BP is important. A rapid rise is poorly tolerated and leads to end-organ damage, whereas a gradual rise in a patient with existent poor BP control is tolerated better.

Conditions that can cause hypertensive emergencies include the following:

> essential hypertension

> renovascular hypertension: atheroma, fibromuscular dysplasia and acute renal occlusion

> renal parenchymal disease: acute glomerulonephritis, vasculitis and scleroderma

> endocrine disorders: phaeochromocytoma, Cushing's syndrome, primary hyperaldosteronism, thyrotoxicosis, hyperparathyroidism, acromegaly and adrenal carcinoma

> eclampsia and pre-eclampsia

> vasculitis

> drugs: cocaine, amphetamines, monoamine oxidase inhibitor (MAOI) interactions, cyclosporine, beta-blocker and clonidine withdrawal

> autonomic hyperactivity in presence of spinal cord injury

> coarctation of the aorta.

Epidemiology

The incidence is around one to two per 100,000 people per year.

Clinical presentation

Hypertensive emergencies can present in a number of ways:

> Hypertensive emergency with retinopathy (previously known as accelerated hypertension) – patients suffering from this often have visual disturbances and retinal haemorrhages.

> Hypertensive emergency with papilloedema (previously called malignant hypertension).

> Hypertensive emergency with encephalopathy – patients present with headaches, drowsiness and epileptic fits. Other ocular complications are also often present.

Physical signs

Common

The diagnosis of a hypertensive emergency cannot be made without high BP and evidence of fibrinoid necrosis of vessels, which can be viewed directly only in the fundi:

> grade III retinopathy – flame-shaped superficial haemorrhages or 'dot-and-blot' haemorrhages deeper within the retina, cotton-wool spots (retinal microinfarcts) and hard exudates (Fig 87)

> grade IV retinopathy – haemorrhages and exudates with papilloedema (Fig 90).

Uncommon

Drowsiness, coma, epileptic fitting, stroke, pulmonary oedema and aortic dissection.

Investigations

Immediate

Check urine for blood, protein and red cell casts. Perform ECG, chest radiograph, FBC, electrolytes, coagulation profile and renal and liver function tests. If there is a clinical suspicion of aortic dissection (Fig 91), an urgent CT scan of the chest or transoesophageal echocardiography is needed. If there is a clinical suspicion of a renal inflammatory condition (eg systemic lupus erythematosus, vasculitis

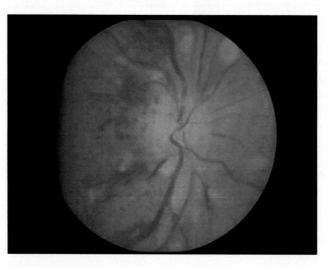

Fig 90 Hypertensive retinopathy: grade IV showing florid papilloedema, haemorrhages and cotton-wool spots. (Courtesy of Mr H Towler.)

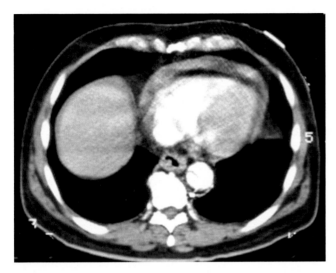

Fig 91 CT scan of aortic dissection. The descending aorta is enlarged and contrast shows a double lumen.

or scleroderma), then specific serological tests will be needed.

Elective

When BP has been controlled, all patients with accelerated phase hypertension require a thorough work-up for secondary causes of hypertension. Renal biopsy may be required.

Differential diagnosis

The differential diagnosis is of acute glomerulonephritis or renal vasculitis, or scleroderma renal crisis.

Treatment

All patients with accelerated phase hypertension should be admitted to hospital for BP control with appropriate drugs and treatment of any complications or secondary cause.

Complications

Stroke, aortic dissection and chronic renal failure.

Prognosis

If untreated, 80% of sufferers will die within 2 years. One recent series reported a 69% survival rate at 12 years.

2.18 Venous thromboembolism

2.18.1 Pulmonary embolism

Embolism can be from any source (eg tumour, air or amniotic fluid), but this section will consider only thrombotic venous thromboembolism.

Aetiology/pathophysiology/pathology

Virchow's triad (local trauma to the vessel wall, hypercoagulability and venous stasis) causes thrombosis in the deep veins of the legs, pelvis or (more rarely) arms, which can propagate and extend proximally. The thrombus may dislodge and embolise to the pulmonary arterial tree. This causes physical obstruction of the vasculature and release of vasoactive substances leading to:

> elevation of pulmonary vascular resistance

> redistribution of blood flow, causing ventilation–perfusion mismatch and impairment of gas exchange

> increased right ventricular (RV) afterload, causing dilatation and dysfunction of the RV.

Often patients have a genetic predisposition to thrombosis but require an environmental stress to elicit overt thrombus formation.

Epidemiology

The incidence of venous thromboembolism is 60–70 cases per 100,000 members of a population. Despite treatment, the 3-month mortality of pulmonary embolism (PE) remains high at 17.5%. The incidence of PE doubles with each 10-year increase in age. It is estimated that PE accounts for 10% of all in-hospital deaths.

Risk factors

These are divided into hypercoagulable states associated with venous thrombosis and acquired conditions that may precipitate venous thrombosis (Table 39).

Table 39	Risk factors for PE	
Hypercoagulable states	**Acquired conditions**
Factor V Leiden mutation	Surgery/trauma/fractures
Protein C abnormalities (mutations and/or resistance)	Immobilisation from any cause
	Obesity
Protein S deficiency	Hypertension
Antithrombin III deficiency	Increasing age
Hyperhomocysteinaemia	Pregnancy/postpartum
Antiphospholipid antibodies (including lupus anticoagulant and anticardiolipin antibodies)	Malignancy
	Chronic cardiorespiratory disease
	Stroke / spinal cord injury
	Indwelling central venous catheter
	Current (not prior) use of combined OCP or hormone replacement therapy (minor risk only)

OCP, oral contraceptive pill; PE, pulmonary embolism.

Clinical presentation

Common

> small and moderate-sized PE:
> > isolated dyspnoea
> > symptoms of pulmonary infarction – pleuritic pain, cough and/or haemoptysis
> massive PE – severe dyspnoea, syncope, haemodynamic collapse and cyanosis
> symptoms of deep venous thrombosis (DVT) – swelling and tenderness in calf.

Uncommon

> progressive ankle oedema and dyspnoea (secondary pulmonary hypertension)
> pyrexia of unknown origin
> atrial fibrillation (AF).

Key point

A young woman with isolated pleuritic chest pain and no risk factors except the oral contraceptive pill (OCP) is extremely unlikely to have a PE if she has a respiratory rate of <20/min and a normal chest radiograph. However, the risk of missing a life-threatening condition means that you should pursue the investigation unless you can make a confident alternative diagnosis.

Physical signs

Common

> tachypnoea
> tachycardia
> crackles on auscultation
> pleural rub.

Uncommon

> cyanosis suggests large PE
> postural hypotension in the presence of a raised JVP

> signs of raised right heart pressure:
> > raised JVP with prominent 'a' wave
> > pansystolic murmur of tricuspid regurgitation
> > loud pulmonary valve (P2) closure sound with wide splitting of S2
> > early diastolic murmur of pulmonary regurgitation
> > left parasternal heave
> swollen, firm calf suggestive of DVT.

Investigations

Investigations must be used in conjunction with an assessment of the clinical probability of PE. The Wells score is often used for this purpose.

Key point

The Wells scoring system for clinical probability of PE

	Score
Clinical signs and symptoms of DVT	+3
Heart rate >100/min	+1.5
Immobilisation >3 days or surgery in previous 4 weeks	+1.5
Previous definite PE or DVT	+1.5
Haemoptysis	+1
Malignancy	+1
PE as likely or more likely than alternative diagnosis	+3

Total score 0/1/2, low probability; 3/4, unlikely; 5, likely; 6, high probability.

ECG

Changes are often non-specific and include sinus tachycardia and anterior T wave inversion. ECG changes of raised right heart pressure are rare and only seen with massive PE. These include right-axis deviation, S1Q3T3, new right bundle branch block, RV hypertrophy and AF.

Chest radiograph

This is often normal. Abnormal findings include pulmonary oligaemia, raised diaphragm, small pleural effusion and segmental collapse.

Arterial blood gases

Hypoxaemia (in larger PEs) and hypocapnia (associated with respiratory alkalosis secondary to hyperventilation) increase suspicion of PE. Normal arterial blood gases do not exclude a diagnosis of PE.

Venous ultrasonography

This is used if there is clinical suspicion of a current DVT, although normal results do not exclude a PE. This can be helpful as a first-line investigation in patients in whom you would want to avoid radiation exposure (eg pregnant females).

Echocardiography

Echocardiography identifies RV pressure overload and dysfunction with large PEs. In patients with non-PE related haemodynamic collapse it can be used to identify alternative cardiac causes for the abnormal haemodynamic state. It is useful as a quick source of information in a critically ill patient, but does not provide a diagnosis of PE.

Plasma D-dimer

This test is sensitive but not specific for the presence of a thrombus (ie it helps to exclude the diagnosis of a thrombus if negative).

Ventilation–perfusion lung scan

A normal scan rules out a PE. Abnormal scans with a high probability of PE must be treated as PE. Medium or low probability scans must be interpreted in the context of the clinical scenario and may require alternative modes of imaging. Perfusion scanning alone gives comparable diagnostic yield (Fig 92). Pre-existing lung disease makes interpretation difficult.

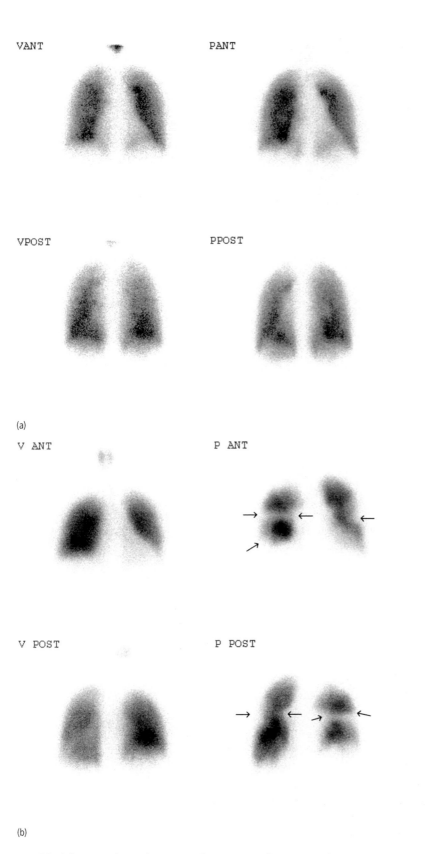

Spiral CT chest with contrast
Increasingly used in the diagnosis of PE (Fig 93). Clearly the imaging technique of choice when there is pre-existing pulmonary disease.

Pulmonary angiography
Historically this was the 'gold standard' investigation but has largely been replaced by CT.

Key point

Consider the following in the differential diagnosis of PE:

> pleurisy/breathlessness

> pneumothorax

> pneumonia

> musculoskeletal pain

> rib fracture

> asthma / chronic airflow obstruction

> other causes of circulatory collapse (myocardial infarction (MI) and cardiac tamponade).

Management
Emergency
General measures are required until a definitive diagnosis is reached:

> Maximal inspired oxygen.

> Analgesia: non-steroidal anti-inflammatory drugs are often very useful. Use opiate analgesia with caution in severe pain as this may depress respiratory efforts and/or cause hypotension secondary to vasodilation.

> Peripheral fluids.

> Give intravenous (IV) loading dose of heparin followed by infusion until a diagnosis is confirmed.

> Monitor cardiac rhythm, pulse, BP, oxygen saturation and respiration rate regularly.

Fig 92 (a) Normal ventilation–perfusion scan. Anterior and posterior views are shown. **(b)** Multiple perfusion defects (indicated by arrows) that are not matched by ventilation defects and therefore indicate a high probability of PE.

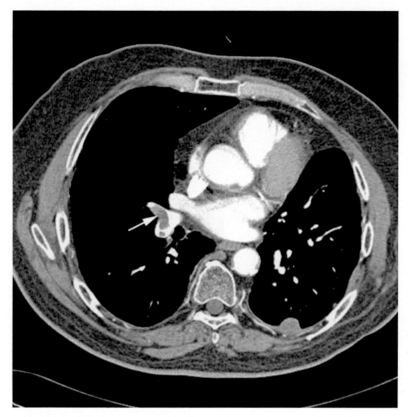

Fig 93 Contrast CT scan of a patient with a large PE visible as a grey filling defect (indicated by arrow) against the white contrast in the pulmonary artery.

The following are often required in cases of massive PE, especially if they are associated with hypotension:

> Thrombolysis. Often recombinant tissue plasminogen activator (rt-PA) is used, but protocol is different from that used in MI. Can be given via a peripheral vein or pulmonary artery (PA) catheter.

> Give colloids if hypotensive and obtain central venous access for monitoring (preferably prior to anticoagulation).

> Inotropes may be required if hypotension persists.

> Discuss case with cardiothoracic team early as surgical embolectomy may be required if the patient does not respond to thrombolysis and colloids and/or if thrombolysis is contraindicated.

Short term

> Analgesia.

> Heparin: unfractionated heparin (UFH) or low-molecular-weight heparin. Prevents further thrombus formation and permits endogenous fibrinolysis. If using UFH continue until international normalised ratio (INR) >2.0.

> Start warfarin or non-vitamin K oral anticoagulant (NOAC) once adequate anticoagulation with heparin is achieved or as per the particular NOAC protocol.

Hazard
Paradoxically, warfarin without heparin may initially increase hypercoagulability.

Long term

> Continue warfarin/NOAC for between 6 weeks and 3 months if the risk factor is temporary and/or it is the patient's first PE.

> Consider long-term anticoagulation for recurrent embolism and persisting risk factors such as thrombophilia.

> Investigate for underlying cause if unknown. Possible investigations include:

> thrombophilia screen

> ultrasound of deep veins in lower limbs and pelvis

> autoimmune screen

> biopsy of suspicious lymph nodes.

> Consider inferior vena cava (IVC) filter for recurrent PE in the presence of adequate anticoagulation or if anticoagulation is contraindicated.

Complications
The most significant longer-term complication is secondary pulmonary hypertension.

Prognosis

This depends on the underlying cause. In general the prognosis is worse for larger PE. Poor prognostic indicators include:

> RV dysfunction on echocardiography

> hypotension

> hypoxia

> significant ECG changes associated with right heart strain.

Prevention

Primary

> consideration of compression stockings and prophylactic heparin in hospitalised patients, especially those with trauma, the critically ill and those

undergoing general and/or orthopaedic surgery

> discourage smoking

> encourage early mobilisation postoperatively.

Secondary

> thrombophilia screening to determine whether prolonged/lifelong anticoagulation is required

> discourage smoking and advise alternatives to the OCP

> weight loss and BP control if necessary

> consideration of IVC filter in selected cases.

2.19 Driving restrictions in cardiology

Driving restrictions are under a process of continued review and can be seen on the Driver and Vehicle Licensing Agency's (DVLA – UK) website (www.dvla.gov.uk/). Many requirements for a Group 2 licence require the completion of an exercise tolerance test (ETT) to specified standards or functional tests such as stress echo or myocardial perfusion imaging.

The current guidelines for major cardiac conditions are outlined in Table 40.

Table 40   Driving regulations issued by the Driver and Vehicle Licensing Agency (DVLA – UK) for driving with cardiovascular disease in the UK

Condition		Group 1 entitlement (cars and motorcycles)	Group 2 entitlement (large lorries and buses)
Syncope (varies according to single or multiple – see DVLA guidelines for further details)	Typical vasovagal syncope with prodrome	Standing – may drive Sitting – must not drive for 1 month and inform the DVLA if solitary	Standing – may drive Sitting – must not drive for 3 months and inform the DVLA if solitary
	Syncope with avoidable trigger or reversible cause	Standing – may drive Sitting – must not drive for 1 month but may resume then if the cause is treated	Standing – may drive Sitting – must not drive for 3 months and may resume then if the cause is treated
	Unexplained syncope	Must not drive and must inform the DVLA If no cause identified, licence revoked for 12 months	Must not drive and must inform the DVLA If no cause identified, licence revoked for 10 years
	Presumed epileptic seizure	Must not drive and must inform the DVLA Need to be seizure free for 5 years for restoration of licence	Must not drive and must inform the DVLA Need to be seizure free for 10 years for restoration of licence
Angina		Permitted unless symptoms occur while driving	Only able to drive when free from angina for 6 weeks and meets ETT / other functional requirements
Angioplasty (elective)		Permitted after 1 week	Permitted after 6 weeks and meets ETT / other functional requirements
Coronary artery bypass grafting, heart valve surgery including TAVI		Permitted after 4 weeks	Permitted after 12 weeks if meets ETT / other functional requirements and LVEF >40%
Acute coronary syndrome		If treated by PCI driving permitted after 1/52 (providing no plan for further urgent revascularisation) and LVEF >40% at discharge If not successfully treated with PCI driving permitted after 4/52	Permitted after 6 weeks if meets ETT / other functional requirements
Arrhythmia		Must cease driving if likely to cause incapacity while driving. May be permitted 4 weeks after cause identified and treated	Must cease driving if likely to cause incapacity while driving. May be permitted 3 months after cause identified and treated and LVEF >40%
Heart failure		Permitted provided no symptoms during driving	Permitted if ETT requirements are met and ejection fraction >40%
ICD – this is a complex area for driving restrictions and so the full guidance should be studied		Implanted for ventricular arrhythmia with incapacity – no driving for 6 months after implant and 6 months after any therapy. If therapy accompanied by incapacity no driving for 2 years Implanted for ventricular arrhythmia but not incapacitated – no driving for 1 month provided LVEF >35% and no fast ventricular tachycardia at electrophysiologic study Prophylactic ICD – permitted after 1 month	Permanently bars from driving
Pacemaker implant (including box change)		Permitted after 1 week	Permitted after 6 weeks
Successful catheter ablation		Permitted after 2 days	Permitted after 2 weeks if arrhythmia did not cause incapacity and after 6 weeks if it did

ECG, electrocardiogram; ETT, exercise tolerance test; ICD, implantable cardioverter defibrillator; LVEF, left ventricular ejection fraction; PCI, percutaneous coronary intervention; TAVI, transcatheter aortic valve implantation.

Cardiology: Section 3

3 Investigations and practical procedures

3.1 ECG

Principle

The ECG is a graphic representation of the electrical potentials of the heart. Each deflection represents electrical activity in the cardiac cycle:

> P wave: atrial depolarisation. A further deflection that represents atrial repolarisation is usually hidden within the QRS complex.

> PR interval: atrioventricular (AV) conduction time.

> QRS complex: ventricular depolarisation. Q is the first negative deflection, R the first positive deflection and S the first negative deflection following a positive deflection.

> ST segment: from the end of the QRS to the start of the T wave.

> T wave: ventricular repolarisation.

> U wave: after or in the end portion of the T wave. Cause unknown.

Adopting a systematic method of interpreting an ECG will enable you to approach the most complex of ECGs with confidence. If you approach all ECGs in this manner then certain patterns will become familiar, enabling rapid diagnosis of arrhythmias and possible structural cardiac abnormalities.

An ECG interpretation scheme should include the following questions. After establishing the basic parameters, start at the P wave, progress through to the QRS and finally examine the T wave:

> What is the rhythm? Is it regular or irregular?

> What is the rate? It should be 300/number of large squares between

each QRS and will identify whether the heart is normal, bradycardic or tachycardic.

> What is the QRS axis?

> What is the P-wave axis?

> Is the P-wave morphology normal?

> Is the PR interval short or long?

> Are there any delta waves?

> Are there any Q waves?

> Is the QRS morphology normal? Are there any signs of right bundle branch block (RBBB) or left bundle branch block (LBBB)?

> Does the ST segment look normal in every lead?

> Are any T waves inverted?

> What is the QT interval?

> Are there any additional features such as U waves?

QRS axis

To establish the QRS axis you need to do the following:

> Identify the limb lead where the QRS is isoelectric: the axis will be 90° from this.

> Look at the limb lead whose axis is at 90° to the lead where the QRS is isoelectric (Fig 94) – if deflection is positive, the axis is directed towards the positive pole of that lead (and if negative, away from it).

The normal axis is from >−30° to <90°. Fig 95 demonstrates examples of the normal axis and right- and left-axis deviation.

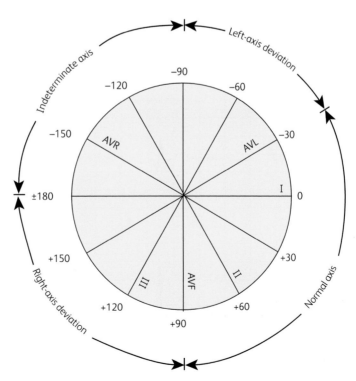

Fig 94 Diagram representing the viewpoint of each limb lead.

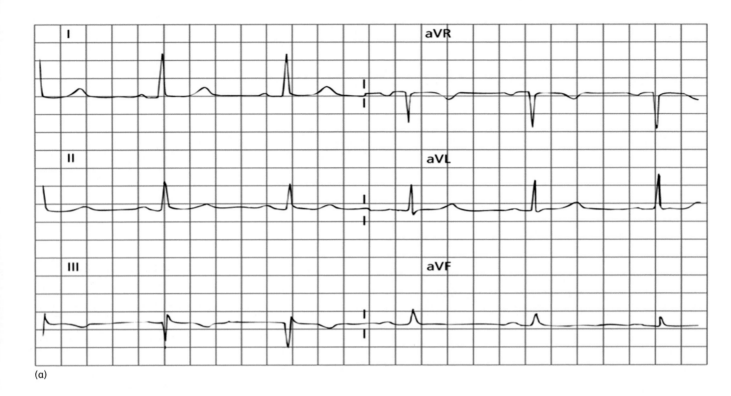

(a)

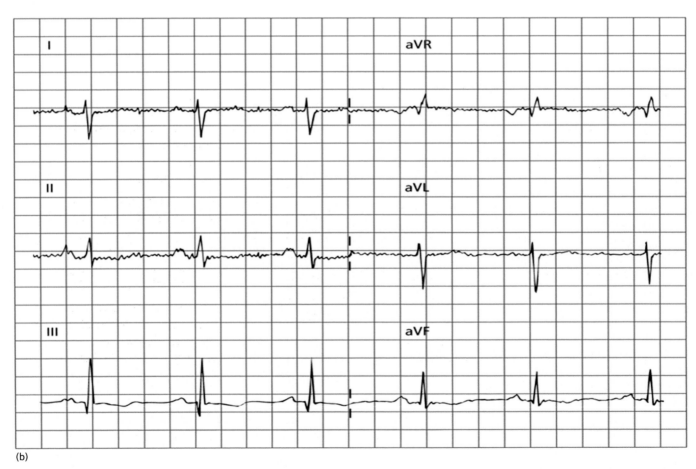

(b)

Fig 95 Examples of **(a)** normal axis and **(b)** right-axis deviation.

Medical Masterclass Third edition

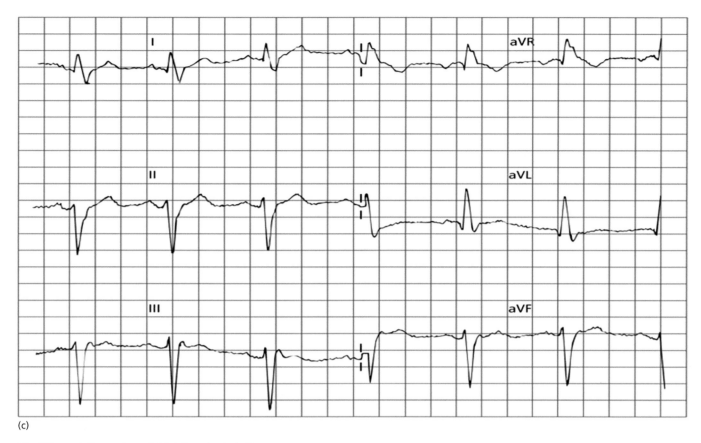

(c)

Fig 95 cont Examples of **(c)** left-axis deviation.

Normal intervals

1 small square = 0.04 seconds.

> PR interval (onset of P wave to first deflection of QRS) = 0.12–<0.20 seconds

> QRS duration (<0.12 seconds)

> QT interval (onset of QRS complex to end of T wave) = 0.35–<0.45 seconds

> QTc = QT adjusted for rate = $(QT/\sqrt{[R\text{–}R}$ interval$])$ = 0.38–<0.42 seconds.

Bradyarrhythmias / conduction disturbances

The key to identification of bradyarrhythmias is in establishing the relative relationship of the P wave and QRS complex. The following are the key features to identify:

> rate

> identify whether there are irregular/regular P waves / QRS complexes

> plot all P waves and all QRS complexes

> no P wave before normal QRS suggests junctional rhythm

> no P wave before wide QRS suggests ventricular escape rhythm.

Figs 96–101 illustrate varying degrees of AV block.

Conduction abnormalities occur because of abnormalities of the normal depolarisation from the AV node to the His bundle and bundle branches.

> Abnormalities in AV node / His bundle conduction lead to degrees of heart block, eg coronary artery disease, myocarditis, digoxin toxicity and electrolyte abnormalities.

> Abnormalities in conduction in the bundle branches lead to widened QRS complexes. Block of both bundles has

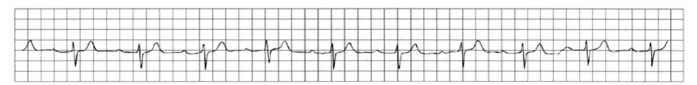

Fig 96 Example of first-degree heart block. The PR interval is in excess of 0.20 seconds.

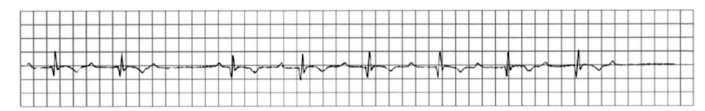

Fig 97 Second-degree heart block (Wenckebach's or Mobitz, type I) with progressively increasing PR interval prior to the failure of conduction with no QRS complex.

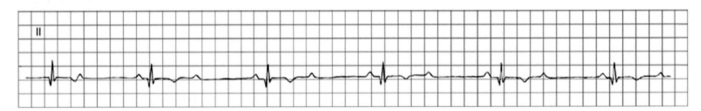

Fig 98 Second-degree heart block (2:1): only alternate P waves are followed by a QRS complex. When there is failure of conduction without progressive increase in the PR interval, this is known as Mobitz, type II.

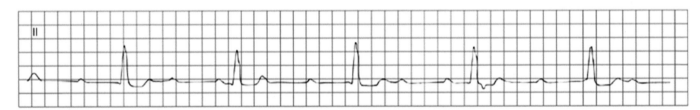

Fig 99 Complete heart block: P waves and QRS complexes are not related. There is a slow ventricular escape rhythm (wider QRS complexes).

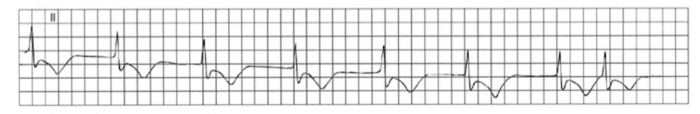

Fig 100 Junctional bradycardia: slow ventricular rate with no discernible P waves.

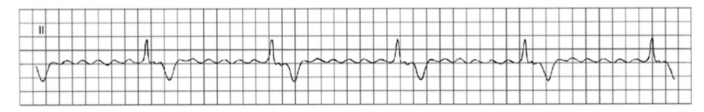

Fig 101 Complete heart block in a patient with atrial fibrillation as the underlying atrial rhythm.

Medical Masterclass Third edition

Table 41	Some key causes of bundle branch block
RBBB	**LBBB**
May be normal Coronary artery disease Cardiomyopathy Atrial septal defect Ebstein's anomaly Massive pulmonary embolism	Coronary artery disease Cardiomyopathy Left ventricular hypertrophy (hypertension and aortic stenosis) Conduction system fibrosis

LBBB: wide (>0.12 seconds) notched, M- or plateau-shaped QRS complex in leads orientated to the left ventricle, ie V5, V6, AVL and I. RBBB: M-shaped QRS complex in leads orientated to the right ventricle, ie V1 and V2.
LBBB, left bundle branch block; RBBB, right bundle branch block.

the same effect as block of the His bundle, causing complete heart block (Table 41).

Tachyarrhythmias

Find out whether there are any of the following:

> Narrow/broad complex?

> Identify whether there are irregular/regular P waves / QRS complexes.

> 'Saw-tooth' appearance of the baseline suggests atrial flutter (ventricular rate may be irregular if there is a variable block).

> Regular narrow complex tachycardia with no P waves seen suggests

AV nodal re-entry tachycardia (see Section 2.2.2).

> Consider differential diagnosis of supraventricular tachycardia (SVT) with aberration (Fig 102) (Table 42).

Specific morphological changes in the ECG

Left ventricular hypertrophy
There are several criteria:

> usually left-axis deviation (>−30°)

> amplitude of V1 or V2 + V5 or V6 >40 mm

> note that in young men with a thin chest wall, these criteria may be met without left ventricular hypertrophy.

Right ventricular hypertrophy
Criteria are the following:

> right-axis deviation (>90°)

> R V1 + S V6 >11 mm

> R V1 or S V6 >7 mm.

Table 42	Differentiating VT and SVT	
Features supporting VT		**Features supporting SVT**
Very broad QRS complexes (>140 ms) Fusion beats Capture beats AV dissociation Significant axis deviation (right or left) Concordance of the QRS deflexions in V16 Onset following R on T		Termination with Valsalva manoeuvre / adenosine Association of 'P' waves and QRS complexes Onset following premature atrial beat

AV, atrioventricular; SVT, supraventricular tachycardia; VT, ventricular tachycardia.

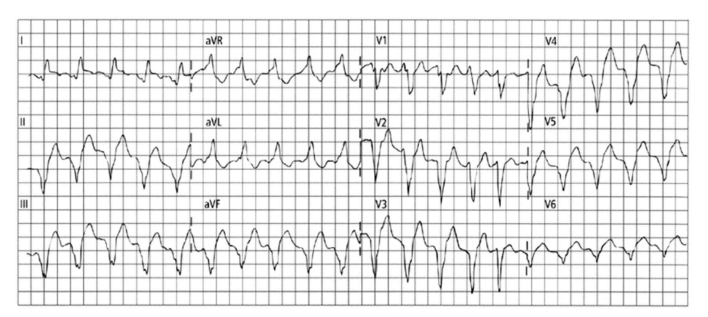

Fig 102 Twelve-lead ECG of ventricular tachycardia (VT) with significant axis deviation, broad complexes and concordance across the chest leads.

Metabolic abnormalities

> hypercalcaemia: short QT and prominent U wave

> hypocalcaemia: long QT

> hyperkalaemia: flat/lost P waves, increased PR interval, wide QRS, tented T wave and arrhythmias

> hypokalaemia: first-degree heart block, ST depression and U waves.

3.1.1 Exercise ECGs

Exercise ECGs can be extremely useful non-invasive investigation in appropriate clinical circumstances, but it is always important to remember that they can produce both false negatives and false positives. They are used less commonly for the diagnosis of coronary artery disease as stress imaging is often more accurate and provides more clinically relevant information. Exercise testing in asymptomatic patients is of limited value.

Principle

The aim of the study is to document the electrophysiological and haemodynamic response to physical stress.

Indications

Exercise ECGs are indicated for the following:

> establishing a diagnosis of angina in a patient with chest pain

> obtaining a measure of exercise tolerance

> evaluating a haemodynamic response to exercise

> evaluation of exercise-induced arrhythmias.

Contraindications

There is a very low mortality if the test is used in appropriate patients: <1:20,000. The following are contraindications:

> significant aortic stenosis

> acute pericarditis/myocarditis

> acute myocardial infarction(MI) / unstable angina

> acute aortic dissection

> systemic infection

> physical impairment that restricts patient from exercising.

Practical details

Before investigation

Omit antianginal medication if the test is for diagnostic reasons. Continue if a functional assessment on treatment is required. Note that beta-blockers and antihypertensives will mask the haemodynamic response.

The investigation

Close observation of the patient is required with full resuscitation facilities to hand. At least two qualified people should supervise the test.

After investigation

Continue to observe the patient closely. Dramatic haemodynamic changes can occur during the recovery period. Terminate the investigation only when all the parameters have returned to their normal level.

Results

Response to exercise

Normal ECG response to exercise:

> Ventricular rate increases.

> P wave increases in amplitude.

> PR shortens.

> QRS: R-wave amplitude decreases.

> ST is sharply up-sloping.

> QT shortens.

> T wave decreases in amplitude.

Abnormal ECG response to exercise (Fig 103):

> No increase in ventricular rate.

> ST depression >1 mm (horizontal/down-sloping): myocardial ischaemia (the greater the degree and the longer it persists into recovery, the greater the probability of coronary heart disease).

> ST elevation (horizontal/up-sloping): where previous MI suggests dyskinetic ventricle / aneurysm.

> QRS: bundle branch block may suggest ischaemia.

> QT: prolongation of QTc (QT adjusted for rate) may be a risk marker for *torsade de pointes*.

> T wave: inversion suggests ischaemia.

> Arrhythmias: ventricular arrhythmia suggests ischaemia.

3.2 Basic electrophysiology studies

Principle

Pace/sense electrodes are placed transvenously via the femoral vein and/or subclavian/internal jugular vein to various intracardiac locations. Electrograms are recorded during sinus rhythm. Arrhythmias are induced using pacing protocols with programmed extra stimuli.

Indications

Electrophysiology studies (EPS) may be helpful in the following circumstances:

> narrow complex tachyarrhythmias: assessing for radiofrequency (RF) ablation

> broad complex arrhythmias: assessing for RF ablation or implantation of an implantable cardioverter defibrillator

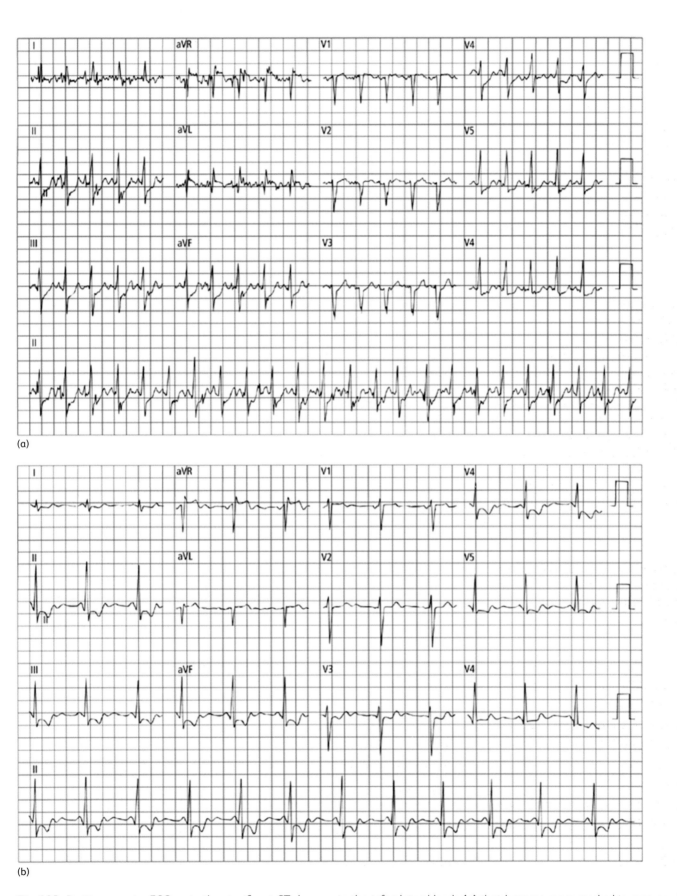

(a)

(b)

Fig 103 Positive exercise ECG: note the significant ST changes in the inferolateral leads **(a)** that become more marked in recovery **(b)**.

- establishing a diagnosis in patients with palpitations/syncope

- assessing bradyarrhythmias (although it is of limited value for this).

Contraindications

Electrophysiology studies are not indicated for patients with the following:

- reversible aetiology for arrhythmia

- severe electrolyte abnormality.

Practical details

Before investigation

Antiarrhythmic medication is usually stopped 48 hours before study.

The investigation

Intravenous sedative (often benzodiazepine) may be used before the procedure because some pacing protocols produce extremely rapid heart rates. Quadrapolar electrodes are placed to obtain intracardiac electrograms (high right atrium, right ventricular apex / outflow tract and His–Purkinje system) (Fig 104). A multipolar electrode placed in the coronary sinus records electrograms from the left atrium and ventricle. Arrhythmias are induced by delivering extra pacing beats after a train of paced beats in the atrium and ventricle. These extra stimuli are timed to occur during the refractory period in an attempt to establish a possible re-entry mechanism (Fig 105). The timing of the individual electrograms will indicate whether there is a possible electrophysiological substrate for arrhythmias. Assessment of the function of the sinoatrial and atrioventricular nodes indicates whether permanent pacing might be required.

After investigation

Patients are observed for a few hours. This investigation is usually performed as a day-case procedure. Drug therapy may be changed as a result of the EPS.

Complications

- femoral vein/subclavian vein (haematoma)

- incessant arrhythmias requiring cardioversion, eg atrial fibrillation.

3.3 Ambulatory monitoring

Principle

Documenting a single-/dual-channel electrocardiogram over 24 hours can provide useful information in the investigation of patients with palpitations, arrhythmias and syncope. It is non-invasive and, with current analysis hardware/software, tapes can be analysed rapidly and accurately. Some devices record the ECG data on a digital card, enabling up to 10 days' continuous monitoring. It is always important when using Holter monitoring to appreciate that this provides only a brief snapshot of the patient's heart rhythm, and that a negative result does not mean that the patient's symptoms are not secondary to an arrhythmia.

Indications

Ambulatory monitoring is indicated for the following:

- evaluation of patients with palpitations and syncope

- monitoring the efficacy of antiarrhythmic therapy

- evaluation of heart rate variability.

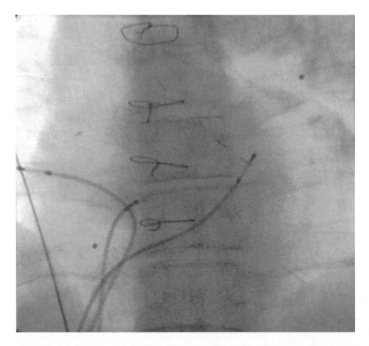

Fig 104 Radiograph demonstrating electrodes placed in the high right atrium, right ventricular outflow tract and His bundle during an electrophysiological test. Sternal wires are present from previous coronary bypass grafting.

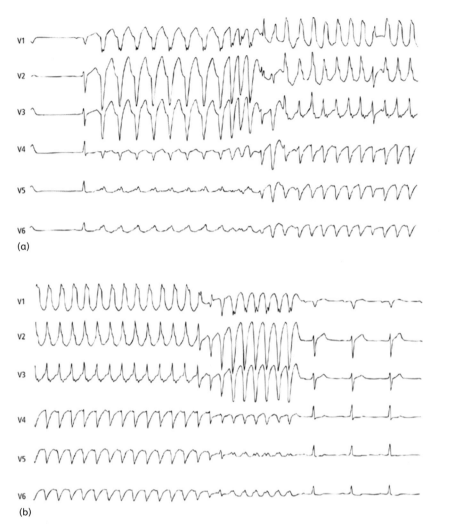

Practical details

There are a number of different methods by which heart rate and rhythm can be observed.

Twenty-four hour Holter monitoring

This is used for patients with frequent symptoms. Even some patients who have infrequent symptoms may have asymptomatic arrhythmic episodes on a 24-hour recording that may provide valuable information (Fig 106).

Patient-activated devices

These are used for less frequent symptoms, eg cardiomemo recorder. However, the efficacy of these devices relies on the patient activating the device, which is not always possible during or shortly after a symptomatic episode.

Implantable loop recorders

These are used for infrequent symptoms. They enable the patient to activate the device up to 40 minutes after the event and still record the heart rhythm (Figs 107 and 108).

Fig 105 Induction of ventricular tachycardia (VT). **(a)** Note the train of paced beats followed by earlier extra stimuli and then the onset of monomorphic (VT). **(b)** VT is then terminated with nine beats of overdrive pacing.

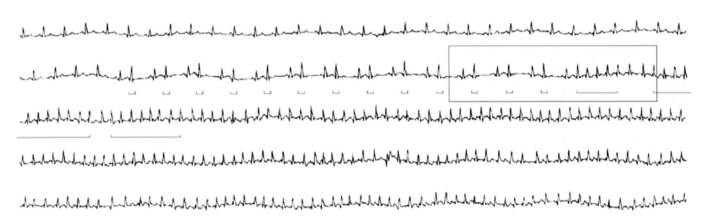

Fig 106 Holter monitor recording demonstrating atrioventricular nodal re-entry tachycardia (AVNRT) / atrioventricular re-entry tachycardia (AVRT). Note the sudden onset after a short period of ventricular bigeminy.

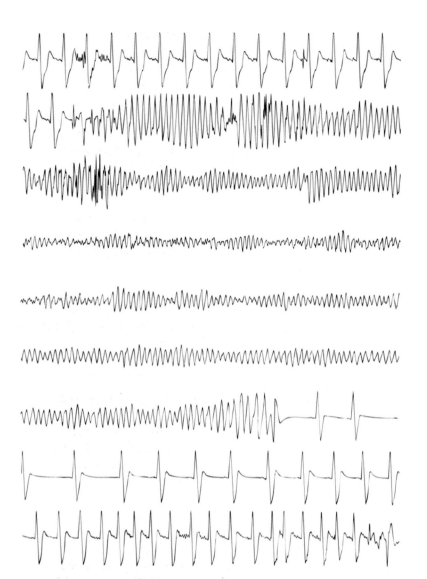

Fig 107 Loop recording showing sinus tachycardia followed by *torsade de pointes* with spontaneous resolution.

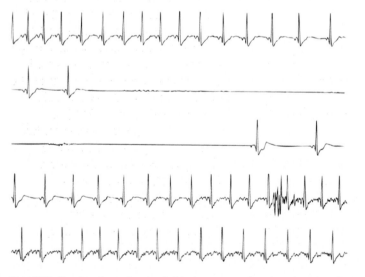

Fig 108 Tracing from implantable loop recorder showing significant pause.

3.4 Radiofrequency ablation and implantable cardioverter defibrillators

3.4.1 Radiofrequency ablation

Principle

The basic idea is to place an electrode in a specific site in the heart and then deliver energy through the electrode to produce a discrete scar. As the scar is electrically inactive, the pathways necessary for tachyarrhythmias may be disrupted. Most tachyarrhythmias can be treated with radiofrequency (RF) ablation:

> atrioventricular (AV) nodal re-entry tachycardia

> Wolff–Parkinson–White syndrome

> concealed accessory pathways (AV re-entry tachycardia)

> ventricular tachycardia (VT)

> focal atrial tachycardias

> atrial fibrillation (AF; AF ablation for paroxysmal/persistent AF or fast rates abolished by ablation of AV node and pacemaker implant for permanent AF)

> Most can be accessed via the right side of the heart from the femoral/subclavian veins; others (left-sided pathways / left-sided VT) have to be approached from either the femoral artery / aorta or via an atrial trans-septal approach.

Indications

Indications include those who have recurrent tachyarrhythmias despite antiarrhythmic therapy. Some patients (eg those with Wolff–Parkinson–White syndrome) who are at high risk should consider RF ablation even if asymptomatic.

Practical details

Before procedure

Antiarrhythmic drug therapy is usually stopped a few days before the procedure as it is usually necessary to induce the arrhythmia prior to delivering RF energy. Be careful: informed consent must be given by the patient before the procedure can go ahead.

The procedure

The treatment is usually performed under sedation.

After procedure

Most patients are discharged on the same day as the procedure or the following day.

Complications

The major complication of RF ablation procedures is the risk of unintentional damage to the AV node and the need for a permanent pacemaker. This occurs in <1% of cases. A rare complication is cardiac perforation which may require pericardiocentesis or surgical repair.

Prognosis

> RF ablation is usually permanent.

> <10% recurrence of the arrhythmia.

3.4.2 Implantable cardioverter defibrillator

Principle

Patients who are at high risk of ventricular arrhythmias may benefit from implantable cardioverter defibrillators (ICDs). Once a ventricular arrhythmia is detected, an ICD can either deliver antitachycardia pacing or shock therapy (electrodes in the right ventricle, superior vena cava and/or casing of the ICD), or a combination of both depending on how the device is programmed.

Indications

In general, indications are becoming broader as larger prospective randomised trials are reported (eg AVID, MADIT, MUSTT, MADIT II and SCDHeFT):

> previous spontaneous ventricular tachycardia (VT) / ventricular fibrillation (VF)

> syncope of undetermined aetiology with VT inducible during electrophysiology studies (EPS) (see Section 3.2)

> severely impaired left ventricular function (ejection fraction <30%).

Contraindications

> reversible cause for VT/VF

> incessant VT/VF

> surgical, medical or psychiatric contraindication.

Practical details

Before procedure

Patients are thoroughly investigated to exclude any reversible cause of arrhythmia (undergoing echocardiography, cardiac catheterisation and CT/MRI). Some will have an EPS to confirm the diagnosis and identify whether the arrhythmia can be pace terminated (see Section 3.2).

The procedure

ICDs are implanted using local anaesthetic and sedation (eg midazolam), or general anaesthesia. The leads are placed transvenously via the subclavian/cephalic veins. The device is implanted either under the pectoralis major muscle or subcutaneously on the left side of the chest wall (Fig 109). In some circumstances VF is produced to ensure that the device can successfully terminate it with shock therapy.

After procedure

On the same or following day the device is checked to ensure correct function of the pacing systems.

Complications

Complications are similar to those associated with pacemaker implantation (see Section 3.5).

Prognosis

Most patients with ICDs die as a result of cardiac pump failure or incessant ventricular arrhythmia. ICDs last between 5 and 10 years, depending on the number of shocks delivered.

3.4.3 Cardiac resynchronisation therapy

Some symptomatic patients who have impaired left ventricular (LV) function (ejection fraction <30%) and left bundle branch block on their ECG will benefit from having an additional pacing lead placed on the epicardial surface of the LV. This is placed through the cardiac veins which are accessed through the coronary sinus via the right atrium. This allows the implantable cardioverter defibrillator (ICD) or pacemaker to synchronise contraction of both the right and left ventricles leading to improved haemodynamic function. This has been shown to improve both symptoms and mortality in selected patients. Cardiac resynchronisation therapy

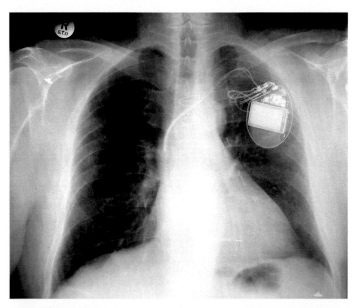

(a)

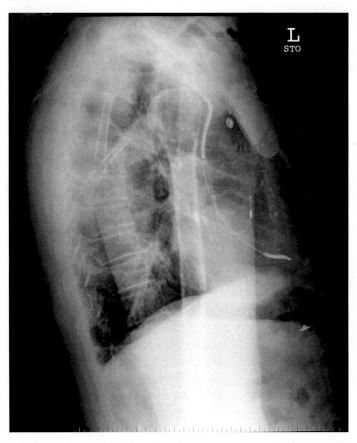

(b)

Fig 109 Chest radiograph of patient with dual-chamber implantable cardioverter defibrillator (pulmonary artery and lateral). Note electrode in right ventricle with defibrillation coil at distal end. A pace/sense electrode is positioned in the right atrial appendage.

(CRT) can be incorporated into ICDs (CRT defibrillator, CRT-D) or stand-alone pacemakers (CRT-P) (Fig 110).

3.5 Pacemakers

Pacing of patients with non-reversible significant bradyarrhythmias can restore life expectancy to close to that of the normal population. Pacemakers have improved considerably over the last two decades. Devices have increased in longevity and reduced in size. In addition, many technical innovations have resulted in pacemakers that are more physiological in their mode of action. NICE has published guidelines (in 2014) regarding the treatment options for patients with heart failure who have left ventricular ejection fraction (LVEF) <35% (Table 43). The simplest of pacemakers consists of a single lead, with its tip in the right ventricular (RV) apex connected to the pulse generator in the subcutaneous tissue of the chest wall. Dual-chamber devices have a further lead with its tip positioned in the right atrial appendage (Fig 111). Pacemakers have a designated terminology which describes the pacing and sensing functions of each device (Table 44).

Indications

Temporary pacemaker

Temporary pacing is useful in the following circumstances:

> as an interim measure before fitting a permanent pacemaker

> inferior myocardial infarction (MI): second-/third-degree block and hypotension/heart failure

> anterior MI: second-/third-degree block (usually large infarct to involve the atrioventricular (AV) node)

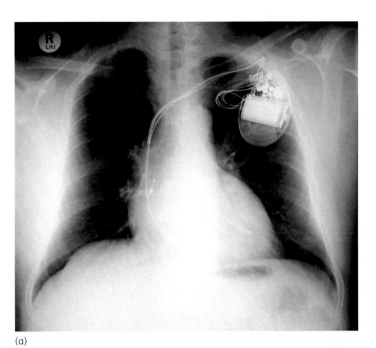

(a)

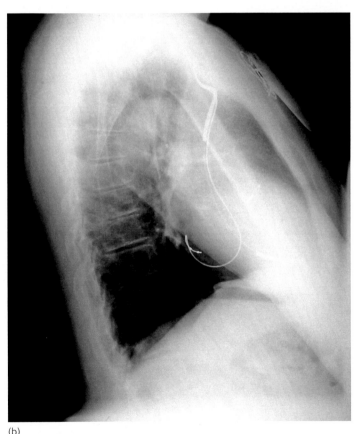

(b)

Fig 110 Posteroanterior (PA) and lateral chest radiograph of patient with CRT-D device. Note the additional lead positioned over the left ventricle.

> symptomatic/asymptomatic patients with trifascicular block undergoing general anaesthesia (should be assessed for a permanent pacemaker)

> drug overdose, eg digoxin, beta-blockers or verapamil.

Temporary pacing is not indicated for asymptomatic patients with bifascicular block who are undergoing general anaesthesia.

Permanent pacemaker
The permanent pacemaker is useful for the following:

> third-degree heart block

> symptomatic, second-degree block

> asymptomatic, type II second-degree block

> atrial fibrillation with pauses >3.0 seconds

> symptomatic documented sinus node dysfunction

> recurrent syncope associated with >3.0 seconds pause with carotid sinus stimulation.

Practical details

Before procedure
Patients should give informed consent and be fasted.

The procedure
The procedure is usually performed under local anaesthesia. The pacemaker leads are placed transvenously via the cephalic/subclavian routes into the RV apex and right atrial appendage under fluoroscopic guidance. The leads are checked to ensure correct pace/sense functions and the pulse generator is implanted subcutaneously.

Table 43 NICE guidelines (2014) regarding treatment options for patients with heart failure who have LVEF<35%

	NYHA class			
QRS interval	I	II	III	IV
<120 milliseconds	ICD if high risk of sudden death			ICD and CRT not indicated
120–149 milliseconds without LBBB	ICD	ICD	ICD	CRT-P
120–149 milliseconds with LBBB	ICD	CRT-D	CRT-P or CRT-D	CRT-P
>150 milliseconds with or without LBBB	CRT-D	CRT-D	CRT-P or CRT-D	CRT-P

CRT-D (P), cardiac resynchronisation therapy defibrillator (pacemaker); ICD, implantable cardioverter defibrillator; LBBB, left bundle branch block; LVEF, left ventricular ejection fraction; NYHA, New York Heart Association.

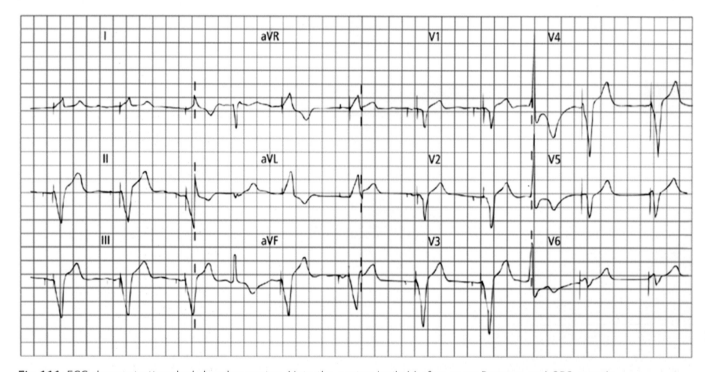

Fig 111 ECG demonstrating dual-chamber pacing. Note the pacing 'spike' before most P waves and QRS complexes.

Table 44 Algorithm used to describe pacemaker function[1]

Paced chamber	Sensed chamber	Effect of sensing	Programming / rate responsiveness
0 = none A = atrium V = ventricle D = dual (A and V)	0 = none A = atrium V = ventricle D = dual (A and V)	0 = none T = triggered I = inhibited D = dual (T and I)	0 = none P = simple M = multiprogrammable C = communicating R = rate responsive

1 For example, a DDDR pacemaker both senses and paces in the atrium and ventricle, and triggers and inhibits, depending on what is or is not sensed. It also has a rate response which means that the heart rate will be paced faster if appropriate, eg during exercise.

After procedure

After a satisfactory pacemaker check the following day, most patients may be discharged from hospital, usually with 5 days of antibiotic therapy and after a lateral and posteroanterior chest radiograph (Fig 112). For driving regulations, see Section 2.19. Pacemakers can be programmed and interrogated by placing a 'wand' over the device; using electromagnetic induction, information can be received or transmitted to the pacemaker. Patients are usually seen every 6–12 months to monitor the pacemaker and re-program it if necessary. The expected life of the battery is 8–12 years.

Complications of pacemakers

Although complications are rare, the following may occur.

Common

> pneumothorax

> pacemaker lead displacement (Fig 113)

> haematoma.

Uncommon

> local infection

> pericardial effusion

> thrombosis and thromboembolism

> infective endocarditis

> pacemaker syndrome: single-chamber pacing, leading to symptoms as a result of loss of AV synchrony.

Rare

> Twiddler's syndrome: patient consciously/subconsciously turns the pacemaker generator, leading to retraction and eventual displacement of the pacing lead.

> Component failure: lead/pulse generator.

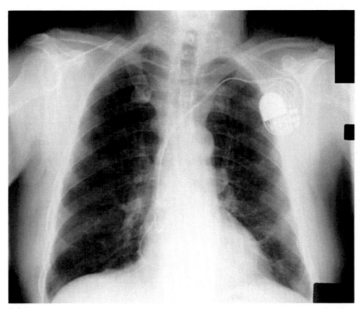

(a)

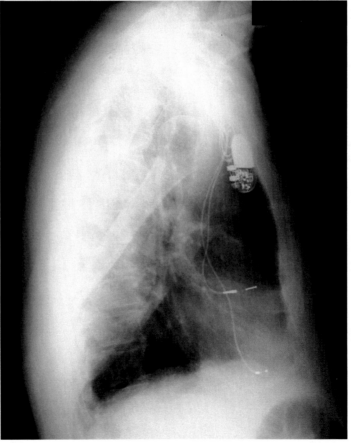

(b)

Fig 112 Chest radiograph of dual-chamber pacemaker: **(a)** posteroanterior (PA) and **(b)** lateral.

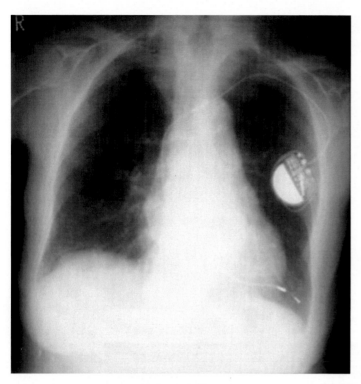

Fig 113 Chest radiograph showing displacement of ventricular lead through ventricle to pericardial space.

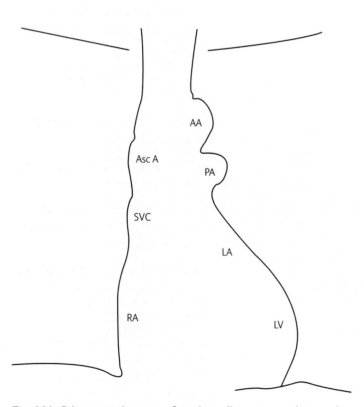

Fig 114 Schematic diagram of cardiac silhouette on chest radiograph. AA, arch aorta; Asc A, ascending aorta; LA, left atrial appendage; LV, left ventricle; PA, pulmonary artery; RA, right atrium; SVC, superior vena cava.

3.6 Chest radiograph in cardiac disease

Abnormalities of cardiac silhouette

The normal cardiac silhouette is shown in Fig 114. Below are the most commonly encountered abnormalities.

Cardiomegaly

Cardiothoracic ratio >0.5 on posteroanterior projection is a fairly specific indicator of cardiac disease, but may be falsely increased in pectus excavatum and very thin patients. The same indication cannot be assumed for anteroposterior projections of the heart. Echocardiography is much more sensitive and enables the direct measurement of ventricular wall thickness, cavity dimensions as well as function.

Aortic enlargement

This is seen in hypertension, aortic aneurysms or aortic regurgitation:

> prominent aortic arch

> ascending aorta protrudes further to the right side

> tortuous descending aorta.

Mediastinal widening

This may indicate an aortic aneurysm and/or aortic dissection.

Enlarged pulmonary artery

This is seen in the following conditions:

> pulmonary hypertension: chronic obstructive pulmonary disease, primary pulmonary hypertension and Eisenmenger's syndrome

> pulmonary stenosis: post stenotic dilatation as a result of turbulent blood flow

> collagen disorders such as Marfan syndrome.

Left atrial enlargement

This is seen in mitral valve (MV) disease (both stenosis and regurgitation), left ventricular (LV) impairment and MV replacement. The left atrium and its appendage are situated in a small concavity immediately below the left main bronchus on the left heart border. Loss of this concavity or a protrusion beyond the normal left heart border is indicative of left atrial enlargement. There is also associated elevation of the left main bronchus increasing the normal carinal angle of 75°. In massive enlargement, the left atrium forms part of the right heart border, giving rise to a double border right heart shadow. Left atrial enlargement may be mimicked by mediastinal or pleural neoplasm.

Left ventricular enlargement
This is often associated with:

> pressure overload – apex elevated and more rounded in shape

> volume overload – widening of the cardiac shadow.

Right ventricular enlargement
The right ventricle does not normally form a cardiac border, but enlargement pushes the LV posteriorly and to the left, causing widening of the heart shadow.

Pericardial effusion
This may produce massive cardiomegaly, giving the cardiac contour a globular appearance, with clear lung fields (Fig 115).

Abnormalities of pulmonary vasculature

Increased pulmonary blood flow

> enlarged pulmonary arteries

> recruitment of upper lobe vessels.

Pulmonary hypertension

> peripheral vasoconstriction (pruning)

> further enlargement of pulmonary arteries

> pulmonary artery calcification.

Pulmonary venous hypertension and pulmonary oedema
In increasing order of severity:

> upper lobe blood diversion

> interlobular septal thickening (Kerley B lines) – thin horizontal lines at lung bases

> alveolar oedema, typically involving the inner two-thirds of the lung ('bat wing' hilar shadowing)

> pleural effusions.

Pulmonary oedema is occasionally unilateral. After treatment, the radiographic appearances often lag behind clinical improvement. Prominent interstitial lines also occur in the following:

> fibrosis

> tumour infiltration

> interstitial pneumonia.

3.7 Cardiac biochemical markers

Principle
Heart muscle damage, usually caused by acute ischaemia, causes release of proteins that can be detected in the bloodstream. Even though cardiac ischaemia/necrosis is the most common cause, there are many other causes of cardiac marker elevation (see below).

Creatine kinase

> Measurement of the cytosolic enzyme creatine kinase (CK) (or more often the cardiospecific myocardial-bound isoenzyme, CK-MB) has been superseded by cardiac troponin for the diagnosis of acute coronary syndrome (ACS).

> Peak value reflects extent of heart muscle damage.

> Has a reasonable specificity, but only a moderate sensitivity.

> Rises 4–6 hours post-myocardial infarction (MI) with peak at around 21–24 hours.

> Used in conjunction with the ECG to make the diagnosis of non-ST elevation myocardial infarction (NSTEMI).

> May give equivocal results and may be uninterpretable in some circumstances, eg very high CK caused by coexisting skeletal muscle damage (Note: CK-MB is also found to a small extent in skeletal muscle).

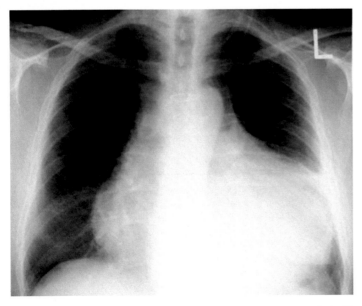

Fig 115 Globular cardiomegaly caused by a large pericardial effusion. Note sternal wires from recent cardiac surgery.

Troponin tests

These tests have now superseded CK-MB assays. Troponins are regulatory elements of the contractile apparatus in muscles; they exist in cardiac-specific isoforms and are highly sensitive. Rapid bedside assays for cardiac troponins T and I are available. They are normally very low/undetectable in the blood and appear 3–4 hours after myocardial damage, peak at 24 hours and persist for up to 14 days. Since they are cardiac specific, skeletal muscle damage does not influence their level. In addition, they are sensitive to the cardiac damage missed by CK.

> Troponins are very useful in differentiating NSTEMI from unstable angina. In patients presenting with ACS, a positive test (ie NSTEMI) is associated with a higher risk of death or MI – the higher level indicating a worse prognosis.

> They may be used to select high-risk patients with ACS likely to benefit from more aggressive treatment, eg low-molecular-weight heparin, glycoprotein IIb/IIIa receptor antagonists and early revascularisation.

> A negative test may be used in conjunction with clinical and ECG criteria to identify low-risk patients suitable for early (12-hour) discharge.

> Due to their long time window they can detect MI up to between 1 and 2 weeks post event.

> While an elevated troponin reflects myocardial necrosis this can occur in situations other than epicardial coronary artery occlusion.

Some non-ACS causes of troponin elevation include:

> tachy/bradyarrhythmias

> hypertensive crisis / hypotension

> myocarditis

> pulmonary embolism

> acute or chronic renal failure (decreased excretion)

> aortic dissection / aortic valve disease or hypertrophic cardiomyopathy

> cardiac contusion / ablation / pacemaker insertion / direct current (DC) cardioversion

> critical illness: sepsis

> rhabdomyolysis.

In view of the above list of non-ACS causes of troponin elevation, be aware when diagnosing MI solely on a troponin elevation. Remember that the diagnosis of MI requires the detection of cardiac marker (troponin) elevation with at least one of the following:

> symptoms consistent with cardiac ischaemia

> ECG changes

> imaging evidence of new loss of viable myocardium or new regional wall motion abnormalities

> identification of an intra-coronary thrombus.

Myoglobin

Myoglobin is present in both skeletal and cardiac muscle, and released about 30 minutes after heart muscle damage. Elevated values may detect infarction much sooner after the onset of chest pain than CK-MB or troponins (Fig 116). It has a short time window and as such can miss late presentations. As a result of the poor specificity of myoglobin measurement, a positive test must be confirmed by troponin or CK-MB.

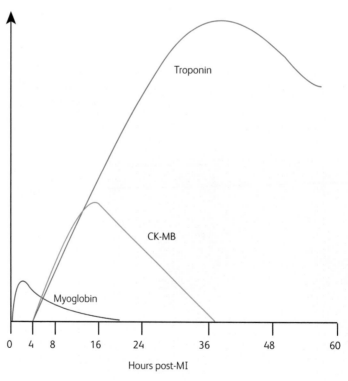

Fig 116 Time course of cardiac markers after heart muscle damage. MI, myocardial infarction.

Brain (B-type) natriuretic peptide

This is a peptide hormone produced by the myocardium (ventricular>atrial) in response to myocardial wall stress. Peripheral blood levels are elevated in patients with left ventricular dysfunction and relate to the severity of heart failure and prognosis. In terms of diagnosis it is most valuable as a 'rule out test' for heart failure where a normal value (in conjunction with ECG and chest X-ray) virtually excludes the presence of left ventricular dysfunction. Levels can be affected by other conditions including myocardial ischaemia (and infarction), severe airways disease and renal impairment.

3.8 Computerised tomography and magnetic resonance imaging

3.8.1 Multi-slice spiral computerised tomography

Principle

In recent years, non-invasive coronary artery imaging has been dramatically changed with advances in computerised tomography (CT) scanning. Modern multi-slice CT scanners (MSCT) can obtain high resolution images from a moving structure such as the heart. This is managed by using a gantry of multiple thin detectors that rotate rapidly around the patient. ECG gating allows the scanner to obtain images during diastole, when cardiac movement is minimal, and reduce motion artefact.

Indications

Investigating chest pain

The overwhelming indication for a coronary CT today is non-invasive assessment of the coronary arteries (Figs 117 and 118). When investigating patients presenting with cardiac-sounding chest pain, formal invasive coronary angiography is associated with a small but serious risk. Coronary CT primarily provides a safe method to exclude significant coronary disease in patients with low risk.

CT calcium scoring is a quick (5 minutes) technique that assesses the presence of calcified plaques in the coronary arteries and gives a numerical score of plaque burden. It does not use any intravenous (IV) contrast. However calcium scoring gives no information about anatomy or distribution of the calcium. Coronary CT angiography uses IV contrast to delineate the coronary anatomy.

NICE (UK) guidelines recommend patients with a high pre-test probability of having coronary disease should undergo invasive coronary angiography and patients with an intermediate risk should undergo functional imaging (such as stress perfusion cardiac MRI see Section 3.8.2). However in patients with a low probability of coronary artery disease, CT calcium scoring and normally a CT coronary angiogram are performed. CT coronary angiography gives no functional information (ie if a stenosis is flow-limiting).

Coronary artery bypass grafts

An increasing use of CT coronary angiography is for assessing presence and patency of coronary artery bypass grafts. Patients who have received bypass grafts in the past often present challenging cases for invasive

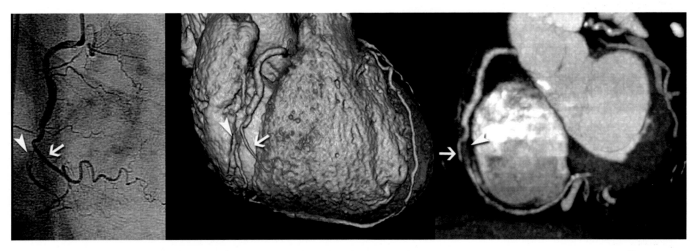

Fig 117 Comparison between angiography (left) and MSCT images of the right coronary artery (expressed in two different processed image modalities, centre and right). (Adapted from Mollet NR, Cademartiri F and de Feyter PJ. Non-invasive multislice CT coronary imaging. *Heart* 2005;91:401–7.)

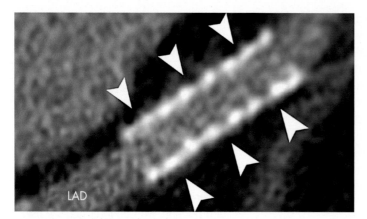

Fig 118 Cross sectional MSCT image of a patent coronary stent. (Adapted from Mollet NR, Cademartiri F and de Feyter PJ. Non-invasive multislice CT coronary imaging. *Heart* 2005;91:401–7.)

angiography, particularly if the details of the grafts used are not known. This can result in a high volume of contrast and a longer procedure. CT enables the operator to know how many grafts are present, where they are and whether they are blocked.

Coronary anatomy

Cardiac MRI is the technique of choice for most intrinsic cardiac anatomy, but CT is useful for pericardial investigation (such as thickening) and anomalous coronary arteries.

Limitations

> Heart rate greater than 70 beats per minute – beta-blockers are often required to achieve this, so patients who are unable to take them may not be suitable.

> Atrial fibrillation or frequent ectopics.

> Severe calcification, the presence of existing coronary stents or metal structures such as valve rings or pacing leads can create sufficient artefact to obscure the coronary anatomy.

> Patients must be able to hold their breath for about 5–10 seconds.

> Small (often distal) coronary arteries cannot be accurately imaged.

Other indications

> Pulmonary disease: CT pulmonary angiography can image the pulmonary vasculature down to the level of the segmental branches. It is the method of choice for investigating thromboembolic disease of the pulmonary arteries.

> Thoraco-abdominal vessels: to detect aortic aneurysm and/or dissection, and renal and carotid stenosis.

3.8.2 Magnetic resonance imaging

Principle

Atomic nuclei with unpaired (an odd number) numbers of protons, neutrons or both have a net charge and therefore a magnetic moment. This magnetic property is exploited in magnetic

resonance imaging (MRI). Hydrogen atoms are a major constituent of the body with a magnetic moment, and are the nuclei imaged by cardiac MRI.

The principle of MRI is simple. A large superconducting magnet produces a very strong external magnetic field (for example, 1.5 tesla equating to a magnetic field 1,500 times stronger than the Earth's magnetic field). Electromagnetic energy is transmitted from coil to nuclei in the body exciting them to a higher energy state. As nuclei return to equilibrium the excess energy is released in the form of electromagnetic waves. This energy is detected by the scanner. As different tissues return to equilibrium at different rates complex mathematical techniques (Fourier transformation) can be used so that the structure made up by the tissues can be reconstructed.

Cardiac MRI (CMR) has revolutionised imaging of the heart as it provides not only anatomical imaging but functional information as well. As for cardiac CT scanning, images are ECG-gated (only acquired during diastole when the heart is relatively still). Irregular rhythms and tachycardia result in a poorer image quality. However, CMR uses no ionising radiation.

Indications

Myocardial disease and viability

CMR allows characterisation of a wide range of myocardial disease such as myocarditis and cardiomyopathies. Using the IV contrast medium gadolinium, fibrosis can be identified in the myocardium. Analysis of the pattern can provide information about whether this is scarring caused by a myocardial infarction or an inflammatory process such as myocarditis, amyloidosis or sarcoidosis.

CMR allows accurate calculation of left ventricular function and size. Regional wall motion abnormalities can be detected. The location and extent of a myocardial infarction can be established and CMR can also be used to assess for viability. Stress perfusion CMR utilises vasoactive agents administered via a peripheral IV cannula, most commonly dobutamine or adenosine. These produce pharmacological stress on the heart, inducing hyperaemia and increasing coronary flow. This is a surrogate for physiological stress and during this period, function of the ventricle can be examined.

Stress perfusion CMR can be used to investigate new patients presenting with cardiac-sounding chest pain and an intermediate risk profile, or patients who have already suffered a myocardial infarction. CMR can then ascertain whether myocardium is irreversibly damaged or whether it is viable. Depending on the amount of myocardium that is salvageable, coronary intervention can be considered. This is of immense use both before and after a diagnosis of ischaemic heart disease is made.

Structural heart disease
CMR is the investigation of choice for diagnosing structural heart disease such as hypertrophic cardiomyopathy, left ventricular non-compaction, arrhythmogenic right ventricular cardiomyopathy etc. It is of use in most congenital disorders and can be used as both a diagnostic and surveillance tool.

Valve assessment
Echocardiography is generally preferred for routine valve assessment, but CMR can be useful.

Aortic disease
CMR can accurately measure dimensions and structure of aortic aneurysms, dissections, abscesses or anomalies like coarctation. It can provide not only spatial measurements but also information about flow. MRI can be used to differentiate between true and false lumina in cases of aortic dissection.

Intracardiac masses
CMR provides unparalleled characterisation of intracardiac masses such as tumours, or most commonly, left ventricular thrombi.

Limitations

> MRI is contraindicated with implanted metal devices such as joint replacements, intracranial clips and some cardiac devices. Most pacemakers/ICDs that are implanted now are 'MRI conditional' and can be used with manufacturer advice, but often adversely affect the results due to artefact anyway. The magnetic field will interfere with most devices and they will need reprogramming after the scan.

> Sternal wires and prosthetic valves (except Starr–Edwards) are safe but will cause artefact.

> Certain coronary stents stipulate a minimum duration of time post implant before they can be imaged.

> Gadolinium cannot be used in moderate to severe renal impairment.

3.9 Ventilation–perfusion imaging

Principle
A comparison of ventilation and perfusion in the lungs to detect areas of mismatch (ie ventilated but not perfused) that occur in acute pulmonary embolism (PE). Many other conditions (eg tumour or consolidation) cause perfusion defects, but these are generally matched by ventilation defects and associated with chest radiograph abnormality.

Indication
CT pulmonary angiography is now the investigation of choice for most suspected PEs. Lung ventilation / perfusion (V/Q) scanning is restricted to patients who cannot undergo a CT scan, such as those with severe renal disease or allergic to contrast, or pregnant patients.

The patient should preferably have a normal chest radiograph. Ventilation–perfusion scan reports are useful if perfusion is normal and PE is therefore excluded, or if definite unmatched defects are seen and the diagnosis is confirmed; however, many scans do not produce clear-cut results and are reported as being of intermediate probability. The diagnostic yield is improved by correlation with clinical suspicion.

Contraindications

There are none. It is safe in pregnancy, although some centres modify the dose.

Practical details

> Inhalation of radioisotope (krypton-81m, xenon-133 or technetium-99m (^{99m}Tc)): patient needs to be able to inhale sufficiently.

> Injection of ^{99m}Tc-labelled albumin macroaggregates or microspheres.

> Scanning after each; some centres only perform a ventilation scan if the perfusion is abnormal.

> Duration of about 40 minutes.

3.10 Echocardiography

Echocardiography is a fundamental part of cardiovascular assessment and is the 'workhorse' of cardiovascular imaging. Its portability, ease of use, lack of side effects and relative inexpense make it indispensable. However, it is highly operator dependent and appropriate training and experience are required for it to be a useful tool.

Principle

A piezoelectric crystal within a transducer generates ultrasonic waves in pulses that travel through tissue. Most of the sound waves are absorbed or scattered within the body but some are reflected back towards the transducer every time an ultrasound wave crosses interfaces of tissues that have different densities – typically the junctions between blood, myocardium and heart valves. Frequencies of 2–5 MHz are required for routine adult cardiac work. Several modes of imaging are recognised.

M-mode

Ultrasonic pulses are transmitted and received along a single scan-line, and the interfaces are displayed as a graph of depth against time. It is especially useful for recording moving structures, timing events within the heart and measuring cardiac dimensions (Fig 119).

Two-dimensional echocardiography

The information is displayed as a fan-shaped image. Detailed information about cardiac structures and their movement can be obtained. Standard transthoracic views include parasternal long and short axes, and two-, three- and four-chamber apical long axes views of the heart (Fig 120).

Doppler echocardiography

Velocity measurements can be derived, using the Doppler principle, from the frequency shift that occurs between transmitted and reflected ultrasound waves from moving red blood cells. Continuous and pulsed-wave Doppler recordings enable direct velocity measurements with the heart and across valves. Intracardiac and valvular pressure gradients are determined from the measured velocities (v) according to the modified Bernoulli equation: $4v^2$.

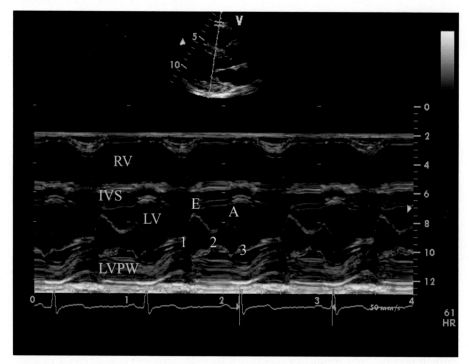

Fig 119 Parasternal long axis M-mode at the level of the mitral valve leaflets.
1, at the end of systole the mitral valve begins to open; E, maximum excursion of anterior mitral leaflet; **2**, initial diastolic closing wave; A, reopening of mitral valve caused by atrial systole; **3**, mitral valve closes at onset of ventricular systole. IVS, interventricular septum; LV, left ventricle; LVPW, left ventricular posterior wall; RV, right ventricle.

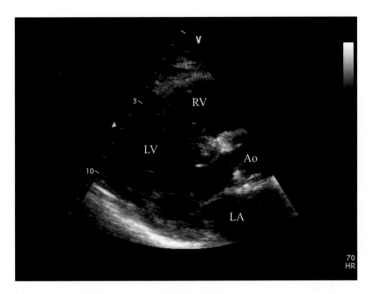

(a)

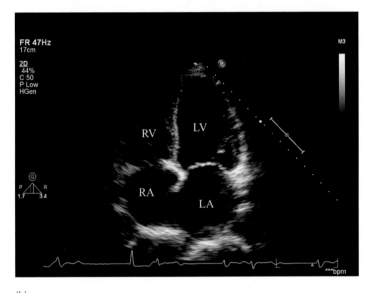

(b)

Fig 120 (a) Parasternal long axis and **(b)** apical four-chamber views of the heart. Ao, aorta; LA, left atrium; LV, left ventricle; RA, right atrium; RV, right ventricle.

An example is shown in Fig 121. Thus, in patients with depressed cardiac function and reduced myocardial blood velocity, valve gradients and therefore stenosis severity may be underestimated with this technique. In this situation, the valve area should be calculated. Colour-encoded Doppler velocity displayed on a two-dimensional image enables semi-quantitative assessment of valve regurgitation severity. Velocities directed towards the transducer are displayed in red and those away in blue.

Increasing velocities are displayed as progressively lighter shades.

Transoesophageal echocardiography
Transoesophageal echocardiography (TOE) consists of a transducer incorporated at the tip of a gastroscope-like instrument. Because of the proximity of the oesophagus to the heart, TOE is especially useful in assessing the interatrial septum, left atrial appendage (usually before DC cardioversion to exclude clot), mitral

valve and aortic pathology. It should also be considered when poor transthoracic views are obtained and for prosthetic valve evaluation. TOE is used during cardiac surgical procedures to assess the functional consequences of valve repair; and also during certain interventional cardiology procedures (eg atrial septal defect closure, transcatheter aortic valve implantation) to guide device delivery.

Stress echocardiography
This technique is comparable to myocardial perfusion imaging and MRI in terms of detection of functional coronary artery disease. It also provides prognostic information in patients with known ischaemic heart disease. It is operator dependent and tends to be used in centres where there is local expertise.

The principle is that under cardiac stress (usually achieved with dobutamine infusion but exercise, dipyridamole or pacing may be used), different echocardiographic windows of the left ventricle are examined looking for inducible changes in regional wall motion under stress. This tends to signify ischaemia in the coronary artery territory supplying that part of the ventricle. The technique can be improved with further use of injectable echo contrast to provide better delineation of the endocardial border of the ventricle. Other applications of stress echocardiography include: determination of myocardial viability in patients with poor left ventricular function and coronary artery disease; assessment of dynamic valve gradients in mitral and aortic stenosis; prediction of functional recovery in patients with severe aortic stenosis and poor left ventricular function; and assessment of dynamic left ventricular outflow tract obstruction in hypertrophic cardiomyopathy.

Other echo imaging techniques
Tissue Doppler imaging enables myocardial motion to be displayed over time, enabling the quantification of regional and global myocardial function

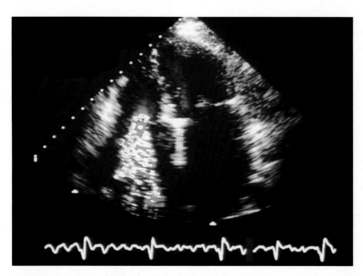

Fig 121 Tricuspid regurgitation: a broad band seen mainly as blue extends back into the right atrium. (Courtesy Dr J Chambers.)

in systole and diastole. This allows diagnosis of complex cardiomyopathies, quantification of ischaemia during dobutamine stress and detection of intracardiac dyssynchrony. Three-dimensional reconstruction of parts of the heart is now possible from a single acquisition of data obtained from three heart beats. This is typically used in imaging valvular lesions and complex shunts. More sensitive measures of left ventricular function include strain imaging which may provide more accurate assessments of left ventricular function than the 'blunt' ejection fraction measurement that is commonly used.

Indications

Echocardiography enables evaluation of regional and global ventricular systolic and diastolic function, assessment of valvular and heart muscle disease, and detection of myocardial ischaemia and viability.

Contraindications

> Stress echocardiography: unstable angina, myocardial infarction in the

preceding 48 hours and ventricular arrhythmia.

> TOE: recent gastro-oesophageal bleed, known pharyngeal pouch or severe oesophageal disease. If there is unexplained dysphagia, arrange investigation before considering TOE.

Practical details

Transoesophageal echocardiography

> Nil by mouth for 4 hours.

> Obtain written consent.

> Insert intravenous cannula.

> Check for loose teeth; remove false teeth and dentures.

> Position patient on left side.

> Give sedation – eg midazolam or diazepam.

> Monitor peripheral oxygen saturation continuously.

> Insert mouth guard and perform test, ensuring that mouth secretions are cleared using suction.

> Monitor recovery; allow the patient home with an escort once they are free of sedation.

Stress echocardiography

The patient should generally omit beta-blockers for 48 hours prior to the test. Intravenous access is required. Dobutamine is administered in stepwise fashion until target rate is achieved or an ischaemic response seen. Images are acquired at baseline, low-dose dobutamine, peak-dose dobutamine and recovery. Images are stored in digital quad screen format for off-line analysis. At each stage of the test, symptoms, 12-lead ECG and BP are recorded. Following the test, the patient is monitored until disappearance of symptoms and resolution of echo and ECG changes.

Complications

Transoesophageal echocardiography

> oesophageal trauma ranging from inflammation to rupture

> aspiration.

Key point

Important information for patients

Explain the following:

> the benefits and risks of the procedure

> the need for sedation, such that they may not remember the test

> that they will be drowsy afterwards, should not drive for the rest of the day and will need to be escorted home

> that they may have a sore throat for the next 1 or 2 days.

Stress echocardiography

> arrhythmias

> allergic reaction to contrast medium

> precipitation of acute coronary syndrome.

Key point

Important information for patients

Stress echocardiography

Stop beta-blockers for 48 hours before the test. Inform patients about the procedure and chosen stress modality. Make sure that they are aware that they may experience chest pain during the test. Explain risk of arrhythmias.

3.11 Nuclear cardiology

3.11.1 Myocardial perfusion imaging

Certain radionuclear tracers (thallium-201 and technetium-99) are actively taken up by myocardial cells in a manner similar to potassium. Their concentration in the myocardium depends on both perfusion (ie blood supply) and integrity of the myocardial cell membrane (ie viable myocardium). A graded colour representation of perfusion is obtained, enabling comparison between regions. Absolute values of blood flow are not obtained.

During exercise or pharmacological stress, the vasodilating capacity of the microcirculation in the heart is maximal and obstruction in the epicardial coronary arteries becomes physiologically significant. A scan after exercise or pharmacological stress with dipyridamole or adenosine is followed by a resting scan at 2–4 hours. Defects seen during stress, which are not present at rest, represent ischaemia. Defects present in both scans ('fixed perfusion defect') usually indicate infarction (Fig 122). The sensitivity for detection of significant coronary artery disease is 80–85% and specificity >90%.

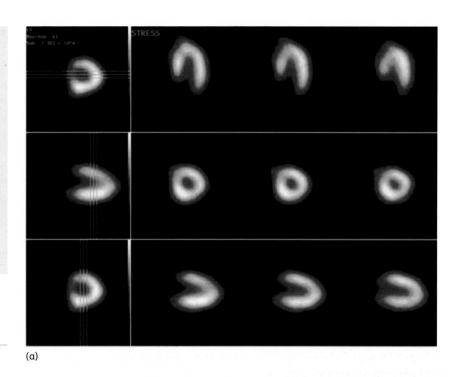

(a)

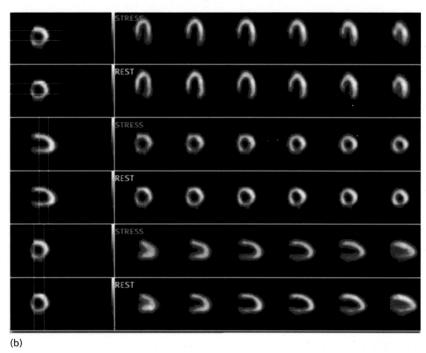

(b)

Fig 122 (a) Normal and **(b)** abnormal stress thallium-201 perfusion scan. Inferior ischaemia is shown in **(b)**. (Courtesy of Dr Jan.)

Indications

Nuclear techniques are non-invasive but reporting is operator dependent. They are commonly used for:

> prognostic stratification after myocardial infarction

> diagnosis of coronary disease, identification of ischaemia and territory of ischaemia in symptomatic patients, especially atypical pain

> risk stratification in patients with known or high risk of coronary

artery disease before non-cardiac surgery

> assessment of myocardial viability; differentiating ischaemia from scar.

3.11.2 Radionuclide ventriculography

Technetium-99m is used to label a patient's red blood pool and can be detected with the use of a gamma camera. The number of counts is linearly related to the blood volume and by using ECG gating to identify different parts of the cardiac cycle the ejection fraction (EF) can be calculated. It is an accurate and reproducible technique for calculating left and right ventricular EFs.

3.11.3 Positron emission tomography

This technique uses positron-emitting radionuclides to produce tomographic images of coronary flow and metabolism. The technique also enables quantification of blood flow within specified regions of the heart. Rest and pharmacological stress scans are performed in a similar manner to thallium imaging. Myocardial viability is suggested by maintained glucose metabolism in an area with a fixed perfusion defect.

3.12 Cardiac catheterisation

Principle

Cardiac catheterisation is the instrumentation of cardiac chambers and/or arteries with catheters to enable pressure measurements, arterial and/or venous blood sampling and performing selective angiography with contrast injection. In addition to diagnostic information, intervention can also be performed to treat coronary or valve lesions.

Catheter-based angiography is performed using a cinefluorographic system consisting of a generator, X-ray tube and image intensifier. The generator delivers electrical power to the X-ray tube, which contains a filament that is heated to ultimately form an X-ray beam. The X-ray beam then projects through the patient at specified angles and is detected by the image intensifier which converts the X-ray beam into a visible light image. This then provides a real-time X-ray image with adequate quality for guiding catheter manipulation within the heart.

Indications

The primary uses of cardiac catheterisation are to assess the presence and/or severity of:

> coronary artery disease
> valvular heart disease
> cardiomyopathy
> congenital heart disease
> pulmonary hypertension
> aortic disease.

The following treatments can delivered in a cardiac catheterisation laboratory:

> percutaneous coronary intervention (PCI) in stable patients for angina as well as in urgent and emergency settings such as primary PCI for ST-elevation myocardial infarction
> balloon valvuloplasty for aortic stenosis, mitral stenosis and pulmonary valve stenosis
> transcatheter valve implantation for aortic stenosis and pulmonary valve stenosis
> percutaneous mitral valve clipping (MitraClip) for mitral regurgitation
> percutaneous 'hole' closures, eg atrial septal defect (ASD), patent foramen ovale (PFO) and ventricular septal defect (VSD)
> left atrial appendage closure for atrial fibrillation in patients unable to tolerate anticoagulation
> interventional treatments in adult congenital heart disease patients.

Practical details

Before procedure

Patients are usually fasted for 3–4 hours pre-procedure. Patients with renal impairment require intravenous fluid pre-hydration. Patients planned for stent implantation require loading with dual antiplatelet therapy, aspirin 300 mg and clopidogrel 300–600 mg (or ticagrelor 180 mg / prasugrel 60 mg in patients with acute coronary syndrome).

During procedure

Procedures are usually performed with local anaesthetic and sedation. Procedures requiring intracardiac imaging with transoesophageal echocardiography are performed under general anaesthetic.

After procedure

Elective patients are usually discharged home on the same day if appropriate. If a coronary stent is implanted patients will require dual antiplatelet therapy for variable time periods (between 1 and 12 months) depending on stent type and clinical situation.

Risks

The potential risks of cardiac catheterisation relate to vascular access, catheter manipulation within the heart and contrast injection. Vascular complications include localised haematoma, retroperitoneal haemorrhage from femoral artery access and pseudo-aneurysm formation. Catheter manipulation could lead to dissection or perforation of coronary arteries or cardiac chambers leading to myocardial infarction, arrhythmia, or pericardial effusion and tamponade. Contrast-related complications include rash, allergy, anaphylaxis and nephropathy. For a diagnostic coronary angiogram patients should in general be consented for a one in 1,000 risk of a major complication.

Cardiology: Section 4

4 Self-assessment

4.1 Self-assessment questions

MRCP(UK) Part 1 examination questions

Question 1

Clinical scenario

A 64-year-old man with diabetes presented to the emergency department with chest pain of 2 hours' duration. His 12-lead electrocardiogram (ECG) showed 3–4 mm of ST elevation in leads V2–V6 and he was diagnosed with an acute anterior ST elevation myocardial infarction (STEMI).

Question

Which is the most appropriate management plan?

Answer

A aspirin, chest X-ray and consider computerised tomography (CT) aortogram

B aspirin, clopidogrel and primary percutaneous coronary intervention (PCI)

C aspirin, clopidogrel, thrombolysis and heparin infusion

D aspirin, enoxaparin and primary PCI

E aspirin, prasugrel and primary PCI

Question 2

Clinical scenario

A 67-year-old man was referred to the cardiology clinic with recent onset symptoms of angina. His past medical history included type 2 diabetes requiring insulin therapy. He underwent coronary angiography, which demonstrated significant three-vessel coronary artery disease with preserved left ventricular function.

Question

What is the best treatment strategy?

Answer

A coronary artery bypass graft surgery (CABG)

B multi-vessel stenting with bare metal stents

C multi-vessel stenting with drug-eluting stents

D optimise medical therapy

E single vessel stenting

Question 3

Clinical scenario

A 60-year-old man presented to the emergency department with retrosternal chest pain radiating to the neck. He had a history of bicuspid aortic valve disease and was under regular follow-up in the cardiology clinic. On examination he was hypotensive and had an early diastolic murmur. His ECG showed inferior ST elevation.

Question

What is the best next step in management?

Answer

A chest X-ray

B CT aorta

C CT pulmonary angiogram (CTPA)

D emergency primary PCI

E thrombolysis

Question 4

Clinical scenario

An 89-year-old man presented to the cardiology clinic with 6-month history of increasing shortness of breath, chest tightness and near syncope on exertion. His past medical history included severe chronic obstructive pulmonary disease (COPD), peripheral vascular disease and previous ischaemic stroke. An echocardiogram showed critical aortic stenosis with peak gradient of 110 mmHg and valve area of 0.5 cm^2. Coronary angiography showed a 60% stenosis in the distal right coronary artery.

Question

What is the best treatment option?

Answer

A aortic valve replacement

B home oxygen

C medical therapy alone

D percutaneous coronary intervention

E transcatheter aortic valve implantation

Question 5

Clinical scenario

A 56-year-old man was admitted with an anterior ST elevation myocardial infarction. He was treated with primary PCI with a single everolimus drug-eluting stent placed in the proximal left anterior descending coronary artery (LAD), and made an uneventful recovery. On day three, prior to discharge, he complained of a new rash. On examination he had well-demarcated palpable patches of red skin with a silvery scale on his knees, elbows and scalp.

Question
Which of his new medications is the likely cause?

Answer
A atorvastatin
B bisoprolol
C everolimus on the stent
D prasugrel
E ramipril

Question 6

Clinical scenario
A 31-year-old woman of Somalian origin, 30 weeks into her first pregnancy, presented to the cardiology clinic with increasing shortness of breath and peripheral oedema. Clinical examination revealed a mid-diastolic murmur consistent with mitral stenosis. An echocardiogram showed restricted mitral valve opening with mean gradient of 14 mmHg and a valve area of 0.8 cm^2. There was minimal calcification with no regurgitation. She remained symptomatic despite being given diuretics and having adequate heart rate control.

Question
What is the best treatment option?

Answer
A further optimisation of medical therapy
B mitral valve replacement
C open valvuloplasty
D percutaneous mitral balloon valvuloplasty
E urgent caesarean section

Question 7

Clinical scenario
A 35-year-old woman was referred to the cardiology clinic to investigate hypertension found on routine screening. She had several blood pressure recordings of >160/95 mmHg. Her body mass index (BMI) was 32 kg/m^2 (normal range 18–25) and she had irregular periods. There was no other significant past medical history.

Question
What is the most likely diagnosis?

Answer
A Conn's syndrome
B Cushing's syndrome
C essential hypertension
D phaeochromocytoma
E renovascular disease

Question 8

Clinical scenario
A 68-year-old man was referred to the cardiology clinic with recent onset chest pain. He described daily retrosternal discomfort on exertion that was relieved by rest. He had a past medical history of type 2 diabetes, for which he took oral medication, and he was a smoker. Clinical examination was normal and a resting 12-lead ECG showed no abnormalities.

Question
What is the best investigation to do next?

Answer
A cardiac magnetic resonance imaging (MRI) with stress perfusion
B coronary angiogram
C echocardiogram
D stress myocardial perfusion test
E treadmill exercise testing

Question 9

Clinical scenario
A 45-year-old woman presented to the emergency department with palpitations. She had been to a wedding the day before. She was anxious, but haemodynamically stable. She reported no previous medical history. Clinically she was in atrial fibrillation with pulse of 130 beats per minute, and this was confirmed on a 12-lead ECG.

Question
What is the most appropriate first-line antiarrhythmic drug for her?

Answer
A amiodarone
B bisoprolol
C digoxin
D esmolol
E flecainide

Question 10

Clinical scenario
A 75-year-old man was brought into the resuscitation room in the emergency department following a head-on collision with another car. His blood pressure was 90/60 mmHg and a chest X-ray showed a widened mediastinum.

Question
What is the most appropriate investigation?

Answer
A abdominal ultrasound
B aortography
C CT
D echocardiography
E MRI

Question 11

Clinical scenario
A 65-year-old man with long-standing severe aortic regurgitation presented to clinic for routine review. He remained asymptomatic.

Question
What investigation finding would be an indication for surgery?

Answer
A left ventricular ejection fraction of 45%
B left ventricular end diastolic diameter of 6 cm
C left ventricular end systolic diameter of 4.5 cm
D pressure half time of <250 ms
E regurgitant volume of 60 mL/beat

Question 12

Clinical scenario

An 18-year-old man presented to the cardiology clinic with a murmur. He had a background of learning disabilities, was of short stature and had a pectus excavatum deformity. An echocardiogram demonstrated pulmonary stenosis and an atrial septal defect.

Question

What is the most likely diagnosis?

Answer

A DiGeorge syndrome

B Down's syndrome

C Duchenne muscular dystrophy

D Noonan's syndrome

E Turner's syndrome

Question 13

Clinical scenario

A 60-year-old man presented with chest pain of 10 hours' duration and the attending paramedic performed an ECG that showed inferior ST elevation myocardial infarction (STEMI). He was admitted directly to the cardiac catheter laboratory and underwent successful stenting of his proximal right coronary artery via radial artery access. He was then admitted to the coronary care unit (CCU). Two-hours post-procedure his vital signs included: pulse 100 beats per minute (regular) and blood pressure 70/50 mmHg. On examination, his jugular venous pressure (JVP) was raised, heart sounds were normal and his chest was clear. A repeat ECG showed good resolution of ST segments.

Question

What is the most likely cause of hypotension?

Answer

A ischaemic mitral regurgitation

B papillary muscle rupture

C post-MI ventricular septal defect

D retroperitoneal haemorrhage

E right ventricular infarct

Question 14

Clinical scenario

A 40-year-old man was referred to the cardiology clinic with hypertension, tachycardia, headaches and sweats. He denied any chest pain or breathlessness on exertion. His past medical history was unremarkable, and he had no relevant family history. His medications included amlodipine 5 mg once daily and ramipril 5 mg once daily. Cardiovascular examination was unremarkable: pulse 70 beats per minute (regular) and blood pressure 150/80 mmHg. Blood tests were all unremarkable. Echocardiography showed mild left ventricular hypertrophy. Ultrasound examination of his kidneys was normal. Three separate 24-hour urine collections for catecholamines were positive, but a CT scan did not identify a phaeochromocytoma.

Question

What is the best next investigation?

Answer

A clonidine suppression test

B metaiodobenzylguanidine (MIBG) scintigraphy

C nothing – reassure that phaeochromocytoma has been excluded

D repeat CT scan

E repeat 24-hour urine collection

Question 15

Clinical scenario

A 55-year-old man presented with sudden onset pleuritic chest pain, breathlessness and a single episode of haemoptysis. He denied any cough or fevers. His past medical history included hypertension, diabetes and bladder cancer, for which he had finished chemotherapy 3 weeks previously.

His vital signs included: pulse 95 beats per minute, blood pressure 130/80 mmHg, temperature 37°C and SaO$_2$ 94% on air (normal range 94–98). His heart sounds were normal and his chest was clear. There was no sign of deep vein thrombosis (DVT). A serum D-dimer was negative, and a 12-lead ECG showed sinus rhythm with no ST/T abnormalities. His chest X-ray was clear.

Question

What is the best next investigation?

Answer

A coronary angiography

B CT pulmonary angiogram (CTPA)

C echocardiogram

D myocardial perfusion scan

E troponin

Question 16

Clinical scenario

An 88-year-old woman presented with a fall. She had been walking with her Zimmer frame when her foot got caught in a carpet and she tripped over. She remembered falling and denied any chest pain, shortness of breath, palpitations or dizziness at any point. She did not lose consciousness. There was no other history of previous falls or dizzy spells. Her past medical history included hypertension and hypercholesterolaemia. Her medications included amlodipine 5 mg od and simvastatin 40 mg od.

Examination was unremarkable, with her vital signs including: temperature 37°C, pulse 90 beats per minute, blood pressure 150/85 mmHg and SaO$_2$ 99% on air (normal range 94–98). Her blood tests were unremarkable, including electrolytes and magnesium. Her ECG, recorded when she was asymptomatic, was as shown (Fig 123). Her chest X-ray was clear.

Question

What is the cause of the abnormality on the ECG?

Answer

A artefact

B atrial tachycardia

C non-sustained VT

D *torsade de pointes*

E transient VF

Question 17

Clinical scenario

A 59-year-old man presented to the emergency department feeling intermittently dizzy. He had been discharged from hospital 10 days previously following an aortic valve replacement for severe aortic stenosis due to a bicuspid valve. He looked well, with a blood pressure of 150/65 mmHg. He was on warfarin for his mechanical valve with an international normalised ratio (INR) of 2.6 and had a normal full blood count, electrolyte and renal function tests. A high-sensitivity troponin-I was elevated at 85 ng/L (normal threshold <34.3 ng/L). His ECG is as shown in Fig 124.

Question

What is the next best management step?

Answer

A antiplatelet therapy

B beta-blockers

C echocardiography

D intravenous amiodarone

E pacemaker implantation

Question 18

Clinical scenario

A 33-year-old African-Caribbean woman presented to the emergency department complaining of progressive shortness of breath, fatigue and ankle swelling for a week. She had given birth to her third child 2 weeks previously via a normal

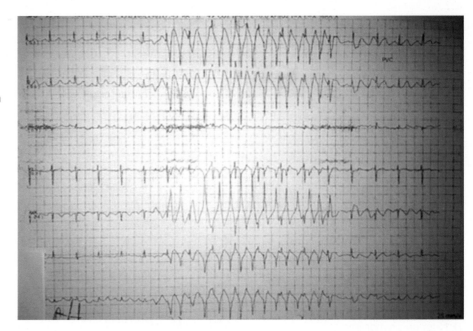

Fig 123

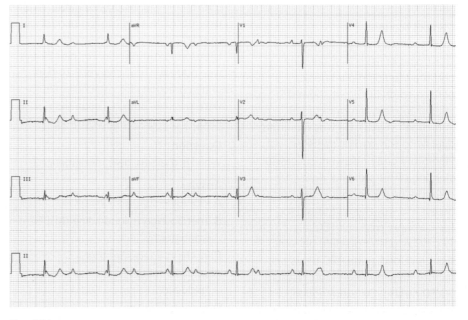

Fig 124

vaginal delivery. She had not had any trouble in her previous pregnancies, had no relevant past medical history, and was on no regular medications. Clinical examination revealed that her pulse was 110 beats per minute, her blood pressure was 110/60 mmHg, her

oxygen saturation on air was 95% (normal range 94–98), she had a soft pansystolic murmur, fine bibasal lung crepitations, and pitting peripheral oedema to the shins. Her blood tests showed haemoglobin 108 g/L (normal range 115–150) and normal renal

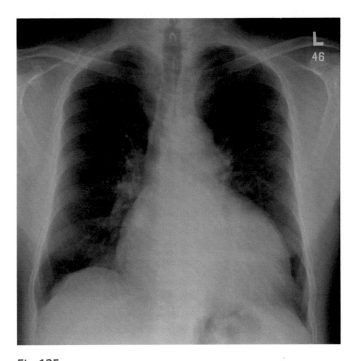

Fig 125

function. Her chest radiograph is as shown in Fig 125.

Question
What is the most likely cause of the presentation?

Answer
A anaemia
B atypical pneumonia
C peripartum cardiomyopathy
D pulmonary embolus
E rheumatic valve disease

Question 19

Clinical scenario
A 45-year-old woman with a background of primary pulmonary arterial hypertension presented with worsening symptoms of breathlessness. Right heart catheterisation had demonstrated she had vasoreactive pulmonary hypertension and she had been prescribed a calcium channel antagonist. A recommendation is made that she should start on bosentan.

Question
What class of agent is bosentan?

Answer
A beta-blocker
B endothelin receptor antagonist
C phosphodiesterase type 5 inhibitor
D prostaglandin analogue
E renin inhibitor

Question 20

Clinical scenario
A 22-year-old man was referred for assessment as part of a diving qualification. His echocardiogram revealed a patent foramen ovale (PFO).

Question
What percentage of the population have a PFO?

Answer
A 5%
B 10%
C 15%
D 25%
E 40%

MRCP(UK) Part 2 examination questions

Question 21

Clinical scenario
A 19-year-old man was seen in the cardiology clinic following an episode of collapse during exertion. His parents described an episode that occurred while playing football in which he suddenly collapsed with what appeared to be seizure activity and urinary incontinence. He was otherwise well, with no significant past medical history, and not taking any medications. His father had suffered a myocardial infarction aged 65 years, but there was no family history of arrhythmia or sudden death.

Question
What is the next step in his care?

Answer
A beta blockade and exercise restrictions
B electrocardiogram (ECG) and additional testing for long QT syndrome
C electrophysiology study
D empiric treatment with an anti-epileptic medication
E referral to neurologist for an electroencephalogram (EEG)

Question 22

Clinical scenario
A 50-year-old woman presented to the emergency department 90 minutes after she suffered sudden onset of left arm weakness, left facial droop and slurred speech. While in the emergency department she complained of chest pain. Her risk factors for vascular disease included being a heavy smoker and having hyperlipidaemia. Physical examination was normal, with the exception of left arm weakness. Her ECG was as shown (see Fig 126). An urgent CT head and CT aorta excluded aortic dissection and did not show any intracranial bleeding or large vessel ischaemia.

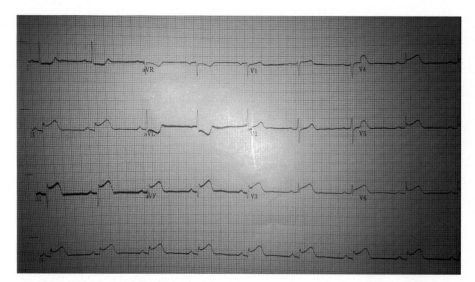

Fig 126

Question
What is the best next management?

Answer
A aspirin and clopidogrel
B aspirin, clopidogrel and fondaparinux
C observe
D primary PCI
E thrombolysis

Question 23

Clinical scenario
A 50-year-old man attended the cardiology clinic for routine review. His past medical history included ischaemic heart disease with myocardial infarction, diabetes, hypertension and cardiac failure. He complained of continuing shortness of breath on exertion, with an exercise tolerance of 50 metres. He denied any chest pain, palpitations, dizziness or collapses. His medications included aspirin 75 mg once daily, bisoprolol 5 mg once daily, ramipril 5 mg once daily, spironolactone 50 mg once daily, furosemide 40 mg once daily, atorvastatin 40 mg once daily and metformin 500 mg three times per day.

On examination his pulse was 65 beats per minute (regular), his blood pressure was 105/65 mmHg and his heart sounds were normal, his chest was clear, and there was minimal ankle oedema only. His ECG showed sinus rhythm with left bundle branch block (LBBB) and QRS duration of 140 ms. His most recent echocardiogram showed an ejection fraction (EF) of 30% with regional wall motion abnormalities, and a recent myocardial perfusion scan showed an inferior infarct but no reversible ischaemia. A recent 48-hour tape did not show any ventricular arrhythmias.

Question
What is the best management plan?

Answer
A angiogram for possible revascularisation
B cardiac resynchronisation therapy defibrillator (CRT-D)
C cardiac resynchronisation therapy pacemaker (CRT-P)
D implantable cardioverter defibrillator (ICD)
E medical management

Question 24

Clinical scenario
A 50-year-old man attended the cardiology clinic for routine review. His past medical history included ischaemic heart disease with myocardial infarction, diabetes, hypertension and cardiac failure. He complained of continuing shortness of breath on exertion, with an exercise tolerance of 100 metres. He denied any chest pain, palpitations, dizziness or collapses. His medications included aspirin 75 mg once daily, bisoprolol 5 mg once daily, ramipril 5 mg once daily, spironolactone 50 mg once daily, furosemide 40 mg once daily, atorvastatin 40 mg once daily and metformin 500 mg three times per day.

On examination his pulse was 70 beats per minute (regular), his blood pressure was 110/65 mmHg and his heart sounds were normal, his chest was clear, and there was minimal ankle oedema only. His ECG showed sinus rhythm without LBBB but QRS duration of 140 ms. His most recent echocardiogram showed an ejection fraction of 30% with regional wall motion abnormalities, and a recent myocardial perfusion scan showed an inferior infarct but no reversible ischaemia. A recent 48-hour tape did not show any ventricular arrhythmias.

Question
What is the best management plan?

Answer
A angiogram for possible revascularisation
B CRT-D
C CRT-P
D ICD
E medical management

Question 25

Clinical scenario
A 50-year-old man was referred for cardiology review because of a murmur. Three months previously he had suffered an episode of syncope, but had not sought medical attention at the time. He denied any chest pain, shortness of breath on exertion, or palpitations. His past medical history included hypertension. On examination his pulse was 75 beats per minute (regular) and his blood pressure was 150/80 mmHg.

His heart sounds were normal, but he had an ejection systolic murmur, loudest at the left sternal edge and in the aortic area. His chest was clear and he had no leg oedema.

His ECG showed anterolateral ST depression and T wave inversion. An echocardiogram raised the possibility of hypertrophic cardiomyopathy (HCM), with maximum left ventricle (LV) thickness of 20 mm and left atrium (LA) diameter of 45 mm. There was a small left ventricular outflow tract (LVOT) gradient of 20 mmHg, but no systolic anterior motion (SAM) of the mitral valve. A 24-hour tape showed one episode of non-sustained ventricular tachycardia (VT) lasting for 10 beats. Cardiac MRI confirmed HCM with maximum LV thickness of 20 mm.

Question
What is the best management plan?

Answer
A alcohol septal ablation
B beta-blockers
C ICD
D surgical myomectomy
E verapamil

Question 26
Clinical scenario
A 65-year-old man presented with a 2-day history of sudden onset of localised pleuritic chest pain and breathlessness. He had no associated sweating, nausea or clamminess. He could usually manage to go out of the house and do his own shopping, limited by his breathing, but he now said that he felt breathless on minimal exertion. His past medical history included myocardial infarction 10 years previously (treated by angioplasty), moderate left ventricular (LV) dysfunction (New York Heart Association (NYHA) class II), obesity, diabetes and hypercholesterolaemia. His medications included aspirin, atorvastatin, amlodipine, ramipril, bisoprolol, metformin and insulin.

On examination his pulse was 90 beats per minute, his blood pressure was 130/80 mmHg, his temperature was 37°C, and his SaO$_2$ was 95% on 2 L of oxygen (normal range 94–98). His heart sounds were normal, his chest clear, and he had mild leg oedema. An ECG showed right bundle branch block (RBBB) with left-axis deviation, both of which were present on previous ECGs. Blood test results were as follows: normal inflammatory markers, 1st troponin 80 ng/L (normal threshold <34.3 ng/L), D-dimer 1,700 ng/mL (normal threshold <250 ng/mL). A chest X-ray showed cardiomegaly but clear lung fields.

Question
What is the best next investigation?

Answer
A coronary angiography
B CT coronary angiography
C CT pulmonary angiogram (CTPA)
D echocardiogram
E myocardial perfusion scan

Question 27
Clinical scenario
A 55-year-old man presented to the emergency department with a 4-week history of exertional chest pain, radiating to the left arm and associated with breathlessness, sweating and clamminess. His symptoms were initially infrequent, but over the preceding week he reported them almost every day on mild exertion. He denied any episodes of chest pain at rest. His risk factors included hypertension, hypercholesterolaemia and the fact he was a lifelong smoker. His father had suffered a myocardial infarction in his 50s. His medications included ramipril 5 mg od and simvastatin 40 mg od. Examination was unremarkable: his temperature was 36.8°C, his pulse was 70 beats per minute, his blood pressure was 130/80 mmHg and his SaO$_2$ was 97% on air (normal range 94–98). His ECG (recorded when

he was not in pain) showed sinus rhythm with no significant ST/T wave abnormalities. A chest X-ray was clear. Two measures of serum troponin were negative.

Question
What is the most appropriate management plan?

Answer
A D-dimer
B discharge and routine outpatient cardiology review
C discharge and urgent outpatient cardiology review
D inpatient coronary angiogram
E outpatient coronary angiogram

Question 28
Clinical scenario
An 84-year-old man presented with a 4-week history of general deterioration, malaise, mild shortness of breath and fevers. He denied any cough, urinary symptoms or rashes. His past medical history included hypertension, diabetes, mild renal dysfunction, chronic obstructive pulmonary disease and a dual-chamber pacemaker first implanted 12 years previously (for sick sinus syndrome), with a first box change 1 year ago. His medications included ramipril 5 mg od, metformin 1 g bd, simvastatin 40 mg od and inhalers.

On examination, his vital signs were: temperature 37.7°C, pulse 80 beats per minute, blood pressure 140/85 mmHg and SaO$_2$ 96% on air (normal range 94–98). His heart sounds were normal with no murmurs. The chest was clear, abdomen was soft and non-tender, and there were no rashes or splinter haemorrhages. The pacemaker site was clean. His ECG showed sinus rhythm, his chest X-ray was clear, and urine dip was negative. He had raised inflammatory markers and was started on broad-spectrum antibiotics.

Twenty-four hours later his blood cultures grew coagulase-negative staphylococci from both bottles. A transthoracic echocardiogram did not show any obvious lead- or valvular vegetations.

Question

What is the most appropriate thing to do next?

Answer

A CT chest
B repeat blood cultures
C screen for cancer
D stop antibiotics
E transoesophageal echocardiogram

Question 29

Clinical scenario

A 45-year-old man presented to the emergency department with sudden onset of severe chest pain. He had a history of hypertension and was known to have a bicuspid aortic valve, for which he was under cardiology follow-up. He was pain-free on arrival.

Clinical examination revealed a loud ejection systolic murmur and an early diastolic murmur. He was mildly hypotensive, with a blood pressure of 95/75 mmHg. His ECG showed a sinus tachycardia at a rate of 106 beats per minute. His chest radiograph showed a small left-sided pleural effusion. Initial blood tests revealed a high-sensitivity troponin I of 62 ng/L (normal threshold <34.3 ng/L) and a D-dimer of 3,600 ng/mL (normal threshold <250 ng/mL).

Question

What is the next most appropriate investigation?

Answer

A coronary angiogram
B CT aortogram
C CT pulmonary angiogram (CTPA)
D ultrasound-guided thoracentesis of pleural fluid
E ventilation–perfusion scan

Question 30

Clinical scenario

A 73-year-old man presented at his wife's request to the emergency department having had a single episode of severe chest pain lasting 2 hours about 3 days previously. He said that he 'hasn't been right since', but was adamant that he had not had any more pain and just felt fatigued. He had no past medical history of note. His blood pressure was 115/85 mmHg. His 12-lead ECG was as shown (Fig 127).

Question

What is the best immediate management plan?

Answer

A arrange a CT pulmonary angiogram (CTPA)
B intravenous thrombolysis
C reassurance
D treatment with antiplatelet agents and monitor on the coronary care unit (CCU)
E urgent transfer for primary percutaneous coronary intervention

Question 31

Clinical scenario

An 82-year-old woman presented with a 5-day history of feeling unwell. She had no significant past medical history and was generally fit and well, but she did admit to some recent mild dysuria. On examination she was febrile (temperature 38.4°C) and she was noted to have an ejection systolic murmur, loudest in the aortic area. Urinary sepsis was suspected and she was admitted for treatment with intravenous antibiotics.

Two days later the laboratory reported that *Escherichia coli* had been grown from urine and blood cultures. She was now feeling better and was afebrile. A transthoracic echocardiogram, requested by the admitting team because of the murmur, was reported as follows:

Left ventricle: normal size, thickness and function.

Right ventricle: normal size and function. Atria: left atrium mildly dilated, right atrium normal sized.

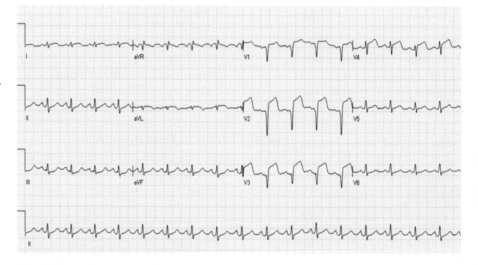

Fig 127

Aortic valve: mild aortic stenosis, peak gradient 30 mmHg, mean gradient 13 mmHg.

Mitral valve: mild central mitral regurgitation, no stenosis.

Pulmonary valve: normal function.

Tricuspid valve: mild regurgitation, right ventricular systolic pressure (RVSP) estimated at 20 mmHg.

Question

What is the most appropriate management?

Answer

A change antibiotic therapy

B continue current treatment

C further blood cultures

D refer for aortic valve surgery

E transoesophageal echocardiography

Question 32

Clinical scenario

A 63-year-old man presented with a 5-week history of feeling unwell. He was obese, with diabetic foot ulcers, and had chronic obstructive pulmonary disease (COPD). Sepsis was suspected and *Staphylococcus aureus* grown on blood cultures. After treatment with appropriate intravenous antibiotics he gradually started improving, both clinically and biochemically. On admission, a systolic murmur had been heard and a transthoracic echocardiogram requested. This was reported as follows:

Left ventricle: normal size, thickness and function.

Right ventricle: normal size and function.

Atria: left atrium moderately dilated, right atrium normal sized.

Aortic valve: normal, no stenosis or regurgitation.

Mitral valve: moderate posteriorly directed jet of mitral regurgitation, no stenosis, no vegetations seen.

Pulmonary valve: normal function.

Tricuspid valve: mild regurgitation, RVSP estimated at 35 mmHg.

Question

What is the best next management step?

Answer

A change antibiotic therapy

B continue current treatment

C further blood cultures

D refer for mitral valve surgery

E transoesophageal echocardiography

Question 33

Clinical scenario

A 52-year-old woman was about to undergo exploratory hysteroscopy under general anaesthesia. She reportedly had a normal ECG at the pre-assessment clinic, but preoperatively her pulse was found to be 50 beats per minute and a medical opinion was sought. She had no prior medical history and was otherwise well, with no cardiac symptoms. Clinical examination was normal. A 12-lead ECG was performed and is as shown in Fig 128.

Question

What is the most appropriate management?

Answer

A continue planned procedure

B delay procedure pending further investigations

C intravenous amiodarone

D oral beta-blocker

E temporary pacing

Question 34

Clinical scenario

A 75-year-old woman attended a follow-up clinic having presented to the acute medical unit with an episode of atypical chest pain at rest some weeks previously. At the time, no ECG abnormalities were noted and serial high-sensitivity troponins were within normal ranges. She had a prior history of a STEMI 5 years previously, for which she had successful PCI to the right coronary artery and was on optimal secondary prevention medication and had been angina free.

Following her recent admission a myocardial perfusion scan had been requested, and she had come to the clinic for the results of this. She had not experienced any further episodes of pain and said that she was well. Part of the report of the myocardial perfusion scan is as follows:

Stress myocardial perfusion scintigraphy Adenosine stress testing was performed with appropriate clinical response. Tc-99 sestamibi was injected and images taken 45 minutes after tracer injection. There was a perfusion defect in the inferior and infero-septal region in the

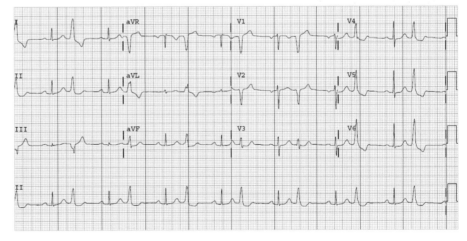

Fig 128

mid and apical segments. There was homogenous tracer uptake elsewhere. The ejection fraction (EF) was estimated at 56%.

The patient was bought back for a rest study that was performed using Tc-99 again and showed similar perfusion defects in the inferior and infero-septal regions in the mid and apical segments. Homogenous tracer uptake elsewhere. The EF was estimated at 55%.

Conclusions

Fixed perfusion defect in the inferior and infero-septal mid and apical regions.

Question

What is the next best management step?

Answer

A antianginal therapy

B coronary angiogram

C discharge from clinic

D heart failure therapy

E stress echocardiography

Question 35

Clinical scenario

A 45-year-old man presented with a 2-day history of worsening sharp, left-sided chest pain, with minimal relief from intravenous opioids prescribed in the emergency department. He was admitted to hospital for investigation. He had a history of depression and was a smoker, but had no significant past medical history.

His vital signs included: pulse 90 beats per minute, blood pressure 135/85 mmHg and oxygen saturation on air 98% (normal range 94–98). Clinical examination was normal, as was a chest radiograph. Serial ECGs were similar to the one shown (Fig 129). Blood tests revealed a normal white cell count and haemoglobin, normal renal function, a CRP of 30 mg/L (normal threshold <10) and serial high-sensitivity troponin I values of 52 ng/L and

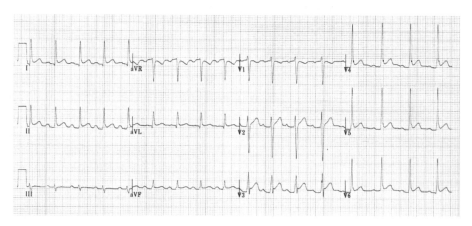

Fig 129

58 ng/L (normal threshold <34.3 ng/L). Subsequent echocardiography was normal.

Question

Once discharged, which medications should he be taking?

Answer

A aspirin

B aspirin, clopidogrel

C aspirin, prednisolone

D aspirin, ticagrelor

E ibuprofen, colchicine

Question 36

Clinical scenario

A 63-year-old man has been seen in the implantable cardioverter defibrillator clinic having had a collapse. The cardiac physiologist has interrogated his device and found that he had an appropriate shock for ventricular fibrillation. He is on appropriate medication and so no changes to this are recommended.

Question

Can the patient continue to drive?

Answer

A he can continue to drive

B he can drive after 1 month

C he can drive after 6 months

D he can drive after 2 years

E he is permanently barred from driving

Question 37

Clinical scenario

A 34-year-old chartered accountant was referred to cardiology clinic following the sudden death of his brother at the age of 28 years. He was otherwise fit and well. The ECG recorded in the clinic was as shown (Fig 130).

Question

Which is the correct interpretation of the ECG?

Answer

A arrhythmogenic cardiomyopathy

B Brugada syndrome

C hypertrophic cardiomyopathy

D long QT syndrome

E normal

Question 38

Clinical scenario

A 46-year-old man presented to clinic with chest pain of recent origin. He described a pressure-type pain in his upper chest that came on with anxiety, lasted for seconds, but had no clear relieving factors. He had no significant past medical history and was a non-smoker. His father had ischaemic heart disease. His ECG was normal.

Question

Which test is most appropriate to investigate this further?

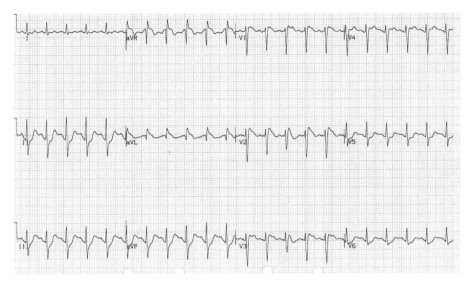

Fig 130

Answer

A cardiac MRI

B coronary angiogram

C CT calcium score

D exercise tolerance test

E myocardial perfusion scan

Question 39

Clinical scenario

A 29-year-old woman presented with breathlessness. Her pulse oximeter saturation was 98% on air (normal range 94–98). She underwent a cardiac catheter which obtained the following results:

Oxygen saturations:

superior vena cava 65%

right atrium 63%

right ventricle 63%

pulmonary artery 88%.

Question

What is the most likely diagnosis?

Answer

A atrial septal defect

B congenitally corrected transposition of the great vessels

C patent ductus arteriosus

D tetralogy of Fallot

E ventricular septal defect

Question 40

Clinical scenario

A 70-year-old man with a background of stroke, hypercholesterolaemia, coronary artery bypass grafting, femoral artery angioplasty, type 2 diabetes and smoking presented to clinic with an irregular pulse. An ECG confirmed atrial fibrillation.

Question

What is his CHA_2DS_2-VASc score?

Answer

A 2

B 3

C 4

D 5

E 6

4.2 Self-assessment answers

Answer to Question 1

E: aspirin, prasugrel and primary PCI

Patients with acute ST elevation myocardial infarction (STEMI) should be treated with emergency primary percutaneous coronary intervention (PCI). All patients should receive loading doses of aspirin 300 mg and a potent P2Y12 inhibiting antiplatelet agent such as prasugrel or ticagrelor. Clopidogrel should only be used if there are contraindications to the more potent agents or if patient is already anticoagulated.

Answer to Question 2

A: coronary artery bypass graft surgery (CABG)

The FREEDOM trial demonstrated that in diabetic patients CABG was superior to PCI in that it significantly reduced rates of death and myocardial infarction.

Answer to Question 3

B: computerised tomography (CT) aorta

Patients with bicuspid aortic valve disease have 10-fold higher risk of aortic dissection compared to the normal population and should be monitored for aortic root dilatation. Dissection of the ascending aorta can involve the ostia of the coronary arteries leading to ST elevation myocardial infarction and can also affect aortic valve function leading to aortic regurgitation.

Answer to Question 4

E: transcatheter aortic valve implantation

Transcatheter aortic valve implantation (TAVI) now offers a treatment option in patients previously deemed inoperable due to significant comorbidities. The PARTNER 1 study showed that in patients with severe aortic stenosis who were not suitable candidates for surgery, TAVI, as compared with standard therapy, significantly reduced the rate of death from any cause, also the composite end point of death from any cause or repeat hospitalisation.

Answer to Question 5

B: bisoprolol

This patient has new-onset psoriasis precipitated by beta-blocker therapy. This is a known association and often resolves completely with discontinuation of the medication.

Answer to Question 6

D: percutaneous mitral balloon valvuloplasty

Percutaneous mitral balloon valvuloplasty (PMBV) should be carried out for severe mitral stenosis in patients who remain symptomatic despite medical therapy, if the valve morphology is suitable on echo. Pregnancy can unmask previously undiagnosed obstructive valvular heart disease and intervention should be performed with adequate shielding of the fetus.

Answer to Question 7

C: essential hypertension

Essential hypertension is by far the most common cause of hypertension. However, young patients with new diagnosis of hypertension should undergo routine investigations to exclude a secondary cause.

Answer to Question 8

B: coronary angiogram

High-risk patients with classic angina symptoms should proceed directly to coronary angiography. Low-risk patients can be evaluated with non-invasive stress imaging. Treadmill exercise is no longer recommended in the work-up of new-onset chest pain.

Answer to Question 9

B: bisoprolol

Cardioselective beta-blockers such as bisoprolol should be considered first line as they will assist rate control in the first instance. In some situations they will aid cardioversion to sinus rhythm. If after rate control a decision is made to try and restore sinus rhythm, then flecainide or amiodarone might be considered.

Answer to Question 10

C: CT

The concern is that he may have trauma to the aorta. This might be reflected in a pericardial effusion seen on echo, but this will not necessarily provide all of the information. He requires cross-sectional imaging and so CT is most appropriate as it is generally quicker to obtain than MRI.

Answer to Question 11

A: left ventricular ejection fraction of 45%

Surgery is indicated in symptomatic patients with severe aortic regurgitation (AR). Indications for surgery in asymptomatic AR are:

> left ventricular (LV) ejection fraction under 50%
> LV end diastolic diameter greater than 7 cm
> LV end systolic diameter greater than 5 cm.

Regurgitant volume of >60 mL/beat and a pressure half time of <250 ms are both echocardiographic markers of severe AR.

Answer to Question 12

D: Noonan's syndrome

Noonan's syndrome is a mutation affecting the RAS-MAPK pathway. It is an autosomal dominant disorder that typically causes short stature, learning disabilities, pectus deformity and congenital cardiac defects (typically pulmonary stenosis, atrial septal defect (ASD) and occasionally hypertrophic cardiomyopathy).

Cardiac associations

DiGeorge syndrome: conotruncal defects (especially tetralogy of Fallot)

Down's syndrome: atrioventricular canal defects

Duchenne muscular dystrophy: conduction abnormalities, cardiomyopathy

Turner's syndrome: coarctation of the aorta and bicuspid aortic valve.

Answer to Question 13

E: right ventricular infarct

Right ventricular infarction can complicate up to 50% of inferior STEMIs. Consider right ventricular involvement in patients who remain hypotensive following inferior STEMI with raised jugular venous pressure (JVP), clear chest and no new murmur. Management includes intravenous fluids to maintain adequate filling pressure.

Answer to Question 14

B: metaiodobenzylguanidine (MIBG) scintigraphy

This patient has clinical features suggestive of phaeochromocytoma (hypertension, tachycardia, sweats, headaches). The three positive 24-hour urinary collections for catecholamines confirm phaeochromocytoma and repeating the test will not add much. CT scan has a very high sensitivity, but in cases where the CT scan is negative and the diagnosis is still considered likely, MIBG scintigraphy is indicated and can detect tumours when the CT scan is negative. There is no role for a clonidine suppression test here, and repeating the CT scan is not likely to be helpful and will simply expose the patient to extra radiation.

Answer to Question 15

B: CT pulmonary angiogram (CTPA)

This patient has a history very suggestive of pulmonary embolism (PE) and is at high risk for deep vein thrombosis (DVT) / PE. A negative D-dimer does not exclude DVT/PE, and in this context it should not have been measured. The definitive diagnostic investigation is a CTPA. Echocardiogram might be useful if it showed right ventricle (RV) dilatation or dysfunction but it cannot exclude PE. If the patient was haemodynamically compromised and CTPA was not readily available, then echocardiogram would be the appropriate next investigation, and if signs of RV overload/dysfunction were seen, then thrombolysis should be considered. Mild elevations of troponin can occur in PE.

Answer to Question 16
A: artefact

This patient presented with a very good history for mechanical fall. At first glance her ECG might be confused for *torsade de pointes*, but looking at it closely the spikes of the QRS complexes can be seen to march through the artefact at the expected regular intervals. Moreover, the morphology of lead III does not get affected by the artefacts, proving that this is just artefact.

Answer to Question 17
E: pacemaker implantation

The ECG shows complete (or 3rd degree) AV block with dissociation between atrial (P-wave) activity and ventricular (QRS) activity. There is a narrow complex, regular escape rhythm. AV block is common following aortic valve surgery.

Answer to Question 18
C: peripartum cardiomyopathy

The clinical presentation is of heart failure with an enlarged cardiac silhouette on the chest radiograph. She is in the peripartum period and has risk factors for peripartum cardiomyopathy in that she is above the age of 30, has had previous pregnancies, and is of African-Caribbean ethnicity. The level of

anaemia is unlikely to have caused such a presentation and there is no evidence of an atypical pneumonia. A pulmonary embolus should be considered but the time course of symptom development goes against this. Rheumatic valve disease is a possibility and an echocardiogram would of course be performed, but she has had two previous pregnancies without trouble so this diagnosis is less likely.

Answer to Question 19
B: endothelin receptor antagonist

Bosentan and ambrisentan inhibit endothelin receptors. Other medications given in pulmonary hypertension include phosphodiesterase type 5 inhibitors (sildenafil, tadalafil) and synthetic prostacyclins (epoprostenol, iloprost).

Answer to Question 20
D: 25%

Patent foramen ovale (PFO) is common, affecting a quarter of the population. The vast majority of patients are unaffected and indeed unaware of the abnormality but in cases where a suspected paradoxical embolus has crossed the PFO, percutaneous closure can be considered.

Answer to Question 21
C: electrophysiology study

Exercise-induced syncope in this young patient requires careful evaluation for malignant cardiac tachyarrhythmia. Patients with long QT1 often present with exertion-related symptoms / syncope.

Answer to Question 22
E: thrombolysis

This is a difficult clinical scenario. The patient has presented with both acute stroke and acute inferoanterolateral myocardial infarction. Primary percutaneous coronary intervention (PPCI) in the context of acute stroke is

high risk in view of further stroke or haemorrhagic transformation. The patient is within the window for thrombolysis, and aortic dissection and intracranial bleed has been excluded, hence thrombolysis for both STEMI and stroke is the best option.

Answer to Question 23
B: cardiac resynchronisation therapy defibrillator (CRT-D)

This patient suffers from cardiac failure New York Heart Association (NYHA) class II/III. He is on appropriate secondary medications and increasing these further will be limited by his blood pressure and heart rate. There is no evidence of significant ischaemia on a recent functional test, hence angiography will probably not show any target for revascularisation of prognostic significance. His ejection fraction is 30% and he has LBBB with QRS = 140 ms. He therefore meets the criteria for device therapy. According to NICE guidelines published in 2014, CRT-D is recommended.

Answer to Question 24
D: implantable cardioverter defibrillator (ICD)

This patient suffers from cardiac failure NYHA II/III. He is on appropriate secondary medications and the dosages should be increased to the maximum tolerated, as blood pressure and heart rate allow. Ivabradine can also be considered. There is no evidence of significant ischaemia on a recent functional test, hence angiography will probably not show any target for revascularisation of prognostic significance. His ejection fraction is 30% and – even though he does not have LBBB – his QRS duration is 140 ms. He meets the criteria for device therapy. According to NICE guidelines published in 2014, ICD is recommended.

Answer to Question 25

C: implantable cardioverter defibrillator (ICD)

This patient with hypertrophic cardiomyopathy (HCM), but without a significant left ventricular outflow tract (LVOT) gradient and with no systolic anterior motion (SAM), had an episode of unexplained syncope and evidence of non-sustained ventricular tachycardia on a 24-hour tape. Beta-blockers are generally indicated for significant LVOT obstruction. Verapamil is not used as a first-line treatment in this scenario. According to the European Society of Cardiology (ESC)-HCM risk calculator, his risk of sudden cardiac death at 5 years is 10.7% and so ICD should be considered. The LVOT gradient is not significant enough for myomectomy to be considered, the usual indication being a gradient >50 mmHg.

Answer to Question 26

C: CT pulmonary angiogram (CTPA)

The history suggests PE rather than MI. He requires oxygen to maintain saturation, he has no crackles and his chest X-ray is clear. There are no new electrocardiogram (ECG) changes. His mild troponin elevation could be due to an underlying PE. Echocardiogram will be useful but unlikely to provide a diagnosis. Given the history, PE should be excluded before further cardiac investigations are considered.

Answer to Question 27

D: inpatient coronary angiogram

This patient has a very good history for crescendo angina. He has multiple risk factors for ischaemic heart disease. Despite his normal ECG and negative troponin it is important to investigate him as an inpatient to exclude significant coronary artery disease. Troponins are very sensitive biomarkers and most patients with normal ECGs and negative troponins could be safely discharged home from a cardiovascular point of view, but negative troponins do not exclude coronary artery disease and if the story is convincing for crescendo angina, the patient should be investigated as an inpatient.

Answer to Question 28

E: transoesophageal echocardiogram

Coagulase-negative staphylococci are often considered contaminants or non-pathogenic micro-organisms. However, they are one of the commonest causes of permanent pacemaker-related infections and they should not be dismissed in patients with indwelling devices who are suspected of having such infection. This patient presented with non-specific symptoms, he has risk factors for infection (diabetes, renal dysfunction and generator change) and has coagulase-negative staphylococci in both bottles. He should proceed to transoesophageal echocardiography. Excluding alternative sources of sepsis and repeating the blood cultures to check progress are also worth doing.

Answer to Question 29

B: CT aortogram

The diagnosis is consistent with an acute aortic syndrome, likely aortic dissection. This is commoner in patients with bicuspid aortic valves and hypertension is a risk factor. The early diastolic murmur suggests aortic regurgitation and the hypotension, left-sided pleural effusion and elevated D-dimer (clot in false lumen of dissection) are classic signs. Where echocardiography is available acutely, this is an appropriate initial investigation, but it requires a skilled operator and may not be diagnostic otherwise.

Answer to Question 30

D: treatment with antiplatelet agents and monitor on the coronary care unit (CCU)

The ECG suggests a late presentation of a completed anterior STEMI. He is pain-free at the moment and wouldn't derive benefit from primary percutaneous coronary intervention. Angiography may well be considered, but acutely he needs good medical therapy. If he has further pain or deteriorates then urgent discussions with the local interventional centre would be warranted.

Answer to Question 31

B: continue current treatment

The clinical suspicion of endocarditis is low. This is likely to be urinary sepsis with consistent organisms grown in both urine and blood. The echocardiographic changes are not suggestive of infective endocarditis and are consistent with the age of the patient.

Answer to Question 32

E: transoesophageal echocardiography

The clinical suspicion of endocarditis is high due to the subacute history and *Staphylococcus aureus* isolated in blood cultures. The transthoracic echocardiogram is not entirely normal given the eccentric mitral regurgitation and may have had suboptimal views given the obesity. Proceeding to a transoesophageal echocardiogram is the best next step in management.

Answer to Question 33

A: continue planned procedure

From the history, it appears that this is an incidental finding in an otherwise asymptomatic and well patient. The 12-lead ECG shows ventricular bigeminy, with alternating sinus beats and monomorphic ventricular ectopics. This is generally a benign condition and provided appropriate monitoring is in place during general anaesthesia, then this shouldn't delay the procedure.

Answer to Question 34

C: discharge from clinic

Atypical pain that is troponin negative and without significant ECG changes is generally very low risk in terms of future likelihood of coronary events. She has had no further pain and the nuclear perfusion scan shows a fixed defect (ie scar) in an area compatible with her previous MI. There is no evidence of inducible ischaemia. Discharge is appropriate.

Answer to Question 35
E: ibuprofen, colchicine

The history and ECG findings suggest a diagnosis of acute pericarditis with an element of myocarditis (sometimes called myopericarditis). Management is with aspirin/NSAIDs along with colchicine as a first-line therapy to prevent recurrences. Corticosteroids are only recommended as a second-line therapy in those who have recurrent symptoms despite initial treatment, and are best used in conjunction with low-dose colchicine.

Answer to Question 36
D: he can drive after 2 years

As the shock was accompanied by incapacity, ie collapse, he cannot drive for 2 years. If there had been

programming changes or medication that would reduce the chance of further VF, then it would have been 6 months.

Answer to Question 37
B: Brugada syndrome

The coved ST elevation in leads V1 and V2 are classical changes seen with Brugada syndrome.

Answer to Question 38
C: CT calcium score

This patient is male, with atypical angina, between 45 and 55 years old, but has no high-risk features for ischaemic heart disease (diabetes, smoking, hyperlipidaemia). This gives him a 22% risk of having coronary disease according to NICE guidelines. Patients who have between 10% and 29% risk should undergo CT calcium scoring. If this is zero, coronary artery disease can be excluded. If the calcium score is 1–400, they should undergo CT coronary angiography, but if greater than 400 they should be offered formal coronary angiography.

Answer to Question 39
C: patent ductus arteriosus

Oxygen saturations for superior vena cava (SVC), right atrium (RA) and right ventricle (RV) are within normal limits with no steps up, ruling out an atrial septal defect (ASD) or ventricular septal defect (VSD). However, there is a marked step up in the pulmonary artery caused by oxygenated blood from the aorta travelling across the patent ductus.

Answer to Question 40
D: 5

Congestive cardiac failure (1 point)

Hypertension (1 point)

Age ≥75 years (2 points)

Diabetes (1 point)

Stroke – stroke or transient ischaemic attack (TIA) in the past (2 points)

Vascular disease (1 point)

Age 65–74 years (1 point)

Sex (female = 1 point)

Respiratory medicine

Authors
Dr J Harper, Dr M Knolle, Dr MG Slade and Dr H Steer

Editor
Dr MG Slade

Editor-in-Chief
Dr JD Firth

The respiratory section of the second edition of Medical Masterclass was written by Dr P Bhatia, Dr S Kaul, Dr DKC Lee, Dr A Pawlowicz and Dr SJ Fowler (editor). This third edition of Medical Masterclass contains entirely new material, but many sections from the second edition have been retained and updated, and we gratefully acknowledge the contribution of these authors.

Respiratory medicine: Section 1

1 PACES stations and acute scenarios

1.1 History taking

1.1.1 New breathlessness

Letter of referral to the respiratory outpatient clinic

Dear Doctor,

Re: Mr Norman Boothroyd, aged 52 years

This man presented with a 2-month history of increasing breathlessness. His appetite has been variable, and he suspects he may be losing weight as his clothes are becoming loose since returning from holiday abroad in the Far East about 6 months ago. He works as a car mechanic in a family-run business and is very worried because his father died of a respiratory complaint. My colleague prescribed some inhalers but these have not helped his breathing. I would be grateful for your expert opinion with regards to diagnosis and management of his breathlessness.

Yours sincerely,

Introduction

Breathlessness or dyspnoea is defined as difficult, laboured or uncomfortable awareness of breathing. It is a feature of many cardiac, respiratory and other conditions. The physician must seek to make a clinical diagnosis before attempting a definitive test. The main diagnostic categories are shown in Table 1.

History of the presenting problem

When and how?
A careful description of the dyspnoea is required. Let the patient tell their story in their own words, but clarify the following points if they do not emerge spontaneously.

> Is the dyspnoea really new or is this a progression of previously mild symptoms? Airways disease in particular often becomes a 'new' problem when the patient is unable to perform a particular task.

> When is it worse? Exertional dyspnoea is a non-specific symptom, but the specific complaint of orthopnoea suggests heart failure (or rarely bilateral diaphragm paralysis) – although any patient with very severe breathlessness will not want to (or be able to) lie down.

> If the symptoms are worse lying on one side then this may suggest unilateral lung disease, eg a patient with right lung collapse may report a preference for sleeping on the left side.

> Nocturnal dyspnoea usually makes the clinician think of heart failure, but asthma is also worse at night.

Is the patient a smoker?
Does the patient smoke now or have they done so previously? These points need to be clarified early. In a smoker, lung cancer requires positive exclusion if there are ominous associated symptoms (particularly weight loss, as seems to have occurred in this case, or haemoptysis). New breathlessness may also indicate a new perception of previously unrecognised airflow obstruction in chronic obstructive pulmonary disease (COPD).

Other substance abuse may also contribute to lung disease and it is important to take a full history, eg smoking of marijuana is associated with bullous lung disease, while alcohol abuse will predispose to pulmonary infections.

Table 1	Causes of slow-onset new breathlessness
Common	Airways disease
	Cardiac disease
	Pleural effusion/disease
	Lobar/lung collapse (caused by obstructing tumour)
Must consider	Thromboembolic disease
	Anaemia
Other conditions	Pulmonary artery hypertension
	Interstitial lung disease
	Neuromuscular disease
	Chest wall disease
	Psychological
	Infections (pneumonia)
	Obesity (though not in this case)
	Sedentary lifestyle

What is the patient's job?

The incidence of mesothelioma is set to peak in 2025. This patient's symptoms could fit, especially if associated with unilateral pain and if their employment history indicates asbestos exposure. Some periods of such employment may have been temporary, hence – when relevant – it is necessary to reconstruct the patient's full work history. Some patients might have been exposed to asbestos during their enrolment in the military, for example.

Other occupations carry their own risks of acquiring occupational lung disease, such as baker's lung or farmer's lung.

Do they have any pets or unusual hobbies?

This question is quick to ask and may be relevant. It sometimes requires some probing: for instance, some people who keep birds do not regard these as pets and will not volunteer their presence in the house.

Is there a family history of lung disease?

In this particular case, the patient has volunteered a family history of lung disease. It is important to explore this further, as there is genetic predisposition for many lung diseases.

Features to suggest infection

Infection would not be a common cause of a dyspnoea of 2 months' duration. The exceptions to this are tuberculosis (TB) or a lung abscess, so you should therefore ask about fever, shivering attacks and sputum production. Is the patient at high risk of TB (eg an immigrant from an endemic area or living on the streets)?

Other relevant history

Previous pulmonary disease

A previous history of asthma, wheeziness or colds 'going to my chest' clearly raises the likelihood of airflow obstruction being the diagnosis. Remember that the patient may have had undiagnosed asthma at school (and therefore been unable to play sport or have disliked the playground in the winter) and grown out of it, only to have it relapse. Alternatively, airway remodelling seen in asthma may continue and cause worsening obstruction.

Cardiac disease

Many cases presenting with breathlessness suffer from cardiac illness. It is important to probe the patient's history thoroughly for any previous cardiac problems. A full cardiac history should be obtained, taking into account symptoms such as chest pain (coronary ischaemia), ankle swelling / paroxysmal nocturnal dyspnoea / orthopnoea (congestive cardiac failure) and palpitations (arrhythmias).

Features to suggest pulmonary embolism

This would not be a common cause of this presentation but needs to be considered, hence ask in particular about any previous known thromboembolism, unilateral leg swelling or discomfort/pain, pleuritic chest pain or haemoptysis (although malignancy would be the immediate concern if this patient had coughed up blood).

Plan for investigation and management

Investigations

Chest radiograph

The chest radiograph is almost an extension of the physical examination; indeed most new patients attending the chest clinic have a chest radiograph before seeing the doctor. Frequently this will show an abnormality that initiates a standard diagnostic pathway, eg pleural effusion, a solitary lung mass or apical alveolar shadowing. It is important to check for cardiac enlargement, and if the chest radiograph appears to be normal then carefully review the apices, the mediastinum and the bony structures.

Blood tests

These are of limited value in the assessment of the slow onset of a new dyspnoea. The haemoglobin will exclude anaemia (and polycythaemia if there has been long-standing hypoxia). Blood tests may be diagnostic where the history and/or examination suggest a specific diagnosis, eg in avian extrinsic alveolitis, and clinical clues of malignancy should be pursued (eg measurement of liver function tests). Sarcoid is notoriously variable in its presentation: measurement of serum angiotensin-converting enzyme (ACE) and calcium are indicated where this diagnosis is entertained. The main value of ACE measurement may be in the monitoring of sarcoid disease activity.

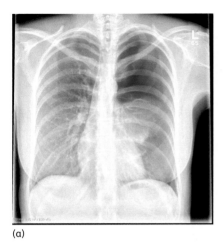
(a)

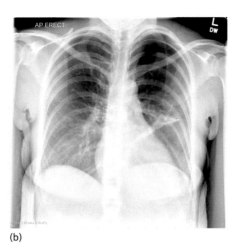
(b)

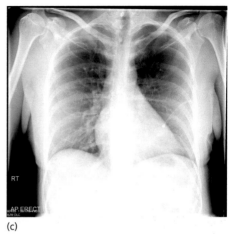
(c)

Fig 1 Radiographs taken in a patient with a left-sided pneumothorax. In this patient with a history of cannabis smoking there is a large pneumothorax at presentation **(a)**, which only partly reinflates after pleural aspiration **(b)**, leading to chest drain insertion **(c)**.

Key point

Brain natriuretic peptide is a good screening test for cardiac failure.

Lung function tests

Lung function measurements are the next investigation for the breathless patient in whom the chest radiograph is non-contributory. Look for evidence of airflow obstruction or a restrictive lung defect. Lung volumes and gas transfer measurements are required where the diagnosis is genuinely uncertain.

Additional investigations

Further investigations are guided by the clinical features and results of the radiograph and lung function tests. They might include:

> computerised tomography (CT) of the thorax
> electrocardiogram (ECG) and echocardiogram (possibly with contrast)
> bronchoscopy
> thoracoscopy
> lung biopsy
> respiratory muscle function tests
> cardiopulmonary exercise testing.

Further discussion

! Hazard

Patients with an inhaled foreign body often have to be prompted to enable this diagnosis, which is suggested by lobar collapse or a persistent cough – 'Have you coughed or choked on anything recently?'.

A patient with dyspnoea and pain may have a pneumothorax. This is usually of sudden onset – but not always – and may be forgotten by the patient. A chest radiograph taken in expiration may demonstrate the condition, as shown in Fig 1.

Consider respiratory muscle weakness if there is a restrictive defect with normal or supernormal gas transfer in the presence of a normal chest radiograph. A good screening test is to compare the erect and supine vital capacity, when a drop of >20% suggests bilateral diaphragm paralysis.

1.1.2 Exertional dyspnoea with daily sputum

Letter of referral to the respiratory outpatient clinic

Dear Doctor,
Re: Mr Kevin Power, aged 24 years
Could you please advise on the further management of this man? Six months ago he took his first job as a hospital physiotherapist and since then he has presented with exertional dyspnoea, and he has been coughing up a cupful of sputum daily. There is no history of wheeze. He also complains of having had intermittent abdominal pain for the last 8 months. Initially this was attributed to the stress of taking his final exams and starting his job. The only other history of relevance is that he has smoked more than 40 cigarettes daily since the age of 15 years.
Physical examination is entirely normal, as is his spirometry.
What is the diagnosis? Do you think that he might be developing chronic bronchitis / COPD?
Yours sincerely,

Introduction

This young man presents with pulmonary and abdominal symptoms, which may or may not be part of the same underlying condition. When considering the differential diagnoses take into account the patient's age. Always rule out ongoing infection first, as this requires prompt investigation and treatment, as well as contagious disorders, so that appropriate steps are taken to protect others.

Causes of a productive cough to be considered in a young patient are:

> COPD (chronic bronchitis) – perhaps associated with α_1-antitrypsin deficiency (see Section 2.3)

> bronchiectasis / cystic fibrosis (CF) (see Sections 2.4 and 2.5)

> lung abscess

> pulmonary TB

> asthma / allergic bronchopulmonary aspergillosis (see Sections 2.2.2 and 2.8.4)

> common variable immunodeficiency.

History of the presenting problem

You must make sure there is no ambiguity regarding the patient's history. Ask:

> Was he really perfectly well prior to his recent episode? Could he play games at school and keep up with his friends when he played football?

> Does he remember frequent visits to his general practitioner (GP) for the treatment of coughs/colds?

> Did he have measles, pertussis (whooping cough) or pneumonia as a child? This may suggest bronchiectasis.

> What is the colour of his sputum? Do the colour and quantity of his sputum change? Has he ever noticed any blood in his sputum? Bronchiectasis and lung abscess can produce purulent sputum,

which may be offensive and blood-tinged. Mucoid or mucopurulent sputum is characteristic of chronic bronchitis.

> Intermittent abdominal pain could be caused by a variety of problems.

Other relevant history

> General health – is there anything to suggest pulmonary TB (eg weight loss or night sweats)? Has he had any recent contact with a person diagnosed with TB?

> Is there any history of nasal/sinus problems? If so, it may suggest common variable immunodeficiency, CF or cilial dysmotility in this case.

> Has he got any symptoms that might suggest diabetes (polydipsia, polyuria or weight loss), which would also suggest CF?

> Is there a family history of similar symptoms? Does he have any brothers/sisters/cousins, and do they (or could they) have CF?

> Is there a family history of COPD / emphysema / cirrhosis of the liver? This might indicate emphysema secondary to α_1-antitrypsin deficiency.

Key point

Do not forget to take a family history – CF or common variable immunodeficiency become the most likely diagnoses in this case if other family members are similarly affected.

Plan for investigation and management

In a patient presenting with exertional dyspnoea and daily sputum production the following should be considered.

Chest radiograph

Perform to help exclude pulmonary TB, lung abscess and heart failure. It may reveal features suggestive of COPD/bronchiectasis/CF and give further clues as to the likely cause of bronchiectasis, for example if dextrocardia is found. Basal emphysematous changes would strongly suggest α_1-antitrypsin deficiency. See Fig 2 for an example of a chest radiograph from a patient with situs inversus and basal bronchiectasis.

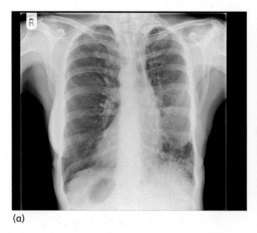
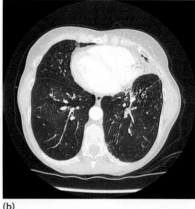

(a)   (b)

Fig 2 (a) This patient has dextrocardia and bilateral lower zone parallel linear shadows or 'tramlines' corresponding to bronchial wall thickening, which is seen on the accompanying computerised tomography (CT) scan **(b)**.

Sputum microbiology examination
Use routine culture and sensitivity, and direct staining and culture to check for acid-fast bacilli.

Lung function tests
These will determine if there is any airway obstruction that may be found in COPD, asthma, bronchiectasis and CF.

Blood tests
A raised white cell count with neutrophilia or raised C-reactive protein suggests an underlying bacterial infection. A low serum α_1-antitrypsin level may suggest hereditary emphysema. Raised fasting glucose may point towards CF-related diabetes. Liver function tests can assess hepatic involvement in both CF and α_1-antitrypsin deficiency. A raised immunoglobulin E (IgE) and *Aspergillus*-specific IgE are seen in allergic bronchopulmonary aspergillosis. Check serum immunoglobulins to look for deficiency.

Arterial blood gases
An arterial blood gas (ABG) test is indicated if arterial oxygen saturation (SaO_2) is <94% in order to check whether there is any evidence of respiratory failure.

Electrocardiogram
Perform this to look for any evidence of cor pulmonale (may also reveal dextrocardia, but this will have been identified by other means!).

Sweat sodium concentration
A value greater than 60 mmol/L is indicative of CF, but a normal test may be observed in approximately 1% of patients with CF who have unusual genotypes.

CT scanning of the chest
This has become the best imaging modality for the detection of bronchial wall thickening and dilatation characteristic of bronchiectasis, with a sensitivity of 97%. It may reveal emphysema and suggest allergic bronchopulmonary aspergillosis if proximal bronchiectasis is seen.

Ultrasound examination of the hepatobiliary system
Conduct to look for any evidence of cirrhosis/gallstones.

Abdominal radiograph
This may show underlying gallstones or a partial intestinal obstruction (meconium ileus equivalent in CF).

Plan to review the patient in clinic when the results of tests are available.

Further discussion

In this scenario the presence of pulmonary and abdominal symptoms in a young man may suggest a late presentation of CF. Up to 7% of patients with CF are diagnosed at age $\geq$18 years, when they are more likely than children to present with gastrointestinal symptoms and diabetes mellitus. Intermittent abdominal pain in CF can be caused by intermittent partial obstruction, low-grade appendicitis, duodenal irritation as a result of failure to buffer gastric acid or cholelithiasis. A further clue may be culture of *Staphylococcus aureus* from the sputum. The most appropriate initial tests should therefore be directed towards the presumed diagnosis of CF in this case.

Common variable immunodeficiency is certainly another possibility, especially since by profession the patient is at increased risk of exposure to bacterial and viral infection.

Pulmonary TB and lung abscess are rather unlikely because of the timescale involved and lack of other systemic symptoms but should be ruled out by a chest radiograph.

The patient is too young to have COPD or even emphysema secondary to α_1-antitrypsin deficiency, because most patients with α_1-antitrypsin deficiency present between 32 years and 41 years and rarely before the age of 25 years. He does not meet the criteria for chronic bronchitis either, which is a diagnosis of exclusion. This is defined as the presence of chronic cough with sputum production that occurs most days of the week, at least 3 months a year, for more than two consecutive years, and in the absence of other specific causes.

1.1.3 Dyspnoea and fine inspiratory crackles

Letter of referral to the respiratory outpatient clinic

Dear Doctor,
Re: Mr Justin Banks, aged 56 years

Thank you for seeing this man who has been complaining of dyspnoea on exertion for the past 8 months. He denies any wheeze or chest pain but also gives a history of having a dry cough for over a year. He has never smoked and works as a clerk in the local council. His past medical history includes appendicectomy, and he was diagnosed with rheumatoid arthritis 3 years ago. Apart from regular non-steroidal anti-inflammatory drugs, he is not on any treatment. Examination reveals fine bibasal crackles only.

Please advise about diagnosis and management.

Yours sincerely,

Introduction

Dyspnoea on exertion with fine inspiratory crackles is a very common symptom and can be due to both cardiac and respiratory causes (Table 2). In this case the most likely diagnosis is interstitial lung disease but it is important to exclude cardiac failure.

History of the presenting problem

Because dyspnoea on exertion with fine inspiratory crackles can be due to congestive cardiac failure or respiratory problems, it is important to pursue both possibilities in your history taking.

Related to the cause of breathlessness

Congestive cardiac failure is suggested by:

> orthopnoea, paroxysmal nocturnal dyspnoea

> peripheral oedema (although can also suggest cor pulmonale due to lung disease)

> exertional chest pain/tightness

> a past history of ischaemic heart disease, hypertension or diabetes.

Airways disease (COPD/bronchiectasis) is suggested by:

> chronic cough productive of purulent sputum

> wheeze

> smoking history.

Diffuse parenchymal lung disease (DPLD, interstitial lung disease) is suggested by:

> progressive breathlessness that is predictable and does not vary

> a dry cough, which is common in DPLD

> the presence of a condition associated with DPLD (in this case rheumatoid arthritis)

> other known causes of DPLD, eg asbestos, drugs (in this case possibly methotrexate for rheumatoid arthritis).

In addition, always ask about symptoms such as haemoptysis, weight loss, etc that may suggest the occurrence of malignancy in patients with underlying DPLD or COPD.

Related to the severity of breathlessness

It is important to assess how disabling the symptoms are by asking how far the patient can walk. A useful objective way of assessing dyspnoea is by using the Medical Research Council (MRC) Dyspnoea Scale.

Key point

The MRC Dyspnoea Scale:

1 Not troubled by breathlessness except on strenuous exercise.

2 Is short of breath when hurrying or walking up a slight hill.

3 Walks slower than contemporaries on the level because of breathlessness or has to stop for breath when walking at own pace.

4 Stops for breath after about 100 metres or after a few minutes on the level.

5 Is too breathless to leave the house, or breathless when dressing or undressing.

Other relevant history

> Relevant past history: childhood respiratory infections, and perhaps also childhood history of measles or pertussis, would suggest bronchiectasis (see Section 2.4). Ask specifically about TB.

Table 2	Causes of breathlessness with fine inspiratory crackles
Cause	**Example**
Cardiac	Congestive cardiac failure
Respiratory	Airways disease (COPD or bronchiectasis) needs to be considered, although crackles are usually coarse DPLD > idiopathic pulmonary fibrosis, sarcoidosis and cryptogenic organising pneumonia > fibrosing alveolitis associated with autoimmune rheumatic disorder: rheumatoid arthritis, scleroderma, SLE, ankylosing spondylitis, mixed connective tissue disorder and polymyositis–dermatomyositis > associated with occupational and environmental exposure: silicosis, asbestosis, berylliosis, aluminium oxide fibrosis, farmer's lung, malt worker's and mushroom worker's lungs, bird fancier's lung and stenosis > autoimmune: primary biliary cirrhosis, granulomatosis with polyangiitis and inflammatory bowel disease > drug induced: amiodarone, methotrexate, penicillamine, busulfan, bleomycin and crack cocaine inhalation > other causes: radiotherapy, amyloidosis, Langerhans' cell histiocytosis, post-infections (eg tuberculosis), pulmonary alveolar proteinosis, lymphangioleiomyomatosis, eosinophilic pneumonia, acute respiratory distress syndrome and lymphangitic carcinomatosis

COPD, chronic obstructive pulmonary disease; DPLD, diffuse parenchymal lung disease; SLE, systemic lupus erythematosus.

> Joint pains: this patient is known to have rheumatoid arthritis, but otherwise joint symptoms would be suggestive of autoimmune rheumatic disorders and sarcoidosis; sacroiliac joints are affected in ankylosing spondylitis (usually upper-zone fibrosis).

> Eyes: hazy vision or decreased acuity, eye pain and photophobia with red eyes all suggest possible uveitis due to sarcoidosis or autoimmune disease.

> Skin problems: a photosensitive rash would suggest systemic lupus erythematosus (SLE).

> Drug history: drugs can cause pulmonary fibrosis. In routine practice check any drug in the *British National Formulary*, but note especially those detailed in Table 2.

> Occupational history: this man now works as a council clerk, but he may not always have done so.

> Hobbies: breeding pigeons can lead to extrinsic allergic alveolitis and cause pulmonary fibrosis in the long run. In routine clinical practice the patient may not mention this because they do not know that it is relevant, or because they fear that it is; in PACES the surrogate's briefing notes are more than likely to say 'Don't mention hobbies unless you are asked directly'.

Key point

Never forget a careful drug history. It's always worth asking specifically about amiodarone: 'Have you been given any drugs to control or steady the heart rate?'.

Plan for investigation and management

Investigation

Having taken a history and (in routine clinical practice, but not in PACES Station 2) examined the patient, the next step is to arrange investigations to confirm the diagnosis and find a cause for the underlying condition.

Chest radiograph

A reticulonodular pattern with loss of volume is seen in idiopathic pulmonary fibrosis. Bilateral hilar lymphadenopathy may be seen in sarcoidosis. In cases of asbestos exposure, pleural plaques may be visible. Look for cardiomegaly and Kerley B lines suggesting congestive cardiac failure. In old healed TB and ankylosing spondylitis, apical fibrosis will be seen.

Blood tests

> full blood count (FBC) to look for polycythaemia (due to hypoxia)

> autoimmune screen including rheumatoid factor, antinuclear antibodies and circulating antineutrophil cytoplasmic antibody (granulomatosis with polyangiitis, previously known as Wegener's)

> serum angiotensin-converting enzyme (ACE) levels (these may be raised in sarcoidosis)

> relevant precipitins (when extrinsic allergic alveolitis is suspected, eg bird fancier's lung).

Electrocardiogram

Look for features of pulmonary hypertension – right axis deviation, P pulmonale in lead II and dominant R in V1 may be seen in pulmonary diseases causing hypoxia. Cardiac sarcoidosis may present with heart block.

Echocardiogram

If cardiac failure is suspected.

Pulmonary function tests

Pulmonary fibrosis leads to a restrictive disorder with reduced forced expiratory volume in 1 second (FEV_1) and reduced forced vital capacity (FVC), but a normal FEV_1:FVC ratio, a reduced carbon monoxide transfer factor, and a reduced total lung capacity and residual volume.

Arterial blood gases

In pulmonary fibrosis an arterial blood gas (ABG) test should be performed if the saturations are less than 92% at rest, to assess for long-term oxygen therapy.

CT scanning

This is the investigation of choice (see Section 3.4.5) and can detect DPLD not visible on the chest radiograph (sensitivity is 94% as opposed to 80%).

Key point

A diagnosis of idiopathic pulmonary fibrosis can be made on CT alone if appearances are typical.

Bronchoscopy and bronchoalveolar lavage

Bronchoalveolar lavage is used to sample cells from the lower respiratory tract. It is not routinely indicated in idiopathic pulmonary fibrosis (where a neutrophilic infiltrate is usually seen) but can be useful in cases of suspected hypersensitivity pneumonitis or non-specific interstitial pneumonia (lymphocytic infiltrate) and in eosinophilic lung disease (eosinophils).

Lung biopsy

A histological diagnosis can be made by lung biopsy. This may be:

> Transbronchial lung biopsy – sampling error is common and samples are often too small to make a diagnosis. It is useful in granulomatous disorders, lymphangitis carcinomatosis, eosinophilic pneumonia, alveolar proteinosis and infections. It is a safe procedure and can be performed as a day case, although pneumothorax occurs in up to 10% of patients.

> Video-assisted thoracoscopic lung biopsy – this is performed under general anaesthesia and provides large, surgical biopsy samples.

Management

Specific management of diffuse parenchymal lung disease will depend upon the underlying cause.

General measures

> withdraw any drugs responsible

> treat any air-flow obstruction with bronchodilators

> stop smoking

> oxygen therapy as per blood gas results

> pulmonary rehabilitation to improve overall fitness

> pneumonia vaccination and yearly influenza vaccination.

Specific treatment

See Section 2.7 for further discussion.

1.1.4 Nocturnal cough

Letter of referral to the respiratory outpatient clinic

Dear Doctor,

Re: Mrs Nicola Cook, aged 36 years

Thank you for seeing this teacher who has a 5-month history of dry nocturnal cough. She has never smoked, is otherwise well and her physical examination is normal. She has tried various over-the-counter cough medications with no relief. I am at a loss as to the diagnosis: can you help?

Yours sincerely,

Introduction

Chronic cough is defined as cough persisting for over 8 weeks. It is the single most common complaint of adult patients to their GPs. It can be a very distressing symptom and may result in conflict with sleeping partners, affect job prospects, disrupt social life, and can generally undermine the patient's confidence. There are many causes (see Table 3): a systematic approach can help reach a diagnosis and hopefully cure this annoying symptom.

In studies of patients referred to tertiary care practices the first three conditions listed in Table 3 are found to be the cause of chronic cough in 65–95% of cases, with combinations of these often present. However, the concept of chronic cough hypersensitivity syndrome is emerging, which may provide an overarching umbrella for patients with chronic cough that may be triggered by various different underlying diseases. Proper history taking, examination and basic investigations can help in diagnosing most cases, but the remainder will need detailed investigations.

History of the presenting problem

An appropriate history will help narrow down the causes. Find out:

> How long has the cough been present for? A very long history is against a sinister cause.

> Did it start after an upper respiratory tract infection? This clearly suggests post-infective bronchial hyperresponsiveness.

> Is the cough worse with exertion? In cough variant asthma, the cough is worse during or after exertion and at night.

> Is there any wheeze? This would indicate asthma or congestive cardiac failure (CCF). In cough variant asthma, there is normally no wheeze or dyspnoea.

> Is there any heartburn, sour belches, indigestion or hoarseness of the voice in the morning? These signs would suggest gastro-oesophageal reflux disease (GORD) or oesophageal dysmotility.

> Has the patient had any headaches/ tenderness over their sinuses, a

Table 3	Causes of chronic cough
Common	Asthma syndromes: cough variant asthma; post-infective bronchial hyperresponsiveness; and eosinophilic bronchitis (see Section 2.8.4) UACS, also known as post-nasal drip syndrome GORD Smoking and COPD Chronic cough hypersensitivity syndrome
Less common	Lung cancer Drug induced (ACEIs and beta-blockers) Bronchiectasis TB Foreign body inhalation Occupational exposure Sarcoidosis Interstitial lung disease CCF Pertussis
Rare	Oesophageal dysmotility syndromes Zenker's diverticulum Tracheobronchomalacia

ACEIs, angiotensin-converting enzyme inhibitors; CCF, congestive cardiac failure; COPD, chronic obstructive pulmonary disease; GORD, gastro-oesophageal reflux disease; TB, tuberculosis; UACS, upper airway cough syndrome.

blocked or running nose, sneezing bouts or a dripping sensation at the back of their throat? These symptoms would indicate upper airway cough syndrome (UACS).

> Is the patient a smoker and is there haemoptysis? Always consider bronchogenic carcinoma in such a case.

> Is the cough accompanied by regular expectoration of phlegm that could be suggestive of bronchiectasis?

> The combination of haemoptysis with weight loss, night fever and chest pain would point towards lung cancer or TB.

> Are the symptoms worse at work? If so this would clearly indicate occupational exposure is an important factor.

> Does the patient have any painful rashes on their legs, with joint pains and itching of the eyes (iritis)? Remember sarcoidosis in such cases.

> Is there dysphagia and recurrent lower respiratory infections? If so, consider oesophageal dysmotility and Zenker's diverticulum.

Other relevant history

Is there any other medical history that could suggest a diagnosis?

> Has the patient been a smoker?

> Do they have a past history of asthma?

> Do they have a past history of rhinitis, sinusitis, nasal polyps or nasal blockage?

> Are the symptoms seasonal? If yes, could this be allergic rhinitis or asthma?

> Has the patient or any close contacts had TB in the past?

> Has the patient had any oesophageal disorder such as Barrett's oesophagus? This can predispose to reflux oesophagitis and cough.

> What is the patient's drug history – enquire about angiotensin-converting enzyme inhibitors (ACEIs), nitrofurantoin and beta-blockers in particular.

> Does the patient suffer from any autoimmune rheumatic disorder?

> Up to 4% of patients with rheumatoid arthritis may have bronchiectasis presenting as cough.

> Is there any history of ankle swelling, orthopnoea, paroxysmal nocturnal dyspnoea and ischaemic heart disease? If so, think of CCF.

Plan for investigation and management

After explaining to the patient that under normal clinical circumstances you would examine her to confirm that there are no abnormalities as stated in the letter from her GP, you would plan as follows.

Chest radiograph

All patients with a chronic cough should have a chest radiograph to look for evidence of malignancy, interstitial lung disease (ILD), infection or CCF. At times a fluid level behind the cardiac shadow will point towards a hiatus hernia with a cough due to associated GORD.

Peak expiratory flow monitoring

A peak expiratory flow (PEF) recording showing diurnal variation is helpful in establishing the diagnosis of asthma as a cause for the chronic cough. If such variation is seen, then a therapeutic trial of inhaled corticosteroid is warranted before proceeding with further investigation.

Pulmonary function tests

These are essential both for diagnosing COPD and assessing its severity. In ILD, lung function tests will show a restrictive pattern.

Sputum examination

Sputum, if present, should be collected for microscopy and bacterial, mycobacterial and fungal culture; it should also be checked to look for differential cell count (eosinophilia in asthma).

Other investigations

Depending on the clinical findings and the results of these investigations, then the following investigations may be appropriate.

Ears/nose/throat opinion, nasendoscopy and imaging (X-ray and/or CT scan of sinuses)

Look for nasal polyps, rhinitis and sinusitis.

Twenty-four hour ambulatory oesophageal pH monitoring

A probe is inserted into the oesophagus to enable monitoring of pH for 24 hours. Patients wear a device called a Digitrapper, through which they record incidents of cough, heartburn, chest pain or other symptoms. When the monitoring period is over analysis seeks to determine how fluctuations in acidity relate to the patient's symptoms.

Oesophageal manometry

Sometimes referred to as an oesophageal function or oesophageal motility study, this test is used to check how well the muscles of the oesophagus are working. It also measures the strength of the lower oesophageal sphincter or 'valve' that prevents the backward flow of food and acid contents from the stomach into the oesophagus. It is helpful in assessing patients with a cough due to oesophageal dysmotility syndrome.

High-resolution CT scan of the lungs

This can identify patients with pulmonary fibrosis and may be diagnostic.

Bronchial challenge test

Using direct bronchoconstrictors such as methacholine or histamine, asthmatics demonstrate both airway hypersensitivity (reacting at a lower dose) and hyperreactivity (greater bronchoconstriction per unit given) than non-asthmatic patients. A bronchial challenge test is indicated when asthma is a possibility but when other tests such as diurnal PEF measurement or bronchodilator reversibility are not diagnostic.

Bronchoscopy / CT staging scan

If there is a lung mass, a staging CT scan of the lungs will establish the extent of disease (stage), which will guide treatment decisions.

Electrocardiogram

Patients with CCF causing a nocturnal cough may have clues to the cause that are evident on the electrocardiogram (ECG), such as old infarcts or left ventricular hypertrophy (due to hypertension). If suspected, then brain natriuretic peptide is a good screening test for cardiac failure.

Echocardiogram

Patients suspected to have CCF on the basis of an elevated brain natriuretic peptide should have an echocardiogram to assess for left ventricular function.

Further discussion

Most causes of nocturnal cough can be diagnosed by a proper history and basic investigations, but some patients may need referral to an ear/nose/throat specialist or a gastroenterologist.

Once a diagnosis is reached patients with GORD may also need advice about lifestyle modifications such as:

> stopping smoking

> losing weight

> eating smaller meals

> avoiding tea, coffee and alcohol

> avoiding foods high in acidity (citrus fruit, tomatoes)

> elevating the head end of their bed by 15 cm

> avoidance of recumbency for 3 hours postprandially

> weight reduction

> decreasing their fat intake.

1.1.5 Lung cancer with asbestos exposure

Letter of referral to the respiratory outpatient clinic

Dear Doctor,
Re: Mr Anthony Edwards, aged 56 years

I would be grateful for your opinion on this taxi driver who came to see me last week with a 4-month history of right-sided nagging chest ache. A chest X-ray was requested and the report indicated that he has right-sided pleural thickening associated with a moderate pleural effusion. He has previously worked in numerous labouring jobs, including as a lagger.

He is an ex-smoker of 6 years. His appetite is poor of late and he has lost a stone in weight in the past 3 months. I fear the worst, but please advise on his further investigation and management.

Yours sincerely,

Introduction

Your main concern is that this patient has mesothelioma as a consequence of asbestos exposure, although asbestos also causes other pathology:

> pleural plaques

> benign, asbestos-related pleural thickening

> benign, asbestos-related pleural effusion

> asbestos-related interstitial fibrosis (asbestosis)

> lung cancer.

It is clearly vitally important to take a detailed occupational history in this case.

Key point

How to take an occupational history

> The easiest way of recording employment is by asking the patient what he or she did immediately after leaving school and then recording positions chronologically; people tend to remember their jobs most easily this way.

> Ask about occupations not asbestos exposure – many workers cannot remember, or deny, specific exposure but mesothelioma is more strongly correlated with particular occupations (especially carpenters, plumbers, shipyard workers and building labourers) than with remembered asbestos exposure.

> Do not forget holiday jobs from school or casual employment (Steve McQueen, the American actor, worked with asbestos for 6 months before he became famous, and he died of asbestos-related lung disease).

> Did anyone in the patient's family work in an asbestos factory and bring the dust home on their clothes?

> On a more short-term basis, particularly if you are worried about the patient's current employment (say in relation to occupational asthma), do the symptoms worsen during the working week and improve at the weekend and during the holidays?

History of the presenting problem

It will clearly be appropriate to take a full history of respiratory symptoms and functional status, as described in previous history scenarios in this book, but the crucial element in this case will be to focus on taking the occupational history.

Occupational history

> If the patient remembers working with asbestos, how long was this for? How close was the contact and for what length of the working day? For example, was the patient working in the holds of ships unloading bags of asbestos? Were the patient's clothes covered in asbestos dust?

> Did the patient wear protective clothing or masks? Were these provided by his employers?

> Record the names of the companies that they worked for (they may be helpful for later reference).

Smoking history

Unless the patient is a never smoker, ask the age at which he started smoking and, for ex-smokers, the age at which he stopped. Ask what he smoked, and the quantity.

Key point

Smoking history
Take an accurate smoking history and record in the notes if and when the patient has stopped smoking. If a patient claims for compensation for an asbestos-related primary lung cancer at a later date, this information will be required, though it is not relevant in claims for mesothelioma.

Symptoms

> Has the patient had any chest pain? If so, how long does it last? Does it keep them awake at night?

> Has the patient been short of breath at rest or during exercise?

> Has it been more difficult of late for the patient to lie down without feeling breathless?

> Has the patient experienced any loss of weight or had a history of anorexia (the details given here suggest that the patient has)?

Persistent pain or rapid progression of symptoms are poor predictive features.

Other relevant history

It is important to ascertain whether there have been any previous episodes of chest problems. Did the patient suffer from chest problems as a child? Many previous chest pathologies can leave pleural thickening (Fig 3):

> asbestos exposure

> trauma

> previous chest infection / empyema

> previous haemothorax

> old TB.

Plan for investigation and management

Investigations
Chest radiograph

In this case, the patient presented with a chest film. In routine clinical practice look carefully for any pleural thickening – it is easy to miss. Is there any calcification, particularly over the diaphragm? Do not forget to look for areas of fibrosis.

CT scan of neck, chest and abdomen

This is invaluable when assessing the extent of disease and checking whether there is pleural thickening, fibrosis or

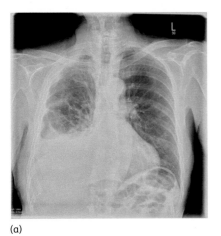
(a)

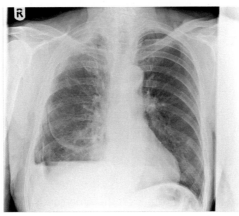
(b)

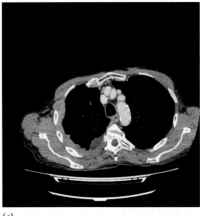
(c)

Fig 3 Chest radiograph showing obvious right-sided pleural thickening and effusion caused by mesothelioma **(a)**. Following pleural fluid drainage, a hydropneumothorax is seen with pleural thickening cranially **(b)**. Pleural thickening is more readily appreciated on CT scans **(c)**.

malignancy (Fig 4). If appropriate, a CT scan may be followed by a CT-guided biopsy. In cases of bronchogenic cancer and asbestos exposure the presence of fibrosis supports the argument that the patient was exposed to significant quantities of asbestos. Where there is parietal pleural thickening, CT features suggestive of malignancy are:

> pleural thickening >1 cm in thickness

> circumferential thickening

> pleural nodularity

> pleural thickening extending onto the mediastinal pleural surface.

In addition, there may be evidence of metastatic disease in other organs on CT scanning, in particular the lungs, liver and bones. Patients with bronchogenic malignancy commonly have enlarged supraclavicular lymph nodes which can be biopsied easily under ultrasound guidance, hence a CT scan covering the lower half of the neck is valuable.

Pleural aspiration

Pleural aspiration is the first diagnostic test for a unilateral pleural effusion.

Hazard

Pleural aspiration has low sensitivity for the diagnosis of malignant mesothelioma. A tissue biopsy is almost always required, and this can be combined with pleural drainage and pleurodesis in thoracoscopy.

Thoracoscopy

This is widely available in specialist centres, where it can be performed by chest physicians, and thoracic or cardiothoracic surgeons. It has a far higher detection rate than blind biopsy (95% in combination with aspiration versus 70% for Abrams' biopsy plus aspiration), and pleurodesis can be performed at the same time if malignancy is confirmed.

Other tests

It will clearly be appropriate to check the patient's full blood count (FBC) (this might reveal anaemia), their electrolytes, renal, liver and bone function tests (for evidence of

metastatic disease); and their lung function tests (to establish baseline).

Management

Specific management will depend on the precise diagnosis, but given the high likelihood of malignant disease referral to a specialist chest physician is required.

1.1.6 Breathlessness with a normal chest radiograph

Dear Doctor,

Re: Mr Colin MacDonald, aged 44 years

I would be grateful for your advice regarding this man who has presented with a 6-month history of breathlessness. He has smoked 20 cigarettes a day since the age of 16, but has recently cut down to five per day. Trials of inhaled steroids and diuretics have been unhelpful. At present his only medication is a steroid nasal spray for his rhinitis. His younger daughter suffers from asthma.

I could not find anything abnormal on physical examination. His chest radiograph is reported as being within normal limits. His spirometry shows forced expiratory volume in 1 second (FEV_1) of 2.6 L (83% predicted), forced vital capacity (FVC) 3.1 L (79% predicted), and an FEV_1:FVC ratio of 83%. Oxygen saturation (on air) is 93%.

I would value your help to make a diagnosis.

Yours sincerely,

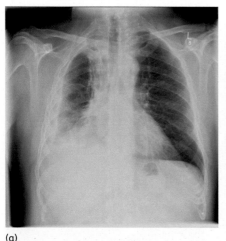
(a)

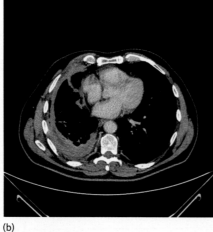
(b)

Fig 4 Chest radiograph **(a)** and CT scan **(b)** of patient with mesothelioma causing right-sided pleural thickening, volume loss and mediastinal shift, with invasion into the right hemithorax.

Introduction

The most likely causes of chronic breathlessness with a normal chest radiograph are shown in Table 4.

Normal spirometry makes COPD unlikely. Asthma as a sole diagnosis would also be improbable given that significantly reduced oxygen saturation is associated with normal spirometry.

Key point

Low oxygenation rules out the possibilities of chronic hyperventilation syndrome or anaemia as the primary cause of dyspnoea.

In diffuse parenchymal lung disease (DPLD), lung function usually shows a restrictive pattern. However, remember that some patients have preserved lung volumes or airflow obstruction, hence it is inappropriate to use restrictive lung function as a criterion to exclude the diagnosis (see Section 2.7). Although most disease would be visible on a high-quality chest radiograph, it is possible to have subtle DPLD that is not.

Although the most common presentation of pulmonary embolism is pleuritic chest pain, with or without haemoptysis, isolated dyspnoea may be the only symptom and the possibility of chronic thromboembolic pulmonary hypertension must be considered in this case. Exertional dyspnoea is also the most common presentation of an early pulmonary hypertension, a rare condition that is frequently underdiagnosed. In view of a history of rhinitis and a family history of asthma, Churg–Strauss syndrome should be also excluded in this case.

History of the presenting problem

A complete history is important to narrow the differential diagnosis. Ask specifically about the following.

Initial presentation

Was it insidious, or did it following any environmental/dust exposure?

Mode of presentation

Was it chronic or episodic? Episodic presentation narrows the diagnostic fields to extrinsic allergic alveolitis (EAA), eosinophilic pneumonia and vasculitis (including Churg–Strauss syndrome). However, there is considerable variation in the time frame of presentation of many DPLDs. For example, eosinophilic pneumonia and Churg–Strauss syndrome may present acutely, episodically or chronically. Others, such as drug-induced DPLDs, may be acute or chronic. Cryptogenic organising pneumonia can occur episodically or seasonally, but would almost always lead to an abnormal chest radiograph.

Other chest symptoms

Patients with DPLDs may have an unproductive cough. A productive cough makes DPLD rather unlikely. Other chest symptoms are uncommon in DPLDs, but if present are of importance as they may further narrow the differential diagnosis. Pleuritic chest pain may occur in DPLDs associated with systemic lupus erythematosus (SLE) (50% of cases), rheumatoid arthritis (25% of cases) and mixed connective tissue disease. Some patients with chronic pulmonary emboli may recall pleuritic chest pain at the time of initial presentation. Substernal discomfort or pain is common in sarcoidosis. Wheezing may occur in chronic eosinophilic pneumonia and Churg–Strauss syndrome. Haemoptysis may be present in chronic pulmonary emboli and vasculitis. Symptoms of recurrent flu-like illness are often a feature of EAA or vasculitis (see Sections 2.7 and 2.8).

Risk factors of pulmonary embolism

Assess the clinical probability of pulmonary embolism (PE) by asking about previous episodes of thromboembolism, risk factors (immobility, etc) and family history.

Drug history

Take a detailed history of all previous and current medication, both prescribed and non-prescribed. Many classes of drugs cause DPLD, hence in routine clinical practice always consult the drug datasheet or *British National Formulary*. The variable timing of onset of symptoms from drug-related DPLD is well known, and some drugs such as cyclophosphamide and amiodarone may have been taken for up to several years before drug-induced alveolitis develops. Do not forget to enquire directly about appetite suppressants, a known cause of pulmonary hypertension.

Prevalence	Cause
Common	COPD Asthma Anaemia
Less common	Pulmonary vascular disorders – pulmonary emboli, pulmonary hypertension DPLD Left heart disease – ischaemic heart disease and aortic stenosis Chronic hyperventilation syndrome
Rare	Pulmonary vasculitis – eg Churg–Strauss syndrome

Table 4 Conditions presenting chronically with breathlessness and a normal chest radiograph

COPD, chronic obstructive pulmonary disease; DPLD, diffuse parenchymal lung disease.

Lifetime occupations

Review in chronological order, including specific duties and known exposures to dust, gases and chemicals. Record details of occupational processes, the exposure level and type of respiratory protection provided.

Recreational interests

Enquire specifically as to exposure to birds.

Family history

Sarcoidosis, idiopathic pulmonary fibrosis (previously known as cryptogenic fibrosing alveolitis) and pulmonary hypertension may rarely be familial.

Travel history

Travelling predisposes to infection with parasites, which may cause pulmonary eosinophilia and is also a risk factor for PE.

Other relevant history

Enquire about other systemic disorders associated with lung diseases and their symptoms (arthralgia or arthritis, rash, dry or red or painful eyes, dry mouth and Raynaud's phenomenon).

A cardiac history is also crucial in this case. This patient had a clear chest, but those with basal crackles due to DPLD are frequently prescribed diuretics for an erroneous diagnosis of heart failure. A lack of response to diuretics is usual in chronic DPLD.

> **! Hazard**
>
> Crackles do not mean that the diagnosis is pulmonary oedema.

A past or current history of asthma and rhinitis may suggest Churg–Strauss syndrome.

A prior history of pulmonary embolus, particularly if it was large or had occurred more than once, would raise concerns about chronic thromboembolic pulmonary hypertension.

A past history of cancer and radiotherapy may explain drug-induced / radiation pneumonitis.

Plan for investigation and management

The priority as always is to decide on the basis of history (and in routine practice the clinical examination) which of the differential diagnoses are most likely in the individual scenario and direct the investigations accordingly.

After explaining to the patient that under normal clinical circumstances you would examine him to confirm his GP's findings, you would consider the following.

Chest radiograph

This should be repeated, particularly if done more than 3 months ago, to assess whether there is any new change.

> **! Hazard**
>
> Remember that the chest radiograph is normal in as many as 10% of patients with some forms of DPLD, particularly those with hypersensitivity pneumonitis.

Lung function tests

Have there been any changes in spirometry? Look for early signs of a restrictive defect such as reduced total lung capacity, residual volume and carbon monoxide transfer factor.

Arterial blood gases

To confirm hypoxaemia as suggested by oximetry.

High-resolution CT

A combination of clinical and high-resolution CT (HRCT) information enables a correct diagnosis in up to 80% of patients with DPLD.

CT pulmonary angiography or ventilation/perfusion lung scanning

Perform if there is high clinical probability of chronic thromboembolic pulmonary hypertension.

Blood tests

Full blood count (FBC) (to check for anaemia and eosinophil count) and urea, creatinine, electrolytes, liver and bone function tests (because calcium may be elevated in sarcoidosis). Check antinuclear antibodies and rheumatoid factor to look for clues to autoimmune rheumatic disease, precipitins (including avian and *Saccharopolyspora rectivirgula*, formerly *Micropolyspora faeni*) if EAA (eg bird fancier's lung or farmer's lung) is suspected, and antineutrophil cytoplasmic and glomerular basement membrane antibodies if vasculitis is possible.

> **Key point**
>
> If there is a high clinical suspicion of pulmonary embolism (PE), do not measure D-dimer levels but proceed directly to appropriate imaging tests – CT pulmonary angiography or ventilation/perfusion lung scanning.

Urine dipstick

To exclude haematuria and proteinuria that might indicate vasculitis or autoimmune rheumatic disease.

Electrocardiogram

This may show features of valvular heart disease or may provide an estimate of pulmonary artery systolic pressure by estimating the pressure gradient across the tricuspid valve in patients with tricuspid regurgitation. It is therefore an important investigation when there is clinical suspicion of pulmonary hypertension or chronic thromboembolic disease.

Echocardiography

Perform if pulmonary hypertension is suspected. Echocardiography can also detect some occult cardiac causes of pulmonary hypertension (shunts, valvular and left ventricular abnormalities).

Further discussion

If DPLD is confirmed by HRCT scan, lung biopsy may not be required if the clinical setting is appropriate and if the appearances are characteristic (see Section 2.7). For patients in whom lung biopsy is required, HRCT images can help to decide whether transbronchial biopsy or open lung biopsy would be the best option, and determine the most appropriate areas from which the biopsy samples should be taken.

If chronic thromboembolic disease is confirmed, a search for an occult malignancy must be considered: women should have a thorough clinical breast examination, all patients should have a pelvic examination, and there should be a low threshold for investigation of gastrointestinal or other symptoms.

If the echocardiogram suggests pulmonary hypertension, further investigations are needed to exclude its known causes, as is right heart catheterisation to determine the patient's prognosis and optimise their treatment. In this situation the patient requires referral to one of the national pulmonary hypertension centres because the management of pulmonary hypertension is highly specialised.

1.2 Clinical examination

1.2.1 Coarse crackles: bronchiectasis

Instruction

This man complains of breathlessness and daily cough with sputum production – please examine his respiratory system.

General features

Look in the sputum pot: note the quantity and character of the patient's sputum.

Is the patient cachexic, of short stature, cyanosed or oedematous (hypoproteinaemic / cor pulmonale)? Does he have clubbing of the fingernails? If these are present in a young patient (<40 years old) consider CF.

Is there an indwelling venous line / 'Portacath'? These are commonly found in patients that require frequent courses of intravenous antibiotics.

Respiratory examination

The auscultatory findings are only part of the picture, but concentrate on the following.

Nasal congestion

Does the patient appear to have a stuffy nose from the character of his voice? Several causes of cough and sputum also lead to chronic rhinosinusitis, including atopy, CF, common variable immunodeficiency and primary ciliary dyskinesia.

Trachea

This is not likely to be deviated, but is there a scar from previous tracheostomy?

Percussion

Areas of dullness are likely to indicate underlying consolidation.

Auscultation

Is expiration prolonged, thereby suggesting chronic airflow obstruction, which could be present in chronic asthma, COPD or bronchiectasis? Bronchial breathing indicates underlying consolidation. Crackles (typically coarse) over a particular area suggests bronchiectasis. Reduced breath sounds over an area are consistent with pleural effusion (lung base) or lung abscess (relatively uncommon).

In routine clinical practice you would clearly perform a full physical examination. This is not possible in the PACES station, but note if the abdomen is swollen (this may indicate cirrhosis/ascites) and if there is a gastrostomy feeding tube (percutaneous endoscopic gastrostomy tube – these are often used to support nutrition of patients with CF).

Further discussion

Diagnosis

In any patient presenting with chronic exertional dyspnoea and sputum production, consider:

> COPD (take a history of smoking, listen for wheeze and check spirometry)

> bronchiectasis (and any condition associated with bronchiectasis) (see Section 2.4)

> bronchial asthma (check history of wheeze, and ask if it is episodic)

> lung abscess and pneumonia (usually of acute onset and accompanied by fever).

In a young patient with chronic exertional dyspnoea and sputum production, consider:

> bronchiectasis (this may be caused by CF)

> α_1-antitrypsin deficiency

> common variable immunodeficiency (this may be suggested by recurrent pneumonia or sinusitis).

Key point

In any patient with breathlessness and clubbing, consider:

> bronchiectasis – look for hyperinflation, prolonged expiration, inhalers, sputum pot

> diffuse parenchymal lung disease (DPLD) (ie usual interstitial pneumonia / cryptogenic fibrosing alveolitis) – look for difficulty breathing *in* with short expiration

> lung abscess (less likely in PACES)

> carcinoma of the lung (less likely in PACES).

Investigations

Chest radiograph

A chest radiograph is helpful to exclude an acute infection. It may also reveal features of COPD, bronchiectasis (Fig 5), interstitial fibrosis, lung abscess or cardiomegaly in congestive cardiac failure. Dextrocardia may be present.

Sputum examination

Send for microscopy, culture and sensitivity, including acid-fast bacilli.

Lung function tests

These will determine if there is airway obstruction, and in cases of COPD will help evaluate treatment. Alternatively they may show a restrictive defect, with reduced gas transfer, consistent with DPLD. It is important to request full lung function tests comprising static lung volumes, spirometry and transfer factor.

CT scanning of the chest

Can diagnose bronchiectasis, interstitial lung diseases, emphysema or presence of bullae.

Arterial blood gases

Indicated if fingertip SaO_2 is <94% to check whether there is respiratory failure (type I or II).

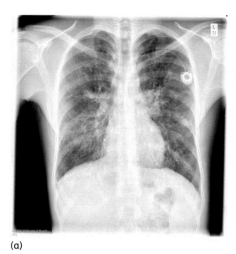
(a)

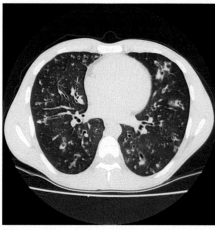
(b)

Fig 5 Chest radiograph **(a)** and CT scan **(b)** from a young male patient with cystic fibrosis, demonstrating bronchiectasis. A subcutaneous central venous port, or Portacath, is seen in the left subclavian vein. In (a) dilated airways with thickened walls can be seen end-on as ring shadows in the right upper zone, and as parallel lines ('tramlines') in the left upper zone, just medial to the Portacath.

Other investigations

Blood tests

A raised white cell count with neutrophilia suggests underlying bacterial infection. Secondary polycythaemia suggests chronic hypoxia. Serum α_1-antitrypsin level may be low, suggesting its deficiency and underlying emphysema. Liver function tests can exclude hepatic involvement in both CF and α_1-antitrypsin deficiency. Test immunoglobulin levels to exclude common variable immunodeficiency.

Electrocardiogram

Is there cor pulmonale?

Sweat sodium concentration

In CF the sweat sodium concentration is usually high (>60 mmol/L).

Ultrasound examination of the hepatobiliary system

Looking for cirrhosis and/or gallstones.

Management

> CF (see Section 2.5)

> bronchiectasis (see Section 2.4)

> COPD (see Section 2.3)

> pulmonary infections (lung abscess / pneumonia)

> common variable immunodeficiency.

1.2.2 Fine crackles: interstitial lung disease

Instruction

This man has had increasing exertional breathlessness and a dry cough for 6 months. Please examine his respiratory system.

General features

Look for cachexia, clubbing and cyanosis. Patients with advanced pulmonary fibrosis have rapid shallow breathing.

Signs of systemic disease:

> skin: look for signs of connective tissue disease (scleroderma/ calcinosis/Raynaud's and signs of dermatomyositis), rheumatoid nodules, sarcoid (erythema nodosum, lupus pernio)

> arthropathy

> eyes: scleritis/uveitis

> lymphadenopathy.

Look also for signs of treatment of a disease such as side effects of steroids.

Respiratory examination

Trachea

This is usually central in diffuse parenchymal lung disease, but may be pulled towards the side if there is severe and asymmetric fibrosis.

Palpation

There will be reduced expansion on affected side(s)/zone(s).

Percussion

This is normal in interstitial lung disease.

Auscultation

Typical crackles suggestive of pulmonary fibrosis are described as fine end-inspiratory 'popping' or a 'shower', and are likened to the sound of Velcro being prised apart or drawing pins falling on to a tiled floor. They will not clear with coughing. The distribution of crackles has some relation to the underlying condition (Table 5).

Further discussion

The terms 'interstitial lung disease' or 'diffuse parenchymal lung disease' are used to describe pathological processes involving the lung parenchyma. If the parenchyma becomes stiff because of fibrosis or infiltration, then the small airways it surrounds may snap open during inspiration – the origin of the typical fine end inspiratory crackles. Many different classification systems have been applied to these diseases, with the result being much confusion. It is easiest to start by dividing them by aetiology, as shown in Table 6, into those of unknown cause (idiopathic interstitial pneumonias) and those with a known cause. Note that it may be difficult clinically and

Table 5   Distribution of crackles as a guide to underlying disease

Distribution	Disease
Upper zones	Inhalational diseases (hypersensitivity pneumonitis, pneumoconiosis, etc)
	Ankylosing spondylitis
Lower zones	Idiopathic pulmonary fibrosis and other idiopathic interstitial pneumonias Asbestosis
	Pulmonary oedema
Anywhere	Sarcoid

Table 6   Classification of diffuse parenchymal lung disease

Class of disease	Example of cause
Idiopathic	Unknown[1]
Drugs[2]	Methotrexate
	Amiodarone
	Bleomycin
	Nitrofurantoin
Autoimmune disease / connective tissue disease	Rheumatoid arthritis
	Systemic sclerosis Dermatomyositis
	Ankylosing spondylitis
Pulmonary eosinophilic syndromes	Acute eosinophilic pneumonia
	Churg–Strauss syndrome
Inhalational injury	Hypersensitivity pneumonitis
	Crack cocaine / heroin / cigarettes
	Inorganic dusts: asbestosis, silicosis and coal worker's pneumoconiosis
Infection	*Pneumocystis jirovecii*, atypical pneumonia, viral pneumonia
Malignancy	Lymphangitis carcinomatosa
	Bronchoalveolar cell carcinoma
Miscellaneous	Sarcoidosis
	Langerhans' cell histiocytosis / histiocytosis X
	Radiation fibrosis

1 Idiopathic interstitial pneumonias include idiopathic pulmonary fibrosis, non-specific interstitial pneumonitis and cryptogenic organising pneumonia, etc (see the list below).

2 This is only a 'top four'; many other drugs have also been implicated. For further details see www.pneumotox.com.

radiographically to differentiate between these conditions and pulmonary oedema, and this should always be considered as an alternative diagnosis.

The idiopathic interstitial pneumonias can be classified in order of frequency as follows:

> idiopathic pulmonary fibrosis (usual interstitial pneumonitis)

> non-specific interstitial pneumonitis

> cryptogenic organising pneumonia

> acute interstitial pneumonitis

> respiratory bronchiolitis interstitial lung disease

> desquamative interstitial pneumonitis

> lymphoid interstitial pneumonitis.

Idiopathic pulmonary fibrosis is the most common idiopathic interstitial pneumonia and is characterised by a progressive fibrosing process with an absence of active inflammation, leading to dense scarring and destruction of the lung parenchyma (histologically this is termed 'usual interstitial pneumonitis').

Other idiopathic interstitial pneumonias contain variable degrees of established fibrosis/scarring and active inflammation. Patients with a significant inflammatory component to their disease may respond to immunosuppressive treatment.

> **Hazard**
> Do not get anxious over the classification of the various forms of interstitial lung disease. Unless there are signs of an associated rheumatological disease, it is usually not possible to make a precise diagnosis on the basis of clinical examination alone.

> If asked by the examiner what the cause of the fine crackles might be, simply say: 'There are a range of conditions that can cause pneumonitis and lung fibrosis: these may be idiopathic, such as idiopathic pulmonary fibrosis; or secondary to other causes, including hypersensitivity pneumonitis, connective tissue disease, sarcoid and drugs.'

Investigations

Chest radiograph
In interstitial lung disease this typically shows reticular and nodular shadowing, perhaps with honeycombing, volume loss and traction bronchiectasis in the worst affected areas. The heart border and diaphragms may give a 'moth-eaten' appearance. In sarcoid there may be hilar lymphadenopathy.

Lung function tests
These typically reveal a restrictive picture with a proportionate decrease in both spirometric (FEV_1 and FVC) and static lung volumes (eg total lung capacity), such that the FEV_1:FVC ratio is preserved. The carbon monoxide transfer factor is also reduced. It is important to establish a baseline.

Pulse oximetry
All patients should have pulse oximetry, leading to a blood gas if oxygen saturations are less than 92% at rest. In the early stages patients with interstitial lung disease may only desaturate on exertion, and a 6-minute walk test with saturation monitoring should be performed to assess this.

High-resolution CT
This is the diagnostic test of choice in patients with suspected interstitial lung disease. This needs to be assessed by a radiologist experienced in assessing parenchymal lung disease. Some conditions, including idiopathic pulmonary fibrosis, sarcoidosis and hypersensitivity pneumonitis, may be diagnosed on the basis of typical CT appearances alone.

> **Key point**
> High-resolution CT is the diagnostic test of choice in patients with suspected interstitial lung disease.

Lung biopsy
The need for tissue sampling in the diagnosis of interstitial lung disease should be addressed by discussion in an interstitial lung disease multidisciplinary team (ILD MDT) meeting. In short, where the combinations of clinical and radiographic features are diagnostic (eg in idiopathic pulmonary fibrosis) then a biopsy is not required. But if this is not the case, then the choice of biopsy technique (transbronchial biopsy versus open lung / video-assisted biopsy) depends again on the likely diagnosis. For example, in sarcoidosis the former is often diagnostic, whereas larger structurally intact (ie surgical) biopsies are required to diagnose idiopathic pulmonary fibrosis.

Other investigations
It is worth considering the following:

> full blood count (FBC)

> inflammatory markers (C-reactive protein (CRP), erythrocyte sedimentation rate (ESR))

> creatinine, electrolytes, and liver and bone function tests (to check for any evidence of multisystem disorder and hypercalcaemia in sarcoid)

> autoimmune and vasculitis screen (rheumatoid factor, antinuclear antibodies, extractable nuclear antigen and antineutrophil cytoplasmic antibodies)

> serum angiotensin-converting enzyme (sarcoid)

> precipitins (including avian and *Saccharopolyspora rectivirgula*, formerly *Micropolyspora faeni*) if hypersensitivity pneumonitis (eg bird fancier's lung or farmer's lung) is suspected

> also check urine dipstick for blood and protein (autoimmune rheumatic or vasculitic disorder).

Management

Treatment, as ever, depends on the underlying condition.

Where inhalational or systemic exposure is implicated, removal of the toxin if possible, or the patient from that environment if not, is necessary.

In idiopathic pulmonary fibrosis, immunosuppression is not beneficial and should not be used. Newer antifibrotic and antiangiogenic drugs (pirfenidone and nintedanib) have been shown to slow the rate of progression of fibrosis, and patients should be assessed by a specialist ILD MDT to determine suitability for these treatments.

Idiopathic pulmonary fibrosis has a poor prognosis (50% of patients die within 3 years of diagnosis) and palliative care services should be involved, preferably before the rapid terminal decline that typically occurs. Opiates provide good palliation of the distressing breathlessness and cough that are often a feature of advanced lung fibrosis. Oxygen therapy may be required (either long-term oxygen therapy or short-burst therapy to improve symptoms and/or exercise tolerance).

Other forms of interstitial lung disease have a much more benign prognosis than idiopathic pulmonary fibrosis, hence the importance of establishing an accurate diagnosis. Some forms of interstitial lung disease do contain a reversible inflammatory component, which may respond to immunosuppressive treatment. The interstitial pneumonitis seen in sarcoidosis, hypersensitivity pneumonitis and with connective tissue diseases often responds well to steroids and other immunosuppressive agents. Eosinophilic lung diseases are highly steroid responsive.

Lung transplantation should be considered, where appropriate, for patients with severe progressive lung fibrosis of any cause.

1.2.3 Stridor

Instruction

This man has had increasing difficulty in breathing. Please examine his respiratory system.

General features

Check for the following:

> From the bedside, note if there is a high-pitched sound with each of the patient's inspirations.

> Look for respiratory distress.

> Look for clues to underlying aetiology:

  > tracheostomy scar

  > goitre and hypothyroidism.

It is unlikely to occur in PACES, but in routine clinical practice look for evidence of malignancy (neck lymph nodes, clubbing, cachexia, tar staining of fingers and superior vena cava obstruction) and in an acute presentation look for signs to suggest anaphylaxis (facial/tongue oedema, erythema and wheeze).

Key point

In a case of stridor, look very carefully at the neck for a tracheostomy scar.

Respiratory examination

> Confirm the patient has stridor (as opposed to wheeze) – 'Open your mouth, and take a deep breath in and out as quickly as you can.'

> Is the trachea deviated?

> There will be no abnormal signs in the chest if the problem is confined to the upper airway.

Further discussion

Stridor and wheeze are both caused by turbulent airflow through the airways. Wheeze is predominantly an expiratory sound, and results from intrathoracic airflow obstruction. Stridor is heard during inspiration and indicates extrathoracic airflow obstruction, which may be fixed or variable (see flow–volume loops in Section 3.4.2).

Investigations

To determine the presence and cause of chronic extrathoracic airway obstruction, check:

> flow–volume loops:

  > fixed obstruction

  > variable extrathoracic obstruction

> laryngoscopy with or without bronchoscopy

> contrast-enhanced CT of the neck and upper mediastinum. In some centres dynamic CT scanning is available, in which continuous scanning of a short section of the airway is performed during the respiratory cycle to demonstrate variation in calibre during different phases of respiration.

Consider the causes of stridor (Table 7).

While a case of acute stridor is extremely unlikely to appear in any postgraduate examination, prompt recognition and appropriate management are life-saving in clinical practice (see Section 1.5.4).

Management

After emergency treatment to ensure the airway is secure and ventilation adequate, further treatment depends on the underlying cause. Specific treatment of the stenosis (for example in malignancy or post-intubation stenosis) may include laser treatment, airway stenting or bypass (ie tracheostomy).

1.2.4 Pleural effusion

Instruction

This man has had increasing difficulty in breathing for the past 2 months. Please examine his respiratory system.

General features

The primary things to check for are respiratory distress, tachypnoea and cyanosis.

Look for clues to underlying aetiology:

> heart failure / fluid overload
> malignancy – there are several signs that would suggest this:
  > sputum pot (haemoptysis)
  > cachexia
  > hoarse voice
  > clubbing
  > tar staining of fingers
  > jaundice (hepatic metastasis)
  > Horner syndrome (ptosis, miosis, anhidrosis and enophthalmos)
  > neck lymphadenopathy
  > superior vena cava obstruction

Table 7	Differential diagnoses of stridor
Acute (see Section 1.5.4)	Angio-oedema > Allergic > C1 esterase deficiency
	Inhaled foreign body
Subacute/chronic, due to progressive obstruction (may also present acutely when stenosis becomes critical)	Extrinsic compression in the neck or upper mediastinum: > Goitre > Lymph node mass > Mediastinal fibrosis > (Obstructive sleep apnoea – see Section 1.4.2)
	Intrinsic: > Tracheal/laryngeal tumour > Vocal cord dysfunction > Gastro-oesophageal reflux > Infection: 　> Epiglottitis 　> Abscess (retropharyngeal or peritonsillar) > Stenosis post-endotracheal intubation or tracheostomy
	Neurogenic: > Myasthenia gravis > Stroke

  > scar (from previous thoracic/breast surgery, CT-guided lung biopsy or pleural biopsy)
  > breast abnormalities (nipple retraction, deviation and mass)
> TB, indicated by:
  > sputum pot
  > lymphadenopathy
> rheumatoid arthritis, indicated by:
  > joint deformity
  > nodules
> other
  > SLE – rash
  > thickened, yellow nails – yellow nail syndrome.

Respiratory examination

General inspection

Look for:

> thoracotomy scar
> scar from previous chest drain / pleural aspiration
> chest wall deformity (thoracoplasty)
> asymmetric chest wall movement (reduced on side of effusion).

Trachea

If deviation is present this will be away from the side of a massive pleural effusion, or towards that side if there is coexisting ipsilateral collapse.

Palpation

> Examine the supraclavicular and cervical nodes as above.
> Expansion may be decreased on the side of the pleural effusion.

Percussion

> Check for dull to percussion on the side of the pleural effusion (it will be 'stony dull' if the effusion is large enough).

Auscultation

> Effusion is indicated by:
  > reduced or absent breath sounds (same area as above)
  > reduced vocal resonance / tactile vocal fremitus (same area as above).
> Bronchial breathing can sometimes be heard just above the effusion due to atelectasis of the overlying lower lobe.

Further discussion

Pleural effusions are divided into exudates and transudates on the basis of Light's criteria (Table 8). Exudates meet at least one criteria, whereas transudates meet none. Light's criteria has a high sensitivity for identifying exudates, but approximately 20% of transudates may be misclassified as (borderline) exudates, usually when patients with heart failure have been treated with diuretics.

The PACES examiner is likely to ask what diagnoses you would consider in a patient with a pleural effusion who presents on the general medical take (Table 9).

General approach to a patient with a pleural effusion

The synchronous aims of initial management are to relieve breathlessness, to elucidate an underlying cause and to minimise invasive investigations.

1 Does the clinical picture suggest a transudate?

> bilateral effusions

> signs of congestive cardiac failure

> hypoproteinaemia

If so, treat underlying cause and re-X-ray.

2 If there is no clear cause or effusion is not resolving, perform ultrasound (US)-guided pleural aspiration and send samples for standard testing. If pleural infection is confirmed, insert chest drain under US guidance and start antibiotics. If transudate, treat underlying cause.

3 If patient is breathless, aspirate up to 1,500 mL for symptomatic relief.

4 If there is no clear cause and exudate is confirmed by Light's criteria, patient will need contrast-enhanced CT.

5 If there is no diagnosis from pleural fluid and CT, consider pleural biopsy:

> thoracoscopy

> CT-guided biopsy if >0.5 cm pleural thickening on CT.

Table 8	Light's criteria for distinguishing exudative and transudative pleural effusions		
Discriminator		Exudate	Transudate
Ratio of pleural fluid protein to serum fluid protein >0.5		Yes	No
Pleural fluid LDH more than two-thirds higher than the normal upper limit for serum LDH		Yes	No
Ratio of pleural fluid LDH to serum fluid LDH >0.6		Yes	No

LDH, lactate dehydrogenase.

Table 9	Causes of a pleural effusion	
Type	Prevalence	Cause
Transudate	Common	Congestive cardiac failure
	Uncommon	Cirrhosis (hepatic hydrothorax) Nephrotic syndrome
	Rare	Myxoedema Peritoneal dialysis
Exudate	Common	Malignancy Bacterial infection (parapneumonic, empyema or TB)
	Uncommon	Pulmonary emboli Haemothorax Autoimmune rheumatic disorder
	Rare	Drug induced Gastrointestinal disease (pancreatitis or subphrenic abscess) Yellow nail syndrome Chylothorax

TB, tuberculosis.

Key point

Chest drain insertion for an undiagnosed pleural effusion is rarely necessary in the absence of suspected pleural infection. Therapeutic aspiration will relieve breathlessness while a diagnosis is established and a definitive management strategy implemented.

Investigations

Chest radiograph
Perform to confirm the presence of an effusion (Fig 6).

Pleural fluid
The following should be sent as standard tests:

> protein and lactate dehydrogenase (LDH) (see Table 8)

> microscopy and culture: both anaerobic and aerobic, and for TB

> cytology (50 mL sample) (Table 10)

> pH: a pH of <7.2 is seen in pleural infection and malignancy

> glucose: a value <1.6 mmol/L typically occurs in pleural infection or rheumatoid arthritis.

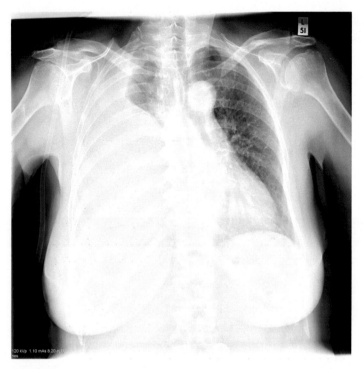

Fig 6 Chest radiograph showing a large right pleural effusion.

Table 10 Cytology of pleural effusions	
Cytological finding	**Possible diagnoses or inference**
Red cells >100 × 10⁹/L	Trauma, malignancy, parapneumonic and pulmonary embolism
White blood cells: neutrophilia (>50%)	Pyogenic infection
White blood cells: lymphocytosis (>80%)	TB, lymphoma and malignancy
White blood cells: eosinophilia (>10%)	Non-diagnostic: can be seen in benign asbestos effusions, drug reactions, pneumothorax, haemothorax, malignancy
Mesothelial cells	Absent in TB
Malignant cells	May be diagnostic of metastatic malignancy if adenocarcinoma confirmed by immunohistochemistry, but reactive mesothelial cells are difficult to distinguish from malignant mesothelial cells, so pleural biopsy is usually required to confirm a diagnosis of mesothelioma
TB, tuberculosis.	

In cases where diagnostic uncertainty remains, consider:

> rheumatoid factor: suggests rheumatoid arthritis is the cause of the effusion

> amylase: suggests pancreatitis

> adenosine deaminase: this is high in cases of TB

> cholesterol and triglycerides if chylothorax suspected.

In the context of sepsis or a parapneumonic effusion, pleural infection is confirmed by the presence of purulent pleural fluid (empyema) or the presence of a non-purulent parapneumonic effusion with a pH of <7.2 (complicated parapneumonic effusion) or a glucose of <1.6 mmol/L. These patients require treatment with a chest drain and antibiotics.

Thoracoscopy

Medical thoracoscopy is primarily a diagnostic procedure, but it can be used for therapeutic purposes. The most common indications in the UK are evaluation of the unknown exudative effusion, staging of diffuse malignant mesothelioma or lung cancer, and treatment by talc pleurodesis of malignant or other recurrent effusions.

Indications for pleurodesis

The indications for pleurodesis are symptomatic recurrent pleural effusion or spontaneous pneumothorax. Many substances have been injected intrapleurally in an attempt to obliterate the pleural space, the mechanism for most being simply to create an inflammatory reaction that leads to the fusion of the visceral and parietal pleura. Talc is the most common agent used in the UK.

1.2.5 Wheeze and crackles: chronic obstructive pulmonary disease

Instruction

This man complains of progressive exertional shortness of breath. Please examine his respiratory system.

General features

Examine for:

> central cyanosis

> bounding pulse and warm palms (signs of carbon dioxide retention)

> tar-stained fingers (if there is finger clubbing then consider concomitant lung cancer)

> tremor:

> > fine finger tremor secondary to β-agonist therapy

> > flapping tremor (indistinguishable from that associated with hepatic failure) due to carbon dioxide retention

> raised jugular venous pressure (JVP) during inspiration (Kussmaul's sign) – this may be observed in the absence of heart failure as a result of the compressive effect of lung inflation on cardiac filling

> signs of right heart failure

> cachexia – 20% of patients with moderate/severe COPD lose weight due to increased muscle protein breakdown as a systemic effect of COPD, but weight loss may be also a sign of concomitant lung cancer.

Look for the additional clues indicating any respiratory problems around the patient: inhalers, nebuliser and oxygen.

Respiratory examination

General inspection
Observe for:

> obvious breathlessness at rest

> tachypnoea

> signs of hyperinflation:

> > chest held near full inspiratory position at end of normal expiration

> > increased anteroposterior diameter of the chest – barrel-shaped chest

> > reduced distance between cricoid cartilage and suprasternal notch (less than three fingers' breadth)

> a 'pump handle' (up and down) movement of the ribs, instead of

normal 'bucket handle' (upwards and outwards) movement

> use of the accessory respiratory muscles of the neck and shoulder girdle

> generalised indrawing of the intercostal muscles and/or supraclavicular spaces on inspiration (Hoover's sign) due to hyperinflation

> pursed-lip breathing – expiration through pursed lips maintains a higher airway pressure, thus keeping the distal airways open longer during expiration and decreasing the work of breathing.

Palpation

> poor bilateral chest movement – expansion <5 cm suggests significant airflow obstruction.

Percussion

> hyperresonant percussion note (but be aware that this is not a robust physical sign)

> obliteration of cardiac and hepatic dullness

> low position of diaphragm with limited caudal motion.

Auscultation

> Breath sounds may be reduced.

> Prolonged expiratory phase of respiration – an excessively prolonged forced expiratory time (longer than 4 seconds, when measured with the stethoscope placed over the trachea) suggests a significant degree of airflow limitation.

> Wheezes – these may be initially heard on forced expiration only and may disappear because of low rate of airflow if this is severely limited.

> Coarse crackles (during early inspiration and often in expiration) – these may clear or alter as the secretions are shifted on coughing or deep breathing.

> Heart sounds may become distant with displacement of the point of maximal intensity to the subxiphoid region.

Further discussion

In early COPD a physical examination may be normal or may show prolonged expiration and/or wheezes on forced expiration only. As the disease progresses, abnormal signs will become apparent and in advanced stages many are almost pathognomonic.

At the time of presentation consider asthma as a differential diagnosis (Table 11) and α_1-antitrypsin deficiency in a patient presenting between the ages of 30 and 45.

Table 11 Clinical features differentiating COPD and asthma		
	COPD	**Asthma**
Smoker or ex-smoker	Nearly all	Possible
Symptoms under age 35	Rare	Common
Chronic productive cough	Common	Uncommon
Breathlessness	Persistent and progressive	Variable
Night-time waking with breathlessness and/or wheeze	Uncommon	Common
Significant diurnal or day-to-day variability of symptoms	Uncommon	Common
COPD, chronic obstructive pulmonary disease.		

Expect to be asked how you would confirm the diagnosis of COPD with lung function tests and how you would treat a patient presenting chronically with the condition or with an acute exacerbation (see Sections 2.2.2 and 2.3).

1.2.6 Cor pulmonale

Instruction

This woman complains of breathlessness on exertion. Please examine her chest.

General features

The key features to establish the diagnosis of cor pulmonale will be cyanosis and a grossly raised jugular venous pressure (JVP). If these are present then look carefully for:

> evidence of COPD

> features of an autoimmune rheumatic disorder, which would suggest the presence of a secondary interstitial lung disease

> obesity, which may indicate obstructive sleep apnoea or alveolar hypoventilation disorder

> severe chest wall deformity such as kyphoscoliosis

> evidence of a neurological disease, such as wasting of the muscles or the presence of muscle fasciculation

> clubbing, which would point towards a diagnosis of interstitial lung disease or bronchiectasis.

Respiratory examination

The findings in the chest will be determined by the underlying pathology, but particularly look for:

> hyperinflation and wheezing, which may indicate COPD

> bibasilar fine inspiratory crackles, which are suggestive of interstitial lung disease

> coarse inspiratory crackles, which are suggestive of bronchiectasis.

In routine clinical practice you would clearly perform a full physical examination. This is not possible in the PACES station, but you should still look at the ankles for oedema, and if asked say that you would particularly like to examine the abdomen to check for the pulsatile hepatomegaly caused by tricuspid incompetence.

Further discussion

The causes of cor pulmonale are shown in Table 12.

Investigation

An appropriate strategy to investigate a patient with suspected cor pulmonale would be as follows.

Respiratory
Conduct chest radiography and lung function tests, proceeding to CT scanning to define pulmonary pathology more clearly (CT pulmonary angiogram with high-resolution reconstruction).

Cardiac
Perform electrocardiogram (ECG) and echocardiography, looking in particular for evidence of right atrial/ventricular dilatation or hypertrophy. Perform right and left heart catheterisation in some cases (for example, where there is no evident respiratory or cardiac diagnosis, or for further estimation of an intracardiac shunt).

Treatment

This will depend on the underlying diagnosis, but be aware of the issues surrounding diuretic treatment. A difficult balance needs to be struck between denying diuretics to a patient with massive uncomfortable peripheral oedema (and perhaps ascites) and rendering the patient exhausted, hypotensive and with advancing renal

Table 12	Causes of cor pulmonale		
General cause	**Prevalence[1]**		**Example**
Lung disease	Common		COPD Cystic fibrosis Interstitial lung disease
Disorder of ventilatory control	Common		Obstructive sleep apnoea
	Uncommon		Primary central hypoventilation
Thoracic cage deformity	Common		Kyphoscoliosis
Neuromuscular disorder	Uncommon		Amyotrophic lateral sclerosis Bilateral diaphragmatic paralysis Poliomyelitis / post-polio syndrome
	Rare		Guillain–Barré syndrome Muscular dystrophy Myasthenia gravis
Disorder of the pulmonary circulation	Uncommon		Chronic recurrent pulmonary thromboembolism Primary pulmonary hypertension
	Rare		Pulmonary veno-occlusive disease Schistosomiasis Sickle cell anaemia

1 Prevalence as cause of cor pulmonale in developed countries.
COPD, chronic obstructive pulmonary disease.

impairment as a result of over-diuresis. In the presence of cor pulmonale a high right-sided filling pressure is required to generate cardiac output.

> **Hazard**
>
> Be aware of the difficulties of managing cor pulmonale with diuretics.

1.2.7 Pneumonectomy/lobectomy

Instruction

This man has long-standing exertional dyspnoea. Please examine his chest.

General features

Look for signs related to chronic hypoxic lung disease (see Sections 1.2.5, 1.2.6 and 2.3):

> cyanosis (central and peripheral), bounding pulse or coarse flap (carbon dioxide retention)

> signs of right-heart failure.

Also, check for signs related to possible underlying malignancy (see Section 1.2.4):

> muscle wasting or signs of weight loss

> tar-stained fingers/moustache

> clubbing (this also occurs in chronic suppurative lung disease – another possible reason for pneumonectomy or lobectomy)

> lymphadenopathy: supraclavicular (especially behind the medial end of the clavicle) and neck nodes

> superior-vena cava obstruction, indicated by:

> > facial and/or upper limb oedema

> > fixed raised JVP

> Horner syndrome, suggested by:

> > unilateral partial ptosis, miosis with or without anhidrosis.

Also take note of oxygen, sputum pot and nebulisers/inhalers.

Respiratory examination

General inspection

Observe for:

> respiratory distress and tachypnoea

> asymmetric chest wall movement

> thoracotomy scars (this may either be a large, single scar approximately along the line of the 7th rib, or a number of small 2–5 cm scars in the case of a thoracoscopic lung resection)

> chest wall deformity (thoracoplasty).

Trachea

Check carefully for deviation.

Palpation

> Examine supraclavicular and neck nodes as above.

> Expansion is decreased on the side of lung resection. It is usually not possible to tell clinically which lobe or lobes have been resected, but there may be reduced expansion of the affected hemithorax.

Percussion

> Dull to percussion – the hemidiaphragm may be raised on the side of the resection and this may lead to basal dullness.

Auscultation

> Breath sounds may be reduced in the affected area, although paradoxically following complete pneumonectomy they may be loud or normal because contralateral breath sounds are transmitted through the fibrosed pleural space and because the normal contralateral lung shifts over and is audible over the affected hemithorax. Bronchial breathing and increased vocal resonance (or tactile vocal fremitus) can sometimes be heard. If you find the breath sounds difficult to interpret think about the scar, tracheal position and percussion note when deciding what is going on.

Further discussion

Consider possible reasons for pneumonectomy or lobectomy (Table 13).

Thoracoplasty, where the hemithoracic cavity was reduced/obliterated by fracturing multiple ribs and moving the anterior and lateral chest wall posteromedially was a common procedure historically for pulmonary TB before the availability of antituberculous medication. The signs are as for upper lobectomy apart from the obvious deformity.

The first investigation that you would request would obviously be a chest radiograph.

Table 13	Reasons for lung resection
Frequency	**Cause**
Common	Lung cancer
Less common	Massive pulmonary haemorrhage Tuberculosis (also thoracoplasty): multidrug-resistant disease in contemporary setting or historic treatment Aspergilloma Bronchiectasis – very rarely treated surgically now Lung abscess / necrotising pneumonia Trauma

1.2.8 Apical signs: old tuberculosis

Instruction

This patient had TB in the past. Please examine his respiratory system.

General features

> If there is bronchiectasis (known to occur with TB) the patient may be bringing up copious sputum with haemoptysis. Look for a sputum pot.

> Scars: before the antibiotic era (approximately 1950 onwards, ie patients likely to be at least 70 years old), various surgical procedures were done to try and treat TB, including phrenic nerve crush, thoracotomy, thoracoplasty and/or plombage (this involved collapse of the affected portion of the lung, usually the upper lobe, and filling the space with 5–18 polystyrene spheres).

Respiratory system examination

Inspection

> There may be a deformity of the upper chest (thoracoplasty).

> Look for reduced movement of the upper chest wall on respiration.

> Look for a scar in the supraclavicular area suggestive of previous phrenic nerve crush.

Trachea

> Is the trachea deviated? In fibrosis it is pulled towards the affected side.

Palpation

> Confirm reduced expansion of the upper chest wall.

Percussion

> The percussion note may be dull at the apex/apices.

> Dullness at the lung base could indicate a TB effusion or a raised hemidiaphragm, which could be due to previous phrenic nerve crush or volume loss due to fibrosis.

Auscultation

> Bronchial breath sounds may be heard, with or without crackles, at the apex/apices.

Further discussion

Old healed TB usually presents as pulmonary nodules in the hilar area or upper lobes, with or without fibrotic scars and volume loss. Bronchiectasis and pleural scarring may be present, with signs localised to the upper chest wall.

Differentiating active TB from inactive TB can be very difficult. The clinical indications of active TB include chronic sputum production, weight loss, fevers and night sweats. However, these symptoms also occur with bronchiectasis, which can be a result of old, inactive TB. It must be remembered that a chest radiograph cannot rule out disease activity accurately. All cases should have sputum examination, and some patients may need a bronchoscopy. Interferon gamma release assays (QuantiFERON and T-Spot) will not help distinguish active from inactive disease.

Hazard

Differentiating active TB from inactive TB can be very difficult.

The signs suggestive of active TB on a chest radiograph are:

> Infiltrate or consolidation – opacification of airspaces within the lung parenchyma. Consolidation or infiltrate can be dense or patchy and might have irregular, ill-defined or hazy borders.

> Any cavitary lesion – ie lucency (darkened area) within the lung parenchyma, with or without the irregular margins that might indicate an area of surrounding airspace consolidation or infiltrates, or surrounding nodular or fibrotic (reticular) densities, or both. Calcification can exist around a cavity.

> Nodule with poorly defined margins – round density within the lung parenchyma, also called a tuberculoma. Nodules included in this category are those with margins that are indistinct or poorly defined. The surrounding haziness can be either subtle or readily apparent, and suggests coexisting airspace consolidation.

> Pleural effusion – this finding must be distinguished from blunting of the costophrenic angle, which may or may not represent a small amount of fluid within the pleural space (except in children when even minor blunting must be considered a finding that can suggest active TB).

> Hilar or mediastinal lymphadenopathy – the enlargement of lymph nodes in one or both hila or within the mediastinum, with or without the associated atelectasis or consolidation.

> Linear, interstitial disease (in children only) – prominence of linear, interstitial (septal) markings.

> Other miliary TB – nodules of 1–2 mm distributed throughout the parenchyma.

The signs suggestive of inactive TB are:

> A discrete fibrotic scar or linear opacity – discrete linear or reticular densities within the lung. Calcification can be present within the lesion and then the lesion is called a 'fibrocalcific' scar.

> Discrete nodule(s) without calcification – one or more nodular densities with distinct borders and without any surrounding airspace opacification. Nodules are generally round or have rounded edges. These features enable them to be distinguished from infiltrates or airspace opacities.

> Discrete fibrotic scar with volume loss or retraction – discrete linear densities with reduction in the space occupied by the upper lobe. Associated signs include upward deviation of the fissure or hilum on the corresponding side, along with asymmetry of the volumes of the two thoracic cavities.

> Discrete nodule(s) with volume loss or retraction – one or more nodular densities with distinct borders and no surrounding airspace opacification, as well as a reduction in the space occupied by the upper lobe.

> Other – any other finding suggestive of prior TB, such as upper lobe bronchiectasis.

Expect to be asked about the management of a case of pulmonary TB and be able to discuss chemotherapy and contact tracing.

1.2.9 Cystic fibrosis

Instruction
This 20-year-old man has been complaining of increasing shortness of breath. Please examine his respiratory system.

General features

Key point
The young patient with a severe chronic respiratory condition is very likely to have CF.

Around the bed, check for:

> non-invasive ventilation (machine, circuit and mask)

> oxygen tubing

> nebulisers/inhalers

> sputum pot (with thick purulent secretions).

When examining the patient, look for the following:

> does he look young for his age? Any chronic debilitating condition retards growth

> cyanosis

> cachexia

> current long-term intravenous access (eg Portacath) or signs of repeated intravenous access attempts

> clubbing

> bruising (insulin injection sites)

> rash (vasculitis or drug-induced)

> proximal myopathy (long-term steroid therapy)

> abdominal scars

> gastrostomy tube / nasogastric tube.

Respiratory examination
Look for:

General inspection

> respiratory distress and tachypnoea

> hyperinflation

> scar (from previous pneumothorax and from previous venous access devices)

> raised JVP: prominent v waves (tricuspid regurgitation)

> abdominal swelling (ascites)

> ankle swelling

> nasal polyps.

Trachea
Deviation may be due to lobar collapse.

Palpation

> Expansion is generally reduced in the presence of hyperexpanded lung fields.

> Can a right ventricular heave be detected?

Percussion

> May be hyperresonant throughout.

> Dullness may be present in case of lobar collapse/consolidation.

Auscultation

> reduced breath sounds and vocal resonance / tactile vocal fremitus generally

> coarse crackles

> wheeze.

In routine clinical practice you would clearly perform a full physical examination. This is not possible in the PACES examination, but look at the ankles for oedema; and if asked say that you would particularly like to examine for signs of cor pulmonale, ie raised JVP, pulsatile liver (if tricuspid regurgitation) and ankle oedema, attributable to CF lung disease. Also check for evidence of other complications of CF: cirrhosis / portal hypertension and diabetic complications (retinopathy, absent pulses / vascular bruits, peripheral neuropathy and proteinuria).

Further discussion
See Section 2.5 for discussion of the diagnosis, complications and treatment of CF.

1.3 Communication skills and ethics

1.3.1 Lifestyle modification

Scenario

Role: you are a junior doctor in a general medical outpatient clinic.

Scenario: Mr Gareth Barnes is a 52-year-old builder who has smoked 10–20 cigarettes per day for many years. He was recently admitted on a general medical take with a 4-month history of exertional shortness of breath, which had got significantly worse during the past few days leading up to admission. He has no significant past medical history except for mild hypertension (150/95 mmHg), for which he has been reluctant to accept medication, and obesity (108 kg; body mass index (BMI) 36.5 kg/m^2 (normal range 18–25)).

A diagnosis of an infective exacerbation of previously undiagnosed chronic obstructive pulmonary disease (COPD) was made, and he improved after treatment with oxygen, nebulised bronchodilators and antibiotics. Spirometry on discharge confirmed moderate COPD.

He now returns to the medical outpatient clinic for review.

Your task: to explain to this reluctant patient that he should stop smoking and lose weight.

Key issue to explore

> Why is the patient reluctant to give up smoking?

> Has he ever made an attempt to give up smoking? If he has tried, then how difficult was it? For how long did he manage to refrain from smoking, and why did his attempt to quit fail?

> Has he tried to lose weight? If so, what lifestyle changes did he make in this respect and did he manage to lose any weight (and why does he think that he was unsuccessful)?

Key points to establish

Introduce yourself appropriately.

Related to smoking

> Explain the patient's spirometry result and the cause of his breathing difficulty.

> Highlight why inhalers alone are not an effective way of treating his shortness of breath in the long term.

> Explain the benefits of quitting smoking, its effect on spirometry and the price he will have to pay if he continues to smoke (he is likely to have gradually decreasing exercise capacity and need repeated hospital admissions, etc). Focus on how smoking affects his health personally (COPD and hypertension) rather than in a general way.

> Balance negative information about harm and risks with positive information about the benefits of smoking cessation.

> Demonstrate active listening skills. Encourage open and non-threatening discussion on how he sees his smoking. Make sure he does not feel pressured and avoid being judgemental. Back off if he appears annoyed. Stay positive and friendly.

> Show understanding of his fears about quitting. Keep avenues open for any changes in his mind.

> Praise him for his past achievements, however small they may seem.

> Explore options available to him to support him in his decision to quit (nicotine replacement therapy, bupropion and smoking cessation clinics).

Related to obesity

> Explain the BMI value, its implication and how obesity contributes to his breathing problem.

> Show understanding regarding the difficulty that he might have experienced while trying to lose weight.

> Suggest various strategies that may help him to lose weight (dietary change, physical activities and drugs such as orlistat).

Appropriate responses to likely questions

Key point

If something is difficult – like giving up smoking or losing weight – then don't pretend to the patient that it is or should be easy.

Patient: I'm not convinced that my breathing difficulty is caused by the cigarettes: I have smoked for 36 years, so why did I become short of breath only 4 months ago?

Doctor: changes related to smoking happen gradually over many years, and may not cause any breathing problems until significant damage is done. Spirometry, the breathing test that you have had done, detects changes in the lungs caused by cigarettes. It measures how quickly you can breathe out and approximately how much you can breathe out, and shows you've now got damage to the lung called chronic obstructive pulmonary disease (COPD). This is irreversible damage caused by smoking, and I'm afraid that that is what you've got. It is not at all uncommon for smokers to first develop breathing difficulties in the way that you have.

Patient: if, as you said, my breathing problem is caused by smoking, why was I not short of breath earlier, all the way along, when my breathing function was getting worse?

Doctor: lots of things affect whether or not you feel breathlessness, such as your general level of fitness, weight, muscle strength, heart function and tolerance of pain and breathlessness. With the same level of problems in their airways, one patient with COPD may complain of extreme breathlessness whereas another gets mild or even no symptoms. In addition, even in a non-smoker function of the lung gets worse over time, and in a smoker this process happens more quickly. It is likely that in your case your lungs have reached a point at which they cannot support your body any more in the way they used to.

Patient: well, I've got to die of something, and besides, it looks as if it is too late for me to give up smoking, anyway. As you said, the damage through smoking has been already done, so what's the point of quitting at this stage?

Doctor: it is true that damage due to smoking is irreversible, so if you give up you won't regain lost function. However, if you keep on smoking it'll get worse much faster. If you stop smoking, your lung function may improve by 5–10% and you may well live longer. Also, smoking doesn't just damage the lungs: it can also damage the heart or cause strokes. If you stop smoking now, you reduce your risk of suffering a heart attack or stroke. So, it is never too late to give up smoking.

Patient: I did try once to give up smoking, but gained over a stone in weight, which I have been unable to lose since then. How am I going to give up smoking and lose weight at the same time?

Doctor: I agree that it may not be easy, but I am sure that you can do it. You have at least two reasons to lose weight. Your weight will certainly make your shortness of breath worse, and it may well be the cause of your raised blood pressure. You are also at high risk of developing other serious medical conditions, in particular diabetes and heart disease. A dietician could help you to choose a diet that is best for you, and you could also consider joining a weight-loss class where you could get advice on both diet and exercise, and work along with other people with the same problems to improve things.

1.3.2 Possible cancer

Scenario

Role: you are a junior doctor in a respiratory clinic.

Scenario: Mr Peter Crisp, a 48-year-old executive, has had a chest radiograph as part of his company's health screening programme (he has never had a chest radiograph before). This has revealed a pulmonary mass in the right upper lobe.

He has no significant past medical history but he smokes 20 cigarettes a day, and he has done so for 30 years.

He has been informed that he has a shadow in his lung and referred to the respiratory clinic.

Your task: to discuss with him the implications of his undiagnosed abnormality, and address his fears that this may be lung cancer.

Key issues to explore

> What is the patient's main worry?

> Is there any particular reason why the patient is worried? In routine

clinical practice patients will often not mention key reasons for their concern, and in PACES the briefing notes for the surrogate will commonly say 'do not mention this unless specifically asked'.

> What further investigations are required?

Key points to establish

Introduce yourself to the patient and say why you have been asked to see them. Explain the proposed outline of your interview by telling them that you wish to go through the history briefly to confirm the information that you have been given, that you would then like to discuss the implications of the findings and finally address any fears or concerns that they may have. Also:

> Ask if the patient would like anyone else to be present during this discussion.

> Be honest – a lung mass is more likely to be lung cancer than any other diagnosis.

> Emphasise that 'something can always be done', even if the diagnosis is serious.

> Always adopt a non-judgemental attitude, eg if this patient continues to smoke despite being informed that there is a shadow in the lung.

Key point

Explain the medical benefits of changing behaviour, but do not be judgemental – even if the patient's behaviour seems to have caused their illness.

Appropriate responses to likely questions

Patient: this was only discovered at a routine check and I feel fine, so surely it can't be serious?

Doctor: it's obviously a good thing that you feel well, because it will mean that the outlook will be better whatever we find … but, I'm afraid it is possible that this is something serious.

Patient: *what could the shadow be caused by?*

Doctor: there are a range of possibilities: it is possible for a shadow like this to be caused by an infection or a rare disease causing inflammation in the lung, but unfortunately it can also be caused by a cancer in the lung.

Patient: *what are the chances that this is cancer?*

Doctor: well, cancer is certainly one of the possible causes, and perhaps the most likely one. What we need to do is to try to find out as soon as possible exactly what this shadow is, the extent of the problem, and what the right treatment would be.

Patient: *how are we going to find out what it is?*

Doctor: we need to do some more tests. In particular we need to organise a CT scan of your lungs. This will show us much more clearly what the abnormal area looks like, and whether there is any enlargement of the lymph glands in the centre of the chest. The CT scan will tell us the best way of taking a tissue sample so that we can confirm exactly what this is. We also need to do some breathing tests to check your lung capacity, because that may affect what the best treatment is. If it looks like a cancer we may also want to do a different kind of scan called a positron emission tomography CT scan (PET-CT).

Patient: *what will you do when you find out what it is?*

Doctor: that very much depends on what we find. If it's an infection, then antibiotics may be needed …

Patient: *but if it's cancer, will you be able to cure it?*

Doctor: I honestly don't know. There are several different sorts of lung cancer, and if it is one of those it will also depend on how far it has spread. I don't think we can really go into too much detail at the moment – because we don't know exactly what we're dealing with here – but some cases of lung cancer can be cured.

1.3.3 Potentially life-threatening illness

Scenario

Role: you are a junior doctor on call.

Scenario: Mrs Angela Warren is a 36-year-old single mother of two who has been brought to the emergency department by ambulance. She developed sudden-onset pleuritic chest pain and breathlessness at rest this evening. On examination her pulse rate is 120 beats per minute regular and her respiratory rate is 24 per minute, but otherwise there are no abnormal findings. Of her initial investigations the electrocardiogram (ECG) shows a sinus tachycardia, the chest radiograph is clear and blood tests are normal except for a raised D-dimer (normal threshold <0.5 mg/L). Arterial blood gases show a normal pH (7.44) (normal range 7.35–7.45), low–normal PO_2 (11.0 kPa) (normal range 11.3–12.6) and reduced PCO_2 (3.0 kPa) (normal range 4.7–6.0).

The pain is easing, she reports feeling less short of breath and she wants to go home.

Your task: to explain to Mrs Warren that PE is a significant possibility and that she should start treatment and be investigated as an inpatient.

Key issues to explore

> Explain the possibility of a potentially life-threatening problem.

> Find out why she is so keen to get home. In routine clinical practice patients will often not mention their reasons for wanting to leave hospital unless specifically asked, and in PACES the briefing notes for the surrogate will commonly indicate that they should do the same.

Key points to establish

Main ethical issue

> The competent patient does have the right to refuse investigation and/or treatment. It is your responsibility to put her into such a position that she is able to make decisions about her management from a well-informed standpoint.

> Is she competent? Does she understand the possible diagnosis and its potential implications? She needs to know that she is at significant risk of deterioration, and even death, from her (presumed) PE.

Key point

The competent patient has a right to decide their treatment.

Practical issue

> Are there childcare issues (for example)? If there are, then offer to make an effort to help in sorting them out. It is unfortunately not uncommon for some doctors to 'wash their hands' of patients seen to be 'refusing treatment', but usually a compromise position can be reached with good negotiation, and the examiners will be looking for your ability to make a workable plan in this scenario.

Willingness to negotiate a reasonable compromise

> Negotiation may result in a treatment plan that is not necessarily ideal, but better than nothing. For example, it may be agreed that the patient is given a dose of low-molecular-weight heparin now, and that they then return in the morning for an appropriate imaging test and review.

Appropriate answers to likely questions

Patient: I'm feeling a bit better, so there can't be anything seriously wrong.

Doctor: I'm obviously pleased that you're feeling a bit better, but I'm afraid that I can't guarantee that there isn't a serious problem here. One of the blood tests – the D-dimer – and one of the tests on the blood from an artery indicate that there may be something serious going on.

Patient: so what do you think the diagnosis is?

Doctor: it is possible that you have had a pulmonary embolus, which is a blood clot in the blood supply to the lung.

Patient: how will you find out if that is what happened?

Doctor: we'll need to perform a scan that enables us to see the blood supply and check if there are any blockages.

Patient: is having a pulmonary embolus dangerous?

Doctor: if this is a clot, then usually the body slowly absorbs it over the next week or so. But the main worry is that either this clot may extend and get bigger, or that more clots may spread to the lung. If this happens then it can be very serious indeed: it can mean that you can't get enough oxygen into your blood, that the heart is sometimes put under too much strain and cannot pump

properly, and in severe cases it may even stop completely.

Patient: what treatment do I need?

Doctor: to help prevent this clot getting worse, or more clots from forming, we need to put you on some blood-thinning medicine. While we are getting the scan to confirm the diagnosis this will be in the form of an injection under the skin. If the scan confirms a clot, you will then be put on blood-thinning tablets for the next 6 months.

Patient: can I go home now?

Doctor: is there some special reason that you want to go home? Is there a problem with looking after the children or something like that – something that we might be able to arrange help for?

Patient: no, I just don't like being in hospital. I want to go home.

Doctor: I'm afraid that I don't think that's a good idea. I think that there's a high chance that you've got clots of blood in the lungs, and from the tests we've done these seem to be affecting your heart and your breathing. I think we should give you the treatment to thin the blood and get the scan done in the morning.

Patient: I hear what you say, but I'm going home. Can't I have the injection and come back for the scan in the morning?

Doctor: OK, as long as you understand that this condition can sometimes be very serious, or even life-threatening, and that is the reason I would strongly advise you to stay in hospital for now. But if you really insist on going home, then I can arrange for you to have an injection of the blood-thinning treatment now before you go. If you do get worse at home, please call an ambulance and come straight back to hospital. I'll make a note in your medical records to say that this is what I've advised.

1.3.4 Sudden-unexplained death

Scenario

Role: you are a junior doctor working on a general medical ward.

Scenario: Mrs Sylvia Dowson, a 56-year-old woman admitted with an exacerbation of COPD 5 days ago, has died suddenly. When seen on the ward round in the morning she seemed to have been gradually improving, and certainly better than she was on admission. She had been on a prophylactic dose of low-molecular-weight heparin, but the most likely cause of death was probably a massive pulmonary embolism.

Her husband has been called into the hospital by the ward sister. He knows that his wife has died, but does not know the circumstances.

Your task: to explain to the husband that his wife died suddenly, probably from a massive pulmonary embolism, and that you will have to discuss the case with the coroner.

Key issues to explore

> The original reason for the patient's admission, and her management.

> What is the patient's husband's understanding of the cause or causes of his wife's death?

> Explain to the husband that his wife was on proper treatment for COPD and that her death was too sudden to be due to that condition, so it is most likely she died due to an underlying pulmonary embolism.

> Explain that there is an increased risk of thromboembolism in acutely ill medical patients, and that a prophylactic dose of low-molecular-weight heparin can reduce this risk but not eliminate it altogether.

Key points to establish

> The uncertainty regarding the cause of death, and that a definite cause of death can only be established by a post-mortem.

> That you will not be able to issue a death certificate without discussion with the coroner or the coroner's officer, who may insist on a post-mortem examination.

Appropriate responses to likely questions

Patient's husband: *it has come as a big shock. I never knew that she was so unwell.*

Doctor: I would first of all like to say how sorry we all are here, especially as her death was so sudden and unexpected. It was a shock to us all. As you know, she was admitted with exacerbation of her chronic bronchitis and emphysema. She was on treatment for this, and when we saw her on the ward round this morning she seemed to be improving.

Patient's husband: *what happened then?*

Doctor: we don't know for sure, but we think that she suffered from a massive clot on the lung. This is the most likely thing to explain her sudden collapse and death.

Key point

Never say that something is certain if it is not.

Patient's husband: *if she had a clot, could it have been prevented?*

Doctor: pulmonary embolism or clots in the lung are known to occur in people who are confined to bed, and your wife had been in bed for much of the last week or so. These clots can be prevented by injections of blood-thinning agents, and we had been giving your wife these injections since her admission.

Patient's husband: *so why did she have a clot if you were giving her injections to stop them?*

Doctor: I'm afraid that the injections aren't 100% effective. Like all treatments they don't always work: they cut down the chances of having clots, but they don't guarantee that you won't.

Patient's husband: *but you said that you are not absolutely sure that she has had a clot in the lungs.*

Doctor: yes, that's true. We think that a massive clot in the lungs is the most likely thing, but we can't prove it and it is possible that she had something else, like a sudden heart attack.

Patient's husband: *so what happens now?*

Doctor: because we are not sure why your wife died, I cannot issue a death certificate. For this reason, and also because she died unexpectedly, I must speak to the coroner's office. It may be that they will decide that a post-mortem examination needs to be done.

Patient's husband: *can't you just sign a death certificate?*

Doctor: I'm afraid that I can't. I can only sign a death certificate if I know the cause of death and, as we've discussed, I'm not absolutely sure here. This is why I must speak to the coroner's office.

Patient's husband: *I'm not keen on her having a post-mortem.*

Doctor: I understand what you're saying, but I am not able to issue a death certificate because I do not know the cause of death. I have to refer the matter to the coroner.

Patient's husband: *what will the coroner do?*

Doctor: I can't say for certain. I will explain what happened: that your wife came into hospital because her chest was bad, that she was on treatment

and seemed to be getting better, and then that she died suddenly and we think from a clot of blood on the lungs. If the coroner is willing to accept that, then I will put it on the death certificate. However, if the coroner says that he wants a post-mortem to try and find out exactly what happened, then that's their decision and we have to accept it.

1.3.5 Intubation for ventilation

Scenario

Role: you are a junior doctor working on a general medical ward.

Scenario: Mr Ian Jones, a 74-year-old man with COPD, is admitted with an acute hypercapnic exacerbation precipitated by a chest infection. He has previously been confined to his home because of exertional dyspnoea, despite the use of domiciliary oxygen and nebulised bronchodilators. Conventional medical therapy is being administered and adjuvant non-invasive ventilation is being set up for him. He still appears mentally alert.

The question of whether or not it would be appropriate to intubate him for ventilation is discussed on the ward round. The view of the medical team is that there would be no guarantee of success, and the process may be unpleasant for the patient. Moreover, even if intubation and ventilation were to be successful and the patient to survive this episode, he is likely to be left with even greater respiratory disability than he had prior to this illness. There is no doubt that whatever is done his medium- to long-term outlook is very poor indeed.

Your task: to approach him with the issue of whether or not he would want to be intubated for ventilation in case the current therapeutic measures are unsuccessful in resolving his ventilatory failure.

Key issues to explore

> What is the patient's understanding of his medical condition and prognosis?

> What is the patient's attitude to invasive procedures such as intubation and ventilation?

> What are the likely attitude(s) of his family members and carers?

Key points to establish

> Is the patient competent to make an informed decision about endotracheal intubation and ventilation? Does the patient have a realistic understanding of the advantages and disadvantages of this treatment? Can he give you an account of them?

> Has the patient discussed these issues with anyone else or written a 'living will'?

Key point

'Prioritising autonomy' means enabling the patient to decide what treatment he or she wants; the doctor's duty being to outline available effective treatments.

Appropriate responses to likely questions

Patient: hello doctor.

Doctor: hello Mr Jones, I would like to have a chat while the mask and equipment to help you with your breathing is being set up.

Patient: by all means.

Doctor: how much do you know about the sort of treatment you are receiving?

Patient: not a lot, really.

Doctor: well, we are going to ask you to breathe through a mask that is connected to a machine that will help you with your breathing. If you breathe normally then the flow of air coming from the machine will help.

Patient: OK doctor, I'll do my best.

Doctor: I hope that the treatment will work for you, but I would also like you to consider what would happen if it doesn't help. Is that something you've ever thought about or talked with anyone about?

Patient: what do you mean?

Doctor: some people with serious medical problems, such as your chest, have thought about exactly what treatments they would want or not want if things got really bad. Some people have talked with their family or friends about it, or have written a 'living will'. Is this something you've done?

Patient: no, what are the treatments you are talking about?

Doctor: if things get worse, we need to think about whether it would be the right thing to take you to the intensive care unit (ICU). There they could put you to sleep, place a tube into your throat and connect you up to a breathing machine, called a ventilator, that will do all the breathing for you. How do you feel about that?

Patient: well doctor, I'm not really sure. What are the pros and cons?

Doctor: the idea would be to help you with your breathing while we try to overcome the infection in your chest, but the treatment has its risks. This includes chest infections that can be very difficult to treat, and there is a strong possibility that you may not be able to come off the breathing machine easily. In that case – if you were going to need the breathing machine for a long time – we would have to make a hole in your neck [show visually], pop a tube down into your wind pipe and use this to connect you to the breathing machine. But to my mind the biggest risk is that even if you do come off the breathing machine and we get you better, you still would not be as good as you were before you came into hospital.

Patient: if I did go onto the breathing machine, would I get better?

Doctor: I'm afraid that this can't be guaranteed. Your chest is very bad and whatever we do it isn't going to get better than it was before you came into hospital. I'm afraid that it's likely that every episode of infection such as this is going to make things worse, even if you do get over it. You may need more help at home, or may be unable to do things for yourself that you were previously able to do.

Patient: what happens if I get worse but do not go on the ventilator?

Doctor: unfortunately, in this scenario the chances would be that you may not make it. We would, of course, continue to treat you as best we can. If you started to suffer more from your shortness of breath or become anxious, we would give you medications to help you deal with those symptoms.

Patient: what's the right thing to do?

Doctor: this isn't the sort of situation where there's a 'right' and a 'wrong' thing to do. Some people will decide that they want to try the ventilator if things get really bad, but they have to recognise that this can be very difficult for them and might not work out. Other people decide that they want to be kept comfortable if they get into that sort of situation. Whatever decision is made, we will look after you as well as we can.

1.3.6 Patient who does not want mechanical ventilation

Scenario

Role: you are a junior doctor on call.

Scenario: you are asked by the nurses to speak to the daughter of a patient who was admitted on the acute medical take a few nights ago. The daughter has told them that she thinks her mother should be sent to ICU for help with her breathing.

Mrs Natalie Cooper, aged 74 years, has presented with type II respiratory failure secondary to exacerbation of a severe COPD that normally limits her exercise tolerance to approximately 50 metres at best. She is well known to the respiratory team because of her recurrent hospital admissions, but on this occasion she has failed to respond to maximal medical treatment that has included a trial of non-invasive ventilation.

During previous admissions the question of escalation of treatment has been discussed with her, and she has consistently said that she would not want to be intubated and ventilated in the event of deterioration. The respiratory team think that this is a reasonable decision for her to have made, that she is competent to make it and this has been recorded in her notes.

Your task: to explain to the daughter that her mother does not want mechanical ventilation and that her views must be respected.

Key issue to explore

> What is the daughter's understanding of her mother's condition? Explain the details: a life-threatening flare-up; a poor response to medical therapy including a trial of non-invasive ventilation; and the progressive character of her underlying lung disease and its complications.

> What is the daughter's understanding of her mother's wishes?

> The impossibility of predicting the outcome of this situation accurately.

Key points to establish

> Demonstrate an understanding of the daughter's wishes, in particular if she wants to do everything to keep her mother alive.

> Ensure that the daughter understands that her mother's decision against mechanical ventilation in the future was her own, and was made on the basis of a full understanding of her condition and the probable consequences of not proceeding to mechanical ventilation.

> Explain that patients have a legal right to decline specific treatment, including treatment that is life-prolonging.

> Demonstrate sympathy with the daughter's difficulty in accepting her mother's decision.

> Reassure her that every effort will be made to keep her mother comfortable in the event that she deteriorates and is dying.

Appropriate responses to likely questions

Daughter: as you said, my mother is very poorly and I feel that she is too ill to make such important decisions as those concerning life-and-death issues.

Doctor: you are right, your mother is probably too ill now to make decisions. However, she has discussed this with the chest team before when she was well. At that time she was fully competent to make decisions on what treatment she would wish to receive in the future.

Daughter: exactly what has been discussed with her in the past?

Doctor: your mother was aware that she has a chronic lung condition, which is progressing, and that her lung reserves are low. She knew that at some point she might end up in a 'do-or-die' situation, because of a flare-up or deterioration, and the possible ways of treating this, with their advantages and disadvantages, were discussed. She made a conscious decision that if such circumstances arose she did not wish to be put on a life-support machine. She had the right to decide what kind of medical treatment to choose or refuse, and made those decisions in advance when she was competent to do so.

Daughter: I still feel that I have the right to overturn my mother's decision, while she is so poorly as not to be able to decide what is best for her.

Doctor: I fully understand what you say and that you want your mother to be kept alive for as long as possible. But your mother took the decision not to be put on a mechanical breathing machine (a ventilator). She has not changed her decision since she's been on the ward so we therefore have to respect her wishes. I am afraid that no one has a legal right to accept or decline treatment on her behalf, and that includes the closest family, however distressing this may be. If we treated her against her express wishes, this might be akin to assault, but I fully understand that it's very difficult for you.

Daughter: if she doesn't go onto a breathing machine, then is it definite that she will die?

Doctor: no, it's not absolutely definite. At the moment she is very ill and we fear that she is going to die, but it's not 100% certain. Patients do sometimes come back from situations as bad as this, but we don't think that's likely, although I'd be delighted to be wrong.

Daughter: if she did go onto a breathing machine, then would she live?

Doctor: again, I'm afraid that's not certain. The machine would help the breathing in the short term, but there can be problems. It can sometimes be very difficult indeed to get someone off the machine and this can lead to a variety of complications. So no, it's not certain she'd live if she went onto the breathing machine.

Daughter: I find it very difficult to accept my mother's decision. She has never told us that she would not want to be put on a life-support machine.

Doctor: I understand that this must be very upsetting for you, but in hospitals we often have these discussions with patients so that we understand their wishes should they get worse. Your mother has been on maximal medication for her chronic lung condition for some time now, and I think that she felt tired of fighting for breath and, more importantly, that the prospect of losing her independence was unacceptable to her. Of course making a decision not to pursue life-prolonging treatment is obviously not an easy one, and she maybe wanted to protect you and others in the family from the responsibility of being involved. Our duty is to respect her values and wishes.

Daughter: it is easy for you to say this – she is not your mother.

Doctor: it's not easy, but I understand your feelings. I have to say that I support your mother's decision, and I would feel the same if she were my own mother. I can assure you that the doctors and nurses will work together to ensure that your mother does not suffer, and that she continues to receive all the treatments needed to relieve her symptoms.

1.4 Brief clinical consultations

1.4.1 Solitary pulmonary nodule

Scenario

Mr Stephen Norman, a 56-year-old man, was found to have an incidental left upper lobe pulmonary nodule on a routine chest X-ray performed during an occupational health screening medical. He is fit and well and has no respiratory symptoms. What is the likely diagnosis, and how should the patient be investigated?

Introduction

There are many causes of a solitary pulmonary nodule (Table 14), the most important of which is lung cancer. Other possible causes include focal infection, a lung secondary, a hamartoma or carcinoid tumour. It is important to look for any external clues that will point towards a diagnosis. Old chest radiographs are extremely helpful in this situation.

Beginning the encounter

Doctor: hello, my name is Dr A, I understand that the problem is that an abnormality was seen on a chest X-ray that you had recently. Is that right?

Patient: yes

Doctor: before we get onto the details of that, can you tell me if you have any major medical problems? Have you ever had any lung problems or been diagnosed with any serious illness such as a cancer?

Patient: [gives list (with doctor politely but firmly discouraging lengthy detail).]

Doctor: and are you on any tablets or medications?

Patient: [gives details (and will probably have been asked to produce a written list).]

These introductory questions will provide useful clinical context and may immediately give a clue to the likely diagnosis, eg if the patient has had any prior history of malignancy, vasculitis or rheumatoid disease.

Focused history

Doctor: was this really just a routine X-ray or did you have any new symptoms before it was done. Any breathlessness, cough, coughing of blood, or discomfort in the chest?

Doctor: have you generally been well in yourself? No weight loss, fevers or loss of appetite? (infection, malignancy, vasculitis)

Doctor: have you ever smoked? When did you stop? How much did you smoke? If the patient is a current or ex-smoker then calculate pack-years, ie (number of cigarettes smoked per day/20) × number of years the patient has been a smoker.

Table 14	Causes of a solitary nodule visible on chest X-ray
Instance	**Cause**
Common	Primary lung cancer, including pulmonary carcinoid tumour Focal infection (bacterial, fungal, or never established but transient nodule) Metastasis from extrathoracic cancer
Less common	Benign tumour (hamartoma) Arteriovenous malformation Active granulomatous disease (TB, sarcoid, vasculitis, rheumatoid nodule, *Aspergillus* infection)

TB, tuberculosis.

Family history

Ask about siblings and parents – is there any history of malignancy, TB or connective tissue diseases?

Social history

Establish the patient's smoking history, occupational history and if there has been any foreign travel to areas of TB prevalence.

With respect to lung cancer it is important to ascertain:

> Occupational history – has the patient had any jobs associated with asbestos exposure (eg carpenter, plumber, lagger, building labourer, electrician)?

> Is there any history of chest wall pain or brachial plexus symptoms (numbness, tingling or weakness in hand muscles)? These are symptoms associated with a superior sulcus tumour.

> Are there any symptoms that might arise from systemic manifestations of cancer and paraneoplastic syndromes? These include loss of balance, dizziness (paraneoplastic cerebellar), bone pain (from hypercalcaemia or metastases), and weakness (Eaton–Lambert syndrome; proximal weakness more than distal).

With respect to TB, consider the following:

> Past history of TB – ask for details of treatment (if possible) and whether any course of treatment was completed.

> Risk factors – has the patient taken steroids or any immunosuppressants, which might increase the risk in a patient with prior TB?

> Travel history – any travel to areas of TB prevalence?

> Alcohol history – does the patient have any history of alcohol abuse, which is associated with TB?

Other considerations:

> lung secondary – enquire into the history of any other tumours the patient may have had (colorectal, renal and, in a woman, breast or ovarian)

> inhaled foreign body or severe respiratory illness – associated with lung abscess

> history of unexplained anaemia or anaemia known to be associated with bleeding from the gastrointestinal tract – arteriovenous malformation

> history of sinusitis, red eyes, hearing loss or renal problems – consider granulomatosis with polyangiitis.

Focused examination

Respiratory system – check the following:

> supraclavicular lymph nodes – palpate carefully

> quickly assess expansion, percussion and auscultation – very likely to be all normal.

Abdominal examination:

> Carefully palpate the liver looking for evidence of metastatic disease, and the kidneys looking for evidence of a primary renal cancer.

Questions from the patient

Patient: *what could this abnormality be due to?*

Doctor: there are a number of possible causes of something looking like this. It could be due to an unusual appearance of an infection, or a condition causing inflammation in the lung, or a tumour within the lung.

Patient: *what will you do next?*

Doctor: what we need to do is to find out what it is (diagnosis), the extent of the problem (staging, if a cancer), and whether there is anything else

about your general health that would influence what treatment we would recommend (fitness for lung resection if cancer). In the first instance we will ask for a CT scan of your body and some blood tests and breathing tests.

Patient: *will those tests tell you exactly what it is?*

Doctor: they may tell us all we need to know, but it's very likely that they won't give us all the information we need … it's very likely we'll need to do a biopsy, where we take a tissue sample to look at down a microscope. The CT scan will tell us the best way of doing that.

Questions from the examiner

Examiner: *how would you manage this man in outpatients?*

Doctor: I would request blood tests including a full blood count (FBC), urea and electrolytes (U&Es), liver function tests (LFTs) and calcium and phosphate to look for anaemia, hypercalcaemia, renal impairment and any evidence of liver metastasis. I would request a CT scan of the neck, chest and upper abdomen to characterise the nodule and to look for supraclavicular, lung, hepatic and adrenal metastasis, or a site of non-lung primary cancer. I would also request full lung-function testing and an electrocardiogram (ECG) to assess fitness for thoracic surgery in case this turns out to be a primary lung cancer.

Examiner: *how could a diagnosis be confirmed?*

Doctor: by appropriate biopsy – possibilities include a CT-guided biopsy of the lung nodule, or sampling of any site of metastasis by, for example, ultrasound-guided lymph node biopsy of the neck, endobronchial ultrasound of the mediastinal lymph nodes, or liver biopsy.

Further discussion

British Thoracic Society guidelines on management of pulmonary nodules are available at: www.brit-thoracic.org.uk/standards-of-care/guidelines/bts-guidelines-for-the-investigation-and-management-of-pulmonary-nodules/

The management of incidentally discovered pulmonary nodules is based upon a baseline assessment of the risk of malignancy. If this is less than 10%, then follow-up CT imaging at intervals of 3 and 12 months is recommended, ideally with computation of nodule volume using volumetry software. Where the risk of malignancy is between 10% and 70% a biopsy is recommended, and for patients with a risk >70% then surgical resection with or without biopsy is advised. The precise recommendations are detailed and depend upon both patient and nodule characteristics, and the interested reader is advised to consult the guidelines for further information.

1.4.2 Daytime sleepiness and morning headache

Scenario

Mrs Sylvia Barclay, a 44-year-old woman, has been complaining of daytime sleepiness and morning headaches for the past 8 months. She has fallen asleep a couple of times at work and her job is at risk. What is the likely diagnosis?

Introduction

Excessive daytime sleepiness is due to abnormal nocturnal sleep, which may be insufficient or inefficient (poor quality sleep). The causes of excessive daytime sleepiness are shown in Table 15. When combined with a morning headache, a sign of

Table 15	Causes of excessive daytime sleepiness
Prevalence	Cause
Common	Insufficient sleep (caffeine use, noise, discomfort, drugs, stressful home circumstances, etc)
	Chronobiologic disorder[1]
	Sleep-disordered breathing disorders[2]
	Restless leg syndrome / periodic limb movement disorder (especially in chronic kidney disease)
Rare	Narcolepsy (symptoms include cataplexy – sudden loss of muscle tone in response to excitement or in anticipation, vivid dreaming, sleep paralysis)
	Idiopathic hypersomnia
	Post-traumatic hypersomnia

1 Jet lag syndrome, shift work, etc.
2 Obstructive sleep apnoea, central sleep apnoea and upper airway resistance syndrome: patients may sleep for the required 7–8 hours every night but there may be frequent arousals preventing slow-wave sleep (stage three and four non-rapid eye movement (REM) and REM sleep) resulting in daytime somnolence.

carbon dioxide retention, the causes can be narrowed down to disorders causing chronic respiratory failure (ventilatory failure).

Causes of chronic respiratory failure resulting in high carbon dioxide that produces morning headaches are shown in Table 16. These can be divided into causes where there is inadequate ventilatory drive, or where the respiratory muscle pump is incapable of maintaining an adequate response. In cases of pump failure, arterial blood gas analysis will usually reveal a normal alveolar–arterial (A–a) gradient (see Section 3.4.1).

Key point

Morning headaches and sleepiness during the day – always consider carbon dioxide retention. OSA alone very rarely causes type II respiratory failure – there has to be some associated obesity, COPD or other explanation.

Obstructive sleep apnoea (OSA) commonly coexists with type 2 diabetes and hypertension, and effective treatment with continuous positive airway pressure (CPAP) significantly reduces blood pressure, particularly in patients receiving antihypertensive medication.

Beginning the encounter

Doctor: hello, my name is Dr A, I understand that you have been troubled by headaches in the morning, and have felt very sleepy during the day. Is that right?

Patient: yes

Doctor: before we get into details of that, can you tell me if you have any significant medical problems? Any problems with your lungs or breathing? Any diabetes or high blood pressure?

Patient: [gives list (with the doctor politely but firmly discouraging lengthy detail).]

Table 16   Causes of chronic respiratory failure causing carbon dioxide retention

Respiratory pump failure

Prevalence	Cause
Common	Airway disease: COPD or severe asthma
	OSA with associated COPD, obesity or muscle weakness
	Obesity
Less common	Other causes of chronic lung disease
	Thoracic cage deformities (kyphosis, scoliosis and thoracotomy)
Rare	MND and motor neuropathies: amyotrophic lateral sclerosis, poliomyelitis, Guillain–Barré syndrome, syringomyelia, phrenic nerve palsies and hereditary sensorimotor neuropathies
	Muscle diseases: congenital myopathies, Duchenne muscular dystrophy, myotonic dystrophy, polymyositis, acid maltase deficiency and limb girdle dystrophy
	Neuromuscular junction disorders: myasthenia gravis

Ventilatory drive failure

Prevalence	Cause
Uncommon	Poliomyelitis and post-polio syndrome (mechanism unknown)
	Sedative drugs
	Metabolic alkalosis
Rare	Brain-stem stroke or tumour
	Arnold–Chiari malformation
	Syringobulbia

COPD, chronic obstructive pulmonary disease; MND, motor neurone disease; OSA, obstructive sleep apnoea.

Doctor: and are you on any tablets, prescription medicines or inhalers at all?

Patient: [gives details (and will probably have been asked to produce a written list).]

These introductory questions will help to establish whether there are any comorbidities likely to increase the risk of, or complicate, OSA, such as type 2 diabetes, hypothyroidism and systemic hypertension. They should also reveal any neuromuscular disease that the patient is already aware of. You will learn whether the patient takes any prescription sedative drugs.

Focused history

Doctor: tell me about your sleeping. What times do you usually go to bed and wake up? Do you wake refreshed? Has anyone ever said that you snore or seem to stop breathing when you are asleep? Is your bedroom quiet, comfortable, well ventilated and not too hot or too cold? Do you have any difficulty falling asleep? Do you take any naps during the day? When is your last caffeinated drink during the day? Do you watch TV / play computer games / use the internet just before sleep?

Doctor: tell me about the headaches. Are they usually in the morning? Do they get better during the day? Any associated nausea, vomiting, visual disturbance, weakness or numbness?

Doctor: do you drink any alcohol? How much? Do you, or have you ever, smoked?

Doctor: do you get breathless when you lie down flat? Is there any swelling of the ankles?

These questions will help to establish whether the patient is sleepy because of:

> unrefreshing sleep – suggestive of OSA

> insomnia – may be due to elements of so-called sleep hygiene (eg use of stimulants such as nicotine, caffeine, other drugs; the bedroom environment; the use of screen-based entertainment prior to sleep, which can be stimulating rather than relaxing).

Headaches due to carbon dioxide retention will usually improve during the day and will not be associated with other neurological disturbance, unless a neuromuscular disorder such as motor neurone disease is causing the hypoventilation. If symptoms of left ventricular failure are present, then the sleep disturbance may be caused by central sleep apnoeas, which occur in 50% of patients with an ejection fraction of <45%.

Focused examination

Observe the patient's general appearance. Is there a high body mass index (BMI), a kyphoscoliosis, any evidence of neuromuscular weakness? Are they breathless?

Mouth – is there plenty of space in the pharynx or do the tongue, uvula and tonsils seem crowded together? If there is a tape measure then measure the neck circumference (>43 cm (17 inches) is associated with OSA).

Check for signs of daytime carbon dioxide retention – flap, warm peripheries, cyanosis.

Cardiorespiratory – check the following:

> jugular venous pressure (JVP) – is this elevated? (right heart failure)

> is there prolonged expiration?

> heart sounds and murmurs (quick auscultation at apex, aortic area and neck – not a full examination) looking particularly for mitral regurgitation in severe left ventricular systolic dysfunction

> auscultate the lungs posteriorly – for crackles (left ventricular failure (LVF)) or wheezes (COPD).

Neurological – check the following:

> Arms out with palms facing up … close your eyes … touch your nose with this finger (touch one of the patient's index fingers) … arm back out … now with this finger (touching the index finger of the patient's other hand) – rapid screening for weakness or sensory disorder in the arms.

> Gait – rapid screening for weakness or sensory disorder in the legs (examiner is likely to tell you that you don't need to do this for reasons of time).

Questions from the patient

[Assuming that the history suggests OSA and the patient is obese:]

Patient: why do I feel so sleepy doctor?

Doctor: in some people, when they fall deeply asleep, the muscles of the neck relax so much that the airway actually closes off at the back of the throat, causing them to choke and eventually to wake up again. I think this is happening to you. It means that you never actually get any properly refreshing sleep, because the moment you begin to do so, you get woken up again.

Patient: what about these headaches?

Doctor: in all of us, when we are asleep, we do not breathe as deeply as when we are awake. In some people who are overweight, this under-breathing is more marked, and it leads to a build-up of carbon dioxide in the bloodstream, which gives you a bad headache. The carbon dioxide level is at its highest at the end of the night so the headache is worst in the morning.

Questions from the examiner

Examiner: what do you think is the likely diagnosis?

Doctor: I think it's very likely that this woman has OSA.

Examiner: how would you investigate this woman's symptoms?

Doctor: the first test I would like is an arterial blood gas to exclude daytime hypercapnia, since if this were present it would require more urgent investigation and treatment.

Examiner: and if the carbon dioxide was normal?

Doctor: I would want some simple blood tests to rule out associated conditions – hypothyroidism, diabetes, hyperlipidaemia – as well as spirometry to assess the nature of any ventilatory defect, and a chest radiograph to look for hyperinflation or diaphragmatic palsy.

Examiner: supposing that was entirely normal.

Doctor: the principal investigation is an overnight sleep study to include oximetry, transcutaneous carbon dioxide monitoring, and some measures of airflow, respiratory muscle effort, arousals and movement. The exact monitoring techniques included in a sleep study vary between centres, but the main

thing is to establish whether the patient has frequent nocturnal arousals disrupting sleep in association with cessation of breathing, and if so whether these are associated with airway obstruction (OSA) or not (central sleep apnoea). In this case we also want to establish whether there is nocturnal hypercapnia to explain her headaches.

Further discussion

Patients with OSA usually require treatment with nasal continuous positive airway pressure (nCPAP) to splint open the airway during sleep and eliminate obstructive apnoeas. In patients in whom there is coexistent respiratory failure treatment with non-invasive ventilation may be necessary, at least initially, to normalise the carbon dioxide before switching to nCPAP thereafter.

1.4.3 Haemoptysis and weight loss

Scenario

Mr Ali, a 35-year-old man originally from Somalia, has presented to the emergency department having coughed up some blood. He also says he has lost some weight recently and is worried about his health. What is the likely diagnosis?

Introduction

Most cases of haemoptysis have a normal chest X-ray and no cause is found, but the risk of a more serious cause such as TB, lung cancer or vasculitis depends critically on the presence or absence of other factors on history and examination. Causes of haemoptysis are shown in Table 17.

Table 17   Causes of haemoptysis

Classification	Causes
Common	Cryptogenic (50%) Acute infection – bronchitis, pneumonia *Mycobacterium tuberculosis* (in some settings) Bronchiectasis Anticoagulant use
Consider	Pulmonary embolus
Uncommon/rare	Vasculitis Tumour (carcinoid, lung cancer, endobronchial metastasis) Aspergilloma Foreign body aspiration

The presence of weight loss in this case is a concerning feature and suggests a serious underlying illness such as TB or aspergilloma. Lung cancer is rare in patients under the age of 40, but clearly a smoking history will be important.

Beginning the encounter

Doctor: hello, my name is Dr A, I understand that the problem is that you coughed up some blood, and that you have been losing weight recently. Is that right?

Patient: *yes*

Doctor: before we get into details of that, can you tell me if you have any significant medical problems? Any problems with your lungs or breathing? Have you ever coughed up blood before? Have you or anyone in your family, or who you live with, ever been treated for tuberculosis?

Patient: [gives list (with the doctor politely but firmly discouraging lengthy detail).]

Doctor: and are you on any tablets, inhalers or prescription medicines at all?

Patient: [gives details (and will probably have been asked to produce a written list).]

These introductory questions will provide clinical context and may immediately provide information about chronic respiratory conditions such as COPD, which may predispose to lung cancer, or treatment with immunosuppressant or anti-HIV medicines, which may suggest a predisposition to TB.

Focused history

Doctor: can you tell me about the coughing of blood? What colour was it (bright red or old, dark blood)? Any clots? And the amount? Did it come out of the blue, or did you have a chest infection with some sputum production at the same time?

Doctor: have you had any other symptoms – chest pain, fevers, sweats? Have you been breathless?

Doctor: I understand that you were born in Somalia. How long have you been in the UK? [The details given in the scenario do not state this, but the differential diagnosis, most notably regarding the likelihood of TB are very different if the patient has been in the UK for 3 months or for 30 years.]

Doctor: [depending on the answer to the previous question] when was the last time you travelled outside the UK? Where did you go?

Doctor: has anyone in your family been unwell recently? Who is at home with you? What sort of place do you live in?

Doctor: have you ever smoked?

Focused examination

Look for evidence of recent weight loss: loose clothes, cachexia. Note any sweating or clubbing. Palpate quickly for obvious lymphadenopathy. Are there any signs of:

> vasculitis

> splinter haemorrhages

> non-blanching rash

> episcleritis?

Respiratory – check the following:

> finger clubbing

> trachea – is it central?

> expansion – equal?

> percussion – any sign of a pleural effusion, which would fit with either TB or a tumour?

> breath sounds may reveal a focal reduction in cases of endobronchial obstruction by tumour, or focal inspiratory crackles in TB or bronchiectasis

> look for a sputum pot (bronchiectasis, TB).

Questions from the patient

[Assuming that there is no definite diagnosis on clinical grounds:]

Patient: *why did I cough the blood doctor? And why am I losing weight?*

Doctor: I'm not sure – we will need to do some more tests to find out exactly what is going on. These symptoms could be caused by infection in the bronchial tubes, including infections like tuberculosis or a mould called *Aspergillus*. They could also be caused by tumours in the chest, but I don't think that's likely – it would be very unusual in a man of your age.

Patient: *can I go home now?*

Doctor: I think it would be wise for us to get a chest X-ray, a test of your phlegm to look for infection, and some blood tests of your general health and get the results of those first, before deciding on the next steps.

Questions from the examiner

Examiner: *how would you distinguish between lung cancer and TB on clinical grounds?*

Doctor: this can be very difficult because both can cause sputum, haemoptysis, fevers, sweats and weight loss. In this case the patient's age and origin from a high-prevalence country make TB most likely.

Examiner: *how would you investigate?*

Doctor: I would like to get a chest X-ray and three sputum samples stained for acid-fast bacilli, as well as a full blood count (anaemia, leucocytosis, high platelet count), liver function tests (to check for coincident hepatitis, liver metastases, and to consider the patient's fitness for anti-TB medication) and, after discussion with the patient, an HIV test.

Examiner: *what would you look for on a chest X-ray?*

Doctor: the things I'd be looking for are a pleural effusion (TB, cancer), multifocal consolidation, with some cavitation (vasculitis, TB), cavity with a fungus ball (aspergilloma), hilar mass – with or without lobar or pulmonary collapse (lung cancer, carcinoid tumour), and mediastinal and/or hilar lymphadenopathy.

Examiner: *if sputum testing was unhelpful, what would you do next?*

Doctor: depending on the results of the chest X-ray, either a CT scan or a bronchoscopy, or both, may be required – the CT scan to aid diagnosis and to guide bronchoscopic sampling.

Examiner: *can the patient go home?*

Doctor: provided he is stable and his haemoptysis is not life-threatening, it would be reasonable to allow him to go home. National Institute for Health and Care Excellence (NICE)

guidance is that patients with suspected TB should not be admitted to hospital unless there is a clear clinical or public-health need to do so, such as homelessness. His immediate contacts will have already been exposed to any risk of TB. He should be advised, however, to avoid public places and unnecessary contact with others until the diagnosis is known. Patients with suspected lung cancer do not generally require admission to hospital for investigation or treatment.

1.4.4 Chronic obstructive pulmonary disease with poor control

Scenario

Mr Geraint Jones, a 71-year-old man with a diagnosis of COPD, has been referred to the respiratory outpatient clinic because of progressive exertional breathlessness and frequent respiratory tract infections. He has lost half a stone in weight over the past year and is underweight. What is the most likely diagnosis, and how would you investigate?

Introduction

Patients with COPD complain of breathlessness, cough, wheeze and recurrent infections/exacerbations. Respiratory failure and cor pulmonale may occur in advanced cases. Many patients with COPD live for years with chronic symptoms, hence it is important to establish what their baseline symptoms and function are, such that one can then determine how far any current symptoms represent a deterioration from normal.

When assessing a patient with uncontrolled symptoms consider the following.

Diagnosis

Is the diagnosis of COPD correct? Do they have additional diagnoses as well as COPD?

> COPD is unlikely if smoking history is minimal (less than 10 pack-years).

> Has the diagnosis of COPD been confirmed with spirometry?

> Asthma – asthma and COPD are overlapping conditions. Around 30% of COPD patients have evidence of eosinophilic (asthmatic) airway inflammation, and these are the patients who get most benefit from inhaled corticosteroids.

> Bronchiectasis – many patients with COPD have coexistent bronchiectasis, which is suggested if chronic sputum production and frequent infections are prominent features.

> Lung cancer – always perform a chest X-ray if a patient with COPD presents with worsening breathlessness, cough, chest pain, weight loss or haemoptysis.

> Interstitial lung disease – progressive breathlessness with bibasal fine inspiratory crackles. Smoking accelerates the course of idiopathic pulmonary fibrosis, which often coexists with COPD.

> Obstructive sleep apnoea – consider if overweight with signs of right heart failure.

> Cardiac disease.

Recent deterioration

What is the cause?

> Is this an acute deterioration, or gradual progression of long-standing disease?

- Infection – the most common cause of acute deterioration in COPD patients. If recurrent or non-resolving infection, then look for resistant organisms (eg *Pseudomonas*).
- Pulmonary embolus (PE) – a stepwise increase in breathlessness from baseline in the absence of increased cough or wheeze should prompt investigation for possible PE.

Other reversible or treatable factors

- Smoking – many patients with COPD continue to smoke, leading to poorly controlled symptoms and progressive lung damage. It is imperative that smoking cessation is discussed with the patient and smoking cessation assistance offered.
- Optimise inhaled therapy.
- Weight loss, deconditioning – weight loss and muscle wasting are features of progressive COPD; refer for pulmonary rehabilitation and discuss nutrition.
- Hypoxia – treatment of chronic hypoxia with long-term oxygen is one of the few interventions shown to improve survival in COPD.

Is this advanced, irreversible disease?
COPD is a progressive condition, even in the absence of ongoing smoking, and many patients will have symptoms that do not respond well to inhaled therapy and require a more holistic, palliative approach. Features in the history suggestive of advanced disease are:

- too breathless to leave the house, or breathless washing/dressing (in stable state)
- admissions to hospital with respiratory failure
- cor pulmonale / right heart failure
- cachexia.

Beginning the encounter

Doctor: hello, my name is Dr A, I understand that the problem is that you have been getting more breathless and having more chest infections. Is that right?

Patient: yes

Doctor: before we get onto the details of that, can you tell me if, apart from your breathing, you have any major medical problems?

Patient: [gives list (with the doctor politely but firmly discouraging lengthy detail).]

Doctor: and are you on any tablets or medications?

Patient: [gives details (and will probably have been asked to produce a written list).]

These introductory questions will provide useful clinical context and will immediately give details of any treatments for COPD.

Focused history

Doctor: I understand that you have a diagnosis of COPD … tell me about that. When was the diagnosis made?

Doctor: do you or have you ever smoked? [calculate pack-year history] When did your breathing problems start? Were you asthmatic as a child / young adult? Do you have good days and bad days? What can you do on a good day? … and on a bad day? Do you have a nocturnal cough or wheeze? Have you ever had to be admitted to hospital because of your breathing?

Key point
Could this be asthma? Patients who suffered with frequent cough and wheeze when young and describe significant day-to-day and diurnal variability to symptoms, may well have underlying chronic asthma, especially if they don't have a huge smoking history.

Doctor: now tell me what has been happening to your breathing recently? What are you able to do? How far can you walk, are you able to leave the house? How does this compare with a week ago … and with 3 months ago? Have you had to stop doing anything because of your breathing? (Establish baseline function and rate of functional decline.)

Specific questions about symptoms that would be helpful in this case are:

- cough/sputum
    - purulence, quantity
    - daily sputum (bronchiectasis?) or only when an exacerbation?
- infections
    - number of infections or courses of antibiotics in the past 6 months
    - did the antibiotics fully clear up the infection? (ie could there be a resistant organism?)
- red flag symptoms for lung cancer, including weight loss, chest pain, haemoptysis
- swollen legs (could indicate cor pulmonale or coexistent biventricular failure).

Focused examination

Concentrate on examining the respiratory system, with particular focus on the pattern of breathing.

Respiratory – check the following:

> sputum pots, inhalers, supplemental oxygen

> general appearance

>> thin patient with emphysematous, hyperexpanded chest ('pink puffer')

>> overweight, peripheral oedema, cyanosed ('blue bloater')

>> pursed lip breathing

> hands – check for clubbing

> chest

>> hyperexpanded chest

>> may be wheezy, or just quiet breath sounds if very emphysematous

>> basal inspiratory crackles are common in COPD.

Cardiac – check the following:

> peripheral oedema

> jugular venous pressure (JVP).

Questions from the patient

[Assuming the likely diagnosis is poorly controlled COPD, with no red flag symptoms, and the patient stopped smoking 2 years ago:]

Patient: why is my breathing getting worse? I stopped smoking a couple of years ago.

Doctor: stopping smoking is the most important thing you could have done to help your breathing, but I'm afraid that there was already significant lung damage by this time. Although cigarettes are no longer damaging your lungs, COPD itself causes chronic lung inflammation and can result in progressive breathlessness, even after you stop smoking.

Patient: how can we improve the COPD?

Doctor: we need to get you on the best combination of inhalers, and it is

important to treat infections promptly to prevent further damage to the lungs.

Patient: why am I losing weight?

Doctor: I'm not sure – I think it's most likely that it's due to the COPD, but we do need to check that there isn't anything more serious going on.

Patient: what do you mean?

Doctor: as I said, I suspect that all of your symptoms are caused by the COPD, but I think we should do a chest X-ray to make sure that there isn't anything like a lung cancer – I don't think there is, but we should check it out.

Patient: if it is all the COPD, then I don't understand why I'm losing weight.

Doctor: COPD doesn't just affect the lungs – it causes generalised inflammation throughout the body, which results in loss of muscle bulk and weight loss. It is important to maintain muscle conditioning and nutrition, and that is why – assuming the chest X-ray and other tests don't show anything surprising – I will refer you for a course of physiotherapy classes called pulmonary rehabilitation.

Questions from the examiner

Examiner: supposing this patient was still very breathless despite optimisation of their inhaled therapy. How would you advise that we treat this?

Doctor: unfortunately many patients with COPD remain breathless despite inhaled bronchodilators and steroids. In this situation I would ensure that they had stopped smoking and had been referred for pulmonary rehabilitation. I would check oxygen saturations and perform a blood gas test if saturations were less than 92% in order to assess for long-term oxygen.

Examiner: and supposing that they still remained symptomatic after those interventions?

Doctor: in that situation, involvement of palliative care would be appropriate, and the patient may get symptomatic relief from low-dose short-acting morphine.

Further discussion

In patients under 65 who have quit smoking and who have disabling symptoms, referral for consideration of lung transplantation may be appropriate.

1.4.5 Asthma with poor control

Scenario

Mrs Anne Smith, a 32-year-old woman, presented with a 2-month history of a dry tickly cough and intermittent breathlessness and chest tightness. She had been diagnosed with asthma as a teenager, but until recently this had been very well controlled, with infrequent use of inhaled salbutamol only. She is a keen sportswoman, but is now struggling to compete at the same level and she has used three salbutamol inhalers in the last month. What management would you recommend?

Introduction

Asthma is an inflammatory condition of the airways characterised by variable airflow obstruction. The history is the key to diagnosis as clinical examination and lung function testing are often normal outside an acute asthma attack. Not all patients conform to the classic pattern of atopic (eosinophilic) inflammation, fully reversible airflow obstruction and responsiveness to inhaled steroids. A subset of asthmatics have symptoms that respond poorly to inhaled steroids and can progress to fixed, irreversible airflow obstruction.

Things to consider:

Diagnosis – is the diagnosis of asthma correct?

> When was asthma diagnosed? By whom? Evidence of variable airflow obstruction?

> Is there a history of atopy?

> Asthma typically causes cough, breathlessness, wheeze and chest tightness, which vary on a diurnal and a day-to-day basis. Ask about nocturnal symptoms – classically these are worse at night or in the morning.

> Consider COPD in older patients who are (ex-) smokers and report little variability to symptoms.

> Consider bronchiectasis if excessive sputum production and frequent infections are prominent features.

How well controlled is their asthma?

> The aim of treatment should be for minimal symptoms, with no restriction to activity using the lowest dose of inhaled steroid.

> Does their asthma restrict their activity?

> Exacerbation history – have there been any admissions to hospital? Any admissions to intensive care?

> Ask about nocturnal symptoms and frequency of reliever medication use. Regular (weekly or more) nocturnal symptoms or use of reliever more than two or three times per week suggests asthma is suboptimally controlled.

Review current treatment:

> Are they taking their medications? Non-compliance with inhalers is common.

> Are they using the inhalers correctly?

Is there anything driving ongoing airway inflammation?

> Smoking

> Atopy/allergy – enquire about potential allergens including pets, pollen, dusts, moulds, etc at home or at work.

> Occupational – are they exposed to substances at work that may be provoking their asthma? Do their symptoms improve at weekends or on holiday?

> Infections – are they getting recurrent infective exacerbations?

> Gastro-oesophageal reflux can drive poorly controlled asthma due to microaspiration.

> Rhinitis/sinusitis – ask about hay fever, nasal congestion, nasal drip.

Beginning the encounter

Doctor: hello, my name is Dr A, I understand that the problem is that you have had a cough and some chest tightness. Is that right?

Patient: yes

Doctor: before we get onto the details of that, can you tell me if you have any major medical problems? Any problems with your breathing before, or hay fever?

Patient: [gives list (with the doctor politely but firmly discouraging lengthy detail).]

Doctor: and are you on any tablets or medications?

Patient: [gives details (and will probably have been asked to produce a written list).]

These introductory questions will provide useful clinical context and may immediately give clues to any relevant comorbidities, although these seem unlikely in a keen sportswoman.

Focused history

Doctor: tell me about your symptoms – ask about cough, breathlessness, wheeze, chest tightness. When do they bother you most (exertional, nocturnal symptoms, diurnal and day-to-day variability)? Do your

symptoms limit your activities? How often do you use your reliever inhaler? How often do you get nocturnal symptoms?

Doctor: is there any history of hay fever, eczema or allergies? Any family history of atopic disease? Have you noticed anything that triggers your symptoms? [Specifically ask about pets, dust, moulds/damp.] What is your job? Are you exposed to dusts or chemicals at work? Are your symptoms better away from work or on weekends/holidays?

Specific questions about symptoms that would be helpful in this case are:

> Cough may be dry or productive. Patients with poorly controlled asthma can produce very thick, rubbery blobs of sputum that are difficult to expectorate.

> Patients often complain of chest tightness and breathlessness, rather than wheeze.

Focused examination

This may be entirely normal since asthma, by definition, is a condition that varies from day to day and diurnally.

Respiratory system – check the following:

> inhalers, sputum pot (if present)

> chest – may well be normal

> > Look for wheeze and hyperexpansion, but these are usually only present during an acute attack.

> > The presence of wheeze when the patient is stable suggests a degree of fixed airflow obstruction or an alternative diagnosis such as COPD.

Other relevant examination:

> perform peak flow measurement (if available)

> suggest that you will check the patient's inhaler technique (examiner is likely to decline).

Questions from the patient

[Assuming the likely diagnosis is poorly controlled asthma:]

Patient: why is my blue inhaler not working any more?

Doctor: your blue inhaler is known as a reliever; it helps to open up the airways and relieves the wheeze and chest tightness during an asthma attack. However, asthma is a condition caused by inflammation in the airways, and although your blue inhaler helps with the symptoms of asthma, it does not treat the underlying inflammation.

Patient: so how can the inflammation be dealt with?

Doctor: the best way of dampening down the inflammation that is causing your asthma is to take an inhaled steroid. This has to be taken regularly, even if your asthma symptoms settle, to stop them coming back.

Patient: I was given a steroid inhaler before, but I stopped taking it because I had heard that steroids have lots of side effects.

Doctor: you're right that steroids can cause problems. High doses of tablet steroids can, over time, cause side effects, but the dose of steroid in an inhaler is much lower that this and is delivered directly to the lungs, meaning the amount that is absorbed into the rest of the body is very low. For most people asthma can be controlled with a very low dose of steroid, which does not cause the same problems seen with tablet steroids, and it's generally better to control asthma with a low dose of a regular inhaled steroid than to have to give much higher doses of tablet steroids if it gets out of control.

Patient: what should I do if I start getting wheezy again in the future?

Doctor: it is important that you have a care plan that will tell you what to do when your asthma becomes less well controlled. I will arrange for you to see our asthma nurse who will draw up an asthma action plan with you. They will give you a peak flow meter that you can use to assess your asthma control at home. If you are waking up at night or using your reliever more than three times a week, or if your peak flow is falling, then you will need to increase the amount of the preventer inhaler you are taking. Your asthma nurse will talk this through with you and provide you with written instructions on what to do and how to seek help if you become unwell again.

Questions from the examiner

Examiner: what investigations would you like to do on this woman?

Doctor: I would start with spirometry to look for airflow obstruction, which would be indicated by a forced expiratory volume in 1 second (FEV_1) to forced vital capacity (FVC) ratio of less than 0.7. If airflow obstruction was present then I would assess reversibility by repeating the spirometry after a bronchodilator. But spirometry is often normal in asthma, so if this was the case, then I would ask the patient to keep a peak flow diary at home to look for diurnal variability.

Examiner: what treatment would you give her?

Doctor: her symptoms are suggestive of asthma and the limitation to her activity and frequency of reliever medication use indicate that this is poorly controlled. Her asthma treatment therefore needs to stepped up, and I would commence her on a regular inhaled corticosteroid in line with British Thoracic Society (BTS) / Scottish Intercollegiate Guidelines Network (SIGN) asthma guidelines. I would also arrange for her to see the asthma nurse to take her through inhaler technique and an asthma management plan.

Examiner: if you suspect that her asthma is being exacerbated by exposure at work, how would you take this further?

Doctor: in this situation it is important to get a very detailed history of exactly what substances she is exposed to at work and how these exposures correlate with her symptoms. As a diagnosis of occupational asthma will have implications for her employment it is important to get objective evidence for this. In the first instance I would ask her to complete a detailed peak-flow monitoring diary, recording her peak flow at home and at work, while documenting her activity at the time. If this confirms that her airflow obstruction is related to her working environment then she will need to see an occupational health physician.

Further discussion

BTS/SIGN asthma treatment guidelines can be found at www.brit-thoracic.org.uk/guidelines-and-quality-standards/asthma-guideline/

1.5 Acute scenarios

1.5.1 Unexplained hypoxia

Scenario

A 44-year-old man has been admitted with a 2-week history of non-specific symptoms of tiredness and being unwell. His chest radiograph is reported as normal but he is found to be hypoxic with a PaO_2 of 8.4 kPa (normal range 11.3–12.6).

Introduction

It is reasonable to assume that the patient has new-onset hypoxia, given that he is experiencing new symptoms. There are five physiological processes that can give rise to hypoxia (Table 18). In this case the finding of a normal chest radiograph makes some of these causes less probable.

History of the presenting problem

As always in acute medicine it is vital to distinguish between genuinely new conditions and acute presentations of chronic conditions. With the chest radiograph reported as normal the main differential diagnoses in this case are shown in Table 19, and the history should pursue these possibilities.

Is the problem really acute? Try to identify whether, with hindsight, the patient has had respiratory symptoms previously, perhaps on exercise. Has the patient had to stop doing anything or slow down recently?

If the problem seems to be long-standing:

> Are there any respiratory or cardiac clues to the diagnosis? Clearly any history of chest pain/tightness, cough, sputum or haemoptysis would be important clues.

> Are there features of untreated asthma (see Section 2.2.2)?

Process	Example
Insufficient inspired oxygen	Altitude and anaesthetic mishaps
Right-to-left shunt	Anatomical (cardiac and pulmonary arteriovenous malformation) Physiological (eg resulting from atelectasis)
Ventilation/perfusion imbalance	Many causes, eg asthma, pneumonia, fibrosis and thromboembolic disease
Alveolar hypoventilation	Severe obstructive sleep apnoea and neurological/neuromuscular disease
Impaired diffusion	Fibrosis

Table 18 Pathophysiological processes leading to hypoxia

Table 19 Differential diagnosis of hypoxia with a 'normal' chest radiograph

	Long-standing problem	New condition
Common	COPD Diffuse parenchymal lung disease Obesity hypoventilation	PE Pneumonic process without chest radiograph changes, eg atypical pneumonia, *Pneumocystis jirovecii* pneumonia and acute aspiration
Rare	Neuromuscular disease Cardiac shunts Pulmonary arteriovenous malformation Hepatopulmonary syndrome Pulmonary hypertension	Extrinsic allergic alveolitis Miliary TB

COPD, chronic obstructive pulmonary disease; PE, pulmonary embolus; TB, tuberculosis.

> Are there features of sleep-disordered breathing? If this is severe enough to cause daytime hypoxia, then it should be associated with excessive daytime somnolence (see Section 2.1.1).

> Is there anything to suggest that there might be a cardiac problem, eg a report of a heart murmur is likely to be innocent, but could be relevant in this context.

> Is the patient at risk of interstitial lung disease? Enquire about occupation and hobbies (see Sections 2.6.2 and 2.7.3).

Key point

Always remember thromboembolic disease, which may not be associated with chest pain when chronic.

What acute conditions is the patient at risk of?

> Pulmonary embolus (PE) may be suggested by recognised risk factors for thromboembolic disease.

> The risk of atypical pneumonia is increased by exposure to air-conditioning systems (*Legionella*) or birds (*Chlamydia*).

> *Pneumocystis jirovecii* (formerly *Pneumocystis carinii*) pneumonia (PJP) may present with isolated hypoxia, at which point risk factors for HIV should be recorded.

> Miliary TB should be considered in high-risk groups.

> Acute aspiration may present without radiographic changes initially and an appropriate history should be sought (eg risk factors for disordered swallow

or reduced level of consciousness), although such a diagnosis could not explain this patient's 2-week history.

Examination: general features

> Does the patient have a fever or look toxic?

> Does the patient look as though they have lost weight? In this case weight loss might suggest miliary TB, or PJP as a complication of acquired immune deficiency syndrome (AIDS).

> Are there any other features to suggest AIDS, eg oral candidiasis?

> Is the patient likely to have obstructive sleep apnoea, eg is he obese or does he have a thick neck?

> Is the patient clubbed? This might suggest interstitial lung disease or a congenital cardiac shunt in this context.

Examination: particular systems

Respiratory and cardiac

> Are there features of airways disease? Are there crackles in the chest? This might suggest interstitial lung disease in this context.

> Are there cardiac features to suggest PE?

> Are there any cardiac murmurs?

> Spirometry should form part of the clinical assessment: COPD is common and should not be overlooked.

Neuromuscular

Is there evidence of neuropathy or myopathy? In particular, does the patient's diaphragm move normally (ie does the abdomen move out as the patient breathes in)? If in doubt, place your hand gently on their epigastrium and ask them to sniff: it should move out as they do.

Investigations

Chest radiograph

Review the chest radiograph carefully. Take it back to the radiologist for further scrutiny with additional clinical information.

> Is the cardiac silhouette really normal?

> Is there subtle evidence of airspace shadowing (Fig 7)? This would suggest interstitial lung disease or a pneumonic process.

> Are both hemidiaphragms clearly visible? Check that you are not overlooking left lower lobe consolidation, which is easy to miss.

> Are both costophrenic angles clearly visible? A small pleural effusion might be caused by a pneumonic process or thromboembolism. Sampling of pleural fluid could be diagnostic (see Section 1.2.4).

Arterial blood gases

An increased $PaCO_2$ (or the demonstration, by calculation, of a normal arterial–alveolar oxygen gradient) would suggest true alveolar hypoventilation. Comparison of arterial blood gases measured on room air and 100% oxygen enables the calculation of the anatomical shunt, which in normal subjects is less than 5%.

Spirometry and flow–volume loop

These measurements should be abnormal if there is occult airways disease of sufficient severity to cause hypoxia. In interstitial lung disease there is usually a restrictive defect. Upper airway obstruction is an extremely unlikely diagnosis in this case, because it only leads to hypoxia as the patient is about to die, but would be revealed by the flow–volume loop (see Section 1.5.4).

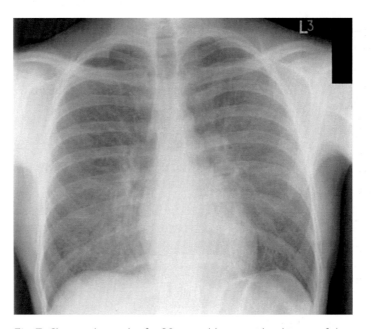

Fig 7 Chest radiograph of a 29-year-old man with a history of dyspnoea and weight loss. Diagnostic possibilities include *Pneumocystis jirovecii* pneumonia.

Blood tests

Routine full blood count (FBC), biochemistry and inflammatory markers are indicated because of the non-specific nature of symptoms in this case. Serum angiotensin-converting enzymes and calcium are indicated if sarcoid is possible. Atypical pneumonia titres or avian precipitins would be indicated if the history is appropriate, as might testing (after discussion) for HIV.

CT scan of thorax

This is likely to be a very helpful investigation, but the way in which the study is performed will depend on what is considered to be the most likely diagnosis. Discussion with the radiologist is required: not just a request form stating 'hypoxia – cause?'

> For suspected thromboembolic disease, or to detect a pulmonary arteriovenous malformation (AVM) a CT pulmonary angiogram is required.

> For suspected interstitial lung disease thin-section reconstructions are helpful. Significant pulmonary fibrosis may be invisible on a plain radiograph, but seen on CT.

Bronchoscopy

Analysis of bronchial lavage fluid is indicated to diagnose PCP. In miliary TB, or if there is CT evidence of interstitial lung disease then transbronchial biopsy is likely to be required. Surgical lung biopsy, usually performed thoracoscopically, may be required in some patients.

Echocardiography

A contrast echocardiogram is the first choice investigation if an intracardiac shunt is suspected (estimation of pulmonary artery pressure is a useful piece of extra data from this study, and should be specifically requested). If there is no cardiac shunt then a CT scan will usually identify a pulmonary arteriovenous malformation (AVM).

Management

Oxygen should be administered to relieve hypoxia, but other aspects of management will depend on the underlying condition.

1.5.2 Pleural effusion and fever

Scenario

A 45-year-old woman is admitted to the hospital with a history of fever for the past 7 days. Her chest radiograph shows a right pleural effusion.

Introduction

Pleural effusion and fever is most likely due to an infective process, but there are other causes (Table 20).

Any pleural effusion associated with a bacterial pneumonia is called a parapneumonic effusion, which if not treated may progress to become an empyema (pus in the pleural space). Pleural infection can also develop without evidence of pneumonia (primary empyema).

History of the presenting problem

It is essential to establish that this effusion is related to an underlying infective process.

> Is there any history of cough with purulent phlegm?

> What is the duration of symptoms? Parapneumonic effusions / empyema usually develop over days–weeks, whereas symptoms lasting weeks–months are more suggestive of TB or malignancy.

> Severe pleuritic chest pain suggests bacterial infection, PE or malignancy.

> Is there any haemoptysis? This could indicate pneumonia, TB, malignancy and PE.

> Is there any history of weight loss? This could suggest TB or a malignancy.

> Has the patient travelled abroad recently? This could suggest pneumonia or PE.

> Is the patient a smoker? Remember: proximal malignancy can present with pneumonia.

> Is there any history of contact with TB or evening rise of temperature with night sweats?

Considering non-infective causes:

> Is there any history of joint pains, rash or red/painful eyes? Rheumatoid arthritis and systemic lupus erythematosus (SLE) may present with an exudative pleural effusion.

> Any past history of extrathoracic malignancy (breast, ovaries or lymphoma)?

> Has there been any exposure to asbestos?

Table 20	Causes of pleural effusion and fever
Frequency (in the UK)	**Condition**
Common	Pneumonia – parapneumonic Empyema – secondary to pneumonia, or (rarely) primary
Less common	TB PE Malignancy – primary bronchial, secondary and mesothelioma
Rare	Autoimmune rheumatic disorder, eg rheumatoid arthritis and systemic lupus erythematosus

PE, pulmonary emboli; TB, tuberculosis.

You should also consider the possibility that the cause of the pleural effusion may not be the same as the cause of the fever:

> Is there a history of congestive cardiac failure or any of the other conditions discussed in Section 1.2.4?

Examination: general features

As always, note immediately how unwell the patient is and check the vital signs – temperature, pulse rate, respiratory rate and blood pressure (watch out for septic shock). Establish if the patient is cyanosed: use pulse oximetry to record SaO_2.

Look for cachexia (suggesting TB or malignancy), clubbing (from malignancy), lymphadenopathy (from TB or malignancy) or any features to suggest autoimmune rheumatic disorder (such as a rash or arthritis).

Examination: respiratory system

> Look at the contents of any sputum pots.

> Palpation: check movements of both sides of the chest (reduced on the side of a big effusion) and look for mediastinal shift by palpating the trachea and the apex beat (both will be shifted away from a big effusion).

> Percussion: will be stony dull on the side of effusion.

> Auscultation: breath sounds will be reduced on the side of effusion, with bronchial breath sounds if it is consolidated or has a collapsed lung above it.

Investigations

Given that pleural effusion is confirmed on the chest radiograph in this case, other appropriate investigations on admission would be:

> FBC – likely to show neutrophilia, with a very high neutrophil count ($>20 \times 10^9$/L) (normal range 1.5–7.0) supporting the diagnosis of empyema

> erythrocyte sedimentation rate / C-reactive protein – very raised inflammatory markers are anticipated in bacterial infection

> blood cultures

> sputum for alcohol- and acid-fast bacilli and bacterial culture

> creatinine and electrolytes – required in any acutely ill patient: impaired renal function may be due to hypoperfusion of the kidneys

> liver function tests – may be abnormal in Legionnaires' disease.

Regarding the pleural effusion itself:

> Thoracic ultrasound can differentiate pleural fluid from pleural thickening. On ultrasound the fluid may be anechoic (may be transudate or exudate), echogenic (exudate) and/or septated (exudate).

> Pleural aspiration: all patients with a pleural effusion in association with sepsis or a pneumonic illness require diagnostic pleural fluid sampling under ultrasound guidance, as the pleural fluid characteristics will determine if there is a need for chest tube insertion. A chest tube should be inserted if the aspirate is purulent, microscopy and culture from the pleural fluid is positive for bacteria, or if the pH of the pleural fluid is less than 7.2. See Section 1.2.4 for further discussion of pleural fluid sampling.

> **Key point**
> In any patient with sepsis and a pleural effusion, a diagnostic pleural aspirate must be performed.

In some patients it may be appropriate to send their blood for an atypical pneumonia screen, test their urine for *Legionella* and pneumococcal antigens, and check their serological tests for autoimmune rheumatic disorder.

Management

General

> oxygen if hypoxic

> ensure adequate hydration and nutrition

> prophylaxis against thromboembolism.

Specific

> Community-acquired pneumonia – appropriate antimicrobials: the bacteriology of parapneumonic effusions and empyema is notably different from that of community-acquired pneumonia (Fig 8). In particular, so-called 'atypical' pathogens are rarely to blame, and anaerobes, members of the family Enterobacteriaceae and staphylococci are much more common. The choice of first-line antibiotic treatment should reflect this.

> TB – appropriate antimicrobials and contact tracing.

> Chest drain insertion and subsequent management (see Section 3.2.4).

> Surgical intervention – patients with persistent sepsis and collections of pus despite antibiotics and appropriate chest tube insertion should be referred to thoracic surgical services.

> **Key point**
> Streptococci, anaerobes, Enterobacteriaceae and staphylococci are the common causes of parapneumonic effusions and empyema – antibiotic choice should reflect this.

Further comments

The use of intrapleural fibrinolytics to break down septations and improve pleural drainage in loculated pleural infection has been the subject of some debate over recent years. However, the most recent evidence suggests that a

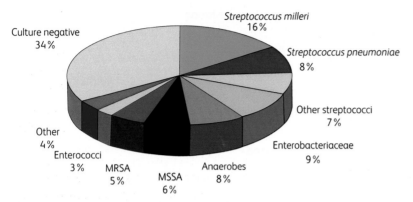

Culture negative 34%

Streptococcus milleri 16%

Streptococcus pneumoniae 8%

Other streptococci 7%

Enterobacteriaceae 9%

Other 4%

Enterococci 3%

MRSA 5%

MSSA 6%

Anaerobes 8%

Fig 8 Bacteriology of parapneumonic effusions (*n* = 430). MRSA, methicillin-resistant Staphylococcus aureus; MSSA, methicillin-sensitive Staphylococcus aureus. Adapted with permission from Maskell NA, Davies CDH and Nunn AJ. UK controlled trial of intrapleural streptokinase for pleural infection. *N Engl J Med* 2005;352(9):865–74.

combination of tissue plasminogen activator (tPA) and dornase alfa (DNase) injected intrapleurally via a chest drain improves pleural drainage and reduces the need for surgical evacuation.

Most pleural effusions associated with pneumonia resolve without any specific therapy directed towards the pleural fluid, but about 10% require specific intervention.

1.5.3 Lobar collapse in a non-smoker

Case history

A 55-year-old woman is referred with a 10-day history of productive cough, gradually increasing shortness of breath and fever. Her symptoms have failed to resolve on oral antibiotics and her chest radiograph shows right upper lobe collapse (Fig 9).

Introduction

The causes of lobar collapse are shown in Table 21.

Is there any concomitant consolidation? If there is, then your initial concern must be to treat infection because a

collapse of the lung may be caused by inflamed and swollen bronchial mucosa, and mucous plugging secondary to lobar pneumonia. Collapse alone, or collapse with concomitant consolidation that is slow to clear (say more than

6 weeks from the onset of symptoms), requires investigation to exclude an endobronchial lesion causing mechanical obstruction.

History of presenting problem

It is important that you get as many specific details as possible regarding this patient's symptoms. Ask her:

> When did the shortness of breath start? Was it before the illness that precipitated admission? If so, how long ago was it? A long history would clearly indicate underlying chronic lung disease, eg COPD in a smoker who has now developed a chest infection or lung cancer.

> Did the shortness of breath start gradually or suddenly? If sudden, then is inhalation of a foreign body a possibility? Infants, children and patients with learning difficulties or dementia are particularly at risk in such circumstances,

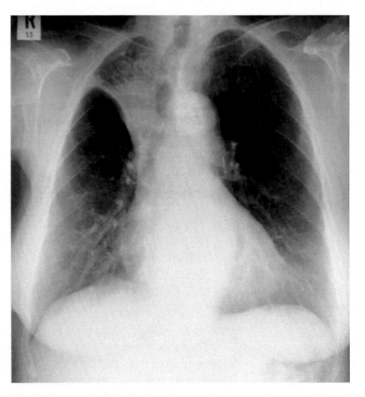

Fig 9 Posteroanterior chest radiograph showing right upper lobe collapse. Note the tenting of the right hemidiaphragm and the raised right hilum. (Courtesy of Dr I Vlahos.)

Table 21	Differential diagnosis of lobar collapse
Classification	**Examples**
Common	Infection (pneumonia and pulmonary tuberculosis)
Other causes	Carcinoma of the lung Inhaled foreign body Asthma Allergic bronchopulmonary aspergillosis Bronchiectasis (particularly cystic fibrosis) Other lung tumours (eg carcinoid)

as well as those with risk factors for reduced level of consciousness (eg epilepsy and alcoholism, etc). Ask for a history of choking while eating food or losing a dental filling.

> How long has she had the fever? Pyogenic pneumonia will typically present with a shorter history than TB.

> What is the colour of her sputum, and has she noticed any blood in it? Haemoptysis can occur in cases of infection, carcinoma of the lung, bronchial carcinoids and pulmonary embolism, although the latter is not a cause of lobar collapse.

> Has she had any associated pains in the chest? Severe pleurisy would be most likely in pneumonia, but pain can be a feature of TB or malignancy.

> Was there a preceding upper respiratory tract infection, which can sometimes precipitate pulmonary infection?

Other relevant history

Ask the patient:

> Is there any history of an underlying lung condition? Patients with chronic chest problems are particularly prone to infection. The thick, tenacious sputum occurring in asthma, allergic bronchopulmonary aspergillosis and cystic fibrosis (CF) may cause mucous plugging resulting in lobar/subsegmental collapse.

> Has she ever smoked? If so, for how long and when did she quit? Lung cancer is relatively uncommon in patients who have never smoked.

> Is there any history of weight loss? Consider carcinoma of the lung and pulmonary TB, as well as the possibility of pulmonary metastases from other primary sites (known or unknown).

> Is there any history of night sweats? Is there any previous history of TB / contact with TB? (See Section 1.4.3 for further discussion.)

> Are there any odd symptoms such as flushing, sweats or diarrhoea that might indicate carcinoid syndrome?

Examination: general features

A full general examination is needed, with particular attention to the following.

> Is the patient acutely unwell? Check her vital signs and note her ability to speak, her use of accessory muscles and whether or not her breathing is laboured or she is cyanosed. Check pulse oximetry.

> Does she look chronically unwell? Evidence of weight loss would support the diagnosis of TB or malignancy, as would the presence of peripheral lymphadenopathy.

> Finger clubbing would most likely indicate lung cancer in this context.

Examination: respiratory system

Check carefully for signs of consolidation (dullness to percussion and bronchial breathing) and for the features of lobar collapse described in Section 1.2.7.

Investigations

Given that lobar collapse is confirmed on the chest radiograph in this case, other appropriate investigations on admission would include the following.

> Blood tests – to look for evidence of infection (raised white cell / neutrophil count or raised C-reactive protein) and establish baseline creatinine, electrolytes, renal, liver and bone function tests (hypercalcaemia would suggest malignancy). Screen for allergic bronchopulmonary aspergillosis (raised eosinophil count, total and specific immunoglobulin E, and precipitins) in (highly) selected cases.

> Sputum and blood cultures – for routine microbiology staining and cultures. If pulmonary TB is suspected special sputum testing for acid-fast bacilli should be requested, as this is not performed routinely.

> CT scan of the chest and upper abdomen – if there is a suspicion of an intrapulmonary lesion you should proceed with a formal staging scan. This includes a search for potential metastases in the liver and adrenal glands, which is where carcinoma of the lung tends to metastasise, and will also sometimes detect the unexpected primary that has metastasised to the bronchial mucosa (cancers that can commonly do this include renal, breast, colorectal and endometrial).

> Bronchoscopy – this should be performed if there is no / poor response to antibiotics, a high suspicion of endobronchial lesion or foreign body inhalation, or if collapse/consolidation persists. CT scanning should be performed first. If an endobronchial lesion is seen, it should be biopsied and sent for histological examination. Bronchial washings and blind brushings should also be taken for cytological and microbiological examination (even if no endobronchial lesion was found).

Management

Give oxygen if the patient's pulse oximetry and/or arterial blood gases reveal hypoxaemia (SaO_2 <94%) together with, in the first instance unless an alternative diagnosis is readily apparent, appropriate antibiotics for community-acquired pneumonia. Further management will depend on the most likely initial diagnoses and response to treatment:

> Chest infection – arrange a repeat chest radiograph in 6 weeks' time to ensure that radiological abnormalities have fully resolved.

> Carcinoma of the lung – see Section 2.9.1.

> Foreign body – this may be removed via flexible or rigid bronchoscopy. Long-term occlusion of bronchi can lead to bronchiectasis, associated with chronic cough and repeated chest infections.

> Pulmonary TB – see Section 1.2.8.

1.5.4 Upper airway obstruction

Scenario

A 56-year-old woman presents with a 5-day history of stridor. She is obese, complains of recent hoarseness of her voice and says that she is tired all the time.

Introduction

Stridor is a musical sound best heard on inspiration, in contrast to wheeze, which is heard on expiration. It is caused by the turbulence of air passing through a narrow glottis or trachea and indicates extrathoracic obstruction. The narrowing of the airway can be intrinsic or extrinsic

(Table 7), and it should be investigated urgently as it may be life-threatening if it proceeds to occlude the airway and may be due to an underlying malignancy.

Hoarseness of the voice that has lasted for more than 6 weeks is an indication for investigation for malignancy in its own right, but in general this is a less worrying symptom than stridor – although in this case they could clearly be due to the same thing.

History of the presenting problem

In taking the history, important issues to explore will include the following.

> Does the patient have any other respiratory symptoms? Is she short of breath, and has she had any cough or haemoptysis?

> Although she is obese, has her weight changed? A loss of weight would suggest a malignancy, while a gain in weight might indicate hypothyroidism.

> Has she always been tired? Tiredness is a non-specific symptom, but along with a change in voice could point to hypothyroidism. Further support for this diagnosis would be obtained if the patient said that she was constipated, did not like the cold or had any other typical symptoms.

> Is there any history of dysphagia? This might be due to an underlying mediastinal tumour pressing on the oesophagus.

> Has the patient noticed any lymphadenopathy or had fevers? These would suggest lymphoma or other malignancy.

> Are there any features of myasthenia gravis? This could be indicated by diplopia or dysphagia.

Relevant past history

Check the following:

> Has the patient ever had any thyroid disorder/surgery?

> Stridor can be due to tracheal stenosis secondary to intubation. Has she ever been intubated, had an operation or been on a breathing machine?

> Has she ever suffered from a lymphoma?

> Does she smoke or has she smoked in the past?

Examination: general features

> Is she acutely unwell? Check vital signs and note her ability to speak, her use of accessory muscles and whether or not her breathing is laboured or she is cyanosed. Check pulse oximetry.

> Does she look chronically unwell? Evidence of weight loss would support the diagnosis of malignancy, as would the presence of peripheral lymphadenopathy.

> Are there any signs of superior vena cava (SVC) obstruction? Swelling of the face and arms, dilated chest wall veins or raised venous pressure would indicate intrathoracic disease pressing upon the SVC.

> Could she be hypothyroid? Look at and palpate for the thyroid gland. Look carefully for the clinical features of sallow complexion, puffy hands and face, and dry skin as well as checking for the most reliable clinical sign of hypothyroidism – slow relaxation of the tendon jerks.

Examination: respiratory system

Confirm the presence of stridor. Note if the trachea is deviated, but remember that there will be no abnormal signs in the chest itself if the problem is confined to the upper airway.

Investigations

Key point

If a patient with stridor is having difficulty in breathing, then the first priority must be to protect the airway. This is easier said than done. Urgent advice from anaesthetic, ear/nose/throat and/or respiratory specialists is required. Cricothyroidotomy or tracheostomy may be needed.

If the patient is well enough, then the following tests would be appropriate.

Flow–volume loop
This is the standard method of showing that there is functional upper airway obstruction (Fig 10).

Bronchoscopy or laryngoscopy
One of these tests is mandatory in cases of undiagnosed upper airway obstruction.

Chest radiograph
This may show a mediastinal mass (including thymoma) or lymphadenopathy.

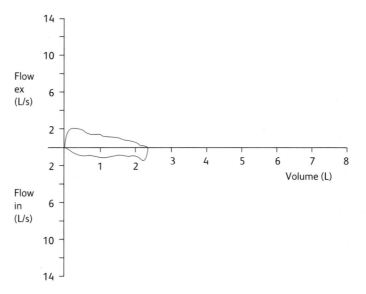

Fig 10 Flow–volume loop of a patient complaining of exertional dyspnoea. Diagnosis: tracheal stenosis.

CT scanning of the neck and thorax
This will show if there is any pathological enlargement of normal structures in the neck or thorax that could be causing tracheal compression.

Other tests
Thyroid function tests, FBC, serum calcium, and renal and liver function tests; use acetylcholine receptor antibodies if there is a suspicion of myasthenia. Thyroid scans can be used to look for retrosternal goitre. A Tensilon test is indicated in suspected myasthenia gravis with underlying thymoma.

Treatment
Definitive management depends, as always, on the diagnosis:

> Laser therapy can be used for post-intubation stenosis.

> If the problem is at the level of the vocal cords, then tracheostomy can be helpful if the problem itself cannot be treated.

> Tracheal stenosis due to malignant disease can be treated with surgery, radiotherapy or airway stenting, or a combination of modalities, depending upon the underlying malignancy and the staging.

2 Diseases and treatments

2.1 Upper airway

2.1.1 Sleep apnoea

The term 'sleep-related apnoea' has been defined as periods of complete absence of breathing during sleep. An apnoea is defined as a cessation of airflow for 10 or more seconds. Based on analysis of breathing patterns, three types of sleep apnoea have been described:

> obstructive apnoea: persistence of the diaphragmatic and intercostal muscle activity

> central apnoea: no diaphragmatic or intercostal muscle activity

> mixed apnoeas central and obstructive apnoeas.

Hypopnoea is defined as a decrease of airflow at the mouth and nose along with a decreased respiratory effort. Some investigators define hypopnoea as a one-third reduction of tidal volume for 10 or more seconds associated with a 4% reduction of oxygen saturation.

Obstructive sleep apnoea syndrome

This is the most common sleep disorder seen in sleep clinics, and is obstructive sleep apnoea (OSA) with excessive daytime somnolence. The prevalence of obstructive sleep apnoea syndrome (OSAS) among middle-aged men and women is estimated at around 5%. The prevalence increases with age partly due to a gain in weight.

OSAS is associated with:

> obesity

> hypertension: the prevalence of OSAS is greater than 25% in hypertensive patients, and in untreated cases of severe OSAS the prevalence of hypertension may be as high as 50%

> gastro-oesophageal reflux disease (GORD)

> smoking.

OSAS results from the narrowing and closure of the upper airway during sleep. This may be due to a combination of factors: reduced upper airway neural reflexes to prevent collapse, decreased upper airway size, increased airway collapsibility, myopathy of upper airway muscles, and fluid shifts from the legs to the torso at night. The pharynx, which lacks supporting cartilage and bone, is the site of occlusion, which can occur at the level of the velopharynx, oropharynx or the hypopharynx. Owing to the relative hypotonia that occurs during sleep there is airway closure, and the patient then attempts to breathe without success, resulting in oxygen desaturation. This results in an arousal (lightening of sleep) and reopening of the airway. Such episodes occur many times each hour during sleep. Arousals can be detected on the electroencephalogram (EEG), and frequent such arousals at the cortical level results in fragmented sleep and excessive daytime somnolence.

Conditions causing a narrow upper airway predispose to OSAS, including:

> mucosal oedema and inflammation, for example in rhinitis

> anatomic deformities such as micrognathia and retrognathia

> enlarged tongue, soft palate or uvula – present in Down's syndrome and hypothyroidism

> infiltration of pharyngeal tissue: obesity and Prader–Willi syndrome

> structural lesions: enlarged tonsils and adenoids

> cranial base abnormalities: achondroplasia and rheumatoid arthritis

> weakness of pharyngeal and laryngeal dilator muscles: congenital myopathies, muscular dystrophies, medullary lesions and vocal-cord paralysis

> increased airway compliance: Marfan syndrome, tracheomalacia and laryngomalacia.

Symptoms

It is essential to take a history from the bed partner, as most symptoms occur during sleep:

> excessive daytime somnolence

> snoring

> apnoeic episodes during sleep

> snorting, gasping and choking sounds during sleep

> restless sleep due to arousals

> nocturnal sweating

> nocturia

> morning headaches

> mood disturbances

> reduced libido

> personality change

> forgetfulness

> symptoms of GORD.

Physical signs

> obesity: body mass index (BMI) of 25 kg/m² or more (normal range 18–25) (BMI is calculated as body weight in kilograms divided by the square of the body height in metres, so BMI is expressed in units of kg/m²)

> collar size: men with a collar size of more than 17 inches (43 cm) and women with one more than 16 inches (41 cm) are at risk of OSAS

> features of hypothyroidism

> anatomic facial deformities

> enlarged tonsils

> large oedematous uvula

> hypertension

> congestive cardiac failure.

Diagnosis

In order to get as accurate a diagnosis as possible, make sure you do the following:

> Take an appropriate history from the patient and their bed partner.

> Assess subjective sleepiness by the Epworth Sleepiness Scale.

> Confirmatory tests:

> Overnight pulse oximetry: this may be normal and, if so, in a patient with a good history and evidence of daytime sleepiness without any other reason, polysomnography should be requested. It is also important to note that overnight pulse oximetry does not confirm OSA, but is merely suggestive of it.

> Polysomnography: this is the investigation of choice. This records the EEG, electrooculogram, submental electromyogram, airflow at the nose and mouth, and thoracic and abdominal wall movement (respiratory effort). At the same time SaO_2, electrocardiogram (ECG), leg movements and snoring sounds can be recorded. Additional sensors can be used to assess the patient's body position (more apnoeas occur in the supine position) and oesophageal pH (respiratory effort against a obstructed airway is associated with gastro-oesophageal reflux). Simultaneous video recording can help in diagnosing apnoea spells with restless sleep due to arousals. Polysomnography helps to determine the presence and type of apnoea, and its relation to sleep stage and body position (more apnoeas occur in the supine position and during rapid eye movement (REM) sleep). The severity of an OSA is determined by the frequency and duration of apnoeas and hypopnoeas (mild: 5–15/hour, moderate: 15–30/hour and severe: >30/hour).

Key point

The Epworth Sleepiness Scale

How likely are you to doze off or fall asleep in the following situations, in contrast to just feeling tired? Use the following scale to choose the most appropriate response for each situation:

0 = would never doze

1 = slight chance of dozing

2 = moderate chance of dozing

3 = high chance of dozing

Situation	Chance of dozing
1 Sitting and reading	_____
2 Watching TV	_____
3 Sitting inactive in a public place	_____
4 As a passenger in a car for an hour without a break	_____
5 Lying down to rest in the afternoon	_____
6 Sitting and talking to someone	_____
7 Sitting quietly after a lunch without alcohol	_____
8 In car while stopped for few minutes in traffic	_____
Total points	_____

If your score adds up to 11 or more, you may have significant sleep deprivation or a sleep disorder.

Treatment

There are three reasons to treat OSA:

> to relieve symptoms

> to reduce the risk of comorbidities associated with OSA

> to provide relief from the effects of OSA on others.

Currently, the best evidence for treatment is symptom relief (achieved by nasal continuous positive airway pressure (nCPAP)). There may be beneficial effects on risks of comorbidities, but this is a field of ongoing investigation.

Weight reduction
Sleep apnoea may be cured by weight loss.

Nasal continuous positive airway pressure
Nasal continuous positive airway pressure (nCPAP), introduced in 1981, is now the treatment of choice. The mask covers the nose and the continuous positive airways pressure delivers pressurised air to keep the upper airway open. The pressure is titrated to achieve the optimum pressure that is needed to reduce the apnoeas. Once a patient is on nCPAP, regular follow-up is needed to monitor compliance, assess the effect on symptoms and for regular machine servicing and mask/tubing replacement.

Dental appliances
In patients who are not able or are unwilling to use nCPAP, dental devices, which advance the tongue or the mandible and hence open the airway, are used. A recent study suggests that they are a reasonable treatment choice in mild-to-moderate sleep apnoea.

Tracheostomy
Prior to nCPAP, this was the treatment of choice. The tube stays capped during the daytime and the person breathes and speaks normally. During the night-time, when the person is about to retire to bed, the plug is removed, allowing the lungs to breathe directly through the tube. This bypasses any previous obstruction in the upper airway, thereby rectifying the problem.

Systemic effects of OSA

> Cognitive and psychosocial function: complaints of poor memory or impaired attention are common in OSA. These improve with treatment.

> Nocturnal hypoxemia: nocturnal hypoxemia is common in OSA and is usually more severe in REM sleep. It leads to increased sympathetic activity, vasoconstriction, raised blood pressure and cardiac arrhythmias.

> Cardiac function: bradycardia, common during apnoeas, is a result of increased vagal tone caused by fluctuations in intrathoracic pressure and stimulation of the carotid body receptors by hypoxemia.

> Cerebral perfusion: intracranial pressure may exceed 50 mmHg during obstructive apnoeas. This is associated with a reduction in cerebral perfusion pressure. Subsequent arousals lower the intracranial pressure and hence increase perfusion. This fluctuation in cerebral blood flow can contribute to chronic vascular stress and stroke.

> Renal function: OSA is associated with an increased release of atrial natriuretic peptide during sleep because of atrial distension. This results in an increase in urine output causing nocturia and enuresis.

> Endocrine function:
  > Reduced nocturnal growth hormone secretion occurs in children with OSA and contributes to growth retardation.
  > Dysmenorrhoea and amenorrhoea can occur in women with OSA and may improve with treatment.

> In some patients with OSA, hyperinsulinemia can occur. Treatment of OSA improves insulin responsiveness in some patients with OSA.

Complications of OSA

> accidents: patients must inform the Driver and Vehicle Licensing Agency (DVLA – UK) once OSA has been diagnosed. For group I (private cars) license holders, driving must cease until satisfactory control of symptoms has been achieved. For group II (heavy goods vehicles), driving must cease until satisfactory control of symptoms has been achieved with ongoing compliance with treatment, which has been confirmed by a specialist

> increased risk of stroke

> increased risk of myocardial infarction

> increased risk of hypertension

> atrial fibrillation

> increased insulin resistance and risk of diabetes mellitus

> anaesthetic complications: due to narrow airway, there may be difficulty in intubation.

2.2 Atopy and asthma

2.2.1 Allergic rhinitis
Aetiology
Allergic rhinitis is defined as a symptomatic nasal disorder brought about by an immunoglobulin E-mediated inflammation of the membranes of the nose following allergen exposure. The classification of allergic rhinitis is based on symptoms and quality of life parameters. It is subdivided according to

duration and severity into 'intermittent' or 'persistent', and 'mild' or 'moderate–severe' (Fig 11).

There is a strong pathophysiological relationship between allergic rhinitis and allergic asthma, with both conditions commonly coexisting. Patients with allergic rhinitis have inflammation of the lower airways and in patients with asthma, the presence of allergic rhinitis is common. Both allergic rhinitis and asthma represent allergic conditions with shared components of airway hyperresponsiveness. Indeed, allergic rhinitis is known to precipitate and exacerbate asthma. Therefore, both allergic rhinitis and asthma represent a spectrum of allergic airway disease extending from the nose to the lung, the so-called unified airway.

Known triggers of allergic rhinitis include:

> aeroallergens – domestic animals, house-dust mites, insects, moulds, plants and pollens

> pollutants – automobile contaminants, diesel exhaust, domestic allergens, gas pollutants, oxides of nitrogen, ozone, sulphur dioxide and tobacco smoke

> drugs – aspirin and non-steroidal anti-inflammatory drugs

> occupational factors

> latex allergy.

Clinical presentation

Patients present with sneezing, itching, watery rhinorrhoea and nasal obstruction.

Physical signs

Look for nasal polyps that can both cause and exacerbate rhinitis.

Investigations

The majority of patients are treated with success empirically; for patients who are refractory to therapy consider the differential diagnosis (below) and also consider occupational history, skin-prick testing, full blood count (FBC) and eosinophil count.

Differential diagnosis

Other non-allergic causes of rhinitis include infection, nasal polyps, foreign bodies or anatomical variants, nasal tumours, granulomatous diseases, and vasomotor (secondary to 'over-the-counter' medication) and idiopathic factors.

Treatment

> Allergen avoidance – although this is not always possible.

> Topical (nasal) steroids – often very effective. Side effects are local irritation and nose bleeds. Check for compliance and technique if there is a failure to improve.

> Oral antihistamines – warn the patient about the sedative side effects of some preparations and interactions with other drugs, eg terfenadine with erythromycin results in prolonged QT intervals.

> Nasal ipratropium bromide may be effective in controlling rhinorrhoea.

> Cromoglycates – no major side effects, but requires frequent use. Eye drops are particularly effective in allergic conjunctivitis.

> Oral leukotriene receptor antagonists.

> Immunotherapy – desensitisation is sometimes possible in selected patients. The technique must be performed in specialist centres.

2.2.2 Asthma

Aetiology

Asthma is defined as reversible airway obstruction associated with airway inflammation and bronchial hyperresponsiveness. The hyperresponsiveness of the airways is caused by a variety of local stimuli including histamine, leukotrienes and prostaglandins. This produces the reversible airflow obstruction that leads to the characteristic symptoms of shortness of breath, chest tightness and wheeze. Risk factors include:

> a genetic predisposition

> a family or personal history of atopy

> obesity

> viral infections (rhinovirus)

> maternal smoking and ethnicity

> socio-economic status.

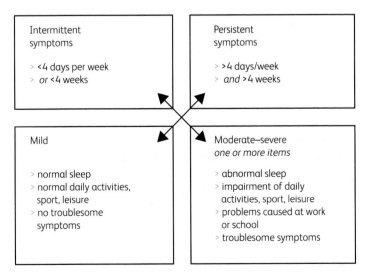

Intermittent symptoms	Persistent symptoms
> <4 days per week > or <4 weeks	> >4 days/week > and >4 weeks

Mild	Moderate–severe one or more items
> normal sleep > normal daily activities, sport, leisure > no troublesome symptoms	> abnormal sleep > impairment of daily activities, sport, leisure > problems caused at work or school > troublesome symptoms

Fig 11 Classification of allergic rhinitis.

The role of other factors such as diet and pollution (black smoke, fine particulate matter, ozone and sulphates) remains controversial. While not directly linked to an increased prevalence of the disease, they certainly exacerbate asthmatic symptoms and there is increased asthma mortality in areas of high industrial pollution. Other precipitants of asthma attacks include house-dust mites, pollens, moulds, fungi, cat and dog dander, aspirin and non-steroidal anti-inflammatory drugs in sensitive patients (approximately10–20%), and occupational exposure.

Epidemiology

The prevalence of asthma continues to rise worldwide, particularly in developed countries. Approximately 15% of the adult population in the UK have asthma and, despite effective medication, there are still approximately 1,500 deaths from the disease each year.

This continued morbidity and mortality highlights the importance of education for both patients and their doctors, with an emphasis on adequate treatment regimens, good compliance and rapid access to medical help when deterioration occurs.

Hazard

Patients are at particular risk of dying from asthma if they:

> are taking more than three classes of drugs

> have required hospital admission in the last year

> have psychosocial problems

> have ever had life-threatening asthma

> use β_2-agonists heavily

> have been inadequately treated for their asthma.

Clinical presentations

> Severe acute attacks – acute breathlessness and wheeze; also hypoxia and/or carbon dioxide retention can lead to stupor and/or confusion.

> Chronic asthma – shortness of breath, wheeze and/or a chronic cough, particularly at night when associated with a disturbed sleep pattern. Symptoms may be produced by exposure to cold air or exercise.

Key point

An isolated dry cough is perhaps the most overlooked symptom of mild asthma (especially in children). Particularly after colds and influenza, patients may be left with an annoying dry cough and are frequently referred to specialists for further investigation. Bronchial hyperresponsiveness is often the cause and responds to a course of low-dose inhaled steroids. Patients should be warned, however, that their symptoms may persist or return with a subsequent cold or chest infection.

Physical signs

Life-threatening asthma

If any one of the features below is present:

> peak flow is <33% of predicted or personal best

> SpO_2 <92%, PaO_2 <8 kPa, 'normal' $PaCO_2$ (4.6–6.0 kPa)

> silent chest

> cyanosis

> altered level of consciousness, confusion or coma

> exhaustion, poor respiratory effort and inability to speak

> hypotension or bradycardia.

Severe acute attack

If any one of the features below is present:

> peak flow is <50% of predicted or personal best

> tachycardia

> increased respiratory rate: ≥25 breaths per minute

> patient cannot complete sentences in one breath

> there is a use of accessory muscles of respiration and intercostal recession (especially children)

> increased pulse rate: >110 beats per minute.

Moderate

If any one of the features below is present:

> peak flow is 50–70% of predicted or personal best

> wheeze

> dyspnoea

> chest tightness.

Key point

The British Thoracic Society (BTS) / Scottish Intercollegiate Guidelines Network (SIGN) guidelines on asthma management are invaluable, but remember: the patient in front of you is an individual. If you are worried in any way about someone with asthma, especially at night – admit him or her. This is particularly the case for those who have an attack that has been going on for some time, if they live alone, do not have a telephone, or would find it difficult to return to the hospital. Do not feel pressurised to send them home.

Medical Masterclass Third edition

Investigations

Key point

Measure arterial blood gases (ABGs) if patient presents with life-threatening signs, or SaO_2 <94%.

Blood gas markers for life-threatening asthma are:

> normal or high $PaCO_2$ (normal range 4.5–6.0 kPa / 35–35 mmHg). Remember, however, that in patients with a low $PaCO_2$ the $PaCO_2$ returns to normal (ie rises) as the patient improves and hyperventilates less

> low pH

> severe hypoxia in spite of oxygen treatment (PaO_2 <8 kPa / 60 mmHg).

Chest radiograph

In outpatients, a chest radiograph helps exclude other causes of wheeze, such as infiltrates resulting from eosinophilia or fibrosis. For patients presenting acutely, a pneumothorax should be excluded and evidence of infection looked for.

Peak flow

This can be used diagnostically to look for morning dips. Motivated patients with chronic asthma can also monitor their progress at home. In patients who clearly do not take measurements on a daily basis, make sure they know their best peak flow and encourage them to at least monitor when they get coughs or a cold.

All patients should be given a management plan based on deterioration of their peak flow: credit-card-sized self-management plans are produced by the National Asthma Campaign (Fig 12).

Lung function tests

These should be performed pre- and post-bronchodilator (eg salbutamol). They are not helpful acutely, but are important as a diagnostic tool to look for evidence of reversibility and to monitor patients with chronic asthma.

Allergy testing

Skin-prick tests can help identify allergens that may precipitate asthma attacks, although in practice many of these are not easily avoided.

NATIONAL **ASTHMA** CAMPAIGN
conquering asthma

name _____

best peak flow _____

zones

	peak flow	treatment
1	_____	continue regular treatment
2	_____	increase dose of _____
3	_____	start steroid tablets and ring doctor
4	_____	call emergency medical help

Asthma Helpline 0345 01 02 03, Monday to Friday, 9am to 7pm
National Asthma Campaign registered charity number 802364

(a)

zones

	symptoms	treatment
1	asthma under control	continue regular treatment
2	getting a cold or waking with asthma symptoms at night	increase dose of _____
3	increasing breathlessness or poor response to reliever inhaler	start steroid tablets and ring doctor
4	severe attack	call emergency medical help

issued by _____   date _____

(b)

Fig 12 Credit-card-sized self-management plan produced by the National Asthma Campaign: **(a)** front; **(b)** back. These cards are available free on request from their offices. (Reproduced with permission of the National Asthma Campaign.)

Differential diagnosis

This includes chronic obstructive pulmonary disease, congestive heart failure, upper airway obstruction (ie foreign body), tumour, pneumothorax, bronchiectasis, pulmonary eosinophilia, granulomatosis with polyangiitis and Churg–Strauss syndrome.

Treatment

The stepwise approach to the treatment of chronic asthma remains the gold standard (Fig 13). For all steps above step 1, inhaled steroids are advocated for controlling airway inflammation and therefore chronic asthma.

The management can be divided into:

> 'relievers' (short-acting β-agonists)

> 'preventers' (inhaled steroids)

> 'controllers' (long-acting β-agonists and leukotriene receptor antagonists).

It is important to explain to patients that the preventers and controllers must be taken regularly, while the relievers are helpful for acute symptomatic relief. Oral preparations include oral steroids, aminophylline and the leukotriene receptor antagonists.

Key point

In acute severe asthma (Fig 14), the patient should not be left sitting in a side room in the emergency department. He or she should be in the resuscitation room and monitored for cardiac rhythm and oxygen saturation. The most senior member of the medical team in the hospital (usually the medical registrar) should be informed of the patient's condition and urgent anaesthetic and intensive care review should be requested if the patient does not improve rapidly or if the presenting symptoms appear life-threatening. Anaesthetists would rather be called to a sick patient than one who has suffered a respiratory arrest.

Summary of management in adults

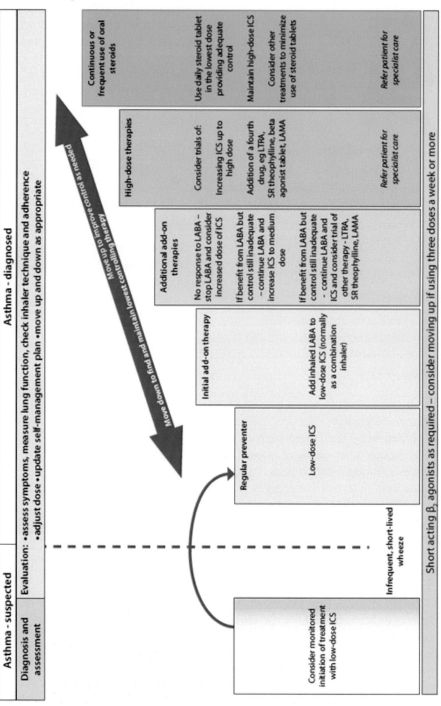

Fig 13 Treatment ladder for asthma in adults. This figure is reproduced from the BTS/SIGN *British Guideline on the management of asthma* by kind permission of the British Thoracic Society. British Thoracic Society (BTS)/Scottish Intercollegiate Guidelines Network (SIGN). *British Guideline on the management of asthma.* Edinburgh: SIGN; 2016. (QRG 153) Quick reference guide. Available from URL: www.sign.ac.uk. ICS, inhaled corticosteroid; LABA, long-acting β₂-agonist; LAMA, long-acting muscarinic antagonist; LTRA, leukotriene receptor antagonist; SR, sustained release.

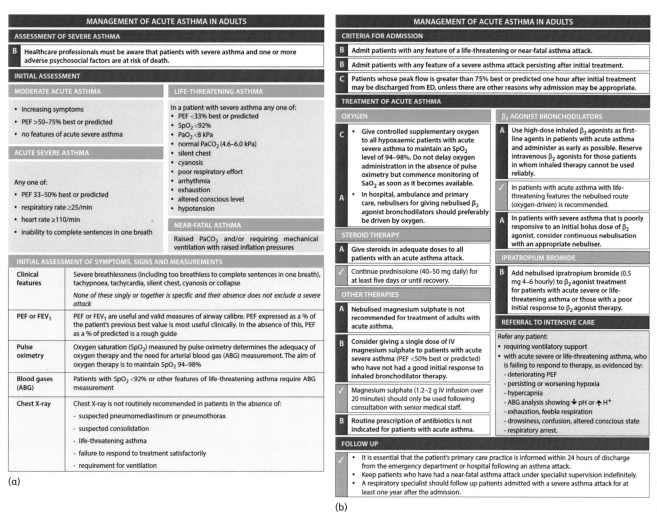

Fig 14 Management of acute asthma in adults. **(a)** Assessment and **(b)** admission, treatment and follow-up. ABG, arterial blood gas; ED, emergency department; FEV₁, forced expiratory volume in 1 second; IV, intravenous; PEF, peak expiratory flow. These figures are reproduced from the BTS/SIGN *British Guideline on the management of asthma* by kind permission of the British Thoracic Society. British Thoracic Society (BTS)/Scottish Intercollegiate Guidelines Network (SIGN). *British Guideline on the management of asthma.* Edinburgh: SIGN; 2016. (QRG 153) Quick reference guide. Available from URL: www.sign.ac.uk.

Other treatments for asthma

Oral theophylline – this is a possible add-on in chronic asthma. It is a methylxanthine and acts as a non-selective phosphodiesterase inhibitor, which leads to bronchodilation. It may also have an anti-inflammatory effect. However, the use of intravenous aminophylline in acute asthma is controversial – while they may help some patients these have not been identified in clinical trial. Intravenous theophylline should thus only be used with extreme caution and with the expert input of senior medical staff.

Leukotriene receptor antagonists – these are the most recent drugs to be added to the therapeutic armamentarium for asthma. They include montelukast and zafirlukast and work by reducing the production of leukotrienes which cause bronchoconstriction, mucus hypersecretion and airway oedema. They may have an anti-inflammatory action. Side effects include abdominal discomfort, diarrhoea and headaches. Their position in the stepwise treatment of asthma has yet to be decided; they may be useful for chronic asthmatics who cannot achieve control with inhaled

steroids (step 3), as well as in cases of exercise-induced and aspirin-sensitive asthma. They have no place in the treatment of acute severe asthma.

Intravenous magnesium sulphate – a single dose may be considered in patients with acute severe life-threatening / near-fatal asthma who fail to respond to initial therapy. The use of repeated dosing with intravenous magnesium sulphate is discouraged as it can potentially lead to muscle weakness and respiratory failure.

Omalizumab – this recombinant humanised anti-immunoglobulin E (IgE) monoclonal antibody has been developed for the treatment of patients with persistent allergic asthma. It is given as a subcutaneous infusion every 2–4 weeks. It can be considered for patients requiring frequent courses of oral corticosteroids (current National Institute for Health and Care Excellence (NICE) guidelines suggest four or more in the preceding 12 months) who suffer from IgE-mediated asthma.

Novel, immunomodulatory therapies (anti-interleukin (IL)-5 and anti-IL-13) are likely to become available in the near future.

2.3 Chronic obstructive pulmonary disease

Aetiology

Tobacco smoking is responsible for 80% of the risk of developing chronic obstructive pulmonary disease (COPD). Other common risks include occupational exposure to environmental dust (eg coal miners), organic antigens (eg farm workers) and α_1-antitrypsin deficiency. Exposure to wood smoke and other biofuels used for cooking is a significant contributor in developing countries. Smokers vary in their susceptibility to smoking: 15–20% develop clinically significant disease.

Pathophysiology

COPD is characterised by airflow obstruction that is usually progressive, not fully reversible and does not change markedly over several months. Airflow obstruction is due to a combination of airway inflammation / fibrosis (chronic bronchitis) and parenchymal lung damage (emphysema), which result from prolonged exposure to noxious particles or gases. COPD also causes systemic inflammatory consequences, including weight loss, decreased muscle mass and ischaemic heart disease.

Epidemiology

The prevalence of COPD among adults is approximately 4–6%.

Clinical presentation

COPD is frequently diagnosed as a result of:

> recurrent respiratory infections or exertional dyspnoea

> an incidental finding during medical assessment for other reasons (eg elective surgery), or during a GP's 'screening' of smokers

> presentation with polycythaemia, cor pulmonale or respiratory failure.

Physical signs

> Early stages – there may be no signs, but look for prolonged expiration, evidence of hyperinflation, bilaterally reduced breath sounds and widespread wheezes.

> Advanced disease – look for use of accessory respiratory muscles of the neck and shoulder girdle, paradoxical inward movement of the intercostal muscles on inspiration (Hoover's sign), expiration through pursed lips, cyanosis, cor pulmonale and weight loss.

> Body mass index – decreasing body mass (observed in 20% of patients with severe COPD) is associated with increasing mortality.

Investigations

Spirometry

This is essential to establish the diagnosis and to assess the severity of the COPD (see Table 22). Airflow obstruction is defined as a reduced FEV_1 to FVC ratio (<70%) post-bronchodilator. In the presence of a reduced FEV_1 to FVC ratio, the severity of the airflow obstruction is then assessed by looking at FEV_1.

Key point

Diagnosis of COPD

> Spirometry is the only method for early diagnosis in asymptomatic patients and should be performed in all over the age of 35 years who have a risk factor (generally smoking).

> Always confirm a clinical suspicion of COPD by spirometry.

Hazard

Diagnosis of COPD

> Do not rely on peak expiratory flow (PEF) measurements: in COPD these may be misleadingly high while FEV_1 is already significantly reduced.

Table 22 Assessment of severity of COPD according to FEV_1 (as a percentage of the predicted value)

Severity	FEV_1
Mild	>80% of predicted
Moderate	50–80% of predicted
Severe	30–49% of predicted
Very severe	<30% of predicted

Reversibility testing

This is not necessary in most patients because acute reversibility testing does not predict a response to long-term therapy. Over-reliance on a single bronchodilator reversibility test may be misleading unless the change in FEV_1 is greater than 400 mL. Testing oral corticosteroid reversibility is no longer recommended because it does not predict response to inhaled corticosteroid therapy.

Chest radiograph

This may show signs of hyperinflation (increased lung height, flat diaphragm, increased retrosternal airspace and narrow heart shadow), parenchymal areas of hypoattenuation and bullae (Fig 15).

Blood tests

Perform a full blood count (FBC) to identify polycythaemia. Measure α_1-antitrypsin level if early onset or a minimal smoking history or family history of COPD.

Arterial/earlobe gases

Test for these if SaO_2 is <92% or there are signs of right heart failure or respiratory failure in order to assess the indication for long-term oxygen therapy.

Transfer factor for carbon monoxide

Check if the patient's symptoms are disproportionate to the spirometric impairment. Some patients can develop significant emphysema but maintain a preserved FEV_1 due to a relative absence of airway inflammation/fibrosis. The low gas transfer seen in these patients usually reflects the true severity of lung damage.

High-resolution CT chest scan

A computerised tomography (CT) scan should be performed if symptoms are disproportionate to the spirometric impairment, if there are unexpected abnormalities on the chest radiograph, if bronchiectasis is suspected, or to assess

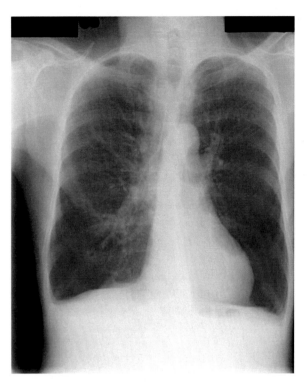

Fig 15 Chest radiograph of a patient with emphysema. Note hyperinflation (low, flat diaphragms).

suitability for lung-volume reduction surgery.

Electrocardiogram and echocardiogram

Perform if features of cor pulmonale are apparent.

Differential diagnosis

The main differential diagnosis is asthma and this should be considered if a patient shows an exceptionally good response to treatment. Bronchodilator reversibility testing, serial domiciliary peak expiratory flow measurements and exhaled nitric oxide may be useful if asthma is suspected (Table 23).

Other common conditions that can present with similar symptoms and signs to COPD include bronchiectasis, congestive cardiac failure and lung cancer. Bear in mind that as well as mimicking COPD, these conditions may also coexist in a patient with COPD.

Table 23	Clinical features differentiating COPD and asthma	
Characteristic	**COPD**	**Asthma**
Smoker/ex-smoker	Nearly all	Possibly
Symptoms under the age of 35	Rare	Often
Chronic productive cough	Common	Uncommon
Breathlessness	Persistent and progressive	Variable
Nocturnal cough/wheeze/breathlessness	Uncommon	Common
Diurnal or day-to-day variability	Uncommon	Common

Treatment

Emergency

See the *Acute medicine* book of Medical Masterclass.

Stable patients

Stop smoking

Key point

All patients regardless of age should be encouraged to stop smoking and offered help (eg nicotine replacement therapy, bupropion, varenicline and smoking cessation clinics) at every opportunity.

Inhaled therapy

> Short-acting bronchodilators (β_2-agonists and/or anticholinergics) – given as an initial treatment, as required, for the relief of exertional dyspnoea.

> Long-acting inhaled bronchodilators (long-acting β_2-agonists (LABA) or long-acting muscarinic receptor antagonists (LAMA)) – given if symptoms persist despite the use of short-acting bronchodilators.

> Inhaled corticosteroids – these are indicated for patients who have an FEV_1 <50% predicted *and* experience two or more exacerbations per year. In patients who do not exacerbate or who have an FEV_1 >50%, inhaled steroids should be added if the patient remains symptomatic despite optimal bronchodilator therapy (LABA + LAMA).

Key point

Inhaled corticosteroids should only be added to long-acting bronchodilators and are not used as monotherapy in COPD. In most patients this would be in the form of a combination steroid and LABA inhaler.

! Hazard

Maintenance use of oral corticosteroid therapy in COPD is not normally recommended.

Theophylline (slow-release formulations)

This should only be used after a trial of short-acting bronchodilators and long-acting bronchodilators.

Mucolytic therapy

Consider in patients with a chronic productive cough. Continue if there is symptomatic improvement (eg reduction in frequency of cough and sputum production).

Pneumococcal vaccination and an influenza vaccination

This should be offered to all patients with COPD.

Nutritional supplementation

Provide this for those who are malnourished.

Antidepressant treatment

Depression is common in patients with COPD and should be actively looked for in those with severe disability.

Pulmonary rehabilitation

This should be offered to all patients who consider themselves functionally disabled by COPD.

Long-term oxygen therapy

See Section 2.12.1.

Non-invasive ventilation

See Section 2.12.3.

Surgery

> Bullectomy – for breathless patients who have a single large bulla on a CT chest scan and FEV_1 <50% predicted.

> Lung-volume reduction surgery – consider if the patient is experiencing marked restrictions of their daily living activities despite maximal medical therapy (including rehabilitation), FEV_1 >20% of predicted, carbon monoxide transfer factor >20% of predicted, $PaCO_2$ <7.3 kPa and there is upper lobe predominant emphysema on high-resolution CT (HRCT) of the chest.

> Lung transplantation – consider if FEV_1 is <25% of predicted, $PaCO_2$ is >7.3 kPa or cor pulmonale is present.

Complications

> common – infection (bacterial and viral) and side effects of corticosteroid treatment

> uncommon – pneumothorax, cor pulmonale and respiratory failure.

Prognosis

In general this is inversely related to age and post-bronchodilator FEV_1. The 5-year survival rate in patients admitted with a hypercapnic exacerbation is 28%.

2.4 Bronchiectasis

Aetiology

Bronchiectasis is a condition that is characterised by the permanent dilatation of bronchi (Figs 16 and 17) from a variety of reasons (Table 24). No definite cause of bronchiectasis is found in over 50% of patients.

Pathology

Recurrent bacterial colonisation and infection lead to progressive airway injury that is mediated by neutrophils, T-lymphocytes and monocyte-driven cytokines. Released inflammatory mediators, elastase and collagenase lead in turn to the inflammation and then destruction of the elastic and muscular components of the bronchial walls, resulting in permanent bronchial wall dilatation.

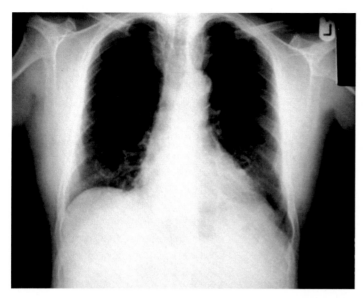

Fig 16 Plain chest radiograph. The tramlines in the right lower lobe are consistent with bronchiectasis.

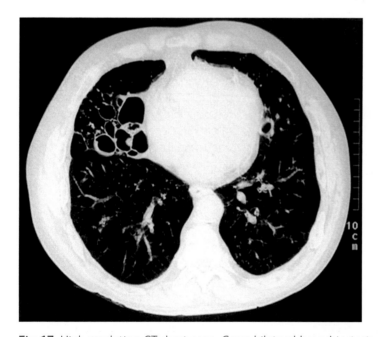

Fig 17 High-resolution CT chest scan. Gross bilateral bronchiectasis, more prominent in the right lung with a classic 'signet ring' appearance generated by an enlarged bronchus and a neighbouring vessel.

Clinical presentation

The classic clinical manifestations of bronchiectasis are a cough and daily production of mucopurulent and tenacious sputum: less than 10 mL/day suggests mild bronchiectasis; more than 150 mL/day indicates severe bronchiectasis. Other symptoms are listed in Table 25.

Signs of bronchiectasis are shown in Table 26.

Investigations

Investigations are carried out to confirm clinical suspicion of bronchiectasis, identify any potentially treatable underlying causes, and assess any functional impairment and the extent of the bronchiectasis (Table 27).

Microbiology
Patients with bronchiectasis usually experience recurrent respiratory tract infections. Prevention of infection and prompt treatment of acute infective exacerbations are cornerstones of management, to minimise lung damage and maintain lung function.

Key point

Exacerbations of bronchiectasis requiring antibiotics are characterised by:

> increasing sputum volume

> increasing sputum purulence

> increased cough, wheeze or systemic upset.

Table 24 Causes of bronchiectasis

Causes	Examples
Idiopathic	
Post-infectious	Respiratory infection in childhood (measles, whooping cough or bronchiolitis), pneumonia, pulmonary TB and non-TB mycobacteria (eg *Mycobacterium avium* complex)
Bronchial obstruction	Inhaled foreign body, endobronchial tumour, extrinsic lymph node / tumour compression and middle lobe syndrome
Mucociliary clearance defects	Genetic: CF and primary ciliary dyskinesia (Kartagener's syndrome) Acquired: Young's syndrome (azoospermia and sinusitis) and toxic gas inhalation
Immune deficiency	Common variable immunodeficiency and HIV
Congenital	α_1-Antitrypsin deficiency, Williams–Campbell syndrome (bronchial cartilage deficiency), McLeod's syndrome (unilateral emphysema) and pulmonary sequestration (non-functioning lung with blood supply from the aorta)
Immunological over-response	ABPA and post-lung transplantation
Others	GORD, rheumatoid arthritis, Sjögren's syndrome, SLE, sarcoidosis, yellow nail syndrome, ulcerative colitis, Marfan syndrome and Ehlers–Danlos syndrome

ABPA, allergic bronchopulmonary aspergillosis; CF, cystic fibrosis; GORD, gastro-oesophageal reflux disease; SLE, systemic lupus erythematosus; TB, tuberculosis.

Table 25 Symptoms of bronchiectasis (frequency of occurrence)

Common	Cough (90%) Daily sputum production (76%) Dyspnoea (72%) Haemoptysis (50%) Recurrent pleuritic pain (46%)
Uncommon	Chronic sinusitis

Table 26 Signs of bronchiectasis (frequency of occurrence)

Common	Crackles (coarse; early inspiratory and late expiratory) (70%) Wheezes (44%) Finger clubbing (30%)
Uncommon	Halitosis Syndrome specific (eg discoloured nails / lymphoedema / pleural effusion in yellow nail syndrome, situs inversus in Kartagener's syndrome)

Sputum culture should be obtained from patients with bronchiectasis in the stable state and at the time of exacerbation, prior to commencing antibiotics. Pathogens that can be cultured are shown in Table 28.

Treatment

Chest physiotherapy
This is the cornerstone of treatment, and it is advised that it should be performed at least twice daily. This includes postural drainage, active cycle of breathing techniques, and oscillating positive expiratory devices.

Adjuncts to sputum clearance
Nebulised saline (normal/hypertonic) assists mucus clearance. Mucolytics (eg carbocisteine) are often used to reduce sputum viscosity, although randomised trial evidence of benefit is limited.

Antibiotics for acute infections
Send sputum for culture. Start empirical antibiotics, treating for 14 days. Adjust antibiotic therapy directed by sputum culture findings if the patient is not responding. Consider intravenous antibiotics if the patient is very unwell, has not responded to oral antibiotics or has resistant organisms (often *Pseudomonas*).

Long-term prophylactic antibiotics
Consider long-term antibiotics if there are more than three exacerbations per year. Send sputum for microscopy, culture and sensitivity (MC&S) and mycobacterial culture. Select a regimen based on sputum microbiology. Macrolides may have anti-inflammatory, disease-modifying effects. Long-term nebulised antibiotics can be considered for patients chronically colonised with *Pseudomonas* (Colomycin/gentamicin/tobramycin).

Table 27 Investigations in bronchiectasis

Test type	Description	Possible findings/indications
Generic	Chest radiograph	In combination with the clinical presentation this may be sufficient to establish the diagnosis, although it is not always abnormal. Look for 'tramlines' (parallel thickened lines representing dilated thickened bronchial walls), ring opacities, band shadows (fluid- or mucous-filled bronchi), crowded bronchial markings resulting from atelectasis and the 'finger in glove' appearance that results from impacted central bronchi
	High-resolution CT chest scan (sensitivity 97%)	Indicated if there is clinical suspicion of bronchiectasis but a normal chest radiograph, there are other abnormalities on a chest radiograph that need clarification, or if surgery may be contemplated. A central (perihilar) distribution suggests ABPA and upper lobe distribution suggests CF / previous pulmonary TB
	Lung function tests	Obstructive pattern
	Arterial blood gases	Hypoxia and/or hypercapnia in advanced disease
	Sputum cultures	*Haemophilus influenzae*, *Streptococcus pneumoniae*, *Staphylococcus aureus* (if recurrent this may indicate an atypical presentation of CF) and *Pseudomonas aeruginosa*
	Bronchoscopy	To exclude foreign body / endobronchial lesion or for assessing and localising the source of haemoptysis
Specific for underlying disease	Serum immunoglobulins	IgG / specific IgG (to pneumococcus and *H influenzae*) / IgA
	Sweat sodium concentration	CF
	CFTR genotyping	CF
	Eosinophils / ABPA screen	ABPA
	ACE / calcium	Sarcoidosis
	RhF / ANA / ANCA	Rheumatoid arthritis / SLE / vasculitis

ABPA, allergic bronchopulmonary aspergillosis; ACE, angiotensin-converting enzyme; ANA, antinuclear antibodies; ANCA, antineutrophil cytoplasmic antibodies; CF, cystic fibrosis; CFTR, cystic fibrosis transmembrane conductance regulator; IgA, immunoglobulin A; IgG, immunoglobulin G; RhF, rheumatoid factor; SLE, systemic lupus erythematosus; TB, tuberculosis.

Table 28 Pathogens cultured from sputum in patients with bronchiectasis

Frequency	Organism
Common	*Streptococcus pneumoniae* *Haemophilus influenzae* *Moraxella catarrhalis* *Staphylococcus aureus* (MSSA or MRSA) Coliforms *Pseudomonas*
Less common	Non-tuberculous mycobacterium *Mycobacterium tuberculosis* Fungi – *Aspergillus*

MRSA, methicillin-resistant *Staphylococcus aureus*; MSSA, methicillin-sensitive *Staphylococcus aureus*.

Other medical treatments

Bronchodilators can be given if there is evidence of airflow obstruction. Inhaled corticosteroids are only indicated if there is coexistent asthma.

Interventional techniques

Bronchoscopy can be used for extraction of mucus (bronchial toilet) if physiotherapy has failed. Bronchial artery embolisation may be used to control severe haemoptysis.

Surgery can be used for symptomatic localised disease (but before doing so it is essential to rule out a systemic disease that may result in bronchiectasis affecting the remaining lung, eg immunodeficiency or aspiration), or massive haemoptysis.

Lung transplantation can be considered for end-stage bilateral disease, usually in patients with cystic fibrosis (CF).

Specific treatments

> immunoglobulin replacement in common variable immunodeficiency

> oral steroids and itraconazole in ABPA (there are no data on the efficacy of voriconazole or other imidazole agents in this condition)

> gastric acid suppression and pro-kinetics for recurrent aspiration associated with gastro-oesophageal reflux disease (GORD).

> recombinant human DNase (rhDNase) in CF.

Complications

> common – recurrent infectious episodes, recurrent pneumonias and cor pulmonale

> uncommon – massive haemoptysis, amyloidosis and brain abscess.

Prognosis

Depends on severity, bacterial colonisation (eg *Pseudomonas* colonisation might be associated with a poorer outcome) and the underlying cause. Deterioration may be due to recurrent and worsening sepsis, or to hypoxia and cor pulmonale.

Prevention

> vaccination against measles, pertussis, influenza and TB

> prompt treatment of bronchopulmonary infections and ABPA

> early removal of foreign body and obstructing lesions.

Key point

Diagnosis
Always pursue the cause of bronchiectasis, as finding the cause may lead to treatment that slows or halts the progression of disease.

Treatment
It is *essential* that the patient's sputum is sent for routine bacterial and mycobacterial microscopy and culture prior to starting antibiotics for exacerbations, although treatment should then not be deferred pending results.

2.5 Cystic fibrosis

Aetiology

Cystic fibrosis (CF) is an autosomal recessive disease caused by a defect in the gene encoding an epithelial cell transmembrane protein termed the cystic fibrosis transmembrane conductance regulator (CFTR). The gene is located on the long arm of chromosome 7 and the most common mutation in the UK is Delta-F508. The function of this protein is to serve as a chloride channel and also as a regulator of an epithelial sodium channel. It is increasingly becoming important to understand the different types of defect a mutation in the CFTR can cause, as this increasingly influences treatment options (Table 29).

There are numerous disease modifiers, currently unknown, that can result in tremendous variation in the presentation of the onset of CF.

Epidemiology

Prevalence in the UK is one in 2,500; it is rare in African-Caribbean people (one in 17,000) and very rare in Asian people (one in 90,000). The age of diagnosis has been dropping because since 2007; CF is screened for after birth, although rare variants may still be missed. Some patients are diagnosed with CF in the sixth or even seventh decade of life.

Clinical presentation

Key point
Consider CF as a potential diagnosis in adult patients with recurrent purulent chest infections.

Presentations of CF are shown in Table 30.

Physical signs

Patients with CF are often short for their age. They may develop clubbing of the fingernails. On chest auscultation, signs of bronchiectasis (coarse inspiratory crackles) and airway obstruction (expiratory wheeze) may be heard. In examination settings, it is not uncommon to see patients with CF who have received liver, lung or kidney transplants.

Investigations

The diagnosis of CF is based on one or more clinical features consistent with the CF phenotype (see above) plus:

> two CF gene mutations (both alleles must be affected to produce disease)

> a positive sweat test

> abnormal nasal potential differences.

Table 29 Types of genetic defect in CF

Class	Type of defect	Example of mutation
I	CFTR is not synthesised	G452X
II	CFTR is synthesised but in abnormal form, and hence retained in the endoplasmic reticulum	Delta-F508
III	CFTR regulation is disrupted	G551D
IV	CFTR chloride conductance is reduced	R117H
V	Reduced CFTR expression	3120+1G→A

CF, cystic fibrosis; CFTR, cystic fibrosis transmembrane conductance regulator.

Table 30 Presentations of CF

Classification	Example
Respiratory disease	Recurrent purulent infections Bronchiectasis
Exocrine pancreatic failure	Malabsorption Failure to thrive Rectal prolapse Intussusception Fatty diarrhoea
Bowel obstruction	Meconium ileus Distal intestinal obstruction syndrome
Endocrine pancreatic failure	Diabetes mellitus
Bone disease	Osteoporosis
Others	Infertility Liver disease (cirrhosis due to intrahepatic obstruction) Arthritis Nasal polyps Sinusitis Complications of antibiotic therapy (hearing loss / renal failure due to aminoglycosides)

CF, cystic fibrosis.

Gene mutations

There are over 1,500 recognised gene mutations. Routine genotyping does not test for all of these, hence it is possible for a patient to have CF without routine genotyping identifying a mutation. Conversely, the finding of one mutation does not diagnose CF because the carrier frequency of a single gene mutation is one in 25.

Sweat test

This should be performed at least twice. High chloride concentrations are suggestive of CF.

Nasal potential differences

Although this can be useful for patients with a borderline sweat test, this test should not be considered diagnostic in isolation (outside of specialist centres).

Key point

Annual review of the patient with CF

In specialist CF centres all patients would undergo annual review. As well as symptomatic enquiry and physical examination this would include, from a physician's perspective:

> a chest radiograph (Fig 18)

> full lung function tests

> full blood count (FBC), along with urea and electrolytes, calcium and liver function tests

> sputum microbiology

> electrocardiogram (ECG).

Treatment

The best care of the CF patient requires multidisciplinary teamwork between a physician, nurse, social worker, physiotherapist, nutritionist, GP and genetic counsellor. In the UK, care for patients with CF is delivered in specialist centres. In CF centres all patients undergo annual review, which enables assessment by this multidisciplinary team as well as the physician.

Avoidance of cross infection

Different bacterial colonisations of the airways of CF patients may carry increased risk of disease. Patients with *Pseudomonas aeruginosa*, specific strains of *P aeruginosa* (Liverpool epidemic strain), *Burkholderia cepacia* and *Mycobacterium abscessus* should be managed separately from each other and patients without the above. Patients with CF are also advised to avoid socialising with each other due to the risk of cross infection.

Respiratory system

Respiratory symptoms should be managed aggressively with the aim being to defend pulmonary function:

> antibiotics

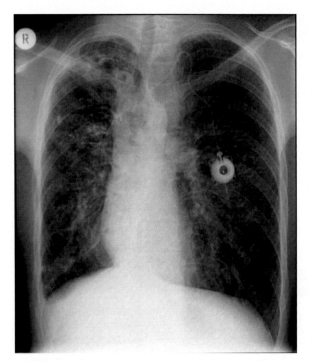

Broadly speaking, patients may be considered suitable for transplantation if the forced expiratory volume in 1 second (FEV_1) is <30% of predicted. Other features favouring transplantation are the development of ventilatory failure and increasing hospitalisations. Because cadaveric organs are in short supply there is increasing interest in living donor bilateral lobar lung transplantation.

Key point

In advanced CF, respiratory failure as a result of overwhelming infection is a common cause of death. Endotracheal ventilation does not alter the outcome in this situation and hence this treatment is not usually offered.

Fig 18 Chest radiograph of an adult patient with CF. Hyperinflation and cystic change (most obvious in the right upper lobe) is evident. A Portacath is seen over the left lung field.

> acute infection

> maintenance therapy in colonised patients (often with nebulised antibiotics)

> sputum clearance:

> nebulised recombinant DNase

> nebulised normal or hypertonic saline

> mannitol powder

> chest physiotherapy

> bronchodilators / inhaled corticosteroids

> oral steroids.

Gastrointestinal disease

Patients must maintain a high calorie diet. Most CF patients have pancreatic insufficiency and receive pancreatic enzymes and supplemental fat-soluble vitamins. All patients with CF should receive specialist nutrition management as part of their multidisciplinary team. Professional dietetic assessment is indicated for all patients.

Ursodeoxycholic acid may be helpful in the management of CF-induced liver disease.

Targeted treatments

Many treatments for specific defects of the CFTR are currently being developed and are in clinical trials. This is a rapidly developing area. The treatments currently available are ivacaftor (which functions as a potentiator of the CFTR in G551D mutations) or combined ivacaftor/lumacaftor (the latter a chaperone to help the CFTR move from the endoplasmic reticulum to the cell surface, for Delta-F508 mutations).

Transplantation

In an advanced case of the disease, lung transplantation (see Section 2.13) offers the best chance of survival. For patients awaiting a transplant, non-invasive positive pressure ventilation can be a useful bridge; endotracheal intubation and ventilation of patients with advanced CF is not usually undertaken, but may be lifesaving in carefully considered individual circumstances.

Complications

Pulmonary disease

The more severe complications occur in more advanced disease:

> sinusitis and nasal polyps

> bacterial respiratory infection

> pneumothorax

> haemoptysis

> aspergillosis

> respiratory failure and pulmonary hypertension.

Gastrointestinal disease

Adults with CF may have abdominal pain, but the cause is seldom appendicitis or other surgically remediable problems. Although surgical advice should be sought where appropriate, most experts have a high threshold for abdominal surgery. Other complications include:

> obstruction

> malabsorption

> glucose intolerance / diabetes

> cirrhosis and portal hypertension.

Other/iatrogenic

The total list of possible complications of CF is enormous but includes:

> infertility in men

> pregnancy (represents a hazard if the FEV_1 is <40–50% of predicted or if there is pulmonary hypertension)

> ototoxicity from repeated aminoglycosides

> Portacath complications.

Prognosis

The median life expectancy is currently 41 years.

Prevention

For parents who are CF gene carriers (eg because a sibling with CF is already identified), prenatal diagnosis is possible. The risks of chorionic villous sampling are roughly equal to those of amniocentesis but with the advantage of giving an earlier result.

Therapy aimed at preventing the phenotypic expression of CF by gene replacement is not yet a practical clinical option.

2.6 Occupational lung disease

2.6.1 Asbestos-related lung disease

Asbestos use was banned in the UK and most other developed countries by 1980, but the latent period between exposure and development of disease is usually several decades. Asbestos usage continues to increase in many developing countries. Occupations associated with high levels of exposure include shipyard workers, foundry workers, carpenters, plumbers, car mechanics (from brake linings) and building labourers. Remember to ask about apprenticeships in the construction industry, which may have been forgotten. Crocidolite fibres (blue asbestos) are more carcinogenic and fibrogenic than chrysotile (white asbestos).

Patterns of disease

Asbestos causes four main patterns of lung disease. Asbestosis occurs only after prolonged asbestos exposure, whereas pleural plaques, mesothelioma and benign asbestos effusions can be seen after relatively light exposure.

1 Pleural plaques / diffuse pleural thickening – fibrous thickening of the parietal pleura, which often calcifies. Pleural plaques themselves are benign and do not usually cause symptoms. If pleural thickening is extensive, leading to a restrictive lung defect and breathlessness, then the patient is classified as having diffuse pleural thickening.

2 Asbestosis – asbestosis specifically means interstitial fibrosis resulting from asbestos exposure and is not the proper term for any asbestos-related disease. Patients have a heavy asbestos exposure and develop progressive breathlessness and dense, irreversible basal lung fibrosis several decades after exposure. High-resolution CT (HRCT) appearances and lung biopsy reveal 'usual interstitial pneumonitis'.

3 Mesothelioma – primary cancer of the pleura.

4 Benign asbestos-related effusions – patients with asbestos exposure and pleural plaques can present with benign, exudative, blood-stained effusions, which may be eosinophilic. It is most important to rule out mesothelioma with a CT scan, thoracoscopic pleural biopsy, and ongoing follow-up before a diagnosis of a benign asbestos-related effusion is made.

Asbestos exposure is also a risk factor for the development of lung cancer, the risk of which is multiplied in those who have a significant smoking history.

Compensation

Mesothelioma, asbestosis and diffuse pleural thickening are compensatable diseases. Lung cancer that develops in the context of asbestosis or prolonged heavy asbestos exposure is also compensatable. Pleural plaques are not compensatable in England, but can be compensatable in Scotland. Potential claimants should be advised to contact their local Citizens Advice Bureau or a solicitor specialising in this field when a diagnosis is made.

2.6.2 Pneumoconioses

Aetiology and pathology

The pneumoconioses are occupational lung diseases caused by inhalation of a variety of industrial dusts. Strictly speaking, asbestosis is a subtype of the pneumoconioses but, because of its relative prevalence, it tends to be considered separately. Likewise, coal worker's pneumoconiosis (CWP) merits its own discussion.

CWP aside, the pneumoconioses can be divided into two subgroups (further details in Table 31):

> Benign forms – these tend to be asymptomatic. They can be recognised by the chest radiograph appearances that they produce: small, round opacities caused by perivascular collections of dust.

Table 31	Industrial substances whose dusts cause pneumoconiosis
Disease type	**Causative agent (disease name)**
Benign disease	Iron (siderosis) Tin (stannosis) Barium (baritosis) Antimony
Fibrotic disease	Asbestos Silica (silicosis) Beryllium (berylliosis) Aluminium ores (Shaver's disease or aluminosis)

> Fibrotic forms – these produce, as the name suggests, pulmonary fibrosis associated with a restrictive lung defect. They may cause symptoms and sometimes progress to respiratory failure.

Coal worker's pneumoconiosis

Coal worker's pneumoconiosis (CWP) is seen in workers exposed to coal dust and accounts for 90% of pneumoconiosis claims for industrial compensation that are not related to asbestos exposure. The condition is generally divided into:

> Simple CWP – based on the chest radiograph appearances of small, round opacities that represent small fibrous nodules in the lung, predominantly in the upper lobes.

> Complicated CWP (progressive massive fibrosis (PMF)) – a patient is said to have advanced to PMF when these fibrous lesions have reached more than 3 cm in diameter. Histologically, these larger lesions commonly undergo necrosis and cavitation.

CWP associated with rheumatoid arthritis is known as Caplan's syndrome. Silicosis can also progress to PMF, and has also been associated with rheumatoid arthritis.

Clinical presentation

This may include:

> breathlessness

> cough

> jet-black sputum production (in CWP only).

Physical signs

There will be few in the early stages of the disease; later the patient may exhibit:

> decreased chest expansion

> inspiratory crackles

> wheeze (in CWP)

> clubbing (asbestosis, but not silicosis; rarely in CWP).

Investigations

Chest radiograph

The International Labour Office has produced a method of classification for the radiographic changes seen in pneumoconiosis. These classifications are largely based on the size and number of opacities seen on the chest radiograph and are used by medical panels when discussing compensation claims:

> For benign pneumoconiosis, small, round opacities are diagnostic of the disease.

> Asbestos can produce a number of changes, including pleural thickening, pleural (holly leaf) plaques, fibrosis and evidence of tumours (Fig 19).

> Silicosis produces classical eggshell calcification around the hilar lymph nodes, as well as peripheral nodules.

> For CWP, see above.

Lung function tests

These show a restrictive picture with decreased forced vital capacity, total lung capacity, residual volume and gas transfer.

High-resolution CT scan

CT scanning will help reveal the extent of the disease, and is particularly helpful when extensive pleural disease masks the lung parenchyma on plain chest radiographs.

Treatment

A priority is avoidance of further dust exposure. The employers of the patient should, if necessary, consider a review of the protective equipment used by their other employees in the workplace. The benign pneumoconioses require no other treatment.

Fibrotic disease is normally considered resistant to therapy, excepting berylliosis, where high-dose prednisolone can produce a clinical improvement. Occasionally, courses of steroids are tried in patients with asbestosis who are showing rapid deterioration of their lung function. Treatment of CWP is largely supportive.

Complications

These may include:

> respiratory failure

> right heart failure

> tuberculosis in silicosis.

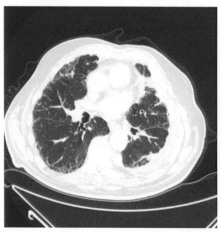

(a)

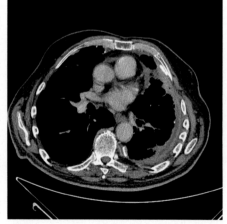

(b)

Fig 19 Asbestos-related CT scans.

Compensation

Through the Industrial Injuries Scheme UK workers can claim compensation for the following diseases: mesothelioma, pneumoconiosis (including CWP, silicosis and asbestosis), diffuse pleural thickening, primary carcinoma of the lung (only if accompanied by asbestosis or diffuse pleural thickening) and byssinosis. Potential claimants should be advised to contact their local Citizens Advice Bureau or a solicitor specialising in this field when a diagnosis is made.

2.7 Diffuse parenchymal lung disease or diffuse interstitial pneumonias

The diffuse parenchymal lung diseases (DPLDs), or diffuse interstitial pneumonias, comprise a wide range of disorders that cause inflammation and/or fibrosis of the lung parenchyma. Where the cause or disease association is known (eg sarcoidosis, connective tissue disease), then these disorders can be easily classified accordingly, but in many cases patients present with an interstitial pneumonitis of an unknown cause (idiopathic).

Within the idiopathic interstitial pneumonias some distinct patterns of disease are apparent and certain histological findings are known to associate with certain patterns of disease behaviour. The idiopathic pneumonias are therefore subdivided into a number of different entities based on histological subtypes and disease behaviour (Fig 20). Idiopathic pulmonary fibrosis (IPF) is one form of idiopathic interstitial pneumonia.

These classifications have undergone a number of different revisions over recent years, with much resultant confusion. It is important not to get too bogged down in trying to memorise all the subtypes of DPLD, which is the preserve of specialised clinicians. All types of DPLD cause thickening of the lung

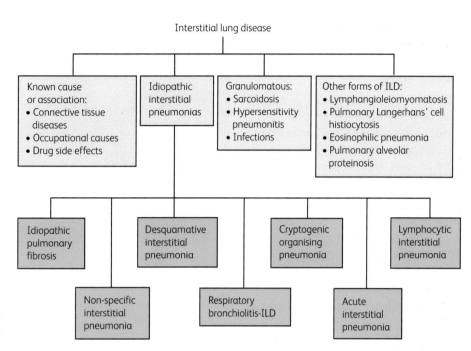

Fig 20 Classification of DPLDs. ILD, interstitial lung disease. (Reproduced with permission from: R M du Bois. Strategies for treating idiopathic pulmonary fibrosis. *Nature Reviews Drug Discovery* 2010;9:129–40.)

interstitium and impairment of gas exchange, leading to breathlessness. A dry cough is often a prominent feature. Patients will need a CT scan and often a lung biopsy to make a diagnosis, and even then precise classification of their DPLD can still be difficult.

For the general physician, the following are the most important of the DPLDs and are discussed below:

> IPF

> cryptogenic organising pneumonia

> hypersensitivity pneumonitis

> sarcoidosis.

2.7.1 Idiopathic pulmonary fibrosis

Idiopathic pulmonary fibrosis (IPF) was previously known as cryptogenic fibrosing alveolitis (CFA).

Aetiology

Not known, but more common in cigarette smokers.

Pathology

For many years the gold standard for diagnosis of IPF was histopathologic evidence from lung biopsy, which shows dense, irreversible fibrosis and destruction of lung architecture, with little or no inflammatory component. This histological pattern is known as usual interstitial pneumonia (UIP). With developments in high-resolution CT (HRCT) scanning, which can diagnose UIP with a high degree of certainty, surgical lung biopsy is now indicated only when diagnostic doubts remain after radiological assessment.

Epidemiology

Most patients are between 40 and 70 years of age at presentation. The incidence of UIP increases with older age from 2.7 per 100,000 people in adults 35–44 years old, to 175 per 100,000 people among those over 75 years old.

Clinical presentation

Insidious onset of breathlessness, often with a dry cough and fatigue. Sputum production is unusual. Haemoptysis is uncommon and suggests malignancy.

Physical signs

Bibasilar late onset inspiratory crackles may be present in the absence of radiographic abnormalities on the chest radiograph. Finger clubbing occurs in 50% of cases. Look for non-pulmonary features that would suggest alternative diagnoses, eg skin rashes, arthritis or lymphadenopathy.

Investigations

Pulmonary function tests
Look for restrictive pattern and/or decreased diffusing capacity of the lung for carbon monoxide (D_LCO). Many patients with UIP are smokers, hence in practice a mixed restrictive and obstructive pattern may be present.

Chest radiograph
Check for peripheral bilateral basilar irregular linear opacities, often with fine nodules, evidence of volume loss, and, in severe cases, honeycombing (Fig 21a). The chest radiograph may be normal in a few cases subsequently shown to have UIP.

High-resolution CT chest scan
Look for peripheral and basal subpleural distribution, honeycombing, irregular linear opacities, septal and intralobular thickening, and traction bronchiectasis with minimal ground-glass shadowing (Fig 21b).

Arterial blood gases
These may be normal at rest, or may reveal hypoxaemia and respiratory alkalosis. Normal resting PaO_2 or SaO_2 do not rule out significant hypoxaemia during exercise or sleep, which is common in diffuse parenchymal lung disease (DPLD).

Differential diagnosis

Other known causes that may give similar HRCT appearances to IPF must be excluded, such as asbestosis, drug reaction, chronic hypersensitivity

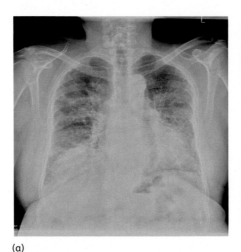
(a)

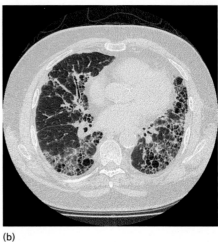
(b)

Fig 21 Chest radiograph **(a)** and CT scan **(b)** in a patient with idiopathic pulmonary fibrosis (IPF).

pneumonitis, chronic sarcoidosis and cryptogenic organising pneumonia.

Treatment

Immunosuppressive agents do not alter the progression of IPF and may actually worsen survival.

Newer antifibrotic and antiangiogenic drugs (pirfenidone and nintedanib) have been shown to slow the rate of progression of fibrosis, hence patients should be assessed by a specialist interstitial lung disease multidisciplinary team (ILD MDT) to determine suitability for these treatments.

Lung transplantation should be considered where appropriate, and patients should be referred well before they reach the terminal phase of their illness.

Long-term oxygen therapy is used in accordance with the criteria established for chronic obstructive pulmonary disease (COPD), and ambulatory oxygen can be of symptomatic benefit for patients who desaturate on exertion.

Pulmonary rehabilitation
Palliative care is of paramount importance. Opiates provide good relief of breathlessness and cough and do not induce respiratory depression when used in palliative doses.

Complications

> cor pulmonale and respiratory failure

> 10-fold increased risk of lung malignancy.

Prognosis

Poor – median survival is 3 years; 10-year survival rate is 5–10%.

2.7.2 Cryptogenic organising pneumonia

Aetiology

Not known, by definition, but organising pneumonia may be a manifestation of, or associated with, various medical conditions. These are predominantly connective tissue diseases, but other reported associations include infection (viral, *Mycoplasma pneumoniae* and HIV), vasculitis, drug toxicity, toxic fume inhalation or smoke inhalation, post-radiation, aspiration and transplantation. The term cryptogenic organising pneumonia (COP) is applied when there is no recognised association.

Pathology

Bronchiolar and alveolar collagenous plugs with surrounding inflammatory cell infiltrate. Lung architecture is preserved.

Epidemiology

COP occurs most commonly in the fifth and sixth decades of life, and has no gender preference.

Clinical presentation

Typically there is a subacute (6–10 weeks) onset with flu-like illness (fever, malaise and weight loss), persistent cough and breathlessness. Occasionally there is fulminant presentation with rapidly progressive severe disease.

Symptoms and chest radiograph changes may wax and wane spontaneously over several months.

Physical signs

Inspiratory crackles are heard in up to 74% of cases, but physical examination may be normal.

Investigations

Blood tests
Neutrophilic leucocytosis in 50% of patients and elevated inflammatory markers (erythrocyte sedimentation rate and C-reactive protein).

Chest radiograph
Patchy, bilateral and variable-sized areas of consolidation, predominantly in the lower lobes and often peripherally (Fig 22a). The infiltrates may be migratory. Unilateral changes occur in 5% of cases. Appearances may be fleeting and resolve spontaneously.

High-resolution CT scan
Bilateral, patchy and asymmetric areas of airspace consolidation with ground-glass opacities. These are mainly in the lower zones with a subpleural or peribronchial distribution (Fig 22b).

Pulmonary function tests
Restrictive defect with reduced diffusing capacity of the lung for carbon monoxide (D_LCO).

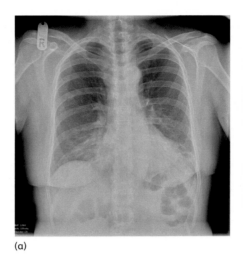
(a)

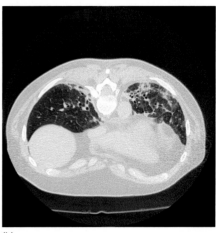
(b)

Fig 22 Chest radiograph (a) and CT scan (b) in a patient with organising pneumonia. In this woman the organising pneumonia occurred in association with anti-polymyositis scleroderma (PM-Scl) antibodies and was not therefore cryptogenic.

Arterial blood gases
Resting or exercise hypoxaemia in 80% of patients.

Bronchoscopy
Bronchoalveolar lavage is often required to exclude infective causes for non-resolving consolidation. Surgical biopsies are preferable to transbronchial biopsies.

Video-assisted thoracoscopic lung biopsy
This is the most helpful examination. A wedge biopsy is required to avoid sampling and interpretation errors related to patchy interstitial changes. As COP often requires lengthy corticosteroid treatment, histopathological confirmation is strongly recommended if clinically feasible.

Differential diagnosis

A variety of other disorders may have similar presentation, such as infections (including the opportunistic), pulmonary lymphoma (beware, as this may initially improve with corticosteroids), usual interstitial pneumonitis, bronchoalveolar carcinoma, chronic eosinophilic pneumonia and sarcoidosis.

Treatment

Oral corticosteroids – these are usually very effective. The optimal regimen is uncertain, but typically a high dose of prednisolone (1.0–1.5 mg/kg/day) is recommended, gradually tapering to zero over several months. Most patients improve within several weeks to 3 months.

Prognosis

Excellent for most patients, but relapses are common (58%), especially within the first 12 months, so close monitoring with chest radiographs and pulmonary function tests is recommended. Patients with frequent recurrences (more than three episodes) may require low-dose maintenance corticosteroid therapy.

> **Key point**
>
> Although COP is uncommon, it should be included in the differential diagnosis in any patient with bilateral airspace radiological changes that are unresponsive to antibiotics.

2.7.3 Hypersensitivity pneumonitis

Hypersensitivity pneumonitis can cause a wide range of presentations, from acute respiratory illness to a chronic, fibrosing lung disease.

Aetiology

Hypersensitivity pneumonitis, also known as extrinsic allergic alveolitis (EAA), is caused by hypersensitivity to inhaled organic dusts. The best-known type is 'farmer's lung', but an enormous range of agents has been reported to cause the condition (see Table 32). There is some evidence that smoking may be protective.

Epidemiology

EAA accounts for 2% of all occupational lung disease. Half of these cases occur in farmers.

Pathology

Histological material is rarely available, but the condition begins as a non-specific diffuse pneumonitis that later develops the characteristic feature of epithelioid non-caseating granulomata. Fibrosis and obstruction/obliteration of bronchioles arises in parallel with inflammatory changes. Honeycombing occurs in advanced cases.

Identification of antigen

A careful history looking for potential antigen exposure should be taken, including exposure to birds, damp/moulds, organic matter such as grasses/hay/compost, and hot tubs. This is of primary importance in identifying culprit antigens.

The demonstration of a serum immunoglobulin G antibody response to the inducing organic antigen (serum precipitins) is widely used to confirm hypersensitivity, but these tests must be employed in the context of a history of exposure to antigen as false-positive reactivity can often be demonstrated due to previous irrelevant exposure.

Furthermore, a negative test does not exclude hypersensitivity pneumonitis.

Prevention

Avoidance of exposure is the counsel of perfection, but is easier said than done in many cases. Patients may be unwilling to put their livelihood (eg farming) or hobbies (eg pigeons) at risk. Exposure can be reduced by changing work practices or the use of industrial respirators. If monitoring suggests that disease is progressive despite these manoeuvres, then exposure must cease. An affected worker may be entitled to compensation.

2.7.3.1 Acute hypersensitivity pneumonitis

Clinical presentation

This occurs within a few hours of exposure. The patient develops a flu-like illness (malaise, fever, headache, and general aches and pains) with a cough and breathlessness, which may be indistinguishable from acute respiratory infection. Wheeze can occur, but it is not a typical feature. Breathing difficulty can range from trivial to life-threatening.

Physical signs

These include fever, respiratory distress and basal crackles. Wheeze may be present, due to bronchiolitis with small airway narrowing.

Investigations

Pulmonary function tests – these can be normal if the patient has not recently been exposed to the precipitant. During the acute illness lung function may be restrictive or obstructive, and gas transfer is reduced.

Chest radiograph – this may be normal, but it characteristically reveals diffuse interstitial shadowing. This is particularly the case in lower and mid-zones, resolving within 24–48 hours after exposure has ceased (Fig 23).

Differential diagnosis

A single episode must be distinguished from other acute respiratory disorders associated with systemic symptoms, the most common of these being infection. Distinction of recurrent episodes from organic dust toxic syndrome (usually caused by fungal toxins) and nitrogen dioxide pneumonitis (silo-filler's disease) can be extremely difficult in those at risk of all of these conditions.

Treatment

In an acute episode, spontaneous recovery begins within 12–24 hours of removing the sensitising antigen. Steroids can hasten improvement, but there is concern that they may increase the risk of recurrence. Respiratory support (oxygen and, rarely, mechanical ventilation) may be needed in severe cases.

Table 32 Aetiology of extrinsic allergic alveolitis

Name	Source	Antigen
Farmer's lung	Mouldy hay	*Saccharopolyspora rectivirgula*, (formerly *Micropolyspora faeni*)
Bird fancier's lung, etc	Pigeons, parakeets, budgerigars, etc	Avian or animal proteins
Malt worker's lung	Mouldy malt	*Aspergillus clavatus*
Cheese worker's lung	Cheese mould	*Penicillium casei*
Bagassosis	Mouldy sugar cane	*Thermoactinomyces sacchari*

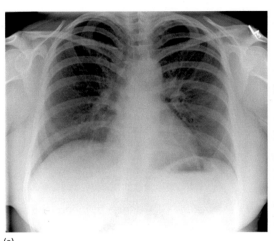
(a)

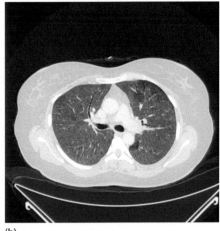
(b)

Fig 23 Chest radiograph **(a)** and CT scan **(b)** in a patient with hypersensitivity pneumonitis. The diffuse, centrilobular, ground-glass nodular infiltrate is difficult to appreciate on a chest radiograph but is more apparent on CT.

2.7.3.2 Subacute hypersensitivity pneumonitis

Clinical presentation and physical signs
Repeated exposure to antigen leads to progressive, persistent coughing and dyspnoea, which develops over weeks to months. Physical examination is similar to acute hypersensitivity pneumonitis, although fever is less common.

Investigations
CT shows inflammatory changes in the form of ground-glass opacities and soft centrilobular nodules. Inflammation and narrowing of the small airways leads to air trapping and mosaic areas of hypoattenuation.

Treatment
Management involves removal of the offending antigen. Steroids are usually given in those with significant symptoms or impairment of gas exchange and, providing antigen exposure ceases, they can usually be weaned off completely over a few weeks.

2.7.3.3 Chronic fibrosing hypersensitivity pneumonitis

Clinical presentation
Continuous low-level antigen exposure over time leads to progressive lung scarring and insidious breathlessness.

Patients may present after many years of exposure with lung fibrosis, but without a prior history of acute episodes. This pattern of exposure and presentation is often seen in those exposed to antigens from pet birds.

Physical signs
These include respiratory distress, widespread crackles, as in other forms of diffuse parenchymal lung disease, but, by contrast, clubbing is uncommon. A high-pitched, apical wheeze can sometimes be heard, reflecting small airway narrowing. The combination of fibrotic crackles and a soft, high-pitched apical wheeze is quite characteristic of chronic hypersensitivity, reflecting both parenchymal lung disease and small airway fibrosis. Signs of pulmonary hypertension and right heart failure may develop.

Investigations
Pulmonary function tests – these reveal restriction (reduced forced vital capacity (FVC)) due to fibrosis and impaired carbon monoxide transfer factor. There may also be a degree of airflow obstruction and increased residual volume due to air trapping.

Chest radiograph – this can show a range of patterns, including diffuse interstitial shadowing, honeycombing and fibrotic changes (in the upper lobes particularly).

High-resolution CT scanning – this is more sensitive than the chest radiograph. It may show findings seen in subacute hypersensitivity pneumonitis (ground-glass opacities, centrilobular nodules and gas trapping), but there is also established fibrosis (traction bronchiectasis, reticulation). Honeycombing resembling idiopathic pulmonary fibrosis (IPF) can occur in advanced cases.

Bronchoscopy / bronchoalveolar lavage – this is useful in excluding infection, and will typically reveal a lymphocytosis. A lung biopsy may be needed to distinguish from other causes of diffuse parenchymal lung disease (DPLD) in some cases.

Differential diagnoses
The main differential diagnosis in many cases is from other forms of DPLD, including sarcoidosis. Advanced fibrosing hypersensitivity pneumonitis can mimic IPF clinically and radiologically.

Treatment/prevention
Avoidance of exposure, as indicated above for acute extrinsic allergic alveolitis (EAA). Steroids and other

immunosuppressive agents are used to treat the inflammatory component of a chronic hypersensitivity pneumonitis and to try to prevent progression to irreversible fibrosis, but the optimum dose and duration of treatment is not known.

Complications/prognosis

Many patients continue their antigenic exposure despite medical advice to the contrary. Some cases develop respiratory failure, but this is relatively uncommon.

2.7.4 Sarcoidosis

Aetiology

Sarcoidosis is a multisystem non-caseating granulomatous disorder of unknown cause but is likely to be due to an exaggerated cellular immune response to an external antigen. Both genetic and environmental factors have been implicated:

> Genetic factors – familial cases are described and some patterns of disease are more prevalent in certain racial groups.

> There is increased incidence in black patients with human leukocyte antigen Bw15.

> Epstein–Barr virus has been implicated.

> *Mycobacterium tuberculosis* may be a trigger.

Pathology

An accumulation of T-helper (CD4) lymphocytes and mononuclear phagocytes in the affected organs, driven by unknown antigens, is followed by the formation of granulomas with an accumulation of macrophages and multinucleated giant cells in active disease. The alveolar macrophages in the lungs release platelet-derived growth factor and fibronectin. These stimulate fibroblast proliferation and result in fibrosis, which is almost always irreversible.

Epidemiology

Sarcoidosis is a common disease and occurs worldwide, but there is great geographical variation. The incidence in the UK is 19 cases per 100,000 people, whereas it is much less common in Japan. Maximum incidence is between 30 and 40 years of age. It is more common in females, and in the USA it is 10–17 times more common in black people than white people.

Clinical presentation

The symptoms and signs depend on the organ(s) involved (Table 33). In over 90% of patients the lungs are affected. Pulmonary involvement may be asymptomatic and detected by a routine chest radiograph. Acute or subacute sarcoidosis may develop over a period of weeks.

Investigations

Chest radiograph

The International Congress on Sarcoidosis established five stages of sarcoidosis based on the chest radiograph:

> stage I – hilar lymph node enlargement only

> stage II – lymph node enlargement and diffuse pulmonary disease

> stage III – diffuse pulmonary disease without lymph node enlargement

> stage IV – pulmonary fibrosis

> stage 0 – a normal chest radiograph.

Serum angiotensin-converting enzyme

Levels are raised in 41–80% of patients. Also raised in hepatitis, miliary TB, HIV and histoplasmosis. If it is raised it

Table 33	Common clinical features of sarcoidosis	
Body system involved	Symptoms	Signs
Respiratory	Cough, dyspnoea and wheeze	Crackles
Skin	Painful dusky blue nodules and shiny raised purple eruption on nose, face, hands or feet	Erythema nodosum and lupus pernio
Eyes	Gritty painful eyes and photophobia	Keratoconjunctivitis, uveitis, iridocyclitis and chorioretinitis
Musculoskeletal	Swollen digits, joint pains and proximal myopathy	Phalangeal bone cysts and proximal muscle weakness
Cardiological	Dyspnoea (cardiac failure) and palpitations	Irregular pulse / rhythm disturbance and crackles at lung bases
Neurological	Headache and paraesthesia	Bell's palsy, mononeuritis and aseptic meningitis
Gastrointestinal	Abdominal pain and disordered LFTs	Pancreatitis and hepatomegaly
Endocrine–metabolic	Polyuria, polydipsia and confusion (caused by hypercalcaemia)	
Renal	Renal colic caused by calculi	
Haematological	Lymphadenopathy	Splenomegaly
Exocrine	Parotid gland enlargement	Parotid enlargement

LFT, liver function test.

may be useful in monitoring disease progression and treatment, but it does not establish or rule out a diagnosis of sarcoidosis.

Serum calcium

Sarcoid tissue produces an abnormal hydroxylating enzyme that converts vitamin D precursors to active 1,25-dihydroxycholecalciferol and leads to hypercalcaemia and hypercalciuria, which respond to corticosteroids.

Heaf or tuberculin test

Very often the main differential diagnosis is TB, either because of the finding of mediastinal lymphadenopathy or because a biopsy obtained elsewhere (eg the liver) has unexpectedly shown granuloma. In this case the finding of anergy in response to Heaf or tuberculin testing would favour sarcoid.

> **Hazard**
>
> There are problems with Heaf or tuberculin testing in sarcoid, as prior BCG (bacillus Calmette–Guérin) makes interpretation difficult, and patients with overwhelming TB can be anergic, particularly if they also have HIV.

Transbronchial biopsy and endobronchial ultrasound fine needle aspiration

Endobronchial ultrasound-guided fine needle aspiration (FNA) has a high diagnostic yield where mediastinal lymphadenopathy is present. If this is not possible, then transbronchial biopsy of the lung parenchyma reveals granuloma in 85–90% of patients. In cases that are clinically clear-cut, biopsy is not necessarily required, but it

is essential to obtain histological material if there is diagnostic doubt.

Tests of disease activity

These will depend on the parameters that were originally abnormal. Good examples might be:

> K_{CO} (transfer coefficient) if there is pulmonary disease
> liver function tests
> serum angiotensin-converting enzyme (ACE), erythrocyte sedimentation rate, serum calcium.

Differential diagnosis

The differential diagnosis depends on the distribution of organ involvement, but might include:

> TB
> lymphoma
> eosinophilic granuloma
> berylliosis
> interstitial fibrosis from other causes.

Treatment

Corticosteroids

The beneficial effects of corticosteroids were first reported in 1951, but many patients do not need treatment: stage 0 and I disease commonly resolve spontaneously. Stage II disease without any symptoms should be monitored for at least 6 months, with treatment offered if symptoms develop (dyspnoea and cough).

Oral prednisolone (0.5 mg/kg/day) is the treatment of choice, given for 4 weeks and then reduced in a stepwise pattern to a maintenance dose of 5–15 mg/day for at least 6–12 months. The disease should be monitored by the patient's symptoms, chest radiography and carbon monoxide transfer factor.

Relapse is common once steroids are withdrawn, and some patients may require long-term treatment.

Topical steroids may be used for cutaneous sarcoid, and with systemic steroids for ocular sarcoid.

Immunosuppressants and other therapies

> Hydroxychloroquine, chlorambucil, methotrexate, azathioprine, cyclophosphamide, cyclosporin and pentoxifylline have been tried in sarcoidosis, often as steroid-sparing agents.
> Anti-tumour necrosis factor (TNF) antibody treatment should be considered in those with severe refractory disease.
> Oxygen should be provided for hypoxaemia.
> Lung transplantation (see Section 2.13).

Complications

These relate to the distribution of organ involvement:

> pulmonary fibrosis with hypoxemia resulting in cor pulmonale
> hypercalcaemia, which can provoke renal failure
> complications related to the affected organ.

Prognosis

> Stages 0 and I disease are usually self-limiting.
> Stage II disease: 60–70% of patients show complete radiographic clearance within 5 years.
> Stage III disease is unlikely to clear and often leads to cor pulmonale if untreated.

2.8 Miscellaneous conditions

2.8.1 Bronchiolitis obliterans

Key point

Do not confuse bronchiolitis obliterans (BO) with cryptogenic organising pneumonia (COP). These conditions differ clinically, radiologically, histologically and in their responsiveness to steroid treatment.

Aetiology

BO is characterised by mainly irreversible airflow obstruction that is usually progressive. It occurs in lung and heart–lung allograft recipients, and is the major cause of lung allograft rejection. The most common cause of non-transplant BO is connective tissue disease (especially rheumatoid arthritis); other less common causes include toxic fume inhalation, infection (viral and *Mycoplasma pneumoniae*), drugs (D-penicillamine), radiation, graft versus host disease (GvHD) in association with allogenic haematopoietic stem cell transplantation, and ulcerative colitis.

Pathology

The hallmark of BO is submucosal bronchiolar fibrosis that is preceded by bronchiolar inflammation resulting in epithelial necrosis. As a result of this the bronchiole will become plugged by granulation tissue. Subsequently, collagen is formed, which may completely obliterate the airway lumen.

Clinical presentation

This is often non-specific and insidious. The most common complaint is exertional dyspnoea, often accompanied by a chronic productive cough. Lung and heart–lung allograft recipients may present with a decline in their forced expiratory volume in 1 second (FEV_1) (see Section 2.13).

Physical signs

These are often unremarkable in the early stages. In more advanced stages there are signs of hyperinflation, end inspiratory crackles, squeaks and wheezes.

Investigations

Pulmonary function tests
Look for an obstructive defect.

Chest radiograph
Initially normal or may show hyperinflation: as the disease progresses subsegmental atelectasis, loss of volume and/or fibrosis may be found.

High-resolution CT chest scan
Radiological appearances are quite distinct from those of COP and reflect underlying airway obstruction. For example, bronchial wall thickening of the segmental and subsegmental bronchi with mosaic perfusion is clearly demonstrated on CT chest scan carried out during expiration.

Lung biopsy
This is the only method of definite diagnosis of BO, but this may be difficult because the diagnostic yield of transbronchial biopsy in BO varies between 15% and 82% due to the patchy nature of the condition and the small size of biopsy samples obtained by this technique. Video-assisted thoracoscopic lung biopsy should be considered if transbronchial biopsy is inconclusive or atypical.

Arterial blood gases
Hypoxaemia and hypercapnia develop only in end-stage disease.

Differential diagnosis

Consider asthma, emphysema, desquamative interstitial pneumonitis and hypersensitivity pneumonitis.

Treatment

Treatment with long-term azithromycin can stabilise lung function and may improve FEV_1 in up to one-third of patients. Patients with BO usually respond poorly to corticosteroids. In lung-transplant recipients ensure adequate levels of immunosuppression are maintained.

Prognosis

BO has a variable course. Some patients present with a rapid decline in FEV_1 and are likely to die within a year of diagnosis, whereas others show progressive slow deterioration. Overall mortality varies from 25% to 56%, and most patients die of infection or respiratory failure.

2.8.2 Respiratory complications of rheumatoid arthritis

Aetiology

The association of rheumatoid arthritis with respiratory disease may be due to:

> rheumatoid-associated lung disease

> drug-related lung disease secondary to drugs used to treat rheumatoid arthritis

> infection secondary to immunosuppression

> coexistent medical conditions.

Epidemiology

Although rheumatoid arthritis is more common in women, rheumatoid lung disease occurs more frequently in men who have long-standing rheumatoid disease, a positive rheumatoid factor and subcutaneous nodules.

Pulmonary involvement is one of the most frequent extra-articular manifestations of rheumatoid arthritis, with the commonest manifestations being interstitial lung disease (ILD) and pleural effusion. Approximately 30–40% of patients with rheumatoid arthritis demonstrate either radiological or pulmonary function abnormalities indicative of interstitial fibrosis or restrictive lung disease.

Although rheumatoid arthritis disease activity is important, smoking is the most consistent independent predictor of radiological and physiological abnormalities suggestive of ILD in rheumatoid arthritis.

Clinical presentations

The range of pulmonary problems is wide and includes the following.

Infection

Respiratory infections account for 15–20% of deaths in rheumatoid patients. Many patients with rheumatoid arthritis are treated with immunosuppression, and atypical infections should always be considered in such cases.

Rheumatoid nodules

Rheumatoid nodules are the only pulmonary manifestation specific to rheumatoid arthritis. These are typically benign but can lead to pleural effusion, pneumothorax, haemoptysis, secondary infection and bronchopulmonary fistula.

Pleural effusions

These are common in rheumatoid arthritis, are exudative and have a low glucose. Chronic rheumatoid effusions can develop into a pseudochylothorax, which contains a 'milky' fluid due to high levels of cholesterol.

Interstitial lung disease

Radiographic findings of ILD occur in 2–5% of patients, while diffusion capacity abnormalities occur in 40%. High-resolution CT scans and histology have shown even higher rates, but clinically significant disease probably occurs in 5–10% of rheumatoid patients.

Bronchiectasis

Of rheumatoid arthritis patients, 10% show radiographic signs of bronchiectasis, which may occur in the absence of ILD. Patients with this complication are more likely to be heterozygous for the transmembrane conductance regulator mutation seen in cystic fibrosis (CF).

Obliterative bronchiolitis

This is rare and usually fatal. It is associated with penicillamine, gold and sulfasalazine treatment and presents with rapid-onset dyspnoea and dry cough. Fever is uncommon.

Caplan's syndrome

This is the combination of rheumatoid arthritis with pneumoconiosis related to mining dust. Look for rapid development of multiple basal peripheral nodules in the rheumatoid arthritis patient who has a history of exposure to mining dusts. This can progress to progressive massive pulmonary fibrosis.

Arteritis

Arteritis of the pulmonary artery and lung is rare; signs of systemic vasculitis are usually present.

Lung cancer

Lung cancer is more common in patients with rheumatoid arthritis than in normal control subjects.

Drug-induced lung disease

Methotrexate pneumonitis is an unpredictable and life-threatening side effect that may occur in 1–5% of patients given this drug. Presentation is often subacute, with symptoms of cough, dyspnoea and fever often present for several weeks or months before diagnosis. Progression to respiratory failure can be rapid. Early diagnosis, cessation of methotrexate, and treatment with corticosteroids and/or cyclophosphamide are important in management. There is a high rate of recurrence of lung injury after rechallenge with methotrexate.

Penicillamine and gold can also cause pulmonary complications.

Other diseases

Patients with rheumatoid arthritis can get apical fibrobullous disease (apical fibrotic cavity lesions similar to ankylosing spondylitis), thoracic cage immobility causing restrictive lung disease and (rarely) primary pulmonary hypertension. Secondary pulmonary hypertension (due to ILD) is more common.

2.8.3 Pulmonary vasculitis

Vasculitides are classified by size of vessel. Small-vessel vasculitides are the commonest form to involve the lung.

Large-vessel vasculitis

Temporal arteritis and Takayasu's arteritis cause large-vessel vasculitis. These do not generally cause pulmonary disease, excepting where there is involvement of the thoracic aorta.

Medium-vessel vasculitis

Churg–Strauss syndrome, polyarteritis nodosa and Kawasaki disease cause medium-vessel vasculitis. Churg–Strauss syndrome involves both small- and medium-sized arteries. Polyarteritis nodosa can involve bronchial arteries.

Small-vessel vasculitis

This group of conditions, most of which produce systemic vasculitis, is characterised by the presence of antineutrophil cytoplasmic antibodies (ANCA). These antibodies are split into two types on the basis of the immunofluorescence pattern, although some ANCA-positive patterns do not fit into either category:

> c-ANCA directed against proteinase-3

> p-ANCA directed against myeloperoxidase.

For practical purposes the two conditions of greatest relevance to the lung are:

> granulomatosis with polyangiitis

> Churg–Strauss syndrome.

Epidemiology

Granulomatosis with polyangiitis

Mean age at presentation is 41 years. No gender predominance. Median time to diagnosis is 5 months.

Churg–Strauss syndrome

Mean age of onset of asthma is 35 years and of vasculitis is 38 years.

Clinical presentation

Granulomatosis with polyangiitis

The majority (90%) of patients present with upper or lower respiratory tract symptoms; 75% of cases involve nasal, sinus or tracheal airways. Respiratory symptoms include cough (50%), haemoptysis (30%) and pleuritis (30%).

Other clinical features include glomerulonephritis (75% within 2 years of onset), arthralgia (70%), ocular symptoms eg proptosis (50%), fever (50%), skin involvement, mononeuritis multiplex and pericarditis.

Churg–Strauss syndrome

This has three distinct phases:

> prodromal phase of asthma/rhinitis

> blood and tissue eosinophilia

> characterised by systemic vasculitis.

In the final phase cardiac (50%) and skin (70%) lesions are characteristic. Glomerulonephritis, mononeuritis, arthropathy and conjunctivitis are also recognised.

Physical signs

These depend on the clinical presentation but could include the following.

Granulomatosis with polyangiitis

Pulmonary signs could include those of consolidation or pleural effusion. Upper airway ulceration may be visible.

Churg–Strauss syndrome

In the prodromal phase wheeze and reduced peak flow are evident. Later skin lesions (erythema, purpura with or

without nodules) and signs of cardiac failure can be seen.

Key point

Consider Churg–Strauss syndrome in patients with asthma whose disease becomes more aggressive and steroid dependent.

Investigations

Full blood count

In granulomatosis with polyangiitis there may be a normochromic anaemia (73%) with leucocytosis and thrombocytosis. A normochromic anaemia may also occur in Churg–Strauss syndrome, but the characteristic abnormality is eosinophilia. The erythrocyte sedimentation rate is usually high in both conditions.

Antineutrophil cytoplasmic antibodies

> Of patients with granulomatosis with polyangiitis, 90% are c-ANCA positive.

> Of those with Churg–Strauss syndrome, 50% are p-ANCA positive.

Radiology

Chest radiograph and CT abnormalities include the following:

> multiple lung nodules (which in granulomatosis with polyangiitis often cavitate)

> patchy consolidation / ground-glass opacities

> diffuse shadowing due to pulmonary haemorrhage

> interstitial shadowing.

Histology

Except in clinically clear-cut cases, histological confirmation is required for diagnosis. However, the yield of diagnostic histology by transbronchial biopsy in patients with granulomatosis with polyangiitis is low – approximately 10%. Alternative possibilities are biopsy

of upper airway lesions, renal biopsy (if there is evidence of nephritis), and open lung biopsy.

Other investigations

Screening blood tests – renal and liver function tests, antinuclear antibodies, rheumatoid (Rh) factor, angiotensin-converting enzymes and autoantibodies.

Urine – look for proteinuria, haematuria and cellular casts as evidence of renal involvement.

Bronchoalveolar lavage – may be required to exclude infective causes for pulmonary infiltrates or cavitating lung nodules. A haemorrhagic lavage suggests pulmonary haemorrhage. The presence of an eosinophilic alveolar lavage suggests Churg–Strauss syndrome or other eosinophilic lung disease.

Differential diagnosis

The differential diagnosis depends on the nature of the presenting symptom. The more difficult differential diagnosis can be of eosinophilia. Where there is significant diagnostic doubt, the case for obtaining biopsy material is strengthened.

Treatment

Granulomatosis with polyangiitis

Steroids with or without cyclophosphamide with or without plasmapheresis. Co-trimoxazole may have a role for patients with disease confined to the upper airway. Azathioprine is often used to maintain remission.

Churg–Strauss syndrome

Steroids with or without cyclophosphamide with or without plasmapheresis.

Complications

Granulomatosis with polyangiitis

Chronic renal insufficiency (in 40%, a quarter of whom will require dialysis), hearing loss (35%), nasal deformities (30%), tracheal stenosis (10%) and visual loss (8%).

Churg–Strauss syndrome
A more benign condition than
granulomatosis with polyangiitis,
but myocardial damage and
gastrointestinal tract involvement
are recognised.

Prognosis

> granulomatosis with polyangiitis:
  13% mortality

> Churg–Strauss syndrome: 11%
  morbidity in long-term follow-up.

2.8.4 Pulmonary eosinophilia
Aetiology/pathology

Pulmonary eosinophilia is the term used
for a group of disorders of different
aetiology, characterised by peripheral
blood eosinophilia and eosinophilic
pulmonary infiltrates. The causes of
pulmonary eosinophilia are:

> allergic bronchopulmonary
  aspergillosis

> drug-induced pulmonary eosinophilia

> tropical pulmonary eosinophilia

> Löffler's syndrome

> Churg–Strauss syndrome

> hypereosinophilic syndrome

> eosinophilic pneumonia.

Allergic bronchopulmonary aspergillosis
This is mainly caused by *Aspergillus
fumigatus*, but may be caused by other
Aspergillus species and *Candida*. Inhaled
spores are deposited in secretions and
then proliferate, resulting in mucus
plugging of the airways. There is
production of immunoglobulin E (IgE)
and immunoglobulin G (IgG) antibodies
and eosinophilic infiltration of the lungs.
Proximal bronchiectasis occurs as a
result of a local immune reaction.

Drug-induced pulmonary eosinophilia
Drugs can cause pulmonary infiltrates,
eosinophilia, fever and pulmonary
symptoms such as wheeze and cough.
It is important to take a full drug

history from any patient presenting
in such a manner, but recognised
causes include:

> aspirin
> methotrexate
> sulfonamides
> captopril
> naproxen
> tetracycline
> carbamazepine
> nitrofurantoin
> tolazamide
> chlorpropamide
> penicillamine
> bleomycin
> chlorpromazine
> penicillin
> gold
> imipramine
> phenytoin
> sulfasalazine.

Tropical pulmonary eosinophilia
The common causes are:

> *Wuchereria bancrofti*
> *Brugia malayi*
> *Ancylostoma duodenale*
> *Strongyloides stercoralis*
> *Toxocara canis*.

Hypereosinophilic syndrome
This is characterised by marked
blood eosinophilia and eosinophilic
infiltration of the heart, lungs, skin,
central nervous system and other
organs. It usually affects men in the
fourth decade of life and has a high
morbidity and mortality.

Chronic eosinophilic pneumonia
This is characterised by blood
eosinophilia with pulmonary eosinophilic
infiltration for which there is no obvious
cause.

Epidemiology

Allergic bronchopulmonary aspergillosis
– is the most common cause of
eosinophilia; occurs worldwide and at
any age.

Drug-induced pulmonary eosinophilia –
is dependent on local patterns of drug
use.

Tropical pulmonary eosinophilia – is
commonly seen in Asia, Africa and
South America.

Chronic eosinophilic pneumonia –
mainly affects middle-aged women with
a history of asthma.

Clinical presentation

Allergic bronchopulmonary aspergillosis
– most patients present with asthma;
10% have night sweats, fever or
malaise.

Drug-induced pulmonary eosinophilia –
cough, dyspnoea and fever may start
within hours of taking the drug.

Tropical pulmonary eosinophilia – most
patients are young adults and present
with cough, which is mainly nocturnal.
Breathlessness, chest pain, fever, weight
loss and anorexia may occur. If
untreated, symptoms may persist or
remit spontaneously and recur later.

Hypereosinophilic syndrome – patients
present with fever, anorexia and weight
loss, along with symptoms secondary to
the organ affected. In 60% of cases the
heart is affected with arrhythmias and
heart failure. In 50% of cases the lungs
are involved and the patient complains
of cough.

Chronic eosinophilic pneumonia –
patients present with cough, dyspnoea,
fever and weight loss.

Physical signs

Allergic bronchopulmonary aspergillosis
– there may be signs of consolidation or
simply wheeze.

Drug-induced pulmonary eosinophilia –
wheeze and respiratory distress.

Tropical pulmonary eosinophilia – wheeze.

Hypereosinophilic syndrome – signs of mitral and tricuspid valve incompetence. Pulmonary consolidation and pleural effusions can occur.

Investigations

Allergic bronchopulmonary aspergillosis
Full blood count – eosinophilia is moderate (0.5–2.0 × 10^9/L).

Skin-prick test – all patients show a positive immediate skin-prick test to *A fumigatus*.

IgE – positive *Aspergillus*-specific IgE (by RAST); total serum IgE is elevated during acute episodes, and serum IgE can be used to monitor treatment.

IgG – precipitating antibodies to *A fumigatus* are found in over 90% of patients.

Chest radiograph – may show segmental or lobar collapse or bronchiectasis. In the acute phase transient, pulmonary infiltrates may be seen.

Drug-induced pulmonary eosinophilia
A chest radiograph may show transient pulmonary infiltrates.

Tropical pulmonary eosinophilia
Full blood count – eosinophilia is high (5–60 × 10^9/L).

IgE – markedly elevated.

Antifilarial antibodies – present in high titre.

Chest radiograph – may be normal, but more typically will show diffuse mottling with lesions 1–3 mm in diameter.

Chronic eosinophilic pneumonia
Blood tests – likely to be peripheral eosinophilia, anaemia, raised erythrocyte sedimentation rate and elevated IgE.

Lung function tests – show a restrictive or mixed defect.

Chest radiograph – shows peripheral pulmonary densities that have been described as 'photograph negative of pulmonary oedema'.

Treatment

Allergic bronchopulmonary aspergillosis
Treatment is with oral corticosteroids during acute episodes. Response to treatment can be monitored by radiologic clearing, resolution of eosinophilia or serum IgE levels. Antifungals (eg itraconazole for 4 months) can be considered in those with persistent symptoms.

Drug-induced pulmonary eosinophilia
Withdrawal of the drug results in resolution of the symptoms, which can be hastened by corticosteroids.

Tropical pulmonary eosinophilia
Treatment of filarial disease is with albendazole with ivermectin or diethylcarbamazine, building up to a dosage of 6 mg/kg/day for 3 weeks. Any marked delay in treatment is associated with a poor clinical response and development of pulmonary fibrosis. Mebendazole, albendazole or pyrantel pamoate are used if *Ascaris* or *Necator* are the cause. Thiabendazole is the drug of choice for *Strongyloides stercoralis*.

Hypereosinophilic syndrome
Treatment is with corticosteroids. Hydroxycarbamide (hydroxyurea) may be helpful in resistant cases.

Chronic eosinophilic pneumonia
This responds rapidly to corticosteroids, and failure to respond within 48–72 hours raises the possibility of alternative diagnosis such as bronchiolitis obliterans (BO) and organising pneumonia. The dosage of corticosteroids is gradually tapered as relapses are common. Most patients regain normal lung function, although a few may develop a persistent obstructive defect, and in rare instances pulmonary fibrosis may occur.

2.8.5 Smoke inhalation

Historically smoke inhalation was described as early as the first century AD, when Pliny reported the execution of prisoners by exposure to the smoke of greenwood fires.

Aetiology/pathology

Smoke inhalation includes the potential of exposure to a wide array of substances because of the complex chemistry of heat decomposition and pyrolysis. Cytotoxic anoxia from carbon monoxide (CO), cyanide and oxidants is a major cause of morbidity, and a number of irritant chemical pyrolysis products have the potential to cause pulmonary damage. Smoke inhalation may cause the following.

Thermal injury
Thermal injury is usually limited to the upper airways, with laryngeal oedema presenting as a major medical management problem. Except in the event of steam inhalation, most heat dissipates in the upper airways, meaning direct thermal injury to the lungs is uncommon.

Irritant/chemical injury
Inhalation of fine particles (particles >10 μm impact in the nasal passages) may cause acute bronchospasm in susceptible individuals.

Smoke contains a number of toxic gases that are soluble in water and cause acute lung injury, including ammonia, sulphur compounds, hydrogen chloride, phosgene and nitrogen oxides.

Asphyxiation
Combustion of plastics, polyurethane, textiles (silk, nylon and wool), rubber and paper products can lead to the production of cyanide gas. Consider cyanide toxicity in all patients with smoke inhalation who have central nervous system or cardiovascular findings. Cyanide interferes with cellular metabolism, subsequently halting cellular respiration: anaerobic

metabolism ensues, with corresponding high lactate acidosis and decreased oxygen consumption.

Clinical presentation

The diagnosis of smoke inhalation is easy as the injury occurs in the presence of smoke and/or a fire. It is very important to find out if any chemicals were involved (eg from factory fires). It is equally important to determine the exact time of exposure and if other people have been involved. Patients with poor respiratory reserve may be seriously ill.

Hoarseness, a change in voice, complaints of throat pain and odynophagia indicate an upper airway injury that may be severe.

Physical signs

Smoke inhalation injury can range from an immediate threat to a patient's airway and respiratory status to only minor mucosal irritation. Relating specifically to respiratory effects, note particularly the following:

> Airway – is this patent?

> Face, mouth and throat – the presence of facial burns or laryngeal oedema indicates a significant inhalation injury.

> Respiratory – wheeze and the use of the accessory muscles of respiration indicates respiratory distress.

Investigations

Arterial blood gases – look for hypoxia and respiratory acidosis.

Carboxyhaemoglobin and methaemoglobin – the pulse oximeter can be misleading in the setting of CO exposure or methaemoglobinaemia, as it detects oxygenated and deoxygenated haemoglobin only and not any other form of haemoglobin. Co-oximeters are capable of detecting methaemoglobin and carboxyhaemoglobin in addition to haemoglobin and oxyhaemoglobin.

Other blood tests – serum lactate (metabolic acidosis secondary to cyanide, methaemoglobinaemia, CO or hypoxia), renal function, creatine kinase.

Chest radiology – in smoke inhalation the chest radiograph is usually normal, but atelectasis, pulmonary oedema and acute respiratory distress syndrome may occur. These changes may take many hours to develop, hence an initial normal chest radiograph does not exclude a significant inhalation injury.

Electrocardiogram (ECG) – may show myocardial ischaemia, as the oxygen carrying capacity of blood is impaired in the presence of carboxyhaemoglobin and methaemoglobin.

Pulmonary function testing – may show a reversible obstructive airway pattern.

Bronchoscopy – can be diagnostic.

Management

Airway – consider intubation, as the risk of developing laryngeal oedema is high.

Oxygen – to correct hypoxia.

Bronchodilators – in patients with bronchospasm.

Antibiotics – if sepsis is present.

Hyperbaric oxygen – in patients with CO toxicity: the half-life of CO is 320 minutes when breathing room air, 90 minutes when breathing 100% oxygen, and 23 minutes in a hyperbaric chamber at 3 atmospheres absolute.

Methylene blue – methaemoglobinaemia is uncommon in smoke inhalation and rarely requires treatment. Levels lower than 30% are usually tolerated, depending on the patient's cardiorespiratory reserve. Indications for treatment with methylene blue are a change in mental status, acidosis, ECG changes and ischaemic chest pain.

2.8.6 Sickle cell disease and the lung

Aetiology

Patients with sickle cell anaemia frequently develop acute pulmonary complications of their illness. The major pulmonary problems that occur in sickle cell disease include asthma, infection, thromboembolism, acute chest syndrome, chronic pulmonary fibrosis and pulmonary hypertension.

Epidemiology

Acute and chronic pulmonary complications of sickle cell anaemia are common, but often underappreciated by healthcare providers. These conditions have clearly emerged as major threats to the well-being and longevity of patients with sickle cell disease, with more than 20% of adult patients likely to have fatal pulmonary complications of sickle cell anaemia. Pulmonary complications account for a large proportion of deaths among adults with sickle cell anaemia.

Acute chest syndrome is the most common cause of death and the second most common cause of hospitalisation of adults with sickle cell anaemia.

Mortality rates for children with sickle cell anaemia have declined because of penicillin prophylaxis, *Haemophilus influenzae* and *Streptococcus pneumoniae* vaccination, widespread implementation of newborn screening programmes for early detection and improvements in parental education.

Despite significant improvements in the life expectancy of patients with sickle cell disease the median age at death is 42 years for men and 48 years for women.

Clinical presentation

Any 'sickler' presenting with fever, pleuritic chest pain and shortness of breath should be carefully assessed and admitted for observation.

Hazard

Aggression and/or confusion should not be mistaken for a psychotic or 'drugged-up' individual; the patient may well be hypoxic and septic.

Key point

The acute chest syndrome is defined as a new pulmonary infiltrate on a chest radiograph accompanied by fever, chest pain and a variety of respiratory symptoms including coughing, wheezing and tachypnoea. Acute chest syndrome often develops after vaso-occlusive crisis.

Multiple factors may contribute to the respiratory distress associated with the acute chest syndrome, including infection, pulmonary fat embolism, iatrogenic fluid overload, hypoxaemia atelectasis secondary to splinting from painful rib and sternal infarctions, and pulmonary vascular obstruction.

Physical signs

Fever, confusion, dyspnoea, crackles in lung fields and evidence of consolidation.

Investigations

Emergency

For acutely ill patients obtain the following.

> Arterial blood gases – looking for hypoxia; acidosis is a marker of the severity of the illness.

> Routine blood tests – severe anaemia may require transfusion or exchange transfusion; renal function (make sure the patient is not dehydrated).

> Chest radiograph – looking for pulmonary shadowing, consolidation and opacities.

> Electrocardiogram (ECG) – check for signs of acute/chronic right heart strain.

Short term

Aimed at identifying reversible disease:

> ventilation/perfusion scan or spiral CT looking for emboli and infarction

> sputum – for microscopy, sensitivity and culture

> echocardiography – to assess for pulmonary hypertension.

Long term

Lung function tests – note that sickle cell patients often have reduced indices, even when in relative good health. Most patients develop abnormal pulmonary function characterised by airway obstruction, restrictive lung disease, reduced gas transfer and hypoxaemia.

Treatment

Emergency

Try to reassure the patient, while:

> administering broad-spectrum intravenous antibiotics and fluids

> administering high-flow oxygen, humidified if possible

> giving adequate analgesia

> anticoagulating as for pulmonary emboli if veno-occlusion is suspected.

Key point

Hypoxia in sickle disease is often ascribed to co-administration of analgesics and/or sedatives. This could be a dangerous assumption and you can check it by measurement of $PaCO_2$. Reduction of respiratory drive should not affect the alveolar–arterial (A–a) gradient.

Short to long term

Close cooperation between haematologist and respiratory physician is helpful. Prophylactic antibiotics will help reduce episodes of infection. The patient may require life-long anticoagulation.

Complications

Repeated pulmonary emboli and infarction may lead to pulmonary hypertension, cor pulmonale and right heart failure in relatively young patients.

2.8.7 Pulmonary disease in the immunocompromised

The most important step in managing patients who are immunocompromised is first recognising that immunodeficiency may be present. Failure to appreciate this situation early enough results in incorrect diagnoses, inadequate treatment and poor outcomes.

Although immunocompromise can often be anticipated and patients forewarned, such as in those with known HIV, or with solid organ or bone marrow transplants, or recipients of cytotoxic chemotherapy, significant immunocompromise can occur in association with other diseases. Patients on medications for rheumatic disease, patients on long-term steroids, and those with concurrent solid or haematological malignancy, should be assumed to have some degree of immunological impairment. Diabetes, liver disease and renal disease can also impair immunological function, which may be clinically relevant.

Key point

Failure to respond appropriately to treatment for infection or presentation with recurrent infections should prompt a search for possible immunodeficiency.

Pulmonary infiltrates in the immunocompromised

Respiratory infection in the immunocompromised usually presents with breathlessness and cough, although some clinical signs can be blunted or atypical. Consolidation on chest radiograph may likewise be reduced in the presence of neutropenia.

Particular immunological deficits predispose to certain infectious agents (Table 34).

Key point

Common pathogens (eg *Streptococcus pneumoniae*) remain the most likely cause of respiratory infection in most patients with immunodeficiency.

History – a short history of symptoms (24 hours) is more common with bacterial or viral infection; subacute presentation (lasting days) may be due to bacterial, viral or fungal disease; a longer duration of symptoms (weeks) suggests mycobacterial or fungal disease.

Differential diagnosis – although infectious causes predominate, non-infectious causes for infiltrates should also be considered and may result from the underlying disease/treatment or from other comorbidities. These include:

> pulmonary oedema – cardiomyopathy is caused by several anticancer agents and is also a complication of HIV

> drug-induced pneumonitis

> lung involvement from underlying disease, eg lymphoma, connective tissue disease, metastatic malignancy, vasculitis

> radiation pneumonitis

> pulmonary embolism (PE)

> graft versus host disease (GvHD) post-bone marrow transplant.

Approach to immunocompromised patient with pulmonary infection

Broad-spectrum antibiotics should be instituted if the patient is unwell or severely immunocompromised as soon as initial blood, urine and sputum cultures have been obtained. If the patient is neutropenic then antibiotics should be in line with the local neutropenic sepsis protocol and the patient should be nursed in isolation.

Further investigations to consider will depend on the clinical situation and the initial response to treatment and include the following:

> throat swabs for viral polymerase chain reaction (PCR)

> blood for viral serology, Epstein–Barr virus (EBV) / cytomegalovirus (CMV) PCR

> high-resolution CT (HRCT) chest – usually shows non-specific infiltrates and consolidation but may show characteristic changes in invasive fungal disease ('halo' sign), tuberculosis (TB), or may demonstrate ground-glass changes in *Pneumocystis* pneumonia (PCP) where the chest radiograph is normal. Also useful prior to bronchoscopy to direct bronchoalveolar lavage

> bronchoscopy and lavage for microscopy, culture and sensitivity (MC&S), TB culture, viral PCR, fungal culture, PCP. This should be considered early in management

> fungal antigens – β-glucan, galactomannan.

If the patient is acutely unwell and unable to undergo bronchoscopy, it may be necessary to treat empirically without definitive microbiological results. Patients with severely compromised immune systems often have co-infection with multiple pathogens and therefore combined treatment with antibacterial, antiviral and antifungal agents may be required depending on the clinical situation.

Table 34 Infection risk in particular types of immunocompromise

Immunocompromise	Cause	Infective vulnerability
Neutropenia	Cytotoxic chemotherapy	Bacteria
	Leukaemia, aplastic anaemia	Fungi (including *Aspergillus*)
T-cell impairment	HIV	Viruses (including CMV, HSV)
	Post-transplant	Fungi (including PCP, *Cryptococcus*)
	Cytotoxic chemotherapy	Mycobacteria, *Nocardia*
	Rheumatological DMARDs	Parasites (*Toxoplasma*)
	Lymphoma	
B-cell impairment / hypogammaglobulinaemia	Myeloma	Encapsulated bacteria (eg *Streptococcus haemophilus*)
	Lymphoma	
	Acute / chronic lymphocytic leukaemia	

CMV, cytomegalovirus; DMARDs, disease-modifying antirheumatic drugs; HIV, human immunodeficiency virus; HSV, herpes simplex virus; PCP, *Pneumocystis jirovecii* pneumonia.

2.8.8 Human immunodeficiency virus and the lung

Aetiology/epidemiology

Lung pathology is common in patients with HIV infection and particularly in those with low CD4 counts. Like the immunocompetent, they are prone to the common viral and bacterial infections, but they are also at risk of atypical infections such as *Pneumocystis jirovecii* pneumonia (PCP). PCP was a common cause of death in acquired immune deficiency syndrome (AIDS) patients until the introduction of co-trimoxazole prophylaxis in those with CD4 counts <200 × 10^6/L (normal range 430–1,690). It now tends to be seen as a first presentation of the disease in previously undiagnosed HIV.

Tuberculosis is a major cause of mortality and morbidity in HIV patients, particularly in developing countries, and non-TB mycobacteria including *Mycobacterium avium intracellulare* (CD4 <100 × 10^6/L), *Mycobacterium kansasii* and *Mycobacterium chelonae* are also seen. Multidrug-resistant TB started to become a substantial problem in the early 1990s, with between 80% and 100% mortality. The relative numbers of patients infected with multidrug resistant TB in Western countries remains small, but the plight of the developing world is uncertain.

Cytomegalovirus (CMV) pulmonary infection rarely occurs alone; if it is found, its presence does not affect the outcome of other lung infections. Fungal infections, eg *Cryptococcus neoformans*, tend to be seen as part of a disseminated syndrome.

Tumours such as Kaposi's sarcoma (KS) commonly occur in the lung as well as the skin, although lymphoma tends to arise in extrapulmonary sites in HIV patients.

Clinical presentation

The management of HIV patients with pulmonary symptoms can be difficult. Do not forget that acute shortness of breath can be caused by bacterial pneumonia, asthma or PE, just as in the immunocompetent. However, patients with HIV more commonly present with a history of gradually increasing breathlessness, fever, mild-to-moderate sputum production, or just a dry cough, and occasionally with haemoptysis.

Physical signs

General features – How unwell is the patient? Are they hypoxic?

Mouth and skin – look closely for KS as well as other stigmata or evidence of immunodeficiency.

Chest – note any intercostal recession; listen for crackles and wheezing.

Investigations

Chest radiograph

This may be virtually diagnostic (Fig 24), but it may appear normal, especially in early cases of PCP or KS.

Hazard

Do not allow a false sense of security if the chest radiograph appears normal.

Oxygen saturation

Check both before and after exercise. Low post-exercise oxygen saturation is typical of PCP.

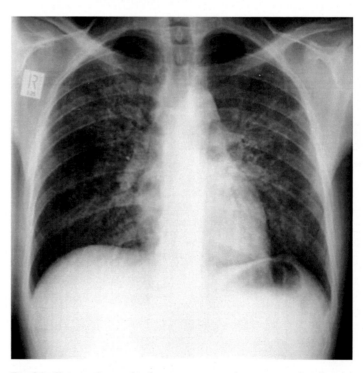

Fig 24 Chest radiograph of a young man who presented with progressive shortness of breath, dry cough and a fever; note the classic bilateral perihilar appearance of the interstitial shadowing that is highly suggestive of PCP, which was later proved on bronchoscopic lavage to be the diagnosis. (Courtesy of Dr I Vlahos.)

CD4 count

Send blood for a CD4 count. Diagnoses to consider are dependent on the level of the CD4 deficiency.

> >750 × 10⁶/L – no increased risk of opportunistic infection

> <750 × 10⁶/L – bacterial pneumonia, oesophageal candidiasis, TB and herpes

> <200 × 10⁶/L – PCP and coccidioidomycosis

> <100 × 10⁶/L – *Cryptococcus, Toxoplasma* and *Mycobacterium avium* complex

> <50 × 10⁶/L – KS, lymphoma, CMV.

Bronchoscopy

Because of the wide range of respiratory pathology seen in the immunosuppressed, bronchoscopy is required in this group of patients if there are new respiratory symptoms and the diagnosis is not obvious. Make sure that samples are sent for the regular investigations, but in particular:

> cytology to look for PCP

> microscopy to look for acid-fast bacilli

> virology to look for CMV.

Intrapulmonary KS is unusual without cutaneous KS, but not impossible.

Other tests

All patients with HIV should be screened for latent TB at the time of diagnosis. Interferon gamma release assays (IGRA) are insensitive with CD4 counts <200 × 10⁶/L, and will therefore need to be repeated once immune reconstitution has occurred. A negative IGRA does not exclude active TB.

Hazard

Sedation in HIV disease
Some newer antiretroviral agents – notably indinavir, efavirenz, nelfinavir, ritonavir and saquinavir – may greatly slow the metabolism of hypnotic agents by interaction with cytochrome P450. Check what your patient is taking, or he or she may stay sleepy for several hours or longer.

CT scan of chest

Useful when other investigations are negative or disease is slow to resolve. Not essential in all patients but can be useful in unexplained hypoxia or fever (you may see lymphadenopathy).

Treatment

Pneumocystis pneumonia
High-dose intravenous co-trimoxazole (Septrin). Steroids (prednisolone 40–80 mg PO) are indicated if the patient is hypoxic (PaO₂ <9.3 kPa). Do not forget to monitor blood tests carefully, including full blood count (FBC) and liver function. Second-line treatment in those unable to tolerate co-trimoxazole is pentamidine or dapsone and trimethoprim.

Supportive care – because of the improved overall prognosis of HIV patients, full supportive care (including intubation and mechanical ventilation) is usually recommended if indicated on physiological grounds.

Hazard
In severe PCP large cysts may form. Pneumothorax could explain a sudden deterioration.

Kaposi's sarcoma

KS may improve in patients with a high viral load who are started on antiviral drugs. Otherwise, refer to an oncologist for intravenous chemotherapy.

Tuberculosis

The frequency of atypical presentations is increased, but management is along conventional lines. Interactions with new-generation antivirals are a problem; specialist advice is required.

Hazard
Do not forget that drug regimens are different for atypical mycobacteria and multidrug-resistant TB.

2.9 Malignancy

2.9.1 Lung cancer

Aetiology/pathology

Smoking remains the chief cause, although other aetiological factors include asbestos, arsenic and some heavy metals. Various histological types are recognised (Table 35).

Table 35 Common histological cell types of lung cancer

Histological classification	Types
NSCLC	Squamous cell Adenocarcinoma Large-cell undifferentiated carcinoma Large-cell neuroendocrine tumour
SCLC	–
Carcinoid tumour	Typical carcinoid tumour Atypical carcinoid tumour

NSCLC, non-small-cell lung cancer; SCLC, small-cell lung cancer.

Epidemiology

Bronchial carcinoma is the leading cause of cancer mortality in the UK, with around 35,000 deaths per year. The male:female ratio is 54:46. Historically men were much more likely to develop lung cancer because of a much higher prevalence of smoking in men after the Second World War, but this gender difference is progressively disappearing.

Clinical presentation

Common

Any persistent change in respiratory symptoms for greater than 3 weeks in a past or current smoker merits investigation:

> cough

> haemoptysis

> shortness of breath (may represent an effusion or lobar collapse)

> chest pain.

Uncommon

Rarer presentations reflect the anatomical site(s) of disease, or the presence of paraneoplastic syndromes (Table 36):

> airway compromise – wheeze or stridor

> oesophageal compression – dysphagia

> neurological

> > nerve involvement, eg hoarseness secondary to recurrent laryngeal nerve palsy

> Horner syndrome

> neuralgic pain as a result of malignant invasion of nerves or roots, eg Pancoast's syndrome and rib involvement

> headaches, clumsiness, diplopia or other neurological symptoms resulting from brain metastasis

> facial swelling – caused by superior vena cava obstruction (SVCO)

> bone pain – caused by metastases

> confusion, abdominal pain and constipation secondary to hypercalcaemia, usually caused by parathyroid hormone-related protein secretion in squamous carcinoma

> confusion secondary to hyponatraemia caused by syndrome of inappropriate antidiuretic hormone (SIADH) secretion in small-cell carcinoma

> Cushingoid features and/or increased pigmentation (ectopic adrenocorticotropic hormone secretion) in small-cell carcinoma.

Physical signs

Examination is often made with the benefit of a chest radiograph.

Common

Look for:

> clubbing

> tobacco-stained fingers

> cachexia

> pallor.

Uncommon

> lymphadenopathy – feel carefully, particularly behind the sternomastoids and deep behind the medial clavicle

> evidence of consolidation or pleural effusion on percussion and auscultation

> hepatomegaly secondary to metastases

> facial swelling and collateral venous circulation.

Rare

> stridor secondary to tracheal or main bronchus involvement

> Horner syndrome

> pigmentation

> skin metastases.

Table 36 Non-metastatic manifestations of lung cancer

Syndrome	Mechanism
Cushing's syndrome	Ectopic adrenocorticotropic hormone
SIADH	Ectopic antidiuretic hormone
Hypercalcaemia	Parathyroid hormone-like peptide
Hypertrophic pulmonary osteoarthropathy	Unknown
Lambert–Eaton myasthenic syndrome	Antibodies against pre-synaptic voltage-gated calcium channels

SIADH, syndrome of inappropriate antidiuretic hormone secretion.

Investigations

Chest radiograph

Most lung cancers are visible on a plain posteroanterior chest radiograph (Figs 25 and 26).

CT scan

For staging the tumour the scan needs to include the neck, thorax, liver and adrenals to look for metastases, as well as the brain if there is evidence of neurological involvement (Fig 27). This should be performed before any invasive biopsy to allow direction of the biopsy to the highest-stage site of disease, which enables diagnosis and staging to be confirmed with a single test. For example, in a patient of good performance status with a lung cancer and left adrenal metastasis, but no other sites of disease, an endoscopic ultrasound will be requested to sample the left adrenal gland.

Positron emission tomography CT scanning

Positron emission tomography (PET)-CT scanning is indicated in patients in whom lung cancer can be treated with radical intent, that is with tumours that are treatable by surgical resection or radical chemoradiotherapy. In general this means those without evidence of metastasis outside the ipsilateral mediastinal lymph nodes. In such patients PET-CT scanning can identify metastases that are not visible on CT alone in about 10% of patients, and can suggest optimal sites for biopsy.

Bronchoscopy

Flexible bronchoscopy is becoming an uncommon test to diagnose lung cancer, being largely replaced by endobronchial ultrasound or image-guided biopsy. This is because sampling of, for example, mediastinal lymph nodes, pleural fluid or liver metastases provides both tissue diagnosis and staging information.

If there is a visible endobronchial lesion then take a biopsy for histology,

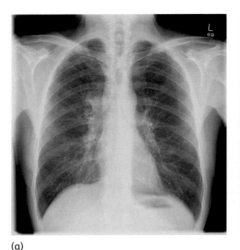
(a)

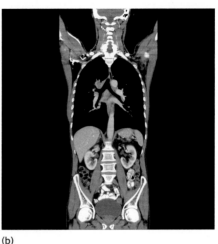
(b)

Fig 25 Chest radiograph **(a)** of a man presenting with a chronic cough and clubbing, who was found to have a right upper lobe lung cancer. A coronal slice from his accompanying CT scan of the chest is shown in **(b)**.

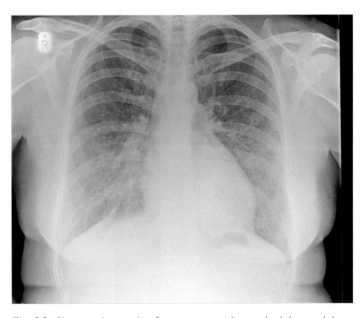

Fig 26 Chest radiograph of a woman with a right hilar nodal mass and nodular shadowing caused by adenocarcinoma of the lung.

brushing for cytology, and washings to microbiology for microscopy, sensitivity and culture, and acid-fast bacilli (remember that rarely infection can mimic carcinoma).

Percutaneous biopsy under CT guidance

This is useful for pulmonary nodules where no evidence of

metastasis is seen on CT or PET scanning. In such patients the pulmonary nodule is the highest-stage disease and therefore the only site for biopsy (Fig 28). The patient should be warned that there is a 10% chance of pneumothorax, hence they must be fit enough to tolerate such a complication.

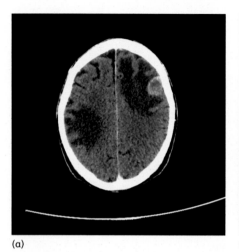
(a)

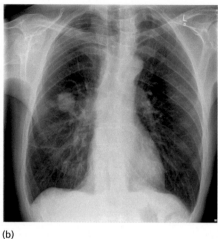
(b)

Fig 27 (a) CT scan of the brain showing bilateral cerebral metastasis in a patient with lung cancer and **(b)** the chest radiograph for the same patient.

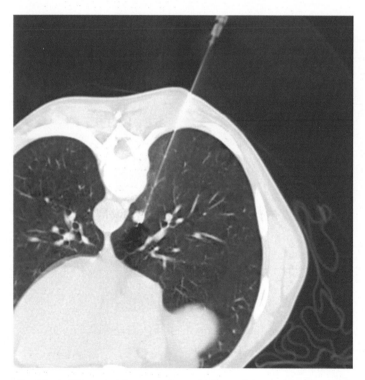

Fig 28 A CT-guided biopsy of a right lower lobe pulmonary nodule. Skilled interventional respiratory radiologists are able to sample nodules of around 10 mm, as shown here. (Image courtesy of Dr Katharine Tweed.)

Endobronchial and endoscopic ultrasound

Endobronchial ultrasound (EBUS) and endoscopic ultrasound (EUS) are techniques that permit the sampling of all mediastinal lymph node areas, as well as centrally placed lung cancers that lie adjacent to but not within the major airways. In addition, EUS can sample the left adrenal gland, which is a common site for lung cancer metastasis.

Mediastinoscopy

This is rarely performed nowadays, having been largely replaced by EBUS and EUS. It can be used, however, to sample some mediastinal lymph node stations in patients where EBUS/EUS is inconclusive.

Sputum cytology

This is no longer recommended as an investigative technique for lung cancer unless the patient is not fit for any active treatment and no other biopsy technique is appropriate.

Blood tests

These are not diagnostic but can identify complications:

> Full blood count (FBC) – anaemia may indicate the progression of disease and/or bone marrow involvement.

> Urea and electrolytes – low sodium may indicate SIADH and raised urea dehydration.

> Liver function tests – if these are deranged it may indicate metastatic disease.

> High calcium with low phosphate is seen in secretion of parathyroid hormone (PTH)-related protein.

Differential diagnosis

This is of the presenting problem but could include:

> infection – consolidation from a pneumonia or tuberculosis

> lung abscess

> vasculitis.

Complications

The vigour with which complications are treated will depend on the patient's general performance status and local expertise (Table 37).

Treatment

Emergency

> SVCO – stenting and/or chemotherapy or radiotherapy

> acute spinal cord compression – surgery or radiotherapy for vertebral body or spinal cord metastasis

> tracheal or main bronchial obstruction – interventional bronchoscopy (diathermy, laser or stenting); requires swift referral to specialist centre; can be followed by radiotherapy, chemotherapy or (rarely) surgery

> pain control – early referral to palliative care team.

Short term

Surgery

Surgery is the treatment most strongly associated with long-term survival and should be offered to all patients whose tumour stage, lung function and performance status permit it. In 2014, 30% of lung resections for lung cancer were performed thoracoscopically, and this proportion is more than 80% in leading centres. Video-assisted thoracoscopic surgery (VATS) is associated with shorter lengths of stay and reduced complications. Patients who have technically operable tumours but are turned down for surgery should be offered a second opinion.

Non-surgical treatment

Radiotherapy with curative intent may be given to patients with non-small-cell lung cancer (NSCLC) without metastases who are not candidates for surgery. Radiotherapy is combined with chemotherapy in the treatment of patients with mediastinal nodal metastasis.

Prophylactic radiotherapy to the brain and hemithorax is given following completion of chemotherapy in small-cell lung cancer (SCLC).

Chemotherapy is the treatment of choice in SCLC, which otherwise has a very poor prognosis. Palliative chemotherapy is also given in metastatic NSCLC because of proven benefits in survival and quality of life.

Targeted therapies – patients with non-squamous carcinoma and activating mutations in the epithelial growth factor receptor (*EGFR*) gene can be treated with the EGFR inhibitors gefitinib, erlotinib or afatinib. Patients' anaplastic lymphoma kinase (*ALK*) gene rearrangements may be treated effectively with crizotinib. At the time of writing there are several promising targeted therapies awaiting technology appraisal decisions from the National Institute for Health and Care Excellence (NICE) on their suitability for use in the NHS.

Pain and symptom control

It is essential to introduce patients and family to support teams as soon as is appropriate.

Prognosis

Overall 5-year survival has doubled in the past decade and is 9.5%, largely because of a doubling in the number of specialist thoracic surgeons and in the number of lung resections for lung cancer.

Prevention

Smoking cessation

Never underestimate your ability to counsel patients about smoking cessation – your words may just be the crucial encouragement the patient needs. All patients who smoke should be pointed in the direction of local smoking cessation services, and ideally followed up immediately at the time of referral. Aids to smoking cessation include counselling, psychological support, nicotine replacement therapy, electronic cigarette use, support groups and antidepressant and other drug treatments.

Table 37 Complications associated with lung cancer

Problem	Treatment
Large airway obstruction	Radiotherapy, endobronchial diathermy, laser or stenting
Pleural effusion	Pleurodesis, tunnelled intrapleural catheter insertion
Bone metastases	Radiotherapy, denosumab
Brain metastases	Solitary metastasis – surgery or stereotactic radiotherapy. Whole brain radiotherapy no longer recommended
SVCO	SVC stent insertion +/- chemotherapy/radiotherapy
Haemoptysis	Radiotherapy and endobronchial diathermy or laser treatment
Electrolyte abnormality	Correct as appropriate

SVC, superior vena cava; SVCO, superior vena cava obstruction.

2.9.2 Mesothelioma

Aetiology

Asbestos fibre has been used extensively for its fire-resistant properties in the building industry, in shipbuilding and for brake and clutch linings in cars. It was mined in countries as far apart as the former USSR, Canada and South Africa, and transported to countries such as the UK by boat. The crocidolite form of asbestos is known to be particularly hazardous in causing lung diseases, but all forms of asbestos are hazardous.

Asbestos fibres are inhaled and become lodged in the alveoli where they are incompletely phagocytosed by macrophages. Some traverse the lung completely to become embedded in the parietal pleura. The resulting inflammatory reaction leads to local tissue damage and fibrosis, and is thought to increase susceptibility to malignant change.

Epidemiology

The effects of asbestos tend to occur 20–40 years after the initial exposure. Therefore, as asbestos controls only became law in the late 1970s, it is predicted that we will continue seeing cases well into the 21st century.

Clinical presentation

> shortness of breath

> weight loss

> chest wall pain.

Physical signs

Evidence of a pleural effusion and/or pleural thickening with:

> decreased expansion on the affected side

> decreased breath sounds on the affected side.

Investigations

Chest X-ray

This will show a pleural effusion or pleural thickening, or both, on the affected side. There may in addition be asbestos-related calcified pleural plaques. Rib erosion or pathological fractures are rare. Pleural thickening that extends onto the mediastinal pleural surface, visible as mediastinal widening, suggests malignant pleural thickening due to mesothelioma.

CT scanning

This will distinguish pleural fluid from enhancing pleural membranes. It will also show mediastinal or hilar lymph node enlargement, if present, as well as the presence of metastases in the lungs, bones or liver.

Pleural thickening is likely to be malignant if it is:

> more than 1 cm thick

> circumferentially thickened around the hemithorax

> nodular

> present on the mediastinal pleural surface.

Obtaining a tissue diagnosis

Pleural fluid alone has a poor sensitivity for diagnosing mesothelioma in most centres, with diagnostic yields of around 25–30%. Blind pleural biopsy with an Abrams' needle is no longer recommended because guided biopsy by thoracoscopy, CT or ultrasound offer much higher diagnostic yields (above 90%). Special stains can help in distinguishing mesothelioma from adenocarcinoma or other tumours.

Differential diagnosis

> lung cancer – there is a synergistic relationship between asbestos and smoking, with lung cancer being five times more common in smokers exposed to asbestos than smokers who have no exposure

> pleural metastasis from non-thoracic cancer, particularly breast, ovary or kidney

> sarcoma

> benign pleural thickening.

Treatment

Emergency

Aspirate the associated pleural effusions if the patient is very short of breath, removing 1–1.5 L of fluid to reduce breathlessness. Only consider pleurodesis once a tissue diagnosis has been obtained.

> **! Hazard**
> Do not insert a chest drain or remove all the fluid because this can hamper attempts at thoracoscopic biopsy later.

Short term

Radical surgery is of no proven benefit and was associated with increased mortality and reduced quality of life in a small pilot randomised controlled trial (RCT). It is no longer offered in the UK outside clinical trials.

Pain can be a major problem and difficult to control, even with opiates. Other agents that can be effective are anti-epileptic drugs (eg gabapentin) or antidepressants.

Talc pleurodesis is effective at preventing recurrent pleural effusion and should be performed as soon as a tissue diagnosis is confirmed. It is not yet known whether talc poudrage, performed thoracoscopically, is more effective than talc slurry pleurodesis.

Recent evidence suggests that drain sites should not be irradiated to prevent chest wall metastasis: it is ineffective at preventing nodules from forming and they are usually not symptomatic in any case.

Long term

Currently the only evidence-based treatment for mesothelioma is palliative chemotherapy with pemetrexed and cisplatin, which has been shown to improve quality of life and increase survival. It is usually well tolerated. Several new targeted treatments show promise but are not yet routinely employed.

Complications

> repeated pleural effusions, which may require placement of an indwelling pleural catheter

> severe pain

> sweats.

Prognosis

This is variable and is strongly influenced by histological subtype. A better prognosis is seen with epithelioid mesothelioma (12–18 months median survival), while sarcomatoid has the worst prognosis (3–5 months). Biphasic mesothelioma shows features of both histologically and is intermediate between the two.

Prevention

There will continue to be a rise in the number of cases in the UK until at least 2025 as the rules controlling the use and handling of asbestos were only enforced in the late 1970s. The 20–40 years' latency from exposure to symptoms means that patients who were young then will continue to present for some time.

Key point

Compensation claims
Patients with mesothelioma, asbestosis, diffuse pleural thickening and lung cancer associated with asbestosis are entitled to state compensation and receive a disability pension. Patients may also be able to make a claim against previous employers for asbestos-related conditions, and may receive compensation if the employer has been negligent in exposing them to asbestos.

If a patient wishes to pursue this course of action, the law generally allows them only 3 years in which to commence legal action after the date on which they first knew they had an asbestos-related condition. It is good practice to record that you advised the patient of this point when you diagnose an asbestos-related condition.

Similar procedures for both state benefits and claims against employers may be followed for coal worker's pneumoconiosis, occupational asthma and a small number of other industrial lung diseases.

Disease associations

Non-pleural mesothelioma tumours may occur as a primary disease on the pericardium, usually presenting as constrictive pericarditis. Diagnosis is normally made by pericardial biopsy.

Peritoneal mesothelioma causes vague symptoms of tiredness, lethargy and loss of appetite, followed by abdominal distension caused by ascites. Diagnosis may be made by laparoscopic omental biopsy.

Mesothelioma may also arise on the tunica vaginalis in the scrotum.

2.9.3 Mediastinal tumours

Aetiology

The mediastinum is the part of the thorax lying between the two pleural sacs and contains the heart and various other thoracic viscera. It is a site where tumours of different pathology are not uncommon: they can occur at any age and may be solid or cystic.

Based on a lateral chest radiograph, the mediastinum can be divided into three compartments (Fig 29). Table 38 shows the normal constituents of the three compartments of the mediastinum as well as the tumours and cysts that may occur in each compartment.

Clinical presentation

Half of all mediastinal masses are asymptomatic, and 90% of these are benign. The likelihood of malignancy is higher in infants and children than in adults. The signs and symptoms of mediastinal masses depend upon the compression and invasion of nearby intrathoracic structures (Table 39). Mediastinal tumours may also be associated with various endocrine syndromes, myasthenia gravis with thymoma being particularly noteworthy.

Investigations

The diagnostic approach to mediastinal masses can be divided into imaging techniques and techniques for obtaining tissue samples.

Imaging techniques

Chest radiograph – most mediastinal tumours are discovered incidentally by posteroanterior or lateral chest radiographs.

CT – this helps evaluate the origin of a mediastinal mass and can some certain lesions confidently, eg teratoma.

MRI – this offers superior definition to CT scanning and may be preferred prior to surgery.

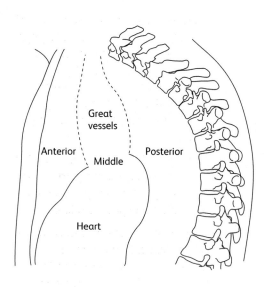

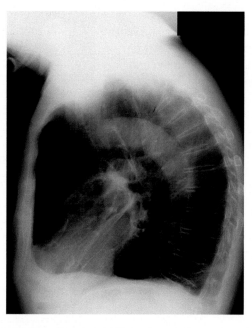

Fig 29 Lateral chest radiograph showing division of the mediastinum into anterior, middle and posterior compartments; the middle compartment containing the heart and great vessels.

Table 38	Normal constituents of the mediastinum and tumours arising from them		
Compartment	**Location**	**Normal contents**	**Examples of mediastinal mass**
Anterior	Superior and anterior to the heart shadow	Thymus gland (remnant), internal mammary arterior and veins, lymph nodes and fat	Thymoma, lymphoma, retrosternal thyroid and parathyroid mass, fibroma, lipoma, teratoma, seminoma and choriocarcinoma
Middle	Posterior and inferior to the anterior compartment	Heart, pericardium, great vessels, trachea, major bronchi and phrenic nerves	Aortic arch aneurysm, pericardial cysts, left ventricular aneurysm and vascular lesions
Posterior	Lies within the margins of the thoracic vertebrae	Oesophagus, thoracic duct, descending thoracic aorta, azygos and hemiazygos veins and sympathetic chain	Oesophageal tumours, neurogenic tumours (neurofibroma, neurilemoma, neurosarcoma, ganglioneuroma, neuroblastoma, chemodectoma and phaeochromocytoma), diaphragmatic hernia and rare tumours (Adkin's tumour, descending aortic aneurysm chordoma and mediastinal sarcoma)

Table 39	Clinical presentation of mediastinal tumours
Structure involved	**Signs and symptoms**
Trachea and main bronchus	Stridor, cough, dyspnoea and recurrent chest infections
Phrenic nerve	Diaphragmatic paralysis (very rare)
Oesophagus	Dysphagia
Sympathetic trunk	Horner syndrome
Superior vena cava	Non-pulsatile distension of neck veins, cyanosis and swelling of the face, neck and upper arm, and dilated veins on chest wall
Pericardium	Pericardial effusion and pericarditis
Left recurrent laryngeal nerve	Left vocal cord palsy with hoarse voice

Medical Masterclass Third edition

Techniques for obtaining mediastinal tissue
Endobronchial ultrasound (EBUS), CT-guided cutting needle biopsy, mediastinoscopy and mediastinotomy can all be used to obtain tissue from mediastinal masses. Surgical approaches are favoured where it is thought likely that a large biopsy will be necessary to arrive at a complete histological diagnosis (eg lymphoma).

Treatment
The treatment of a mediastinal mass would depend on the nature and location of the lesion.

2.10 Disorders of the chest wall and diaphragm

Normal respiration requires the chest wall and diaphragm to work as a pump, enabling airflow into the lung and expiration of air from the lung. In order for the muscles to work effectively, it is essential that the bone structure of the thorax (principally vertebrae and ribs) maintain their intact structure.

The diaphragm is the principal muscle of inspiration, and is innervated by the phrenic nerve, which leaves the spinal cord above the thorax at C3/4/5. The external intercostal muscles, scalene and sternocleidomastoid are considered accessory muscles for inspiration. Expiration is largely a passive process, but can be aided by abdominal muscles and the internal intercostal muscles.

Aetiology
Neuromuscular disorders
Patients with congenital muscular diseases, eg Duchenne muscular dystrophy or myotonic dystrophy, are at risk of developing respiratory failure and should be monitored for this. Acquired neuromuscular conditions, eg myositis, Guillain–Barré syndrome, motor neurone disease and myasthenia gravis, also require close monitoring.

The diaphragm and phrenic nerve may be affected by the conditions detailed above. Diaphragmatic paralysis is sometimes an incidental finding, or may be discovered during investigation of respiratory failure. The phrenic nerve may be injured during trauma: it may also be compressed in its passage through the thorax (malignancies, aneurysm, thyroid disease) or affected by infections (herpes zoster) or mononeuropathies. Diaphragmatic weakness may develop decades after poliomyelitis.

Structural
The principal condition affecting the thoracic skeleton leading to respiratory failure is kyphoscoliosis, but in the acute trauma setting patients should be assessed for flail segments of ribs. Kyphoscoliosis can be caused by a large number of conditions, including neuromuscular disease (eg muscular dystrophy / cerebral palsy), diseases of the vertebrae (eg osteoporosis or Pott's disease) or connective tissue disease. In older people, patients may also develop respiratory failure secondary to previous thoracoplasty.

Herniation of abdominal contents into the diaphragm can effectively reduce lung volume.

Hazard
Obesity may mimic diseases of the chest wall by producing a restrictive defect.

Key point
Note that patients with neuromuscular diseases may be at increased risk of aspiration and aspiration pneumonia secondary to impaired swallowing mechanism.

Investigations
Imaging – investigation of thoracic wall disease should include chest radiograph or CT, particularly if there is concern about compressive causes of phrenic nerve paralysis such as malignancy. Imaging of the diaphragm through ultrasound may also be used to assess paralysis.

Blood gases – These should be sampled (ideally in the early morning) to assess for respiratory failure; sleep studies may reveal nocturnal hypoventilation.

Lung function testing – this may show a restrictive defect. In addition to spirometry and lung volumes, tests of respiratory muscle strength may be helpful. This may be achieved through measuring mouth pressures or sniff testing.

Key point
It is important to monitor respiratory function of patients with acute neurological illnesses (Guillain–Barré syndrome / myasthenia gravis) closely. They may require 4-hourly monitoring of FEV$_1$.

Other – complications such as polycythaemia and right heart failure / cor pulmonale should be assessed in patients with established respiratory failure secondary to chest wall disease.

Management
Management of chest wall and neuromuscular disease is largely supportive. There are specific interventions for some of the underlying neurological disorders, which may impact on respiratory function.

Patients may require supplemental oxygen therapy or management with non-invasive ventilation. Surgical options are limited.

2.11 Complications of respiratory disease

2.11.1 Chronic respiratory failure

Aetiology

In health, the arterial partial pressure of carbon dioxide ($PaCO_2$) is maintained within a narrow range by adjusting alveolar ventilation to match the fluctuating rate of carbon dioxide production. Respiratory failure results from a disorder in which lung function is inadequate for the metabolic requirements of the individual. It can be classified into two types:

> Type I respiratory failure: this is characterised by a low PaO_2 (<8 kPa) and normal or low $PaCO_2$. It is mainly due to diseases that affect lung parenchyma with hypoxaemia due to right-to-left shunts or ventilation/ perfusion mismatch. Such conditions include pneumonia, pulmonary oedema, acute respiratory distress syndrome, fibrosing alveolitis and pulmonary embolism (PE).

> Type II respiratory failure: also called ventilatory failure, this is characterised by a low PaO_2 and a high $PaCO_2$. This occurs when alveolar ventilation is insufficient to excrete the carbon dioxide produced by tissue metabolism. The most common conditions include chronic obstructive pulmonary disease (COPD), obesity, chest wall disorders, respiratory muscle weakness and depression of the respiratory centre.

Both types of respiratory failure may be acute or chronic, depending on the speed of their development.

Inadequate ventilation occurring acutely will result in a low PaO_2 and a rising $PaCO_2$, which will result in the lowering of blood pH (respiratory acidosis). A chronically raised $PaCO_2$ is compensated for by the renal retention of bicarbonate and as a result the pH returns towards normal (compensated type II failure). This can be called

chronic respiratory failure (CRF), which can be the end result of any chronic lung disease.

Assessment of patients with chronic respiratory failure

Patients with CRF may have one or more of the following features:

> use of accessory muscles of respiration

> tachypnoea

> tachycardia

> sweating

> pulsus paradox

> inability to speak

> signs of carbon dioxide retention (bounding pulse, headaches, peripheral vasodilatation, flapping tremor of the outstretched hands, confusion, drowsiness and papilloedema).

Investigations

An arterial blood gas measurement will establish the diagnosis, but it is essential to arrange appropriate tests to find an underlying cause if this is not apparent. These include chest radiograph, lung function testing, high-resolution CT scan and (in selected cases) ultrasound of the diaphragm.

Treatment

> treat underlying disorder

> controlled oxygen therapy (see Section 2.12.1)

> non-invasive ventilation (see Section 2.12.3).

2.11.2 Cor pulmonale

This is defined as enlargement of the right ventricle (dilatation and/or hypertrophy) due to increased right ventricular afterload from diseases of the lungs, chest wall or ventilation control centre. Right ventricular failure is not necessary for a diagnosis of cor

pulmonale. Primary diseases of the pulmonary circulation (eg chronic pulmonary thromboembolism, vasculitis and idiopathic pulmonary arterial hypertension) are included by some, but in the Medical Masterclass are discussed in the *Cardiology* book.

Physiology

The pulmonary circulation lies between the right ventricle and the left side of the heart. It carries deoxygenated blood, which takes part in gas exchange in the lungs. Blood flow through the pulmonary circulation depends on the left ventricle and respiratory movements (the negative intrathoracic pressure during inspiration sucks blood into the pulmonary circulation, while the positive pressure on expiration pushes it forwards). The right ventricle acts as a pump only when there is obstruction to pulmonary blood flow.

Cor pulmonale is due to an increase in right ventricular afterload that occurs secondary to an increase in pulmonary artery pressure (pulmonary arterial hypertension (PAH)).

Pathophysiology

Hypoxic vasoconstriction is the most common cause of PAH. Hypoxia may be episodic as seen in obstructive sleep apnoea (OSA), or chronic as seen in many other chronic lung conditions. Once PAH is present, there is an increase in right ventricular workload to maintain an adequate cardiac output. PAH may be worsened by the increase in blood viscosity that accompanies polycythaemia, which in turn is due to hypoxaemia. It may also occur in some people who live at high altitudes and is known as chronic mountain sickness (Monge's disease).

Clinical presentation

The symptoms of PAH are non-specific in the early stages of the disease and may not be apparent for months or even years. As the disease progresses, symptoms become more noticeable. They include:

> general – fatigue

> respiratory – dyspnoea (initially on exertion), cough, haemoptysis

> cardiac – presyncope or syncope on exertion (due to the inability to increase cardiac output during exercise), chest pain (may be due to ventricular ischaemia), leg swelling, palpitations

> hoarseness of the voice – a rare complication due to compression of the left recurrent laryngeal nerve by the dilated pulmonary artery

> right upper quadrant abdominal pain and jaundice – can be seen in advanced cases due to passive hepatic congestion.

Examination

Check for:

> features of underlying conditions

> respiratory – cyanosis (central and peripheral), tachypnoea

> cardiac – distended neck veins with a prominent v wave (tricuspid regurgitation in right ventricular failure), left parasternal heave (due to right ventricular hypertrophy), ejection systolic murmur over the pulmonary area, pansystolic murmur at the left sternal edge (tricuspid regurgitation in right ventricular failure), splitting of the second heart sound with accentuation of the pulmonary component, pulsatile hepatomegaly, peripheral oedema.

Diagnosis

Perform the following to establish a case of cor pulmonale:

> full blood count (FBC) – may show polycythaemia

> electrocardiogram (ECG) – may show right axis deviation, P pulmonale, rhythm disturbances and right bundle block

> arterial blood gases

> lung function tests

> imaging – chest radiograph; high-resolution CT-scan (HRCT), CT pulmonary angiography (if recurrent pulmonary embolism is suspected)

> overnight testing – pulse oximetry may demonstrate nocturnal hypoxaemia; polysomnography if OSA is suspected.

Treatment

> specific – treat the underlying condition (COPD, DPLD, etc)

> general – maximise oxygenation; diuresis (but note that patients may depend on high right-sided pressures to sustain cardiac output); consider preventative anticoagulation, even if the PAH is not caused by thromboembolism.

2.12 Treatments in respiratory disease

2.12.1 Domiciliary oxygen therapy

Blood returning to the heart from the tissues has a low PO_2 and travels to the lungs via the pulmonary arteries. The pulmonary arteries form pulmonary capillaries, which surround alveoli. Oxygen diffuses from the high pressure in the alveoli to the area of lower pressure of the blood in the pulmonary capillaries. After oxygenation blood moves into the pulmonary veins which return to the left side of the heart to be pumped to the systemic tissues. In a 'perfect lung' the PO_2 of pulmonary venous blood would be equal to the PO_2 in the alveolus. Three factors may cause the PO_2 in the pulmonary veins to be less than the alveolar PO_2:

> Ventilation/perfusion mismatch: in a 'perfect lung' all alveoli would receive an equal share of alveolar ventilation and the pulmonary capillaries that surround different alveoli would

receive an equal share of cardiac output (ventilation and perfusion would be perfectly matched). Diseased lungs may have a marked mismatch between ventilation and perfusion. Some alveoli are relatively over-ventilated while others are relatively over-perfused (the most extreme form of this is a shunt).

> Shunt: occurs when deoxygenated venous blood from the body passes unventilated alveoli to enter the pulmonary veins and the systemic arterial system with an unchanged PO_2.

> Slow diffusion: in the normal lung, the diffusion of oxygen into the blood is very rapid and is complete, even if the cardiac output is increased (exercise) and the blood spends less time in contact with the alveolus. This may not happen when the alveolar capillary network is abnormal (if there is lung fibrosis and emphysema).

Domiciliary oxygen therapy has the aim of correcting hypoxia while maintaining the $PaCO_2$ and subsequently the pH within an acceptable range. The advantages of domiciliary oxygen therapy are:

> Increased survival: two studies have established a place for prolonged oxygen treatment in the management of COPD: the British Medical Research Council trial, which evaluated oxygen for 15 hours/day versus no oxygen, and the National Institutes of Health nocturnal oxygen therapy trial (NIH NOT Trial), which compared 12 versus 24 hours of oxygen/day. Both studies showed a survival benefit in selected patients with cor pulmonale. In addition, the NIH NOT Trial showed better survival in patients with continuous oxygen therapy as compared with nocturnal oxygen therapy only.

> Reduction in haematocrit: this leads to improved pulmonary and systemic blood flow.

> Neuropsychological improvement.

Indications for long-term oxygen therapy

> chronic hypoxaemia due to COPD, chronic asthma, DPLD, bronchiectasis, pulmonary vascular disease, CF, idiopathic pulmonary arterial hypertension, pulmonary malignancy and heart failure

> nocturnal hypoventilation due to obesity, neuromuscular disease, chest wall disorders and obstructive sleep apnoea (OSA)

> palliative use.

Patient selection

The need of oxygen therapy should be assessed in:

> all patients with cyanosis

> patients with polycythaemia

> patients with cor pulmonale (oedema)

> in COPD, patients with a forced expiratory volume in 1 second (FEV_1) is <30% of predicted.

All patients should be on optimum medical treatment prior to assessment for long-term oxygen therapy (LTOT).

LTOT is indicated in patients with:

> daytime PaO_2 of <7.3 kPa on two occasions, 3 weeks apart during a period of clinical stability

> daytime PaO_2 between 7.3 kPa and 8 kPa, in the presence of cor pulmonale (oedema), polycythaemia or nocturnal hypoxaemia (SaO_2 <90% for more than 30% of the time).

Once a patient fulfils the criteria for LTOT, the appropriate flow rate that can achieve a PaO_2 above 7.3 kPa should be determined by checking the arterial blood gases on oxygen. Most patients in the NIH NOT Trial needed 1–2 L of oxygen/minute delivered by nasal cannulae. Patients will need an additional 1 L of oxygen during exercise and while sleeping.

Ambulatory oxygen

All patients with chronic lung disorders should be assessed for ambulatory oxygen requirement. The 6-minute walk test is a simple and widely used stress test that makes it possible to evaluate the functional status of patients with lung disorders and their ability to carry out activities of daily living. The test measures the distance walked on a flat surface in 6 minutes and requires a constant level of effort, similar to that needed by the patient to carry out activities of daily living. The test has also been used to assess exercise-induced desaturation.

The American Thoracic Society guidelines for domiciliary oxygen state that 'ambulatory O_2 should be prescribed to patients normoxaemic at rest with evidence of exertional desaturation to 88% or less'. Short-term ambulatory oxygen is associated with significant improvements in health-related quality of life. Ambulatory oxygen can be prescribed in three groups of patients:

> patients on LTOT who are mobile and need to / can leave the home on a regular basis

> patients on LTOT who are housebound and unable to leave the home unaided, but may use ambulatory oxygen for short, intermittent periods only

> patients without chronic hypoxaemia but who show evidence of arterial oxygen desaturation on exercise.

Short-burst oxygen therapy

Short-burst oxygen therapy, usually provided from cylinders, is commonly prescribed for patients who do not fit the criteria for LTOT but remain breathless after minimal exertion. Its use either before or after exercise is probably of no benefit for most patients with moderately severe COPD who exercise for more than a very short period of time.

Modes of administration of oxygen

> oxygen cylinders

> oxygen concentrator

> portable small lightweight cylinders for ambulatory oxygen delivering liquid oxygen.

2.12.2 Continuous positive airways pressure

Continuous positive airways pressure (CPAP) is delivered by a machine that delivers a constant pressure to the airway, via a tube and a mask, thus acting as a pneumatic splint preventing upper airway collapse. Colin Sullivan introduced it in the early 1980s for the treatment of OSA, before which the treatment of choice was tracheostomy. The pressure delivered can be titrated to achieve adequate upper airway patency. The interface delivering the pressure can be nasal, full face or nasal pillows. The advantage of the nasal pillow is that no headgear is needed to keep it in place. If needed, oxygen can be delivered via the CPAP.

Indications for continuous positive airways pressure

Obstructive sleep apnoea

The treatment of choice for OSA is nasal CPAP. This prevents the nocturnal collapse of the upper airway that occurs at night (causing apnoea and hypopnoea), thus preventing sleep fragmentation and daytime somnolence. The pressure needed to achieve this can be titrated by repeating sleep studies on CPAP. However, autotitrating machines are now available, thus avoiding repeated sleep studies.

Neuromuscular diseases

Inspiratory upper airway collapse can complicate neuromuscular diseases affecting the chest wall, but CPAP can prevent these episodes of upper airway collapse. CPAP also prevents atelectasis in neuromuscular and chest wall diseases, hence nasal CPAP should be considered in such patients with type I respiratory failure.

Paralysed hemidiaphragm

CPAP can prevent the flail action of a paralysed hemidiaphragm and thus improve the efficiency of inspiration.

Other pulmonary conditions

CPAP may be indicated in any pulmonary disorder that results in severe oxygenation abnormalities (a fraction of inspired oxygen greater than 0.6 is needed to maintain a PaO_2 greater than 60 mmHg) in the presence of a normal $PaCO_2$.

Pulmonary oedema

CPAP in patients with severe cardiogenic pulmonary oedema can result in early physiologic improvement and reduce the need for intubation and mechanical ventilation.

Central sleep apnoea

Up to 50% of patients with severe heart failure (ejection fraction <45%) suffer from nocturnal central sleep apnoea, presenting with daytime somnolence and paroxysmal nocturnal dyspnoea. These patients have increased morbidity in comparison with patients who have congestive cardiac failure without central sleep apnoea. CPAP can help relieve their daytime symptoms.

Complications

> dry nose, nosebleeds and sore throat

> nasal congestion, runny nose and sneezing

> irritation of the eyes and the skin on the face

> abdominal bloating

> headaches

> leaks around the mask because it does not fit properly.

2.12.3 Non-invasive ventilation

Respiratory failure results from an imbalance between the capacity of the 'ventilatory apparatus' (including respiratory centre, spinal cord, intercostal nerves, chest wall, bronchi and lungs) and the load placed upon it. This imbalance can be acute or chronic. In acute respiratory failure leading to respiratory acidosis, some form of transient ventilatory support is needed while medical therapy corrects the insult.

Non-invasive ventilation (NIV) is the delivery of ventilatory support without the need for an invasive artificial airway. It has a role in the management of acute or chronic respiratory failure in many patients, and may have a role for some patients with heart failure. NIV can often eliminate the need for intubation or tracheostomy, and preserve normal swallowing, speech and cough mechanisms. There are two types of NIV: non-invasive positive pressure ventilation (NIPPV) or negative pressure ventilation.

Non-invasive positive pressure ventilation

Non-invasive positive pressure ventilation (NIPPV) is usually delivered nasally or via a face mask, thereby eliminating the need for intubation or tracheostomy. It can be administered in a volume-controlled or pressure-controlled manner. A bi-level positive airway pressure device is used, which delivers different pressures during inspiration (inspiratory positive airway pressure (IPAP)) and expiration (expiratory positive airway pressure (EPAP)). Volume ventilators are often not tolerated because they generate high inspiratory pressures that result in discomfort and mouth leaks. Although positive-pressure support is usually well tolerated by patients, mouth leaks or other difficulties are sometimes encountered. Supplementary oxygen can be given via the mask.

Negative pressure ventilation

This can be provided by devices such as the iron lung, tortoise shell or cuirass. The concept of mechanical ventilation first evolved with negative pressure ventilation. In the late 1920s, Philip Drinker introduced negative pressure ventilation and popularised the iron lung. He maintained an 8-year-old girl with acute poliomyelitis on artificial respiration continuously for 122 hours. The polio epidemics of the 1930s, 1940s and 1950s led to the development of pulmonary medicine as a specialty and the iron lung as a workhorse. Ventilators delivering negative pressure ventilation fell out of favour as the use of NIPPV increased during the 1960s, primarily due to an improvement in anaesthetic procedures.

Negative pressure ventilators support ventilation by lowering the pressure surrounding the chest wall during inspiration and reversing the pressure to atmospheric level during expiration, thereby augmenting the tidal volume by generating negative extrathoracic pressure. Body ventilators and iron lungs either cover the whole body below the neck, or apply negative pressure to the thorax and abdomen.

Studies of body ventilators have shown benefit in patients with COPD, neuromuscular disease and chest wall deformities who develop acute respiratory failure, but prospective and controlled studies are lacking. In chronic respiratory failure resulting from chest wall, neuromuscular or central hypoventilation, several uncontrolled studies reported benefits of intermittent negative pressure ventilation, but no benefit was demonstrated in patients with stable but severe COPD.

Because of their awkward size and their tendency to cause upper airway obstructions in some patients, negative pressure ventilators are not readily acceptable and NIPPV is the modality of choice for NIV.

Mechanism of action

NIPPV decreases the work of breathing and the IPAP improves alveolar ventilation while simultaneously resting the respiratory musculature, which helps in blowing out carbon dioxide. It also prevents atelectasis and hence recruits alveoli in gas exchange.

Externally applied EPAP decreases the work of breathing by partially overcoming the auto-positive end-expiratory pressure, which is frequently present in these patients. Patients therefore have to generate a less negative inspiratory force to initiate a breathing cycle.

Indications

Acute respiratory failure leading to respiratory acidosis

Acute respiratory failure with respiratory acidosis (pH<7.35 with a raised $PaCO_2$) may be due to exacerbation of COPD, cystic fibrosis (CF) or bronchiectasis, or pulmonary oedema or pneumonia.

Chronic respiratory failure

Patients with neuromuscular and chest wall diseases, obesity hypoventilation syndrome, OSA with hypoventilation, COPD with hypoventilation or any other respiratory disorder with hypoventilation, may not be able to breathe out carbon dioxide normally, causing respiratory acidosis. Initially this occurs during the night and can be detected by overnight transcutaneous carbon dioxide monitoring. A 7am arterial blood gas analysis is helpful as it reflects nocturnal gas exchange. Nocturnal NIPPV can improve their gas exchange and symptoms. With disease progression, their need for NIPPV will increase.

Contraindications

> respiratory arrest

> inability to use a mask because of trauma or surgery

> excessive secretions

> haemodynamic instability or life-threatening arrhythmia

> high risk of aspiration

> impaired mental status

> a non-cooperative or agitated patient

> life-threatening refractory hypoxaemia.

Complications

> ulceration of the nasal bridge due to a tight mask – this can be avoided by choosing the correct size mask and applying gel foam at pressure points

> gastric distension

> hypotension

> barotrauma.

Practical details

If NIPPV is indicated, it should be started as soon as possible because respiratory acidosis worsens with time. Prior to starting this treatment on someone with acute respiratory failure, a plan should be made for whether the patient will be a candidate for intubation and mechanical ventilation if NIPPV fails. If so, the ICU team should be informed as soon as possible.

The initial IPAP and EPAP should be set up as per the hospital guidelines.

Once NIPPV is started, measurement of arterial blood gases (ABG) should be repeated in approximately 1 hour (earlier if there is clinical deterioration). If there is an improvement, treatment should continue on the same inspiratory and expiratory pressures. If $PaCO_2$ is increasing, IPAP can be increased to help blow it out.

If the ABG is improving, they should be checked at increasing intervals. Once the acidosis is corrected, the NIPPV can be stopped. However, if this occurs in late evening, it will be prudent to continue the NIPPV overnight and stop it next morning.

Always remember to optimise medical treatment for the underlying condition.

Though NIPPV may be effective in respiratory acidosis due to exacerbation of asthma, such patients should be managed in an ICU with access to immediate intubation.

2.13 Lung transplantation

Lung transplantation is a potential treatment for end-stage lung disease of many causes. The most common underlying illness resulting in lung transplantation is CF, followed by pulmonary fibrosis and then pulmonary arterial hypertension. Patients are considered if they are limited by shortness of breath in activities of daily living and have an estimated 2-year survival of <50%.

Referral criteria

Age – there is no arbitrary age cut off, but as a general guideline patients who are younger than 65 years will be considered for single lung transplants, younger than 60 years for a double lung transplant, and younger than 55 years for a heart–lung transplant.

Other – patients should have good rehabilitation potential and (importantly) a good psychosocial support network. They should be ambulatory and of average body weight (body mass index (BMI) normal range 18–25).

Specific – these exist for CF/bronchiectasis, chronic obstructive pulmonary disease (COPD), pulmonary fibrosis and pulmonary arterial hypertension (PAH).

Contraindications

These include untreatable second organ failure (renal disease with an estimated glomerular filtration rate (eGFR) <50 mL/min, coronary artery disease, left ventricular failure), non-curable extra-pulmonary infections (HIV, hepatitis B / hepatitis C), malignancy within the past 5 years (except for certain skin tumours), or indicators of poor compliance (substance abuse including tobacco smoking in the past 6 months, documented non-compliance, untreatable psychiatric illness interfering with compliance).

Relative contraindications

These include age above the threshold, chronic conditions with end organ failure (hypertension, diabetes mellitus), osteoporosis, severe gastro-oesophageal reflux, steroid use of >15 mg prednisolone/day and weight outside the BMI of 18–25. Pulmonary infections with specific organisms also have worse outcomes than those without, something that is of particular importance in CF patients.

Outcomes

Receiving a lung transplant may sometimes be perceived as replacing one illness with another, albeit a less severe one. Patients receive immunosuppressive treatment and prophylactic antimicrobial cover. Mean 1-year survival is around 80%, and 50% 5-year survival is quoted to patients.

Complications

Complications arising after lung transplant are principally due to the immune responses and immunosuppression, and the difficult balance between maintaining a functioning immune system and preventing complications from immunosuppressive therapies or rejection.

Rejection

This can occur in three stages: hyperacute, acute and chronic. Hyperacute rejection is IgG mediated and occurs within minutes of transplant. Acute rejection is due to cell-mediated rejection and occurs up to 3 months post-transplant. It is managed by increasing immunosuppression and steroids. Chronic rejection is a slow process that occurs over years through the development of bronchiolitis obliterans, which affects most lung transplants over the years and is a considerable management challenge.

Infection

Due to immunosuppression and disrupted lung defences (reduced mucus clearance, reduced cough reflex, loss of lymphatic drainage), patients are at increased risk of infection following lung transplant. Bacterial pneumonias, especially those caused by Gram-negative bacteria, account for most postoperative infection, but viral pneumonias (eg caused by cytomegalovirus (CMV)), fungal pneumonias and *Pneumocystis jirovecii* infection also occur. Patients typically receive antimicrobial prophylaxis to prevent infections.

Other

The reduced immune response may also manifest itself in the development of cancers. Among these, lymphoproliferative disorders are particularly common after lung transplant. Other complications are due to the long-term side effects of immunosuppressive (and antimicrobial) treatments and include renal dysfunction, osteoporosis and hypertension.

3 Investigations and practical procedures

3.1 Arterial blood gas sampling

Principle

To measure the oxygen and carbon dioxide tensions and acid–base status of arterial blood.

Indications

Arterial blood gas (ABG) sampling was a research procedure until the mid-1960s. It is now widely performed, either by direct arterial puncture or from indwelling arterial lines. Indications include:

> respiratory failure (type I or II)

> renal failure

> hepatic failure

> cardiac failure

> drug intoxication (aspirin and narcotics)

> endogenous acid overproduction (ketoacidosis or lactic acidosis)

> severe illness, cause unknown.

Contraindications

Care should be taken in the presence of bleeding disorders. Renal physicians will be appropriately unimpressed if an ABG sample is taken from an arteriovenous fistula.

Important information for patients

The procedure should be explained to the patient. The possibility of requiring more than one attempt should be mentioned.

Practical details

Before the investigation
The patient should be lying or sitting comfortably and an appropriate site selected. The radial artery of the non-dominant arm is most commonly used, but the brachial or femoral arteries can be used. Make sure you have enough sterile gauze to apply immediate pressure after the procedure.

The investigation

> Clean the skin over the wrist with an antiseptic solution. Palpate the artery between the tips of the forefinger and the middle finger of one hand.

> Holding it between your fingers, introduce the needle (with the heparinised syringe attached) at an angle of 45°, and slowly advance the needle along the line of the artery. On puncturing the artery, a small spurt of blood entering the syringe will be seen.

> Withdraw 3–4 mL of blood and press a sterile dressing over the site of puncture.

> Expel any air bubbles and cap the syringe. The syringe should be labelled and sent to the lab immediately on ice if a blood gas machine is not available at the 'bedside'.

The role of local anaesthesia remains controversial. Although used by some, especially in paediatric practice, skilled operators maintain that it adds unnecessary complexity to the procedure.

After the investigation
It is best if an assistant or the patient can apply direct pressure for the required minimum 5 minutes.

Complications

In practice, complications are rare but include:

> haematoma

> arterial spasm leading to distal ischaemia

> nerve damage:

> the femoral nerve lies lateral to the femoral artery

> the median nerve lies medial to the brachial artery.

3.2 Pleural procedures

General points

Pleural procedures should be performed only by suitably trained individuals and in an appropriate clinical area under sterile conditions. It is best to avoid doing pleural procedures out of hours unless the clinical situation requires urgent intervention.

Ultrasound is of little practical use in guiding procedures for pneumothorax.

Key point

Drainage of pleural fluid

The use of ultrasound to guide any pleural procedure for the purposes of draining fluid should be considered mandatory, except in exceptional circumstances. This should be performed at the bedside at the time of the procedure: distant 'X marks the spot' ultrasound marking is not recommended as the complication rate from this is equivalent to a blind, non-ultrasound-guided procedure.

3.2.1 Indications for pleural procedures

3.2.1.1 Diagnostic aspirations

Pleural aspiration of up to 50 mL of fluid is utilised for diagnostic evaluation of unilateral pleural effusions.

3.2.1.2 Therapeutic aspirations

Pleural effusion – therapeutic aspiration of up to a maximum of 1.5 L of fluid is usually sufficient to relieve acute breathlessness in patients with pleural effusions. Aspiration, rather than insertion of a chest drain, should be considered the first line in patients who do not have suspected pleural infection and do not need a drain for other reasons (see Section 3.2.1.3). It is also preferable out of hours, when chest drain insertion is best avoided unless necessary.

Pneumothorax – therapeutic aspiration is used in patients with symptomatic pneumothorax, and should be considered the first line in symptomatic patients with spontaneous primary pneumothorax of any size. No more than 2.5 L of air should be aspirated before reassessment with a chest radiograph.

3.2.1.3 Chest drain insertion

A chest drain should be inserted in the following instances:

> empyema and complicated parapneumonic effusions

> traumatic haemo/pneumothorax

> during surgery in certain instances (video-assisted thoracoscopic surgery (VATS), thoracotomy, oesophagectomy, cardiac surgery)

> malignant effusions for the purpose of talc pleurodesis.

Chest drains should be inserted for patients with pneumothorax in the following situations:

> in any ventilated patient

> in tension pneumothorax after initial needle decompression

> persistent or recurrent pneumothorax after initial aspiration

> secondary pneumothorax

> traumatic pneumothorax

> bilateral pneumothoraces.

A pneumothorax in a patient over 50 years old with a significant smoking history should be treated as a secondary pneumothorax.

3.2.2 Pleural procedures, common features

Consent

Full consent should be obtained for patients, with documented written consent for chest drains. The risks of pleural procedures are as follows.

Risks of pleural aspirations

> pain

> failure of procedure

> pneumothorax (about 3% with ultrasound guidance, 5–15% without ultrasound guidance)

> visceral injury, haemothorax, pleural infection (rare).

Risks of chest drain insertion

> pain

> pneumothorax (5%)

> bleeding/haemothorax (2%)

> intrapleural infection (2%)

> drain dislodgement or blockage (15%)

> organ puncture (rare)

> failure of procedure.

Patient position

There are two usual positions for a patient to be sat for a pleural procedure (Fig 30). Providing there is sufficient depth of fluid visible on ultrasound, an alternative is with the patient lying flat in the lateral position with arms up in front of the face.

Site of needle insertion

The site of needle insertion should ideally be within the triangle of safety to minimise the risk to underlying structures and reduce the risk of visible scarring (Fig 31). Alternatively, the second intercostal space in the

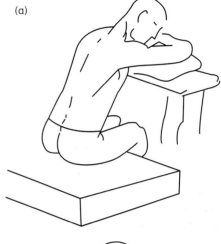

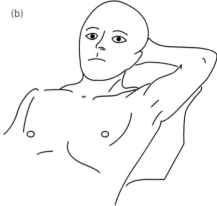

Fig 30 Positioning of the patient for a pleural procedure. **(a)** Upright position while leaning forwards with arms resting on a table or bed. **(b)** Lying on the bed while slightly rotated with the arm on the side of the lesion behind the patient's head.

midclavicular line may be used in the case of pneumothorax.

A posterior approach may be used for drainage of fluid under ultrasound guidance. However, inserting the needle more posteriorly gives greater risk of damage to the intercostal artery, hence this must be avoided (Fig 32).

Anaesthetising the pleura

Achieving good anaesthesia of the pleura is an essential skill for anyone undertaking pleural procedures. The parietal pleura is richly innervated and is the main source of pain during pleural

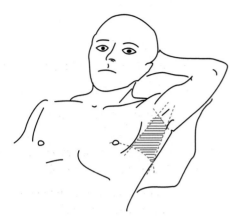

Fig 31 The triangle of safety is bordered by the lateral edge of latissimus dorsi, the lateral border of pectoralis major and superior to the fifth intercostal space.

Fig 32 When using a posterior approach the needle should be inserted lateral to the angle of the rib posteriorly (at least 10 cm from the spine).

puncture. Liberal use of 1% lignocaine is recommended.

> First anaesthetise the skin using a 26G needle.

> Next use an 18G needle to inject lignocaine into the subcutaneous tissues more deeply, onto the periosteum of the superior border of the underlying rib and into the intercostal muscles.

> While maintaining suction on the needle, slowly advance until air/fluid is aspirated. The tip of the needle is now just inside the pleural space.

> Withdraw the needle slightly until air/fluid can no longer be aspirated. The tip of the needle is now lying just outside the parietal pleura.

> Inject several millilitres of lignocaine onto the parietal pleura.

3.2.3 Pleural aspiration

Diagnostic pleural aspiration is usually performed with a small-bore needle that is similar in size to the needle used to infiltrate lignocaine, hence the use of lignocaine prior to the procedure is not routinely necessary (dependent on operator and patient preference).

Local anaesthesia should be utilised when performing therapeutic pleural aspiration.

Important points to consider when performing pleural aspiration are:

> Ultrasound guidance for all fluid aspirates is strongly advised.

> Ensure the patient is in an appropriate position.

> Use a small-bore needle to reduce the risk of complications.

> Insert the needle above the superior border of the rib to avoid the neurovascular bundle.

> For diagnostic aspirations, 50 mL of fluid is sufficient.

> For therapeutic aspirations:

> > After confirming the depth of the pleural space using initial needle aspiration, the cannula should be advanced into the chest while aspirating continuously until the pleura is breached and air or fluid is withdrawn.

> > Attach the cannula to a three-way tap to enable easy expulsion of fluid or air. This can be attached to an intravenous giving set, although

many clinicians now use dedicated pleural aspiration kits.

> Stop when no more air/fluid can be withdrawn *or* 1.5 L has been withdrawn *or* until the patient develops symptoms of cough / chest discomfort.

3.2.4 Chest drain insertion

Chest drain insertion is painful, hence premedication with opioids and benzodiazepines should be considered. It is essential to achieve good local anaesthesia of the chest wall and pleura.

Small-bore (12–18F) drains inserted using the Seldinger technique are adequate in most situations, including pleural effusion, pneumothorax and empyema.

Large-bore, blunt dissection chest drains should be used in cases of haemothorax/ trauma, or if there is a risk of lung perforation with the Seldinger technique (ie where the lung is tethered close to the chest wall), or in cases of severe surgical emphysema / large air leak.

Important points to consider are as follows.

Before the procedure

> Written consent should be obtained for all chest drains.

> Use direct ultrasound guidance for pleural effusions.

> Ensure the patient is in the appropriate position and is provided with appropriate analgesia.

During the procedure

> The procedure should be carried out with full aseptic technique (including gown, sterile drapes, mask, sterile field and sterile gloves).

> Insert drain above the superior border of the rib to avoid the neurovascular bundle.

> Before fully inserting the drain, fluid (or air in the case of pneumothorax) from the site of drain insertion should

be obtained. If no fluid (or air) can be drained, the procedure should be abandoned.

> For drains inserted with the Seldinger technique:

>> It is imperative that the wire is not left inside the chest cavity.

>> The dilator should not be inserted further than 1 cm beyond the depth from skin to pleural space. The marker on the dilator should be set to the correct depth needed to access the pleural space, as determined with the introducer needle.

> Drains should never be inserted with substantial force.

After the procedure

> Do not drain more than 1.5 L of fluid at a time. A suitable regime for rate of drainage should be provided by the doctor inserting the drain – a typical recommendation would be to drain 1–1.5 L, clamp for 4 hours, drain 1 L, clamp for 4 hours, then repeat.

> Obtain a chest radiograph to check the position of the drain.

> Underwater seal system – always maintain the level of water above the bottom of the tube in the system; the bottle should be kept below the level of the chest.

> Check daily if the drain is draining, bubbling or swinging.

> **!** **Hazard**
> Never clamp a bubbling chest drain as there is a risk of tension pneumothorax.

3.3 Flexible bronchoscopy

Principle

Fibre-optic bronchoscopy allows inspection of the bronchial tree, sampling of bronchial and alveolar fluids for microscopy and culture, and the biopsy of the bronchial mucosa, abnormal lesions, or (by transbronchial biopsy) alveolar tissue. In specialist centres it can also be used therapeutically for the removal of foreign bodies or the administration of treatments for asthma, chronic obstructive pulmonary disease (COPD) and thoracic malignancy. When performed using a bronchoscope equipped with endobronchial ultrasound (EBUS) it can permit fine needle aspiration of mediastinal and hilar lymph nodes for the diagnosis of granulomatous disease and the combined diagnosis and staging of thoracic malignancy.

Indications

Diagnostic

> evaluate lung lesions seen on a chest radiograph

> assess airway patency

> investigate unexplained haemoptysis

> search for the origin of suspicious or positive sputum cytology

> obtain specimens for microbiological examination in suspected infections

> evaluate a suspected tracheoesophageal fistula

> evaluate the airways for a suspected bronchial tear after thoracic trauma

> determine the extent of respiratory injury after the inhalation of noxious fumes or aspiration of gastric juice.

Therapeutic

> remove foreign bodies

> remove secretions or mucous plugs

> perform difficult intubations

> bronchial thermoplasty in the treatment of asthma

> insertion of endobronchial valves or coils for the treatment of COPD

> debulking of endobronchial tumour in lung cancer or endobronchial metastasis

> insertion of self-expanding metallic airway stents for the treatment of malignant central airway obstruction.

3.3.1 Transbronchial biopsy
Principle

To obtain diagnostic tissue, usually in cases of suspected diffuse parenchymal lung disease (DPLD).

Indications

Although the samples obtained are small and sometimes crushed, transbronchial biopsy achieves a high diagnostic yield in DPLDs that have centrilobular accentuation, such as granulomatous and metastatic diseases. These include:

> sarcoidosis: 75–89% diagnostic yield

> carcinoma: 64–68% diagnostic yield

> infection

> eosinophilic pneumonia

> alveolar proteinosis.

Complications

The risk of developing a pneumothorax is around 5%, although only a third of such patients then require pleural aspiration or drainage. Significant haemorrhage probably occurs in 2–5% of cases.

3.3.2 Endobronchial ultrasound and mediastinal lymph node biopsy

A small curvilinear ultrasound probe is attached to a modified flexible bronchoscope, allowing visualisation of mediastinal structures through the walls of the trachea, main and lobar bronchi. The technique is mainly used for sampling mediastinal lymph nodes in proven or suspected lung cancer, but it is also good for diagnosing tuberculosis or sarcoidosis where the mediastinal lymph nodes appear to offer the best site for biopsy. The technique can also biopsy extrabronchial masses in the mediastinum or lungs provided they are within 2 cm of the central airways. Samples are taken by fine needle aspiration, guided by real-time ultrasound.

3.4 Interpretation of clinical data

3.4.1 Arterial blood gases

What is measured

Key point

Whenever you take a set of blood gases, make sure that you clearly record the date, time, patient's name and their inspired concentration of oxygen. This is crucial for interpretation and comparison with other results: a PO_2 of 12 kPa is normal (normal range 11.3–12.6) if the patient is breathing air but grossly abnormal if they are on 60% oxygen!

Blood gas machines record various data (Table 40).

Many blood gas machines also give a value for base excess/deficit, which makes it easy to separate metabolic from respiratory causes of pH disturbance. Various algorithms are used

in these calculations, the principles being as follows.

> Predict the pH that would arise in normal blood in the presence of the PCO_2 actually measured. If the PCO_2 is high, then the predicted pH is low; if the PCO_2 is low, then the predicted pH is high.

> Calculate the amount of acid or base that would have to be added to the blood to change the predicted pH into the pH as actually measured. This is the base deficit/excess (in mmol/L) and a measure of the degree of 'metabolic', as opposed to 'respiratory', disturbance. A normal value is between −2 and +2.

If a particular blood gas machine does not provide the base deficit/excess, then a useful rule of thumb is as follows: in uncompensated metabolic disorders, the steady-state PCO_2 (measured in mmHg, where 1 kPa = 7.6 mmHg) should be numerically equal to the last two digits of the pH. For example, a normal PCO_2 is 5.3 kPa or 40 mmHg, and a normal pH is 7.40. If this picture is not observed, then either: the problem is not simply metabolic – there is a primary respiratory element to the acid–base disorder; or the metabolic change is very acute and respiratory compensation has not had time to develop (unlikely, because respiratory compensation is very rapid).

Interpreting results

The Alveolar–arterial oxygen (A–a) gradient

This is a very useful equation for assessing how well the lungs are working in terms of gas exchange, and therefore whether hypoxia is due to a problem within the lungs (eg ventilation/perfusion mismatch, right-to-left shunt, reduced diffusing capacity) or outside them (eg respiratory muscle weakness, coma). It is the difference between the partial pressures of oxygen in the alveoli and in the systemic arteries. The latter can be directly measured, but the former has to be estimated. The equation for the A–a gradient is:

> $PAO_2 - PaO_2 = (FiO_2(P_{atm} - P_{H2O}) - PaCO_2/0.8) - PaO_2$

For a subject breathing room air the equation is:

> $PAO_2 - PaO_2 = 20 - (PaCO_2/0.8 + PaO_2)$

The A–a gradient in normal subjects is less than 2 kPa, although this increases slowly with age so that for an 80-year-old a value of up to 3 is normal.

If hypoxia is caused purely by hypoventilation, for example following an opioid overdose, then the A–a gradient will remain normal, because the $PaCO_2$ will rise as the PaO_2 falls. By contrast, the $PaCO_2$ will be low in a patient with hypoxia due to impaired ventilation/perfusion (V/Q) matching.

Table 40	Measurements made by blood gas machines		
	Normal range		**Notes**
PO_2	>11.2 kPa (breathing air)		
pH	7.35–7.45		
H^+	35–45 nmol/L		
PCO_2	4.7–6.0 kPa		Respiratory failure = PO_2 <8 kPa, with PCO_2 <6.5 kPa = Type I PCO_2 >6.5 kPa = Type II
HCO_3^-	21–29 mmol/L		The plasma bicarbonate is not measured by the machine but calculated from the pH and PCO_2

Abnormalities of PO₂
Low PO₂

Because it is not possible to specify the precise concentration of oxygen that a patient receives, unless they are intubated and ventilated, normal values for PO_2 cannot be quoted for those breathing on 24%, 28% or other oxygen masks. As a very rough guide, the 'hypoxaemia score' can be calculated as follows:

> Hypoxaemia score = PO_2/FiO_2 (where FiO_2 is the fraction of oxygen inspired, in air 0.21).

If the patient were breathing air, then applying the lower limit of normal PO_2 (11.3 kPa) would give a score of 54, and the value of PO_2 taken conventionally to define hypoxia (8 kPa) would score 38. In assessing a patient breathing supplementary oxygen, a value of <38 is usually taken as indicating significant compromise.

High PO₂

Air has a PO_2 of 21 kPa. Allowing for the PCO_2, the highest PO_2 that can be achieved breathing air is around 15 kPa. If a value higher than this is obtained, then the patient must have been breathing supplementary oxygen.

Abnormalities of PCO₂
Low PCO₂

Hyperventilation may be:

> primary – most commonly caused by anxiety

> secondary – to metabolic acidosis (respiratory compensation), or when attempting to maintain normoxia (eg in pulmonary embolus, acute severe asthma, pneumonia).

Key point

How can you tell if the patient has a metabolic acidosis?

Look for reduction in pH and increased 'negative base excess', ie a base excess more negative than −2.

High PCO₂

Hypoventilation may be caused by problems with the respiratory (airway, lungs, respiratory muscles and chest wall) or neurological (central and neuropathic) components of respiration.

How can you tell if this is acute or chronic? In chronic carbon dioxide retention the bicarbonate (HCO_3^-) rises (secondary metabolic compensation) and the chloride falls.

Much more rarely a high PCO_2 is secondary to metabolic alkalosis, which would be known as respiratory compensation.

Key point

How can you tell if the patient has a metabolic alkalosis?

Look for elevation in pH and an increased 'base excess', ie a base excess more positive than +2.

Abnormalities of acid–base status
pH or H⁺?

Alterations in acid–base status can result from changes in PCO_2, bicarbonate concentration or both:

> Respiratory acidosis/alkalosis – means that the primary process affects PCO_2.

> Metabolic acidosis/alkalosis – means that the primary process affects bicarbonate.

> 'Mixed' disorders – arise as a result of more than one 'primary' process.

Whatever the primary process, it will usually be accompanied by secondary change in either PCO_2 or bicarbonate concentration, such that change in blood pH is minimised.

Putting the values for PCO_2, pH and bicarbonate for any particular patient onto the nomograms shown in Figs 33 and 34 will define the type of any acid–base disturbance, as is done by calculation of the base deficit/excess shown above.

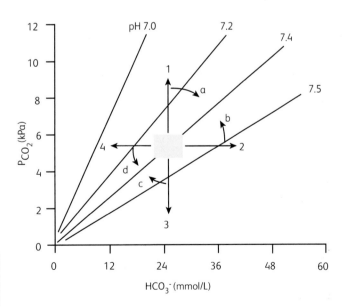

Fig 33 Nomogram showing relationships between PCO_2, pH and bicarbonate. Shaded area depicts normal range. Perturbations: **(1)** respiratory acidosis, with **(a)** secondary metabolic alkalosis; **(2)** metabolic alkalosis, with **(b)** secondary respiratory acidosis; **(3)** respiratory alkalosis, with **(c)** secondary metabolic acidosis; and **(4)** metabolic acidosis, with **(d)** secondary respiratory alkalosis.

3.4.2 Lung function tests

See Table 41.

Peak flow

This is a valuable guide to airway obstruction, but it is also influenced by patient aptitude and lung volume among other factors.

Spirometry

The vital capacity may be reduced by many disorders, but the forced expiratory volume in 1 second (FEV_1) is disproportionately reduced in obstructive conditions. This may be quantified from the FEV_1:forced vital capacity (FVC) ratio (Table 42 and Fig 35). This ratio is normally 80% (range 70–85%), although the 'normal ratio' tends to decline with age.

> A decreased ratio indicates an obstructive lung defect.

> A raised or normal ratio in the presence of a reduced FVC is suggestive of a restrictive defect, but this diagnosis can only be made definitively by measurement of total lung capacity (TLC).

Laboratory lung function

These tests can only be performed in a patient who is relatively well. They record lung volumes (TLC and residual volume (RV)), flow–volume loops and estimate the efficiency of gas transfer within the lung using carbon monoxide (carbon monoxide transfer factor (T_{LCO}) and transfer coefficient (K_{CO})). After looking at the FEV_1 and FVC, lung volumes are helpful in further interpretation of the underlying pathology.

Gas transfer

T_{LCO} and K_{CO} are measurements of gas diffusion across the alveolar membrane. K_{CO} is corrected for lung volume as $K_{CO} = T_{LCO}/Va$, where Va is the alveolar volume available for gas exchange. In the laboratory, carbon monoxide is used to calculate this diffusion capacity, hence the 'CO' after the terms.

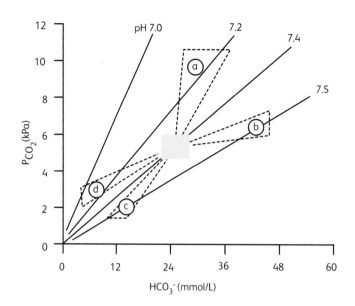

Fig 34 Relationships between PCO_2, pH and bicarbonate seen clinically in the four simple types of acid–base disturbance. Shaded area depicts normal range. Perturbations: **(a)** respiratory acidosis; **(b)** metabolic alkalosis; **(c)** respiratory alkalosis; and **(d)** metabolic acidosis.

Table 41	Definitions of lung function	
Abbreviation	**Meaning and units**	**Description**
PEF	Peak expiratory flow (L/s)	Maximum rate of expiratory airflow during maximum forced expiration
FEV_1	Forced expiratory volume in 1 second (L)	Volume of air expired during first second of a forced expiration
FVC	Forced vital capacity (L)	Volume of air expired by a forceful expiration after taking a full inflation
FEV_1:FVC	Ratio (%)	
TLC	Total lung capacity (L)	Total volume of air in the lungs after maximum inspiration
RV	Residual volume (L)	Volume of air remaining in the lung after a maximum expiration
FRC	Functional residual capacity (L)	Volume of air remaining in the lungs at the end of normal expiration without any muscle activity. The 'neutral point' of the respiratory system

Table 42	Causes of restrictive and obstructive lung defects	
Type of defect	**Spirometric pattern**	**Examples**
Restrictive	Increased FEV_1:FVC ratio	Pulmonary fibrosis, respiratory muscle weakness, obesity, pleural disease, chest wall and skeletal disorders
Obstructive	Decreased FEV_1:FVC ratio	COPD and asthma, tracheobronchomalacia

COPD, chronic obstructive pulmonary disease; FEV_1, forced expiratory volume in 1 second; FVC, forced vital capacity.

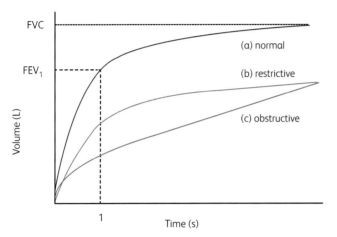

Fig 35 Spirometry curves for **(a)** a normal patient, **(b)** a patient with a restrictive lung defect and **(c)** a patient with an obstructive lung defect.

If you imagine the alveolar membrane in its healthy state as being thin and permeable, say like a sheet of tissue paper, any pathological process that causes it to become thickened and coarse will slow down the movement of carbon monoxide (or oxygen) from the lung into the bloodstream. Conversely, increased levels of blood and therefore haemoglobin, either in the bloodstream or in the alveoli, will cause an increase in the uptake of oxygen (Table 43).

Flow–volume loops

These measure the expiratory and inspiratory flow of air (L/s) against actual volume exhaled or inhaled.

The upper, expiratory curve starts with the patient at maximum/forced inhalation (TLC) and ends at residual volume (RV).

The curves have characteristic shapes according to the underlying disease process and whether the pathology is causing intra- or extrathoracic obstruction to the airflow, thus distorting the shape of the curve from the normal. The most important patterns are those of expiratory flow limitation (Fig 36).

3.4.3 Overnight oximetry

This relatively cheap and easy test can be used as a baseline investigation to

screen for possible sleep apnoea in patients who report disturbed sleep and/or daytime somnolence. The patient's SaO_2 is continuously recorded via a finger probe while they rest.

Analysis of the results looks for drops in the saturation (SaO_2) and the frequency of these events, which may represent episodes of apnoea (see Section 2.1.1). Patients with recurrent hypoxic episodes and/or large dips in their oxygen should be referred for formal assessment by a physician who is an expert in sleep disorders.

3.4.4 Chest radiograph

Before interpreting a chest radiograph check the name, date, side label and projection: usually posteroanterior (PA) or anteroposterior (AP). Then stand back and take a long hard look. Does anything strike you straight away? If so, fine, but do not ignore the rest. Always examine the various parts of a chest radiograph in a systematic manner. The following routine is suggested.

Check for patient rotation – this causes asymmetry of the soft tissue shadows and may produce apparent increased density in one lung or simulate mediastinal shift.

Tracheobronchial tree

Follow the trachea and main bronchi (study for displacement, narrowing or intraluminal masses). If the trachea is not central it may be pushed across by superior mediastinal mass (eg retrosternal goitre) or pulled over to the side of the lesion by fibrosis or collapsed lung.

Assess the mediastinal contour. Are there any abnormal shadows (tumour, goitre or paratracheal lymphadenopathy)?

Look at the position, outline and density of the hilar shadow. Displacement of the hila is common in collapse, fibrosis or resection of the lung. Enlarged and

Change in K_{CO}	Mechanism	Examples
Increased	Reduced alveolar volume Increased pulmonary capillary blood volume	Skeletal deformity, pleural disease and respiratory muscle weakness Left-to-right shunt, lung haemorrhage and polycythaemia
Reduced	Destruction of lung capillaries Impairment to diffusion by disease Reduced pulmonary capillary blood volume Reduced uptake by blood	Emphysema Fibrosing alveolitis Pulmonary vascular disease, pulmonary hypertension and right-to-left shunt Anaemia

Table 43 Causes of increased and decreased K_{CO}

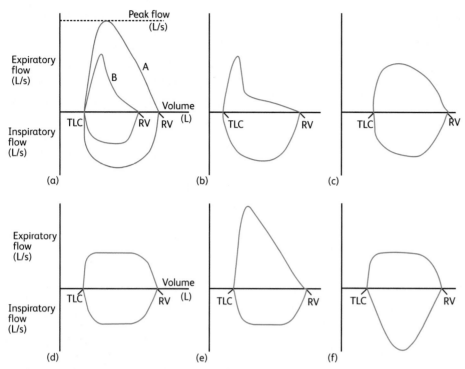

Fig 36 Flow–volume loops: **(a)** normal patient **(A)** and obstructive lung disease **(B)**, eg asthma or chronic obstructive pulmonary disease (COPD); **(b)** emphysema; **(c)** restrictive lung defect, eg pulmonary fibrosis; **(d)** fixed intrathoracic or extrathoracic obstruction, eg tracheal tumour; **(e)** variable extrathoracic obstruction, eg tracheal stenosis outside the thoracic cavity, works like a one-way valve, opening on expiration while collapsing on inspiration; and **(f)** variable intrathoracic obstruction. RV, residual volume; TLC, total lung capacity.

lobulated hila are characteristic of hilar adenopathy. Enlarged, but otherwise normal hila occur with dilatation of the pulmonary arteries. Unilateral enlargement of a pulmonary artery (distended by a thrombus) may be seen in massive embolism. Perihilar haze is an early sign of pulmonary oedema. Check whether both hilar shadows are of equal density; increased density of the hilum is the most common manifestation of a hilar mass – do not miss it!

Cardiac shadow

Is the heart size normal, enlarged or narrow (COPD)? Estimate the cardiothoracic ratio; the heart should fill less than half the thoracic width.

Follow the contours of the heart. Are all heart borders well defined?

> Right middle lobe collapse – hazy (blurred) right heart border.

> Lingular collapse – hazy left heart border.

> Right lower lobe collapse – the heart border is preserved, and there is an additional wedge-shaped density and a blurred medial diaphragm.

> Left lower lobe collapse – there is a wedge-shaped density behind the heart ('sail sign', or an apparent double heart border) that obscures the medial diaphragm, which is elevated.

Check the areas behind the heart. Do not miss hiatus hernia, tumour of the oesophagus or lung collapse.

Diaphragm

In full inspiration the mid-point of the right diaphragm lies at the level of the anterior end of the sixth rib. The dome of the right diaphragm is normally up to 1 cm higher than the left.

> Is the diaphragm elevated (suggesting paralysis, eventration or infrapulmonary effusion)?

> Are both diaphragms, the costophrenic angles and the cardiophrenic angles well defined? A blurring of the diaphragm indicates either pleural fluid or disease in the adjacent lung field. A minimal pleural effusion or pleural thickening obliterates the costophrenic angle.

> Is there any calcification over the diaphragm (this would indicate asbestos plaques)?

Soft tissues and bones

Abnormalities here may give a false impression of pulmonary disease and should be examined before analysing the lung fields.

> Look at the breast shadow (mastectomy produces ipsilateral hyperlucency – a 'blacker' lung).

> Examine the clavicles, ribs and scapula for evidence of metastasis (indicates lytic or sclerotic lesions) and fractures, old/new (suggests it is pathological). Turning the chest radiograph on its side (which is possible in most picture archiving and communication systems (PACS)) often helps you to study the ribs as it distracts the attention from everything else.

> Look for subcutaneous emphysema.

Pleura

Ignore the lung fields and take a good look around the edge of the lung at the pleura. Is it thickened (pleural plaques) or calcified? Do not miss a small pneumothorax (especially apical).

Lung fields

> Assess the size of the lungs: if they are small the problem could be poor inspiration, respiratory muscle weakness or fibrosis, whereas if they are large then this suggests COPD.

> Is the transradiancy of each zone equal? Compare the relative parts of the opposite lung to detect more subtle parenchymal changes. If there is any abnormally increased or decreased density, describe its location, size (localised or diffuse), shape (irregular, round, wedge-shaped or linear) and texture (reticulonodular or solid).

> Are all the pulmonary lobes and fissures intact or are they distorted (Fig 37)?

Key point

If any abnormality is identified on a chest radiograph, compare its appearance with that on previous films. The sequence and pattern of abnormalities may give important clues to the most likely cause. Recognition that changes are long standing often prevents unnecessary investigations. If in doubt, ask a radiologist!

3.4.5 Computed tomography scan of the thorax

There are a number of indications for CT scans of the thorax. As with all investigations, the more detail that is provided on the request form then the better able the radiology team is to provide a scan that will answer the clinical question. A variety of techniques are used.

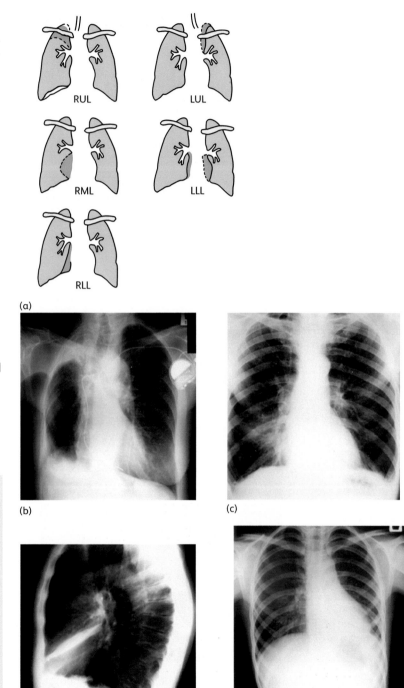

Fig 37 Radiological signs of lobar collapses. Note alterations to the positions of the fissures, trachea and diaphragms. (**a**) Diagrammatic representation of the radiographic patterns of lobar collapse – right upper lobe (RUL), left upper lobe (LUL), right middle lobe (RML), left lower lobe (LLL) and right lower lobe (RLL); (**b**) RUL collapse secondary to tuberculosis infection (also pacemaker); (**c**) RML collapse, which can be difficult to diagnose; (**d**) RML collapse, which is clearly demonstrated on a lateral chest radiograph; and (**e**) LLL collapse, with the 'sail sign' where the collapsed lobe lies behind the heart and the mediastinum is shifted to the left, straightening the right heart border.

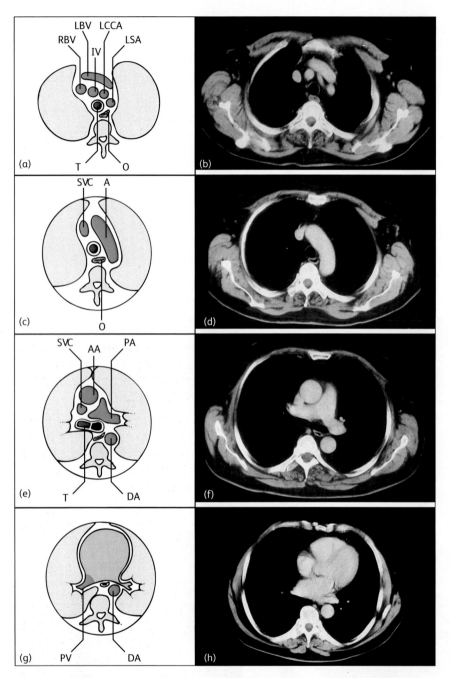

Fig 38 Principal mediastinal structures on CT scanning of the thorax. Remember that you are viewing the sections from below, ie the left of the thorax is on the right of the figure. **(a, b)** Section above the aortic arch. The trachea (T), oesophagus (O), right brachiocephalic vein (RBV), left brachiocephalic vein (LBV), innominate vein (IV), left common carotid artery (LCCA) and left subclavian artery (LSA) are visible. **(c, d)** Section at the level of the aortic arch (A). The superior vena cava (SVC) is visible. **(e, f)** Section below the aortic arch. Both ascending (AA) and descending (DA) aortas are visible. The trachea (T) is bifurcated and pulmonary arteries (PA) are seen. Note in **(f)** that the bifurcation of the trachea is present behind the pulmonary arteries, but it is difficult to see in cross-section. **(g, h)** Section at the level of the pulmonary veins (PV). Lower lobe intrapulmonary arteries and bronchi are not shown in the diagram. DA, descending aorta. (CT scans courtesy of Dr I Vlahos.)

Fig 38 shows the principal mediastinal structures seen on CT scanning of the thorax.

Types of scan

Modern multidetector CT scanners continuously acquire data from contiguous slices through the body. The ability to acquire multiple slices at once – 'volumetric data acquisition' – makes scanning fast and of high resolution. The data obtained can be processed and reformatted post-acquisition to provide images in multiple orientations and to highlight particular features.

High-resolution scans

These are often invaluable in the diagnosis of parenchymal lung disease and can be diagnostic of certain conditions, thus avoiding the need for further more invasive investigations, eg in sarcoidosis or usual interstitial pneumonia (Table 44).

If the changes are subtle, the radiologist may perform a scan with the patient lying prone, to ensure that pulmonary interstitial fluid is not mimicking the changes of fibrosis: fluid will move downwards, while fibrosis remains in the same area of the lung on both views (Fig 39).

Lung cancer staging

Staging scans for suspected lung cancer (or other discrete lesions like abscesses) cover the neck, chest and upper abdomen to include everything from the supraclavicular nodes to the kidneys. These images can be viewed on different window settings using PACS workstation software:

> Soft-tissue windows – these highlight mediastinal structures, lymph node enlargement, soft-tissue invasion and metastases in liver or eg adrenal glands.

Table 44 Typical high-resolution CT appearances of some diffuse parenchymal lung diseases

Disorder	High-resolution CT appearances
UIP	Patchy abnormalities that are mainly peripheral and basal. Also look for reticular and honeycomb changes with ground-glass opacification and traction bronchiectasis
Asbestosis	Similar to UIP. Reticular nodular opacities and thickened interlobular septa. Pleural plaques are often present
Sarcoidosis	Lymph node enlargement and micronodules with bronchovascular and subpleural distribution. Abnormalities mainly in the upper and mid-zones
Lymphangitic carcinomatosis	Irregular thickening of the interlobular septa, peribronchial cuffing and thickening of fissures. No architectural distortion
Extrinsic allergic alveolitis	Ground-glass opacification and poorly defined centrilobular micronodules. Air trapping on expiratory scans
Langerhans' cell histiocytosis	Cysts of bizarre shape associated with nodules. Lung bases usually not affected
Lymphangioleiomyomatosis	Thin-walled cysts surrounded by normal lung

UIP, usual interstitial pneumonia.

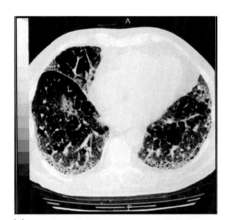

(a)

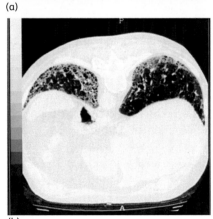

(b)

Fig 39 CT scan of the thorax of a man with pulmonary fibrosis in **(a)** supine and **(b)** prone positions. Note the different positioning of the patient on the scanning table (at the bottom of both films). The honeycombing appearance of the lungs remains posterior in both views.

> Lung windows – these concentrate on the lung parenchyma, producing images of the tumour as well as the condition of the surrounding lung, eg lymphangitis carcinomatosa, or pathology affecting the surrounding lung such as coexisting emphysema or fibrosis.

CT pulmonary angiography

CT pulmonary angiography (CTPA) has become the imaging modality of choice in suspected pulmonary embolus. Rapidly acquired volumetric data using multidetector scanners permit sharp imaging of the pulmonary arteries, which can be viewed in various reconstructions, typically axial, coronal and sagittal.

Reading a scan

When you assess a CT scan, remember that you are viewing it as though you are standing at the patient's feet looking upwards, so the patient's liver is on the left of the picture and the spleen on the right, etc. Like the chest radiograph, try to follow a system through the scans.

> Follow the main vessels such as the descending and ascending aorta and its arch.

> Look carefully for enlargement of the hilar and paratracheal lymph nodes and any other soft-tissue changes (Fig 40).

> Look at the lung windows – study the lung parenchyma and run your eye carefully around the pleura looking for any thickening, plaques and/or adjacent fibrosis.

> Finally, show a radiologist and, for your education, ask them to talk you through the scan.

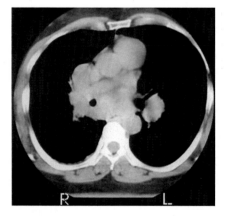

Fig 40 CT of the thorax: note the mass of lymph nodes that is distorting the normal architecture of the mediastinum. This patient was subsequently diagnosed as having sarcoidosis.

4 Self-assessment

4.1 Self-assessment questions

MRCP(UK) Part 1 examination questions

Question 1

Clinical scenario

A 73-year-old semi-retired plumbing and heating engineer was referred to the respiratory outpatient service with a 3-month history of gradually worsening breathlessness on exertion. This was associated with a nagging left-sided chest pain that sometimes woke him from sleep. He thought he had lost a little weight. His past medical history included only hypertension, for which he took amlodipine 5 mg od. He had smoked 20 cigarettes daily between the ages of 19 and 30. He was not aware of having worked with asbestos in the past.

His chest X-ray showed a left-sided moderate pleural effusion, and a calcified pleural plaque on the right hemidiaphragm.

Question

What is the most likely diagnosis?

Answer

A lung cancer with malignant pleural effusion

B mesothelioma

C pneumonia with parapneumonic effusion

D rheumatoid arthritis

E tuberculosis

Question 2

Clinical scenario

A 43-year-old man was admitted to hospital with a fever, cough, breathlessness and left-sided pleuritic chest pain. A diagnosis of left lower lobe community-acquired pneumonia was made. He was treated with intravenous benzylpenicillin 2.4 g qds for 48 hours, followed by oral amoxicillin 500 mg tds. He became afebrile on the second hospital day. However, on the sixth hospital day he complained of worsening fevers and breathlessness, and a chest radiograph showed a left pleural effusion. Ultrasound-guided pleural aspiration revealed a multi-septated effusion of slightly turbid, straw-coloured fluid. Pleural fluid analysis revealed:

> Gram stain – no organisms seen
> protein – 56 g/L
> lactate dehydrogenase (LDH) – 1,540 IU/L
> glucose – low
> pH – 7.15.

Question

What is the appropriate initial management?

Answer

A addition of clarithromycin

B insertion of a chest drain

C insertion of a chest drain and intrapleural administration of vancomycin

D referral for video-assisted thoracoscopic surgery

E repeat blood cultures

Question 3

Clinical scenario

An 83-year-old woman was referred urgently to the respiratory outpatient service with a cough and worsening breathlessness. She had a past history of hypertension, type 2 diabetes, osteoporosis and recurrent urinary tract infection. She was taking the following medications regularly: amlodipine, aspirin, calcitriol, metformin and nitrofurantoin. Her chest radiograph and computerised tomography (CT) scan showed focal, symmetrical, peripheral, predominantly lower zone, peribronchial consolidation in a pattern suggestive of organising pneumonia.

Question

Which medication is most likely to account for these appearances?

Answer

A amlodipine

B aspirin

C calcitriol

D metformin

E nitrofurantoin

Question 4

Clinical scenario

A 57-year-old man was referred to the respiratory outpatient service with breathlessness, which had been gradually developing over many months. He was a smoker of 40 pack-years.

Question

What lung function parameter would be most characteristic of emphysema?

Answer

A a forced expiratory volume in 1 second (FEV_1):forced vital capacity (FVC) ratio of 70%

B an FEV_1 of 65% predicted

C an FVC of 85% predicted

D a residual volume (RV) of 170% predicted

E a transfer coefficient (K_{CO}) of 68% predicted

Question 5

Clinical scenario

A 73-year-old woman, an ex-smoker of 20 pack-years, was admitted to the medical assessment unit as an emergency with fever and breathlessness. Physical examination was consistent with lobar pneumonia, which was confirmed by her chest radiograph.

Question
Which parameter is a predictor of severity of her pneumonia?

Answer
A a diastolic blood pressure of 65 mmHg

B a heart rate of 110 beats per minute

C a respiratory rate of 32 breaths per minute

D a systolic blood pressure of 95 mmHg

E an oxygen saturation of 92% on air (normal range 94–98%)

Question 6

Clinical scenario
A 72-year-old woman presented with rapid weight gain, easy bruising and muscle wasting. Her chest radiograph showed a right upper lobe mass with paratracheal lymphadenopathy.

Question
What is the most likely underlying cause of her symptoms?

Answer
A adenocarcinoma of the lung

B large cell undifferentiated carcinoma

C pituitary Cushing's syndrome

D small-cell lung carcinoma

E squamous-cell lung carcinoma

Question 7

Clinical scenario
A 28-year-old woman presented to the emergency department with a 24-hour history of breathlessness, cough and wheeze. She had a past medical history of asthma, normally well controlled on formoterol/budesonide combination inhaler. On examination she was dyspnoeic at rest and able to talk in short sentences. Her SpO$_2$ (peripheral capillary oxygen saturation) was 90% on air (normal range 94–98%) with a respiratory rate of 30 breaths per

minute and heart rate of 130 beats per minute. There was widespread expiratory polyphonic wheeze throughout both lung fields. An arterial blood gas (ABG) test on air revealed PaO$_2$ 7.5 kPa (normal range 11.3–12.6), PaCO$_2$ 3.5 kPa (normal range 4.7–6.0) and bicarbonate (HCO$_3^-$) 25.0 mmol/L (normal range 21–29).

Question
What is the severity of her asthma exacerbation?

Answer
A acute severe asthma

B life-threatening asthma

C mild acute asthma

D moderate acute asthma

E near-fatal asthma

Question 8

Clinical scenario
A 25-year-old woman with eosinophilic asthma was seen in the respiratory outpatient clinic following two severe exacerbations requiring hospital admission. She was receiving maximal dose inhaled therapy with a combination inhaler of long-acting β$_2$-agonist and inhaled corticosteroid, inhaled long-acting antimuscarinic, montelukast and a maintenance dose of 15 mg prednisolone daily. She had a persistently elevated serum total immunoglobulin E (IgE), with strongly positive specific IgE to house-dust mite and tree pollen. She was being considered for treatment with omalizumab.

Question
What is the mechanism of action of omalizumab?

Answer
A anti-CD20 monoclonal antibody

B anti-immunoglobulin E (IgE) monoclonal antibody

C anti-interleukin (IL)-5 monoclonal antibody

D anti-IL13 monoclonal antibody

E Th2 cytotoxic agent

Question 9

Clinical scenario
A 74-year-old man with chronic obstructive pulmonary disease (COPD) was reviewed in the respiratory outpatient clinic. He was an ex-smoker. He was receiving treatment with a long-acting β$_2$-agonist / long-acting muscarinic antagonist combination inhaler. He was independent in his activities of daily living and walked his dog regularly. He became breathless when walking up an incline or walking upstairs.

Question
What was his score on the Medical Research Council (MRC) Dyspnoea Scale?

Answer
A 1

B 2

C 3

D 4

E 5

Question 10

Clinical scenario
A 45-year-old smoker was referred to the respiratory clinic with breathlessness. His CT scan showed emphysema.

Question
Which radiological pattern would be suggestive of α$_1$-antitrypsin deficiency?

Answer
A apical bullae

B basal predominant panlobular emphysema

C homogenous centrilobular emphysema

D paraseptal emphysema

E upper lobe predominant centrilobular emphysema

Question 11

Clinical scenario
An 82-year-old man was admitted on the acute medical unit with a 5-day history of cough that was productive of green sputum, breathlessness and

wheeze. He had a past medical history of COPD. He was treated with nebulised salbutamol, ipratropium and oral antibiotics.

Question
Which organism is most likely to be responsible for his presentation?

Answer
A *Chlamydia psittaci*

B *Haemophilus influenzae*

C *Legionella pneumophila*

D *Mycoplasma pneumoniae*

E *Pseudomonas aeruginosa*

Question 12

Clinical scenario
A 45-year-old man was evaluated in the respiratory outpatient clinic for possible obstructive sleep apnoea syndrome. He had completed the answers to the questions on the Epworth Sleepiness Scale as part of his assessment. His score was 19.

Question
What value on the Epworth Sleepiness Scale indicates excessive daytime sleepiness?

Answer
A ≥ 8

B ≥ 10

C ≥ 11

D ≥ 15

E ≥ 19

Question 13

Clinical scenario
A 25-year-old man presented acutely with a 1-day history of right-sided pleuritic chest pain. He had no other respiratory symptoms. He had no significant past medical history and was a non-smoker. Examination of the respiratory system revealed a central (normal) trachea, with hyper-resonance on percussion and reduced air entry over the right hemithorax. A chest X-ray showed a right pneumothorax with a 1.5 cm margin at the level of the hilum.

Question
What is the most appropriate management option?

Answer
A aspiration

B discharge with outpatient follow-up in 2–4 weeks

C intercostal chest drain

D observation for 24 hours

E observation for 24 hours with high-flow supplemental oxygen

Question 14

Clinical scenario
A 65-year-old man presented acutely with a productive cough. He had no other respiratory or constitutional symptoms. He was an ex-smoker of 10-pack-year history. Examination of the respiratory system showed right basal bronchial breath sounds. A chest X-ray showed evidence of consolidation in this area. He was treated for community-acquired pneumonia and improved clinically.

Question
What follow-up arrangement would this man require upon discharge?

Answer
A CT chest

B none

C repeat chest X-ray in 2 weeks

D repeat chest X-ray in 6 weeks

E repeat chest X-ray in 12 weeks

Question 15

Clinical scenario
A previously healthy 34-year-old African-Caribbean woman presented with a 6-month history of non-productive cough and a tender erythematous rash on her shins. There was no history of night sweats or weight loss. There was no history of any foreign travel. There was no significant abnormality on respiratory examination. Her chest radiograph showed bilateral hilar lymphadenopathy.

Question
What is the most likely diagnosis?

Answer
A carcinoid syndrome

B lymphoma

C *Mycobacterium tuberculosis* infection

D sarcoidosis

E systemic lupus erythematosus

Question 16

Clinical scenario
A 38-year-old man presented acutely with pyrexia and a productive cough. His past medical history included renal transplantation, and he had been treated by his primary care physician with levofloxacin with no effect. Examination of the respiratory system revealed bilateral widespread coarse inspiratory crepitations. A CT scan of the chest revealed widespread nodular shadowing with indistinct margins and lesions with halo signs. Serology showed positive galactomannan.

Question
What is the most likely diagnosis?

Answer
A aspergilloma

B invasive aspergillosis

C *Mycobacterium avium* infection

D *Mycobacterium tuberculosis* infection

E *Pneumocystis jirovecii* pneumonia

Question 17

Clinical scenario
A 65-year-old man with a history of COPD presented to the respiratory clinic with symptoms of chronic dyspnoea and swollen legs. Examination revealed a raised jugular venous pressure, a right ventricular heave and pitting oedema to the knees. Arterial blood gas analysis was performed to assess the patient for long-term oxygen therapy (LTOT).

Question
What level of arterial partial pressure of oxygen (PaO_2) when breathing air would be an indication for LTOT in this man?

Answer

A PaO$_2$ <6.0 kPa

B PaO$_2$ <6.5 kPa

C PaO$_2$ <7.3 kPa

D PaO$_2$ <8.0 kPa

E PaO$_2$ <8.5 kPa

Question 18

Clinical scenario

A 35-year-old man presented acutely with a history of rigors, productive cough and purulent sputum. On examination he was found to have signs consistent with a pleural effusion. A diagnostic aspiration of the pleural effusion was performed.

Question

Which finding on testing of the pleural aspirate would suggest the diagnosis of empyema?

Answer

A glucose 0.5 mmol/L

B LDH 15 IU/L

C pH 7.25

D pH 7.30

E protein 20 g/L

Question 19

Clinical scenario

A 23-year-old woman presented with chronic rhinitis and shortness of breath. She also described paraesthesia in her right hand and persistent diarrhoea. There was no family history of atopy. Examination of her respiratory system was unremarkable. Her serology showed an eosinophilia and her auto-immune screen showed a positive p-ANCA (antineutrophil cytoplasmic antibodies).

Question

What is the most likely diagnosis?

Answer

A allergic bronchopulmonary aspergillosis

B asthma

C Churg–Strauss syndrome

D eosinophilic pneumonia

E granulomatosis with polyangiitis (Wegener's)

Question 20

Clinical scenario

A 30-year-old man presented with a history of recurrent lower respiratory tract infections. He had no other medical history of note, excepting that he and his partner were undergoing investigations for infertility. On examination of the chest there were bibasal inspiratory crepitations that altered on coughing.

Question

What is the most likely unifying diagnosis?

Answer

A cystic fibrosis

B Kartagener's syndrome

C primary hypogammaglobulinaemia

D Sjögren's syndrome

E whooping cough

MRCP(UK) Part 2 examination questions

Question 21

Clinical scenario

A 64-year-old woman presented as an emergency with breathlessness, which had been worsening over the preceding 4 weeks. She reported that she could now climb a flight of stairs with difficulty, having been able to run in a 10 km fun-run 6 months earlier. She had been treated for breast cancer at the age of 41 but had no other past medical history and took no regular medication. She lived with her husband who was in good health. Physical examination revealed stony dullness to percussion and reduced breath sounds over the right hemithorax. A chest radiograph revealed a large right pleural effusion.

Question

What is the most appropriate initial intervention?

Answer

A diagnostic pleural aspiration of 50 mL fluid under ultrasound guidance, with specimens sent for cytology, microbiology and biochemical analysis

B immediate admission to hospital for insertion of a chest drain under ultrasound guidance and talc pleurodesis

C insertion of a tunnelled intrapleural catheter under ultrasound guidance to permit outpatient pleural drainage

D non-ultrasound-guided diagnostic pleural aspiration with specimens sent for cytology, microbiology and biochemical analysis

E therapeutic pleural aspiration of 1,000–1,500 mL fluid under ultrasound guidance, with specimens sent for cytology, microbiology and biochemical analysis

Question 22

Clinical scenario

A 19-year-old university student presented as an emergency to hospital with left-sided pleuritic chest pain and breathlessness. She had no past medical history and took no regular medication. She smoked 20 cigarettes daily. A chest radiograph revealed a 50% left pneumothorax.

Question

What is the most appropriate initial management?

Answer

A aspiration of the left pleural cavity followed by repeat chest radiograph

B chest drain insertion and admission for observation

C chest drain insertion and discharge home with a one-way drainage (Heimlich) valve

D referral for thoracoscopic left pleurectomy and pleurodesis

E smoking cessation advice

Question 23

Clinical scenario

A 47-year-old building labourer, a smoker of 25 pack-years, was referred to the respiratory outpatient service with a cough and breathlessness. He had noticed a little loss of weight. His past medical history was notable for a myocardial infarction 3 years ago, from which he had made a good recovery such that he remained able to work.

On physical examination he had clubbing of the fingernails, but there were no other abnormal signs. A CT scan of the chest and upper abdomen revealed a 2.3 cm right upper lobe nodule and enlarged (1.5 cm short axis) lymph nodes in the right hilar and right paratracheal stations, but no other abnormalities. His lung function tests, full blood count, urea and electrolytes (U/E), liver function tests (LFTs) and calcium were normal.

Question

Which is the most appropriate next investigation?

Answer

A a cardiopulmonary exercise test

B a CT-guided needle biopsy of the right upper lobe nodule

C a flexible bronchoscopy

D a positron emission tomography (PET)-CT scan

E an endobronchial ultrasound and mediastinal lymph node biopsy

Question 24

Clinical scenario

A 65-year-old woman, a smoker of 45 pack-years, was reviewed in an outpatient clinic during work-up for suspected lung cancer after she presented with a cough that had persisted for 3 months. She was otherwise fit and well and took no regular medication. On physical examination there was clubbing of the fingernails, but there were no other abnormal signs.

Lung function testing revealed FEV$_1$ 1.5 L (67% predicted), FVC 2.1 L (69% predicted) and transfer coefficient (K$_{CO}$) 55% predicted. Following abnormal results from chest radiography and CT scanning of the chest and abdomen, a whole-body PET-CT scan was performed. The only abnormalities visible on PET-CT are shown in Fig 41.

Question

What is the most appropriate next investigation?

Answer

A bronchoscopy and biopsy

B CT-guided percutaneous right lung biopsy

C endobronchial ultrasound and mediastinal lymph node biopsy

D mediastinoscopy

E surgical wedge resection of the right upper lobe and mediastinal lymph node sampling

Question 25

Clinical scenario

A 44-year-old woman was referred to the respiratory outpatient service with a 6-week history of worsening breathlessness on exertion and noisy breathing. She had previously been extremely fit and was a competitive triathlete. She had had a melanoma removed from her leg 4 years previously. There was a family history of asthma in her mother and hay fever in her younger daughter. She had never smoked. On physical examination the cardiovascular system and respiratory systems were normal at rest. The results of spirometry and a flow–volume loop were as follows:

> FEV$_1$ 3.1 L (104% predicted)
> FVC 3.6 L (106% predicted)

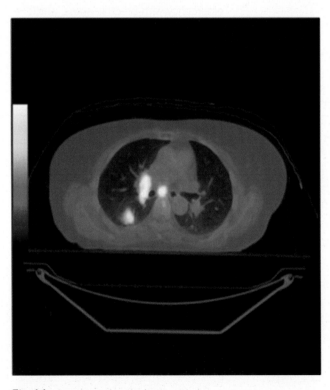

Fig 41

> peak expiratory flow rate 350 L/min (85% predicted)
> in the flow–volume loop expiratory flow is shown as positive and inspiratory flow as negative (Fig 42).

Question

What is the most likely cause of her breathlessness?

Answer

A asthma

B extrathoracic compression of the trachea

C intrathoracic large airway obstruction

D pleural effusion

E tracheobronchomalacia

Question 26

Clinical scenario

A 46-year-old woman with long-standing asthma was seen in the respiratory outpatient clinic with increased wheeze, cough and sputum production. She was found to have an elevated serum total IgE and moderate eosinophilia. A high-resolution (HR) CT showed central bronchiectasis with mucus plugging.

Flow volume

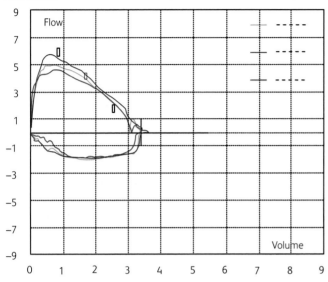

Fig 42

Question
Which test would help confirm a diagnosis of allergic bronchopulmonary aspergillosis (ABPA)?

Answer
A fungal hyphae seen in bronchial lavage fluid

B negative *Aspergillus* immunoglobulin G (IgG)

C positive ANCA

D positive *Aspergillus*-specific IgE

E positive serum β-glucan

Question 27

Clinical scenario
An 18-year-old woman with asthma was seen in the emergency department with a 24-hour history of breathlessness and wheeze. She had a history of poorly controlled asthma and took her inhaled therapy intermittently.

On examination she was dyspnoeic and distressed at rest. Her SpO_2 (peripheral capillary oxygen saturation) was 89% on air (normal range 94–98%), improving to 95% on 15 L per minute oxygen via a non-rebreathe mask. Her heart rate was 130 beats per minute and her breath sounds were quiet on auscultation of her chest. She had been given nebulised salbutamol and ipratropium, intravenous magnesium, and she had been started on an intravenous aminophylline infusion. An arterial blood gas (ABG) after treatment on 15 L per minute oxygen showed PaO_2 9.1 kPa (normal range 11.3–12.6), $PaCO_2$ 6.0 kPa (normal range 4.7–6.0) and pH 7.35, with serum total bicarbonate 20 mmol/L (normal range 21–29).

Question
Which intervention is most appropriate at this stage?

Answer
A admission to the intensive care unit

B give a further dose of intravenous magnesium

C start an intravenous ketamine infusion

D start an intravenous salbutamol infusion

E start non-invasive ventilation (NIV)

Question 28

Clinical scenario
An 82-year-old woman was reviewed in the respiratory outpatient clinic. She had a past medical history of COPD and peripheral vascular disease. She was receiving inhaled treatment with tiotropium and budesonide/formoterol. Her post-bronchodilator spirometry showed FEV_1 38% predicted, FVC 87% predicted and an FEV_1:FVC ratio of 0.45.

Question
According to the GOLD (Global Initiative for Chronic Obstructive Lung Disease) classification, what is the severity of her airflow limitation?

Answer
A mild

B moderate

C severe

D unable to tell from the above information

E very severe

Question 29

Clinical scenario
An 80-year-old man with COPD was seen in the respiratory outpatient clinic. He was an ex-smoker and had a poor exercise tolerance of around 100 metres on the flat. His past medical history included localised prostate cancer. He was on treatment with inhaled umeclidinium/vilanterol (long-acting muscarinic antagonist / long-acting $β_2$-agonist) for his COPD.

He had evidence of significant hyperinflation and gas trapping according to his pulmonary function tests, and a thoracic CT scan revealed severe upper zone predominant centrilobular emphysema. His ABG on air at rest showed PaO_2 8.1 kPa (normal range 11.3–12.6), $PaCO_2$ 5.3 kPa (normal range 4.7–6.0) and pH 7.4 (normal range 7.35–7.45).

Question
Which treatment should be considered next?

Answer
A long-term oxygen therapy

B lung transplantation

C lung volume reduction surgery

D nocturnal non-invasive ventilation

E pulmonary rehabilitation

Question 30

Clinical scenario

A 65-year-old man was admitted to the acute medical unit with an exacerbation of COPD. An ABG test taken on 2 L per minute oxygen delivered by nasal cannulae showed PO_2 7.9 kPa (normal range 11.3–12.6), PCO_2 11.5 kPa (normal range 4.7–6.0), pH 7.29 and serum bicarbonate 32 mmol/L (normal range 21–29).

He was treated with nebulised bronchodilators and prednisolone, and started on NIV with inspiratory positive airway pressure (IPAP) 12 cmH$_2$O, expiratory positive airway pressure (EPAP) 4 cmH$_2$O, with 5 L per minute of oxygen entrained into the inspiratory circuit. The mask fitted well with minimal leak, and there was no apparent patient–ventilator lack of synchrony.

A repeat ABG test in 1 hour showed PO_2 8.5 kPa, PCO_2 11.6 kPa, pH 7.30 and serum bicarbonate 31 mmol/L.

Question

What is the most appropriate intervention now?

Answer

A increase the EPAP to a target of 10 cmH$_2$O as tolerated

B increase the IPAP and EPAP to a target of 20 cmH$_2$O and 10 cmH$_2$O, respectively

C increase the IPAP to a target of 20 cmH$_2$O as tolerated

D start an aminophylline infusion

E transfer to the intensive care unit for intubation and mechanical ventilation

Question 31

Clinical scenario

An 81-year-old woman was admitted to the acute medical unit with type II respiratory failure secondary to an exacerbation of COPD. She was known to have severe emphysema with upper lobe bullae. She was started on NIV at settings of IPAP 20 cmH$_2$O, EPAP 4 cmH$_2$O, with 2 L/min of oxygen.

Twenty minutes after starting NIV she deteriorated acutely, complaining of left-sided chest pain. She was centrally cyanosed and in respiratory distress. Her oxygen saturation was unrecordable (normal range 94–98%) and her blood pressure (BP) was 60/40 mmHg. On examination she had absent breath sounds over her left hemithorax with tracheal deviation to the right.

Question

What course of action should be taken?

Answer

A increase inspiratory positive airway pressure (IPAP) to 25 cmH$_2$O

B insert a cannula into the second intercostal space in the mid-clavicular line on the left

C order an urgent chest X-ray

D start intravenous infusion of salbutamol

E transfer to the intensive care unit for intubation and mechanical ventilation

Question 32

Clinical scenario

A 74-year-old man with COPD was admitted to the emergency department with breathlessness. After receiving optimal medical treatment his oxygen saturations were within the range 88–92% (normal range 94–98%). The respiratory nurse specialist enquired whether or not he should be started on NIV.

Question

Which finding on ABG analysis would lead you to advise that he should be started on NIV?

Answer

A pH 7.29, PCO_2 5.5 kPa

B pH 7.30, PCO_2 6.7 kPa

C pH 7.33, PCO_2 6.2 kPa

D pH 7.37, PCO_2 7.0 kPa

E pH 7.40, PCO_2 10.0 kPa

Question 33

Clinical scenario

A 69-year-old man was seen in the respiratory outpatient clinic with daytime sleepiness. His past medical history included type 2 diabetes and ischaemic heart disease. His body mass index (BMI) was 29 and his score on the Epworth Sleepiness Scale was 18 (elevated). He had an overnight sleep study that showed an apnoea–hypopnoea index of 35 (elevated). Mean oxygen saturation was 92% (normal range 94–98%) and a waking capillary blood gas showed PCO_2 5.5 kPa (normal range 4.7–6.0), pH 7.39 (normal range 7.35–7.45).

Question

Which initial therapy should be recommended?

Answer

A mandibular advancement device

B overnight continuous positive airway pressure (CPAP)

C overnight non-invasive ventilation (NIV)

D uvulopalatopharyngoplasty

E weight loss surgery

Question 34

Clinical scenario

A 42-year-old woman was admitted to the respiratory ward with a 6-month history of breathlessness, increasing peripheral oedema, daytime somnolence and waking headache. She had a past medical history of type 2 diabetes, hypothyroidism and hypertension.

On examination her BMI was 33, her chest was clear to auscultation, there was pitting oedema up to her abdominal wall, and her jugular venous pressure was elevated. She had peripheral capillary oxygen saturation of 89% on air (normal range 94–98%). Her chest X-ray showed normal lung fields. An ABG test on air showed PO_2 7.7 kPa (normal range 11.3–12.6), PCO_2 9.8 kPa (normal range 4.7–6.0), pH 7.36 (normal range 7.35–7.45) and serum bicarbonate 39 mmol/L (normal range 21–29).

Question
Which intervention is most likely to lead to long-term clinical improvement?

Answer

A acetazolamide

B high-dose diuretic therapy

C long-term oxygen therapy (LTOT)

D nocturnal continuous positive airway pressure treatment

E nocturnal non-invasive ventilation (NIV)

Question 35
Clinical scenario
A 72-year-old man presented to the emergency department with a 2-day history of fever and cough. His past medical history included hypertension and gastro-oesophageal reflux. On examination he was alert and orientated. His vital signs included temperature 38.7°C, pulse 120 beats per minute, blood pressure (BP) 75/40 mm/Hg and respiratory rate 30 breaths per minute. There were bronchial breath sounds at the right base. His blood tests included C-reactive protein (CRP) 280 mg/L (normal threshold <10 mg/L), white cell count (WCC) 18×10^9/L (normal range 4–11), urea 17 mmol/L (normal range 2.5–7.0), creatinine 220 µmol/L (normal range 60–110). His chest radiograph showed right lower lobe consolidation.

Question
What is his CURB-65 score?

Answer

A 1

B 2

C 3

D 4

E 5

Question 36
Clinical scenario
A 55-year-old man was admitted with a community-acquired pneumonia. He had no significant past medical history and was taking no regular medications. His CURB-65 score on admission was 4. He was treated with intravenous

antibiotics and transferred to the intensive care unit for haemodynamic support.

Question
Which investigation is most indicated within the first 24 hours of treatment?

Answer

A serum for β-glucan

B serum for mycoplasma serology

C sputum for acid-fast bacilli (AFB) smear and culture

D throat swab for viral polymerase chain reaction (PCR)

E urine for *Legionella* and pneumococcal antigen

Question 37
Clinical scenario
A 27-year-old man was admitted to the respiratory ward with cough, fever and purulent sputum production. In the weeks prior to his admission he had suffered from a sore throat and had difficulty swallowing. He had no relevant past medical history and took no regular medication. On examination the right side of his neck was tender, and ultrasound with Doppler revealed a right internal jugular vein thrombus. His chest radiograph showed several cavitating lesions in both lung fields.

Question
What is the most likely responsible organism?

Answer

A *Fusobacterium necrophorum*

B *Klebsiella pneumoniae*

C *Mycobacterium tuberculosis*

D *Staphylococcus aureus*

E *Streptococcus pneumoniae*

Question 38
Clinical scenario
A 47-year-old man was admitted with community-acquired pneumonia. His chest X-ray showed right middle lobe consolidation. Blood cultures were positive for *Streptococcus pneumoniae* and his urinary pneumococcal antigen was positive. He was treated with intravenous

benzylpenicillin. On day 3 of treatment his C-reactive protein (CRP) had not fallen and he continued to be pyrexial.

Question
What is the most appropriate course of action?

Answer

A change antibiotics to piperacillin/ tazobactam

B perform a lumbar puncture

C request a chest X-ray

D request a CT pulmonary angiogram

E request an echocardiogram

Question 39
Clinical scenario
A 67-year-old retired stonemason presented with a 9-month history of non-productive cough and gradually worsening shortness of breath. He described no other respiratory or constitutional symptoms. He was an ex-smoker of 10 pack-years. Examination of the respiratory system revealed bibasal fine inspiratory crepitations that did not alter on coughing. A chest X-ray showed upper and middle zones nodules with evidence of calcification. His spirometry showed an FEV_1 at 60% of predicted and an FVC at 65% of predicted.

Question
What is the most likely diagnosis?

Answer

A bronchiectasis

B Caplan's syndrome

C COPD

D siderosis

E silicosis

Question 40
Clinical scenario
A 75-year-old man presented with anorexia and haemoptysis. He was a smoker of 40-pack-year history. Examination revealed signs consistent with a right pleural effusion. A diagnostic aspiration was performed on the pleural effusion.

Question

Which feature would indicate an exudative pleural effusion?

Answer

A pleural fluid lactate dehydrogenase (LDH): serum LDH ratio >0.5

B pleural fluid LDH more than two-thirds of the value of the upper limit of normal serum LDH

C pleural fluid protein:pleural fluid LDH ratio >0.5

D pleural fluid protein:serum protein ratio >0.4

E pleural fluid protein of 29 g/L

4.2 Self-assessment answers

Answer to Question 1
B: mesothelioma

The combination of chest wall pain and pleural effusion, persisting over several weeks and present in a man likely to have been exposed to asbestos is highly suggestive of mesothelioma. A history of having worked in a high-risk occupation (carpenters, shipyard workers, boilermen, plumbing and heating engineers, roofers) is much more predictive of mesothelioma risk than the patient being able (or not) to remember having worked with asbestos.

Answer to Question 2
B: insertion of a chest drain

A parapneumonic effusion with a pH of less than 7.2 requires pleural drainage. There is no evidence supporting the use of intrapleural antibiotics, and parapneumonic effusions commonly involve anaerobic organisms for which metronidazole would be a better choice than clarithromycin. Immediate referral for thoracic surgery without attempting drainage first would be premature.

Answer to Question 3
E: nitrofurantoin

Nitrofurantoin is commonly associated with pulmonary toxicity, which can take many different forms, including organising pneumonia. The other medications are not associated with parenchymal pulmonary toxicity, although aspirin can be implicated in exacerbating asthma.

Answer to Question 4
D: a residual volume (RV) of 170% predicted

Emphysema characteristically produces hyperinflation of the lungs leading to a markedly increased RV. Airflow obstruction leads to a forced expiratory volume in 1 second (FEV_1):forced vital capacity (FVC) ratio of less than 70%. Isolated reduction of FEV_1, FVC or the transfer coefficient (K_{CO}) alone, without further information, is not specific to emphysema.

Answer to Question 5
C: a respiratory rate of 32 breaths per minute

A raised respiratory rate is one of the factors most strongly associated with a poor prognosis in pneumonia, and when greater than or equal to 30 breaths per minute adds a point to the CURB-65 prognostic score for pneumonia severity. The other points are scored if there is confusion, if the blood urea is >7 mmol/L (normal range 2.5–7.0), if the systolic blood pressure (BP) is <90 mmHg or the diastolic BP is ≤60 mmHg, and if the patient's age is ≥65 years.

Answer to Question 6
D: small cell lung carcinoma

The most likely explanation for her symptoms is paraneoplastic secretion of adrenocorticotropic hormone (ACTH). In the context of a lung mass the most likely explanation is small-cell lung carcinoma.

Answer to Question 7
B: life-threatening asthma

The SpO_2 (peripheral capillary oxygen saturation) of <92% (normal range 94–98%) and a PaO_2 of <8 kPa indicates that this is life-threatening asthma. An elevated $PaCO_2$ or the requirement for mechanical ventilation with raised inflation pressures would indicate near-fatal asthma.

Answer to Question 8
B: anti-immunoglobulin E (IgE) monoclonal antibody

Omalizumab is an anti-IgE monoclonal antibody, which has been approved by the National Institute for Health and Care Excellence (NICE) for the treatment of patients with allergic IgE-mediated asthma who need continuous or frequent (four or more courses in the previous year) treatment with oral corticosteroids.

Answer to Question 9
B: 2

Medical Research Council (MRC) Dyspnoea Scale:

1 – breathless on strenuous exercise only
2 – breathless when hurrying or walking up a slight hill
3 – walks slower than contemporaries on level ground due to breathlessness or has to stop for breath when walking at own pace
4 – stops for breath after walking for about 100 metres or a few minutes on level ground
5 – too breathless to leave the house or breathless when washing and dressing.

Answer to Question 10
B: basal predominant panlobular emphysema

α_1-Antitrypsin deficiency is an inherited autosomal co-dominant disorder characterised by a deficiency of the glycoprotein protease inhibitor α_1-antitrypsin. The clinical manifestations include early development of emphysema, which characteristically has a basal predominance and panlobular pattern. The emphysema is more severe in smokers. There may also be associated liver dysfunction.

Answer to Question 11

B: *Haemophilus influenzae*

The most common organisms responsible for infective exacerbations of COPD are *Haemophilus influenzae*, *Moraxella catarrhalis*, *Streptococcus pneumoniae* and viruses such as respiratory syncytial virus (RSV), influenza and parainfluenza. *Pseudomonas aeruginosa* is commonly seen as a colonising organism in chronic lung disease with structural airway abnormalities such as bronchiectasis and cystic fibrosis. *Chlamydia psittaci*, *Legionella pneumophila* and *Mycoplasma pneumoniae* are all atypical organisms that can cause pneumonia.

Answer to Question 12

C: ≥11

The Epworth Sleepiness Scale comprises a series of eight questions, which ask the patient to rate the likelihood of them falling asleep in a variety of situations with a score of 0–3 for each question. The patient is given a total score of between 0 and 24, with a score of ≥11 considered to represent excessive daytime sleepiness.

Answer to Question 13

B: discharge with outpatient follow-up in 2–4 weeks

The man suffered from a primary spontaneous pneumothorax, and British Thoracic Society guidelines on pneumothorax advises that a primary spontaneous pneumothorax with no symptom of shortness of breath and of a size <2 cm at the level of the hilum can be managed in the community with outpatient follow-up in 2–4 weeks.

Answer to Question 14

D: repeat chest X-ray in 6 weeks

A repeat chest X-ray is recommended in patients with community-acquired pneumonia when there are persistent symptoms or signs or when the patients are at risk of lung malignancy (current or ex-smoker or over the age of 50). A study has shown that radiological resolution of consolidation occurs in 51% of patients at 2 weeks and 74% of patients at 6 weeks. The recommendation is therefore to repeat a chest X-ray at 6 weeks.

Answer to Question 15

D: sarcoidosis

The description of the rash is suggestive of erythema nodosum. The bilateral hilar lymphadenopathy (BHL) on the chest radiograph is suggestive of sarcoidosis, tuberculosis or lymphoma. The symptoms do not suggest lymphoma, while the lack of night sweats, weight loss and foreign travel make a *Mycobacterium tuberculosis* infection less likely. BHL on chest radiography is not commonly seen in systemic lupus erythematosus (SLE) or carcinoid syndrome.

Answer to Question 16

B: invasive aspergillosis

The clinical picture and radiological findings are typical for invasive aspergillosis. The disease is usually only seen in those who are immunocompromised. Galactomannan is a serological test for the disease, although it is commonly false positive, especially after the use of piperacillin/tazobactam. Aspergilloma does not present with systemic involvement.

Answer to Question 17

D: PaO_2 <8.0 kPa

Patients with COPD who have a PaO_2 of less than 7.3 kPa (normal range 11.3–12.6) fulfil the criterion in terms of PaO_2 for long-term oxygen therapy

(LTOT). However, the PaO_2 criterion is reduced to that of less than 8.0 kPa in those who have symptoms and signs of cor pulmonale. The peripheral oedema, raised jugular venous pressure (JVP) and right ventricular heave are all suggestive of cor pulmonale.

Answer to Question 18

A: glucose 0.5 mmol/L

A parapneumonic effusion by definition is an exudative effusion. The lactate dehydrogenase (LDH) and protein values quoted above would not fulfil the criteria for an exudative effusion (see Light's criteria (Section 1.2.4, Table 8) for more details). An empyema has a pH <7.2 and a glucose of <1.6 mmol/L.

Answer to Question 19

C: Churg–Strauss syndrome

The upper respiratory symptoms along with multi-system involvement suggest Churg–Strauss syndrome. Asthma and allergic bronchopulmonary aspergillosis (ABPA) would not cause neurological symptoms. With regards to antineutrophil cytoplasmic antibodies (ANCAs) it is c-ANCA (anti-proteinase-3 (PR3)) which is associated with granulomatosis with polyangiitis (previously known as Wegener's). Churg–Strauss syndrome is associated with p-ANCA (anti-myeloperoxidase (MPO)).

Answer to Question 20

A: cystic fibrosis

The history and examination findings are typical of bronchiectasis. Cystic fibrosis is associated with infertility. Kartagener's syndrome is very much rarer, but it also causes bronchiectasis and infertility and is sometimes associated with situs inversus. It is a primary ciliary dyskinesia (PCD) that is an autosomal recessive disease. Cilia are involved in organ rotation embryologically, thus situs inversus occurs in ~30% of patients with PCD.

Answer to Question 21

E: therapeutic pleural aspiration of 1,000–1,500 mL fluid under ultrasound guidance, with specimens sent for cytology, microbiology and biochemical analysis

The patient is highly likely to have a malignant pleural effusion. The priorities in her management, in order, are: rapid relief of current symptoms; rapid diagnosis of the cause of her effusion; an intervention to prevent further effusion-related breathlessness in future; and the avoidance of unnecessary bed-days in a patient likely to have limited life expectancy. Options B and C are appropriate for longer-term management of her effusion once a diagnosis is established but do not offer a diagnosis. Options A and D do not offer symptom relief and it is no longer considered appropriate to carry out pleural interventions without ultrasound guidance.

Answer to Question 22

A: aspiration of the left pleural cavity followed by repeat chest radiograph

In a young, previously fit person, pleural aspiration may be all that is required to relieve symptoms and is the initial treatment of choice. Surgery is usually reserved for patients with recurrent pneumothorax. Smoking cessation advice, while highly relevant, is not the most appropriate initial management option.

Answer to Question 23

D: a positron emission tomography (PET)-CT scan

The priority is to establish diagnosis and staging as rapidly as possible and with the minimum number of invasive tests. This man has potentially operable lung cancer. A PET-CT scan will identify extrathoracic metastasis in approximately 10% of patients and should be performed in all radically

treatable patients with lung cancer. By performing the PET-CT scan first, a biopsy of the highest-stage disease can be performed, thus minimising invasive testing.

Answer to Question 24

C: endobronchial ultrasound and mediastinal lymph node biopsy

This woman has a PET-avid lesion in the right lung lower lobe together with PET-avid right hilar and subcarinal lymph nodes. The most appropriate diagnostic test is one that will provide accurate histological diagnosis and staging in the least invasive manner. Endobronchial ultrasound permits the fine needle aspiration of hilar, subcarinal and paratracheal lymph nodes bilaterally and will confirm a tissue diagnosis and reveal to which lymph nodes the cancer has metastasised. The likely best treatment will be combined chemo-radiotherapy, and accurate staging will permit the appropriate planning of radiotherapy fields to encompass all of the tumour.

Answer to Question 25

B: extrathoracic compression of the trachea

The flow–volume loop shows normal expiratory flow but significant limitation of inspiratory flow: the inspiratory graph should be semi-circular and concave upwards, whereas it is considerably flattened in this example. In addition, the mid-inspiratory flow should be approximately equal to the mid-expiratory flow of 4 L per second, whereas here it is approximately 2 L per second. Extrathoracic large airway narrowing is typically worse on inspiration, whereas intrathoracic large airway obstruction (for example, due to tracheobronchomalacia or other cause) is worse on expiration. The flow–volume loop findings and spirometry are not suggestive of asthma or pleural effusion.

Answer to Question 26

D: positive *Aspergillus*-specific IgE

A diagnosis of allergic bronchopulmonary aspergillosis (ABPA) with bronchiectasis is made based upon an elevated total IgE, eosinophilia, positive *Aspergillus*-specific IgE or skin-prick test, positive *Aspergillus* immunoglobulin G (IgG) / precipitins and CT findings of central bronchiectasis. β-Glucan is a pan-fungal marker that is detected in serum in cases of invasive fungal disease.

Answer to Question 27

A: admission to the intensive care unit

This patient has near fatal asthma as defined by the high-normal $PaCO_2$ on analysis of her arterial blood gas. She should be admitted to the intensive care unit as it is likely she will need intubation and mechanical ventilation having already received maximal medical therapy. Intravenous salbutamol and a repeated dose of intravenous magnesium are unlikely to provide any additional bronchodilation over and above the treatment she has already received. Intravenous ketamine has a bronchodilator effect but should not be used outside an intensive care setting. Non-invasive ventilation should not be used in this situation because of the risk of worsening hyperinflation.

Answer to Question 28

C: severe

The GOLD (Global Initiative for Chronic Obstructive Lung Disease) classification of airflow obstruction in COPD is based upon the post-bronchodilator FEV_1:

> mild – FEV_1 ≥80% predicted

> moderate – FEV_1 ≤50% to <80% predicted

> severe – FEV_1 ≤30% to <50% predicted

> very severe – FEV_1 <30% predicted.

Answer to Question 29

E: pulmonary rehabilitation

Pulmonary rehabilitation has been shown to improve dyspnoea, health status and exercise tolerance in stable patients with COPD, as well as reducing hospitalisation for patients with a recent exacerbation. This patient may be a candidate for lung volume reduction surgery, but he would need to complete a pulmonary rehabilitation course first. His age and history of malignancy indicate he would not be a candidate for lung transplantation. His PaO_2 is above the cut-off value for consideration of LTOT.

Answer to Question 30

C: increase the IPAP to a target of 20 cmH₂O as tolerated

In this case there has been minimal improvement in the arterial blood gas after starting NIV. Good medical therapy has already been given and there is no mask leak or patient asynchrony. The NIV settings in this case are sub-therapeutic and the IPAP should be increased towards a target of 20 cmH₂O in order to improve minute ventilation and CO_2 clearance. Intravenous aminophylline could be considered, but this patient will gain the most therapeutic benefit from optimising the NIV settings.

Answer to Question 31

B: insert a cannula into the second intercostal space in the mid-clavicular line on the left

This patient is likely to have developed a left-sided tension pneumothorax, which is a recognised complication of NIV, particularly for patients with emphysema and bullous disease. The immediate life-saving course of action is to insert a large-bore cannula in the second intercostal space in the mid-clavicular line to decompress the tension pneumothorax. The NIV should be stopped at this stage as positive pressure ventilation will worsen the

pneumothorax. NIV can safely be recommenced once an intercostal drain has been inserted and connected to an underwater seal.

Answer to Question 32

B: pH 7.30, PCO₂ 6.7 kPa

NIV should be started in the context of an acute exacerbation of COPD if the arterial blood gas shows pH <7.35 (normal range 7.35–7.45) and PCO_2 >6.5 kPa (normal range 4.7–6.0) despite optimal medical therapy. The other arterial blood gas (ABG) results in this question are either not sufficiently acidotic to meet the requirements for NIV or show an acidosis without hypercapnia, implying a metabolic acidosis in which case NIV is not indicated.

Answer to Question 33

B: overnight continuous positive airway pressure (CPAP)

This patient has evidence of severe obstructive sleep apnoea (OSA) syndrome as evidenced by his markedly elevated apnoea–hypopnoea index in combination with a high score on the Epworth Sleepiness Scale and elevated body mass index (BMI). The normal waking capillary blood gas and mean oxygen saturation of 92% (normal range 94–98%) indicates the predominant picture is of OSA rather than of hypoventilation. Nocturnal CPAP is the most appropriate therapy in this circumstance. A mandibular advancement device is unlikely to be successful in this situation of severe OSA. Weight loss surgery could also be considered, but CPAP should be started in the first instance.

Answer to Question 34

E: nocturnal non-invasive ventilation (NIV)

This patient has signs and symptoms of obesity hypoventilation syndrome (OHS) with subsequent right ventricular

failure and a chronic compensated hypercapnia. Nocturnal NIV will treat her overnight hypoventilation and will improve her right ventricular dysfunction. Diuretic therapy alone will not treat the underlying problem. CPAP is used to treat obstructive sleep apnoea (OSA): it can be used in cases of OSA/OHS overlap, but the situation here is more suggestive of OHS. LTOT alone should not be used here as without additional ventilatory support oxygen therapy may exacerbate type II respiratory failure.

Answer to Question 35

D: 4

The CURB-65 score is used to assess the severity of community-acquired pneumonia. A point is scored if each of the following is present: confusion (Abbreviated Mental Test score ≤8), urea >7 mmol/L, respiratory rate ≥30 breaths per minute, systolic BP <90 mmHg and/or diastolic BP ≤60 mmHg, age ≥65. This patient therefore scores 4, which gives him a predicted mortality of 28% at 30 days, signifying severe pneumonia.

Answer to Question 36

E: urine for *Legionella* and pneumococcal antigen

This man has a severe pneumonia according to his CURB-65 score. The National Institute for Health and Care Excellence (NICE) and the British Thoracic Society (BTS) guidelines in this situation recommend blood cultures, sputum for bacterial culture, and urine for *Legionella* and pneumococcal antigen analysis. Further investigations such as serology or PCR to look for atypical, viral or fungal pathogens may be indicated if he does not respond to standard antibiotic therapy.

Answer to Question 37

A: *Fusobacterium necrophorum*

Fusobacterium necrophorum causes Lemierre's syndrome. This is a pharyngeal infection most commonly occurring in young adults. The infection spreads through the soft tissues of the neck and carotid sheath causing jugular vein thrombosis. Embolisation to the lung can occur, causing cavitation and abscess formation.

Answer to Question 38
C: request a chest X-ray

High-level penicillin resistance is rare in *Streptococcus pneumoniae*. The failure to improve with appropriate antibiotic therapy suggests that the patient may have developed a complication of his pneumonia. The most likely cause is a parapneumonic effusion, which may have become infected. The most appropriate investigation is therefore a chest radiograph. If this confirmed the presence of a pleural effusion he would then require an ultrasound-guided pleural aspiration.

Answer to Question 39
E: silicosis

The clinical and radiological findings are typical for subacute silicosis. The smoking history is not substantial and the spirometry showed a restrictive pattern, thus making COPD unlikely. Siderosis is associated with exposure to iron oxide and is commonly associated with welding work. Caplan's syndrome occurs in miners with seropositive rheumatic arthritis or positive serum rheumatoid factor.

Answer to Question 40
B: pleural fluid lactate dehydrogenase (LDH) more than two-thirds of the value of the upper limit of normal serum LDH

Light's criteria states that a pleural effusion is exudative when any one of the following conditions is fulfilled:

> pleural fluid LDH:serum LDH ratio >0.6

> pleural fluid protein:serum protein ratio >0.5

> pleural fluid LDH more than two-thirds of the value of the upper limit of normal serum LDH.

Index

Note: page numbers in *italics* refer to figures, those in **bold** refer to tables.

novel oral anticoagulant (NOAC),
　tachycardia 90
NSAIDs *see* non-steroidal
　anti-inflammatory drugs (NSAIDs)
NSTEMI (non-ST elevation MI) 57, 72,
　171, 172
　unstable angina and *see* unstable
　　angina and NSTEMI
nuclear cardiology 179–80
nutritional supplementation, COPD 262

O

obesity hypoventilation syndrome
　(OHS) 325
obesity, lifestyle modification 226
obliterative bronchiolitis, rheumatoid
　arthritis 279
obstructive sleep apnoea (OSA) 235,
　236, 237, 296, 298
obstructive sleep apnoea syndrome
　252–4, 325
occupational aspects, HCM 98
occupational lung disease 269–71
oedema 21, 69, 171
oesophageal manometry, nocturnal
　cough 207
oesophageal pain 58
omalizumab
　asthma 260
　mechanism of action 322
opioids 217, 304
orthopnoea, exertional presyncope
　and 10
OSA *see* obstructive sleep apnoea
　(OSA)
outcomes, lung transplantation 301
overnight oximetry, interpretation of
　clinical data 309
overzealous fluid removal 13
oxygen saturation 10, 13, 286
oxygen therapy
　interstitial lung disease 217
　long-term, IPF 272

P

pacemakers 166, 167–70
　coagulase-negative staphylococci
　　187–8, 194
　complications 169, *170*
　implantation 193
　indications 166, 167
　related infections 187–8, 194
PACES stations and acute scenarios,
　cardiology 3–77
PACES stations and acute scenarios,
　respiratory 199–251
palliative chemotherapy, cardiac
　tumours 130
palpitations
　causes 40, 41, **41**
　with dizziness 3–5
　paroxysmal *see* paroxysmal
　　palpitations
Pancoast's syndrome 288
pansystolic murmur 23–4
PAP (pulmonary artery pressure)
　elevation 135, 138
　estimation 104
paralysed hemidiaphragm,
　management 299
parapneumonic effusion, defined
　246
paratracheal lymphadenopathy 315
paroxysmal nocturnal dyspnoea,
　exertional presyncope and 10
paroxysmal palpitations 41–3
patent ductus arteriosus (PDA) 118,
　195
patent foramen ovale (PFO) 65, 67, *67*,
　142, 193
patterns of lung disease, asbestos 269
PCI *see* percutaneous coronary
　intervention (PCI)
PDA *see* patent ductus arteriosus (PDA)
PE *see* pulmonary embolism (PE)
peak expiratory flow (PEF) monitoring
　COPD 260
　nocturnal cough 207

peak flow
　asthma 257, *257*
　lung function tests 308
penicillamine 279, 281
penicillin130, 281
pentamidine, *Pneumocystis* pneumonia
　287
pentoxifylline, sarcoidosis 277
percussion
　bronchiectasis 213
　of chest 61
　COPD 221
　cystic fibrosis 225
　interstitial lung disease 215
　pleural effusion 218
　pleural effusion and fever 247
　pneumonectomy/lobectomy 223
　tuberculosis 224
percutaneous biopsy under CT guidance,
　lung cancer 289, *290*
percutaneous coronary intervention
　(PCI)
　acute stroke 193
　diabetes 140
　GA in heart disease 144
　recommendation for 39–40
　stable angina 79, *79*
　in stable patients for angina 180
　STEMI 191
percutaneous mitral balloon
　valvuloplasty (PMBV) 105, 192
perfusion defect 189–90
pericardial disease 108–13
　acute pericarditis 108–10
　constrictive pericarditis 112–13
　effusion 110–12
pericardial effusion 110–1, 112, 171,
　171
pericarditis 63, 64, 84
peripartum cardiomyopathy 144, 193
peripheral vascular system, hypertension
　19
permanent pacemaker, indications 167
persisting pain without ECG
　abnormalities 58

ritonavir, HIV 287
Rosenbach's sign **26**
routine screening, hypertension at *see* hypertension

S

Saccharopolyspora rectivirgula 212, 217
salbutamol 316
salicylates, rheumatic fever 130
saquinavir, HIV 287
sarcoid disease activity, monitoring of 200
sarcoidosis 276–7
screening relatives for inherited condition, discussion 32–3
secondary prevention, STEMI 84
secondary pulmonary hypertension 138, **139**
seizures, syncope and 52, 53
Seldinger technique 304, 305
Senning procedure 122
septal alcohol ablation, HCM 96, *97*
septrin, *Pneumocystis* pneumonia 287
serum 276, 277
short-burst oxygen therapy 298
shunts, secondary pulmonary hypertension, management 139
SIADH (syndrome of inappropriate antidiuretic hormone secretion) 288, **288**
sickle cell disease, lung and 283–4
sick sinus syndrome 187
siderosis 326
sildenafil 138, 193
silicosis, clinical and radiological findings 326
simvastatin 183, 187
sinoatrial dysfunction, bradycardia 85
sinus tachycardia
    causes 62
    irregular pulse 49
    symptoms 43
site of needle insertion, pleural procedures 303, *304*

skin-prick tests
    asthma 257
    pulmonary eosinophilia 282
SLE (systemic lupus erythematosus)
    autoimmune rheumatic disease 140
    DPLDs and 211
sleep apnoea 252–4
sleep study, PPH 137
small-cell lung cancer (SCLC) 291
small cell lung carcinoma 322
small-vessel vasculitis, pulmonary vasculitis 279
smoke inhalation 282–3
smoking
    cessation, lung cancer 291–2
    COPD 240–1, 260, 262
    history 200
        lung cancer and 209
    lifestyle modification 226
    of marijuana 199
social history
    breathlessness and exertional presyncope 10
    solitary pulmonary nodule 234
soft tissues and bones, chest radiograph 310
solitary pulmonary nodule 233–5
sotalol, tachycardia 90
spiral CT chest with contrast, PE 151, *152*
spirometry
    COPD 260, **260**
    hypoxia 245
    lung function tests 308, **308**, *309*
spironolactone 186
    breathlessness and ankle swelling 8
    cardiac failure 93, 94
sputum culture
    bronchiectasis 214, 264, **265**
    clearance, bronchiectasis 264
    cytology, lung cancer 290
    exertional dyspnoea with *see* exertional dyspnoea
    exertional presyncope and 9
    lobar collapse 249

microbiology examination 203
nocturnal cough 207
pleural effusion and fever 247
pleuritic chest pain 62
stable angina 78–80
staging, lung cancer 312–13
Stanford classification, of aortic dissection 133, *134*
staphylococci 247
Staphylococcus aureus 23, 107, 189, 194, 203, **265**
Starr–Edwards valves 23
statins
    stable angina 79
    STEMI 83, 84
    unstable angina and NSTEMI 80
ST elevation myocardial infarction (STEMI) 72, 81–5, 192
STEMI *see* ST elevation myocardial infarction (STEMI)
stenotic aortic valve 16, *16*
steroids
    acute hypersensitivity pneumonitis 274
    allergic rhinitis 255
    asthma 259
    autoimmune rheumatic diseases 141
    bronchiectasis 266
    hypertension 50
    pneumoconioses 270
    pulmonary vasculitis 280
    rheumatic fever 130
    sarcoidosis 277
    subacute hypersensitivity pneumonitis 275
Streptococcus pneumoniae **265**, 283, 285, 323, 326
stress echocardiography 177, 178, 179
stress imaging 78, 98
stress myocardial perfusion scintigraphy 189–90
stridor 217–18
stroke and murmur 64–8